THE MACABRESQUE

The Macabresque

HUMAN VIOLATION AND HATE IN GENOCIDE, MASS
ATROCITY, AND ENEMY-MAKING

Edward Weisband

OXFORD
UNIVERSITY PRESS

OXFORD
UNIVERSITY PRESS

Oxford University Press is a department of the University of Oxford. It furthers
the University's objective of excellence in research, scholarship, and education
by publishing worldwide. Oxford is a registered trade mark of Oxford University
Press in the UK and certain other countries.

Published in the United States of America by Oxford University Press
198 Madison Avenue, New York, NY 10016, United States of America.

© Oxford University Press 2018

"Wall Poem" by Thomas Krampf was published in *Taking Time Out: Poems in Remembrance of Madness*
(Salmon Poetry LTD., 2004), 60, and is reprinted with permission.

Library of Congress Cataloging-in-Publication Data
Names: Weisband, Edward, 1939– author.
Title: The macabresque : human violation and hate in genocide, mass atrocity,
and enemy-making / Edward Weisband.
Description: New York, NY : Oxford University Press, [2018] |
Includes bibliographical references and index.
Identifiers: LCCN 2017010034| ISBN 9780190677886 (hardcover : alk. paper) |
ISBN 9780190677909 (epub)
Subjects: LCSH: Genocide. | Political atrocities. | Massacres.
Classification: LCC HV6322.7 .W436 2017 | DDC 304.6/63—dc23
LC record available at https://lccn.loc.gov/2017010034

9 8 7 6 5 4 3 2 1
Printed by Sheridan Books, Inc., United States of America

In homage to Tzvetan Todorov,
this book is written in loving memory of my parents, Mark and Edith,
who once asked that I ask why genocides occur;
and is dedicated with all my love and gratitude,
to my wife,
Joan Elizabeth Weisband,
who shared the answers, as they came.

Contents

Preface

AT SOME POINT, collective human suffering turns into numbed silence or a sustained scream. Access to verbal expression, even intelligibility, fails in agony. As this book is released, the echoes of such agony bellow from out of the homes, streets, and prisons of Syria, Yemen, and South Sudan. The scales of inhumanity plunder new depths as the world watches and shields its eyes. Many reasons may be adduced for why evil arises and wends its ways. What follows ponders not so much why evil occurs but rather how it happens. Much is said and written about lethality in genocide and mass atrocity, as well it should. Yet the very focus on the numbers of dead or on the seemingly strategic aims or objectives of perpetrators disregards the significance of how victims are made to suffer, in particular, the means, modes, and methods of dying imposed upon them prior to their death. Overwhelmingly, perpetrators revel in the harms, hurts, and pains they instill on the bodies, minds, and spirits of others reified as different, precisely on account of their similarity, and tend to fixate on the immediacies of humiliation, torture, and physical and often sexual violation. Death alone, it appears, is insufficient to satisfy perpetrator desire for a kind of diabolical absolution in the desecration of victim personhood. The central question raised here is why. To kill is relatively easy. Why pursue human suffering as an end in itself if all that is wanted are the objectives of political victory? Thus we are compelled to veer from explanations of collective violence toward examination of the problematics of human violation in enemy-making, that is, how and in what ways collective human violation in genocide and mass atrocity originate in defiance of all precepts of moral order, normative practice, or ethical principle—despite the often repeated protestations by perpetrators to the contrary.

Such inquiry is made all the more perplexing by virtue of the fact time and again, as demonstrated by the case studies depicted here, perpetrators and victims are not strangers in relation to each other but citizens, neighbors as it were, of a common land or society. In instances of genocide, mass atrocity, and enemy-making, one after the other, a national government devours its own citizens by rendering them stateless: thus degrading their civil status thereby demeaning their very personhood through what I designate as "the macabresque." Human violations in genocide and mass atrocity, or whenever hatred fuels enemy-making are everywhere the same but invariably different. As a conceptual problematic, human violation differs from collective violence in its theatricality with respect to the persistence of performative transgression. The macabresque emerges in and through the dramaturgical styles of human violation. The styles of dramaturgical performativity in human violation reflect cultural norms and practices, ideological illogics, motivational drives, and attitudinal predispositions, as well as psychosocial and emotional desires. Ultimately, how the macabresque plays out is shaped according to the theatricalities that appeal to the preferences of perpetrators who act not out of banal thoughtlessness or even obedience or conformity, as is so often theoretically alleged. They act out the macabresque on ludic stages of performativity keyed to lurid delusions shaped by admixtures of cultural belief and sadistic, often perverse, desire that once triggered collectively give vent to a cruelty beyond words and a suffering beyond measure.

Acknowledgments

MANY COLLEAGUES, FRIENDS, FORMER STUDENTS, AND ASSOCIATES in the field have contributed to the development and completion of this book. All members of the Virginia Tech Department of Political Science create a genuinely supportive scholarly and intellectual community in which to explore difficult theoretical questions and complex analytical issues. I am grateful to Karen M. Hult, Professor and Chair, Department of Political Science, for her many scholarly contributions and current departmental leadership. I am especially indebted to Timothy W. Luke, University Distinguished Professor and former Chair, Scott G. Nelson, Associate Professor and Director of Graduate Studies, and Ioannis A. Stivachtis, Associate Professor of Political Science and Director of the Virginia Tech International Studies Program for their exceptional contributions to our discipline, department, and instructional programs, so beneficial to our students. Their friendship means so much to me. Thanks go as well to François Debrix, Professor of Political Science and Director of the Virginia Tech Alliance for Social, Political, Ethical, and Cultural Thought (ASPECT) for his scholarship on violence and for his pursuit of cross departmental interdisciplinary activities. I wish to recognize with warm appreciation, our years of collegial friendship with: Clair Apodaca, Priya Dixit, Bettina Koch, Deborah J. Milly, Wayne D. Moore, Charles L. Taylor, and Laura Zanotti. I remain deeply grateful to numerous former and present Virginia Tech colleagues for their warm and nurturing friendship, including E. Fred Carlisle, William E. Lavery Professor and Senior Vice President and Provost Emeritus; A. Roger Ekirch, Professor of History; Thomas Gardner, Alumni Distinguished Professor of English; Joseph Pitt, Professor of Philosophy; Robert Siegle, Professor Emeritus, Department of English. I am blessed by successive generations of former students, resulting from over fifty years of teaching. In particular, I gratefully thank my former SUNY Binghamton students, including: Paul Contino, Christian Davenport, Michael Eisenstadt, Jami Floyd, Matthew Krain, Nadia Rubaii, Eric P. Schwartz, Alan E. Steinweis, and Owen Pell; each of whom have pursued such brilliant careers. I also wish to recognize with affectionate regard my former Virginia Tech students: Christopher J. Colvin, David Dansereau, Elana DeLozier, Amber Newell, Robert Ralston, Joel Shelton, Valerie Szybala, and Courtney I. P. Thomas; who are having such an important impact in their respective careers. I thank Daniel P. Neville for his devotion that means so much and for his technical support at a critical juncture. Thanks also go to Josette Torres for her assistance in enabling me to keep track of my passwords. Special thanks also goes to Hirbohd Hedayat for working shoulder to shoulder with me at the conclusion of this project to ensure editorial accuracy in endnotes and bibliographic references. Many former teachers and mentors inform the analytical spirit of this project. I note in this regard the late Professor Majid Khadduri who, while teaching at the Johns Hopkins School of Advanced International Affairs (SAIS), inspired several generations of students to pursue academic and diplomatic careers focused on Islamic cultures and institutions. I also wish to extend my abiding appreciation to the late Thomas M. Franck, whose distinguished career in international legal scholarship and as President of the American Association of International Law ultimately contributed to international institutional building, especially to the development of UN peacekeeping programs. In addition, I want to thank my many friends in the American Political Science Association as well as in the International Studies Association, in particular Naeem Inayatullah, Richard Ned Lebow, Nicholas Onuf, R. B. J. Walker, and especially Stephen K. White. I want to extend personal gratitude to the dedicated scholars across the globe who contribute to the deliberations of International Association of Genocide Scholars, especially Alexander Laban Hinton and to those professional scholars and practitioners who regularly participate in the Politics and Psychoanalysis Symposia, especially Lene Auestad, Pina Antinucci, Jay Frankel, Amal Treacher Kabesh, and Julianna Vamos. I gladly acknowledge my gratitude and esteem for my cherished friends Maria Speck, and Alnoor Ebrahim, Professor of Management, Tufts University. Daniel J. and Helen Neville, David and Donna Snover, and Brian and Annette Davie bring constant joy and love, for which I am profoundly grateful. Finally, I wish to thank Angela Chnapko, Political Science Editor at Oxford University Press, for her never failing faith in the value of this project and for her support in bringing it to fruition.

THE MACABRESQUE

Falange sky
and mud
sequence
and the blood of the angels
who cry
for their children
in doorways
who hold their eyes
in their hands.

Thomas Krampf
"Wall Poem", Taking Time Out: Poems in Remembrance of Madness, 60

Evil involves precisely the blurring of distinctions between Good and Evil—that is, the elevation of Evil into a consistent ethical Principle.

Slavoj Žižek
The Plague of Fantasies, 303

The response to evil is not justice but love . . . . Accordingly, evil is not injustice, nor is it banal. Like love, evil is metaphysical before it is psychological. It is a way of being in the world, of locating an ultimate meaning, for a finite subject. Neither the lover nor the evil person can live with the knowledge of his or her own separation from others. Both love and evil are responses to shame, which is the experience of finitude in a subject with aspirations for the infinite.

Paul W. Kahn
Out of Eden, 138–139

To abandon the attempt to comprehend evil is to abandon every basis for confronting it, in thought as in practice. The thinkers who returned to the problem of evil while knowing the limits of any discussion of it were driven by moral demands. For creatures endowed with reason, love of the world cannot be blind. The intellectual struggle is more important than any particular results that emerge from it.

Susan Neiman
Evil in Modern Thought, 325

PART I

The Macabresque of Human Violation

Introduction

TAKING PERFORMATIVITY SERIOUSLY

THE LINKAGES BETWEEN violence and spectacle extend back to biblical and classical times and even before that, to the cultures of prerecorded history. The contemporary digital world has become all too familiar with media displays of graphic violence. In many cases, what might once have seemed images of unimaginable horror have become living-room realities. This study focuses on the related performativity in genocide and mass atrocity, or the staging, dramaturgy, and aesthetics of collective violence, in particular, during the twentieth century. Studies of genocide and mass atrocity often point toward their causes and consequences, their aims and effects, in measures denominated by numbers of those killed and how the violence occurred. In contrast, this study examines why and how so many victims are violated before their murders. In this perspective, genocide and mass atrocity provide a kind of "cover" for the sustained and systematic torture, torment, and agony of victims beyond, and thus in addition to, their purposive death. This is what taking performativity in transgression seriously signifies, a reversal in analytical focus from death in collective violence to the study of genocide and mass atrocity *as a means* to pursue the performativity of large-scale human violation *as the end* sought by perpetrators.

Many questions arise as a result of this shift in perspective. Why do different sets of perpetrators adopt contrasting performative methods and instrumentalities? What is the relationship between cultural milieu and the aesthetics and dramaturgies of sadistic cruelty? Why do perpetrators often pursue interrogational torture to elicit confessions from hapless victims who have nothing to confess? Performativity in human violation illustrates the ways perpetrators force victims to participate in processes of their own *torture as a performative act to get the victim to participate in depersonalizing themselves & the perp as a recognition of an affective agent of pain*

42 The Macabresque of Human Violation

depersonalization and debasement. In case after case, victims endure not only extreme forms of physical degradation; they are, in addition, forced to experience mental and psychological, emotional and spiritual humiliation. In many instances victims are made to become agents of their own self-betrayal by being forced into forsaking what they most cherish. Conversely, perpetrators often compete among themselves for recognition and status as effective agents of the excruciating pain they cause in quests for absolute power. The method, means, and modes of performative violation may often appear redundant or secondary to whatever the specific murderous objectives of genocide and mass atrocity may be. But they are as critical to an understanding of perpetrator behavior relative both to culture and the psychodynamics of perpetrator motivation as any accounting of the strategic ends pursued in collective violence.

Performativities of human violation, moreover, tend to occur within demarcated times and spaces, whether on roads during long marches or at roadblock ditches or in the pits of killing fields; in prisons and detention centers; in concentration, death, work, or rape camps; or within torture chambers or in often targeted indigenous villages; at laboratories or documentary archives; or during show trials and so-called great purges. All are established for the purposes of performative transgression, but each assumes a distinct cultural, political, and psychological character. Generalizations do emerge, however, across the relevant case studies presented here. The most important is the consistency of the macabre leitmotif on account of the contrast between the indescribable sufferings of victims and the indifferent contempt exuded by perpetrators. Performativity of human violation in the spatialities and temporalities of performative transgression may thus be said to give rise to *the macabresque*. This usage derives from another, *carnivalesque*, one that sometimes refers to the festivality at play during intersessional times of debauchery and killing.

The macabresque as a concept differs somewhat, since human violations accompanying genocide and mass atrocity tend not to be orgiastic in implementation but, rather, the result of deliberate actions in circumstances under the control of power and command structures. Yet to attribute the macabresque to political or strategic rationale is to belie the superfluous or, for want of a better term, its utterly gratuitous nature, even in cases of "ethnic cleansing." So the question arises as to why it occurs repeatedly. Indeed, the study of the macabresque culminates in nothing less than the history of extreme violence during the past century. This history is linked to, but remains distinct from, onsets of warfare.

No single set of answers, no single theoretical or analytical perspective, suffices to explain the macabresque of performative transgression in genocide and mass atrocity. The task is readily beset by its complexity given the range of factors relevant to explanations. Thus a constellation of approaches, themes, and concepts from a multiplicity of theoretical perspectives, especially cultural studies and political science and social and political psychology, becomes a necessary antidote to the false mystification of perpetrators, their demonization as larger than life, or their banalization as less than merely ordinary. To say that perpetrators are "ordinary," as is so often done, is to beg the question of what is *ordinary* in ordinary. At issue here is nothing less than how perpetrators as theorized political subjects are constructed. The answers given here underscore the influences of desire, envy, and mimetic rivalry.

But to refer to such conceptual units of analysis requires further elaboration to determine their explanatory value or use in contexts that are framed by both group and individual behaviors. This, too, represents a critical challenge in evaluating the macabresque as a form of political and social behavior. How does one explain its persistence across time and cultures? Its very repetitions, however, are suggestive of psychosocial theory that stresses the individuality of social phenomena against the analytical background of theories based on the repetitious nature of human desires and demands. To feature this element of behavior in the macabresque, an entire theoretical perspective and an attendant vocabulary must be applied using such terms as *akrasia* and *akratic willfulness, disorders of will; self-deception; ideological reification* and the *logics of illogic*; and *sadism* and *narcissism*. Several of such terms have entered everyday vocabulary, as if their theoretical or explanatory meanings and import were self-evident. They are not. On the contrary, their applications require precise delineation in theoretical terms if they are to serve as necessary and sufficient in explaining the macabresque.

Sadism and narcissism, among others, entail precise analytical meanings, but only once they are framed by the theoretical logic that sustains them as explanatory concepts. This represents a paramount exercise within the context of psychosocial theory throughout what follows. Pride of place is given to the formulations of Lacanian and, to a lesser extent, Kleinian theory, since these perspectives provide insights into the constitutive character of human subjectivity and mental developmental processes in human personality or that of subjectivation. Desire and desiring represent critical components of subjectivity. This gives rise to analytical emphasis on what persons desire, how they learn to desire, what they yearn for in desire, how they seek *to be* the desire of what is deemed desirable. These psychodynamics are compounded by what Lacanian theory also represents as loss in terms of Oedipal separation and the consequent quest for substitution in desire that is driven by what is represented as the interiority of psychic images or maternal and paternal images, with emphasis on *learned* or mimetic desire.

Much appropriate skepticism greets such propositions within the social sciences with respect to their explanatory validity regarding large-group behaviors. The question of levels of analysis looms as a significant methodological or analytical problem. Here again, it becomes important not to assign causal explanations in cases in which multifarious factors are clearly relevant to episodes of genocide and mass atrocity. That said, the macabresque represents a form of performativity that permits the applications of psychosocial theory informed by such concepts as ego-ideal and the dread of "theft-enjoyment." The case studies here demonstrate the possibilities of psychosocial analysis focused on the psychodynamics of desire and how these help to explain what otherwise remains inexplicable—the unrelenting cruelty of perpetrators of genocide and mass atrocity in the macabresque, again and again.

Sadistic cruelty, depraved perpetrator behaviors in the macabresque as demonstrated by numerous examples, including several of the major case studies presented here, reveal an additional phenomenon. It is linked to the techniques of interrogational torture, as well as to the methods of torment and agony that are clearly imposed on victims for the purpose of their humiliation. This process of humiliation consistently assumes an epistemological tone, as if the victims possessed a truth or fundament made accessible only by means of their debasement. Victims in the macabresque confront perpetrator demands for what E. Valentine Daniel has called *informativeness*, a kind of information with no basis in verity but nonetheless held out as necessary for victims to provide.[1]

The forms vary across the macabresque terrains of torture, torment, and agony, but they remain persistent with respect to perpetrator demand for some form of yielding, some kind of offering, on the part of victims. But victims cannot offer what they do not possess. It is as if perpetrators demand what Jacques Lacan referred to as the *agalma*, a term he derived from the ancient Greek in relation to the notion of a wondrous gift to the gods endowed with mystical powers that functioned as a votive offering. Perpetrators, by means of human violation, seek from victims the magic of their absolutized pleasure but in so doing destroy the vitality that lies at the very core of human relationship and interaction.

Tzvetan Todorov, a wise and acute observer of totalitarian systems, comments on the relationship of totalized power to scientism to the effect that it "as a doctrine starts from the hypothesis that the real world is an entirely coherent structure." He adds, "It follows that the world is transparent, that it can be known entirely and without residue by the human mind."[2] Scientism represents the conversion of scientific method imbued by critical method and theoretical contestation with certitude regarding the capacity of knowledge to know all that can be discovered, and to dominate the future with power in the present that controls all that moves history, including thought itself. As Todorov states, "Scientism derives from the existence of scientific practice, but it is not itself scientific. Its basic postulate—the complete transparency of the real—cannot be proved; the same is true of its implementation in the construction of ultimate ends through the process of knowledge."[3] The macabresque emerges from within the core of genocidal and mass atrocity not by accident, as it were, or as an auxiliary contingent relative to mass murder, annihilation, or death. On the contrary, it demonstrates how perpetrator self-deceptions demand that truth become a function of their will, once what they will, in the words of Leslie Farber, is the unwillable.[4]

1

From Collective Violence to Human Violation

DARK DESIRES IN DISORDERS OF WILL

THE PSYCHODYNAMICS OF DESIRE

In any realm of formal inquiry, effective investigation depends on getting the "correct" questions "right." Whether the research approach is defined as analytical or diagnostic, exploratory or theoretical, speculative or scientific, the imaginative task turns on the questions raised: why, and on what logical or methodological basis? Sometimes, inquiry permits interrogative discovery. At those moments, new questions, even with respect to old problems, appear. This compels new formats of investigation, and opens the way for renewed analytical perspectives and revised conceptual frames. The present study is situated in a long tradition of psychosocial analysis. The specific objective here is to extend this theoretical orientation by focusing on the psychodynamics of desire relative to explanations of genocide and mass atrocity. The aim is to demonstrate how at times, under certain conditions, and in particular situations, desire as an element in the human psyche and emotion work in ways that appear to embolden subjects to become perpetrators and thus behave in the service of what I describe as the *macabresque*, that is, the performative transgression, dramaturgies, and aesthetics of human violation in genocide and mass atrocity.

My basic argument is that the psychodynamics of desire contribute to the transformation of "ordinary" individuals into those who directly and indirectly undertake to support or engage in genocide, mass atrocity, and their performative dramaturgies. It has now become commonplace to assert that it is mostly ordinary citizens who are the main practitioners of genocide and mass atrocity. But the question arises as to what is "ordinary" in ordinary persons who engage in mass atrocity during genocidal or near-genocidal events. The answer given here is desire, particularly as it is conceived and theorized in the psychoanalytic work of a number of seminal theorists, including Melanie Klein and Jacques Lacan, as well as by an important group of psychosocial theorists. This is not meant to suggest a kind of mono-causal approach to mass atrocity or genocidal violence. My claim is much more restrained. Namely, the question of perpetrator motivations is robbed of a robust explanatory perspective in the absence of a theoretical framework that is focused on the psychodynamics of desire as manifested by and through the dramaturgy and aesthetics of performative transgression that are so often present during episodes of genocide and mass atrocity. The aim here is to interrogate why so many seemingly normal or "ordinary" people participate in mass atrocity across numerous cultures and during many historic episodes of egregious violence. The answers focus on specific key behavioral dimensions of human relations and self-esteem as they relate to perpetrator choice and volition within a psychosocial framework focused on merciless mass atrocity and how human violation is stylistically implemented as a separate problematic, over and beyond mass killing, in genocide or near-genocidal episodes.

The essential question raised here concerns not only the phenomenon of genocide and mass atrocity as a discrete issue over and above that of mass violence, murder, or death; it also concerns the ways in which genocide and mass atrocity occur. The shift from collective violence to human violation through performative transgression assumes a kind of style each time and in each circumstance it arises. I explore this in terms of aesthetic or dramaturgical style, specifically what I call the *macabreseque* in order to emphasize its sadistic theatrical character. This is, indeed, to borrow from Joseph Conrad's immortal title, "the heart of darkness" which we are beholden to understand and explain, however preliminarily and however speculative our psychosocial tools. One observation that does present itself consistently is that when genocide and mass atrocity occur, the macabresque differs from culture to culture. I infer from this that it is not merely accidental that certain images capture our memory as emblematic of specific genocides or mass atrocities; for example, the predation and death marches into the desert of the Armenian genocide; mass starvation in the Ukraine, *dekulakization* and the destruction of peasant farming in favor of collectivization during the Stalinist period, leading to the Great Party Purges and Show Trials of the 1930s; the killing apparatus of the death camps and the diabolical "scientistic" laboratories of the Holocaust; mass starvation and the village trials perpetrated by the Red Guard movement during the Maoist cultural revolution; the killing fields and prisons for purposes of torture, confession, and archival record in the Cambodian genocide; the torture and disappearance of the Argentinean "Dirty War"; the roadblocks and dismemberment by macheté in the Rwanda genocide; the shame-camps, mass graves, and mass rape in the Bosnian War. Even in cases of authoritarian or military dictatorships, mass atrocity tends to take on its own instrumental dramaturgy and aesthetic: the electric shocks of the Brazilian and Chilean torture and interrogation centers, the "necklaces" of burning tires in South African townships, the waterboarding tortures in South African detention centers, and the forced digging of graves by victims prior to being gunned down across decimated villages in East Timor under Indonesia's brutal occupation; each and all signify the sadistic horrors of performative transgression and human violation over and beyond mass murder. Nonetheless, these images are often taken to represent the numbers killed or dead, not *how* victims died or how they were made to suffer. This, then, is the issue taken up here: why do genocide and mass atrocity assume different modes of performative transgression in different cultural environments?

Genocide and mass atrocity occur both within open and carceral spaces of collective or group torture, agony, and torment, sometimes slowly, but also during frenzied outbreaks under conditions of carnivalesque "festivality." In this, we confront reasons why the macabresque of performative transgressions becomes suggestive for psychosocial inquiry in the study of large-group violence. Specific examples of the macabresque of performative transgression in political violence abound: Auschwitz and other killing camps and the torture and labor concentration camps during the Holocaust; the torture, maiming, and killing sites of the Cambodian genocide during the Khmer Rouge era, typified by the infamous Tuol Sleng S-21 prison; the brutal detention centers of interrogation, sexual abuse, and torture at ESMA (Escuela Superior de Mecánica de la Armada), "the Argentine Auschwitz," as well as at "La Perla" (centro de detención) during the Argentine "Dirty War"; the beating and killing grounds of the Omarska concentration camp, along with numerous others, during the era of ethnic cleansing in Bosnia-Herzegovina; the highways and roadblocks of mutilation and dismemberment during the Rwandan genocide; the mountain villages of Guatemala that witnessed diabolical violations of villagers, especially women, children, and the elderly; the forests and plantations of Tamil regions of Sri Lanka, with its ensembles of innocents suffering the systematic brutalization of families taken together, violated together by intolerable pain; and other sites, including those in Chile, Brazil, Indonesia, India, southern Sudan, and today as one writes, in the makeshift basements of bombed-out apartment complexes in the urban neighborhoods of Assad's Syria. All represent instances of macabresque cruelty performed differently, episode to episode, culture to culture; but all retain the tints of perpetrator desires to project shame and humiliation onto victims in depraved and repulsive ways commensurate with attacks against the dignity of personhood.

THE MACABRESQUE OF GENOCIDE AND MASS ATROCITY

The concept of macabresque as an analytical perspective underscores the analytical linkages between willful or disordered perpetrator desire and the sometime influences of supererogatory moralism, self-sacrifice, and a perverted sense of heroism that function both consciously and unconsciously. Such behaviors and psychodynamic influences demonstrate what I take to be the disorders of will that cast perpetrators and their behaviors in ways that are reflective of their desire to humiliate victims and to do so absolutely. The consequence is macabresque theaters of political evil: dramaturgical and aestheticized forms of surplus cruelty instrumentalized by means of forced displays of performative human transgression.

The French speak of the *plaisanterie macabre,* a ghastly dance performed by skeletons whose shivering bones rattle to the sways of demonic music, as the ghostly figures *laugh* in the face of death. Performative transgression resides in the noir ecstasy of derisive contempt for the victims, who are made to perform in the production of their own torments and agony, while the perpetrators participate in the production of "surplus enjoyment" that is key to the macabresque as demonic entertainment. Even in cases of ethnic cleansing, when the ostensible purpose is the forced removal of large segments of local populations, violence tends to take on the surplus qualities beyond whatever might be required in accordance with strategic necessity, as evidenced by how mass murder and rape became organized during the disintegration of Yugoslavia. Mass human violations become contoured around an aesthetic of performative dramaturgy to allow perpetrator enjoyment of shame entertainments designed to humiliate victims. Macabresque dramaturgy assumes many aesthetic forms, all designed to inflict hideous pain and humiliating punishments, sometimes in controlled environments such as torture "chambers," but also during frenzied moments of staged public horror. These kinds of applied performative violations permit perpetrators to revel in their absolute power, but, simultaneously, to project hatred, revenge, and revulsion onto their victims, who are reified and thus made to appear, at first in fantasy but eventually in ideological constructions, as the very incarnations of the shame, humiliation, and loss against which the perpetrators also seek to defend.

To specify the modalities of the macabresque, painful as the task most certainly is, is to pay homage to indescribable suffering, agony, and torment produced theatrically. Macabresque atrocity in performative transgression demonstrating surplus or sadistic cruelty includes displays of group massacres, occasionally involving group or collective burnings and public hangings; widespread geographic displacement; inhumane marches; inhuman treatment and degrading unsanitary conditions; the brutal separation of families; attacks against the elderly, women and children, against parents, against members of families forced to witness the violations against other family members; coerced victim laughter during instances of intrafamilial torture; ritualized dismemberment; disemboweling before family witnesses; confinement in starvation camps; forced labor; momentum killings, sometimes frenzied, occasionally ritualized, seemingly spontaneous yet often the result of premeditated execution; public hangings; group incineration; victims digging their own graves before their mass execution; various forms of performed enactment and reenactment of the power over life and death by means of staged inflictions of pain and "slow" suffering; lurid, lewd, and lethal forms of victimization display; mechanisms and methods to humiliate and to humiliate absolutely, such as bodily exposure and brutal nudity before moments of ritualized death; sexual violation, abuse, and mutilation; systematic torture using a range of instruments and methodologies; forced release of alive victims from airplanes; simulated forms of "etiquette" or

"propriety" to induce victim agony; during torture, the juxtaposition of cultural artifacts, such as the presence of music, religious, or culturally recognized symbolic artifacts, in scenes involving depraved forms of cruelty; shared semantic euphemisms that
refer to the victims, means, or instruments of their torment, in a series of vernacular or
slang terms in order to suffuse the dramaturgy of transgression with the "spirit" of sar-
donic/derisive irony.

The macabresque assumes aesthetic form by means of language, the language of euphemistic reification. These performative processes define the very nature of the macabresque: its aesthetics, its theatricality, its frenzy, its ferocity—all to drain the blood of
sufferers, whose participation in the agonies of their own transgression becomes the
mark of macabresque violation. Daniel Jonah Goldhagen, in his study of eliminationist
practices, states "cruelty is a common feature of eliminationist assaults. Cruelty is also
an enormously significant aspect of them. It is significant foremost because the victims
endure violence and suffering at their tormentors' hands. It is also significant because its
perpetration tells us much about the perpetrators. Yet such cruelty remains little analyzed
and poorly understood." Later he adds, "When a person's task is to kill someone, he need
not gratuitously beat, torture, or degrade that person first. He need not take initiative to
augment her suffering. Yet perpetrators routinely do, so much so that just in the killing
act itself in one of the eliminationist assaults where it is most frequently said the perpetrators were conscripted and had no choice, the perpetrators subjected an amazingly high
percentage of the victims to enormous gratuitous cruelty and suffering."[1]

Macabresque practices attack victims by means of systematic campaigns of depersonalization that include, for example, elimination of the distinguishing marks of human
faciality. Victims discover themselves in the macabresque by recognizing the "faceless-
ness," the namelessness, of their condition. Often, they hide from each other in the very
shamefulness of defacialized anonymous existence. Ruth Minsky Sender recounts her
experience of defacialization in Auschwitz as follows: "We walk hurriedly into the huge
barrack. It is filled with triple-decker bunks. On most decks lie five shriveled bodies with
hungry, horror-stricken eyes . . . a strange mass of weird-looking creatures, wrapped in
rags, barefooted, with shaven heads and eyes bulging from hunger, horror, bewilderment."[2] This sense of shame and humiliation lingered even after the liberation of the
camp, as the liberators confessed, "When you see them, there's nothing to distinguish
them, you know. Shaved heads and sunken cheeks. There's no way. It's hard to even
see them as human. Under the circumstances you try to avoid seeing them too much."[3]
Another Holocaust survivor, remembering her liberation, confessed:

> The soldiers came up to the fence and just stood there, looking at us. I couldn't
> understand their behavior at all . . . but then I saw one of the soldiers double over and
> throw up. Soon another was doing the same and then another. And then I under-
> stood. They were looking at us in disgust. A deep despair came over me. I felt like
> Adam when he first knew he was naked, horrible and ashamed. I looked around

me and saw myself and the other prisoners for the first time through the eyes of those soldiers. We were disgusting to look at, no doubt about it . . . a moment after that first soldier threw up a strange thing happened among the prisoners. We began turning away from them. We turned our backs to them; we didn't want them to see us.[4]

This speaks to the fundamental character of shame, the yearning to hide, to run away from the body and the self and to escape under a mask of anonymity, that is, of depersonalized identity.

Defacialization and namelessness demonstrate the linkages between depersonalization and the dynamics of shame and humiliation in influencing the cast given to surplus or sadistic cruelties in the macabresque. Primo Levi poetically described the mortification of fellow prisoners as a process of transforming the sense of body and name into the null experience of being but a number, "*Null Achtzehn*. He is not called anything except that, Zero Eighteen, the last three figures of his entry number; as if everyone was aware that only a man is worthy of a name, and that *Null Achtzehn* is no longer a man. I think that even he has forgotten his name."[5] Anne Applebaum's history of the Soviet Gulag similarly explains that

throughout the Gulag's existence, the prisoners always reserved a place at the very bottom of the camp hierarchy for the dying—or rather, for the living dead . . . a whole sub-dialect of camp slang was invented to describe them . . . most often they were called *dokhodyagi* . . . put simply, the *dokhodyagi* were starving to death . . . in the final stages . . . [they] took on a bizarre and inhuman appearance, becoming the physical fulfillment of the dehumanizing rhetoric used by the state: in their dying days, enemies of the people ceased, in other words, to be people at all.[6]

Arne Johan Vetlesen, in his analysis of "collective evildoing" writes:

Corporeal torment, therefore, "aims at the obliteration of the subjectivity of the subject . . . at the elimination of all powers of agency . . . at absolutizing the power of the torturer by way of silencing the voice and crushing the world . . . that used to belong to the victim now demonstrably reduced to sheer animality."[7]

Giorgio Agamben describes the ultimate victims as those who lose the will to survive and surrender to despair, anguish, and hopelessness. They are the *Muselmann*, the "living dead" who have experienced "desubjectification."[8]

The curse of such dying is to make death its own blessing. This is made all the more incomprehensible, however, like a death scream too quiet to hear, for its non-utilitarian or end-in-itself character. This is the macabresque in political evil: decreative dramaturgical spaces plied with the blood and skin, the bones and flesh of sufferers who are made to agonize death (and life) <u>by experiencing the agonies of dying performatively—for</u> <u>the "enjoyment" of perpetrators</u>. The catacombs of torment, agony, torture, and death "decreate" an aesthetics of surplus cruelty by means of performative transgression as an end in itself. There are many such theaters, and they appear, by definition, wherever political evil arises. The communal suffocations of the gas showers in Nazi killing camps and vans represent the prototypical case. To bear witness to the pain and suffering, it becomes necessary to state that to those made to breathe Xyklon B, death did not come instantaneously or even quickly. Death came, but in durations experienced as endless, a sequence of minutes ticking slowly in units of unlimited pain, by levels of excruciation that evince the essences, literally, of crucifixion—that is, a slow dying by asphyxiation. As in other killing camps, one hears the dying gasps of others as one gasps one's own final breaths. Performative transgression is not cruelty, pure and simple; it is cruelty of a special kind, in how sufferers are made to die by means of sadistic supplements obscenely applied to the bodies of victims, whose beings must be violated so that their very personhood is degraded. This is the "surplus" in surplus cruelty, and it is an essential element in the overall designs and specific aims of the perpetrators of the macabresque. Every instance is both calamity and catastrophe, a turning point that leaves catacoustic echoes resounding in the resonances of memory.

Each calls forth the historic obligation to memorialize and understand, a task fraught with critical problems and issues. Inga Clendinnen, for one, writes of "the Gorgon effect," the nauseating sensations, weaknesses of imagination that deplete the capacity to analyze perpetrators' actions. With bewilderment, she recounts numerous stories of obscene violation and surplus cruelty. She enters a kind of dialogue with Primo Levi's attempt to understand the macabresque theatricality of Nazi guards, "this choreography of their creation, the dance of dead men." Methodologically, she places the problematic of performative transgression into an analytical frame focused on "what it does" for perpetrators. "For the historian," she writes, "such participatory rituals are most usefully thought about as texts-in-performance; and these acted texts . . . are invaluable, because they are . . . the heart-made creation of whatever group it is we are trying to understand."[9] In the specific case of the guards in Nazi concentration camps, she underscores the role of staged performance and theatricality during the prewar Nuremburg rallies. "Even the most brutish of the SS had played their parts in the mass theater of party rallies and national celebrations," she writes. "They had been sensitized to the transformative power of theatre long before their arrival at the camps, and they brought that predilection with them. . . . Theater was everywhere in Auschwitz."[10] She describes the ritualized brutalities and choreographed beatings to ponder why punitive theatricality was so central, constant, and unremittingly present given the docility of the inmates in the face of overwhelming force. Her analysis stresses the extent to which <u>Nazi camp guards were fully immersed in the dramaturgical</u> aesthetics of death and dying: <u>the theatricality of performative transgression reflected in</u> their desires for <u>"glamour" and for "self-image" among themselves</u>. <u>Transgressive theatricality provided a space to "enjoy" group self-deception on the part of perpetrators,</u> one that allowed them to participate collectively in the social fantasies of their own making. Clendinnen observes:

> These pieces of SS theatre, constructed and enacted daily, reanimated the SS sense of high purpose and invincibility, authenticated the realism of their absurd ideology, and sustained both morale and self-image in what was, indubitably but inadmissibly, psychologically a hardship post.

The surplus cruelty exerted on the bodies and spirits of victims appeased the guards' desire to share in each other's desire. Desire for commonality in desire propelled surplus cruelty forward among the ranks of perpetrators, who perceived (or tried to see) in each other the same ardent supererogatory or heroic desire that they wanted to believe kept them together—but which also set them apart. So the allures of noir ecstasy had to be revitalized in spectacles of ghoulish horror. Clendinnen adds:

> I would further claim that the excitements of those enactments and entertainments worked to maintain the glamour still attaching to their gruesome calling, and that the manic theatricality imposed on inmates was primarily addressed not to its cowering audience, but to its SS impresarios.[11]

Cruelty in the macabresque theaters of performative transgression is always a *surplus*, always beyond strategic necessity, because it originates in the perpetrators' unconscious and disordered desires. Slavoj Žižek comments on Nazi "surplus enjoyment" as a case in point. He states that contrary to Nazi calls for rough but cool discipline, "the relationship between the two levels, the text of the public ideology and its 'obscene' superego supplement, remained fully operative."[12] The macabresque of performative transgression came to serve as a kind of "dirty" secret. The purpose was to shield from view the noir ecstasy the Nazi guards sought by means of comedic ritualizing of administrative routines to the point of victim agony. "This fact not only posed no obstacle to the execution of the Holocaust—it precisely served as its libidinal support, since the very awareness that 'we are all together in it' . . . served as a 'cement' to the Nazi collective coherence."[13] Theaters exist for the enjoyment of the audiences and participants; theaters of performative transgression are no different. Noir ecstasy in the macabresque seeks its own set of enjoyments that conceal the sources of desiring from those who are the desiring subjects, the perpetrators themselves. Žižek hints at this when he comments, "It was precisely this 'transgressive' character" that contradicted the explicit norms of Nazi propaganda that "accounted for the 'surplus-enjoyment' one got from excessively torturing the victims."[14] Shame may have resulted, but "this shame was the unmistakable sign of the excess of *enjoyment* they got from their acts."[15] Enjoyment refers not to mere or simple pleasure but to obscene *surplus* enjoyment, obscene for being in psychic contact with what is forbidden.

Herein lies the noir ecstasy, the lust that connects desire for what is prohibited to the strictures that demand desires be fulfilled precisely because they are forbidden. As Žižek declares, "Power thus relies on an obscene supplement—that is to say, the obscene 'nightly' law (superego) necessarily accompanies, as its shadowy double, the 'public law.'"[16] The macabresque aesthetics in performative transgression seek to satisfy the quest for noir ecstasy by giving way to obscene desire for surplus cruelty as a mode of coming near to what is openly forbidden—but secretly obliged or demanded. This is the beginning of an understanding of political perversity and its relationship to sadism, so much to the core of the macabresque aesthetics of surplus cruelty in performative transgression. And the critical dimension is shame, the shamefulness of shame in the psychodynamics of the macabresque manifested so brutally by perpetrators in their drive to humiliate victims.

LICENSE FOR MASS ATROCITY ON A SMALL AS WELL AS LARGE SCALE

Here I develop a psychosocial framework to suggest that desire inheres in a willfulness that seeks to lend "positivity" to the negativity of psychic absence or emptiness that Lacanian theory situates at the center of human personality. Macabresque theatricality sustains the illusions and willful self-deceptions of existential meaning in the political reifications of collective purity (social or ethnic exclusivism) and absolute freedom (state supremacism). But this occurs on the pyres of a psychic abyss, ones seemingly attached to disordered demand for supererogatory self-sacrifice and heroism to satisfy unconscious desires for what, ultimately, is unattainable. In this sense, the macabresque demonstrates the psychodynamics of a kind of metaphysical eschatology, giving way to what Aristotle Kallis has described as the "license" for frenzied cruelty. Such license lends concrete release to the psychic drama of macabresque desires. The macabresque thus assumes dramaturgical elements for purposes of the surplus obscene enjoyment of perpetrators even for those acting as spectators, literally, witnesses to the spectacle of torment and agony.

MACABRESQUE SITES OF PERFORMATIVE TRANSGRESSION

Kallis's political history of genocide and fascism emphasizes the "license" to hate and "license" to kill. His stress on the combinations of the transgressive and the performative, specifically, in the murderous campaigns pursued by *Einsatzgruppen* troops in the East European occupied states between 1941 and 1944, is highly suggestive. It applies the concept of "frenzy" as a unit of analysis to illustrate the role and influence of desire in the psychodynamics of macabresque theatricality. In particular, it moves the focus beyond the extermination camps to demonstrate how performative transgression operates "in open air." Kallis stresses the sense of total release and abandon, the ecstatic sensations of ritualized horror that transform mass slaughter into what he calls, borrowing Bakhtin's term, the "carnivalesque." In the process, surplus cruelty devolves into the macabresque of performative theatricality for the purposes of staging a calamitous moment in political time that permits corporeal violation without limits or controls, a surrender to political evil for the sheer transgressive obscenity of it, sometimes witnessed and often applauded by crowds. Kallis writes, for example, "This format of discharging violence created an exceptional psychological space where ritual, transgression, and the anonymity of the crowd produced the illusion of an extraordinary experience of unbound permissibility, governed by the emphatic lapse of conventional norms." Surplus cruelty became regularized, routinized by the ritualized carnival, temporary in its moment, but momentous in its power. "During these rituals taboos could be broken and new borderline ('liminal') moral spaces could be accessed for a finite period of time and only in the context of ritualized action."[17]

Such "moral spaces" represent the theaters of performative transgression in which the supererogatory sadomasochism of perpetrators is revealed in and by means of their surplus cruelty. Their aim, their desire, is to suspend time so that the agonies of death and dying can be prolonged, sustained by methods and levels of unspeakable cruelty, to heighten the perverse "enjoyment" of the macabre spectacle for the witnessing audiences and crowds, but most of all for the sadistic enjoyment of the participating perpetrators themselves.

> Depending of [*sic*] the situation and nature of the *Aktionen*, Jews, Poles, and Romani were tortured and humiliated by their guards, forced to perform perverse rituals and ridicule their customs, hit with rifle butts or wooden sticks, dismembered and paraded. Crushed skulls would sometimes be preserved by members of the auxiliary police members as proud mementos and prizes from the executions. Some of these rituals would last for many hours or even days, or would be repeated with chilling regularity over a period of time.[18]

Clues regarding the disordered, akratic, and unconscious motivations of perpetrators derive from such demands that victims perform rituals of utter humiliation and in doing so ridicule their own cultural mores or traditions before they die. Perpetrator depravity has nothing to do with strategic political objectives but everything to do with perverse, indeed, disordered will and desire. And what is wanted most of all is that the victims participate in their own demise and degradation as a practice in the sport of humiliation.

Kallis speaks of the frenzy that gripped the cadres of perpetrators as they swept through Eastern Europe under the deathly aegis of Nazi commanders. But the phenomenon becomes transmogrified according to place, time, and culture. At certain times and under specific conditions, macabresque violence attacks victims using ideologically constructed grounds of political, ideological, and identitarian reifications as justification. "Rage, license, and performance created a continuum of murderous violence, in which horrendous excesses were legitimized by their public enactment and entire groups were reduced to a loathsome subhuman form of existence that ostensibly justified more—and more extreme—violence."[19] A kind of spectrum emerges in which various instances of performative transgression appear to unroll in the momentum of greater and greater frenzy.

Frenzy in the Macabresque of the Guatemalan Civil War (1960–1996)

The macabresque in frenzied cruelty represents the definitive character of savage violence by the Guatemalan government against its Mayan indigenous peoples. As in the Sri Lankan Civil War and the Timorese war of independence mercilessly suppressed by the Indonesian paramilitary Kopassus, the context was set by the Guatemalan Civil War, fought between 1960 and 1996, in which government forces committed genocidal atrocities against the Mayan population and widespread, gross violations of human and civil rights. The victims of the governmental onslaught, presumed to be leftist and subversive, included politicians in opposition, social movement activists, trade union representatives, academics and students, journalists, religionists, and slum children; but most of all, it targeted indigenous Mayan and Ladino peasants. The Guatemalan Commission for Historical Clarification (Comisión para el Esclarecimiento Histórico [CEH]) in its final report, "Guatemala Memoria del silencio" ("Guatemala: Memory of Silence"), published in 1999, estimated that of the hundreds of massacres perpetrated by Guatemalan military and paramilitary armed forces, the vast majority (by some estimates nearly 400) occurred in rural Mayan villages between late 1981 and 1983, including in such village areas as Chajul, Nebaj, and Ixcan in the Franja Transversal del Norte, as well as in such villages as El Quiche. It is estimated that tens of thousands of children lost at least one parent to the violence perpetrated by the army and in the province of El Quiche. The armed organizations that perpetrated the mass atrocities included military and counterinsurgency forces, death squads, special commando units, and the National and Treasury Police, all under governmental control, as well as landowners deputized with police functions.[20] The direct role of the central government in the war against its own citizens was underscored during the 2013 trial and conviction of former Guatemalan president Efrain Rios Montt for the murder and forced disappearances of approximately 1,400 indigenous Ixil Mayans during his time in office, between 1982 and 1983. During Montt's tenure, the macabresque reached its saturation point in the course of deadly and brutal military "pacification" campaigns against the Mayans, including Victoria 82 and Operation Sofia. Montt's trial represents a landmark in the history of international transitional justice in that it was first time a former head or chief of state had been tried in domestic courts for crimes of genocide. This stands as a precedent, though his initial conviction was overturned on the grounds of judicial technicalities.

In all, the Guatemalan Civil War accounts for the loss of approximately 200,000 lives. Additionally, the CEH reported that human rights violations perpetrated against [ethnic Mayans] demostrat[ed] an *aggressive racist component* of *extreme cruelty* that led to the *extermination en masse* of defenseless Mayan communities purportedly linked to the guerrillas—including children, women, and the elderly—through methods whose cruelty has outraged the moral conscience of the civilized world . . . these massacres and so-called scorched earth operations, *as planned by the State* . . . [and] *committed by agents of the State, especially members of the Army,* resulted in the *complete extermination* of many Mayan communities, along with their homes, cattle, crops, and other elements essential to survival.[21]

The Commission concluded that the massacres against the Mayan peoples between 1981 and 1983 constituted "acts of genocide" in which there was "evidence of . . . savagery which preceded, accompanied, or occurred after the deaths of victims."[22] Massacres included

the killing of defenseless children, often by beating them against walls or throwing them alive into pits where corpses of adults were later thrown; the amputation of limbs; the impaling of victims; the killing of persons by covering them in petrol and burning them alive; the extraction, in the presence of others, of the viscera of victims who were still alive; the confinement of people who had been mortally tortured, in agony for days; the opening of the wombs of pregnant women, and other similar atrocious acts.[23]

Atrocities included mass rape. This is the macabresque in the lurid detail of *inhuman* violation done in a frenzy, village to village, throughout the Guatemalan highlands. The shift from collective violence to human violation is detected in the escalation of death and the performativity of violation, year after year, from selected killings to scorched earth, from mass murder to making victims become witness to the desecration of family members, from sporadic campaigns to the devastation of entire regions, massacre after massacre, in unrelenting waves of sheer sadistic cruelty.

A major feature of the macabresque of the Guatemalan genocide were the systematic disappearances of persons. This came to be a core feature of the macabresque imposed during the Argentinean "Dirty War," described in chapter 6 and during the military dictatorship of Chile during the period 1973–1990. The Guatemalan government is acknowledged to have been the first to initiate widespread forced disappearances of citizens, numbering between 40,000 to 50,000 over the course of the war. The Guatemalan judicial system is also the first to have tried and convicted a former official, Felipe Cusanero, of the crime of ordering the forced disappearances.

And yet there remains a further dimension to the macabresque, <u>the violating of what persons hold dearest and making them complicit in such crimes</u>. Cultural desecration paralleled the physical atrocity leveled at individuals and individual families in village communities.

> The Army destroyed [Mayan] ceremonial centers, sacred places, and cultural symbols . . . language and dress, as well as other elements of cultural identification, were targets of repression . . . the legitimate authority structure of the communities was broken; the use of their own norms and procedures to regulate social life and resolve conflicts was prevented; the exercise of Mayan spirituality and the Catholic religion was obstructed, prevented, or repressed; the maintenance and development of the indigenous peoples' way of life and their system of social organization was upset . . . displacement and refuge exacerbated the difficulties of practicing their own culture.[24]

In many instances, soldiers forcibly removed villagers from their homes. As Greg Grandin observes, this devastated "the highland's agricultural cycle, leading to hunger and widespread deprivation."[25] Grandin adds that on this basis the CEH report concluded that the genocidal campaign against the Mayan peoples unfolded "not as state decomposition but state formation, a carefully calibrated stage in the military's plan to establish national stability through an incorporation of Mayan peasants into government institutions and a return to constitutional rule." But one must wonder about the relationship of such means to such ends. The physical pain and spiritual abuse suffered will be remembered as part of the corrosive guilt and shame Mayan victims were made to experience. Perpetrators of the Guatemalan genocide, as well as in other instances of the macabresque, acted to ensure that victims were humiliated to the point of degradation by forcing them to act in ways that were *supportive* of the violations against what they loved or valued most in the world: other family members, cherished friends, treasured principles.

This places the meaning of the concept of "frenzy" into a different analytical perspective. This underscores the design in the frenzy at the core of the macabresque to make victims experience not only violence but a sense of self-violation that derives from the admixtures of guilt and shame in self-betrayal. And shame is critical here as distinct from guilt; for guilt arises from something one has done; in the present case, shame emerges from something one is and, as a result, *could not do*—to protect or defend. Diane M. Nelson, in her study of the Guatemalan genocide and its aftermath, describes this process when she writes, "This is further complicated in Guatemala by the war's mixing of the public theaters of cruelty with the enforced privatization of pain and guilt."[26] She adds, "The massive repression—leaving whole villages, along with those who didn't flee, in smoking ruins and dumping tortured bodies in public spaces . . . taught private repression. Keep the secrets, never speak out. It made every witness a collaborator, especially when they could do nothing to save the victim." This is suggestive of the primary aim of the macabresque—not merely to attack the body of victims but also to assail their psychic and emotional spirit by making them feel *guilty on account of the shame of self-betrayal*, despite their innocence and inability to act against the onslaughts of frenzied sadistic cruelty perpetrated by armed military and paramilitary forces. That this is the case helps to explain why the macabresque emerges during instances of genocide and mass atrocity. It is designed to devastate victims from the inside out, as it were, by making them feel shame for who they are as much as for what they do. As Nelson concludes, "Guilt and horror paralyzingly combine."[27]

This dynamic is hardly unique to Guatemala and its mostly Mayan peasant victims. The attempt to force victims into actions that foment their sense of having betrayed themselves runs across the entire history of the macabresque throughout the twentieth century. Stalin, Mao, Pol Pot, and members of the Argentinean junta, as we shall see, were among its masters. Foucault has written, "The body is . . . directly involved in a political field; power relations have an immediate hold upon it; they invest it, mark it, train it, torture it, force it to carry out tasks, to perform ceremonies, to emit signs."[28] Perhaps it is to mark the body with power, a power that forces the body of the violated to betray the self and the beloved. This becomes central to the macabresque. Agamben refers to the *thanatopolitics*, or the politics of death. In being forced into the moral doom of a nightmare of self-betrayal, victims are made to experience thanatopolitics under the conditions of deepest desecration, the inversion of morality and ethical love into the instrumentalities of self-annihilation.

Frenzy in the Macabresque of the Military Dictatorship of Chile (1973–1990)

Complicity with evil is evil, and the United States bears a historic burden of responsibility for supporting the overthrow of the democratically elected government of Salvador Allende, on September 11, 1973, and for aiding the installation of a military junta and dictatorship headed by General Augusto Pinochet. The dramatic events following the coup immediately took on the cast of frenzy in the macabresque: mass murder; large-scale arrests; concentration of prisoners; and the systematic deployment of depraved techniques of torture and thus the infliction of grotesque suffering on citizens, who were often bound together while they were being tortured—but who were guilty of nothing except political commitment to democratic processes and dialogue. Mass atrocity erupted during the initial months of the regime, but the macabresque lingered until its end. For the seventeen years the junta ruled Chile, all democratic institutions, civic rights, and civil protections were nonexistent. Several thousand victims vanished. In a formulation that arose, victims were said to become "made to disappear"—that is, being made to join the ranks of the "mysteriously" vanished, the *desaparecidos*. Chilean citizens were summarily rounded up and detained, imprisoned, interrogated, and tortured at sites of the macabresque: in the Victor Jara Stadium, on the ship *Esmeralda*, and at many other satellite detention and torture centers, including the notorious Colonia Dignidad. Tens of thousands were displaced from Chile in a purification process that sent them into Argentina and other state jurisdictions under a cloud of criminal suspicion from which they could and did not escape.

Once mass atrocity began, the identities of citizens became classified by the regime in accordance with a taxonomic social system that had been politically constructed not merely to divide but for purposes of onslaught as well. The Pinochet regime, in this regard, applied a quasi-legal technique. Many of the passports of those leaving Chile became "blacklisted" with the letter *L*, standing for *lista nacional*. The consequence for the exiled individuals involved was cross-border surveillance by secret police maintained by the Chilean government in conjunction with several other Latin American dictator-ships, in what is known as Operation Condor.

Fascist regimes tend to convert the values of liberty and freedom into totalized ver-sions of sacred truth. The macabresque perpetrated by the Pinochet regime against the Chilean nation was unique in its ideological tenor that turned economic philos-ophy into a state religion in order to justify all manner and forms of human viola-tion. The Pinochet regime uniquely pursued a neoliberal agenda as justification for mass atrocity. Its libertarianism advocated the values of market exchange and systems, free enterprise, and private property. Its nemesis or mimetic rival was anyone of a presumed socialist or left-leaning persuasion whom the junta chose to reify as devils incarnate. The result was that economic "truth" quickly became the device of politi-cal fiction. To defend economic freedom, the junta destroyed political liberty in the name of supply-side economics that were now transformed into immutable if not, indeed, metaphysical significance. Perhaps for these reasons, former British prime minister Margaret Thatcher supported Pinochet to the very end of his life. Certainly for such reasons, several members of the American economic profession associated with neoliberalism and free-market reform participated in the transformations of the Chilean economy at the very behest of the regime. Once economic policy became applied as a form of political religion, however, the gates of Chilean society opened to the evils of the macabresque.

Frenzy in the Macabresque of the Sri Lankan Civil War (1983–2009)

Frenzy is a crowd phenomenon, a kind of stampede that feeds on transgressive impulses to destroy limits defined by what is prohibited. It tends to snowball into larger and larger fulminations against the "other," and it leads to compulsive forms of violence, at once intense and, at other times, quiescent, but always at the trigger's edge of inhuman brutal-ity. It demonstrates a capacity for hatred embedded in envy and mimetic rivalry that seeks the annihilation of the other, an aim that defies both reason and reasonableness. What is "willed" is the death of the "other," in particular, the demise of the culture of the "other."

This includes destruction of any cultural form and all that is representative of the social groups that appear to "relativize" perpetrators' cultural, social, and political status or that threaten imminent loss of territory and thus diminution of what is deemed as integral to "the body politic." Especially virulent in this context is the attempt to secede in a war of liberation or separation, one combining ethnic or cultural distinctions with threats to the "integrity" of the settled boundaries of a sovereign state.

These factors were present during the Sri Lankan Civil War, a conflict waged over the establishment of an independent Tamil state, called Tamil Eelam, in the north and east of the island, between the Singhalese majority and Tamil minority, beginning in July 1983 and lasting twenty-six years. On May 17, 2009, the Sri Lankan Ministry of Defense finally announced the end of armed conflict.[29] The war was fought over the course of several phases that witnessed intense violence, efforts at mediation, retaliations over attacks, and resumptions of the intense violence. These phases included the initial outbreak, which witnessed brutal massacres, assassinations, and attacks on cultural artifacts; it was succeeded by Eelam War II (1990–1995) and the Eelam War III, which ended in the defeat of the Tamil insurrection. War, especially civil war, begets mass atrocity and this was clearly demonstrated throughout the Sri Lankan Civil War. The United Nations has estimated that from 80,000 to 100,000 people were killed during 1982–2009, more than half of them noncombatant civilians. The final months of the war, between January and May 2009, were among the deadliest; the numbers of people killed are still in dispute. That the mass atrocities committed at that time represented a frenzy of macabresque proportions is not in doubt.

Mass atrocities were perpetrated by both Tamil paramilitary and terrorist organizations as well as by the Sri Lankan military, which was dominated by Sinhala combatants. In mid-September 2015, the United Nations Human Rights Council called for the establishment of a special tribunal to bring to justice those responsible for Sri Lankan war crimes, in which it alleged that both sides had committed war crimes. Domestic efforts in Sri Lanka to impanel a truth and reconciliation commission have been sporadically underway, along with increasing recognition that former president Mahinda Rajapaksa, his brother, the former defense minister Gotabaya Rajapaksa, and other members of the family should not enjoy immunity from prosecution. Although Sri Lankan government forces and the Liberation Tigers of Tamil Eelam (LTTE, aka the Tamil Tigers) were each culpable of crimes against humanity, major human rights agencies have declared that the Sri Lankan army, navy, and air force engaged in "state terrorism" against Tamil civilians, supporters, and sympathizers.[30] The depth and extent of the violations against Tamil civilians and the ways in which violence was perpetrated are indicative of a form of the macabresque gripped by a frenzied release of contempt and hatred seen as justification for sustained human violation. Tamil victims have testified that Sri Lankan military forces and government-backed paramilitary organizations perpetrated mass atrocities, including the indiscriminate shelling of Tamil communities; aerial bombardments of schools, hospitals, and Tamil homes;

forcible conscription of child soldiers into their ranks; mass rape of Tamil women and forced abortion; widespread displacement of Tamil families; and torture and rape of Tamil refugees in the camps established for civilians fleeing war zones. In July 1983, memorialized as "Black July," frenzied violence carried out by Sinhala mobs killed at least four hundred Tamils, destroyed tens of thousands of houses, and initiated a diasporic "scattering" of Tamil's populations.

What was peculiar to the macabresque of the Sri Lankan Civil War, however, was the central government's deployment of military forces, weapons, and attacks against civilians in villages or in specially demarcated areas such as safe zones. Assault weapons, anti-personnel mines, rocket-propelled missiles, aerial bombardments, and the like represent the instrumentalities by which collective violence gradually, but seemingly inexorably, shifted into the outrages of human violation. The frenzy was clear under conditions of war and armed conflict. The battle was under control of the central government, which still chose to use the macabresque against Tamil citizens to make them pay the price for the violence wrought in their name, whether they sought it or not.

Sexual Violation in the Democratic Republic of the Congo and in the Darfur of South Sudan

No act, no form of violence, no kind of human violation combines the frenzy of brutal violence with lingering ravages of guilt and self-revulsion in the aftermath of human violation more than rape; and no population has been more subjected to this form of horrific abuse and humiliation than the people of the Democratic Republic of the Congo and of the southern Sudanese region of Darfur. Rape as an instrumentality of genocide destroys belief in life, in the courage of personality, and in a genderized self. Such suffering also corrodes cultural, social, or communal bonding, any sense of collective belonging. Mass atrocity targets natality as an expression of male womb envy and dread of the feminine. Perpetrators of macabresque transgression in mass atrocity attack women: women as mothers, as potential mothers, and as pregnant mothers in waiting. They do so by targeting the reproductive organs of victims or by means of barbaric and inhuman treatment of fetuses and the newly born, or both.

In Darfur, survivors testified that the *Janjawiid* "targeted women with sexual violence . . . rape was so ubiquitous that it appeared to be an instrument of policy to destroy the fabric of the targeted communities and perhaps even to create a new generation with 'Arab' paternity." Some observers go on to suggest that "these rapes are . . . orchestrated to create a dynamic where the African tribal groups are destroyed . . . they want to make Arab babies . . . It's systematic.'" Sadistic violation of female fecundity and capacities for neonatal caregiving is perpetrated in the Eastern Congo in ways that recalibrate depictions of how obscene surplus cruelty operates. In 2003, for example, a survivor reported that she was "forced to watch rebels kill and eat two of her children."[31] In some cases "vital organs were . . . cut off and used as magic charms . . . ethnic Hema children were thrown onto arrows stuck in the ground."[32] A corroborating UN report indicated that victims were butchered so that their organs could be harvested and force fed to members of their families.[33] Across the many cases of political evil, defilement of a person's (mostly but not exclusively of women's) sexuality, the utter debasement of even the will or spiritual freedom to experience physical intimacy and to do so without dread, represents the repeated subtext of performative transgression in mass atrocity.

Rape in the DRC has become so prevalent and common that healthcare providers treating survivors conclude that it is "a cheap, simple weapon for all parties in the war . . . designed to exterminate the population."[34] The normalization of the rape perpetrated by a number of paramilitary groups has been a predominating form of macabresque violation, especially in the eastern regions including North Kivu and South Kivu, and Province Oriental. One study provides a taxonomy of rape in the DRC that depicts variations with respect to the cultural and socioeconomic contexts wherever it is perpetrated, with significant consequences for the victims. Patricia Rozee distinguishes rape in the DRC as follows: "primitive rape," used for purposes of control or punishment, or to enforce silence in its aftermath; "status rape," used to humiliate the victim based on presumed "rank" or status; "ceremonial rape," perpetrated as part of socially prescribed or tolerated rituals; "exchange rape," when intimate contact is used as an instrument of economic or social bargaining; "theft rape," or involuntary sexual abduction or enslavement or both; "prostitution and survival rape" used by victims without access to the resources necessary to sustain their lives.[35] Rape violence against women, men, and children has attained pandemic proportions in the past fifteen years. According to some accounts, no less than a quarter of the male population and nearly 65 percent of children reported that at some point they had been exposed to some form of sexual violence. As a senior researcher for Human Rights Watch reports:

> Rape is the norm . . . what's different in Congo is the scale and the systematic nature of it, indeed, as well, the brutality. This is not rape because soldiers have got bored and have nothing to do. It is a way to ensure that communities accept the power and authority of that particular armed group. This is about showing terror. This is about using it as a weapon of war.[36]

A director of Panzi Hospital in Eastern Congo has suggested that rape is "a show of force, of power . . . done to destroy the person . . . [In the Congo] sex is being used to commit evil."[37] Victims suffer depression, anxiety, insomnia, and despair, often compounded by physical mutilation: "crippled or missing limbs, blindness, damaged or destroyed internal organs and/or genitals, and sexually transmitted disease."[38] Moreover, rape in the Congo is so brutal, so violent, that tens of thousands of survivors[39] are too physically damaged to bear children. Such transgressive violations are often performative, as communal circles of communities are forced to witness violations of victims in efforts that are clearly aimed at their utter humiliation. This compounds the shame cast on victims in the aftermath. In traditional communities, where honor and shame represent prevailing values, rape erodes, even destroys, the status of women, making it impossible for them to ever again function with dignity. This, too, is the purpose of the macabresque in its dia-bolical aims to destroy communities: by leaving those who remain alive to suffer living death, *as if* it were their own fault.

RITUALIZED TRANSGRESSIONS OF RAGE AND FRENZY: TOWARD PSYCHOSOCIAL ANALYSIS

In studying mass atrocity, concepts such as perverse desire or sadistic cruelty are typi-cally applied devoid of theory; that is, they are applied as psychological terms without a psychology. I have suggested that surplus cruelty exerted theatrically by means of per-formative transgression represents an end sought by perpetrators on account of its own enticements. The absent explanatory dimension lies in perpetrator motivations driven by disorders of will. In unconscious ways, perpetrators willfully demand a kind of existential transcendence by "fraudulent" psychic means. Perpetrators may well yearn for a form of strange existential permanence and continuity in the face of finitude in bonding with each other through forgeries of "iron will." What perpetrators apparently seek is desire to share in desire, to share in shared desire with those of the same blood, race, and cultural or political identity, not for ideological reasons as such, but as an unconscious means of attaining transcendence beyond finitude and mortality. Kallis recognizes this when he observes that mass atrocity stands as "a ritual of perverse self-affirmation through the performative annihilation of 'the other.' "[40] Transgressive violations are vitalized macabr-esque theaters not intended for lascivious satisfaction alone, although obscene enjoyment and the search for noir ecstasy are ever present. The frenzy that Kallis depicts partially explains the stampeding, not only of crowds, but of perpetrators tempted into inhuman brutality in no small measure on account of the illusions of totalized gratification held together by the promise, in fantasy as well as ideology, that shared blood belonging is made possible through the commonalities of depraved honor. But blood bonding and honor exist only for as long as the "enemy," "the other," "the unwashed," and "impure" live. Frenzy is a mechanism of hatred and fraudulent purification of self and society charged by the animus stemming from envy and mimetic rivalry.

This is evidenced by the mimetic quality of noir ecstasy in the macabresque of perfor-mative transgression that was mimicked by the fascist legions in states occupied by the Nazis during the war and led to the successive official declarations of the statelessness of the Jews and other populations selected for concentration and extermination. Nazi-inspired transgressions became the model for perpetrators operating under the aegis of other national authorities. As Kallis points out, the Iron Guards of the Legionary State in Romania, for example, adopted the perverse performative techniques initially demon-strated by Nazi Einsatzkommando, "such as tying their victims to a column for hours or even days in full public view and dissecting them whilst still being alive."[41] During such instances of mass atrocity, the psychodynamics of desire appear to adhere to a repetitive claim to the right and obligation to display human violation in the ghoulish theatricality of the macabresque.

THINGS OF FANTASY/PHANTASY

To explain this requires a language and theoretical perspective focused ultimately on the psychodynamics of desire and envy, mimetic rivalry and cruelty, and on shame and humiliation—all relative to human violation in the macabresque. Sadistic cruelty in the macabresque reveals the dread in the social fantasy that the mimetic rival or the "other" will steal, rob, or tear asunder common capacities to know desire in blood and belonging. But this, too, is a substitute for a drive toward and against a sense of ultimate gratification stemming from what Lacan theorizes as *jouissance*, a psychic force that is tantalizing, even titillating, but also shocking and repulsive given its power to destroy the sense of individuation, even personality.[42] The more one has of *jouissance*, the closer one comes to it, the less one can bear or support it. For these reasons, the fundamental law or phantasy (as opposed to fantasy) in Lacanian theory underscores the primordial drives toward incestuous return to totalized security and the phallic prohibition, discussed in the next section, that represents the paternalized refusal or rejection to permit access to *jouissance*. This produces a primordial yearning in surrogacy for what Lacan calls *objet a*, that is, objects of desire alternative to *jouissance* comprising psychic modes of desire and desiring, not merely in terms of acquisition but, rather, in terms of subjectivation and human development.

Jouissance and *Objet A* of Fantasy

The fundamental fantasy will be traversed but in various ways and degrees. It leaves a residue from which "obscene supplements" emerge in Lacan's *objet a*. *Objet a* helps to shape infantile fantasy and influences various formats of social fantasy whenever it counters the dread of breakdown, disintegration, and, especially, loss. Fink describes *objet a* "as the *remainder* produced when that hypothetical unity breaks down, as the last trace of that unity, a last reminder thereof."[43] It is a remainder and a reminder that maintains its retentive capacity to attract the subject and to entice desire. "By cleaving to that rem(a)inder, the split subject, though expulsed . . . can sustain the illusion of wholeness: by clinging to object *a*, the subject is able to ignore his or her division." Fink also adds, "That is precisely what Lacan means by fantasy."[44] *Objet a* is the guide to the desire that offers the temptation to walk the path toward lost ecstasy and enchantment, in endless cycles of self-deception that hold out the possibilities not only of individuated wholeness but also of conjoined unity with "the Thing" that is the maternalizing principle, the barred signifier of the (m)Other. Arguably, in this reside the ideological and eschatological sources of the quest for the desire to give material form to ecstasy and rapturous enchantment;

the congenital reifications beholden to images of absolute purity and power; slavish obeisance to artifacts of charisma and sacrality; the sense of immortality through exclusivism and supremacism; and the lifelong yearning for return to *das Ding* or "the Thing."
Objet a readily turns toward desire as a block against *jouissance* and yet is chastened in
the process. *Objet a* thus represents the "play dough" of fantasy, to be manipulated and
enjoyed but also prohibited and thus feared. Fink observes that "the subject casts the
Other's desire in the role most exciting to the subject."[45] Excitement in fantasy is always
a double-edged sword; the pleasure and thrill to the excitement in fantasy is the other
side of the ever-present risk of theft and loss. An injunction to enjoy is always about
the compunction to resist and desist. Here again, we see the mediations between *objet
a* and *jouissance*. As Fink writes, "This pleasure—this excitation due to sex, seeing and/
or violence, whether positively or negatively viewed by conscience, whether considered
innocently pleasurable or disgustingly repulsive—is termed jouissance, and that is what
the subject orchestrates for him or herself in fantasy."[46] This represents a critical factor in
explaining the macabresque in genocide and mass atrocity. The psychodynamics of *jouissance* and *objet a* under conditions of mimetic rivalry and extreme anxiety over threatened social loss or political dissolution influences the disciples and disciplines of desire to
enter darker diabolical realms, where *objet a* travels psychically ever nearer emotionally to
the forbidden territories of lost ecstasy and proscribed enchantment. The macabresque
in political evil constitutes just such a forbidden realm, where sacrality turns in against
itself in frenetic fevers of dissolute narcissism and sadistic cruelty, all in the name of what
becomes unspeakable horror and ultimate sin against personhood.

    Violations of others begin to appear as lawful, once the legitimacy of law itself seems
threatened by the proximity of unwanted but desperately desired *jouissance*. In this regard,
Žižek observes, "Does not Lacan perform the same anamorphic shift of perspective in his
famous reversal of Dostoyevsky ('If there is no God, nothing at all is permitted') . . . in his
reversal of . . . Law as the agency which represses desire into (the concept of) Law as that
which effectively *sustains* desire?"[47] He continues, "The relationship between Law and its
transgression: far from undermining the rule of the Law, its 'transgression' in fact serves
as its ultimate support." Law and its transgression enter into a kind of psychically forged
fantasmatic conspiracy whenever social order is permeated by constructed images of loss,
lack, and depletion, especially those provoking sensations of shame and guilt. Žižek states
in this regard, "Law itself relies on its inherent transgression, so that when we suspend
this transgression, the Law itself disintegrates."[48] In such instances and under the right
circumstances, including political leadership, power constellations, and ideological reifications, the macabresque is never far removed. For his part, Kallis concludes:

> The combination of extreme scope of change, recurring order collapse, and very
> short intervening periods between those painful breakdowns (1917–20, 1939,
> 1941) embedded a particularly poisonous sense of transience and reversibility to
> any arrangement. This, in turn, sustained feelings of resentment and fed excessive

ambitions for recapturing pure, "cleansed" identities from the ruins of fractured historical space and time.[49]

For such reasons, it becomes necessary from a methodological standpoint to historicize applications of psychosocial interpretation in the study of genocide and mass atrocity. Thus the concept of the macabresque enters as a unit of analysis suggestive of a theoretical approach combining psychosocial analysis and exploration of the causes and dynamics of the macabresque that reside in reminiscences of times past and resentments of the present.

"THE GOOD OLD DAYS"

Many examples exist to demonstrate how collective violence becomes transformed into a dramaturgy of human violation, discussed briefly here and in greater detail in subsequent chapters, within the context of case studies of the macabresque. For the moment, I begin with an illustration, one among many that occurred across Eastern Europe and the Baltic region in such towns as Liepaja, Latvia, and the surrounding areas, in 1941–1942. So many public executions and mass murders happened here during this brief period that the region became widely "visited by scores of German spectators," giving rise to what came to be called "execution tourism."[50]

A volume entitled *The Good Old Days* (*Schone Zeiten*), a phrase lifted from Kurt Franz's personal memoir recalling his days as commandant of Treblinka, documents, with reference to letters, diaries, memoranda, and photographs mostly written by Germans, event after event when Jews were clubbed to death or hanged, but not before being forced to undress and then summarily murdered with firearms and dropped into "death trenches," in public and to the cheers and applause of the witnessing crowds. Hugh Trevor-Roper comments in the book's foreword, "The most horrible photographs, and some of the most horrible narratives, in this book record . . . massacres, especially those in the Baltic states [that] were carried out in public. In Kaunas, Lithuania, where Einsatzkommando 3 operated, the Jews were clubbed to death with crowbars, before cheering crowds, mothers holding up their children to see the fun, and German soldiers clustering around like spectators at a football match."[51] The sense of public entertainment was further enhanced by music. Trevor-Roper observed, "At the end, while the streets ran with blood, the chief murderer stood on the pile of corpses as a triumphant hero and played the Lithuanian national anthem on an accordion."[52] In reference to another typical event, a German officer wrote in his diary that in Zhitomir, Ukraine, "Soldiers were sitting on rooftops and platforms watching the show. The execution was arranged as a form of popular entertainment." Another witness wrote that vehicles on which loudspeakers were mounted had driven through Zhitomir, announcing that "Jews would be shot in the market-place or something to that effect."[53] Many similar accounts follow on these, underscoring the juxtaposition of brutality and glee, massacre and entertainment, executions and beatings taking place at close proximity, previously scheduled and publicly announced in their entirety for purposes of macabresque spectacle.

WHEN VIOLENCE IS NOT ENOUGH

Genocide and near-genocidal violence tend to spin out of war and major conflict, and they mostly entail domestic outbreaks of violence when governmental and quasi-governmental agents attack segments of their own civilian populations. The question I explore, therefore, concerns the ways in which this influences how mass atrocity becomes implemented. Answers focus on identity and the ways in which identities become "constructed" during periods of genocide and mass atrocity. Repeatedly, identities become "invented" to suit the ostensible political and strategic objectives of the perpetrators. This speaks to perpetrator disorders of will and mimetic desire. Such psychodynamics are released in the macabresque. A critical dimension of the macabresque is its exhibitionism, the fact that when genocide and mass atrocity unfold, the perpetrators set the stage for each other to witness their sadistic practices of humiliating their victims and making them suffer torture, torment, and agony.

To refer to this as the macabresque is not to endow it with the aura of imaginative inventiveness. On the contrary, there is a thuggish and unimaginative quality to the sadism of perpetrators across cultural domains. Watching victims suffer as they are killed transfixes how perpetrators see themselves and thus transforms their self-identity and identifications with each other. I explore this from various vantage points, including the cultural, political, social, psychological, and psychosocial. Voyeuristic exhibitionism, shame, and humiliation play major roles in how the macabresque becomes executed.

The question next arises as to the explanatory perspectives relevant to an analysis of the reasons. Questions thus arise about the analytical "fit" between topic and method in examining the psychodynamics of desire as a contributing factor in cases of genocide and mass atrocity. As a response, let us follow the lead suggested by a series of clues. Together, these help to establish the relevance of psychosocial perspectives applied to cases of extreme violence in political contexts in which genocide and mass atrocity occur as a consequence of perpetrators acting, sometimes under orders as military personnel or as members of organized paramilitary forces, including security police, but at other times, as civilians who are all too willing to lend a helping hand, without glimmers of mercy or compassion, in implementing extreme systematic human violation.

Clues relate to the frequency of the phenomenon. Genocide and mass atrocity are not "sometime things." To the contrary, they represent a pandemic scourge, one that happens almost wherever the cartographies of political power or state sovereignty "territorialize" national boundaries and engage in war, or even subnational conflict. Manifestations of this are virtually endless in a modern world that was brutally forged under the historic conditions of global colonialism and that remains skewed by the chronic atrophies produced as a consequence of nationalism, postcolonialism, and political and ideological extremism: from US actions against Native American tribes since pre-Revolutionary days and in the Philippines and in Cuba at the turn of the century to Anglo-Australian genocidal policies against indigenous aboriginals; from German brutalities against the Herero and the Nama in southwestern Africa to Nazi diabolical exterminationism against the Jewish people during the Holocaust; from the post-Ottoman assault against the Armenian and Greek Christian communities, which included starvation and performative violations as instrumentalities of genocide and atrocity, to the Russian and Chinese "civil" wars, both of which involved genocidal famine as a political instrumentality; from British policies toward Mau Mau and honor/kinship segmentary cultures of Kenya to the paramilitary intercommunal violence against Muslim and Hindu peoples during Operation Searchlight in East Pakistan, later to become Bangladesh; from the internecine Burundian, Rwandan, and Cambodian genocides to state crimes against humanity leveled against the indigenous Mayan people of Guatemala; as well as against the Tamils in Sri Lanka; against the Igbo in Nigeria; against the Christians of East Timor-Este; against children and youth in Liberia; against the entire population in (Anglophonic) Sierra Leone under Charles Taylor; against the Sara, Hadjerai, and Zaghawa in (Francophonic) Chad under Hissène Habré; against the Baganda and other kinship groups in Uganda; and against (all) women in East Congo, and so on. This litany of pain goes on and on: in Iraq during the chemical attacks against the Anfal Kurds and in contemporary Syria against the people of Aleppo, among other locations. The present study asks why and, more than this, it demonstrates how the psychodynamics of desire function as motivational compulsions in the violent behaviors of perpetrators. Thus it concentrates on why perpetrators, including the minions who had lived "normal" lives until the outbreak of mass violence, enter the realm of mass atrocity and participate in it, often with the appearances of "enjoyment." And why is it, as well, that once political violence subsides or is terminated, former perpetrators, including some of the most monstrous, such as Josef Mengele and Klaus Barbie, return to normality both in terms of personality displays and in terms of the normalcy of their ways of life—as if nothing had happened.

The frequency of episodes, the chameleon-like behaviors of perpetrators, represent only the first set of clues as to why the motivations of perpetrators pertain to the psychic and emotional dynamics of desire as envisioned within a framework embedded in psychosocial analysis.

When mass atrocity occurs, the methods, means, and instrumentalities of violence extend beyond "mere" mass murder done in extrajudicial ways. The problematic that requires examination in psychosocial perspectives grows not from mass murder or killing alone, or even from the fact that the actual numbers of people killed in episodes of genocide and mass atrocity can and do attain such stunning magnitudes. What is especially perplexing originates in the fact that perpetrators of mass atrocity have since the Armenian genocide tended to be agents of state authority, whether their actions appear to be officially or unofficially sanctioned or not; and, correlatively, victims tend to be citizens of the very sovereign state or system that inflicts the harm. When mass atrocities occur, perpetrators act under the aegis of law, of legality; that is, they act under the guises of officially prescribed and politically sanctioned authority. Think only of Nazi Germany, Maoist China, the Soviet Union under Stalin, Sukarno's anti-communist purge in Indonesia and Suharto's ravaging of East Timor, Pol Pot's Cambodia, or of "Hutu Rwanda" and "Serbian Bosnia." Genocide and mass atrocity, in addition to all the rest that may be said about them, represent profound political betrayals by governments relative to their *own* populations or segments within them—but why? What is in the "nature" of the political, that is, in the psychosocial formations of nation-states, and thus in the character of modern political culture, that prompts governments across a wide range of political cultures to inflict unspeakable suffering against their own populations. What is implied in this question points not to mass murder alone but to mass torment as an aim in itself, and not one that is merely a means to any discernible set of political objectives. Mass atrocity, it seems, is pursued by certain governments or quasi-governmental authorities and their agents as an end in itself, but why?

An additional clue is the sheer sadistic cruelty of perpetrators, the unrelenting viciousness aimed at victims. Psychosocial perspectives permit the examination of perpetrator motivations in ways that illuminate why mass atrocity is ever present in cases of genocide but inexplicable if the metric of interpretation is the achievement of political objectives or strategic goals. Hatred and violation are released in degrees and at levels difficult or impossible to comprehend except through psychosocial perspectives. Whenever, wherever, mass atrocity occurs, the measure of perpetrator malevolence lies not in numbers of deaths alone. Rather, it resides in the torments and agony of dying they inflict on innocent victims, mostly hapless citizens, whose bodies and souls are brought to the point of cadaverous near-death by the very horrors of the collective human violation they are forced to bear before or as they are killed. Stephen Frosh, among others, ruminates on the excessive features of collective violence, which are theorized in later chapters as performative transgression and "surplus cruelty." He writes, "What, if there is no element of fantasy involved, what can explain the frenzy, the willingness to demolish the self as the other, and the escalating hatred so evident in the contemporary political scene."[54] And Frosh leaves little doubt as to the scars. As he has recently reminded us, memories of such human trauma linger and take on a life of their own, often, like chimera, haunting history never to be forgotten nor fully vanquished.[55]

When genocide and mass atrocity crimes are perpetrated, the instrumental processes of implementation function performatively, theatrically, and aesthetically, with victims often made to participate in their own humiliation. *Violence*, it appears, is not enough to satisfy perpetrators. Genocide and near-genocidal violence must be transformed into *violation*. As Adriana Cavarero, following Julia Kristeva, indicates that "the horror of violation"[56] petrifies those made witness to it. This is in contrast to the "terror" of violence from which human beings run. The horror of physical violation paralyzes victims before they die. During scenes of violation in instances of mass atrocity, victims become witness to their own disembodiment and to the evisceration of other victims, who are often kin, even neighbors. Victims become petrified prior to death by being made to see what is not ordinarily meant for them to see: the human body fragmented, torn into parcel parts and dismembered. They become enfeebled by shock, unable to escape from intolerability of horror, the very essence of trauma. These effects, however, appear to be what many perpetrators actually do desire. This underscores the voyeuristic and exhibitionist behaviors of perpetrators. When they act, they wish to be seen, by other perpetrators, by the victims themselves, and in some cases, by bystanders. This is not to suggest that this is the "cause" of genocide or mass violence; nor are these necessarily the aims that perpetrators consciously pursue before or during episodes of killing. The macabresque appears to be the incidental occurrence of murder. But its consistent presence suggests a pattern of desire among perpetrators to bond, a desire to share in a common fate, a destiny borne by mutual recognition of having entered into the forbidden realms of manufactured hell.

Let me cite an observation that was made at the conclusion of a systematic overview of the psychoanalytic studies on Nazis that challenge the notion of "a Nazi personality." "One of the many myths about the Nazi personality has centered around the Nazis being interpersonally cold and socially aloof. Although many of them showed signs of social skill deficits, we also found, however, that a majority of them were not unresponsive to close, supportive interpersonal relationships." The report continues, "In fact, many may have actually felt deprived of close, personal affiliations . . . . Thus, the 'brotherhood' of many of the Nazi sponsored organizations may have served as a substitute for this perceived need for interpersonal intimacy."[57] The desire for such brotherhood in bonding demands common action that distinguishes the "brethren" from all others. I suggest that this includes the macabresque in and through which perpetrators are able to stage, execute, witness, and reaffirm each other in relation to themselves.

From Festivality and the Carnivalesque to the Macabresque

The aesthetic details of macabresque theatricality rarely comport with our understanding of what the perpetrators actually want. Their motivations become reduced to a sterile hollowness, a kind of shrill "thoughtlessness." Survivors sometimes give testimony but always in ways that express their bewilderment and sense of utter betrayal. Primo Levi gave brave witness, but once he was done, he plunged to his death in the very building where he had lived before and after the war. What Levi knew and struggled so valiantly against was the poverty of language, the inexpressibility of words, a tonal flatness in the cadences used to describe surplus cruelty, to interpret what perpetrators "intend." Analytical language languishes in semantic thickets of distress and denial, contradiction and avoidance. Memory is scabbed over, never healed or transcended. There do exist attempts at comprehension in an intellectual tradition that looks to "festival" as the culturally prescribed moments of collective release: from psychic suppressions of guilt and shame; and from the moral oppressions of honor, duty, and obligation. In the Christian tradition, "carnival" refers to the eating of meat before abstinence; and Mardi Gras is "Fat Tuesday" before the first lean Wednesday of Lent. By means of their festivality, cultural communities test the limits of permissibility between the profane and sacred, the flesh and the spirit, and thus give expression to the tensions between sensuality and renunciation. The scandal in carnival arises as a consequence of the excessive sacrifice of one's own being to the once forbidden fruits of desire. In festivality, scandalous displacements occur: the psychic forces that may have required abstinence and restraint now demand release of desire. But the carnal spirits of desire embody cruel disciplines as well as joyous ones.

As Nancy Jay has shown, rituals of sacrifice across cultures represent the blood bonding of men.[58] Calls to sacrifice give meaning and moment to male bonding. Festivality provides an invitation for masculine enjoyment of shared release. But during the performativity of the macabresque, festivality and masculinity combine self-sacrifice with the desire for shared desire in blood bonding. Through the macabresque, perpetrators are able to give concrete form to a sadomasochistic desire that bonds them to each other in a kind of blood brotherhood conjoined by death, dying, and the rituals of unspeakable cruelty that is their "secret" alone. This is the allure of "absolute power." It bestows on perpetrators, not merely the rights to demean and degrade the personhood of victims, but also the "obligation" to do so. At such times, the most depraved forms of human behavior seem, to those who undertake to perpetrate them, to represent the heights of human possibility. Dan Stone examines the carnivalesque and observes, "Durkheim and Caillois talk of the 'transport' of collective rituals as festivals and war as though they are states of ecstasy. Something of this sense is captured too in Saul Friedländer's term '*Rausch*,' the ecstatic aspect of which also connotes frenzy, rapture, intoxication, inebriation, and euphoria."[59] Stone defines ecstasy as a "stretching out" between permissibility and prohibition in ways linking ecstasy to external law, "to reinforce the law (this is the frisson of transgression)."[60] He refers to "ecstatic communities," in a conceptual way that is similar to Clendinnen, in that he points to the shared sense of desire and the yearning for a sense of shared commonality among perpetrators who have "transgressed together."[61] This is what it means to enact the diabolical aesthetics of performative transgression. The shared noir ecstasy of the macabresque descends into the sadistic depravity of mass atrocity. This occurs in part through the voyeuristic and exhibitionist behavioral aspects of the macabresque and is thus suggestive of why it so often becomes integral to the unfolding of mass atrocity. Psychosocial explanations offer some tentative explanations, including those focused on shame and sadism, along with Lacanian emphases on desire. And thus, two reservations are required at this juncture: many women entered the ranks of perpetrators and thus the masculinization of absolute power in the macabresque is subject to analytical modification; secondly, sadistic cruelty in the macabresque is as often as not systematically applied in deliberate ways and thus belies the notion of carnivalesque frenzy. But the allures and enticements of power remain constant.

THE POWER OF POWER TO ATTRACT

That power has the power to attract is implicitly suggested by Mark Levene, who finds evidence for the "power" of power to attract certain state elites and their adherents to engage in genocide.[62] He suggests that there is a distorted desire at work during such moments, one that demands satisfaction, but only at enormous human cost that are doomed to fail precisely as a consequence. Levene reviews various situational permutations leading to genocide, for example: late consolidation of national sovereignty and statehood and consequent mimetic desire or ideology to "catch up" through exertions of military power, as in the prototypical case of pre–World War I Germany; political elites in postcolonialist nation-states torn domestically by ethno-grievances; or ideologically driven regimes that embolden paramilitary armed power organizations to use mass atrocity in struggles to ensure political legitimacy. Pressures may be varied and function as a consequence of multiple factors, such as ecological, economic, cultural, and demographic. But these material features of conflict provoke manifest drives for power, altogether familiar to students of genocide and mass atrocity. Levene observes, "As the demands of the system intensify, the drive of the relatively weaker states to more rapid, fast-speed development will also intensify; so in turn will the limiting factors, economic competition, demographic explosion, resource scarcity and mass ecological degradation, conspire to wreck their ambition." This combination of power drive and constraint produces, he suggests, "the temptation to overleap the limiting factors by short-cuts, even one 'great leap forward.'"[63] The mystiques of legitimacy, power, glory, purity, supreme security expressed in multiple formats of ideology and political rhetoric reveal and revel in the psychodynamics of both conscious but also unconscious desire. Levene implies the fantasmatic influences of desire at work in genocide when he declares, "Genocide in the future is likely to become a function and all too regular by-product of attempts to attain the unattainable."[64] My claim is that such disordered will is a function of the psychodynamics of desire. To interpret disorders of will in genocide, to grasp how and why political will becomes disordered in mass atrocity, to grasp why certain political elites would act to devastate their own children all requires an analysis of desire in influencing social fantasy and mimetic rivalries.

Desire and disorders of will or akratic willfulness operate in particular ways in the macabresque under the conditions of genocide and mass atrocity; conversely, disordered will spins out from the psychodynamics of desire. This underscores the relevance of psychosocial explanations of perpetrator motivations, not only in cases of genocide, but especially in instances of mass atrocity in which performative transgressions of victims appear as ends in themselves.

Levene's analysis demonstrates that genocide and mass atrocity tend to arise in cases of perceived loss that are ideologically constructed as historic wrongs demanding a collective obligation to resist. This often results in ideological incantations shaped around manufactured logics of illogic anchored to notions of collective or personal self-sacrifice. These, too, function in support of social fantasies captivated by the yearnings of desire but also suffused by the corrosive influences of shame and guilt. Levene implies the relevance of the psychodynamics of desire with reference to social fantasies of loss and ideologies of self-righteous power, so prevalent among perpetrators of genocide and mass atrocity. He refers to perpetrators' tendencies to deceive themselves into believing that they, and they alone, are engaged in a process of righting a historic wrong. Levene writes, for example:

> Yet, on another level, one could equally propose that the contours and trajectory of the Nazis' "never again" fixation are quite relateable and comparable with that of many other perpetrators. For instance, in all of our archetypical cases, Cambodia's included, the genocidaire perception of a particular moment or moments of previous societal trauma when the 'enemy' group almost succeeds in sabotaging the state's initial drive to achievement are more broadly linked to some more general wrong-turn in the country's history.[65]

Mimetic desire is an ever-present component of such psychosocial ideological constructions. As Levene observes, "In each of these instances, the charge is, in effect, the same: these historic enemies of the true, authentic, grass-roots and 'pure' forces of national or societal progress, the ones, in other words, who ought to be kept out, down, or preferably both, are actually given an unfair advantage with which not only to challenge but even undermine true society's heroic even Herculean path towards independence and salvation." When fantasies of loss, the alien other, and self-righteous indignation congeal around political reifications of difference in otherness, ideologies of sacrifice and shame, supremacism and exclusion emerge in ways conducive to genocide and mass atrocity. The psychodynamics of desire lead to demands for retribution over the historic loss that is perceived and socially propagandized as "truth" but in disordered formats of collective will and self-deception. Levene implicitly refers to the psychodynamics of desire and disordered will with reference to the contributions of Ronald Aronson, specifically the latter's "phraseology, the classic case of 'realizing the unrealizable', the ultimate expression of an entirely self-willed audacity directed towards overturning the intrinsic framework of contemporary reality."

Akrasia: Weakness of Will in Disordered Desire

This concept of disordered will, or akratic willfulness, originates in an Aristotelian concept of *akrasia,* traditionally defined as weakness of the will. I suggest that calling it weakness of will is conceptually misleading in that instances of akrasia manifest disordered willfulness, a kind of willfulness that demands precisely *what is not available on demand* or that inflames desires in a manner not accessible to gratification on the basis of human choice, action, or behavior. Prime examples include the end of creature death or the attainments of "divine" genius. The *akratic,* a term applied in modern philosophy to refer to the

psychic or mental condition of volitional weakness, in the present context, points analytically to the disordered willfulness on the part of perpetrators in the macabresque of genocide and mass atrocity. Akrasia may be said to inhere in disordered willfulness, patterns
of cognition, decision-making, and behaviors that demonstrate attempts to impose will
upon reality. Such designs often reveal political imaginaries grounded in social fantasies
of desire. The psychodynamics of political imaginaries and semiotics, of disordered will
and willfulness, and of unconscious desire are never far apart. Linda A. W. Brakel examines the tensions in akrasia between "rational" thought and desire with respect to "the
philosophy of action." She states, "Accompanying every omnipotent wish (and thought)
and many akratic acts are *unconscious* desires, often forbidden or unacceptable." Akratic
disorders of will demonstrate the role and influences of desire during emotional states or
under psychological conditions when agents act out in sadistic or narcissistic ways. Brakel
continues, "It becomes clear that understanding the role of unconscious desire, constitutively functioning to aid in the production of readiness-to-act toward fulfillment of its
own content, is central to an increased understanding of various problem cases in psychoanalysis and in the philosophy of action." This is pertinent to agential action of perpetrators, whose behaviors manifest varying degrees of self-deception, as well as akratic
willfulness in "willing" or desiring "the unwillable" as is the case with various supremacist or purification ideologies used to justify genocide or mass atrocity. Brakel concludes
that analytical focus on akratic disorders of will permits systematic analysis of a range of
subsequent akratic behaviors or tendencies. These include "(1) the repetitive nature of
symptomatic acts, (2) the need for symptomatic external actions when it seems that internally gratifying phantasies should suffice, (3) why 'harmless' wishes occasion symptoms,
and (4) the complex relation between omnipotent wishes (and thoughts) and unconscious desires."[66] Brakel's observations concerning akrasia are framed within the context
of philosophy and psychoanalysis but are equally germane to psychosocial examination
of perpetrator behaviors in various settings of the macabresque. They clearly distinguish between vague "wishes" or dreams and "desires" with respect to what she names
"action-readiness."

Akratic disorders feature collective self-deceptions motivated by fantasized, idealized,
or demonized political imaginaries bound to the "action-readiness" of perpetrators. A. O.
Rorty writes suggestively of "characterological akrasia" to emphasize collective rather
than individualistic patterns of dysfunctional behavior that are reflective of disordered
will and motivation over time. Rorty indicates that akratic disorders tend to arise within
specific cultural, social, and political contexts. She states, "Akrasia is not always a solitary
activity; it often works through sustaining social support."[67] She also states that "akrasia as
a species of character disorder is typically not episodic [and] often indicates a widespread
epidemic pattern of character disorders." In addition, she observes that its "long-range
sources lie in political and social practices; and its most effective cures may be political
rather than personal . . . individual akrasia may indicate social disorder."[68] Rorty's hypoth-
esized linkage between individual disordered motivation, on the one hand, and social,

political and collective disorders of will, on the other, implicitly theorizes the connection between akratic or disordered willfulness and perpetrator behaviors compelled by political ideology and reification, on the other.

Disorders of will often cluster in and around the group behaviors of perpetrators who seek to participate in bonds forged among themselves by means of what they share in each other, a common desire for bonding or recognition. These psychosocial dynamics also hold true during instances of mass atrocity: when surplus cruelty is justified in ways that "will" the malevolence in the macabresque to be manifestations of the "good." As Rorty observes, "As standard ordinary beliefs are elicited and reinforced by our fellows, so too are many of our favorite akratic failures . . . the canny akrate puts herself in situations where her actions receive social support . . . she need now always initiate her akrasia."[69] This is another way of suggesting the prevailing role of imagistic capture and political reification in the psychodynamics of large groups, particularly those that appear to reinforce in-group paranoia against threats reified ideologically as rivalrous and potentially destructive. Disorders of will thus simultaneously become realized through patterns of individual "normalcy" while revealing a specific pathology in the ethnographies of groups. For such reasons, studies of genocide and mass atrocity often turn to perpetrators acting in groups and to group dynamics. Within the context of disordered will, Leslie Farber observes, "will is the category through which we examine that portion of our life that is the mover of our life in a certain direction or toward an objective in time."[70] He posits the existence of a realm of motivation and volition that represents a substratum of unconsciousness that forms a "seamless whole enclosing me that pushes in a particular direction at the same time that the direction in the world enlists my will and the faculties wedded to it."[71] He associates this realm of will with "direction," which he understands "not as an ideal goal toward which we press, however much we falter, but rather as a way interspersed with, yet not obstructed by, worldly detail and worldly objectives." The theoretical implication of this is that psychosocial manifestations of akrasia form around "ego-idealized" versions of inclusivity, exclusivity, and supremacy—that is, around identitarian constructions permeated by infantile narcissism and aggression in formats disfigured by reification. Hatred, insecurity, and violence as a consequence are never far away. Farber, like Rorty, implicitly recognizes the relevant significance of those cultural supports that give rise to, nurture, and sustain behavioral motivations during episodes of mass atrocity. He underscores the ways in which culture and cultural environments permeate the shaping of perpetrator motivations. In this sense, Farber's psychosocial perspective is profoundly ethnographic and sociological in its emphasis on the primacy of external influences or alterity in the development of human unconsciousness and, ultimately, in terms of what motivates perpetrators engaged in practices of mass atrocity. Farber also emphasizes the ways in which human beings seek "direction" as a defense against the anxiety of non-being and nothingness, another way of implicitly theorizing the role of "ego-ideals" in social fantasy. He refers to modernity as the "Age of the Disordered Will" and to the "myriad varieties of willing what cannot be willed that enslave us."[72] He writes, "If anxiety is more prominent in our time, such anxiety is the product of our particular modern disability of the will."[73] Here, too, his analysis of human motivation and volition is suggestive of the psychodynamics of reification in mass atrocity and the macabresque.

This theoretical framework permits us to examine the volitional state and subjectivities of perpetrators in ways that demonstrate the strains of their own self-deceptions. A standard definition of self-deception reads as follows: "self-deception is the acquisition and maintenance of a belief (or, at least, the avowal of that belief) in the face of strong evidence to the contrary motivated by desires or emotions favoring the acquisition and retention of that belief."[74] Self-deception may thus be interpreted as a disorder of motivation and will that "facilitates harm to others and to oneself, undermines autonomy, corrupts conscience, violates authenticity, and manifests a vicious lack of courage and self-control that undermine the capacity for compassionate action."[75] Self-deception reveals itself in those who act on the basis of disordered will in denial of analytical contradiction or critical self-reflection. Such motivations reflect rationalizations fostered by internal emotional or psychological needs and narcissist desires as well as by external cultural supports. On account of akratic or disordered willfulness embedded in reifications, perpetrators readily conjure fixed and frozen images of adversarial "others." Victims thereby become susceptible to the dread-filled images of out-groups "willed" to "be" whatever ideological reification demands they "be" or "are." The masquerade of self-deception in the dynamics of akratic willfulness tends to shield perpetrators from themselves. What is hidden or denied, in particular, are the self-reifications projected outward.

"LITTLE MEN GONE WILD": POWER AS
FANTASY AND AS SELF-DECEPTION

Ronald Aronson describes genocidal moments as fantasy states gripped by power as an end for itself, but also seeking power as a means to re-create reality in its own image. In this, Aronson connects the dots, so to speak, that link power, the political formations of the nation-state, and genocide by showing how fantasy, self-deception, and denial arise at moments of perceived collective or state political weakness in the name of total or absolute power. This also points toward the theoretical frameworks of "political opportunity" models of power stressing the influential factors of threatened loss of power as critical to the pathways of mass murder. Aronson, moreover, partially addresses these issues in psychosocial terms. Genocide represents, Aronson declares, a "fantasy-solution." "The guiding principle," he writes, ". . . has been that evil is a praxis, and is therefore intelligible." Genocidal regimes are "fantasy-states, amalgams of madness and reality," in which, he adds, "mass murder became the denial-solution of an otherwise insoluble situation."[76] Aronson argues that the delusions of power become wrapped in willful self-deceptions transformed into public policy. "A paramount fact of each case we have studied is the effort by the ruling group to turn state power into power to create 'a world after its own image.'"[77] Aronson, in effect, is lifting analysis of genocide out of the circuits of social psychological, rationalist, or purposive conceptions of motivation to include irrational, noncognitive forms of ideation and fantasy, thus embracing volitional concepts of power beyond the notions of strict utilitarian motivation grounded in disordered will and desire. This perspective is echoed by Dan Stone, who writes, "Instead of seeing fantasy thinking and means-ends rationality as irreconcilable opposites, it is important to see here how the rationalized structures of modernity can themselves not only channel but even create forms of thinking that are utopian and ultra-violent."[78] Much of what has happened in the macabresque of twentieth-century genocide and mass atrocity bears witness to Stone's observations that specifically refer to Aronson's psychosocial perspective. As Stone indicates, "In these processes of state building, colonization, and development the role of fantasy, fear of pollution, and what Aronson calls 'social madness' must also be accounted for."[79] This represents precisely the objective of the study here.

In this, Aronson and Stone and others who adopt similar perspectives are in effect outlining a psychosocial analysis by indicating that in willful self-deception, political regimes bent on evil want to believe their own lies. They adhere to cheap and cheapening epistemologies that "will" themselves into truth by demanding too little of reality, in order to "will" their possession of it. Aronson writes, "Evil, for example, is not directly reducible to or derivable from prior suffering. It is not just that a given social group has been oppressed or brutalized and subsequently does the same to others in equal degree." He later observes, "What is frightening to confront in such evil is that it is indeed rage, fury, destructiveness; but now organized in such a way as to keep itself out of touch with its origins, and with all ways of being remedied." The language of strategic, purposive, or even rational motivation thus becomes strangely out of place if the analytical context is the political evil of mass atrocity. "Evil is not functional, then, except in this mad sense, and so cannot be derived from the usual determinisms. It appears demonic precisely because of its quality of being out of control and madly purposive, especially when that purposiveness expresses a social system that can only devour its people to keep itself functioning."[80] Genocidal actions may reveal political evil intent, but such evil intentionality is not motivated by impulse-cognitive-strategic calculations except to use power to deny reality in its own willful self-deceptions and fantasized self-imaginaries. The evidence for this claim as an analytic problematic is the often seemingly coincidental presence of mass atrocity, specifically the dramaturgical staging of performative transgression beyond the mass murder and killing.

In psychosocial frames focused on mass atrocity, the "will to power" translates into disordered willfulness for power as an end in itself for itself. Theodor Adorno put it similarly when he commented that

the Fascists raised to an absolute the basic idea of strategy: to exploit the temporary discrepancy between one nation with a leadership organized for murder, and the total potential of the rest. Yet by taking this idea to its logical conclusion in inventing total war, and by erasing the distinction between army and industry, they themselves liquidated strategy.[81]

Mass atrocity especially in genocidal violence has no political purpose other than to satisfy the insatiable desires that convert perceived "need" into unconscious "demand," as Lacan understood so well. Pathways to mass atrocity in genocide reveal a form of psychic and emotional fixation in the sense of "willed" reification in the political imaginaries of political evil. Such reifications are created specifically to deny "reality" its epistemological dimensions of perspective, contradiction, limitation, and so forth. As Aronson writes, "Evil is the human out of touch with itself, driven there by extreme circumstances out of its control, finding the power to strike blindly even while unable to strike truly. It is mad, frozen, impotent human praxis, striving to lose touch with its source."[82] But there is, in what Aronson insists on calling "madness," a kind of non-motivated motivation that blinds evil doers in their willfulness: to pump up their omnipotence at the very instant when they are most narcissistically infantile. Aronson refers to the Nazis as "'*wildgewordene spiessburger*'—little men gone wild." He concludes, "Evil is a 'natural' product, we might say, of the dialectic of impotence and power."[83] The pathway to genocide and mass atrocity thus demonstrates not so much madness as the disordered or akratic and thus "willed" attempt to make what is "unwillable" attainable, power in itself as such, that is, as an end for itself unto itself. Aronson is right to observe it is impotence masquerading as omnipotence, omnipotence in search of its own demise.

THE "EXTRAORDINARY" IN NORMALIZED BIOPOWER

Who else but Michel Foucault could capture the rapacious, essentialist, and ultimately depraved essence of genocidal power, bent on its own self-annihilation while caught in the fantasies of absolute power and totalized freedom made real or felt to be possible through the mechanisms of unchecked cruelty in mass atrocity? This is the inner side, the introjected side of akratic willfulness, to transform what is often ideologized as identitarian difference into the grounds of sadistic reification, and to deploy biopower as way of exposing one's body politic to masochistic self-destruction. But Foucault's project, now integral to the history of Western letters, is in a sense to invert Aronson's concept of "madness" by depicting it as "normal," that is, by demonstrating how the history of the "modern" is a history that "might be called power's hold over life" and its grip over death.[84] Foucault in his summative lecture declares, "The right of life and death is always exercised in an unbalanced way: the balance is always tipped in favor of death. Sovereign power's effect on life is exercised only when the sovereign can kill."[85] In Foucauldian perspective, the pathway to genocide is central to the political history of the sovereign nation-state. This history comprises what Foucault calls "two series: the body-organism-discipline-institutions series, and the population-biological processes-regulatory mechanisms" ostensibly aimed at protecting the now-disciplined citizen as a living breathing organism and entire populations as regularized entities. Foucault represents these processes of bio-power discipline and regulation as being fixated on statistical facticity, on sanity and the sanitary, on sexuality and security. But the corporeality of biopower readily devolves into essentialized reification, "to fragment, to create caesuras within the biological continuum addressed by bio-power."[86] If biopower is to function at all, it must "inscribe" "hierar-chical" differences among "species" in ways that conjure "biological threats" as a "nor-malizing precondition that makes killing possible."[87] War becomes not merely political but eugenic: "war is about two things: it is not simply a matter of destroying a political adversary, but of destroying that [sort] of biological threat."[88] Foucault thus theorizes that identitarian reification, racism, war, and death represent complementary technologies of biopower. "Racism justifies the death-function" of sovereign power and thus the "work-ings of a State that is obliged to use race, the elimination of races and the purification of the race, to exercise its sovereign power."[89] For Foucault, the culmination of these historic trends lies in totalized power, the Nazi state, and the racist socialist state of the Stalinist type.

But even Foucault now appears to shudder. His, after all, is a history of the process of "normalizing" biopower. Yet, for once, he uses the word, "extraordinary" to describe Nazi society. "We have, then, in Nazi society something that is really quite extraordinary," he comments. "We have an absolutely racist State, an absolutely murderous State, and an absolutely suicidal State." And it is this latter phenomenon, the willful exposure of the entire population of Germany to violent death at the hands of their own government, that Foucault appears to find so extraordinary. He dwells on the famous "Telegram 71," sent by Hitler in April 1945, which ordered the destruction of the "German people's own living conditions" as retribution for their "betrayal" of him.[90] Sovereign biopower, racist and sanitizing, absolute and normalizing, thus turns against itself in the form of a gen-ocidal regime that would devour its own people rather than fail in its "malgenic" racist "madness." Herein lies the metric of disordered or akratic willfulness in the distorted psychodynamics of desire. Foucault concludes by observing, "The Nazi State makes the field of life it manages, protects, guarantees, and cultivates in biological terms absolutely coextensive with the sovereign right to kill anyone, meaning not only other people, but its own people."[91] The disordered desires of genocidal regimes viewed from the perspec-tive of the psychosocial thus link the more or less conscious sadism of its instrumentali-ties with the unconscious masochism of its aims.

In a sense, mass atrocity in genocide whenever, wherever it occurs, represents the site that fuses collective sadomasochism. Armed organized power regimes that pursue mass atrocity in genocide and near-genocidal violence seek satisfaction in giving vent to fanta-sies of total power often conjured around the mystifications of absolute state supremacy or social exclusion and purification. In psychosocial contexts, such quests for omnipotent power reveal themselves to be quests for power for itself in itself alone; all other objec-tives are secondary, in some sense, not "real," however strategically aimed and ideolog-ically represented. Mass atrocities serve ostensibly as the instrumentality of a regime's power and objectives. But they also represent supports to cover the unconscious depth of self-contempt and self-abnegation, dread, doom, and anxiety that fuels desire as it becomes transformed into demands for the macabresque in performative transgression. Mass atrocity may seem purposive in some political contexts, such as those associated with ethnic cleansing, but it is hardly purposeful in any rational or strategic, let alone, cognitive sense if for no other reasoning than it tends to be self-defeating. Foucault brings us closer to an understanding of how normalizing sovereign biopower becomes not only racist but profoundly suicidal once it becomes genocidal and engages in mass atrocity. Mass murder, systematic devastation of domestic society and economy, the destruction of the cultural fabric within a polity on pathways to genocide underscore the basic contradiction: total power in the name of social and cultural absolutes represents a delusional form of self-deception in which power becomes its own worst enemy and nightmare.

Self-Deception: Ignorance as Power, the Power to Know Nothing

Performative transgression and supererogatory obligation—often delusional forms of behavior and motivation—march together in the self-deceptions of fraudulent self-sacrifice and heroism so often present in genocide and shared among those who participate in mass atrocity. Walter Kaufmann, the great student of existentialism, once distinguished falsehood from self-deception with reference to "bad faith"—that is, a form of fraudulent belief maintained by those duped by it in ways that allow them to remain content to will themselves into states of self-delusion by demanding too little of themselves with respect to truth or evidence. They want to believe what they believe. More than this, they "will" truth into what they desire to be true. "With self-deception a truth appears, a method of thinking, a type of being which is like that of objects; the ontological characteristic of the world of self-deception, with which the subject suddenly surrounds himself, is that here being is what it is not, and is not what it is."[92] Self-deception, like all reification, undertakes to "*will what it is.*" It is a decision to determine what "truth" is or is not on the basis of what one "wants" or wishes to be, thereby to reduce the meaning of truth to mere preference and in the process to avoid self-interrogation in imaginative understanding or by means of critical reasoning with respect to the metrics of objectivity, however conceived. Self-deception inheres in meager kinds of wishful thinking. Kaufmann links such lack of epistemological rigor in self-deception to moral/ontological debility. He speaks of the willing acceptance of "non-persuasive evidence." Self-deception "stands forth in the firm resolution *not to demand too much*, to count itself satisfied when it is barely persuaded, to force itself in decisions to adhere to uncertain truths." But Kaufmann refers to self-deception as more than ideological self-mystification; it is an implosive assault against the ontological integrity of human presence by means of a chronic diminution of one's own volition, especially with respect to moral and ethical judgment. But this is what is wanted in self-deception, to will what is not, to will what one can never be. He concludes, "One *puts oneself* in self-deception as one goes to sleep, and one is in self-deception as one dreams. Once this mode of being has been realized, it is as difficult to get out of it as to wake oneself up."[93] Many Germans in the immediate aftermath of the Second World War emerged from the bunkers and the places of hiding to view their cityscapes in rubble, and their economies in ruin. As they did so, many experienced this sad emergence into the reality of what they had done, as if wakening up from a nightmare. And so it is of genocidal societies.

It is thus sometimes suggested that German society behaved in the immediate aftermath of the Second World War in a postdream like state of mind somehow alive to immediate surface sensations, but simultaneously numb on the inside. In the sense that Kaufmann means, it was. The dream was in self-deception, the reality was in the nightmare of genocide and mass atrocity. Such self-deceptions congeal into formats of demonic but supererogatory hate during times gripped by genocidal intent. The orchestrators, the perpetrators, the compliant ranks of bystanders all tend to proclaim their heroism at the very moments when they manifest nothing more than the vanity of self-deceptions. This speaks to the core of what desire and ideology do as support for the fantasies of grandeur at the very instant perpetrators demonstrate utter conformity to delusional artifacts of power.

Herein lies the methodological appropriateness of psychosocial analysis of desire in examining disordered genocidal intent recursively linking the mystifications of hate with the delusions of heroism. As Jason J. Campbell observes, "The only thing that remains is hate. Hate fuels genocide. It breeds anger and festers with indignation. It fuels willful ignorance and misology."[94] In this, he gestures not merely to the nature of self-deception but toward what stands behind and within it in the forms of motivation: desire for the unwillable.

Toward a Theory of Absolute Power: The Normalization of the Anti-normative or Anomic

A core problem in the study of politics and the political is power, what it is, how it functions, whether it acts as the means to the ends, let's say, of domination or defense, or, to the contrary, whether it serves merely as an end in itself. Power operates at all levels of the social, as well as the political, personal, and interpersonal, within groups and across collective aggregations. To the extent that power appears to encourage perpetrators to pursue tactical objectives, it may be deemed as a means to an end, or sets of ends, along a means-ends chain of strategic calculation. This would appear plausible relative to the genocidal violence the historic evidence suggests often takes place in the aftermath of wars or civil conflicts when elites struggle over position and in relation to postwar, postconflict settlements. The very concept of genocide, however, loses meaning as strategic policy once it is laden by the macabresque of mass atrocity that is altogether superfluous to rational objectives, as is so often the case. Macabresque aesthetics and dramaturgies of performative transgression in mass atrocity serve little or no rational purpose, even if genocidal murder and crimes against humanity become justified by their perpetrators on seemingly rational grounds. During episodes of the macabresque, power becomes the remit in search for its own absoluteness, and the shaming and humiliation of victims, the means.

If mass atrocities lead nowhere but to torment and suffering as ends in themselves, why do they so often occur? What does it mean to say that the exercise of absolute power represents an end in itself for itself alone? What are the manifestations of absolute power; how does it function, how is it exercised, and, above all, why does it exist?

Answers are suggestive for the psychosocial analysis of desire in mass atrocity, as indicated in Wolfgang Sofsky's study of concentration camp guard behaviors, in which he outlines what is, in effect, a theory of absolute power. Sofsky does so in sociological terms focused on Auschwitz and Majdanek and other "intermediate" concentration camps that were morbidly situated between work or labor camps, on the one hand, and death or extermination camps, on the other. "Concentration" in this universe signified impermanent prolongation of life in a death-world of living agony in which the exercise of power was indeed absolute. His perspective explicitly focuses on sociality and situation. For methodological reasons, he abjures psychological explanations of perpetrator motivations. To do otherwise, he suggests, would entail a kind of analytical reductionism. Such an approach "reduces" absolute power to perpetrator motivations by making each the equivalent of the other. Sofsky rejects this. Motivations do not bring about or "cause" reality. Concentration camps did not exist because perpetrators psychologically sought after them; perpetrators became perpetrators once the camps existed. "If one foregrounds the psychology of the perpetrators and their victims," he writes, "social reality is reduced to the motivations and experiences of the individuals involved."[95] Sofsky etches out a kind of meso-level analysis of the power structures and relational dynamics in the concentration camps. In this, he is clear regarding the level of analysis his methodological procedure requires, one that does not operate "above" the camps in the methodological sense that his efforts aim at an overarching political, strategic, ideological, or social history of the camps; nor does it function analytically "below" camp conditions by assessing the motivational psychology of perpetrators. On the contrary, his aim is to hone in on the concentration camp as a social formation, a unique end-state condition with its own features in the methodological "middle" grounds of meso-level analysis. Sofsky thus explicitly wishes to avoid the perils of both macro- and micro-level analysis. With a gesture toward Hannah Arendt's theme concerning the banality of evil, that is, the enormity of the historic crime and the minuscule motivations of individual perpetrators, Sofsky writes:

The topos of incomprehensibility has, first and foremost, a moral meaning. Manifestly, the customary moral criteria geared to the actions of individuals break down in the face of collective crime. In describing such crime in terms of responsibility or "criminal energy," individual psychopathology or ideological blindness necessarily leads to a banalization of the concrete deeds.[96]

But the methodological question that arises concerns whether such rejections of criminality, pathology, ideology, and so on, as explanations necessarily entail total avoidance of attempts to apply motivation and intentionality as units of analysis with respect to perpetrators in their capacities as individuals and as members of groups.

I suggest, to the contrary, psychosocial theoretical frameworks bridge levels of analysis at macro, meso, and micro levels, a possibility Sofsky denies. He states, "There is an unbridgeable gap between the perpetrators and their actions. The organized crime was monstrous—not the perpetrators."[97] He adds, "Yet, this should not mislead the analyst into orienting the investigation toward the genesis of political and macrosocial structures. The alternative to criminology or psychology is not a general theory of society. Between the two poles lies the true and distinctive field for the analysis of power: the organization of the camp, and the situated actions and suffering within it."[98] Sofsky underscores the recursivity connecting situation and perpetrator, perpetrator to situation: "Social relations exist only in the regular behavior of individuals interacting, organizations only in the actions of their personnel. Collective crimes, in the final analysis, are individual crimes in a collective."[99] That said, Sofsky rejects the functionality of concentration camps and evaluation of perpetrators in terms of impulsive-cognitive-strategic or purposive motivations. "Just as the interpretive recourse to individual intentions and plans is blinkered and inadequate," he declares, "little light is shed by the functional perspective: it degrades the perpetrators, debasing them into the attendants of a terror machine running seemingly by itself."[100] His interpretation of recursivity, however, runs the methodological risk of representing "situation" as the "cause" of perpetrator action, while motivation becomes a mere function of situation. "The camp system functioned because the murderers actually took on their roles; they were only too willing to carry out the work of terror. They exploited the opportunities offered by the absolute power to kill, and expanded its scope."[101] What is missing here are the psychodynamic linkages that extend from psychic interiority to situational exteriority and back across the permeabilities of culture and consciousness, fantasy and ideology, group dynamics and individual behaviors. Sofsky's depiction of the surplus cruelty imposed on victims to illuminate the substantive meaning of absolute power is theoretically weakened by avoidance of the psychodynamics of perpetrators, an analytical orientation on which his very concept of absolute power ultimately depends.

Sofsky's analysis applies a phenomenological approach to situational sociology composed of an in-depth or "thick description" of the daily lifeworld of the camps as experienced by those who were in them. This perspective obviates any suggestion of goals or aims, ends or objectives beyond the exercise of absolute power. "To speculate about a teleological explanation is to confuse the intentions of a group with the structures that crystallize in a social field."[102] The concentration camps constituted a "social world" "not a rational system with an unambiguous, purposeful orientation" but rather a hermetic space in which time slowed to accommodate the quickening pace of power on display for itself to behold. To "craft a thick sociological description," Sofsky declares, requires "explications of structures and processes," intensive detailed depictions of social situations, and systematic interpretations of meanings based on microscopic examination of relational interactions gripped by the designs and devices (as well as the disgraces) of absolute power. Sofsky's definition of absolute power, his depiction of how it became organized and structured, his portrayal of who wielded it and how, and his examination of its effects, all bear direct relevance to the very psychodynamics of motivation, will and desire he is so keen to exclude. Sofsky writes, "Absolute power is not bent on achieving blind obedience or discipline, but desires to generate a universe of total uncertainty, one in which submissiveness is no shield against even worse outcomes."[103] The pathway to genocide is not paved by death alone, it is strewn with the detritus of mass atrocity; and the universe of atrocity becomes lethal once death becomes insufficient to satisfy perpetrators functioning at ground levels on the pathways to genocide.

Sofsky rightly differentiates absolute power from social rule, despotism, punitive power, and disciplinary power. Absolute power inheres in total control over death and dying, over life as it is lived from moment to moment, day by day; it is absolute in its unfettered capacity not only to murder but to exert excruciating pain and torment instantaneously, without cause, reason, purpose or aim—except for itself as an act in itself. But does this not suggest the presence of a distorted volition, a demand for power to satisfy a desire, which like all desire, functions never to be satisfied, but in this case to be unrelenting in its extremes. Sofsky declares, "Even killing, that final reference point of all power, is not sufficient."[104] The cases in point here are Nazi concentration camps. No generalization about them diminishes their unique horrific character. But attempted exertions of absolute power on the part of perpetrators of mass atrocity speak not merely to situation but to the psychodynamics of desire and volition in human personality and character, however malleable such character appears to be relative to "situation." Sofsky indicates, "Absolute power transforms the universal structures of human relatedness to the world: space and time, social relations, the connection with work, the relation to the self."[105] Absolute power resides in unconscious constellations of desire, fantasy, reified identitarian constructions, disordered willfulness. It functions within normative relationships; more than this, it enters a transactional realm that might be described as the anti-normative. This, too, is reflective of the psychodynamics of unconscious desire. He describes how it operates in the camps: it "dissolves the link between transgression and punitive sanction"; "requires neither occasions nor reasons, and has no interest in obligating itself by threat"; "goes on a rampage whenever it so desires"; "does not wish to limit freedom, but to destroy it"; "does not seek to guide action, but to demolish it."[106] Absolute power reifies all identity constructions.

Identitarian categories become fixed and fixated, closed and frozen, spatialized as well as naturalized. As identity is naturalized, it becomes spatialized. This is the phenomenological significance of concentration in the context of mass atrocity. Concentration spatializes identity by destroying space within the camp, between individuals, across groups, among the entire collectivity of victims. This becomes a means toward their degradation, a process that involves theatricality, performative transgression, a dramaturgy of victim suffering and torment so as to permit the violations borne by the demands of absolute power to take place. The *spatialization* of *reified identity* by means of absolute power concentrates people in order to demean their individuality, to destroy even the semblance of their dignity, to deny them a sense of individuation, initiative or autonomy. Absolute power works to erode the minimal basis of privacy. This is denoted by the unrelenting assault against the epidermal borders separating one body from another, each person from the other. In so doing, it "massifies" humanity by attacking the possibilities of distinction, intimacy, and subjectivity. All personal distinctions are distilled out from soul or spirit of victims to be replaced with camp labeling and/or recast racialized identity constructions. Camp labeling "branded its victims with stigmata, guiding the prisoners' behavior by its stamp."[107] But, again, neither rational purpose nor situational contingencies explain the behaviors, the motivations, the subjective impulses or even the group compulsions of camp guards. The compelling theoretical question that defies either rational or situational explanations, one that challenges the probity of utilitarian logic or even deontological normative morality is this: once prisoners are concentrated, why torment them with the absolute power that transforms life into living hell? If collective fantasy or ideological self-deception demonizes the existence of the targeted victims, as the Nazi did in relation to the Jews, why are mass killing, mass murder, mass death, and the like, insufficient in themselves? If the pathway to genocide is extermination, why not simply exterminate? Why the need for absolute power? Why the concentration of victims for purposes of exerting these modalities of gratuitous nonstrategic surplus cruelty in the most excessive sadistic manner conceivable, when all of this serves no apparent *purposive* objective?

Given this problematic, rationally conceived notions of "motivation" seem grossly inadequate to the task of methodologically framed explanation. This is the core issue and one that goes undertheorized throughout much of contemporary analysis of genocide and mass atrocity. The answer points to perpetrators not as the agents of politics but *as carriers of agentic desire*. Might absolute power be explainable on the grounds that its excessive, superfluous cruelty serves no other motivational purpose than to satisfy perpetrators' desire, however defined? And if so, might desire as a psychic and emotional phenomenon require theoretical explanation in psychosocial frameworks or perspectives?

Sofsky's own methodological sociology is suggestive in this regard. It implies the dynamics of self-esteem based on notions of "mirror images," that is, on self-reflective dynamics encapsulated by the formulation, "I am what I think you think I am." The key here is not merely what the other thinks of a subject but, rather, how and in what ways a subject thinks of itself as it perceives how or in what ways others perceive or objectify it. This spectral dynamic generates self-reflexive constructions of how others see the self relative to how subjects apperceive themselves. This is the meaning of "the gaze" central to Sartre's interpretation of the shame and reification so critical to psychodynamics of desire in situational contexts that attempt to link prejudice and reification with humiliation and violation.[108]

This appears to be implied by Sofsky's interpretation of why concentration camp guards became transformed into the perpetrators of mass atrocity reflective of absolute power. Mass atrocity resides in the excesses of violence, in the surpluses of violation, in the excesses of torment, agony, and suffering beyond any rational objective, and thus in the *psychosocial* desire for particular kinds of "enjoyment" that the camp guards shared—and recognized that they shared. Sofsky describes the dynamics of desire and the mirror image in methodological frames that obviate both but stress the relevance of self-esteem in explaining perpetrators' behaviors. He states, "The camp was a laboratory of violence. Absolute power in action liberates a perpetrator from all inhibitions; cruelty becomes unhinged."[109] One consequence is a kind of anti-normative normativity. "Virtually anything can be ventured, repeated, intensified, or halted, without reference to norms or goals." Sofsky associates the libertine quality of absolute power with "absolute freedom" to perform with "barbaric ingenuity."[110] And it is from this strange satanic ingenuity in the demonic instrumentalities of absolute power that aestheticized but decreative performativity emerged. Sofsky implies that transgressive performativity as theater, game, and ritual, played not only for individual perpetrator entertainment but as competitive processes of wager with ritualized rules subject to revision and violation at will. Perpetrators jousted for reputational status up the scales of deranged standing. Prestige was granted to perpetrators according to how exquisite the modalities of suffering they designed and with what degrees of horror the diabolical implementations occurred. In the *Gehenna* of concentration camps, perpetrator rank depended on how total the pain, how deep the agony, how high the pitch of screams they extracted.

Sofsky, to his scholarly credit, describes in unwanted but ethically necessary detail the methods of absolute power in concentration camps.[111] In this, he gives precise meaning to ludic power in performative transgression. He presents in painstaking detail the methods and techniques applied by perpetrators to ensure seething pain, smoldering agony, searing torment. But rarely was the process aimed at victims in their singularity as individuals. "By contrast, demonstrative excess was a performance, a spectacle directed to an audience. It was a staging to spread fear and earn respect. The more brutal the SS officers, the higher their standing among their superiors and accomplices."[112] He further elaborates, "In this atmosphere, the atrocities involved are not even directed primarily against the victims. For the perpetrators, the victims are nothing more than stage props in the performance, trophies for their self-aggrandizement."[113] In Sofsky's analysis, perpetrator self-expansion and self-aggrandizement emerge as the conceptual artifacts of motivation. These motivations pivoted on reputational recognition among perpetrators who judged each other on the basis of standards benchmarked by degrees of ferocious brutality and the extent this proved entertaining. Sofsky refers to these dynamics as the manifestations of "subculture." "The more dead bodies subculture members could chalk up, the greater was their fame; the more adroit and imaginative their brutality, the higher their rankings in the in-group pecking order."[114]

Sofsky proceeds to draw a critical inference here that resonates with social psychological analysis of in-group dynamics. It is based on methodological assumptions stemming from his sociological orientations with stress on structural arrangements conditioning perpetrator motivations. He states, "Both for perpetrators and for spectators, the humiliation, harassment, and killing of victims provided a distraction and source of amusement. *This had nothing to do with anger, hatred, or rage. The identity of the victim was totally immaterial.*"[115] Sofsky combines explanations of "prototypicality" within groups based on the alleged importance of conformity relative to majoritarian opinion with reputational status of members within the context of in-groups to develop a theory of absolute power. He then frames the dramaturgies and aesthetics of performative transgression of the most sadistic kind to indicate that desire, hate, emotionality, relationality as a whole, are irrelevant to theoretical explanation. His argument is that "performance is aimed at the audience. Its significance derives from the personal distinction of the perpetrator. Its function is the distribution of prestige, the confirmation of collective *habitus*."[116] The psychodynamics of perpetrator fantasy, desire, ideology, volitional orientation, even anxiety, and so on, are all methodologically circumscribed to emphasize the internal forces at work prompting perpetrators to behave primarily in relation to each other. Motivation is defined as the epiphenomenal outcomes of self-presentation strategies. This speaks to the psychosocial dimensions of mass atrocity and how it occurs. Sofsky remains consistent in his methodological orientations framed by a phenomenological sociology. As a result, motivations appear as the consequences of situational arrangements or structural conditions; and thus habitus stands as the critical component influencing perpetrators behaviors.

Perpetrators are mostly indifferent to victims as bearers of specific cultural, social, or political identity; similarly, they are indifferent to victim suffering, Primarily, they are concerned about how each perceives other perpetrators perceiving each other within the context of the social milieu in which their roles are defined and reputations made. Here he implicitly rejects mindless obedience as an explanation of perpetrator behavior contrary to social psychological simulations associated with Philip Zimbardo or Stanley Milgram in favor of conformity and reputational status. Sofsky avers, "Obedience, loyalty, comradeship, and 'steeled severity' determined the guiding image of the SS."[117] He suggests, however, that this subcultural value system was hardly sustained by meager displays of obedience. Rather, the hellish environment in which perpetrators operated demanded independent initiative in the exercise of invented cruelties. "Thus, excess did not spring from mechanical obedience. On the contrary; its matrix was a group structure." Sofsky thus stresses how the role of *habitus* generated the impacts useful in explaining the cruelties of absolute power. He observes, "The collective *habitus* is more than a mere disposition to act in a customary way. At the same time, it is a normative demand addressed to the members of the organization. It calls for conformity with the values and habitual practices of the group."[118] On this basis, Sofsky lists the "motives for violence." His outline is meant to underscore the triviality and randomness of perpetrator motivation. He observes, for example, "Many deeds were perpetrated on the basis of a momentary mood or lark, a sense of boredom, during a contest, or because a person wanted to pocket a few cigarettes as a reward. Side by side with sadistic aggression stand habitual tormenting, indifferent killing, collective massacre under the influence of alcohol, or killing under specific orders."[119] But are phenomenological descriptions such as indifference, inebriation, mood, and boredom forms of motivation; are they not descriptions of behavioral or life experiences that in turn require motivational analysis?

Killing under orders may be motivation enough, but orders in themselves do not explain what Sofsky describes as violence given over to patterns of "sadistic aggression." This is Sofsky's very point: perpetrators invented a reality of a totalized power to torment. This led them into desires for the release of sadistic aggression *to impress themselves and each other* simply that they could do whatever they desired in a group-constructed race to the bottom. This is highly suggestive for understanding the determinative motivations arising from within the psychic and emotional interiorities of concentration camp guards. But it does not lead to the conclusion that there existed a single Nazi mind or a camp guard personality. What counted was the bond created among perpetrators in that each sought what the other in the group had to give, status recognition granted on the basis of wonton cruelty. This suggests the relevance of the mirror image by underscoring the explanatory significance of the psychodynamics and sociology of self-reflexive presentations of the self. Ultimately, this points toward the reasons why the macabresque emerges in cases of mass atrocity: *it stages these instances of self-representation.*

These observations also situate Sofsky's interpretation within the frames of social psychological theories pertaining to the dynamics of self-categorization, self-identity and prototypicality. As he concludes, "But excess provides the perpetrator with a distinctive sense of self-esteem . . . the culprits gain the certainty that they are capable of anything, any outrage. *Excess is an act of uninhibited self-expansion.*"[120] Sofsky's sociological approach thus veers methodologically toward the social psychological, from absolute power to sadistic aggression, and from self-representation to perpetrators' self-expansion as sadists. An analytical step remains, however—namely, careful delineation of what self-representation indicates about human development and personality and how it becomes seized by perverse desire for displays of sadistic cruelty in the contexts of mass atrocity.

DISORDERS OF WILL BY OTHER NAMES: OBJECTIFICATION, ESSENTIALIZATION, DEHUMANIZATION, AND DEMONIZATION

Is it imaginatively possible to understand what perpetrators perceive, sense, know or feel about those victims whose humanity they violate in the instants of mass atrocity? A language exists to denote the processes of perpetrator reification applied to suborned victims: *objectification, essentialization, dehumanization,* and *demonization.* These are the "ization" dynamics that transform the status of personhood denoted by freedom, singularity, and spirituality into a thing-like substance thus attributing substantiality to the human condition. But freedom, individuality and spirituality do not possess thing-like qualities. They are defined by their effervescent qualities, such as imagination and crea- tivity, and by capacities such as compassion, care and love, empathy, understanding, integ- rity, morality, and so on. What, then, does it mean to dehumanize, essentialize, demonize human beings? How do reifications relate to the staged dynamics of mass atrocity and performative transgression in cases of mass atrocity? What do these processes indicate about the psychodynamics of desire and disordered will?

In thinking about what Sofsky calls the sadistic aggression at the core of performative transgression in mass atrocity, one is assailed by the inhumanity of perpetrators in their *humanhood*. How can perpetrators—as human beings—do evil unto others? What are the portals of absolute power? What is the relationship of perpetrator-to-victim in the rawness of the agony? How do perpetrators interpret their own behaviors? Motivational analysis features *relationality* in genocide and mass atrocity: first, perpetrators in relation to themselves in terms of *self-deception*; second, perpetrators in relation to each other in terms of *mirror images*; third, perpetrators in relation to victims in terms of *sadistic aggression* and *performative transgression*. Often, victims are reified as subhuman or less than human, as in cases of dehumanization; or, alternatively, they are demonized as exis- tential threats to immediate survival and also to the very survivability of the in-group(s). Dehumanization was rampant during the historical era of colonialist domination, often entailing economic exploitation and forced geographic displacement. Aboriginal and pri- mordial communities in various regions of Africa and Asia, but also in precolonial North America, were typically reified as subhumans. Often, settlers treated them as "deserving" of subjugation. If and whenever indigenes resisted, they were subjected to massive assault, to the point of decimation, even extermination, as demonstrated, for example, by the colonialist histories of Tasmania and Southwest Africa.[121] Similarly, in cases of demoni- zation, victimized groups become perceived as the vectors of disease, decay, decadence, and demise, as were the Jews during the Holocaust, or Muslim Bosniaks in the course of ethnic cleansing during the disintegration of the former Yugoslavia.

What such patterns of reification demonstrate are the influential roles played by unconscious self-deceptions often entertained by perpetrators who demand of them- selves that *they believe what they want to believe* and thus in turn deny, reject, or condemn contradictory evidence. Self-deceptions embedded in psychosocial akrasia function to promote objectified identitarian constructions of many kinds and stripes: blood, caste, or kinship honors nativism, majority nationalism, the ethnicization of nationality, the racialization of race, the spatialization of difference, gendered forms of social or class exclusivism, misogyny, sexism, fascist supremacism, and so on. This is in the nature of the "see one, see all" kinds of stereotypes operating on the basis of prejudged mark- ers. Martha Nussbaum, among others, has outlined the dimensions of objectification in the context of feminist theory. Objectification may be said to occur when persons are spectrally viewed and treated in terms of the following: their instrumentality (as a means to further utilitarian ends); less than deserving of autonomy or self-governance;

inert or unable to pursue independent agency or ends of their own; fungible or less than unique and singular and thus interchangeable with others; violability and thus open to violation; chattel labor to be traded; unable to experience imaginative forms of subjective understanding.[122] Objectification, along with dehumanization, demonization, and essentialization, thus represents the way of depicting relationships devoid of benevolence, sympathy, empathy, or even pity. The possibilities of imaginative exchange embodied in the privileging of the moral status of "the other," as in Levinasian concepts of the "ontological supplement" and "faciality," disappear in favor of interrelational opacity.[123] But does objectification add up to dehumanization or dehumanization, to demonization, and why might such distinctions matter with respect to the motivations of perpetrators in wielding absolute power?

Related to this issue is the question of narcissism and of "minor differences" long familiar to students of Freudian psychoanalysis. Some of the most horrendous outbreaks of genocidal outrage appear to emerge in political cultures assailed by "minor" identitarian differences. This serves to underscore the relevance of psychosocial analysis in the study of genocide and mass atrocity because it opens up the possibilities of exploring the unconscious emotional forces at work relative to jealousy, envy, and other such psychic conditions in which political identity appears disfigured by reification. Karl Figlio presents a suggestive argument for why when extreme political violence against some in a society occurs at the hands of others, the "others" are national or cultural "brothers" and "sisters" who share overwhelmingly in identitarian commonalities or "sameness" except for "minor" differences. "Consciously," he writes, "we exclude others who are different, but unconsciously, we hate sameness, and avoid it by creating delusional differences." He adds, "Hatred drives the projection of these delusional differences into the other that it creates, there to be exterminated. Overt differences, to which the delusional differences can be attached, mask the delusional projection, and the source of hatred in sameness."[124] This appears to be the case. The victims of mass atrocity who suffer grotesque pain are frequently distinguishable from perpetrators only by minor identitarian contrasts, differences so minor they are appropriately contextualized as delusional. But why? Identitarian identicality and/or sameness in identity politics, not identity difference as such, comprises a critical vector in genocide and mass atrocity. A prime example is that of the Bosniak victims who suffered ethnic cleansing and atrocity at the hands of perpetrators who were Slavic compatriots but not co-religionists.

Reifying prejudices thus play out in various ways in the course of mass atrocity. This has provoked controversy over the conceptual applications of such terms as "dehumanization" and "demonization." Both processes involve the psychodynamics of desire and reification. They demonstrate disordered motivations to "*will*" difference into becoming alien, to subordinate difference in "otherness" by attributing categorical substantiality to the personhood of those being reified. The question arises as to whether this psychodynamic of willful reification eviscerates the humanity of victims or, alternatively, demands that victims retain their humanness as they are violated.

ON RELATIONALITY IN ABSOLUTE POWER

Johannes Lang's critique of the concept "dehumanization" illustrates the problem.[125] He accepts the concept of absolute power as valid. But he does so in order to resurrect the theoretical importance of relationality; secondly, he shifts emphasis from situation to personality. He thus recalibrates the methodological perspective from sociology to social psychology. In my view, however, his analysis stops at the very point where it should begin, with a psychosocial framing of the disorders of will. Lang's immediate concern is conceptually to reject dehumanization as a way of describing what perpetrators "do" to victims on the grounds that to do so distorts the behavioral elements of absolute power critical to an understanding or interpretation of their relationality. Lang suggests that an emphasis on how perpetrators *dehumanize* their victims in mass atrocity theoretically strips analysis of perpetrator desires and motivations from their fundamental compulsions, the effort to exact extreme pain to disembody the subjectivity of victims—so as to experience the power to torment the humanity of others. Lang argues that what this requires, however, is that victims remain human in their *human* spirit and subjectivity; otherwise, perpetrators would no longer desire the absoluteness of absolute power. Lang argues that although mass atrocity is embedded in the asymmetries of objectified relationality between perpetrator and victim, such relationships demand that victims as well as perpetrators retain their ontological status as "human." Perpetrators must "experience" victims as partaking of human subjectivity so as to be "worthy" of serving as objects of excruciation. In Lang's perspective, this very quality of humanness would be undermined if victims were to be perceived as dehumanized, the very point suggested analytically by the term "dehumanization." As he comments, "The victim is instrumentalized, but not dehumanized; he becomes an instrument in the hands of the perpetrator, but an instrument whose humanity—or, more precisely, subjectivity—is a centrally important element of its instrumentality." He adds, "To make people the object of one's power is not necessarily to objectify them, but can be to subordinate their subjectivity to one's own."[126]

Lang then adopts Sofsky's interpretation of the influences of social identity in explaining perpetrator behaviors; excess violence becomes the insignia of belonging to an in-group, its values and expectations. He explicitly aligns his approach within the methodological frames of social psychology by recontextualizing Sofsky's phenomenological sociology to accommodate John C. Turner's concepts of social identity and self-categorization. This is critical to social psychological conceptions of group dynamics. In my view, however, these tend to equate motivational forces with impulsive-cognitive-strategic processes of in-group homogenization and out-group discrimination and hostility, as well as actions that accede to the prototypical benchmarks of in-group behaviors and normative expectations.

To emphasize his brand of social psychology, Lang criticizes Sofsky's sociology for being insufficiently psychological. Lang states, "Sofsky effectively separates the psychological from the sociological inquiries into the realities of the Nazi concentration camp. This is an unfortunate move," he continues, "because it severs social action from its motivational dimensions." Lang continues his criticism on the grounds that "psychology and sociology must be united in any investigation into the camps . . . . Social psychology provides the needed bridge between psychology and sociology; it occupies the borderland between the two disciplines."[127] But the contiguous methodologies of each, social psychology and phenomenological sociology, incapacitate explorations of perpetrator motivations once they eschew psychosocial analysis. Lang comments on Sofsky's apparent disregard for the *social* in social psychology. "Sofsky's objections regarding psychology can be interpreted as merely emphasizing that we should focus on situations; when he discards psychology on such grounds, he seems to be guided by a rather outdated conception of psychology as a thoroughly intrapsychic, individualistic discipline."[128] Lang concludes, "This narrow view of psychology ignores social psychology, which is, after all, essentially situation-oriented."[129] Lang thus criticizes Sofsky on the methodological grounds of social psychology; faults him for failing to emphasize the psychological dimensions of in-group social dynamics; and alleges that Sofsky ignores the methodological stress on sociality in contemporary social psychology. The question arises, however, as to how Lang develops his own approach to the dynamics of objectification, which he methodologically approves as a unit of analysis as opposed to the analytical concept of dehumanization that he rejects, the very starting point of his effort to reposition the psychological dimension in examining sadistic aggression.

Lang claims that dehumanization is invalid as a formulation in describing perpetrator to victim relations precisely because it tends to obscure the subject-to-subject relationship that applies in such cases. He favorably cites Alexander L. Hinton's approach, which abjures application of the term *dehumanization* in favor of "production of subjectivities." This neo-Foucauldian formulation is applicable when, to quote Hinton within the frames of Lang's critique, the psychicalities of victims, " 'serve as the symbolic templates through which their subjectivity and that of the perpetrator may be manufactured.' "[130] But Lang also finds fault with Hinton's assessment that the relationship between subjectivities, perpetrator to victim, in the process of "manufacturing difference, comprises dehumanization." Lang prefers instead the standard social psychological formulations, including "depersonalization," "desensitization," and "emotional hardening" as well as the normalization of violence and the "routinization" of self-aggrandizing sadism. As to the victimized, most especially the hapless Jews in the Nazi concentration camps, Lang depicts how the camp guards reified them in terms of "de-individualization" and "essentialization."[131] But Lang, given the methodological constraints framed by his adaptations of social psychology, is unable to explain essentialization or de-individualization beyond the fact that they occurred and perpetrators, as members of in-groups, gave rise to behaviors that manifested them.

THE CONFLATION OF MOTIVATION WITH PURPOSE:
ON METHODOLOGICAL CIRCULARITY

Social and political behavioral theories explain by reframing descriptive concepts and nominalist categories into explanations of why and how certain sets of processes and occurrences do or do not happen and in what ways. Throughout this exercise, I have found fault with various theoretical perspectives that purport to explain pathways to genocide and mass atrocity by inscribing perpetrator motivations on the basis of in-group normative prescriptions or purposes. The problem emerges in the absence of value-added dimensions in explanations of motivations and intentionality. This is brought on by a fateful conflation of what *motivates* perpetrators, on the one hand, and their *purposes*, especially in groups, on the other. Perpetrator motivations, alone, in groups and as participants in collective social and political orders, inhere in multiple overlays of psychic and emotional consciousness and unconsciousness defined by concepts focused on non-purposive phenomena: desire and longing; anxiety and fantasy; abjection and paranoia; sadistic obsession and disorders of will.

The psychodynamics of introjection and projection help to illustrate how non-purposive unconscious motivations explain perpetrator behaviors, for example, with respect to reification, dehumanization, and essentialization. The concept of motivation thus methodologically situates analysis of the pathways to genocide and mass atrocity on a spectrum from perpetrators' interiority to situational exteriority, and thus external purposive behaviors back to motivational interiority—but in noncircular ways. The very social psychological concepts typically applied in explaining perpetrator behaviors themselves become problematicized analytically. Concepts such as self-identity, self-categorization, obedience, conformity—all become amendable to theoretical explanations in psychodynamic frames that provide further insight into why sadistic violence and performative transgression occur. Perpetrators are given to infusing their motivations with a wide range of extraneous purposes they represent as compelling, from love of country to national glory to fears of lethal infection brought on by members of suborned groups. Self-deceptions permit perpetrators to conflate unconscious motivations with declared purposes. Failure to draw distinction between unconscious motivation and conscious intentionality results in analytical, methodological, and theoretical circularities in analytical logic: *(perpetrator) roles are said to explain behavioral motivations (absolute power, sadistic aggression, surplus cruelty, performative transgression, and lurid theatricality) reflective of purposes attached to role-playing (self-identity, self-categorization) that derive from the purposive objectives of groups (objectification, essentialization, dehumanization, and demonization); in turn, these purposes serve as motivations stemming from role-playing in groups (obeisance, obedience, conformity) that explain perpetrator purposes in groups and thus their motivations prompting sadistic aggression and absolute power, and so forth.*

Admittedly, group dynamics influence the purposive behaviors of individuals as members of groups at micro levels of analysis, groups in relation to each other at meso levels of analysis, and groups within social structures as a whole at macro levels. Theories adequate to the task of explaining motivations in genocide and mass atrocity must provide "bridge frameworks" of analysis that embed motivations in explanations beyond purpose. As Abraham Kaplan once stated in his classic study of theory and methodology, " 'Theoretical' thus means abstract, selecting from the materials of experience; but it also means conceptual (in a narrow sense), constructing from the selected materials something with no counterpart in experience at all."[132] Purposive behaviors represent the "materials of experience"; unconscious motivations do not in the sense since they remain analytically elusive. This helps to define the theoretical challenges of applying psychosocial perspectives to collective behaviors involved in mass atrocity. This is underscored by Kaplan's reflection on theory as "bridge." To cite Kaplan's discourse once more, "We may say to start with that a theory is a system of laws. But the laws are altered by being brought into systematic connection with one another, as marriage relates two people who are never the same again. Each law takes up into itself something of the substance of the others. It is generalized, reformulated, or at any rate, reinterpreted." He adds, "The theory is not the aggregate of the new laws but their connectedness, as a bridge consists of girders only in that the girders are joined together in a particular way. The theory explains the laws, not as something over and above them, but by giving each the strength and purpose which derives from the other."[133] Such an informed methodological inquiry recomposes how motivations "to perform" atrocity become theoretically problematicized over and above their utilitarian purposes except in the limited sense of desire and its psychodynamics of ludic, transgressive performance.

The Macabresque of Performative Derision and Faux Irony

Victims rarely suffer alone or in isolation. They are made to die in groups to ensure that they become aware of others dying—as they themselves die. The psychosocial processes that provoke political reification and hatred become transformed into hellish aesthetics of human mortification. This is what the term *mass atrocity* signifies. The systematic debasement of victims proceeds by means of an aesthetic "style"—that is, an "art form" at once perverse in its exhibitionism and voyeuristically sadistic in its instrumental methods. The term *evil* is used in many ways and in many contexts. I would suggest that it be reserved for these very instances of mass atrocity when egregious agonies are inflicted on groups of people at the hands of other human beings who have descended into the status of perpetrators. Why does death by killing alone appear insufficient to gratify perpetrators? Why are victims made to endure staged, ludic, or performative transgression; why the ever-present dramaturgical or aesthetically performed atrocities, when political violence becomes transformed into human violation? The study of the psychodynamics of perpetrator motivations during large group violence (violation), in particular, mass atrocity in genocide focuses on what I depict as the aesthetics of *the macabresque of performative transgression*.

Perpetrators of mass atrocity often revel in the perverse or exhibitionist dramaturgies of the macabresque. They create "theaters of horror" that demand abhorrent displays of sadistic or surplus cruelty be made to occur. Performative transgression, what Marguerite Feitlowitz poignantly described as "sinister theatrics," inheres in the suffering of victims made to "perform" theatrically while being subjected to torment and humiliation.[134] At times, victims are made to be complicit in their own and others' defilement or to bear witness to the agony and debasement of loved ones, friends, neighbors, fellow co-religionists, and even strangers who share common ethnic affinities or cultural affiliations. The sadistic motivation is perverse in its desire for display. For the exhibitionism here does not put the human body on public display in "excited" defiance of the norms of social decency; rather, it seeks to devastate the very social norms that distinguish the decent from the indecent. It does this by means of the macabresque, the production of horror frozen into morbidity by means of displayed or performative violation, often involving sexual violation, physical dismemberment, or both. The perversity is in the theatricality but also in perpetrators' desire to transform obscene agony into the sadistically "enjoyable" by virtue of derisive or ironic aesthetics, by means, for example, of strains of classical music being played while electronic shocks are being applied. Concentration camp guards insisted on the Women's Orchestra of Auschwitz, when female inmates were forced to play symphonic performances as a way of delaying their own deaths, but at what emotional cost? The macabresque aesthetics of transgressive violation typically include such elements of derisive "non-humor" seething with acidic "non-irony" as an accompaniment to sadistic cruelty. Such is the measure of the macabresque to have victims reincarnate either the comedic, so as to force them into a "pathetic" parody of their own suffering, or to make victims embody the tragedy of their own and other victims' deaths, thereby transforming victim torment into the pathos of an agonic anti-comedy. This represents the import of the "surplus supplement" in the macabresque of performative transgression.

Students of acute racist prejudice and violence, including Adorno and Max Horkheimer and, more recently, Michael Billig, have shown that hatred and political reification, on the one hand, and demeaning humor, on the other, often march together. Billig states, for example, "As Freud suggested, the joke provides a setting in which one can be freed from the demands of pity. If the ultimate word is an emblem of extreme racism, then enjoyment might be gained through a lack of restraint, which permits the racist to treat humans as animals."[135] For such reasons, certain subsets of slave owners in the American South festooned their chattel laborers with names from Greek and Roman classical literature or from the Shakespearean repertory, such as Cassius, Brutus, and Macbeth. More relevantly, as in the case of the Argentinean Dirty War, the instruments, methods, and chambers of torture were bestowed with funny or "endearing" euphemisms designed to transform the horror of their implementation into a bond of solidarity among perpetrators. It was perhaps Lucy S. Dawidowicz who most poignantly understood the power of laughter in the perpetration of Nazi evil. She points to Hitler's speech to the Reichstag on January 30, 1939, in which he declared, "I have often been a prophet in my life and was generally *laughed* at. During my struggle for power, the Jews received with *laughter* my prophecies .... *I suppose ... the then resounding laughter of Jewry in Germany is now choking in their throats.*[136] Ron Rosenbaum comments on the acuity of Dawidowicz's scholarship identifying Hitler's repeated reference to this speech, which she describes as a "declaration of war against the Jews." Dawidowicz also compared the speech Hitler delivered on September 1, 1939, in declaring war against Poland in which he omitted all reference to the Jews. Dawidowicz observed that Hitler subsequently conflated the two speeches by repeatedly referring to the September speech as the one that had focused on the "laughter" of the Jews instead of one that he had delivered in January. Dawidowicz infers from this a series of "slips" demonstrating that Hitler's genuine aim in invading Poland was the destruction of European Jewry.

But Rosenbaum goes beyond this to suggest that the ultimate significance of Dawidowicz's finding pertains to the repeated references to Jewish laughter as such. He suggests that Hitler's objective in seeking the extermination of the Jews was to eliminate their laughter from the face of the earth. Rosenbaum thus refers to the concept of "displacement," a psychoanalytic term (although he subsequently abjured the validity of psychoanalytic examinations of Hitler). The displacement occurs by means of the "last laugh" that Hitler is said now to experience by "savoring a secretive triumph, whose pleasure is clearly enhanced by an awareness of its profoundly *illicit* nature."[137] Rosenbaum rejects theory that would suggest that the Holocaust demonstrated self-sacrificial supererogatory obligations on the part of perpetrators, although he admits that national humiliation and shame, as well as a desire for revenge, were and remain plausible factors. The point he stresses in the context of laughter, however, is that it became an emotional and outward expression featuring the *innermost* sense of shared complicity between Hitler and those closest to him in his immediate entourage. Laughter at the Jews became an element of the desire they shared and felt bound by, but a desire for what? In Rosenbaum's interpretation the answer is not only a desire for transgression in and for itself but also to enjoy its mechanisms and means, its modes and methods—that is, its artfulness, craft, ingenuity, and inventiveness. Rosenbaum links Berel Lang's and Lucy Dawidowicz's analyses by stating with reference to Hitler and the circle immediately around him, "And what exactly is he relishing so deeply? Not merely the thing in itself, the mass murder but the delicious—to him—irony of it, the exquisite—to him—literary irony that those who laughed are now having their murders measured out in the sound of their subsiding laughter by the very one they laughed at." Rosenbaum adds, "In a way, it is a confirmation . . . of the slaughter as an aesthetic experience, in the perpetrators' relishing its piquant artful ironies, that the highest degree of conscious evil discloses itself."[138] In this analytical light, the macabresque as a perspective on the aesthetics of mass atrocity thus enables us to frame an approach to the sado-intimacies which inevitably arise during episodes of performative transgression when mass violence becomes converted into mass human violation. It stresses the often intimate or direct forms of violence imposed on victims on the part of perpetrators who, time and again, case upon case, give every appearance of surplus or sadistic enjoyment of their own dramaturgical performance. This, too, is suggestive of the psychosocial applications of concepts pertaining to desire, particularly Lacanian conceptions of *jouissance*.

Such efforts at demeaning victims by means of overlaying or conjoining the opposites—malevolence, on the one hand, and euphemism, on the other—during episodes that combine perverse exhibitionism with sadistic brutality help to define the dark aesthetic features of performative transgression. These in turn point to the psychodynamics of political reification and desire, even hatred, as nodal points in mass atrocity. The shibboleth at the entry to Auschwitz, *Arbeit Macht Frei*, the pretense to labor socialism at the gates of hell, makes the point all too clearly. Mass atrocity, performativity of violation, and transgressive humor of non-comedic humor are integral to the political evil that is the macabresque and never so close as when they operate as the hands in the gloves of perpetrators. Rosenbaum, following the thoughts of Berel Lang stresses the sheer enjoyment gleaned by Hitler and fellow Nazis from the moral outrages perpetrated against Jewish victims, a sense of enjoyment tantamount to acts of an aesthetic anti-imagination. "There is a conscious *relish* in the horrific transgressiveness of the dehumanization process—a kind of artistic process in reverse, a decreation, in which humans are reconfigured, resculpted into subhumans—a relish in the process that cannot be defended as a self-sacrificial descent to ruthless methods for an idealistic cause. The methods *were* the essence, the methods were the madness."[139] From this perspective, the self-deception that sustained Nazi evil was not simply that perpetrators wanted to believe the lie that what they were doing was "good" in some ideological sense; rather it stemmed from the fact that they knew what they were doing to be evil and did so on this precise account and in a psychosocial sense, as "artists" called to the desecration of life rather than to the creative life of the imagination. This helps to explain the aesthetic qualities with which it was done. Rosenbaum comments, "The notion of an art of evil implies a knowing awareness of wrongdoing. If the locus of evil is in the degree of consciousness of the evil nature of an act, artistic consciousness is almost, by definition, the most elaborate, the deepest kind of consciousness."[140] This desire for what is evil as a form of aesthetic enjoyment combines pain with pleasure, cruelty with laughter, and death with art. Thus, mass violence does not attain the status of art by means of lethality alone, additionally, it requires a desire to engage in "evil as an art, the art of evil."[141] Art is a method, an act of the imagination, and a form of representation. Its purpose is in itself for itself, as a means of self-expression, as an end to be valued, but also as a means to enjoyment of a particular kind, one that is amenable to interpretation by means of such psychosocial concepts and perspectives as sadism and *jouissance*. This demonstrates the critical linkages I wish to establish among the disordered desire for absolute power as an end in and for itself in mass atrocity in consonance with the sadistic cruelties designed and given expression within the universes of the macabresque. It is the macabresque in mass atrocity that is critical to a psychosocial interpretation of mass murder and genocide. Again, this is because the macabresque allows us to examine disorders of will and desire partially explainable within psychosocial perspectives.

The question thus becomes, why the hatred, the humor, and the routine violation played out performatively, often theatrically, in the most depraved manner available to the diabolical imagination. Macabresque aesthetics of performative transgression tend to become spatialized into "theaters." Such theatrical, dramaturgical, or ludic spaces readily become transformed into the lurid "geographies" of concentrated (in)humanity. Here, inhuman torments run rampant, untrammeled by empathetic reserve or sympathy of any kind or degree. Here, again, we confront the allures and enticements of absolute power. Spatialized dramaturgies in mass atrocity create the macabresque in multiple ways across the instances when it occurs. Events may be premeditated or spontaneous, orgiastic or in deliberative slow motion. Time as a sequence of moments withers in the spaces of mass atrocity, however, to allow the macabresque dramaturgies of performative transgression to proceed; time must stop so that the liminal boundaries between social civility and political depravity become defaced or disappear altogether.

A critical component of performative transgression is systematic debasement of physical modesty. Any attempt at social privacy or personal intimacy is destroyed—absolutely. All that is personal becomes denuded. Life as it is lived in the interstitial gaps of sociality or interpersonal relations becomes transmogrified into naked compressions. Here, again, I find evidence for the voyeuristic and exhibitionist qualities in perpetrator behaviors. In the Omarska killing camp, dozens of Bosniak men and boys were forcibly pressed together within the cramped quarters designated by Serb guards as "the White House" so that the prisoners would suffocate slowly against each other and in the others' sweat. Why are victims made to sing but to the tune of death and dying; why are they forced to dance as their spirits wither; why are they made to laugh while their souls dissolve into numbness and decay; why are they required to share such decreative experiences collectively among other victims as the macabresque violations perpetrated against them petrify their minds and spirits even before the rigor mortis of the body sets in. Such totalized vulnerability is made all the starker, all the more shame-filled for victims themselves, as their souls become tokenized by placing their bodies on display, as it were, smack against each other. Why does it appear "necessary" for perpetrator regimes and their agents to exact spiritual agony and physical torment often from fellow and sister citizen-victims, by means of their mental, psychic, or emotional humiliation, their corporeal degradation, even the attempted demise of their very personhood? The psychodynamics of political reification and desire provide conceptual tools with which to engage these questions.

PART II

On the "Normality" of Perpetrators

HOW WE KNOW THEM, HOW THEY KNOW THEMSELVES

2

Perpetrators Alone and Together

ANALYTICAL PERSPECTIVES,

METHODOLOGICAL CRITIQUES

Whenever persons act alone to engage in acts of vicious cruelty, it becomes readily straightforward to pathologize their behaviors. They are categorized as psychopathic in cases in which diagnostic emphasis is placed on their interior compulsions; or, alternatively, they are considered as sociopathic if it appears that exterior impulsions had contributed to their anomic acts. Cruelty as such is not considered the normal disposition of individual persons. In analyzing the pathologies of violence, the question becomes one of determining the nature and origins of the abnormality, what drove the perpetrator to engage in deviant or antisocial behaviors and why. Simon Baron-Cohen,[1] for example, has recently presented findings that demonstrate how internal neurological circuitries within the brains of certain individuals contribute to developmental abnormalities and thus behavioral psychopathologies evident in what he calls their "zero negative" or "congenital incapacity" to experience empathy. As such, they manifest psychopathic tendencies. On the other hand, Russell Jacoby,[2] in his examination of the "roots of violence" follows on the work of both Freud and René Girard by stressing the social dynamics of mimetic desire in human violence. Girard's account emphasizes the sociopathologies generated by conflicts among "fraternal brothers," groups steeped in violence not on account of the magnitudes of the differences separating them, but rather driven by conditions provoked by fears over the loss of these identitarian distinctions (what I discuss with respect to identitarian identicality). Jacoby shows how misogynist sociopathic fantasies stoke these fears by becoming laminated by unconscious male anxieties over the procreativity and fecundity of women and over unconscious masculine dread of feminization. In such cases, pathologies reside in the social composition of competing masculinities/patriarchies and take shape or form in the personal or communal or both.

Examinations of the etiologies of genocide or of mass atrocity, however, tend to emphasize neither psychopathology nor sociopathology. On the contrary, the analytical languages of sickness and abnormality, and thus of pathology, tend to be avoided entirely. When evaluating the behaviors of perpetrators and what "causes" them to act in such extremist and abhorrent ways, the answers tend to emphasize perpetrator normality—that is, what renders them "ordinary" and thus indistinguishable from most other individuals. Explanations thus turn not so much toward individual pathology but, rather, to the distortionary influences of the "situations" in which groups of perpetrators are seen to operate. Perpetrators, their psychological or emotional states, their beliefs and attitudes as motivational forces, their backgrounds and capacities for empathy and information processing, and other such, all tend to become analytically subsumed under situational factors seen to be so extraordinary that they can convert "ordinary" persons into "extraordinary" perpetrators. This is not to suggest that such approaches either deny the essential importance of human choice and volition in the execution of atrocity crimes and violence. Nor do such analytical approaches lump all perpetrators together without attempting to differentiate subsets among them. Analytical focus on the relationships that pertain between perpetrators as persons acting in groups and often under certain command structures, on the one hand, and the situational factors that variously permit, support or, even, compel the implementation of mass atrocity, on the other, is clearly appropriate given emphasis on the causes of genocide, mass violence or large group conflicts.

But the theoretical argument I make here is that situations of mass atrocity raise the curtains on the performative. To relate perpetrators to their behaviors and their behaviors to the situations in which they function requires a psychosocial framework of analysis featuring the dramaturgical and aesthetic nature of these fateful relationships. Such so-called situations resemble the features of "scenes" staged and performed in part for exhibitionist and voyeuristic purposes. When perpetrators act, they become witness to the degradation of victims. Thus they serve as actors but also an audience unto themselves. The macabresque readily yields to perpetrator variations in theatophilic and scopophilic exhibitionism, states of self-exhibitionism on the part of perpetrators and their voyeuristic fascination and grandiose fantasy guided by akratic dreams of omnipotence.[3] Exhibitionism and voyeurism do not cause genocide nor do they exclusively explain mass atrocity; rather they help to contribute to an understanding of the macabre components of mass atrocity that emerge by and through the dramaturgies and aesthetics of the macabresque. As I also go on to suggest, sadomasochistic behaviors are integral to exhibitionist desires. The desires for voyeuristic exhibition are not causal in the sense that they provide answers about why mass atrocities occur. They do suggest, however, why under certain conditions perpetrators across many cultures and in multiple settings appear susceptible to the dramaturgical and aesthetic lures (and allures) embodied in the macabresque.

I suggest, therefore, that self-exhibitionism provides a theoretical basis for interpreting the macabresque as a discrete phenomenon in mass atrocity violence. The desire among perpetrators to bond together is forged by means of their desire for shared self-exhibition and for voyeuristic power and control over the bodies of others in the process. These desires can, and do, function among perpetrators who are appropriately considered to be normal and ordinary. But these desires may as well progressively become *more, not less* insistent as perpetrators perform their excesses and outrages. The "appetite grows with eating"; the more desire is satisfied the less it is satisfied. This provides a basis for interpreting why perpetrators in war or conflict, especially those deemed normal at the onset of hostilities, so often appear to become inured to its violence and cruelties. Study after study has shown that perpetrators become used to plying their task the more they do it. But why? That they do so is not self-explanatory. No single answer suffices. But I argue that explanations in part derive from the sense of absolute power, as has been suggested by Sofsky and others. But, again, power is a concept that insufficiently explains perpetrator desire. Once the quest for absolute power becomes linked to self-exhibitionism and given complete mandate by the "situations" calling for mass atrocity, the stage is set for the "scenic," the macabresque, to be enjoyed by its audience of perpetrators as viewers who gaze unto themselves as they denude their victims of human dignity.

But first, I wish to review several treatments of perpetrators that have focused on the perplexing question of "normality." To what extent is perpetrator normality a function of their being no more and no less than "ordinary." If "situations" are thought to be determinative, analytical emphasis is placed on how and why the transformation of ordinarily normal persons into such extraordinary killers occurs. The answers often tend to emphasize the extraordinary character of the situations, including wars. When the focus turns to the perpetrators themselves, analysis concentrates on motivations defined in relation to group dynamics or situational norms. Some degree of rationality is assumed, in particular with respect to group behaviors. As we have seen, even discussions regarding the drive for absolute power situate perpetrator actions within analytical perspectives that underscore the role of their group dynamics: their desire for recognition, self-esteem, and bonding but on the basis of conceptions of rationality that stress human capacities for self-rationalization.

POLITICAL ANALYSIS OF WAR AND CIVIL CONFLICT AS VECTORS

In the sections that follow, I encapsulate several studies that examine war as a causal factor in genocide and mass atrocity. These establish certain correlated relationships among a range of empirical indicators that are predictive of high levels of death. The strengths of these analyses are clear and hardly need defense here. But their methodological rigor disables their capacities to grapple with measures that remain inaccessible or irrelevant to quantitative analysis. Interpretations of the unconscious in emotion and desire are sometimes analytically construed as "perceptions." Perceptions are conceived or represented as "rational" or as rationalized reactions to external phenomena, as in, for example, perceptions of territorial loss or of historic events prompting national humiliation. Ethno-grievances on the part of insurgent groups or demands on the part of power regimes calling for the purification of the homeland tend to be framed in perceptual, strategic, and, ultimately, rationalized terms. Even self-styled rationalizations suffused with ideological constructions linked to calls for restoration of historic wrongs or irredentist calls for land and return to glory are examined as cognitively framed ideological articulations to which I have referred here as the logics of illogic: romanticized, sometimes racialized, either utopian or dystopian, invariably fascist or collectivist. The macabresque as an explanatory perspective demonstrates the analytical limitations of these approaches to extreme violence. Their conceptual analysis remains beholden to cognitive constructions of mind, perception, rationality, and ideology. Put alternatively, the question pertains to the extent to which political analysis of war and collective violence would discover validity in expanding its theoretical perspectives to include qualitative psychosocial analysis of the macabresque by methodologically embracing the unconscious, in particular, collective social fantasy as units of analysis in the study of war, conflict, and violence with emphasis on efforts to explain organized human violation.

FACTORS IN EXPLANATIONS OF WAR

That there exist direct, positive, or causal relationships between war, civil war, and genocidal violence is implicitly borne out by Greg Cashman. In encapsulating a vast literature on the "paths" to war, he indicates, for example, that "although there is as yet no psychological theory of war, we find cognitive, personality, and emotional factors important to the understanding of war."[4] Cashman also points to "a few empirical regularities" in war, including, "when interstate war happens, it almost always involves contiguous neighbors." He adds, "The most likely underlying cause of fighting between contiguous states is a dispute over territory."[5] Cashman also indicates that wars disproportionately occur between "enduring rivals or strategic rivals," and that "most wars are preceded by militarized disputes or crises that involve escalatory behavior preceding the outbreak of war that looks like a conflict spiral."[6] If interstate war represents a major predictor of genocide and mass atrocity, such factors as territoriality, contiguity, rivalry, and escalating spiral thus become relevant not only in terms of objectives in war but also to the psychodynamics of mimetic desire or envy.

Armed Power Organizations and the Domestic Fallacy

Additionally, the inducements of regime power in both international and domestic conflicts prevail over other explanations of the causes of genocide and mass atrocity. Martin Shaw outlines arguments linking armed power within domestic and international or cross-border political contexts to explain the causes of genocide and mass atrocity.[7] Shaw's approach also helps to frame a case-study approach to mimetic desire in the macabresque. Shaw declares, "Genocide is always a deliberate policy and organized action and so needs to be explained primarily within political conflict." Shaw stresses the role of "regimes" or organized power and of insurgent forces that take over the institutional/administrative apparatus of the national state. He observes that regime type and legitimacy become critical variables in linking war and conflict dynamics to genocide.[8] Shaw stresses the impacts of "armed power organizations" within nation-states. Such armed-power organizations tend to use and abuse identitarian or social categories to manipulate intergroup violence. He states, "Thus genocide is not ethnic conflict but conflict between armed power organizations and civilian groups that *mobilizes* social differences as ethnicity."[9] Shaw thus emphasizes analytical linkages between power and culture. Within Shaw's theoretical perspective, "power" methodologically emerges as the critical dimension in fomenting genocidal violence since power regimes reinforce ethnic, sectarian, or racialized divisions as rationales for their own designs. In Shaw's analysis, therefore, it is not war so much as it is *the exercises of power in war* against targeted civilian populations that drive accelerated paths to genocide and mass atrocity.

What I take to be implied here is that selected segments of civilian populations become scapegoated and essentialized and, ultimately, made to suffer in the macabresque. Power dynamics fuel the flames of identitarian reifications rather than the obverse, during episodes of genocide and mass atrocity. This is borne out, for example, by Fujii's examination of the vectors of power and identity as causal factors during the Rwanda genocide, discussed later in this chapter.

Shaw indicates that the linkages between war and its "degeneration" into genocide occur as a result of the expanding victimization of civilian populations. He suggests that genocide is a kind of "anti-war"[10] against *"civilian groups as enemies."*[11] Shaw continues, *"We should focus on what all genocidal campaigns have in common: not the destruction of a particular group type (the groups attacked vary greatly between the cases) but the civilian character of the attacked population."*[12] Shaw thus envisions the instrumental causes of genocide and mass atrocity as a relationship between government (armed power organizations) and the military or paramilitary in relation to civilian populations and thus civil society. He adds, "Genocide, like war, involves constant feedback from the 'military' direct perpetrators to the 'political' central organizers." Shaw infers from this that *"the most common direct causal context is not simply political conflict, but conflict that has already become violent."*[13] On these grounds, Shaw admonishes against too great an emphasis on domestic factors in provoking genocide and mass atrocity in favor of stress on the international and cross-border elements provoking the violence. This leads him to suggest that genocidal forms of collective violence tend to be prompted by international as well as domestic factors and influences. *"Generally it is a particular combination of national and international circumstances that provides the contexts for genocidal escalation,"* Shaw asserts. "When one thinks of the origins of the concept of genocide, in *world* wars and *international* law, this should be obvious."[14] This, too, is confirmed by specific references to the role played by Vietnamese intrusions on Cambodian territory in the ideologies of the genocidal Pol Pot regime, and by the Burundian Tutsi in the mindset or fantasies of the Rwandan genocidal regime. Shaw adds, "Yet the deep-rootedness of the domestic fallacy means that genocide studies will not escape from it without a conscious commitment to global and international understanding."[15]

The domestic fallacy arises as a consequence of misappropriated interpretations of the causes, purposes, and the consequences of cross-border violence among sovereign states at macro levels of analysis. It is impossible to assess the causes of the Cambodian genocide in the absence of a history of intervention in that country on the part of many powers, including the French but, in particular, the Vietnamese, who become "racialized" and victimized during the Cambodian genocide. Similarly, it is not possible to comprehend the origins of "Hutu power" during the Rwandan genocide without an examination of the Tutsi incursions and the earlier attacks on the Hutu from and within Burundi. Shaw is correct to point out the levels-of-analysis problem associated with the domestic fallacy. But the domestic fallacy as such also represents a failure to examine how power translates into motivations for sadistic cruelty and victim suffering. In this precise sense, war, civil conflict, and even genocide and mass atrocity as forms of collective violence become excuses permitting macabresque sadism and cruelty to press forward toward human violation.

Civil War, Land, and "Political Opportunity"

Matthew Krain, in his empirical study of the causes of genocide and mass atrocity, stresses this very state-centric or domestic viewpoint Shaw would some years later reject. Nonetheless, Krain's analysis retains its relevance given its focus on what he calls "state-sponsored mass murder" and his emphasis on "onset and severity." Krain's immediate objective is to discount a theory of "democide" proposed by R. J. Rummel. This suggested that it was high power concentrations within sovereign states that represented the major predictor of democide and politicide. Krain demonstrates that the "political opportunities" theoretical model provides a more robust perspective in explaining mass murder. As we shall see in the context of the Chinese Cultural Revolution, conditions defined by "political opportunity" include challenges to established political elites or order; resistance to the political status quo or regime continuity; and the signals indicative of elite vulnerability or regime weakness. "Political opportunity" as an explanatory focus links perceived threats to regime stability on the part of challengers, real or imagined, and subsequent elite responses. Krain embeds his research in a literature that theorizes "political opportunity" variously as situations that involve "big opportunity," in which the domestic governing structure seems on the verge of collapse; transformations in the international political system, especially those caused by war and interstate conflict; civil war and revolutions; regime changes as a result of secessionist movements, decolonization, and so forth. Wars, civil wars, extraconstitutional changes, processes of decolonization, thus create "windows of political opportunity."[16]

But the methodological question Krain raises is, which factor or which combination of factors best predicts for mass murder? Krain explains, "New elites taking power or old elites trying to hold onto power can and must reconsolidate power quickly and efficiently."[17] But under what conditions will they resort to mass murder? Krain's objective, then, is to test empirically which of these factors or circumstances constituting political opportunity consistently predict for mass murder and by extension mass atrocity. Krain's conclusion is clear: "civil war involvement is the most consistent predictor of the onset of state-sponsored mass murder."[18] Krain hastens to confirm the argument made by others, including Robert Melson, to the effect that internal and international wars together, whether they occur in succession or simultaneously, enhance the probabilities of mass murder at exponential rates.[19] Krain thus argues that analytical approaches that factor in war, revolution, and decolonization in combination with civil war have the greatest predictive effects on the outbreak of mass murder. This is certainly borne out by the Cambodian genocide. These combinations of variables underscore the significance of regime stability, continuity, legitimacy, and, ultimately, the importance not only of power as such, but particularly of *threatened loss or diminution of power* in explaining genocide and mass atrocity. Power as a variable thus remains at the center of explanatory perspectives on the causes of genocide and mass atrocity. It now becomes modified to emphasize the explanatory significance of threatened loss of power. Civil wars in post–World War II China and in post–World War I Bolshevik/Soviet Russia illustrate how political opportunity models enable us to explain high death levels. On this basis, Krain concludes that it is not the "mere status of a state" or even power concentration as such that explains outbreaks of mass murder; rather it is civil war as "events that open the political opportunity structure" that are more robust. These propositions emphasizing the combination of civil war and threats to power status also imply the salience of mimetic desires among rivals, especially among those who for whatever reasons are deemed different. This too becomes relevant to applications of mimetic desire, rivalry and envy in the study of the macabresque during genocide and mass atrocity.

Insurgency as Ressentiment, Ressentiment as Powerlessness

In an often-cited article, James D. Fearon and David D. Laitin empirically establish the central role of rural insurgency in combination with poverty and administratively weak government as sources of instability that predict for high levels of civil war conflict. The particular relevance of their analysis for the study of genocide and mass atrocity is that it discounts the influences of ethnic, sectarian, and religious cleavages as primary causes of collective violence when such factors function alone. Rather, these cultural factors appear to play out in secondary ways, but mainly only after violence has started. They state, for example, "It appears *not* to be true that a greater degree of ethnic or religious diversity—or indeed any particular cultural demography—by itself makes a country more prone to civil war."[20] Put in an alternative way, they indicate, "[t]he estimates for the effect of ethnic and religious fractionalization are substantively and statistically insignificant."[21] Fearon and Laitin also found "little evidence that one can predict where a civil war will break out by looking for where ethnic or broad political grievances are strongest."[22] This suggests that the relationship of perpetrators to victims does not depend on any particular social or cultural configuration at macro levels of analysis.

What appears to be more significant is the frequency of rural guerilla warfare and the specific policy pursuits or political aims of such insurgent groups relative to the society as a whole. As Fearon and Laitin show, these vary across their sample. Poverty plays an important role and carries higher predictive weight than social divisions or cultural cleavages. Fearon and Laitin indicate, for example, "Among the poorest countries where we observe the highest rates of civil war, the data indicate a tendency for more homogeneous countries to be more civil-war prone."[23] Fearon and Laitin's broad conclusion is that "state weakness marked by poverty, a large population, and instability—are better predictors of which countries are at risk for civil war."[24] *If* war and civil war promote further violence on pathways to genocide and atrocity, and *if* civil war is a function of structural forms of state weakness in combination with rural poverty, instability, and, above all, insurgency, what are the methodological as well as theoretical implications? Fearon and Laitin indicate, "We find little evidence that civil war is predicted by large cultural divisions or broadly held divisions. But it seems quite clear that intense grievances *are produced by* civil war—indeed, this is often a central objective of rebel strategy."[25] Powerlessness is as much a factor as absolute power on the pathways to genocide and mass atrocity; secondly, identitarian issues, challenges, and conflicts serve as covers for the drive to violence and power but in epiphenomenal ways. This is confirmed indirectly by the fact that once a regime starts out toward fomenting the macabresque, it must "invent" or accentuate identity differences among the population, as in the case of the Cambodian genocide, which delineated a classification scheme dividing so-called "new" people from "base" people. Identitarian markers and cleavages thus become relevant to explanations of collective violence given their relevance to how insurgent groups become galvanized into action. Identitarian conflicts also remain central to explanations of genocide and mass atrocity, since they demonstrate the influences of social fantasies and mimetic rivalries, especially regarding how power structures "position" rival groups in relation to each other.

Quantitative vs. Qualitative Methodologies: A Brief Contrast

In recent years, empirical studies have factored in a range of other variables in explaining genocide and mass atrocity. These include land, specifically land size, population densities, and ethnic compositions relative to geographical regions. Hannibal Travis, for example, has focused on the characteristics of political formations manifesting or experiencing significant death tolls in the course of genocide. He encapsulates the findings of several teams of scholars, including Monty Marshall and Monica Duffy Toft, among others, in order to stress the relationship of land size and population density: in general, the larger the size, the greater the likelihood of genocide. Travis writes, "Surveying a variety of data sets, strong relationships emerge between country size and mass violence. . . . Without being a necessary or sufficient cause of genocide or other episodes of mass killing, country size plays a role in it along with other factors."[26] Land size and population density factor into higher death tolls along with ethnic composition or what Travis calls "ethnic variation." He states, "A possible mechanism for explaining the relationship between conflict and country size is ethnic variation. The protagonists in most civil wars between 1946 and 2000 waged them on account of ethnic, racial, or religious identity."[27] Regime power, landmass, population density, ethnic divisions thus all contribute to levels of lethality. This suggests that mimetic rivalries in genocide often revolve around regime power and status with respect to land, its control and loss, the ethnicity of domestic populations in certain geographic regions, and the presence of external risks. The methodological issue here thus concerns levels of analysis and how to link the correlated quantitative factors specified by Travis at macro levels to the micro level behaviors of agents.

Alternatively, Ben Kiernan, in a paper focused on the Holocaust, the Cambodian genocide, and the Rwandan genocide, stresses how mimetic desires function as predictors of genocidal violence at levels of analysis focused on regime behaviors.[28] Kiernan's approach is qualitative and historical, in contrast to the methodological empiricism presented by Travis and the studies he cites. Quantitative and qualitative approaches diverge with respect to the role and influences of identitarian constructions or reifications. Kiernan states, "Leaders of all three regimes held visions of the future partly inspired by ancient pasts—mythical and pristine—in which they imagined members of their original, pure, agrarian race, farming once larger territories that contained no Jews, no Vietnamese, and no Tutsi." This depiction delineates the basic characteristics of mimetic desires; they are dreamlike, intense, rivalrous, and in the context of genocide, as Kiernan comments, "racialist, reactionary, rural and irredentist." Land and memory come together in such desiring. Kiernan notes, "The perpetrators of genocide against those victim groups shared preoccupations not only with ethnic purity but also with antiquity, agriculture, and expansionism," the very factors so often present in mimetic desire. In this sense, quantitative and qualitative analyses veer more closely together in finding that mimetic desires tend to provoke sadistic drives for mastery over those who have been culturally constructed and ideologically reified as rivals or rivalrous claimants to power and land. Political opportunity models and empirical studies of land size and population density help to explain why genocide and mass atrocity occur especially whenever dissolution of the political or social order is threatened. Identitarian differences also tend to appear, sometimes to justify political and strategic objectives as justifications for collective violence, but also as the reasons for pursuing the transitions to sustained forms of human violation culminating in the macabresque. Explanations of genocide and mass atrocity are thus called on to confront the phenomenon of the macabresque on its own terms and to do so, in part, as the manifestation of mimetic desire in social fantasy and an influence in political ideology, as well as in war and civil conflict.

Defensive Violence in Wartime

Richard Rhodes provides a systematic framework for examining perpetrator transformation from soldier to "defensive" perpetrator and from defensive perpetrator to "virulent" killer. His case study analyzes the SS-Einsatzgruppen, "special forces" organized and commanded by Heinrich Himmler and Reinhard Heydrich, along with a string of officers from varied backgrounds ranging from professional careers, including lawyers, to former police. The ranks of these paramilitary security forces were supplemented by members of the *Totenkopf* or "death-head" concentration camp guard regiments as well as the Waffen-SS. Together they were tasked with the single objective, "to murder Jews, not indirectly by herding them into gas chambers but directly, by shooting them into antitank ditches, natural ravines or pits freshly dug by Russian prisoners of war."[29] The Einsatzgruppen were divided into four Einsatzkommando units and were deployed throughout a vast region east of Germany, mostly in areas bordering Russia. These were the forces at work in hundreds of killing sites throughout the Baltic region and in the Ukraine and Belarus, from Tallinn on the Baltic Sea in Estonia to Odessa on the Black Sea. Rhodes, as so many scholars and observers before and since, asks the fundamental question, "What made it possible for men, some of them 'ordinary men,' to kill so ruthlessly?" He bases his response on a criminological assessment of the emergence of violence in the human personality by adopting what he calls the "violent socialization process" model. This emphasizes a sequential set of phases in the development of capacities for violence beginning with "brutalization" and "belligerency" and ending with "violent performances" and "virulency."[30] These phases revolve around the violence experienced by individuals with effects that alternately become internalized and projected outward. Rhodes focuses on training and specifically on the kinds and degrees of brutality beaten into recruits designed to transform them into mass killers. Although his framework emphasizes situational factors, such as the violence experienced by those he describes as "novices," he stresses the significance of choice and discretion available to recruits in response to "brutalization." He writes, "Brutalization is inflicted on novices and is thus involuntary, but passage through the three later stages results from *decisions* the subject makes. So people become violent by choice, not by chances."[31] That said, brutalization does succeed in transforming most recruits from civilians into murderers.

The fulcrum on which such transformations occur is self-identification or self-representation combined with self-rationalization. Rhodes recounts a kind of internal dialogue experienced by those now chastened by brutalization and about to enter the next phase of "belligerency." He suggests that at this stage, their critical aim is to survive while assuming their new mantle of identity as killers. The quest from one phase to another provokes self-rationalization on the part of perpetrators: to survive one must kill; not to kill is to threaten one's own survival. Thus violence is envisioned as "defensive." This leads to a third phase Rhodes describes as follows: "But success with defensive violence marks a turning point in the subject's violence development. He has proven his resolve, which gives him great personal satisfaction. He has also answered the painful question he identified during the belligerency stage of how to protect himself and the people he values from violent subjugation."[32] The psychodynamics at work during this putative tertiary phase thus involve sets of both conscious and unconscious forces in which perpetrators judge themselves against the background of the values and institutions they appear to want to extol.

This is suggestive of the psychic phenomenon I encapsulate with reference to the rival self-other, the unconscious aspects of self in relation to the self at the base of a range of insecurities and doubts that prompt individuals consciously to seek forms of social confirmation or meritorious affirmation. In the context of performative violence, this appears to facilitate the transitions from defensive killing to violent performativity. Rhodes observes, "But stage three can be a slippery slope, since it already encompasses the majority of the violent experiences necessary to become fully, malefically violent."[33] And at this point, situational factors truly become determinative or governing in the sense that "All that is missing is social reinforcement of a violent identity and a widening resolution to use violence."

At this psychic and emotional juncture, the shift into phase four, or virulence, turns on what I suggest are the exhibitionist factors of self-display, perpetrator to perpetrator. Rhodes addresses the importance of peer perceptions in the process. "However personally satisfied a violent performer may be with his defensive victories, they will not change his fundamental view of himself—his self conception, his identity—unless other people acknowledge them and demonstrate their full significance to him by their actions."[34] Rhodes's language of performativity and the role the immediate "audience" of perpetrators among themselves plays in the transition away from defensive violence to offensive or activist underscores the linkages of exhibitionist/voyeuristic desire and the macabresque in mass atrocity. "The heady experiences of violent notoriety, especially combined with his painful memories of feeling powerless and inadequate during brutalization and belligerency," Rhodes writes, "encourage the subject to believe that violence works, that he has discovered a way not only to reliably protect himself . . . but also to dominate other people just as he was once dominated."[35] The consequence is perpetrator entry into the final stage of virulent killing. But such a phase would not serve the desires of these killers who had experienced all that had come before if it were to involve sanitized forms of instantaneous victim death. As previously suggested, death does not come to victims of mass atrocity in the absence of gruesome patterns of killing. Such practices are demanded as the price of "allowing" victims to die. Victims experience exhibitionist and voyeuristic outrages because they serve as opportunities for those fully initiated into the "death-head" battalions to display their hardened calls to violence. Rhodes correctly introduces the concept of "violent performances" as critical to an understanding of perpetrators.

But he fails to take full advantage of the analytical significance his conceptual insight allows. Performativity is a means to a form of self-enhancement, a way of aggrandizing the self in relation to other subjects engaged in the same kinds of performativity. The answer to why "ordinary" men kill lies in *how* they kill: performatively for the benefit of each other but to make each look "more" especially in the aftermath of shame, humiliation as well as powerlessness in the face of political loss. The collective gaze among the Einsatzgruppen thus became a critical factor in determining how the rival self-other in each perpetrator encouraged each to perceive himself as a self-object unto itself relative to other perpetrators.

ENTER POLITICAL PSYCHOLOGY: SELF-RATIONALIZATION AS "IDEALS"

Political psychology has largely incorporated the discourses of social and cognitive psychology with special emphasis on agent or actor judgments defined conceptually as cognitive exercises of the political subject with respect to assessments of the probabilities of certain processes, events, end-state conditions and consequences for political decision making. Political psychology also concentrates on decision-making relative to various behavioral taxonomic or classification schemes and distinctions. The focus is thus on how one person, a cluster of persons, large subsets of individuals, and so on, partake of the qualities deemed definitive or characteristic of general or broad categories of persons acting collectively. Prejudice and stereotypes, for example, fall well within the analytical domains of political psychology whenever questions arise as to the political implications of identity constructions or of categories of identity that influence political outcomes. Time sequences or temporality is heuristically important as well in studies emphasizing changes across certain time periods, first, in terms of how initial values and perceptions are expressed, but secondly, in terms of how they are altered under changing conditions or remembered in their aftermath. Stanley A. Renshon notes the inadequate incorporation of culture and of cultural variables as units of analysis in political psychology. "Psychology permeates political life. Yet each alone, and both collectively, are embedded in numerous cultural contexts." He adds, "Yet, paradoxically, although political psychology has made substantial substantive and institutional progress in the past seven decades, little of the field's theory and less of its research has examined culture explicitly."[36]

Kristen Renwick Monroe, in a groundbreaking study of "the psychology of genocide," combined the analytical frameworks of political psychology with the methodologies of ethnography to examine first-person narratives in stories told by witness-participants in the Holocaust, each of whom is represented as characteristic of "archetypal behavior" personified by a typology that includes: "Rescuer"; "Bystander"; "Soldier for the Nazi"; "Nazi Propagandist"; and "Unrepentant Political Nazi."[37] Monroe devotes much methodological attention to the process of gathering and evaluating interviews. "I think of the stories in this book," she writes," as acting like flashes of lightning, illuminating the cognitive landscape and helping us to understand how people see themselves, how they see others and the world around them, and how their cognitive perceptions influence their political acts."[38] Of central interest is "cognitive scaffolding" combining self-images, world views, ethical standpoints, and "cognitive classifications involving the speaker's expectations about what is normal behavior toward others."[39] Monroe situates her approach within the methodological frames of the "Bristol School" of social psychology. Established by Henri Tajfel and colleagues in the course of extensive empirical analysis of group dynamics, it advanced "social identity theory" on the basis of what proved to be compelling evidence demonstrating consistent tendencies on the part of members of groups to categorize themselves, each other, and the members of other groups. But such categories tended not to be neutral but connoted "distinctions" of worth, value, meaning, or merit that eventually reflected comparative baselines of self-worth and self-esteem. Monroe comments, "Social identity theory thus roots prejudice, discrimination, and the violence that can result from it in an innate psychological need for distinctiveness. We desire our identity to be both distinct from and compared positively with that of other groups."[40] Social identity theory thus stresses situational influences alongside psychological demands for recognition. "The critical intellectual traction of social identity theory lies in establishing a clear link between the psychological and sociological aspects of group behavior, in effectively linking the microlevel psychological need to distinguish, categorize, and compare groups with the broader, social phenomenon of group behavior."[41] On this basis, Monroe references the literature on genocide that stresses: psychological distancing or numbing; the hardening of ethnic categories or group boundaries; the fundamental role of categorization, particularly of self and others; and "cognitive stretching" or the process of treating as normal or normative what would have been "unimaginable."[42]

Monroe encapsulated her findings to conclude that, first, "Self-image is the central psychological variable," and secondly, her prototypes each evidenced "dramatically different self-concepts."[43] Monroe notes that Nazi supporters depict themselves as on the defensive, basically reactive, to the dangers presented by the Jews. "This self image is heavy with victim mentality . . . describing the Nazis as people who are 'too open,' too nice, too good to protect themselves effectively against the tricks of the unscrupulous Jews."[44] Monroe stresses the extent to which Nazis and Nazi supporters revealed a metaphysical worldview gripped by a deep fatalism, a kind of moral or ethical paralysis born of a pervasive sense of personal "helplessness," and subsequent acquiescence in the face of state authority or power. Monroe, in effect, confirms the consistency of the patterns of self-deception at work in mass atrocity. She observes, "The real powerlessness grew out of an identity perception in which people saw themselves as people who were helpless; a critical part of this helplessness was ignorance. Their lack of knowledge somehow excused people for not acting . . . . [T]he state was somehow not just all powerful but also all knowing and hence not to be questioned."[45] Monroe links self-image and identity to relationships, that is, "self in relation to others and the way the speaker views him- or herself in relation to the world."[46] At the core of Nazi self-identity was adoration of culture against the forces that would dissipate the racial purity of the traditional Aryan and Germanic in-groups. Monroe underscores the centrality of values and of explicit value-commitments manifested by the unrepentant Nazi and Nazi sympathizer. These values include "racial purity," "cultural separatism," as well as what was called, " 'old values and old religion,' an Aryan way of doing things that excludes people who are judged 'different.' "[47] This set of ethical commitments, indeed, these demonstrations of moral capacity, perplexes Monroe. Methodologically, she writes in consonance with those who envision the possibility that supererogatory obligations based on self-images of moral "idealism influenced Nazi behaviors no matter how immoral those behaviors were in fact." Monroe outlines this moral conundrum as follows: "Ironically, it was the rancorous Nazi (Florentine) who spoke about values more than anyone else. She described herself as idealistic, and her life certainly demonstrates an incredible commitment to the ideals she holds dear."

Herein lies what Eric Hoffer once described as the "True Believer," the fanatic who makes claims to heroic truth through self-abnegation. For Monroe, "This highlights the difficulties in thinking about values—in general terms—as influences on moral choice." How, one wonders? Monroe continues, "Ordinarily, we think of being an idealist as a positive thing. But if the ideals are Nazi ideals, this is something most of us would consider negative from an ethical point of view."[48] In this regard, however, I would challenge a basic assumption implied by Monroe's logic and language to the effect that "Nazi ideals are ideals."

This veers toward an implicit ethical relativism, not with respect to the values themselves, but regarding the psychological and, thus, moral status of the person uttering them. Monroe's entire project is devoted to showing how self-image determines moral viewpoint. But are all self-images morally and thus psychologically equivalent? Is it not necessary to delve into the sources of "self-images"? The term, "Nazi ideals," as a unit of analysis represents a misnomer generated by the very nature of Monroe's methodology to treat, for example, the manifestations of self-deception as morally equivalent to genuine forms of altruism. What her Nazi speaker is issuing are not Nazi "ideals" born of self-images but self-rationalizations borne by the delusions of disordered will. This is not meant to require a distortion of Monroe's methodological or empirical neutrality, but it is to suggest that the "neutrality" she adopts skews her findings from the start. Monroe compounds this problem in ethical reasoning by drawing a series of misleading inferences. To repeat, she claims, "But if the ideals are Nazi ideals, this is something most of us would consider negative from an ethical point of view. Considering Nazis and their values thus reveals the difficulty in speaking generally about values. We need to know the content and specificity of values."[49] Monroe proceeds to state her thesis of moral equivalency. "When we take such an approach, there seems surprisingly little significant difference on the dimension of expressed values among rescuers, bystanders, and Nazi supporters. This suggests the obvious. Most people want to feel they're doing good, *even genocidalists*. People do not consciously arrange themselves along a moral continuum with the goal of defining themselves as evildoers or people who ignore the needs of others."[50] We have already seen in the context of our discussion of laughter within the macabresque that some evidence suggests that Hitler and his entourage did implement their exterminatory policies precisely because they knew them to be evil. Additionally, the relationship of any subject to moral values of "good" is grounded in the moral qualities and features of the subject. The evil done by perpetrators in mass atrocity is not "good"; perpetrators are hardly in positions to make claims that it is. This was the claim that Eichmann made, that he only wanted to do good, and on the basis of Kantian ethics no less. To accept this within the frameworks of an empirical methodology in *political* psychology that purports to relate self-image and/or self-identity to presumed moral stances even in cases of profound immorality or ideological extremism not surprisingly culminates with a set of findings that sheds little light about how perpetrators "think," let alone why they think as they do, and even less about practical ethics or moral theory.

ENTER THE POLITICAL

Recognition of contested analytical terrains becomes methodologically important when exploring the political contexts of mass atrocity. Such perspectives include focus on situational factors fostered by a range of influences: nation-state; sovereignty; territoriality; nationality; nationalism; ethnicity; class; religion and sectarian ideology; patrimonial legitimacy; and patriarchy. Postcolonial pathways to genocide and mass atrocity, in particular, often lead to the cultural transformations of honor-kinship, descent or segmented lineage into ethnicized, sometimes racialized identities. Such political concepts as nationhood, nationality and nationalism, statehood and sovereignty, ethnicity and ethnic conflict, sectarianism and sectionalism, are deemed to play out in war, war crimes, crimes against humanity, massacres, ethnic cleansing, mass killing, mass murder, genocide, etc. Each case, every instance, is different. I shall explore various approaches to genocide and mass atrocity, emphasizing the explanatory linkages between perpetrator behaviors to group dynamics in various political and social contexts. The major methodological issue concerns the relationships between individuals and groups and how to theorize the influences of each in explaining collective violence.

Leaders and Followers in Groups: "The Fundamental Attribution Error"

Benjamin A. Valentino offers a taxonomic classification, or what he calls a "typology of mass killing," defined as *"the intentional killing of a massive number of noncombatants."*[51] Valentino focuses on mass atrocity since he indicates that most episodes of mass killing occur in the absence of genocidal objectives. Valentino criticizes several situational theories applied to explanations of mass killing, including "social cleavages and dehumanization," and "the scapegoat theory," as well as "political opportunity" models. The latter tend to suggest that national crises including sub-national conflicts become tantamount to those situations that "provide the incentives, opportunity and cover for revolutionary elites seeking to consolidate political power" by means of genocide and mass atrocity.[52] Valentino acknowledges that "political opportunity" explanations may be relevant, but only if precise factors of such situations are specified. Valentino's typology of mass killing divides into six types: "communist," "ethnic," "territorial," "counterguerrilla," "terrorist," and "imperialist."[53] Two subsets imply the macabresque presence of transgressive violence in addition to killing as evidenced by the terms, "dispossessive mass killing" and "coercive mass killing." Dispossessive mass killings "strip large groups of people of their possessions, their homes, or their way of life"; the mass killing that results is a consequence of such aims that include mass collectivization, ethnic cleansing, "colonial enlargement" or the "territorial ambitions of colonial or expansionist powers." Coercive mass killing is defined as a function of war that targets large numbers of civilian populations once "conventional military techniques" no longer appear able to achieve their strategic objectives. "Submission" to the force of perpetrator military might or political will rather than extermination as such is what is sought. Valentino represents "guerilla wars," "terror bombing," "starvation blockades/siege," "sub-state/insurgent terrorism" and "imperial conquests and rebellions" as falling under this category. In a methodological note, Valentino comments that these dynamics account for the situations in which most mass killing in the twentieth century occurs.[54] Valentino's review of the transgressive violation in mass atrocity thus provides theoretical and conceptual space for an analysis of the dramaturgical and aesthetic implementation strategies and tactics deployed by perpetrators: as underscored by his theoretical interests in ethnic cleansing and mass starvation. Valentino positions his analysis well within the explanatory constructs that underscore the personality traits or features of perpetrators, on the one hand, as well as those, on the other, that point to situational variables as critical features to why mass killing occurs.[55]

Valentino thus straddles a major theoretical and methodological divide between those featuring interior features of personality as opposed to those foregrounding the impacts of situational factors, including "horizontal" peer pressures as well "vertical" command structures. Valentino states, for example, that "the search for the causes of mass killing should begin with the capabilities, interests, ideas, and strategies of groups and individuals in positions of political and military power *and not with factors that predispose societies to produce such leaders.*" He divides perpetrators into two broad categories. He declares, "I believe that two distinct social and psychological processes go a long way toward explaining the recruitment and motivation of most perpetrators of mass killing. The first process involves the concerted or self-selected recruitment of sadistic or fanatic individuals. The second process relies on situational pressures, including authority and peer pressure, to induce otherwise ordinary human beings to participate in acts of extreme violence."[56] Valentino concludes that so-called sadists and fanatics tend to be in the minority, whereas "ordinary" persons constitute the majority on pathways to "mass killing: intrinsic traits like fanaticism and sadism may influence a few perpetrators toward extremism; extrinsic situational variables are the main predictors of how large numbers of 'ordinary' persons will in time undertake behaviors that perpetrate mass killing." He states, "The individuals charged with carrying out such violence may do so even in the absence of a deeply held prior commitment to its goals or a profound hatred of their victims."[57] This leads Valentino to infer a fundamental role for the influences of groups on individual perpetrators. Valentino writes, for example, "These findings have powerful implications for our understanding of mass killing. In particular, they highlight the decisive role that small groups or even individual leaders can play in the causal process of these episodes of violence."[58] To conflate the external impacts of groups on their members with the internal features of individual personality traits represents what Valentino, along with a carefully researched body of findings in social psychology, labels the "fundamental attribution error." This emerges, he avers, as a consequence of "a general human tendency to discount the effect of situational pressures in influencing the behavior of others."[59] Valentino underscores the role of leaders as critical to the behaviors of individuals with groups especially those positioned with command or hierarchical structures. He concludes, "The unique ideas, beliefs, strategies, even personalities of these leaders . . . often constitute the necessary conditions for mass killing."[60] From the perspective of the macabresque, this observation supports the conclusion that even staged events and exhibitionist performances require the role of "directors" to engage effectively in the dramatic mise en scène.

Lingering Malignancies of Commemoration: Fantasized Losses in the Political Imaginary

Michael Mann's analysis of Nazi perpetrators emphasizes the role and impact of political imaginaries in a typology that identifies at least eight main types: "ideological, disturbed, bigoted, fearful, conformist, bureaucratic, materialist, careerist."[61] Mann, in a subsequent study focused on ethnic cleansing, distinguishes nine ideal-types of perpetrators: "ideological, bigoted, violent, fearful, careerist, materialist, disciplined, comradely, and bureaucratic."[62] Mann underscores the importance of political territory in combination with regionalized identitarian constructions. With respect to Nazi perpetrators, Mann points to regional identity or geographic background in relation to the genesis of perpetrators who became committed Nazis, a point subsequently made by Manus I. Midlarsky in theorizing the relationship of political extremism to imagined or constructed sense of historic "losses." Mann notes the "over-representation" of ideological Nazis from German regions lost and regained within Germany, in particular, from "Alsace-Lorraine and areas lost to Denmark and Belgium." Midlarsky's research supports this argument.[63] He constructs an analysis of revanchism by theoretically postulating a timeline in national, including, German history, that is demarcated by a series of phases: "subordination, gain and loss." Midlarsky's analysis begins by extrapolating on the fact that the highest proportion of Nazi perpetrators and war criminals in Mann's sample originated in the highly contested region of Alsace-Lorraine and Malmedy. Midlarsky notes the significance of the back and forth phases in territorial possession that occurred with respect to Alsace-Lorraine between Germany and France.[64] According to Midlarsky this entailed a fateful sequence, "German subordination (1648–1871), gain (1871–1919), and loss (1919–1940)." These processes eventuated in mystified collective memories of historic losses for which the Jews were ultimately blamed. These losses provoked the sense of humiliation that helped set in motion the social fantasies of subordination and loss. In this view, these make up "the situation" that fostered mass atrocity. Mann and Midlarsky, each in their way, but in complementary fashion, effectively posit a theoretical framework germane to psycho-social analysis. National territory, its "domination," alleged "protection," the "purity" of populations who occupy it, the ideological myths of loss and return, etc., and the fantasies of what Midlarsky calls "ephemeral losses" all serve as vectors on the pathways to genocide and mass atrocity. I describe this in terms of the personification of the nation. Mann summarizes the data by indicating, "The perpetrators were also drawn disproportionately from core 'nation-statist' Nazi constituencies—from 'threatened' or 'lost' border regions"—that is, from contiguous and disputed areas as well.[65] Mann emphasizes "a shift from *kleindeutsch* to *grossdeutsch* racial nationalism in Nazism." In a subsequent study, Mann examines how identitarian conflicts play out in relation to territorial disputes that are defined as "ethnic cleansing." Mann indicates that perpetrators of ethnic cleansing divide into three basic categories: "*radical elites running party-states*"; "*bands of militants forming violent paramilitaries*"; and "*core constituencies providing mass though not majority popular support.*"[66] This emphasis on the mix involving territory and identitarian conflict underscores the centrality of the territorial sovereign nation-state in relation to situational explanations of genocide and mass atrocity. Mann devises eight arguments in theorizing ethnic cleansing, the core of which are as follows: "*The danger zone of murderous cleansing is reached when (a) movements claiming to represent two fairly old ethnic groups both lay claim to their own state over all or part of the same territory and (b) this claim seems to them to have substantial legitimacy and some plausible chance of being implemented.*"[67] Mann's combination of terms and insights suggestive of factors that advance the pathways to genocide and mass atrocity, include references to legitimacy, control over the territorial boundaries and land of the national state, identitarian rivalries, real or imagined over the same or nearly identical territory, in combination with calculations of feasibility. Mann also introduces the elements of asymmetrical power in terms of strategic and tactical calculations, with the "*less powerful side*" determined to fight rather than submit and the "*stronger side*" convinced of its "*overwhelming military power and ideological legitimacy.*"[68] Mann's perspective also stresses the role of civil war and domestic factionalization and/or radicalization in the process of generating "*an unstable geopolitical environment that usually leads to war.*"[69]

ENTER THE SOCIETAL IN SOCIAL PSYCHOLOGY

In the sections that follow, I trace some of the basic assumptions that I take to be representative of theoretical currencies in the field of social psychology as applied to the study of genocide and mass atrocity. Social psychological approaches have sought to categorize perpetrators relative to motivation, have famously undertaken a range of simulation studies to provide inferential evidence regarding situational forces, and, above all, have developed a vocabulary to describe group dynamics in ways presumed to be relevant to explaining how and why perpetrators behave as they do in groups. My aim is to demonstrate both the value and limitations of this working lexicon in order to build toward my representation of the theoretical efficacy of psychosocial perspectives. I suggest the most salient "saddle point" aligning social psychology with psychosocial theory occurs when the social psychological concept of "prototypicality" is viewed alongside psychosocial concepts of "ego-ideal." This discussion, in turn, sets the stage for further elaboration of the meaning and significance of the macabresque. I indicate that the value-added contributions of psychosocial theory derive from applications of the performative as a unit of analysis, and I offer a defense of this. Emphasis on the performative enables us to associate the politics of theatricality with the situational factors at play in the psychodynamics of groups, including of perpetrators. The contrast between social psychology and psychosocial theory suggests alternative perspectives on performativity.

Whenever genocide and mass atrocity occur, it happens in groups. Collective intent results from group agency and thus from perpetrators acting together in groups. Perhaps no discipline is more attuned to the study of groups and group dynamics than social psychology. But with major exceptions, it has tended to demur in relation to the study of genocide and mass atrocity. This reflects a disciplinary orientation Daniel Bar-Tal describes as "individualistic-cognitive social psychology with some emphasis on interpersonal interaction and small group behavior." He states, "Societies do not exist in isolation from society members, but the meaning of the society can only be understood when the cognitive-affective repertoire of the society members is taken into account." Bar-Tal emphasizes the mediational effects on group actors that derive from macro and micro level influences. He concludes, "There is a continuous interaction and reciprocal influence between society members' repertoires, on the one hand, and societal institutions, structures, culture, and other societal characteristics, on the other."[70]

MOTIVATIONS OF PERPETRATORS ACCORDING TO IDEAL-TYPES: TAXONOMIC CATEGORIES AT MICRO LEVELS OF "LEGALIZED" CRIMINALITY

One of the most systematic recent typologies of perpetrators within the frames of social psychology has been developed by Alette Smeulers. Her methodological framework is configured around the concept of international crimes committed by "ordinary" individuals who but for the genocidal or mass atrocity situations confronting them would probably have remained law-abiding citizens. Smeulers thus refers paradoxically to "law-abiding criminals." Smeulers accepts the Milgram findings (discussed later) and adapts them for purposes of analysis to indicate that it is the violence that drives the carts of hate and ideology, not the converse. She speaks of "psychological entrapment."[71] "Many people do not start to kill and torture because they hate their victims or perceive killing and torturing them as justifiable but they start to hate their victims and start to believe in the ideology because it justifies the killing and torture in which they have become involved."[72] In terms of her analysis, therefore, genocide and mass atrocity become a kind of ex post facto along the pathways to officially sanctioned or legitimated collective violence. Smeulers suggests that people come to believe their own lies as well as to the well-known concept initially advanced by Robert Jay Lifton referred to as "doubling" in which perpetrators cauterize the universe of agony in which they operate from their own habitual life and living circumstances that proceed normally.[73] Smeulers's own bibliographic methodology includes close examination of what she refers to as "ego documents, biographies and case law." On the basis of her evidentiary archive, she classifies perpetrators according to the extent to which individuals before genocide or mass atrocity stood to gain or to lose in the restructured society as a consequence of violence. She concludes that some had a lot to gain, others a lot to lose, and that these sets of calculations became realized in perpetrator motivations and strategies *before and after* collective violence. Smeulers thus stresses social psychological processes of "adaptation and transformation." She applies this heuristic framework by classifying perpetrators according to a taxonomy featuring "ideal-types." This representation of ideal-types permits her to assess how different categories of individuals respond to situations of violence in a variety of ways. She lists the ideal-types *before* collective violence has ensued: "law-abiding citizens," "borderline types," and "criminals/sadists," either actively or non-actively engaged. *After* collective violence has unfolded, individuals who have been law-abiding tend to join in collective violence, she avers, for reasons of "careerism," conformity and "fear of rejection," or on account of a willingness to become an "authoritarian follower" or, even, a "devoted warrior" and, finally, because of "fear" over "direct" or "internalized threats." Borderline types become engaged for reasons of opportunism or "greed" and "profit"; alternatively, they become fanatical as a consequence of "dogmatic ideology." And criminal or sadistic types turn into "masterminds of evil" or simply criminals for personal gain or sadistic and fanatic for purposes of "sexual satisfaction" or for reasons of "hatred and resentment."[74]

Smeulers thus alleges that these transformations and adaptations demonstrate the impacts exerted by extrinsic circumstances, external pressures, and exterior dynamics of collective violence as opposed to intrinsic trait consistencies or interior psychodynamics. Smeulers's ideal-types are framed in sets of assumptions regarding human personality, normality, emotional adjustment, psychic stability, capacities for imaginative distantiation, ethical and critical symbolism, and so forth, all of which ground her typology. Smeulers, however, adds an important dimension to her taxonomic exercise by seeking to show that "law-abiding criminals" get swept up in a spiral of escalation during what she describes, citing Ervin Staub, as a "continuum of destructiveness."[75] Smeulers emphasizes the fact that the pathways to genocide and mass atrocity tend overwhelmingly to be authorized, sanctioned and thus in effect legitimated by state regimes or government elites thus providing an aura of legality to what would otherwise be classified as criminal behavior. "But within such a malignant governmental system, military organization or police unit, it is those who do not break the rules but those who *abide by* the rules who become the perpetrators."[76] This holds major implications for research in terms of psychosocial analysis. As she concludes, "A common feature of all perpetrators is that they submit themselves to the dominant social order and adapt to these extraordinary circumstances and as such get progressively involved in an evil system."[77]

SOCIALITY AND SITUATIONISM, SELF-IDENTITY AND SELF-CATEGORIZATION

Social psychological studies of groups deemed relevant to explanations of mass atrocity often emphasize either "sociality" and/or "situation" as critical perspectives. *Sociality* refers to *horizontal* relationships among members of groups. Conceptual units of analysis that are often applied include "self-categorization," "social identity," "peer pressures," "in-group" and "out-group pressures," "social exclusions" and "conformity." *Situationism* is often cast in terms of *verticality* and involves examination of hierarchy and command, orders and obedience; social psychological explanations of group behavior thus focus on "self-stereotyping," "identification processes," "group perceptions of diversity and homogenization," "cohesion and solidarity," and the "cognitive dynamics" of identitarian categories. The concept of behavioral motivation tends to be envisioned as a kind of force or energy contributing to how persons alone, or in groups, pursue certain objectives— that is, either as cognitions or perceptions, or, alternatively, as influences. Both cognitions and influences enable persons to establish forms of self-identity or self-categorizations. Controlled experiments employing either survey data or simulated responses often depict behavioral consistencies as well as anomalies said to be indicative of motivations, cognitive or perceptual or against the background of situational influences. Motivations are described accordingly: they are said to pulsate in varying ways; they operate under variable conditions of sociality and situation; they function with different effects; they impel, compel, or repel; they proscribe, prohibit or prevent; they are discernible across manifold textures of the human lifeworld, in moments and meetings, in memory, and in the myriads of purposive aims driving social objectives. Social psychological methods stress inductive methods in analytical contexts. These postulate either "inner," or "intrinsic," dimensionalities in social behaviors, on the one hand, or behavioral responses to external, or "extrinsic," stimuli, on the other. Social psychological methods then proceed to evaluate how relationships among interior motivational drives and exterior incentives operate in multiple settings and circumstances, and with what outcomes or consequences. Such examinations feature "inner" motivation to assess how and to what extent behaviors manifest the intrinsic character of drives, needs, or perceived interests; these intrinsic elements are viewed as providing evidence of motivational autonomy and capacities for self-direction, or lack thereof, particularly in learning and educational environments and with respect to "attitudinal orientations." Conversely, extrinsic or "incentive theories" examine how and to what extent rewards and punishments influence personal behaviors or social interactions. Incentive theories emphasize the external "pulls" of carrots and sticks and thus stand methodologically in contrast to "drive theories" focusing on intrinsic "needs" or inner determinants that "push" behaviors toward or away from fulfillments of need, defined in biological, physiological, or emotional terms.

Many of the signal achievements in social psychology (and in psychological sociology) relate intrinsic and extrinsic phenomena. This includes, for example, Abraham Maslow's "hierarchies of needs," Leon Festinger's theory of "cognitive dissonance," and Jerome Bruner's theory of "social interactionism," as well as the symbolic interaction theory initiated by George Herbert Mead. All purport to show how social meanings and behavioral responses derive from the ways in which persons alone and in groups mediate across inner, interior and/or intrinsic motivations relative to external, exterior, and extrinsic influences, and vice versa. Parallel research in social psychology focuses on categories of individual behaviors within groups or on classes of group behaviors relative to their members. This yields certain analytical concepts showing how persons realign their self-representations—that is, actions, choices, attitudes, and so on—to accommodate to group preferences, earmarked normatively to what is often referred to "prototypicality." "Social identity" theories, for example, stress the role of status perceptions and status seeking in groups. Individuals in groups often attempt to influence their status-image. They do so, however, through divergent strategies. Some individuals choose to accentuate their distinctiveness; others tend to submerge their persona within groups.

PROTOTYPICALITY: SOCIAL CONSTRUCTIONISM IN GROUP DYNAMICS

The battery of social psychological concepts applied to the study of group dynamics that include, "social identity," "social identification," "self-categorization," "self-concepts," "self-depersonalization," and "self-stereotyping" are often benchmarked to the notion of "prototypicality." *Prototypicality* may be defined as behaviors within groups adjusted to the attitudes or values that members perceive, intuit, or accept as primary reference points. Often the dynamics of prototypicality demonstrate efforts by individual members to accommodate to their perceptions of what the group leaders desire or what other group members collectively believe, admire, or seek. These dynamics are often said to be strengthened by the presence of "out-groups." Processes such as self-categorization and self-stereotyping tend to reinforce in-group solidarities when countervailing "out-groups" are perceived especially in cases in which members of out-groups are seen both as homogeneous within themselves as in instances of stereotyping, as well as adversarial to the in-group itself. Objective features or markers are not critical to such perceptions. Given the influences of prototypicality, in-group members are often purported to renounce some degree of autonomy to adopt the attitudes or behaviors of their in-groups, a process also conceived within social psychology as "self-depersonalization."

The dynamics of prototypicality are often alleged as explanations of how "ordinary" persons become enticed to act as perpetrators or serve in supportive capacities or remain indifferent to atrocities as "by-standers." Such perspectives have generated important observations regarding genocide and mass atrocity: once interstate war and/or domestic civil war have functioned to create conditions tantamount to "normalizing" conflict, prototypicality functions to "normalize" extensions of violence to include genocide and mass atrocity against civilian populations; secondly, once governmental, military, paramilitary, and police agencies become armed with absolute power, they will readily engage in genocidal violence and mass atrocity crimes. The pathways to genocide are seen to be paved by unchecked or absolute power and its legitimization through command, and by group cultures of violence that alter previously proscribed behaviors against mass atrocity and transform them into acceptable ones, if and when—and this is the key catalytic ingredient—these dynamics take on the semblances of prototypicality. Normalizing genocide and mass atrocity among group members in terms of "horizontal sociality" on account of command authority and legitimacy and, conversely, in terms of "vertical situationism" on account of peer pressures and "self-identification" behaviors, each illustrate the dynamics of prototypicality. These approaches emphasize how groups construct meanings, frame perceived realities, and become tethered to behaviors, attitudes, and orders seeking to "normalize" violence.

THE PROTOTYPICAL CONDITIONS OF EVIL:
TWO APPROACHES—SIMULATION AND "ROOTS"

Analysis of situational influences in social psychology often proceeds on the basis of controlled simulation. Social psychology applies inductive methodological approaches suggestive of how groups function under controlled conditions of duress. One theoretical cluster in social psychology has predominated in the research focused on genocide: simulated experimentation. A second orientation has recently developed that is focused on the social pathologies or "roots" of what is described as "evil." Inferences advanced by the findings of this entire body of social psychological research are taken to illustrate how "ordinary" individuals, when placed in untenable group environments or in authoritarian situations, act in defiance of moral decency or conscience. These social psychological approaches divide into two subsets: the first, the simulations of Solomon Asch, Stanley Milgram, and Philip Zimbardo; the second, the behavioral studies of Roy F. Baumeister and Ervin Staub. The first subset deployed controlled experimental methods to simulate situations of peer pressure or of command authority, including prison situations; the second approach includes large and complex taxonomic tapestries that seek to classify the "roots" of evil. What unifies this research is the emphasis on peer pressures and command structures—to conform or obey, whatever the cost to others.

Three sets of experiments in group psychology and obedience, initiated ten years apart, generated conclusions that have been highly influential in genocide studies. The 1951 Asch experiments on conformity or obeisance at Swarthmore College, the 1961 Milgram experiments on obedience to authority at Yale University, and the 1971 Zimbardo prison experiments at Stanford University adopted simulation designs to illustrate person-situational interactions.

The Asch-Swarthmore Experiments: Obeisance

The Asch experiments on conformity revealed the importance of extrinsic influences on status seeking based on self-categorizations. Subjects sought to maintain or to enhance their status among members of their in-groups by calibrating their views to suit the majority opinion, even when they were informed that such positions were incorrect. Subjects' reactions to various situations differed, however, throughout the progression of Asch's experiments. Some held firm to their opinion or viewpoint; others wavered in a variety of ways. But in numerous instances, subjects demonstrated the effects of peer pressures by acting in conformity to observations, values, or opinions held or expressed by the majority of participants and, thus, in conformity with the pressures exerted under conditions of prototypicality. Asch's simulated experiments demonstrated how subjects veered away from their initial positions—indeed, tried to hide their original opinions or personal observations, even when they were objectively accurate—once confronted with disagreement on the part of other group member(s).

The Milgram-Yale Experiments: Obedience

Milgram's experiments, initiated in July 1961, were undertaken in conjunction with the opening of the Adolph Eichmann trial in Jerusalem and were specifically designed to test the "chain of command" or obedience defense. Milgram concluded that his simulations did confirm that ordinary persons, not necessarily motivated by intrinsic personality traits like sadistic desire or by extrinsic pressures like rewards, would demonstrate destructive behaviors, once ordered to do so. Specifically, he claimed to have shown how ordinary persons are capable of becoming accomplices to cruelty simply as a function of "going along to get along," that is, by renouncing accountability for the consequences of actions taken under command or in accordance with peer pressure. Milgram associated these behaviors with pathways to the Holocaust. He stressed that his experiments demonstrated willingness to conform; depraved subservience; mindless abdication of any personal responsibility; moral blindness in the face of manifest cruelty; and ethical indifference to egregious harm, pain and torment suffered by others as a direct result of one's own actions. Milgram's theory of obedience is a variation on the theme of proto-typicality: at moments of pressure or duress, individuals transfer decisional responsibility to reference groups and their leaders. Thus, psychological boundaries between individuality and group membership disappear. Milgram's study of obedience thus advances an "agentic state" theory of obedience by attesting to the proclivity of individuals to change their cognitive perceptions and strategic perspectives in order to situate themselves in groups as the instruments or agents of the principals, that is, as the agents of "figures" of power and authority on whom they bestow deferential obedience. Milgram's research purported to confirm the validity of the dynamics of overriding prototypicality in groups in shaping the moral behaviors and ethical considerations of actors in groups. His methodological approach left much open to question, particularly in light of its universalist claims. James E. Waller, in his overview of motivational research in studies of genocide, observes, "The lack of empirical support makes it clear that the agentic shift is not essential to all acts of obedience. At times, people will obey authority without relinquishing a sense of personal responsibility for the action to a superior. This begs the question, however, as to the sources of obedience in the first place."[78]

C. Fred Alford drew very different conclusions from the Milgram experiments. In his view, Milgram's simulations demonstrated not so much capacities for craven obedience or conformity but the "intrusion of doom and dread into modernity."[79] Alford references the now long-familiar disagreement that ranged between Zygmunt Bauman and Daniel Jonah Goldhagen over modernism, anti-Semitism, and the Holocaust. These differences included disagreement over the meaning and significance of the Milgram findings with respect to the Holocaust: did "Germans" kill Jews because they were ordered to do so, as alleged by Bauman, or because they sought relief in the sadistic pleasure of anti-Semitism, as alleged by Goldhagen? Alford notes that Milgram vehemently denied that his experiments revealed such sadistic desires. "This is not how Milgram, and most others, interpret the classic experiment," Alford observed. "Milgram argues that the experiment, has nothing to do with sadism, and everything with obedience."[80] Alford disagreed, referring to behaviors filmed during Milgram's simulation when the experimental subjects experienced "grotesque laughter, the giggling fits at the shock generator"—that is, fits of laughter while inflicting what they were led to believe was excessive pain on others. Alford asks, "What if these men are giggling in embarrassed pleasure at being given permission to inflict great pain and suffering . . . . Milgram rejects this interpretation, but offers no reason."[81] Alford stressed that the Milgram instructors told subjects beforehand that they alone—not the subjects—were responsible for the pain induced in the victims. Alford wonders whether this lent psychological cover to the manifest sadism. Alford suggests, "The structure of the Milgram experiment protects them [the subjects] from knowledge of their own sadism, while allowing them to express it." He adds, "Could it be the psychological function of leaders to provide plausible psychological deniability to their followers, as well as to shelter them from the consequences of their desires?" But what is the significance of a desire to enjoy causing pain and suffering?

This question turns not so much on pain and suffering but on the desire to enjoy causing it. Alford locates the answer in the dread of finitude, mortality salience, the fear of death and dying, and anxiety over doom. Alford states, "*Sadism is the form aggression takes when it seeks to inflict its doom on* others."[82] Alford thus explains the behaviors provoked by Milgram's simulation experiments in ways that reject Milgram's own conclusions. He does so by reframing the possible inferences to be drawn from obedience to sadistic desires.

The Zimbardo-Stanford Prison Studies: Obsequiousness

The Stanford Prison Experiment, conducted by Philip Zimbardo in August 1971, and subsequently replicated in other experimental work, has been widely accepted as reinforcing Milgram's obedience thesis. To both renown and notoriety, Zimbardo has focused on guard-prisoner psychological interactions in a range of prison and correctional settings, some real, as in the case of the infamous Abu Ghraib prison, others experimentally contrived, as in the case of his original Stanford Prison Experiment. In general, Zimbardo rejects dispositional or psychological trait theories; but his inferential logics are based on presumptions concerning the nature of human character. The results of his experimentations are mixed in that his methods preclude certain sets of questions, while his conclusions render those questions essential but moot. Zimbardo's summative overview is delineated in his book, *The Lucifer Effect*. "The Lucifer effect" refers to the "situational" effect and "incremental" dynamics. These are said to lead to "transformations of good, ordinary people, not angels, into perpetrators of evil in response to the corrosive influence of powerful situational forces."[83] On the basis of his simulated prison findings, Zimbardo concludes that "situational power is most salient in novel settings, those in which people cannot control for their new behavioral options . . . In such situations the usual reward structures are different and expectations are violated."[84] Such observations, however, raise a host of further issues. What provokes "the Lucifer effect" that predicts for "evil": is it the external mechanisms of reward and punishment at the micro level of the prisoner; is it the mesopower of guards acting within authority or command structures; is it the interaction between guard authorities and experimental subjects relative to expected outcomes within delimited contexts or situations, or some combination of them together at macro levels of prison environments? Zimbardo's situationism based in *symbolic interactionism* and *social constructivism* does not respond. This is the case despite the empiricism implied by his operationalized methodology.

　　Zimbardo's emphasis on constructions of reality conflates "belief" with "ideology" and assumes that both alone constitute human subjectivity. He declares,

> [I]t is the meaning that people assign to various components of the situation that creates its social reality . . . Social reality is more than a situation's physical features.

It is the way actors view their situation, their current behavioral stage, which engages a variety of psychological processes.[85]

On what basis do people come to "view" their situation, their "behavioral stage"? Zimbardo responds by referring to the social effects of "mental representations" or beliefs that "can modify how any situation is perceived, usually to make it fit or be assimilated into the actor's expectations and personal values."[86] How do such beliefs relate to social or situational effects? Zimbardo's answer is that beliefs "create expectations, which in turn can gain strength when they become self-fulfilling prophecies."[87] How and why do socially constructed images of what Zimbardo describes as "the images of the enemy," "hostile imagination" or propaganda, arise?[88] Might interior dispositional character traits predict for certain belief structures or render certain ideological beliefs more attitudinally acceptable in some personalities as opposed to others? Might the need for social approval and fear of loss of status in the peer group refer to anterior personality traits or interior modes of dispositional character, even to motivations? Such analytical effort to demonstrate the impact of situation on the psychological behaviors of persons in groups excludes reference to the elements of psychic interiority or emotional subjectivity, the very dimensions Zimbardo's theoretical models appear to assume.

Zimbardo's methodology discounts trait consistency or dispositional "densities" as predictive factors in favor of the importance of teams and of the influences of role-playing in teams. In his schema, teams exert powerful pressures on persons, who respond to them in a double-edged way, not only by pursuing the "need for social approval," but as the result of the fears of being socially excluded or even ostracized.[89] Zimbardo refers to C. S. Lewis's concept of the "terror of being left outside" in describing how the "motivational force" of social approval becomes "doubly energized" by the "fear of rejection."[90] "This fear," Zimbardo concludes, "can cripple initiative and negate personal autonomy."[91] Zimbardo's analysis envisions evildoing whenever the pressures of social situations force individuals in command structures to do what they otherwise might not do by way of repressive or violent behavior. He describes systemic power as a mix of "institutional support, authority, and resources" that together "gives validation to playing new roles, following new rules, and taking actions that would ordinarily be constrained by preexisting laws, norms, morals and ethics."[92]

Such generalizations, however, methodologically conflate "systemic power" with "ideology." Zimbardo, for example, defines ideology as "a slogan or proposition that usually legitimizes whatever means are necessary to attain an ultimate goal."[93] Ideology emerges whenever "those in authority present the program as good and virtuous, as a highly valuable moral imperative."[94] But, as before, this raises conceptual and methodological issues that remain unanswered: is ideology a function of leaders, of momentary slogans, of policy, of goal-oriented behavioral patterns over and beyond those exerted by "ideology"; why, in particular, are leaders so important in validating the goals and objectives taken up by groups as they commit to evil if ideological conformity exerts its own set of pressures on groups? In the end, the independent variables that Zimbardo specifies as causal of the Lucifer effect, including such motivations as "ideology," "situational leadership," and "systemic power," slide together in combined sets of influences said to operate on persons, groups, and social settings, particularly in fluid situations. Zimbardo shows how human autonomy and volitional will can be influenced, even taken over, by the fears of social exclusion. But his approach does not fully explain how group sociality and personality mutually interact in ways that infuse behavior with a propensity toward the extreme violence he associates with the Lucifer effect. Many of the participants in Zimbardo's simulation exercise subsequently averred that they were simply assuming roles designated in advance but ill-defined and without advance training or definition. Any such systematic effort to extrapolate to real life on the basis of the dynamics generated by a simulation experience that appears closer to that of kidnapping or hostage taking as opposed to prison conditions, and in the absence of a control group, remains deeply flawed. The consequence is that the study's findings cannot and, indeed, must not be used to generalize human behaviors under prison conditions. Thus, Zimbardo's prison experiment demonstrates low ecological validity. Given the fact that the student participants were from a highly select population sample, the experiment also suffers from low population validity.

Zimbardo is certainly right to stress the theoretical significance of the concept of systemic power in explaining how carceral settings readily devolve into group dynamics of "correctional" brutality. Waller draws critical conclusions that theoretically problematize simulated prison studies in ways that emphasize the analytical significance of relating internal and external factors. Waller, wonders, "Why do our external behaviors and roles so dramatically affect our internal psychological framework?"[95] He responds, "Primarily because we tend toward integration between the external and internal. In other words, we are troubled by inconsistencies between *what* we do and *who* we think we are. We are motivated to alleviate these inconsistencies to preserve the integrity of the self."[96] Zimbardo's analysis offers a social psychology of motivation in groups on the basis of assumed conceptions of human subjectivity but does not specify the dimensions of human motivation on which such assumptions depend. Zimbardo's heurism proceeds devoid of theorized psychological motivation as an adjunct to ground his experimental analysis of situational power. His methodology purports to demonstrate the need for social approval as motivation within prison structures of power and authority but in ways that render power and authority motivational influences unto themselves and thus redundantly, if not tortuously, self-explanatory.

INDOCTRINATION AND BELIEF IN ONE'S OWN LIES

Christopher R. Browning's study on Reserve Police Battalion 101 reviews a range of explanations for why this cohort, so "ordinary" in so many ways, became galvanized to implement the Nazi policy of systematic extermination of the Jews.[97] In so doing, he finds numerous parallels with the findings presented both by Zimbardo and by Milgram. He discounts "frenzy" as an explanation since most in his cohort sample had not previously been submerged in the horrors of war. They did experience "brutalization" but as an effect, not cause, of their behaviors. The rank and file were ordinary in the sense that most were "middle-aged" and from working-class backgrounds from Hamburg, some of whom in the years leading up to the war had manifested political and ideological support for the Nazi Party by becoming members. In his search for answers, Browning examines the now well-trodden set of debates regarding human personality: Theodor Adorno's "F-Scale" approach to "authoritarian personality" emphasizing characterological factors such as "rigidity," "submissiveness," "aggressiveness," "toughness," "opposition" to inner reflection, "destructiveness," "projection outward of unconscious emotional impulses," and a tendency toward prejudice and stereotyping; Zygmunt Bauman's criticism of the F-scale authoritarian personality approach is that it implies personality dysfunction as the basis for explaining why individuals undertake mass violence, as opposed to what Bauman argues is appropriate stress on social roles and the impacts of social forces; John Steiner's concept of "sleeper" that suggests that certain individuals retain latent violent tendencies provoked under the right circumstances; Staub's critique of this "sleeper" thesis on the grounds that to be a normal human being is to maintain the "motivations," "thoughts" and "feelings" necessary for "mass destruction." Browning appears to give pride of place to Zimbardo's findings with respect to tripartite variations among the original eleven guards in Zimbardo's prison guard simulation: "cruel and tough," "tough but fair," and "good guards." Browning comments:

> Zimbardo's spectrum of guard behavior bears an uncanny resemblance to the groupings that emerged within Reserve Police Battalion 101: a nucleus of increasingly enthusiastic killers . . . a larger group . . . who performed as shooters and ghetto clearers . . . and a small group (less than 20 percent) of refusers and evaders.[98]

Similarly, Browning finds resonance with "many of Milgram's insights" that "find graphic confirmation in the behavior and testimony of the men of Reserve Police Battalion 101," in particular, "the mutual reinforcement of authority and conformity . . . render considerable support to his [Milgram's] conclusions."[99]

But Browning indicates that a critical explanatory factor was indoctrination. He cites approvingly Milgram's hypothesis that "the more destructive behavior of people in Nazi Germany, under much less direct surveillance, was a consequence of an internalization of authority achieved 'through relatively long processes of indoctrination, of a sort not possible within the course of a laboratory hour.' "[100] On this basis, Browning examines the documentary record to show the extent to which ideological indoctrination did occur in Nazi Germany and leaves little doubt of its effectiveness with respect to those whose behavior he examined. Daniel Jonah Goldhagen criticized this aspect of Browning's thesis by arguing that the ideological grip of anti-Semitism was so deeply ingrained, so profoundly integral to German culture, that the indoctrination of police and security forces played a secondary role in mobilizing the perpetrators to kill Jews. In response, Browning refers to both his "multilayered portrayal of the battalion" in terms of the segments that emerged within it, regarding the actual killing, as well as his "multicausal explanation of motivation."[101] Browning refutes the "one mind" thesis he associates with Goldhagen that alleges all Germans were seized by "the demonological nature of the Jews" or that, alternatively, they were committed to "the greatest crime in history." What Browning does concede is that he might have "emphasized more explicitly the legitimizing capacities of government."[102] He later adds, "It was precisely the Nazis' demolition of democracy and the restoration of an authoritarian political system, emphasizing communal obligations over individual rights, that gave them legitimacy and popularity among significant segments of the German population."[103]

Browning's mention of "communal rights" in the context of why "ordinary" men became perpetrators deserves greater emphasis than it ultimately receives. Germany's political culture under the Nazi regime did return to its historic stress on "communal rights." But to what does this refer and why is it relevant to these debates purporting to resolve questions concerning motivations for killing and Nazi Party ideology and legitimacy? I emphasize this issue here because it anticipates the central element of what is absent from these debates: focus on communal honor. What often remains missing from these explanatory perspectives and many others of a similar nature is focus on the traditions of honor within German political culture throughout the nineteenth century and its role and impact in Nazi ideological constructions. These emphasize shame, humiliation and the "stab-in-the-back" (*Dolchstoßlegende*) notion by the Jews that Hitler repeatedly alleged was the cause of German defeat in World War I. Browning, like many other scholars, recognizes the importance of humiliation in galvanizing Nazi Germany for purposes of war and the "final solution." Loss and humiliation represent essential dimensions of the theoretical perspective advanced by Midlarsky, for example, in his "ephemeral gain and loss" model of political extremism. But the reference to "communal rights" as a core component of Nazi authoritarianism does not gather explanatory significance until it is linked to a systematic discussion of honor and shame in German political culture. This applies as well to other cultures that have witnessed mass atrocity, including Cambodia and Rwanda. This situates the question as to what is "honor" and how does honor relate to shame and shame disciplines as core factors in applications of psychosocial perspectives sensitive to comparative anthropology in the study of honor codes and shame disciplines.

This focus elevates the explanatory importance of culture as a dimension that is not necessarily causal but one that intervenes in how, as well as why, perpetrators such as those in Battalion 101 behave as they do. Shame and honor, therefore, play out as important factors in explaining the very behaviors to which Browning gives powerful testimony. In the end, Browning gestures toward the macabresque by referring to the perspective of Fred E. Katz, who, Browning declares, "argues that in a killing environment the creation of 'a culture of cruelty' is a 'powerful phenomenon' that provides many satisfactions—individualized reputation and enhanced standing among one's peers, alleviation of boredom, and a sense of joy and festivity, of artistry and creativity—to those who flaunt their gratuitous and inventive cruelties."[104] Browning thus embraces the argument presented by Katz indicating that dramaturgy and aesthetics are integral to mass atrocity. He concludes with a question pertaining to the nature of political culture. "But we are still left with an unresolved question that cannot be solved by simple assertion: Is a culture of hatred the necessary precondition for such a culture of cruelty?"[105] To get the answer right, however, one must ask the right question. In the present instance, the question is whether or not a culture of honor and shame is necessary? And as I attempt to demonstrate in succeeding chapters, the answer for the most part is in the affirmative.

THE SEARCH FOR "ROOTS"

A small corner of research in social psychology has concentrated on relationships between motivation and violence framed as "evil." Motivations tend to be presented along a psychological continuum comprising impulsive-cognitive-strategic responses relative to a range of external conditions created by groups. Questions concerning pathways to genocide thus become converted into inquiries over "evil" motivations in groups. A prime example is that of Roy F. Baumeister's analysis of "prototypes of human evil" engaged in "actions that intentionally harm other people" with evil defined as "intentional interpersonal harm." In Baumeister's approach, evil stems from loss of self-restraint.[106] He adds, "Therefore, regardless of the *root* causes of violence, the *immediate* cause is often a breakdown of self-control."[107] His approach turns to genocide once he portrays "evil" as motivated by "true belief" and "idealism." Baumeister writes, for example, "Idealistic perpetrators believe they have a license, even a duty, to hate. They perceive the victim in terms of the myth of pure evil: as fundamentally opposed to the good, for no valid reason or even for the sheer joy of evil."[108] Baumeister's conclusions purport to reveal that members of groups relate internally to other members around prototypical norms and expectations, values and attitudes; these are established *outside-in*. Groups impose themselves on members so that individuals calibrate who they "are," what they "believe" to what they perceive to be group demand or preference. Baumeister's concept of "idealistic evil" brings together a kind of oxymoronic contradiction in order to illustrate the "self-denying" even "puritanical" nature of a number of genocidal regimes, including the Maoist, the Khmer Rouge, and the Nazis. With respect to the latter, for example, he observes, "It was not the dregs and thugs, but the finest flower, who committed the most horrible deeds."[109] Idealism in depravity, puritanical self-denial, and absolute loss of self-control in mass murder and killing—this is what motivates perpetrators. Why and how do "idealism" and puritanical "self-control" motivate evil perpetrators? Baumeister's response is suggestive of self-categorization and prototypicality in groups, in particular, the fusional tendency to want to become one with majority opinion. He writes, "This pattern of deferring to the group's moral authority is seen over and over again in violent groups." Baumeister identifies groups and group dynamics as the core condition on the pathway to genocide. He does so on the grounds that the "moral authority" of groups provides "sufficient justification to perform wicked actions."[110] In idealistic evil, "no greater fault" or "crime" arises than defection from group standards. "Keeping the group together with a strong sense of separateness and commitment is in many cases a more fundamental and urgent goal that accomplishing its stated purposes."[111] But if evil is done in the name of the good, as Baumeister alleges, the question is why. The answer is not self-evident if it only refers to group dynamics. For if groups do cause "evil" in the delusional self-deceptions that evil is "good," the issue remains as to what motivates this.

THE TAXONOMIC SEARCH FOR ROOT CONDITIONS

Ervin Staub has examined pathways to genocide by positioning motivation as the central unit of analysis.[112] He applies the concept of "evil" to the study of group violence by delineating both the precise circumstances as well as the general conditions contributing to motivations during episodes of mass violence. His methodological thrust tacks on broad analytical generalizations to social psychological explanations of human motivation in groups. His theoretical framework is limited to the study of how impulsive-cognitive-strategic psychological influences function as "motivations." What does Staub mean by "motivation"? His application of the term "motivation" appears to privilege a kind of methodological exteriority in the study of human behavior but in ways that demonstrate internal factors depicted as *impulsive-cognitive-strategic*. In his earlier work, Staub states the following: "I will use several motivational concepts, some in part interchangeably. Motivation designates an active psychological state that makes an outcome or end desirable . . . ." He adds the circular definition, "A *motive* is a characteristic of the individual or culture out of which active motivation arises."[113] Staub then lists "needs," "goals," and "aims" as ways of distinguishing motives. Staub adopts what he calls a "personal goal theory" of motivations, arranged and rearranged according to the changing salience of motives located along what he calls a "hierarchy" of motives."

On the basis of a complex array of forces and factors, Staub summarizes his findings, stating:

> Motives of control and comprehension are important all along. Scapegoating, subordinating the self to authorities, joining a movement and adopting an ideology, assuming power over others through dominance and violence can all provide people with feelings of comprehension, control, and power.[114]

Staub thus inches analytically closer to the theoretical centrality of self-reflexive feelings of power and control. His methodological assumption, however, is that perpetrators attain their "feelings of comprehension, control and power," by means of submission to authority, ideology and group peer pressures. Power and control are taken to operate at various levels. But the basic methodological problem Staub's hierarchy produces is its failure to specify how power at one level intersects with the dynamics of power at the other levels, if they do at all. He writes, "Characteristic psychological processes operate in groups. The boundaries of the self are weakened. The 'I' becomes embedded, enveloped, and defined by the 'we.' This makes emotional contagion easier." He adds, "Emotional contagion is both a means of mutual influence and a source of satisfaction for group members."[115] But here again, a contradiction seems to arise in that power and control are critical to what is said to motivate individuals to do "evil." When they do so, however, they become especially amenable to emotional contagion within groups in which the self is said to be "embedded, enveloped and defined by the 'we.'"

Staub indicates that motivation to engage in violence may serve as an end itself, that is, designed to cause "hurt or harm" as an end, or as an instrumental means to other aims or objectives. He elaborates this psychological approach to motivation by indicating that material as well as identitarian values come into play during conflicts. He suggests that the dynamics of group identity in conflicts manifest certain features: "categorization," defined as "who we are and who they are"; "identification," a process of "defining one-self and others as belonging to particular groups"; and, finally, "social comparison," that is, "people evaluating their worth relative to others belonging to particular groups."[116] In Staub's view, identities are multiple and shifting. But he also avers, "As members of an identity group come together around shared beliefs, as commitments to ideology and group intensify" ethnic, religious, and racial identity groups "become increasingly fixed."[117] Staub introduces the important elements of culture, political organization, economic status and rewards, territorial sovereignty, into the equations of violence and intergroup competition and conflict grounded in identitarian constructions. He goes further to suggest that loss of status or standing, shame and humiliation, all based on a sense of "powerlessness," particularly relative to group identities, represent important elements. He states, "Shame and humiliation give rise to the motivation to reassert identity and dignity, often by violent means."[118] He adds, "This may be especially so in cultures that prize honor."[119] Cultures beholden to saving face and to honor-bound traditions disciplined by shame punishments may indeed seek "revenge" as a price for return to social peace and equilibrium. But revenge is a complex phenomenon that comes at a high price on the roads to genocide, as witnessed in Cambodia, Rwanda and within other shame cultures. But why? Staub's schema is ultimately unable to generate answers.

ON EMOTIONALITY, OR WHAT'S LOVE GOT TO DO WITH IT?

James E. Waller provides a taxonomy of "extraordinary human evil" in search of root causes. His notion of motivation is suggested by, "What forces shape our responses to authority?" His inquiry focuses on three nodal points: "actor," "context of the action," and "definition of the target." Under actor, he presents motivation as emerging from what he calls "our ancestral shadows," a category that includes "ethnocentrism," "xenophobia," and "desire for social dominance"; in addition, he adds "identities of the perpetrators," depicted in terms of "cultural belief systems," "moral disengagement," "rational self-interest." Context of the action disaggregates what he calls "a culture of cruelty" culled from three factors, alone and together, that include "professional socialization," "binding factors of the group," and "merger of role and person"; finally, his schematic outline stresses the "social death of the victims, characterized by "us-them thinking," "dehumanization," and blaming the victims."[120] But Waller appears ultimately unconvinced that extraordinary human evil can be explained by applying models of behavior based on assumptions of the "ordinary" in everyone. He concludes, "Understanding the universal dispositional nature of human nature, however, tells us only that we all are *capable* of extraordinary evil. It does not explain why only *some* of us actually perpetrate extraordinary evil and, in fact, why the great majority of us never do."[121] Waller's analysis thus emphasizes situational conditions in framing explanations of such behaviors.

Daniel Chirot and Clark McCauley methodologically apply the concept of "psychological foundations" in ways suggestive of human emotions. Chirot and McCauley inquire as to "What are those 'durable' passions that lead to so much horror?"[122] In their perspective, "emotions" appear and dissipate. They act as grips; they predict behaviors: but not consistently or for extended periods of time. Emotions reflect "situations:" and situations depend on a range of fleeting factors, not the least of which is defined by leaders and their emotions. Chirot and McCauley introduce aspects of human emotionality that they regard as constants. They write, for example, "Fear is perhaps the key emotion for understanding genocide."[123] They add, "The most powerful fear is fear of extinction, the fear that 'our' people, 'our' cause, 'our' culture, 'our' history may not survive."[124] Clearly, Chirot and McCauley are stressing the strength of identitarian attachments related to group survival. Their interpretation of the perceptual nature of emotionality leads them to develop a theory of fear based on the social psychological concept of "negativity bias." Questions arise: why the salience of loss; how does loss sensed by individuals translate into cultural traditions, ideological perceptions, collective memories of loss; when and under what sets of conditions does memory of collective loss become transformed into factors that predict for genocide and mass atrocity? As if to respond, Chirot and McCauley consider "hate" as a composite of multifarious emotional states. Hate, they write, "seems to us best understood as an extreme form of negative identification."[125] In their view, hate represents a function of the object or external stimulus that provokes it whenever present. It is all in the perception of the external object or situation that is determinative. "When the target of hate prospers and succeeds, we feel negative emotions; when the target of hate fails and suffers, we feel positive emotions. Whatever combination of contempt, disgust, anger, and fear are at work, and however different various combinations might be, the origin is the same in that we have a persistent negative appraisal of the object."[126] Such emphasis on the object as cause of hate prompts Chirot and McCauley to emphasize how situations or conditions prompt emotions, but in ways subject to dramatic change and fleeting variations. Chirot and McCauley define "love" against the background of their definition of hate. "Our conceptualization makes hate directly the opposite of love."[127] They suggest, "Love is an extreme form of positive identification, whereas hate is an extreme form of negative identification."[128] If emotionality is always epiphenomenal and thus secondary to or caused by primary factors outside or external to persons, emotions such as love and hate might indeed be methodologically constructed as comparable "opposites." But to do so runs the risk of depleting the analytical categories indicative of how human emotional experiences are integral to self-reflexive understandings.

This, too, demonstrates how the levels of analysis problem can lead to conceptual as well as methodological fallacies. Chirot and McCauley illustrate this by treating the emotionalities of love and hate as merely opposites of each other, in analytical contexts focused on group behaviors in genocidal situations. Their conception of love remains undertheorized; but it appears to function as a form of positive attachment or identification. This stands within their scheme as contrasted to the negative forms of emotionality once hate is experienced. They indicate, "At the individual level it is love of self and individuals close to us, while at the group level it is love for a collectivity that can be as large as an ethnicity, religion, culture, or nation."[129]

It would seem as if Chirot and McCauley conflate narcissism with love. Do groups of perpetrators of mass atrocity acting as collective actors or agents "love" in any meaningful sense of the term? Is it theoretically useful or conceptually sound to impute to perpetrators actions and behaviors that under any set of circumstances whatsoever demonstrate anything that relates to the emotionality properly associated with "love," even if "love," by definition, is to include "love of country." Chirot and McCauley appear to hold to love as an explanatory approach. "This perspective," they claim, "contrasts with the common association of genocide as a manifestation of irrational hatred. Hatred of targeted groups is no more irrational than love of groups with which we identify."[130] To an extent, the issue is semantic; clearly, one can call anything by any label. But the semantic horizons adumbrated by the concept of love become inexact and inappropriate, to say the least, if the claim is that groups or perpetrators act out of "love" for the objects with which they identify. To suggest otherwise is to deplete the humanness of love that renders love what it is. Notwithstanding this, Chirot and McCauley state, "the obverse of genocide is identification with a loved group—friends, family, village, clan, tribe, class, nation, or religion on whose behalf the massacres are carried out."[131] There is no love, properly conceived, along the pathways of why perpetrators commit genocide and mass atrocity. And the reasons point toward the incapacities for full emotionality and away from abilities to empathize discussed later by Fonagy and colleagues. Love may not be interpreted as the obverse of hate, but even if it were so considered, the question arises as to whether all perpetrators actually do hate their victims. Sofsky's claim is precisely that they do not, given their indifference toward victims. Thus, the argument from a conceptual perspective configured around love and hate seems highly suspect.

WHAT IS THEORETICALLY "PERMISSIBLE" IN SOCIAL PSYCHOLOGY?

Theodor Adorno once wisely articulated the problem of conflating love with narcissism when he wrote, "In repressive society the concept of man is itself a parody of divine likeness. The mechanism of 'pathic projection' determines those in power perceive as human only their own reflected image, instead of reflecting back the human as precisely what is different."[132] Adorno understands how this translates into the patterns of self-deception and rationalization. "Murder is thus the repeated attempt, by yet greater madness, to distort the madness of such false perception into reason: what was not seen as human and yet is human, is made a thing, so that its stirrings can no longer refute the manic gaze."[133] In so writing, Adorno stakes out the methodological claim for a systematic examination of disordered will or akrasia and the processes of reification in collective violence, a critical component of psychosocial theory. Much has been written about the causes of genocide and mass atrocity and especially about the relationships between individual perpetrators and groups. Most of the social psychological literature reveals a combination of circularity and redundancy by attempting to explain behaviors on the basis of rationality, rationalization and prototypicality in groups. It would seem that there exists a systematic avoidance of anything pertaining to the interiorities of the human psyche or mentalized structures of human emotionality. Freudian and post-Freudian discourses have become so discredited, it would appear, among the empirical social sciences; and the methodological boundaries between psychoanalytical theory, sociology, and social psychology so firm, that studies of genocide and mass atrocity falter on the failures of *interdisciplinarity* over apparent fears of *multidisciplinarity*. And yet, in the absence of psychosocial theory, the macabresque remains inexplicable specifically in frameworks that appear theoretically permissible in social psychology.

3

One Mind, Heart, and Spirit

REDUCTIONIST TRAPS IN PSYCHOSOCIAL THEORY

ON THE PROBLEM OF THE SINGLE MIND

How, then, does one resolve theoretical contestations with respect to genocide and mass atrocity? The study of perpetrator behaviors requires methodological latitude attuned to the recursive dynamics between interior and exterior dimensions of individual and group behaviors. This recognizes the singularity of individuals in groups, as well as the impacts of groups on perpetrators. It helps to frame an understanding of why perpetrators engage in acts of performative transgression. Terms such as *mass annihilation, mass murder, democide*, and *policide* are theoretically misleading in that they imply the analytical separation between the modes, means, methods, and instrumentalities of dying from the numerics of deaths. But torturous and tormented dying is the rabid signature of mass atrocity. Mass atrocity stages funereal defilements of victims so that as death approaches it comes to victims in the dramaturgical darkness of performative transgression. The question is why; and the answers depend on disciplinary context and perspective. But throughout, much evidence points toward perpetrators in relation to other perpetrators—as each perceives themselves and the others in frames theorized by social psychology as the dynamics of prototypicality. Perpetrators seldom act alone in isolation from other perpetrators. Their roles are sealed in the blood bonds of honor that transform absolute power as an end itself into the badge of duty beyond the normal call of obligation—that is, into a realm of self-deception in which the vilest forms of cruelty loom as the heights of supererogatory heroism. This pattern of self-deception does not function one perpetrator at a time. It requires collective group confirmation. Power "absolutized" in this fashion requires submersion into group norms; but submersion is not only about processes of fusion, peer pressures, or obedience. These may play out in the routines of abject normalized violence. But the exercise of absolute power requires staging, and such staging demands an audience or witnesses. These factors represent the beginning of an understanding of what motivates perpetrators to pursue genocide and mass atrocity as the ends, but also as the means of the macabresque.

A focus on the relations between psychology and culture, among other probes, turns to the question of "meanings," how they are made or forged, how they are reaffirmed, altered, delegitimated, and reconstituted. To what extent are such processes of "meaning-making," or sense-making universal as opposed to variable and how or on what grounds? As we approach the quest for an understanding of genocide and mass atrocity and its connections to the macabresque, questions arise pertaining to culture. Psychoanalytic theory has often been alleged to be indifferent to the dimensions of culture and support-ive of universalist claims regarding the Oedipal model of development. But as Freud's own interest in comparative anthropology reveals, anthropology from the very begin-ning stands at the crossroads of psychosocial theory. In the present context, the question that arises pertains to the relationships between cultural factors and the styles of drama-turgy and aesthetics adopted within the macabresque. If we are to treat the macabresque seriously as a cultural phenomenon, variations as well as commonalities become critical. Here, we focus on variations in political cultures as they appear to bear on how the maca-bresque becomes organized and executed. Discussions of culture within psychosocial perspectives fall into a number of analytical and methodological traps. These tend to equate mindsets of cultural values as "single mind" or analytically treat groups of persons acting within groups as a single person. Levels and units of analysis readily become equiv-alent in reductionist fashion to the detriment of interpretation and analysis.

MASS MIND IN METHODOLOGICAL CONTEXT: ANALYTICAL CONSTRUCT OR MYTHICAL ILLUSION

Daniel Pick, in a scathing critique of psychoanalytic theory, recounts what he regards as errors once "the Nazi mind" is methodologically constructed as a unit of analysis. "Much of the wartime clinical literature on Nazism exemplified such suspect 'psychologism,'" he writes, "assuming the universality of certain key models in psychoanalysis such as the Oedipus complex or the death drive."[1] Pick critically dismisses collective mind and related efforts to theorize the Holocaust. Pick writes, psychoanalysis was thus "couched as though it was obvious that minds always in the end struggled with the same 'univer-sal' problems . . . that the most basic features of identity formation (most notably the negotiation of the Oedipus complex) were timeless . . . across time and space, and what changes through and through remains a matter of debate."[2] For these reasons, Pick dis-counts efforts to explain Nazi motivations using Freudian concepts, particularly "narcis-sism, sadism, identification, idealization, or the superego" as analytical guideposts.[3] Pick argues that psychoanalytic concepts with emphasis on psychic personality assumed that "power was secured through whips, clubs, guns, tanks, and planes, but also through the psycho-political manipulations of love and desire, hatred, envy, and anxiety."[4] Pick adds, "The sources of those feelings and passions, it was said, lay not only in culture, politics, and society, nor even in innate personal endowments, but in the unconscious meanings associated with the experiences of infancy, the nature of parent-child relations, and the complex milieu of the family." Pick raises the methodological gauntlet against what he envisions is a misguided attempt to perceive the making of an authoritarian personality in every adult citizen in Nazi Germany. "Each infant, in short," he writes, "was a political subject in the making."[5] The methodological problems detected by Pick stem in his view not only from the universalizing/dehistoricizing psychoanalytic methodologies, but from applying them across layers of behavioral agency, from individuals to groups and from groups to societies as a whole. "On occasion, analysts focused upon the psychopathology of particular individuals; at others, upon the mentality that was said to be typical in particular organizations (such as the SS), or even upon the entirety of those who became enthralled by Hitler."[6] Pick thus offers a countercritique that deplores theoretical mystifications of a universalized unconscious purportedly formed in infancy and indiscriminately applied to all persons and to groups and to Nazi Germany. He applauds the fact that gradually psychological theories received skeptical acceptance and in many instances outright rejection. "In one sense psychological factors receded into the background: in the vast post-war literature that emerged on the Third Reich historians increasingly concerned themselves with the particular structural conditions or systemic features of German society, rather than psychoanalytical accounts of the individual or inquiries into the dynamics of groups."[7]

Pick bestows particular authority on Foucault and Foucauldian influences for having brought about the methodological rejection of psychoanalytic notions of the "self," identity, knowledge, culture, and so forth. Foucault, writes Pick, "lyrically described 'man' as an historical construction, a figure in the sand who might be washed away."[8] Pick adds, "Foucault's work . . . contributed to the view that the endeavor to use psychoanalysis or other psychological approaches to understand key aspects of culture and society, or even the minds of individual people in the past, was an antiquated approach, and categories of such as 'the abnormal' should not be reproduced but rather historicized and analyzed."[9] This, Pick suggests, helped generate new forms of historiography. "Instead of assuming that people always return to the same deep intra-psychic problems, historians were to investigate how the most apparently timeless beliefs or structuring assumptions of life are constituted in and through history itself."[10] In his view, the methodological quandary posed by the "mind," the psyche, remains insurmountable if applied within contexts that aim to explain collective behaviors on the basis of individual biographies or that use individual abnormalities as analytical pathways to explain mass violence. Pick concedes that "the more subtle psychoanalytical accounts, as well as historical and fictionalized biographies of particular Nazis, invite us to speculate about the remote and proximate psychological causes of murderous political practices." But he rejects efforts to shift meth-odologically from the levels of analysis that in effect move from the study of "one" to the analysis of the "many" and, conversely, from the many to the one. "Some psychohistorical literature on the Third Reich, however, assumes in advance," Pick writes, "that individual events cause much later ideological outcomes, or suggests that evidence of, say, psychosex-ual 'deviance' in childhood or adolescence carries obvious explanatory weight in under-standing later 'perverse' political attitudes."[11] In this regard, Pick uses as his example that of Hitler himself. Pick supports the methodological assertions of Ron Rosenbaum that discount psychic and psychological efforts to "explain" why Hitler "became" what he "is" historically.[12] Much has been written about the presumed causal factors that prompted Hitler to become "Hitler."[13] Here again, motivation is said to explain behavior but on grounds that allege monocausal explanations of complex outcomes. As Pick declares, "All of these aspects of Hitler's life are intriguing, but it is wrong to claim that it was any one of them that definitively twisted Hitler's mind into a different shape."[14]

Ron Rosenbaum, like Pick, reckons with psychohistorical attempts to "psychologize" the evil that Hitler wrought by reference to perverse psychosexual dynamics internal to Hitler's own psyche. Rosenbaum writes, for example, "It mattered to Freudians as a vindication of the belief that the defining truth about the unanalyzed person can be found in what is hidden rather than what is apparent; that the important truths are always beneath the surface and that they are almost always sexual truths."[15] Rosenbaum is avowedly skeptical. "And so, from the beginning, psychoanalytic writers . . . have had a go at Hitler, most trying to locate the source of his problems in infantile erotic life, the preferred breeding ground for problems in Freudian theory."[16] Rosenbaum, in particu-lar, calls into question the theoretical validity of attempting to attribute Hitler's *political* pathology to his *sexual* pathology, as Rosenbaum sees it outlined in a study by Norbert Bromberg and Verna Volz Small entitled *Hitler's Psychopathology*.[17] This study features Hitler's well-known calamitous sexual relationship to Geli Raubal and represents it as critical to the development of Hitler's psychopathology. Rosenbaum disapprovingly dis-misses the conclusions offered by Bromberg and Small regarding Hitler's demonic anti-Semitism with the following comment, "The anger *he projected* outward at the Jews was, they conclude, derived from the hatred of the sexual predator, the predatory Jew within himself. He had to exterminate them because he *was* them."[18] Rosenbaum criticizes Bromberg and Small for revealing "an eagerness to explain everything" in this manner, a proclivity Rosenbaum associates with psychoanalysis as a whole and with psychohistory in particular.[19] He observes, "As overcomplicated, uncorroborated and speculative as it seems, it was this self-hating dynamic that, the psychoanalytic authors maintain, gener-ated the Holocaust."[20]

Rosenbaum raises an important methodological issue. Although particular historic leaders may help to determine the pathways to genocide and mass atrocity in particu-lar ways at particular times, their "mind" or psyche is not equivalent methodologically to causality in terms of collective dynamics. This underscores the importance of levels of analysis in examining collective violence. That said, the psychodynamics of introjection and projection indicated by the plausible suggestion of Hitler's sense of shame and humiliation is, in my view, theoretically tenable. This is given some degree of credence by Rosenbaum himself. Rosenbaum applies this precise formula of introjection and projection to explain the rabid anti-Semitism of Reinhard Heydrich, the very figure who presided over the Wannsee Conference that embarked on the Final Solution. It was Heydrich who, until his assassination, directed exterminatory policies, second only to Himmler and to Hitler himself. Rosenbaum is well aware of the parallel he is drawing between the Heydrich and Hitler cases. He writes, "But, also like Hitler, Heydrich was rumored to have had a special *Jewish* doppelgänger haunting *him*: a shadowy alleged Jewish ancestor, rumors of whose existence gave rise to the widespread reports that Heydrich felt personally plagued by a putative Hebrew shadow."[21] Rosenbaum refers to the fact that "to some, Heydrich was not only a potential successor to Hitler, he might be a possible explanation—in the sense that his struggle with this Jewish-blood shadow might be a clue to a similar dynamic in Hitler's psyche."[22] Rosenbaum thus wrestles with the levels of analysis problem that arises once systematic study of large-scale violence is explained against the background of not only the biography of a specific political leader but also in terms of the psychoanalytic dimensions of that leader's psychic and emotional personality. The emphasis on the role and impacts of single leaders that is central to many such studies on genocide and mass atrocity renders this analytical issue more, rather than less, acute. On the one hand, it is readily understood that facile explanations of the behavior of many individuals alone or in groups on the basis of the presence and personality of one leader must be avoided; on the other hand, numerous studies demonstrate the essential significance of the single leader in pathways to genocide and mass atrocity, with respect to both small and large group dynamics.

Rosenbaum[23] concludes with a cautionary admonition that advises against methodological efforts framed by singular explanations—that is, theories that confuse or conflate levels of analysis: "I cite this not for its persuasive power (it falls far short of convincing me) but as an example of the way explainers strain for the ultimate explanatory prize, the missing link, the key hidden variable in Hitler studies: the link between his purportedly aberrant personal pathology and his abhorrent political ideology—between his sexuality and his anti-Semitism."[24] Pick and Rosenbaum each in their way, therefore, in effect, outline what to avoid methodologically in all theoretical frameworks of psychosocial analysis. I encapsulate these suggested traps to be avoided as follows:

- cultural values or predispositions represented as a single mind or psyche;
- collective mental states treated as universal and unchanging;
- constructions of a singular mind or psyche as a collective form of causality;
- conflation of the mind of a leader with the mind or mentality of a people;
- singular trait selection as the basis for explaining behavior, with respect to specific leaders but also in regard to groups;

- psychopathological depictions of individual abnormality as explanations of malevolent forms of collective behavior;
- universalized and methodologically dehistoricized explanations of collective behavior on the basis of immutable psychosocial forces;
- psychosocial frameworks that "psychologize" violent behaviors on the basis of speculative theories devoid of explanations linking macro, meso and micro levels of analysis.

PSYCHOLOGIZING GROUPS AND SOCIOLOGIZING INDIVIDUALS: ON METHODOLOGICAL FALLACIES

The methodological risk here is to lend individual personality to collective actors or, conversely, group personality to individual actors. Numerous theorists have commented on the perilous dangers of conflating persons with groups, groups with individuals. Elisabeth Young-Bruehl put it succinctly when she wrote, "It is just as methodologically suspect to psychologize society as it is to sociologize individuals. The first fallacy presumes that a society can be understood as a large diagnosable individual . . . . The second fallacy treats an individual as no more than a function of or player in a group, as only a tablet on which social order is stamped." The problem that arises is one in which "Intrapsychic processes become products of social imprinting, as though the unconscious were the society at large beamed into an individual's brain."[25]

Ideologies of Desire and "Orectic" Obsessions

Young-Bruehl attempts to resolve the methodological problem of the one in the many and the many "ones" in the psychodynamics of groups. She links historic or political situations with personality traits defined by desire. "In complicated modern societies, many social characters prevail in different subsocieties, regions and local and translocal institutions," she writes. "There is no such thing as 'the culture of narcissism.' But at particular historical moments—especially moments of crisis—a dominating set of social character traits may emerge, affecting the whole society, making some individuals desire to connect with the dominative configuration and making others feel alien or alienated."[26] Young-Bruehl emphasizes desire or patterns of desire realized in groups under varying conditions. She describes these conditions as "orectic ideologies of desire." She writes, "I am going to call an ideology of desire an 'orecticism,' from the Greek word *orektikos*, meaning desirous or pertaining to the desires."[27] She adds, "An orecticism is a worldview shaped by a desire, a desire that has produced an ideology or articulated itself into an ideology."[28] Orectic ideologies grounded in the psychodynamics of desire are realized through individual but collective behaviors in groups at different times and in distinct ways. From this perspective, the origins or sources of ideologies including those that legitimate mass atrocity derive from orectic desires. Young-Bruehl indicates that orecticism experienced individually but within groups leads to collective projections of guilt onto scapegoated or objectified (reified) victims. She writes, "Orecticists feel guilt, and then repress their guilt *with their prejudices.*"[29] Orectic desire is thus theorized as a defense against certain psychic and emotional processes realized concretely by prejudices, ultimately, by hatred.[30] The mechanisms and modalities of surplus cruelty are thus hardly random. They take on specific form reflective of the orectic desires from which they emerge. Young-Bruehl observes, "Orecticists cannot be satisfied to exercise power or enjoy the prerogatives of power, their 'others' must be marked, literally, on the areas of their bodies that signify the type of dominance desired or on the symbols for those areas."[31] She draws a parallel between how orecticists inflict kinds of torments against victims to how Dante depicted the ways sinners are punished "in the inferno of Hades" according to the nature of their sins.

Young-Bruehl aligns her understanding of the orectic relations between the reifications of hatred and performative transgression. In this, she points to the psycho-aesthetics of group leadership and followership in moments of orectic desire that take on the semblances of human physicality. Envy plays a critical role. Whatever is most hated in reified groups represents what is most desired and thus the most envied. This generates a kind of need to be in denial, to eliminate any reservation or doubt that may percolate within perpetrators as a group formation. "One of the key functions of leadership in a group where obsessionality is rife: the leader must never waver, never turn back, never reconsider, never be anything less that hard, steely, a beacon in any darkness."[32] But the role of followers is no less than important. They, too, must demonstrate absolute and unreserved commitment through what Young-Bruehl describes as "metaphors that are psychoanatomically precise—their backbones, their sphincter control."[33] She interprets the aesthetics of performativity and in effect the macabresque with reference to the parades, the demonstrations, the "feats of muscular clenching and releasing—like the Nazi goose-step march, many other forms of parade drill, and various forms of ceremonial saluting and bowing." In surplus cruelty and performative transgression, "Hypertonicity is the obsessional mode of dependency."[34]

Orectic desires thus evoke fantasies of absolute physical purity that in turn revel in ideologies of total exclusion. In this perspective, essentialized physicality is the operative principle of perpetrators acting within the macabresque. She observes, "Orectic prejudices are monodirectional: they always move from the body to other group characteristics, which are said to derive from the body."[35] The spheres of orectic desire in the macabresques move from the body to the world and from the world back into the body. "World conquest goes hand-in-hand with preservation of control over the details of bodily life." The aim in orecticism is always "to protect their intimate, bodily assertion of control and to fortify the private spheres in which they originally exercised such control."[36] Young-Bruehl understands that the linkages between group dynamics, on the one hand, and prejudice and desire, on the other, are tethered to social fantasies regarding the human body, its shapes and qualities, its vulnerabilities and its idealized perfection. What she implies but does not elaborate is the critical influences of shame, or rather, the shame of shamefulness, in orectic desires and ideologies. Shamefulness is what must be denied by such social groups and in such cultures. For shamefulness emerges out from bodily functions that bespeak of physical weakness and frailty, the very features of physicality that stem from whatever is taken as disfigurative and ugly, "effeminate" and thus vulnerable, all of which are denied or disavowed by the theatricality Young-Bruehl describes. This is the hidden step or linkage between orectic desire and hatred that she fails fully to examine and yet represents as the one element that is critical to her analysis.

Young-Bruehl thus applies a psychoanalytic interpretation of "projection" in a methodological context framed by desire and orectic ideologies. This represents a crucial step in forging a psychosocial framework of analysis. Young-Bruehl speaks of "orectic projection" as a way of understanding the psychodynamics of projected hatred. She implicitly refers to the permeable nature of psychic and/or emotional boundaries operating between inner psychodynamics of will and emotionality and exterior reality. "Hatred that has been projected is then felt by the projector to be coming from the outside, from the group that received the projection."[37] Projection theory in the framework of Young-Bruehl's examination of orectic desire helps to explain the virulence of genocide and mass atrocity. In this analytical perspective, hatred represents the consequence of resisting guilt: the more the guilt, the deeper the projected hatred and reification. As in the case of some forms of cancer, cells that kill originate in the immune system. The greater, the more prevailing the guilt, the deeper, the more driving the orecticism becomes. "Orecticists are more recalcitrant," she writes, "because their prejudices *are* their defenses—against acknowledging their wishes and against their own guilt feelings, the voices of their superegos."[38] I suggest that the emotional impulses Young-Bruehl depicts as "guilt" stem every bit as much from those of shamefulness. *It is shamefulness that provides the need for defensive barriers, for it is the shamefulness of shame that must be denied more vehemently the more shame is fantasmatically experienced as present.* Young-Bruehl notes how "internal enemies" come to be "represented in the external world. She envisions these orectic processes within methodological frames shaped by assumptions concerning permeability of psychic boundaries between what is perceived as external fact and what resists recognition in the psychic interiorities of fantasy and desire. She gradually moves toward a definition of motivation that relates not only to what is wanted or sought after as desirable in a purposive sense, but also to an understanding of motivation subject to the will to power in the psychodynamics of desire. And it in such orectic contexts, combining ideologies of desire and fantasies of power, that groups play such a critical role in sadistic aggression. Orecticists, Young-Bruehl writes, "work constantly, in fantasy or fact, at getting their world to conform to their visions, the images of their desires. The instrument of their work is their imaginary group, the group they bring into being by wishing it so." She adds poetically, "They are always hammering away at the hot metal of their hopes for 'us.'"[39] And that hot metal is the fantasmatic force that seeks to keep shamefulness away by virtue of prejudice and power, honor, and obligation, sometimes transmuted into hideous cruelty in collective moments of self-deception.

INDIVIDUALISM AND COLLECTIVE OBJECT RELATIONS

At issue is the extent to which behavioral outcomes in groups depend on the traits of individuals or on the situational dynamics of both, what Fred Weinstein calls the drive for "omnipotent mastery and control" relative to "wishful thinking." This takes hold in what Fonagy and his colleagues described as "representations." Weinstein refers to this as interiorized psychic "objects." He suggests that they tend to become exteriorized. Once they do so they emerge in forms of ideological expression and behavior. What methodological language might we adapt for purposes of linking interior "object" formation with exterior political culture; conversely, what is the role and influence of political culture when groups of individuals acting under the rubric of large group identity perpetrate egregious violations? Weinstein stresses "the persistently heterogeneous composition of groups that even the most ruthless dictatorships could neither absorb or repress."[40] He points toward efforts to "connect the inner world of 'wishes, feelings, memories, percepts, and symbols,' to the outer world of cultural perspectives, social locations, so long they do not obligate any sense of unity of unconscious motivation, of collective identity or memory, or of shared predispositions to behavior." What counts in Weinstein's inquiry, therefore, are the linkages connecting exterior influences with internal "objects" in the mind; secondly, his analysis raises questions pertaining to how interiorized objects and fantasies become projected or established as exteriorized "realities." In so doing, Weinstein warns, like Young-Bruehl, against methodological reductionism that deduces individual personality from group or collective behaviors, and *vice versa*. He writes, for example "It is therefore best not to think in terms of collective (in the sense of unified) identity, collective memory, unity of motive, fixity of character, 'core personality,' or continuity of events over time."[41] He calls for an approach that privileges "unique, idiosyncratic perceptions" that demonstrate how "primacies shift within and among these locations."[42] The analytical issue in psychosocial theory turns into the challenge of responding to methodological individualism. Weinstein, for his part, does not march toward analytical nihilism by rejecting psychosocial theory altogether. Instead, he applies the concept, "wishful thinking" as a unit of analysis in the study of group dynamics.

Weinstein defines *wishful thinking* as follows:

> Wishful (or fantasy) thinking as it affects contact with the social world refers here to an imagined omnipotent mastery and control of some portion of the world in pursuit of a goal that is beyond anyone else's capacity to obstruct, regardless of how their interests and moral perspectives are affected, so that whatever outcome one imagines for oneself is realized, because in wishful thinking there are no insurmountable obstacles.[43]

In this, Weinstein appears to be echoing Kaufmann's discussion of self-deception and Farber's interpretation of disordered or akratic will, discussed earlier. He indicates that, "Wishful thinking plays an important role in social relationships and should be valued similarly in social theory as well, because it is the originating sources of novel forms of ideological expression and authoritative leadership."[44] He thus leads inquiry out of the quagmires of methodological individualism, but delivers it into the quandaries of how "wishful thinking," in so many ways parallel or consonant with the concept of "self-deception" influences collective behaviors. His answer stresses the roles played by normative concepts in the exercise of judgment and decision-making. He continues, "What must be emphasized rather is the way that people, codes, rules, objects, come to be represented in the mind, the way that these things come to constitute knowledge for people, and the different ways that people come to think and to feel about them."[45] Weinstein thus emphasizes the phenomenological lifeworlds in which subjects operate and their exercise of judgment, choice, and intent—especially with contexts framed by wishful thinking.

> Thus rather than conceive of wishful thinking in the familiar structural ('id') terms, as a determinative, undergirding, third sphere or realm of mental activity, along with ego and superego, it makes better heuristic sense to conceive of emotional commitments to mental representations of people and things based on real experiences in two culturally legitimate spheres, self-interested or material activity and moral activity, and to conceive of wishful thinking as occurring in either sphere, in terms of shifting primacies and priorities.[46]

Emphasis on material and moral activity underscores the relationship between mind and society, psyche and sociality, social fantasy and cultural constructions of the macabresque. The influences of honor and shame in the psychodynamics of the macabresque loom as significant as well.

Political cultures influence how mimetic desires operate in collective contexts and help to drive how sadistic cruelties become weaponized in the macabresque but differently in specific political cultures. To demonstrate this, I turn to how the psychodynamics of mimetic desire operate. In so doing, I delineate conceptual themes pertaining to social fantasy, "thing-enjoyment" and sadistic cruelty. This discussion is designed to connect psychosocial analysis of the unconscious to the macabresque; as demonstrated by various case studies of theaters of transgression that illustrate cultural styles of the macabresque. Again, the focus is not on the etiologies of genocidal murder or killing in mass atrocity. Our interest remains concentrated on the sources of the macabresque. The objective is to explore how political culture and ideological reifications or logics of illogic help to create the specific forms of living hell before death that is the macabresque but also how the macabresque emerges from the fantasmatic energies and unconscious emotionality inherent within the psychodynamics of mimetic desire.

4

The Modalities of Desire in Mimetic Rivalry

SIN, SIGN, AND SYMBOL

MIMETIC DESIRES, MIMETIC RIVALRIES

Desires are forged in imitative processes. Mimesis influences the contents of desire but also how desires arise and take form in desiring. Desire is always about the desire to live experientially in shared desire; "one" desires what the "many" desire. Through mimesis cultures and their agents influence what causes desire, that is, how to desire whatever is deemed as desirable. Lacanian perspectives in psychosocial theory suggest that political culture and ideology represent the conscious effects in the Symbolic realm of desires provoked by social fantasies in the Imaginary that convert libidinal drives in what Lacan calls the register of the Real into the displacements of *jouissance*, leading to desires for *objet a,* that is, object alternatives for thing-enjoyment.[1] How these metonymic psychic displacements become culturally and thus mimetically disciplined are often examined by focusing on processes of acculturation or on socialization dynamics, "schema" narratives, rituals of liminality or sacramental rites of passage. All instruct human subjects not only on what to desire, but how to desire. Desires thus tend to be intermediated: they appear to derive from internal wants, but they originate in mimesis and thus from cultural influences and social dynamics. But *jouissance* is always barred; and thus desires function according to the constitutive dictates of absence.

Envy and jealousy, honor and shame are never far apart. Driven by inaccessibility, desires exist in comparison to what others have, are, or do. Mimetic desires do not remain innocent for very long at any level of social interaction, but tend to become transformed into mimetic rivalry. Sometimes this applies to individuals, but more often it applies to groups, however they become clustered together in identity constructions. The relevance of this is straightforward: victims in the macabresque become so because they represent in psychodynamic ways, the mimetic rival that in fantasy threatens to steal the thing-enjoyments of perpetrators. For this they must not only be punished but also be *seen to be punished*. Thus the performativity of transgression becomes converted into the dramaturgical and aesthetic stages of the macabresque so that sadistically infused desires can be inscribed onto the flesh, mind, and spirits of mimetic rivals.

MIMETIC DESIRES IN MOTION AND RIVALRY: PAULINE NYIRAMASUHUKO AND THE METHODOLOGICAL ISSUES OF GROUP MIND

Jean-Michel Oughourlian demonstrates the ways in which mimetic desire degrades social relationships, from within interpersonal relations and across families to cataclysmic outbreaks of collective violence and mass atrocity. Oughourlian argues that mimetic desire galvanizes psychic and emotional resources of individuals and social groups in a tri-modal dynamic: "mimetic incorporation"; "interdiction"; and "the presence of a rival."[2] Mimetic desires provoke efforts to incorporate the desires of others, to become the incarnation of what is taken as their mystery. In the emotionality of hatred and contempt, there is often the clandestine or fantasmatic envy or jealousy leveled against the mimetic rival, for example, on the part of the Nazis toward the Jews, by the Cambodian elite against the Vietnamese and others racialized as Vietnamese, or on the part of extremist Hutu against the Tutsi. "We want to dispossess him which is to say, to possess him entirely," Oughourlian writes. "By taking possession of what the other is, the subject hopes to derive an increase in existence and of power that will guarantee him a final and exclusive happiness and the perfect enjoyment of his object."[3] Oughourlian adds that mimetic desires are "always drawn by the desire of others rather than by the object it pursues."[4] The mimetic rival becomes caught in an aporetic predicament: at once existentially desirable and endowed with a powerful presence, a paragon of "plenitude," a protagonist imputed to have the capacity for total freedom in terms of access to desire; yet, on the other hand, a despicable figure or despised group. The mimetic rival is seen to prevent consummation of what it—as the mimetic rival—is alleged to be able to possess, to do or to be. Oughourlian indicates that the hatred and contempt, the rage-filled ardor with which perpetrators pursue victims is but the "reversed image of a fervent adoration, a secret adulation yoked to unconscious depreciation of oneself."[5] Mimetic rivalries thus operate with "an extreme intensity: we want to melt into the other, take his place, rob him of his very being, of the secret of his luminous aura, of the autonomy that we dream of and that seems to be his."[6] In a figurative sense, literally, perpetrator sadism seeks to devour the body and the spirit of mimetic rivals. This is the purpose of the macabresque and staged performative transgression.

The objective in mimetic desire is "always a desire 'to be,' to exist in greater measure, a desire for an achievement or a dreamed of completeness that one might feel stands before one *but is being held onto by the other.*"[7] Mimetic desire is always a response to a felt deprivation that resists presence. "Desire can bear upon any object, any being, any idea, any project," so long as it is promoted by what others desire—as influenced by what subjects sense or fantasize as lacking or lost. "We are led to detach ourselves from one model in order to adopt another, in whom we always believe we see a 'surplus' of being that we lack," Oughourlian comments.[8] Ineffable in nature, inaccessible to human consciousness, the Lacanian Real represents a theorized existential abyss known to psychic experience through anxiety. But anxiety, too, is a cover, a shield from the Real. What the unconscious fantasizes are only tremors of the Real, the void or vacancy at the core of psychic experience in proximity with the "lack" that permeates human existence. How does the lack come to be known? Its manifestations inhere in phobia, antipathies and disgust, in the fear of fainting and in the dread of nothingness, in the diaphanous horrors over self-dissolution and emptiness. Mimetic desires function as a powerful motor force in human encounters because they suppress anxiety and sequester the "lack" by nurturing the self-deceptions that the lack would dissipate if only one were able to "possess" the rivalrous other, their freedom, their *jouissance.*

In extreme cases, mimetic rivalry transmutes into mimetic frenzies of violence. The "license" that Kallis describes as a frenzy to perform mass atrocity takes on a kind of reality of its own. This is the import of what the studies of war, conflict, and violence I mentioned earlier indicate: violence breeds greater violence. Mimetic ideologies emerge to justify not mere violence but sadistic violations of the bodies of rival "others." Mimetic desire in rivalry is driven by fantasized demands for possession of victims. Mimetic rivalry demands violation as the price that must be paid if desire of the other is to be captured or destroyed. What transforms the *jouissance* of the mimetic rival from something coveted to that which must be captured and utterly consumed through sadistic violation? The answer is power and resistance to submission on the part of rivals. This bestows mimetic value to the rival by seeming to make it difficult for perpetrators to devour or eliminate their rivals. The macabresque arises in the midst of these mimetic dynamics. The paragon's unwillingness to give up its *jouissance*, its capacity for thing-enjoyment, to cede it to those caught by mimetic rivalry, drives ardor into frenzy. This represents an alternative perspective on the psychodynamics of disordered will. The paragon resists the willfulness of the perpetrator and becomes all the more desirable as a mimetic rival.

I selectively trace the case history of Pauline Nyiramasuhuko, the Minister of Family Affairs and Women' Development in the Interim Government of Rwanda headed by Jean Kambanda, which presided over the genocide. Her career is defined by the fact that International Criminal Tribunal for Rwanda (ICTR) Trial Chamber II, on June 24, 2011, found Nyiramasuhuko guilty of the following: conspiracy to commit genocide; genocide; extermination, persecution, and rape as crimes against humanity; violence to life and outrages upon personal dignity as war crimes. She is the first woman to have been indicted by the ICTR; the first woman convicted of genocide; the first woman in the history of transitional or international criminal law to be convicted of rape as a crime against humanity; and the first woman sentenced to life in prison on the basis of such charges. The methodological issue that arises is how to frame the case history and political agency of a genocidal leader beyond micro level attributes in ways that are informed by meso- and macro level variables so as to resolve the reductionism inherent in the methodological traps of conflating the group mind with individuals, or individual motivation with group behavior.

Envy, at the individual/personal level, and the struggle for recognition among groups represent levels of analysis, the one focused on micro level individual agency, the other on meso level situational variables, processual, and structural. Together, these help to establish the scaffolding conditions from which the Rwandan genocide unfolded.

Recent comparative analyses of genocide discount the causal influences of cultural or social constructions of large-group identities as direct factors in fomenting paroxysms of mass killing. Overall, findings suggest that essentialized categories of collective identity represent the secondary effects of genocide. Deployed by perpetrators to justify mass atrocities, reified images of subaltern or targeted groups are symptomatic of outcomes rather than determinative of the underlying causes of genocide. Given Rwandan history leading up to the genocide, intersectionality as an analytical concept serves to underscore the complex composite of factors prompting extreme violence. These include, in addition to ethnicity and gender, political power, social class, and the history of economic and educational discrimination. Although actual causes of genocides differ from case to case, they often emerge in the course of elite struggles over power and the control of economic resources.

Our inquiry, therefore, devolves into a quest for such a macro level "canopy" theory attentive to levels of analysis that provide an overlay of macro-analysis in explaining genocidal mass rape; relative to micro level attributes that include perpetrator identitarian attributes, such as gender or ethnicity, as well as motivational factors, such as envy; and, finally, that enfold interactional or structural variables at meso levels of analysis, in the present analysis, framed by the struggle for recognition between Hutu and Tutsi. Such a theoretical perspective must also concentrate on the catalytic elements that contributed at macro levels to the actual outbreak of genocidal violence.

For his part, Scott Straus, in a recent comparative study of conflicts leading to or avoiding genocide, underlines the theoretical importance of macro level variables.[9] Straus states, "I conclude that the strongest commonality among the mass categorical violence cases, and the factor that the negative cases lack, is the ideological dominance among the political elite of a hierarchical, nationalist founding narrative."[10] The content of this founding narrative was "the Hutu social revolution."[11] How, then, does "the Hutu social revolution," molded and recast according to the transfigurations of a hierarchical, nationalist founding narrative, represent the crucial macro level factor or dimension in explaining genocidal violence? Straus suggests the answer. "The founding narrative thus shapes how military elites define the stakes of the conflict, for whom they are fighting and against whom they are fighting."[12] He continues, "The narrative also shapes threat perception.

The war is not a simple military one between armed groups, but a war between those *who would take away* Hutu freedom and those who would protect it."[13] What is at work here is not merely envy or a reciprocal struggle for recognition but a zero-sum game in which winners take all. This element points to an intrinsic feature of what Girard has designated theoretically as mimetic desire and rivalry, *the dimension of all or nothing at all,* in keeping with theories of mimetic rivalry. Straus further elaborates how this component became articulated by and through the Hutu founding narrative. He writes, "Finally, the claim is also that the Tutsis of the past want the same things as the Tutsis of the present. That claim—Tutsis have the same preferences across generations—is essential to the logic of genocide because it allows Tutsis to be constructed as unwinnable."[14] It is, therefore, not merely the mystifications of Tutsi ethnic identity that transform them into mimetic rivals of Hutu. Rather, it is the portents of threatened displacement by the Tutsis of Hutu desire to be the exclusive embodiment of Rwandan national peoplehood. It is the reification of Tutsi *desire to desire* that accentuates Hutu demands for their elimination from Rwanda. In the Hutu genocidal social and political imaginary, Tutsis desire *"desires"* to be the incarnation of Rwanda. As Mamdani declared, "Because for Hutu Power, the Hutu were not just the majority, *they were the nation."*[15] For this, Tutsis bodies, that of women and men, girls and boys, were raped, mutilated, and destroyed. And Hutu women participated in the physicality of the violations sometimes with abandon as illustrated by the case history of Pauline Nyiramasuhuko.

The case history of Pauline Nyiramasuhuko illustrates how the behavior of one perpetrator at the micro level of analysis illustrates the dynamics of group behaviors at the meso level of analysis, in ways that demonstrate the theoretical/explanatory relevance of macro- or canopy-level perspectives. Attention to the overlays among these three levels of analysis pays due deference to the analytical importance of avoiding methodological reductionism intrinsic to the notion of group mind. These observations implicitly refer to the three levels of analysis linking micro level motivations with meso level processes of interaction framed not only by gender and ethnicity but also by political agency, class status, and recognition. In addition, they implicitly serve to introduce canopy or macro level variables such as mimetic desire and rivalry.

These factors underscore the determining influences of her institutional and policy role within the context of Rwandan honor, kinship and patriarchal traditions. They provide a basis for demonstrating the dynamics of mimetic desire and rivalry inflamed by the threatened loss of class status and political power set in motion on April 6, 1995, by the precipitous death of President Juvénal Habyarimana. I argue, therefore, that the analytical route to an understanding of Pauline Nyiramasuhuko runs through her career, her attained class status, her power as a member of the central government, and thus by means of emphasis on her political agency. To be sure, this makes her more, not less, culpable in the sordid Rwandan history of sexual violence and genocidal brutality against women.

During instances of mass atrocity, it is not only the mimetic rival that acts as the object of desire, it is the perpetrators' mimetic desire for victims' desire—as the cause of desire—that becomes the objective.[16] What perpetrators seek by means of the macabresque is to possess the desire of what the rival desires. The performativity of transgression originates in such fantasized demand. "Mimetic desire is born from the imitation of the model's desire," Oughourlian observes. "The objects that are most desired by the model, to which he holds on most tightly, are those he is keeping for himself, that he forbids."[17] Mimetic desires of perpetrators, impeded in fantasy by those about to become victimized, prompts perpetrators into seeking their violation. Oughourlian outlines this starkly when he writes that "the more the obstacle resists, the more frenzied the desire becomes."[18] The stage is set for performative transgression so that the frenzy of mimetic desire can be released violently and thus realized in mimetic spaces of agony and horror. Oughourlian describes the consequences of mimesis turned to frenzy in terms of "passional pathology," "paroxysm of violence," "mimetic epidemic," "mimetic crisis," "metaphysical desire," "hallucinatory sacrality," and of "savage, vampire-like desire."[19] Mimetic desire turns into a kind of black religion permeated by social fantasies of "hallucinatory sacrality." The result is mimesis driven to the extremes of "metaphysical desire" that is so fixated on the rival that it releases "unrestrained passions, destructive love, masochism and sadism, raging violence."[20]

Mimesis carried to the point where desire propels demands for an evacuation of the rival by installing the self into the bodies and spirits of victims indicates how mimesis in desire becomes transformed into macabresque sadism. Oughourlian describes the resulting psychodynamics as "a veritable pathology of fusion."[21] Such "desires are always contagious: a copied desire transmits itself from person to person in a kind of mimetic epidemic," he writes.[22] Oughourlian describes these as the "phenomena of mob psychology, which can be as sudden as they are unforeseen: lynchings, explosions of violence, running berserk, mass movements, or collective furies." The functional role of mimetic ideology is to confirm such self-deceptions. In such a manner, perpetrators can entertain the "illusion of the anteriority."[23] During these instances, the tyranny of small differences looms large. The threats of identitarian identicality, at the very core of mimetic rivalry in mimesis, must be destroyed; if all are equal or the same, rivals would enjoy equal access to *jouissance*. At such times, contrasting differences become accentuated on the part of perpetrators; this allows them to sense in fantasy and to self-deceive themselves in conscious belief that they alone possess the power to desire. Mimetic rivalry turns toward macabresque sadism in mass atrocity whenever the demand for eliminating human identicality becomes transformed by pursuit of totalized forms of supremacism and exclusivism, each a fantasy of power over desire. For in mimetic rivalry, alterity in desire speaks through the illogics of exclusivism and supremacism.

Comparison is mimetic to its core, and desire is its power to influence conscious behaviors. The psychodynamics of power and desire reverberate across the boundaries of self and otherness. Whenever it is projected outward, reification of the differences of others also appear to pulsate with rage against the self, against fantasized inadequacies of the "freedom" of the self. This has previously been referred to as the psychodynamics of the rival self-other. Such psychic processes are often described in terms of introjection and projection, the capacity of the human psyche and emotional spirit to propel outward onto others the inner worlds of self-contempt; this explains the behavior of perpetrators who are perhaps sometimes assailed by unconscious feelings of shame over defaults of honor, however these may be construed or culturally constructed. These psychic and emotional dynamics adhere to volitional processes that demonstrate disordered will or akratic intentionality: to despise others in their otherness as an unconscious strategy for deflecting shame and self-hatred, the inner sense of sullied presence or stained being. The *charnière* or the psychic hinge veering from introjection to projection is mimetic rivalry based on comparison, subject to subject, split subject or rival self-other relative to itself as subject, rival self-other relative to others as reified, concretized, essentialized objects. In the psychic flows of mimetic rivalry, mimetic desire turns from introjection toward projection in disordered or akratic attempts to attribute fixity and axiomatic or naturalized "givenness" to ontological as well as political categories of difference—that is, to project the elements of certainty or necessity onto the contingent problematics of human freedom so as to displace the self as inner victim with the outer victims now depicted as apparitions of disgust.

The transmutational processes between and mimetic desire and ideology across the psychic pathways from introjection to projection, and vice versa, stream back and forth in mimetic rivalry: reification of the self and its capacities for "freedom" relative to the "freedom" of others in their difference; disordered willfulness in akratic intentionality and extremist forms of moral masochism; displaced concreteness, substantiality, fixity, and closure in imagistic reifications of the self relative to others in mimetic desire; logics of illogic in mimetic ideology; projection of the stains of self-contempt onto displaced or surrogate "others" on the basis of "naturalized" categories of difference; "thingification" and false concreteness of otherness leading to dehumanization and demonization; sadistic rage and the ravages of surplus cruelty in the macabresques theaters of performative transgression; and mimetic rivalry in political evil.

FROM MIMETIC RIVALRY TO SOCIAL ANTAGONISM

Theoretical efforts to apply psychosocial perspectives, in particular Lacanian perspectives, in explaining macabresque sadism and performativity in human violation must perforce do so on the basis of a single building-block assumption on which the entire explanatory edifice regarding social fantasy depends. I have referred to this in terms of loss of ecstasy, the surrendering of symbiosis with *das Ding*, "The Thing," the elemental or primordial bonding between mother and child that must be given up or renounced to permit entry into language and the possibilities of a life lived according to symbolic meanings and values. This analytical presumption, that unconscious fantasy exists and that it influences social and political behavior, initiates a series of methodological concerns. Discussion of fantasy and loss and lack underscore the role played by the unconscious in social and political collective life. The analytical problem that results concerns how to frame studies of politics and the political once this assumption becomes methodologically incorporated. Jason Glynos frames this issue as an epistemological plight or tension with respect to the empirical representability of politics. He underscores discursive conceptions of society grounded in understandings of "the failure of representation."[24] He comments, "Here, in other words, epistemological incapacity is transformed into the positive ontological condition of politics and political subjectivities. It is because our symbolic representations of society are constitutively lacking that politico-hegemonic struggle is made possible."[25]

Glynos thus demonstrates the epistemological significance of Lacanian conceptions of the unconscious for the study of politics in general, and as I argue, for the systematic examination of the macabresque in genocide and mass atrocity. Distinctions between psychology and psychosocial analysis ride on these assumptions. This carries profound methodological consequences for interpreting the causes and processes of genocide and mass atrocity. Numerous formulations of these guiding principles or similar propositions with respect to the unconscious have been articulated by numerous authors who emphasize the primordial character of lack and loss in the unconscious as the critical dimension from which symbolic meanings in society derive. It is as if from the negativity of loss and lack in the Real of libidinal *non*-reality, the positivity of desires emerges, as manifested in culture. This perspective provides an initial step toward theorizing the relationship of social fantasy to the macabresque, a linkage that reveals the constitutive role played by the psychodynamics of loss and its restoration, of lack and its restitution. Once this is established, it becomes possible to examine social fantasy in relation to what Margarita Palacios calls "social antagonism." This represents the initial phases of a psychosocial rendering of the macabresque, specifically with respect to its cultural variations.

FROM PHANTASY TO FANTASY, AGAIN

The conceptual and semantic question arises of how to differentiate the fundamental Oedipal phantasy from its spinoffs manifested by the fantasies of daily living. References to "thing-enjoyment" in Lacanian perspectives tend to refer to Oedipal or libidinal drives toward *jouissance* or maternalized ecstasy, and thus pertain to the fundamental phantasy. For purposes below that apply the concepts of *jouissance* and thing-enjoyment in psychosocial perspectives, the term, fantasy, covers both forms of psychic experience; since their effects are the same within the context of the following analysis in the section that follows, with reference to several authors who link fantasy to political analysis, in terms of loss and lack. Lorenzo Chiesa following Lacan indicates, for example, "The primordial object that was lost has thus a *causally* determinative value with respect to the structurally insatiable nature of the subject's desire."[26] The primordial object so called is more a condition of "union" that "precedes primordial frustration." Chiesa adds, "We are dealing here with a mythical undifferentiated whole—an 'unlimited totality' in which . . . any subject-to-come is located."[27] Chiesa describes the phenomena of lack and loss as follows: "the Thing (the mother) as a transcendent lack which is the primordial object as *always* already *lost* for the subject; one realizes that one 'had' the primordial object only after one has lost it."[28] Chiesa thus sets out the basic framework assumption with respect to the origins of fantasy that in turn help explain the dynamics through which human desires and desiring originate.

Just as it is spurious to base explanations of human behavior, let alone collective violence, on psychoanalytic assumptions regarding psychic development and early human maturation, so is it specious to reject explanations that feature primordial psychodynamics in shaping the dimensions of human personality fixated on the gravitational lock of lack and loss in the unconscious. Disagreements arise over the extent to which the unconscious may be said to determine behaviors. The contention that generates much discussion pertains to the issue of "overdetermination," that is, the extent to which primordial psychic experience is alleged to "determine" actions, a return perhaps to more traditional meta-ethical concerns over the status of free will with respect to human autonomy. Attempts at resolution vary, but the fantasmatic, even chronic delusionary character of desire remains a theoretical constant in Lacanian psychosocial theory. The theoretical implications are, therefore, clear: first, human desiring is constituted by its quest for substitutions and displaced forms of surrogacy; secondly, whatever becomes symbolically available or accessible does not ultimately gratify lest the quest for desiring cease; thirdly, chronic dissatisfactions foster tendencies to repetition; and, finally, the psychodynamics of lack and loss veer toward social fantasies of *stolen* thing-enjoyment, that is, psychic loss or lack by virtue of fantasmatically experienced sensations of theft.

In this sense, the human condition is that of Prometheus bound but, as Kleinian theory suggests, congenitally paranoid. Adrian Johnston encapsulates this in referring to the law prohibiting access to the *jouissance* of maternalized union, that is, the law of phallic prohibition, sometimes also referred to in terms of "castration." He writes, "Desire, which exists in the absence of *das Ding*, is preserved by making the Other (i.e., the Symbolic locus of the Law, the source of restrictions) into a 'metaphor of this prohibition', into a scapegoat for the structurally determined loss of the Real *an sich* ('The Other stole my *jouissance*!'—the falsity here resides in the fact that something one never possessed in the first place cannot be stolen)."[29] But fantasmatic "stolenness" fosters human desiring on positive and negative terms. Herein lies the basis of response to the question of the status of human existential freedom. Johnston declares, "Thus, the Law, in all its incarnate forms, enables the subject to continue desiring, rather than undergoing the traumatic destitution that would result from a full apprehension of the inherent deadlock of the libidinal economy." He further states,

> The introduction of the Law generates desire ex nihilo. Instead of forbidding a preexistent set of urges in the individual, it teaches the subject what to covet, if only as an inaccessible vanishing point whose appearance of possible accessibility

is a mirage engendered by the seemingly contingent nature of the Law and its authority.[30]

What, then, are the possibilities of moral freedom if morality itself is cast under the shadows of "mirage" and delusion? Self-deceptions of perpetrators often make claims to ideals or ideational constructions of principled norms and behaviors, but does any of it constitute morality properly so named? What is so often accepted as morality is in fact ideological not only in an ideational sense but also, even more to the point, in ontological ways. Reasons point toward the relationship of psychic fantasy to ideology. This becomes critical to the examination of the macabresque that is typically represented by perpetrators as the very essence of morality, the search for truth, goodness, and meaning, but predicated on narcissist self-delusions and paranoid forms of sadism. What Lacanian theory suggests, however, and what Freud and Lacan both consistently averred, was that such sadistic and narcissistic behaviors are not to be analytically construed as abnormal or psychopathological in the specific sense that those who undertake them remain fully responsible.

Such is suggested by Derek Hook and Calum Neill in their review of Lacanian notions of human subjectivity.[31] In relation to the macabresque of South African apartheid, they write, "This, then, is perhaps the most paradoxical aspect of fantasy: that, more than anything else, it constitutes what is irreducible about us despite the fact that it cannot be fully separated from the field of the Other." Fantasies of loss and lack, of *jouissance* and *objet a* in desiring all may influence, even, constrict, possibilities in cultural constructions of identity, but, and this is critical, they do not *overly* determine collective processes of social or political identifications in a moral or ethical sense. Perpetrators remain morally culpable even for their self-delusions, especially when articulated in fraudulent epistemological terms as the search for truth or in false axiological terms as the quest for moral ideals. As Hook and Neill comment,

> What this means is that while there certainly is an element of symbolic determination at play within the persistence of apartheid ideology . . . this ideology is ultimately held aloft, recreated and reanimated by the fantasies and enjoyments of its beneficiaries, for which, to emphasize, such subjects remain fully accountable.[32]

I shall return to this problem of how the conflation of fantasy, ideology, and morality plays out with respect to perpetrators and the macabresque.

Lacanian conceptions of lack and loss in the unconscious thus bear on how collective conceptions of social and political life become framed and vitalized. These unconscious dynamics are envisioned as mechanisms that foster what Jason Glynos and Yannis Stavrakakis indicate is "the fantasy support for many of our political projects, social roles, and consumer choices."[33] They stress the relationship of discursivity to thing-enjoyment. They observe, for example, "A good portion of political discourse focuses on the delivery of 'the good life' or a 'just society', both fictions (*imaginarizations*) of a future state in which the current limitations thwarting our enjoyment will be overcome."[34] Glynos and Stavrakakis suggest, moreover, that collective designs enlisted in the recapture of thing-enjoyment go beyond mere discursivity. They demand performativity as well. In so doing, by implication they outline the pathway to the macabresque. They write:

> The logic peculiar to fantasy, then, entails the staging of a relation between the sub-
> ject (as lack) and the object (as that which always escapes socio-symbolic capture),
> thereby organizing the affective dimension of the subject. The way it desires and
> enjoys the paradigmatic form of such a staging, of course, involves transgressions
> of public norms and ideals. For in transgressing prohibitions or officially affirmed
> ideals subjects aim at that which appears to lie beyond the socio-symbolic horizon
> and which holds out the promise of a full enjoyment.[35]

The theoretical progression from Lacanian conceptions of the unconscious to thing-enjoyment and lack and loss now come full circle in psychosocial frames emphasizing the staging of transgressive actions in order to pierce the symbolic universe of political culture: in the name of reacquiring the lost ecstasy that was stolen but never was. Many forms, modes, and means exist that demonstrate such social and political exercises. But as we have seen, certain sets of conditions do occasionally emerge, such as war and violence combined with threatened erosions of elite power or symbolic standing, that prompt genocidal campaigns and mass atrocity crimes. But at these critical junctures demands for the staging of performativity relative to thing-enjoyment are rarely far removed, for the reasons suggested here. It is the very staging of transgressions that counts in the schemes of those driven by the unconscious quests to recapture stolen thing-enjoyment. The consequence is sadistic cruelty and performative transgression in the macabresque.

FROM SOCIAL EXCLUSION TO SOCIAL ANTAGONISM

The unfolding of the macabresque tends to begin with exclusions, the reifications of otherness, the amplifications of difference, especially in cases in which small contrasts only serve to highlight loss of distinctions or to exaggerate the dread stemming from the identicalities shared among members of a society. Margarita Palacios calls this dynamic "social antagonism" and indicates that "only by adding the category of enjoyment (pleasure-derived from transgression), can we begin grasping what collective violence—at least in modern societies—is about."[36] Palacios emphasizes exclusion as the critical dimension of social antagonism. "Social antagonism, as different from social disorganization and episodic violence, is the act of exclusion of those who are considered to threaten the fragile/contingent symbolic integrity of society."[37] She underscores the "aggressive jealousy" that is aroused by social antagonisms precisely because what is experienced in the interiority of unconscious fantasy is projected outward and in effect put onto "the excluded other who appears (this time) as 'stealing enjoyment' from the self." This intensifies "existential" competition and becomes transformed into "libidinal" conflict. At such moments, "only the destruction (or suffering) of the other seems to satisfy the self."[38] Palacios recognizes the ease with which the dynamics of social antagonism as she describes them devolves into moralistic self-justifications on the part of perpetrators. She writes, "Ethical claims (usually about the restoration of the symbolic-moral order) go hand in hand with what appears to be a clear denial of that very same symbolic order (enjoyment of the exclusion of the other)."[39] Her examples include reference to the torture of those deemed to represent threats to moral or social order. She adds, "Indeed, I would argue that whenever there is a moral discourse accompanying collective violence, some sort of social antagonism is at play."[40] This is demonstrated by the examples below that reveal, first, how such discourses depend on political culture but also how these fraudulent moral discourses influence how human violations become executed or performed.

The presence of so-called moral discourses whenever the macabresque emerges is not coincidental to the purposes of causing suffering before death. Palacios observes, "Indeed, ethical claims that attempt to give legitimacy to violence go together with a perverse eroticization of death." This is a key to the macabresque, its perversity and its sadism. She explains, "Excess of violence aiming at nothing but suffering and humiliation shows the presence of a libidinal link between the self and the other."[41] This libidinal link entails sadistic cruelty since perpetrators seek ways to make victims renounce desire or fantasized thing-enjoyment as a consequence of inflictions of pain often directly administered by perpetrators on the bodies of victims. Fantasy is an ever-present influence during episodes of social antagonism whenever it comes to be played out in the macabresque. From a methodological standpoint, its avoidance by social scientists and circumvention as a unit of analysis in theoretical efforts to explain organized cruelty leads to a faltering inability to grapple with why genocide and mass atrocity occur. "Fantasy functions as a construction," Palacios writes, "as an overproduction of meaning. It is an imaginary scenario filling out the void, the opening of *the desire of the other*."[42] The psychic opening unto the desire of the other must be staged if fantasy is to serve as an imaginary scenario. Such fantasy is performed in such a way as to "establish the law" that keeps *jouissance* or thing-enjoyment away while simultaneously giving into the sense that the recapture of the "others'" capacity to desire is a way to return to *jouissance*. This process of transgression is both lurid and ludic and leads directly to the infliction of indescribable pain onto victims who are made to pay the price for fantasmatic lack and loss and theft of thing-enjoyment. During episodes of social antagonism, what is most dreaded is also simultaneously most coveted—that is, the reanimation of *jouissance* by means of sadistic cruelty in the macabresque. The phantoms of thing-enjoyment seem forever relentless in their pursuits.

Torture, Torment, and Agony: All Pain, Different Kinds of Suffering

In broad measure, collective violence is political in origins and outcomes whereas human violation is socially, culturally and ideologically constructed. Whenever the macabresque becomes staged or enacted the politics of collective violence intersect with the cultural. For such reasons, one is able to associate aesthetic and dramaturgical "styles" with the systematic infliction of pain. Elaine Scarry, in a classic discussion of torture, examines the inexpressibility of pain, the isolation of the body in pain, the separation of those in pain from the world at large. But she notes how certain "avenues" or realms of representation permit the personal portrayal and general depiction of pain in ways leading to its signification through "shared discourse" including scientific and legal.[43] She writes, "Nowhere is the sadistic potential of a language built on agency so visible as in torture." Such weapons represent the means by which to demonstrate the "convincing spectacle of power." She adds, "It is, of course, precisely because the reality of that power is so highly contestable, the regime so unstable, that torture is being used."[44] Scarry emphasizes display of absolute power as a critical component of all sites of torture. "What assists the conversion of absolute pain into the fiction of absolute power is an obsessive, self-conscious display of agency." In this, she broaches the performativity at the core of the macabresque.

Scarry outlines a tri-modal structure of torture: intensification of pain; its objectification outside the prisoner's body as it is experienced within; and how "the objectified pain is denied as pain and read as power, a translation made possible by the obsessive mediation of agency."[45] Scarry implies the relationship of the macabresque to mass atrocity. She observes, "Physical pain always mimes death and the infliction of physical pain is always a mock execution."[46] Her analysis lists the spatiality of torture; the rooms where infliction occurs; the names bestowed on such rooms within the culture in which torture occurs and the weapons used are also given names in ways that stress how they are made known to their victims. All this is intrinsic to the macabresque. Spaces collapse, physical interiority becomes psychically externalized; material exteriority becomes intensely invasive; strange, horrible instruments become transformed as elements of intimate sensation; conversely, familiar household objects like doors and refrigerators become "de-objectified" into mechanisms by which the "world" "disintegrates" into sheer pain, made all the more excruciating by virtue of a prevailing sense of spiritual self-disintegration.[47]

Sofsky's analysis of the competition among Nazi concentration camp guards emphasizes "innovation and artifice" in the displays of absolute power. Scarry's analysis provides an additional dimension, one that points in the direction of shame and self-humiliation, that of perpetrators as well as of victims. The "games" of torture and of absolute power are not only about the physicality of pain, horrible as it is, but about, for want of a better term, the devouring of the human spirit. The macabresque exists for such purposes, to allow perpetrator desire for another's desire, what Lacan would call their *jouissance*, to dissolve into shame, that is, victim shame at their utter humiliation wrought by the sense of self-betrayal. In the macabresque, performativity, or what Scarry implies by "agency," is designed to make victims complicit in their own suffering. They must see what is done to them, feel and make known that they *understand* why what is happening to them is occurring; they must be made to acknowledge that they *deserve* the pain and the humiliation accorded them. And the reasons for this reside in the psychodynamics of sadistic cruelty, shame and, ultimately, honor. Collective violence in genocide and mass atrocity represents an ultimate form of betrayal on the part of a government or regime toward its own mostly civilian and non-combatant population. But the identitarian constructions that attend such instances reflect subjective reifications that inhere in unconscious forms of shame sometimes given over to ideological or cultural expressions of honor or glory.

It is as if the shame of perpetrators unconsciously demands that they sadistically exact from victims the manifestations of shame as psychological or emotional recompense through the displays of victim self-betrayal. Such is the case with the *Sonderkommando*, the Jewish corps in Nazi death camps who were enlisted to assist in the disposal of remains, but who on a regular basis were themselves exterminated; it also applies to those tortured to obtain their forced confessions. The design of absolute power in the macabresque is not to merely paralyze victims before death but to "*empower*" victims, in their very powerlessness, *not to be able* to defend themselves against the ultimate shame and sense of humiliation wrought by self-betrayal. Here, too, the negativity of theft of thing-enjoyment and of lack and loss become manifested by the "positive" performativity of cruelty and sadistic transgression.

This is to the core of the dramaturgy and aesthetics of macabresque sadism. It is as if in their self-betrayal, victims are able to bestow the magic or mystery of their *jouissance* into the life-blood of perpetrators who live in the social fantasies of willed self-deception. Scarry states of victims, "He is to understand his confession as it will be understood by others, as an act of self-betrayal. In forcing him to confess . . . the torturers are producing a mime in which the one annihilated shifts to being the agent of his own annihilation."[48] Herein lies one connection between collective violence in genocide and mass atrocity and the macabresque as a cultural and social phenomenon aimed at human violation. "This unseen sense of self-betrayal in pain, objectified in forced confession, is also objectified in forced exercises that make the prisoner's body an *active* agent, an actual cause of pain."[49] Pain and self-betrayal in the macabresque become mutually implicated, reciprocally infused. "If self-hatred, self-alienation, and self-betrayal (as well as the hatred of, and alienation from, and betrayal of all this is contained in the self—friends, family ideas, ideology) were translated out of the psychological realm where it has content and is accessible to language into the unspeakable and contentless realm of physical sensation," Scarry observes, "it would be intense pain."[50]

Scarry recognizes the role and influence of culture in fostering stylistic variations in how torture and, by implication, how the aesthetics in macabresque sadism become actualized. Her examples include the "nomenclature for torture": how pain becomes euphemistically referenced as "mimetic of a particular invention or technological feat," such as "the telephone" in Brazil or the "motorola" in Greece; or in accordance with "cultural events, ceremonies and games," for example, "the dance" in Argentina, or "the birthday party" in the Philippines; and thirdly, words based in "nature or nature civilized" in ways that stress features that are "dainty, diminutive, or mythologized", for example, "the parrot's perch" in Brazil or Uruguay and "the little hare" in Greece.[51] The question thus arises as to the status of such euphemistic language; how to interpret its presence in the macabresque, its relationship to perpetrators, specifically what is says about them.

THE LANGUAGE OF PERPETRATORS: LIES AND EMPTY EUPHEMISM

The dramaturgy and aesthetics of the macabresque, however, adhere to empty forms of euphemism, derisive irony, tropes of comedic metaphor, all for the purpose of install-ing absolute power by erasing the elements of "pleasure," joy, and humor to be found in authentic metaphoric euphemism, comedy and irony. In relation to the macabresque, "sadistic pleasure" stands as a contradiction of terms. Macabresque engagements that involve performative uses of sadistic cruelty retain a quality of frightful indifference to the pain of others. Such profound indifference is belied by the very notion of "pleasure" if pleasure as a concept is semantically associated with human relationships involving the sensual, funny, vital, spontaneous, joyous, creative, life-affirming, and so on. Sadism is not passionate, it is empty, although often systematic. Its design is to separate victims from desire, to eliminate their capacities to and for desire. Sadistic cruelty in torture and macabresque torment and agony aim at establishing what in the French language is some-times referred as the *dispositif*, that is, mechanisms of control over controls, in the present instance, control over victims' control of desire. One way to accomplish this diabolical objectivity is to link performativity in the macabresque to process of making victims complicit in their own or other victims' physical suffering.

What perpetrators in their sadistic drives want or demand of victims is that in their bodily pain they are made to experience the absence of desire, along with the accom-panying sense of spiritual disarray, moral disintegration, and emotional decline that signifies the end of personality. This is what the self-betrayal of victims in the context of the macabresque entails, renunciation of what persons value the most, including their capacity to love and to know emotion. Ervand Abrahamian, in his study of "tor-tured confessions," describes self-betrayals of recantation as suicide. For those forced to recant, "One's mere presence on the stage is itself a form of suicide," he writes, "for it signifies the explicit rejection of oneself as well as the implicit betrayal of one's own friends, colleagues and beliefs."[52] He describes this as "grand theater," designed to con-firm what "the targeted audience" wants to believe "innocent of the stage preparations that precede the show," "that their society is mortally threatened by omnipotent exter-nal forces," and that the confessions themselves result from "truth, guilt, redemption, and moral conscience" and are thus "voluntary," rather than the consequence of tor-ture or coercion.[53] Victims thus "come onto the stage to humiliate, dehumanize, and demonize themselves as well as their associates."[54] But is even this sufficient to meet the desires provoked by mimetic rivalry?

Envy, jealously and mimetic desire influence how pain becomes extracted from victims, but in specific ways. For perpetrators do envy and become jealous of victims in mimetic desire but not by reifying the objects of *what* victims desire. Rather, what perpetrators reify are *the causes* of victim desire. Euphemistic language in torture and the macabresque serves the purpose of allowing perpetrators to revel in their self-deceptions: first, that it is possible to reify the freedom of others thereby to attribute substantiality to it; and, secondly, as a consequence, to extract, capture, and reincorporate the freedom (the *jouissance*) into perpetrators' own collective being. In their semantic applications of euphemistic usage, perpetrators reveal not their humor but, rather, their deadly self-delusions to the effect that the cause of victims' desire is mobile, transferable, and fungible in the sense that the less victims are able to cause desire, the more the perpetrators become empowered to do so. Euphemism demonstrates the fundamental internal contradiction of all sadistic cruelty, that in the ostensible name of pleasure in desire, one finds only hollow shells of desire encrusted with the slime of indifference to pleasure. And the reasons for this pertain to the perpetrators' self-deceptions in the macabresque, that they are the servants of higher causes, greater ends, and absolute truths or principles. Such delusions are born in fantasy and take shape in ideology, but an ideology that is not ideational alone but, rather, comes alive in a kind of political ontology that appears to demand of perpetrators all the gravity and seriousness of intent necessary for heroic or supererogatory action. Given such ideologies that foster moralistic self-righteousness, especially in forms that become culturally anchored to strict disciplines of honor and shame, such notions as joy, pleasure, humor, irony, comedy, let alone, self-criticism or self-deprecation, are nonexistent.

EUPHEMISM AS ANTI-IRONIC

How, then, might we consider euphemistic language in the macabresque? In raising this question, the lexical status of euphemism as a literary device becomes in itself analytically problematicized. Once euphemism no longer serves as a means for perpetrators to lace cruelty with pleasure beyond the experience of sadistic indifference, why do they so often deploy its dramaturgical and aesthetic leitmotifs? In part, the answer derives from what perpetrators hide from themselves: their unconscious efforts to transform social fantasy into ideological truth and make "truth" (as well as beauty) the function of power. Euphemistic language connects perpetrators in their shared desire for defense against recognizing the social fantasy and thus the ideologies that beguile them. The major bulwarks of such psychic defense become manifested in ideological constructions of "truth" or "beauty" behind which all perpetrators ultimately hide. If the purpose of torture or victims' suffering in the macabresque is to bring about their sense of self-betrayal, the role of euphemism in macabresque language and theatricality is to permit perpetrators to distort the meaning of truth, but even more than this, to falsify the very nature of epistemology as a method for deriving what truth means or requires in any context, including scientific. So, too, does euphemism in the macabresque function as a challenge to the philosophical character of aesthetics to reveal and explicate the meaning, import and character of art. Euphemism in the macabresque represents a kind of anti-lexicon that demonstrates perpetrator indifference and lack of empathy not only in relation to victims as persons but also to the status of truth and art in the human condition. The consequence is to conflate ideology with morality. Simply put, perpetrators come to believe their own lies, leading many observers to grant them a degree of legitimacy in moral terms they absolutely do not deserve. The memory of genocide and mass atrocity is derogated by such fallacious interpretations of moral discourses and reasoning. Perpetrators willfully and narcissistically deceive themselves by adopting a euphemistic language; observers should not be misled by this. Such language may serve as a temporary means to confirm perpetrator belief in their right to exercise absolute power. Ultimately, what it reveals is the difficulties perpetrators have in recognizing the fragility of their inner capacities to process reality.

Berel Lang usefully reflects on the implications of the non-ironic in Nazi signifying semantics. He indicates that "the Nazi would not only contrive a language *of* domination, but they intended to demonstrate that language itself was subject to political authority."[55] To demonstrate this, Lang focuses on the Nazi term to describe their program of genocidal extermination, *Endlösung*, or Final Solution. He focuses on the juxtaposition between the terms "final" and "solution" in the semantic context of irony. Lang states, "The characteristic feature in irony of 'double vision,' of language reiterating itself with a difference—and with a negation at that, to be supplied by the reader—makes irony an unlikely feature of totalitarian discourse at any time." He adds, "irony underscores the possibility of nonliteral meaning and impels the reader beyond the apparent text (thus beyond censorship)—both of those affording to the writer and to the reader a measure of freedom that would undoubtedly be seen by totalitarianism as subversive."[56] Lang's reference to "writer" and "reader" could as well refer to perpetrator and victim in that he underscores the profound absence of criticality in Nazi euphemistic usage. The Nazis intended to subvert language in the strict sense of rendering linguistic formulations formulaic and thus subservient to social fantasies that were grounded in perverse desire disciplined by power in concert with ideological illogics of logic. It is not so much that speakers lie as it is an example in which speech itself becomes constituted by linguistic and figurative constructions designed to conceal the fraudulence of the lie relative to those who speak in concert with each other. Lang comments, first, in relation to the phrase, "final solution" but, more generally across the Nazi-inspired vernacular, that "the language of genocide has contrived a distinctive literary figure." This feature, intrinsic to the phrase "final solution," signifies the lexical distortion of the Holocaust as a style of the macabresque in that "denotation of the term, although logically consistent with it . . . substantively contradicts it . . . the figurative term is meant to draw attention away from both this change and from the individual aspects of its referent, thus concealing what is denoted (and attempting to conceal the fact of concealment as well)."[57] Lang's observations regarding the term "final solution" is aligned with a fundamental precept in psychoanalytic theory to the effect that speech does not convey what it purports to say but rather obfuscates motivation with respect to speaker intentionality and meaning.

The macabresque transforms this into a psychosocial phenomenon, linking social fantasy, ideological reification, and political power to create a cultural and social order unto itself by virtue of a kind of Orwellian language-speak.

Lang's analysis links vacuous language, or what he refers to as "the lie," with perpetrator self-deception, on the one hand, and shows how self-deception demonstrates the disorders of will and akratic willfulness analytically associated with Farber's concept of "willing the unwillable." In so doing, Lang helps to illustrate the fundamental character of the macabresque. "As people live by representation in the present and by memory in the past, moreover, the role of language in the genocide remains a cogent representation of the event more generally. We find it, in this role, replete with evidence of the will to do evil, the power of the imagination to enlarge on that will, and the capacity for violence which such impulses nourish, inside language or out."[58] Language thus becomes more than a mere lie, it is transmuted into a weaponized instrumentality of violation. "It is not only, then, that language becomes morally culpable by its figurative device of the lie—but that elements of the lie are also themselves effective causes in the deliberate act of genocide."[59]

Lang's examination thus parallels Scarry's interpretation of how pain becomes instrumentalized in torture. Additionally, Lang examines the logic of illogic in what he calls "Nazi rules of language" from the vantage point of will and willfulness in perspectives that parallel the analytical frameworks of Mark Levene, Ronald Aronson, Allen Feldman, and Leslie Farber, as well as Walter Kaufmann. With respect to genocide and the instrumental role of language, Lang writes, "On both sides of that analogy, distinctions based on evidence and moral principle are obliterated; categories and distinctions devised and *willed* by the agent are made to seem natural and necessary, and this is itself part of the intention."[60] In political reification and ideological constructions, "will" dominates truth, meaning and signification. Social contingency or what is historically derived or driven must become "naturalized" and rendered necessary in accordance with doctrinal dictates. This too accords with the psychosocial analytic perspectives framed by Lacanian theory.

The attack against epistemology and aesthetics attempts to defy limits, moreover, precisely because of the basic sadistic impulses to define "law" and to inscribe it onto the bodies of victims as they are made to renounce the sources of their desiring, as illustrated by Feldman relative to those incarcerated in the H-Block of Belfast's prison for political prisoners. But Lang's analysis underscores how language in the macabresque becomes an instrumentality of human violation in a process that renders even the possibility of truth itself "a lie." What greater human violation exists than to devastate the hope of truth's ultimate victory in the vanquishing of a language that offers no alternative but the expressions of lies? As Lang observes, "Not only language but logic is brought inside history by these efforts, moreover"; and, later, he adds, "There is nothing in language, or in humanity, more generally, that is exempt from the controlling intention. The will to do evil through the medium of genocide is in fact the will to transcend *all* limits or restrictions, and this intention, which includes language among its objects, produces a lie of even a larger order than does the use of language specifically tied to the act of genocide."[61]

This then is the role and significance of the macabresque, to transform truth into fantasy and to make fantasy the benchmark of collective meaning in the ideological expressions of what now is made to appear as "truth."

To return to the question of euphemism, the euphemistic language of torture in the macabresque is not ironic as such but the reflections of disordered will seeking to destroy all play, even that of ironic chicanery, in the vacuity of theatrical performativity dedicated to cadaverous speech and address. "The moral lie comes close to being absolute, denying the figurative representation of truth in all its forms and even the possibility of truth itself; the moral lie chooses evil as its good on grounds of principles, and this means that no subordinate purpose which is not evil is acknowledged or chosen by the agent of genocide."[62] Speech becomes accessory to a kind of linguistic non-speech, the voice of perpetrators, a mere catacoustic echo of sustained systemic prevarication. Fantasy is elevated to the status of morality, and ideology to the status of political ontology. To enact this, to make this come alive, is why performativity in the macabresque, including speech act performativity, is as critical to an understanding of genocide and mass atrocity as are efforts to explain the killing on the basis of strategic or political purposes alone. In political cultures in which honor codes and shame disciplines operate, assertive rules, or what Austinian language theory classifies as instructional speech act performatives, tend to become predominant in instances of conflict and redress. The immediate implication of this for the study of the macabresque is that much of the human violation that occurs as a consequence of sadistic cruelty is designed to "teach" victims lessons, that is, to exact revenge for fantasized wrongs thereby returning social order to whatever is ideologically constructed as "just," "good," or "right." For these reasons, fantasies of shame and humiliation play a far greater role in fomenting the macabresque than is generally recognized.

A CRITIQUE AND CAUTION

Methodological disagreements arise within this context. Will is about volition. Volition is about choosing, and both bear consequences for interpretations of moral/ethical responsibility in the aftermath of genocide and mass atrocity. Liah Greenfeld, in a review of Andreas Musolff's study of the metaphor "body politic" as applied by the Nazi, warns against the analytic dangers of confusing signs with symbols. The effect, she admonishes, is that metaphors such as *body-illness-parasite* become construed as virtually self-determining in political action, that is, they are deemed to be causal in themselves. She refers to such an error as "cognitivist." Greenfeld avers that metaphors are symbols not signs. Thus, they are "necessarily interpreted by every user and recipient, and so cannot be *imposed*."[63] She continues, "To disregard this crucial difference between signs and symbols is, indeed, to commit a weird categorical mistake, indeed implying as it does that the mental functioning of the German public was, literally, no different from that of non-human animals living in the world of signs that do not lend themselves to interpretation, that, in other words, German people had no more responsibility for their actions, no more moral agency behind them, than the dogs trained for guard duty in the concentration camps."[64] In a sense both Musolff and Greenfeld are correct, however, in stressing what Lang calls Nazi language rules and what they attempted to do: first, transform symbolic meanings into a sign language of lies and distortions; and, secondly, to cover over this effort so as to eliminate ethical responsibility in the name of higher purposes. Metaphors are not sui generis, as Greenfeld rightly claims, but as Musolff also suggests, metaphors in Nazi syntax and semantics were advanced as the axiomatic truth beyond the possibilities of critical interpretation. This is in the character of sadism in the macabresque—that is, to wish, indeed, to will oneself into believing that one acts without discretion as the agency of law. Morality becomes discursively construed as normative principle beyond modification. The "word" becomes the law and the law is to afflict pain on others so that victims yield themselves up to the alters of truth-making in the macabresque.

KANTIAN FORMS OF BEAUTY, PEIRCEAN "ANTHROPOSEMEIOSIS" AND INFORMATIVENESS WITHOUT INFORMATION: EXTRAPOLATIONS BASED ON VIOLENCE/VIOLATIONS IN SRI LANKA

In his poignant study of violence/violation during the Sri Lankan civil war, aptly entitled *Charred Lullabies*, E. Valentine Daniel dwells on the relationships of language and meaning, voice and silence, at moments of inhumane cruelty and inhuman suffering such as that experienced in Sri Lanka during the 1980s, and beyond.[65] To proceed, he borrows from the "semeiosic terminology" of the linguistic philosopher Charles Sanders Peirce. In so doing, he refers to the Greek meaning of *semeion*, or signs to emphasize the relationship of any cultural universe to the diffusion of signs by which order becomes constituted. Here, too, Daniel distinguishes the realm of silence from the realm of speech as, in effect, the separation between the macabresque of human violation and the realm of legal and discursive accountability relative to it. He writes, for example, "Whereas silence or speechlessness is one of the main and pervasive effects of violence, the juridical legal apparatus demands words (or other signs) so that justice may be done."[66] He associates the voice, the speech of such legal accountability, with what he, following Peirce, calls "anthroposemeiosis." He declares, "Anthroposemeiosis is such a cumbersome word. But none other better describes what it is to be human." Later, he adds, "Anthroposemeiosis entails practices that contain an interpretation of what it is to be a human being, to belong to a discursive community, a community with a more or less shared horizon."[67] Daniel thus depicts a realm of performativity and discourse opposite that of the macabresque in which voice resonates with communal meaning through signs or semeiosis, that is, through "the growth and spread of symbols," by means of human sharing and caring.[68] But the question arises as to the relationship of signs to intentionality in representation, the very problem that confronted Scarry as she sought to examine weapons of torture and the pain of victims in what seemed to be their intrinsic condition of "unrepresentability." To respond to this problem, Daniel turns to Peirce's tri-modal structure of signs and signification that distinguishes sign in its material or objective state, the representation of that materiality, and the interpreter undertaking the representation. He is particularly interested in adopting Peirce's notion of a "qualisign" applied to the labeling of signs in ways that presume signs stand for their own representation alone, as it were, divorced from their materiality as objects, and thus removed from interpretive signification. "In other words, a qualisign is a sign that admits to the inexhaustibility of its representational mission; one never gets to the bottom of it."[69] To illustrate the point, Daniel turns to beauty as a qualisign; that is, "beauty is best represented by something that represents beauty's unrepresentability."[70] He adds, "A sign of beauty bulks large with qualisignification."[71] To link this aesthetic perspective with the pain produced by violation, Daniel counterintuitively turns to the Kantian formulation of beauty as *"the form of the purposiveness of an object so far as this is perceived in it without any representation of a purpose."*[72] Daniel thus calls attention to the Kantian distinction between the non-purposive nature and status of an object of beauty as opposed to the *"form* of that purposiveness."[73] The form of beauty serves as an end itself, not a means to another purposive end; in this sense, therefore, beauty stands for itself, beyond purpose.

On the basis of Kantian conceptions of beauty as form for itself, not form for other purpose, Daniel asserts, "The sensory mode called the aesthetic ought not to be limited to the beautiful but must be ready to admit a most unwelcome member into its domain, pain."[74] Earlier, I referred to absolute power in the macabresque of genocidal and mass atrocity as an end in itself for itself without purpose. Daniel, in effect, frames a parallel analysis by reformulating the Kantian definition of beauty and applying it to the pain and suffering stemming from what he, following the work of Henry Shue, calls "interrogational torture." He states, "Pain is the form of the *informativeness* of a victim so far as this is perceived in him without representation of information."[75] Yet, again, we confront the problem of self-deception on the part of perpetrators who attribute "informativeness" to victims who are entirely devoid of any kind of veritable information. The form becomes the end in itself, even though it is represented as a means to another purpose—that is, information or "truth." That informativeness is imputed to victims in the absence of information and in the void of its representation is the very basis of performativity in the macabresque. Informativeness devoid of information is precisely what the macabresque dramatizes, not for purposes of ludic pleasure as such, but because of the sadistic demands of perpetrators that they themselves act as the moral servants of truth, indeed, the moral agents of desire. Victims are thus forced to perform the truth of nontruth; they become the "qualisigns" of perpetrator reification in which dramaturgical and aesthetic forms of pain, torment, and agony substitute for the very veracity of truth. As a result, truth is now brutally discounted; the means by which this is done is the verisimilitude in the chambers of the macabresque, sadistically enacted in multiple forms and settings.

The core meaning of *non-sense* thus acquires a new cast. Daniel portrays perpetrators' self-deception in this regard in the following way: "But this harmony (the torturer's sense that the victim in pain makes sense, is coherent) is achieved without use of concepts, and without a concept the torturer cannot be regarding the object in terms of any determinate information." Daniel continues, "And yet, the torturer finds the victim-in-pain informative." Daniel extracts the significance of this by connecting the "informativeness" of victims, the epistemological and aesthetic know-nothingness of perpetrators' self-deceptions, and the performativity of pain and suffering in the macabresque. He concludes that what the perpetrator "encounters is mere sense, mere suitability. Mere suitability of x without any definite y which x is suitable for, is suitability without material content: x displays only the *form* of informativeness."[76] The interpretation of signs, symbols, and metaphors as elements in self-deception thus becomes a critical perspective in examining the devices of the macabresque. The forms of suffering, that is, torture, torment, agony, become instrumentalized in the macabresque to transform victims into sources of *informativeness void of information*. Their disfigurement is what is wanted as the form of truth and beauty but only as a form and thus devoid of purpose. Perpetrators mystify their roles by believing that extraction from victims of informativeness void of information serves a higher purpose, and is suffused by moral principle and utopian objectives rather than mechanisms for performative transgression, and thus human violation. But the ghosts of Immanuel Kant know better, call it what perpetrators will, the effects are systemic sin in political evil, the essence of depravity in the human condition.

5

Human Development and the Political Subject

THE LACANIAN SCAFFOLDING

IN PSYCHOSOCIAL PERSPECTIVES

ᴒ

THE LACANIAN SCAFFOLDING: AN INITIAL GLANCE
AT IDEAL EGO AND EGO-IDEAL

Systematic examination of the macabresque in mass atrocity "theorizes" that self-deceptions, disordered will, and the psychodynamics of desire represent critical components of sadistic cruelty that is deployed as a political weapon. Psychosocial inquiry thus concentrates on efforts to illuminate why perpetrators desire or give into the psychic and emotional blandishments of sadistic cruelty; why when this occurs it manifests a kind of excessive, one might say, depraved "enjoyment" on the part of perpetrators that seeks satisfaction (however unavailing) through dramaturgical exhibitionism, in particular, the performative aesthetics of the macabresque. Psychosocial perspectives turn to the ludic dimensions of mass atrocity, fueled by disorders of will and motivation that often appear captivated by reified identitarian constructions. These analytical approaches interrogate the relationships between disordered perpetrator motivations and their self-deceptions that develop around collective political reifications and ideology.

Unconscious social fantasy and primary psychic representations are seen to lend support to the kinds of ideological logics of illogic in constructions of collective identity that become culturally fixed and frozen. Political reification represents an overlay of conscious imagery said to reveal the influences of primary psychic phenomena or representations theorized as ideal ego, ego-ideal, and superego. The theoretical challenge is to frame psychosocial analysis in ways relevant to explanations of the macabresque incorporating these largely psychoanalytic units of analysis. Multiple psychosocial perspectives loom as appropriate analytical venues for such an endeavor. In my view, certain Lacanian precepts pertaining to the psychodynamics of desire, especially *jouissance* and *objet a*, provide a basis for explaining why collective forms of violence turn toward performative transgression and macabresque human violations once genocide or mass atrocity is initiated. Relatedly, Lacanian perspectives provide a basis for theorizing the relationship of Gestalt or imagistic formations characterizing the "ideal ego" in the unconscious, or what Lacan termed the Imaginary, to what I suggest is the grip of "primary representations." In Lacanian perspectives, desire as a primal motivation is initially held in the grip of imagistic or primary psychic formations or representations. These make up the ego unconscious during infancy. They retain their hold throughout adulthood, in various ways and to varying degree. A kind of symbolic "emptiness," as theorized by Peter Fonagy and his colleagues and by Hanna Segal, among others, sometimes results.[1] This generates consequences for an understanding of the psychodynamics of political reification and transgressive performativity in the macabresque. The basic theoretical proposition is that primary psychic formations or representations can and do delimit collective or cultural modes of symbolic imagination and expression, and that this has broad implications for the study of collective violence and international politics, as evidenced by mass human violation as a discrete phenomenon in genocide and during outbreaks of mass atrocity. Richard K. Ashley envisions the symbolic process in terms of a "spectro-poetics" of international relations. He conjures up the image of the "itinerate condottiere" applicable to the exigencies of realism; but his metaphoric imaginary applies as well to the paradoxical nature of perpetrator agency and the macro level semeiosis of genocide and mass atrocity. Ashley writes, for example, "This figure of the itinerate condottiere is paradoxical ... He would position himself as the one who, in the ordeal against death, would bear the power born of a life of a paradigm he reflects, and as the one who, in mirroring this life, would offer himself as a window on the forces of death it necessarily confronts."[2] Ashley adds, "The failure of the IC's historical reality to make manifest the power of his privileged ideal constitutes for him a definite, if abstract, will to compensate for the lack by effecting here or there whatever can be made effectively to *count* as a territory of pure paradigmatic being where the word's authority would be absolute." He continues, "It [mass symbolism] constitutes for him a will to give proof to the historical power of his ideal of faithful being by working to cultivate and effect some concept of person, people, blood, race, nation, community, tradition, class, discipline, civilization, Europe, Christendom, or some other paradigm of faith in the word—some construct that, as concept, can be accorded the status of a bounded representable territory signified by a name—and make it function as a verisimilar historical experience of this ideal."[3] For such reasons, whenever political violence turns into genocide, mass atrocity, and, as often as not, into the dynamics of enemy-making as a consequence of hatred, the shift toward human violation occurs within the signified boundedness of sovereignty and nationally constituted states.

SELF-REPRESENTATION IN KILLING COMPARTMENTS

Abram de Swaan, in an attempt to offer a comprehensive review of theory applied to explanations of perpetrator behavior, begins with the arresting title *The Killing Compartments: The Mentality of Mass Murder* to emphasize that whenever mass murder occurs, it happens within a sequestered realm of time and of space.[4] Societies given to what de Swaan refers to as "mass annihilation" become compartmentalized, in part, as an avoidance scheme in semeiosis permitting perpetrators to perform their mission while simultaneously protecting the ability of the rest of society to proclaim not merely its ignorance but also its innocence. De Swaan envisions various processes of compartmentalization at "all" levels and in multiple realms. He lists mental forms in which "the dominant group" coheres more tightly while becoming increasingly distant from others emotionally, intellectually and morally. Compartmentalization also occurs socially as the in-group separates from others. The process alters human and social relations across all institutions. Finally, compartmentalization advances and is reinforced through the "propagation, legitimation and enforcement" of the "political regime."[5] In a sense, de Swaan's conceptual portrayal of compartmentalization runs parallel to my depiction of the macabresque; the macabresque is performed in the temporal and spatial sequesters of compartmentalized reality.

De Swaan's descriptive sweep of the situational factors at work in mass annihilation are broad, but ultimately, he concentrates his analytical focus on the micro level of perpetrator behaviors. His depiction of the mental state of perpetrators features the self-representational state of unity and bonding, similar to what Stanley Milgram had several years earlier called "the agentic state." This is a condition of self-representation in which self and group become ideologically forged together and emotionally fused as a singular unity. The dynamic takes place within the economies of social fantasy as well, as suggested by Sofsky in his analysis of perpetrator group dynamics and their displays of absolute power. De Swaan grounds his analysis in psychoanalytic and psychosocial theory, in particular, by referring to the psychoanalytic work of Peter Fonagy and his colleagues that examines infantile and child development. De Swaan places particular emphasis on their concepts of "mentalization" and "dysmentalization." De Swaan describes the reconstructed "realities" that perpetrators commonly share, from which they nurture the belief that they are justified to do whatever other perpetrators believe is justified, no matter how deep the harm to victims. De Swaan pursues what he calls "the itinerary of dysmentalization" operating within the "mentality" of perpetrators.[6] This consists of "a strong attachment to close relatives, a remnant of early mentalization." He adds the familiar dimensions of "unquestioning" obedience to superiors and "unconditional loyalty" to other in-group members. But he interprets these as the consequences of "a superimposed form of primitive mentalization," or "'emotional contagion.'" De Swaan then draws on a recent literature to suggest that the perpetrators of the Gestapo or the Nazi secret police "were shackled with 'symbiotic ties' to a 'bureaucracy of comrades,'" that they acted "in a transient, quasi-delusional state; their moral conscience has been transferred to the commander and turned into a 'superego' in uniform." De Swaan stresses the fusion of perpetrators as subject and object, perpetrators alone and together in groups, fantasized as one agent. "For the elite fighting units, the platoon is one, it marches in step, its single goal is shared by all."[7] De Swaan appears to emphasize the fantasmatic quality of this order of bonding. He comments, "This is reminiscent of the recurrent fantasy of being absorbed in a perfect unity." Fantasmatic unity brooks no sense of autonomy, choice, or volition, providing an example of extreme "group think" that consists of a mindset *willfully* determined to obviate the need for will or choice.[8] Here, again, played out in terms of obedience and conformity is the combination of self-deception and disorders of will that "excludes any reflection, any distinction between the order and its execution, between the superior's desire and the inferior's act." De Swaan adds, "This is the meaning of *Befehl ist Befehl* (Orders are orders). Loyalty is equally unconditional: an attack on a comrade is an attack on oneself and an attack on the unit as a whole." What sustains such mental, emotional, even spiritual closures? It is as if the subject becomes evacuated as a self, unable to represent itself as an independently volitional subject. This, indeed, is suggestive of the very meaning of "dysmentalization." It would seem that the delusions of ethical norms or superordinate conceptions of morality play out in ways that deplete capacities for either ethical or moral responsibility and action. These psychodynamics reside at the core of akrasia, the weakness of will that masquerades as strength of will in its willfulness and self-deceptions. Willfulness sustained by dysmentalization inheres in social fantasy. De Swaan concludes, "This may not correspond to the realities of an army platoon, but it does represent the shared fantasy of its members in a male-bonding, military subculture." The shared fantasy attaches to the desire for shared desire represented in the shared fantasy of self and group in compartments of mass annihilation, compartments of the macabresque for the very reasons de Swaan delineates, perpetrator desire for bonding and recognition played out in social striving for absolute unity.

Desire emerges in the course of human development, in parental or caregiver relationships with infants and children, in the economies of unconscious drive disciplined in complex ways by guilt and shame. In some cases, particularly with respect to perpetrators, desires for shared desire appear as supererogatory flames that burn especially during moments of the macabresque. For such reasons, elites bent on genocide or mass atrocity repeatedly spew ideological incantations of collective humiliation to mobilize their minions and to justify mass violence. But the illusions reside in self-representations that Fonagy and his colleagues have suggested emerge as dysfunctions of "mentalization" or of the "dysmentalization" to which de Swaan lends so much emphasis. Thus, I turn to this concept briefly, for it indicates the connections between psychoanalytic and psychosocial theory in ways relevant to an interpretation of the relationship between mass atrocity and the macabresque.

MENTALIZATION AND NORMALITY: THE NAZI AMBITENT

Efforts to understand the "unthinkable" behaviors of perpetrators almost inevitably turn to the question of how perpetrators represent "who" they are to themselves as they inflict such pain on others. Self-representation becomes a critical component of attempts to examine perpetrators. Neither pathological nor criminological explanations suffice with respect to these forms of mass anomic behaviors. But this provokes a perplexing issue. If perpetrators acting in groups demonstrate "normality," what is in the nature of normalcy that permits those who perpetrate the macabresque to be considered "normal"? And if what perpetrators do is to be considered part of normal human personality, how do perpetrators envision or represent themselves to themselves—in their normality? Research undertaken by Peter Fonagy and his colleagues is helpful to students of genocide and mass atrocity because it postulates self-representation in mentalization as a core feature of human development. Just as "the psyche" refers to the materiality of the brain and the entire somatic composition of human physicality as related to consciousness and the unconscious, mentalization is more than mere cognition or neurology. It refers to interior processes of imaginative and emotional development that reflect psychic relations with external "objects," most especially parents and caregivers, *and* how these exteriorities come to be represented as interiorities in the psychic and emotional organization of any human being. In this view, the entire process of mentalization spins on the axles of agency and self-representation. Fonagy and colleagues state, "Our main focus throughout is on the development of representations of psychological states in the minds of infants, children, adolescents, and adults. Mentalization . . . is the process by which we realize that having a mind mediates our experience of the world. Mentalization is intrinsically linked to the development of the self, to its gradually elaborated inner organization, and to its participation in human society."[9] Mentalization provides a conceptual framework for examining not only cognitive development but also imaginative and emotional development through a series of infantile and early childhood phases that include "the self as a 'physical agent'"; "the self as a 'social agent'"; "the self as 'a teleological agent'"; "the self as an 'intentional mental agent'"; and "the self as 'a representational agent.'" The latter phase, associated with ages four to five years, initiates what Fonagy and his associates refer to as "the autobiographical self." They describe this as "the ability to comprehend the 'representational' and 'causally self-referential' properties of intentional mind states, leading, among other things, to the establishment of an abstract, temporally extended, historical-causal concept of the 'autobiographical self.'"[10] External realities constituted by parents and caregivers thus come to be represented in the interiority of infantile and child consciousness and are critical factors in influencing how mentalization develops. The essential feature is, literally, the interplays of "play" between a child and a parent or caregiver, during which "the child can see his fantasy or idea represented in the adult's mind, reintroject this, and use it as a representation of his own thinking."[11] The internal and external become mutually implicated. The adult must "live" in the fantasies of the child to enable him to develop capacities for "representation of his own representations." "By entering into the child's world in a playful way, the child sees the adult adopting an 'as if' attitude to his intentional state. The frame is present so that he knows that his thoughts or feelings are not 'for real,' yet he perceives them outside, in the parent's mind." At his juncture, mentalized capacities for representation become possible for a child. "Linking his internal state to a perception of that state outside offers a representation—a symbol of the internal state: it corresponds to, yet it is not equivalent to, the state. The playful attitude of the parent is crucial." The child must incorporate his or her own psychic and emotional conditions in fantasy, play, or cognition and all three together, as reflected in the minds and responses of parents. This is essential to the developmental processes that are integral to representation. "In this way he can ultimately use the parent's representation of his internal reality as the seed for his own symbolic thought, the representation of his own representations."[12]

Developmental pathways in human consciousness are fraught with risk and disability. At issue is self-representation as a capacity: the connectedness with one's subjectivity, imagination, and emotional state or condition, measured in terms of autonomy, on the one hand, and its opposite, overdetermination by psychic constellations that Freud described as "thought-reality" as opposed to "external reality," on the other.[13] Fonagy and associates declare, "If the adult's attitude precludes the duality of holding the frame of external reality while offering mirroring or reflection, the child's transition toward integration and mentalization may be jeopardized. He may not feel free—secure—to explore the adult's mind and find himself in it, or what he finds there may be a distorted picture of his mental state, which the child cannot safely use to represent his experience."[14] Play and capacities for playfulness provide a kind of baseline for evaluating the developmental aspects of mentalization. And play is more than strict cognition but presents itself in capacities for imagination, creativity, discovery, and, in forms of courage, hope, and empathy.

This sheds light on the findings produced by psychoanalytic and cognitive study of large numbers of Nazis referred to earlier that described both the rank-and-file and the Nazi elite as manifesting the characteristics of what they termed the "ambitent." "The ambitent individual is particularly inefficient in their problem-solving style and is associated with people who have no 'mind of their own' or are lacking 'an internal compass.' Ambitents rely heavily on others and on an external structure for guidance in problem solving." The report confirmed "the normality thesis" by stressing that no evidence was found to suggest Nazis were "psychotic, bizarre, or severely disturbed," nor were they "overwhelmed with sadism and aggression." Rather, under scrutiny, what they did reveal was a "rigid, eccentric, or inefficient" pattern of thinking and that "such a cognitive style draws on inaccurate stereotypes that may take the form of prejudice."[15] It is methodologically perilous to extrapolate psychosocial explanations of collective or group adult behaviors on the basis of psychological or psychoanalytic theories of childhood development. But such characteristics as rigidity and prejudice parallel the inability to experience "play" or to express complex thoughts imaginatively. In this view, "dullness" is a matter not of intelligence alone, but of abstract mind, empathetic heart, and compassionate spirit, as well. Disabilities with respect to what Fonagy and his colleagues depicted as mentalization and representation become manifest in patterns of thinking, reasoning, and classifying that are overly determined by interior constellations of "thought-reality."

Lene Auestad describes this as follows: "We could think of an emotion or affect as pointing in two directions, inwards and outwards, so to speak. Furthermore, in terms of object-relations theory, the internal and the external are not necessarily psychic reality vs. outer, observable reality, but could also be thought of as referring to what is conceived of as 'me' vs. 'not-me', where both of these are internal in the sense of being unconsciously fantasized constructs."[16] The macabresque does not open onto the staging of creative play or inventiveness. Its ludic forms give rise to a darkness that has nothing to do with comedic laughter or tragic grief. What it does allow is the externalized expression of internal psychic and emotional "object constellations in the past"[17] that overly determine how perpetrators in the macabresque envision and act on identitarian constructions. I shall refer to these object constellations as primordial reifications and theorize their emergence in human personality in terms of ego-ideal, social fantasies built around mimetic forms of desire, and so on.

No more powerful object constellation arises within the psychodrama of mentalization, moreover, than that of parents or caregivers. It is the very point of the entire object-relations approach to human development to assert that a mirror imaging occurs in which infants and children come to relate, see, know, and accept themselves as parents relate, see, know, and accept them, but not before dissections and intersections occur that distort and recombine the imageries. In this context, Fonagy and his colleagues speak of the etiologies of "narcissistic personality disorder." This emerges in cases in which caregivers misinterpret or counter a child's psychic and emotional state or condition. They describe the effects of this as follows: "However, as this mirrored display is incongruent with the infant's actual feeling, the secondary representation created will be distorted. The infant will mislabel the primary, constitutional emotional state. The self-representation will not have strong ties to the underlying emotional state. The individual may convey an impression of reality, but . . . the self will feel empty because it reflects the activation of secondary representations of affect that lack the corresponding connections within the constitutional self." This emptiness, the hollow shells of emotional disconnect, a psychic condition framed by secondary representations or primordial reifications, lingers into maturity well within the ranges of behavioral normalcy. So much is made of intellectual intelligence. But there exists as well emotional and moral intelligence grounded in the fullness of imagination, in the joys of spontaneity and the delights and satisfactions of disciplined flexibility, including that necessary for purposes of creativity. Infantile secondary representations in mentalization, object constellations in consciously fantasized constructs that *con-fuse* external realities with internal objects, primordial reifications patterned around the psychodynamics of ego-ideal, all provide explanatory approaches to the rigidities of human personality that some observers have pejoratively described as the condition of being an "emptity." Such psychodynamic sources contribute emptity to dysmentalization and basic lack of empathy, as de Swaan indicates. They may also foster adult desires for narcissistic omnipotence and absolute power through the bonding mechanisms triggered by and in the macabresque.

This does not suggest a universal feature in human personality that explains the behaviors of perpetrators. What these developmental concepts do underscore is variability of culture and child-rearing practices and their influences on adult personality. They also serve to underscore the importance in human development of capacities for self-understanding and general awareness, as well as the relevance of environmental factors conducive to the disabilities of narcissistic self-deception and disordered will, which have implications for psychosocial explanations of perpetrator behaviors. The question, again, concerns self-representation and the psychic and emotional latitudes conferred on human personalities as a result. Fonagy and colleagues demonstrated how primordial mentalized constructions arise and become highly influential, if not determinative, in emotional forms of rigidity that can influence how attitudinal prejudice arises in adult behavior. To anticipate this discussion, I cite Fonagy and colleagues with respect to secondary representations. "We have attempted to specify in greater detail the psychological mechanism that underpins the processes by which parental affect-mirroring deviates from its normal course in terms of our concept of the *alien self*." They add, "Where parental care-giving is extremely insensitive and misattuned, we assume that a fault is created in the construction of the psychological self . . . . *The infant, failing to find himself in the mother's mind, finds the mother instead.* The infant is forced to internalize her representation of the object's state of mind as a core part of himself. But in such cases the internalized other remains *alien* and unconnected to the structures of the constitutional self."[18] This statement, with its emphasis on "internalized other that remains alien," is suggestive of the psychodynamics of "transposed alterity" central to Lacanian concepts of the Imaginary and its structural role in social fantasy. These structural processes and psychodynamics do not predict for perpetrator behaviors, or even for their inclinations. They do not determine the personalities of perpetrators, let alone cause genocide or mass atrocity. Their relevance is not causal but incidental to mass atrocity insofar as they foster the rigid, cold, indifferent, nonempathic stance that is repeatedly evidenced by and through the behaviors of perpetrators and typically on display in the macabresque.

Hatred reveals a psychic and emotional construction of indifference, not of genuine passion; and attitudinal indifference *in part* results from secondary representations and subsequent disconnects between the self as subject unto itself and the subject as a rival self-other—that is, the subject as rival self-object unto itself. Such a self-object becomes not so much "captured" by secondary representations of an internalized alien self as it is *captivated* by internal mentalized constructions. Under situational influences, including command and peer in-group pressures during mass atrocity, these occlude empathetic vision. Sight becomes beholden to social fantasies that transform external realities into ghosts and internal apparitions that perpetrators flail against. Here, too, the macabresque is the means that allows these interior demons to take shape in material reality, particularly around the identitarian forms cast around innocent victims. As this happens, the bodies of victims become demonized. They are reified as the containers and purveyors of infectious risk: disease, decay, disintegration, disarray, decadence, and so forth. Much of what occurs in the drama/trauma killing processes of the macabresque is engaged in a hellish process of expurgation from what is fantasized, reified, and ideologically constituted as the execrable and the excremental. This is suggestive of the role played by shame and honor in the organization of the macabresque. Shame is both universal as psychological experience and culturally shaped and individually determined. Under certain sets of conditions, shame turns to rage, as well as into a wide range of emotional and cognitive constructions, including envy and jealousy. The psychodynamics generate perverse desires for relief and/or release. Often these culminate with dramaturgical displays of honor embodying fantasmatic masculine power. Sometimes these dynamics lead to calls for supererogatory obligation based on self-sacrifice. When perpetrators act, they experience masculinized bonding in excessive forms aimed against the bodies and blood of victims. It is as if shame must be projected outward so that honor can return. The macabresque demonstrates profound yearning for the security against the shame that derives from threats to the social order whenever masculine power itself has become problematic. As Frosh has shown, much German anti-Semitism derived in part from a fantasized form of demonization to the effect that the Jews were feminizing the Germans, their honor, their power. Shame readily translated into the demand for honor displayed. Such yearnings devolve into perverse desires incarnated in what is properly interpreted as sadistic drive—that is, demand for displays of sado-intimacy.

The critical element is not cruelty alone, but rather cruelty on display as performative transgression. I relate the reasons for this in a psychosocial perspective by linking shame and performative transgression to sadistic demand that the "laws" of prohibited ecstasy, or what Lacanian theory suggests as *jouissance,* be declared and staged by means of displays of perverse desire. The lines connecting the psychic and the political, the individual and the collective, in macabresque dramaturgies of transgression cross from the psychodynamics of desire to the laws of phallic prohibition, from *jouissance* to *objet a.* For these reasons, mass atrocity takes hold as a discrete phenomenon when genocide or near genocide becomes normalized as the orders of the day. Social disintegration, the absence of principles of human decency, the license to undertake mass murder, releases unrestrained desire for something over and above mere killing. The hunt of desire turns to existential decay beyond mere decadence; what is psychically prohibited now becomes emotionally accessible. In terms of Lacanian theory extrapolated and applied to explanations of the macabresque, the sadomasochism of perpetrators reaches beyond ontological loss and lack to grasp at the most forbidden of all fruits, the return to existential ecstasy—the ecstasy that never was—in surrogacies of human violations. Before outlining Lacanian theory, however, I refer back to the largely social psychological literature on perpetrators of genocide and mass atrocity. I do so to present the strengths of this research but also to demonstrate its limitations given its nearly exclusive explanatory reliance on perpetrator self-identifications and, especially, on their cognitive self-rationalizations.

PERSPECTIVES ON EGO-FORMATIONS AND THE PSYCHODYNAMICS
OF SELF-REPRESENTATION

On the basis of clinical research and experience, these theoretical perspectives indicate that primary representations emerge in the course of pre-Oedipal infantile ego development, and feature psychic formations of ideal ego and ego-ideals. Ideal ego develops during infancy under highly variable conditions; thus these psychic formations are different for each human being. Environmental factors of nurture are critical. As Stijn Vanheule and Paul Verhaeghe suggest, the ego forms in and around interactive relations, and thus never as the consequence of an "a priori identity."[19] They continue, "The Ego starts with an original identification and is subsequently enlarged by successive identificatory layers, each one going back to a specific object relation." Such putative identificatory layers constitute critical overlays in ego formation. They provoke the imagistic configurations Freud terms as primary "representations," of which the ideal ego is among the first.[20] Lacan builds on this theoretical framework by featuring the primacy of early self-representations in fostering the multiple defensive and aggressive functions of the ego. Culture, its images and imaginaries, its symbolic meanings, values, and, in particular, language, its signifiers and semiotics, pave the ways for unique as well as universal psychic development. In an elaboration, Vanheule suggests, "Lacan argues that, in a similar way, *Gestalts* guide human development but are embedded and transmitted within a cultural context. Culture and familial history help mold the images with which humans identify, and it is primarily within the family context that they are expressed. Lacan therefore prefers the Latin term, 'imago' or image over *Gestalt*."[21] And the Lacanian concept of "imago," or mental representation, anticipates the findings proposed by Fonagy and colleagues regarding "mentalization," "self-representation," and "secondary representation." Together these form the "primary formations or representations" within the psychic register Lacan refers to as the Imaginary. As theoretical constructs, they help guide our understanding of the psychic mechanisms that process mentalized trajectories leading to self-individuation.[22]

Lacan, early in his career, initiated a theory framed by the psychodynamics of infantile self-imagery. He later revised or repudiated some aspects of this. He suggested, in particular, that critical to ego development during early childhood was how and to what extent possibilities of self-recognition were presented to infants and the degree to which these included images of physical wholeness or integrity. Self-perception, according to this perspective, represents the rudimentary and indispensable vehicle for human development in ways that lend analytical primacy to the psychodynamics of primary or self-representation. In this view, the ideal ego immediately assumes the character of something external to the self, an image of the self that is introjected from the self as subject onto the self as object and, as it were, from outside the self. Imagistic and audial features experienced as exterior thus serve as the central formative features of ideal ego. Vanheule and Verhaeghe indicate that Lacanian theory suggests how ideal ego formations arise out from these refractory infantile images. Of crucial import is the theoretical weight carried by the imputed relationship of any subject relative to itself as "subject" but also as "object." "Mirroring is the process that calls the Ego into existence and comes down to the adoption of a body image that was first actively captured by the subject in the external world as something ideal—as an Ideal Ego." And one dimension of this is the extent to which ideal ego as the early outcome of infantile psychic development is shaped by primary unconscious configurations of physical unity and embodied wholeness. As Vanheule and Verhaeghe indicate, "It is only to the extent that the alien image has a value in integrating inner chaos that a subject discerns this image as something ideal with which it is favorable to identify."[23] This also underscores the illusory, and some suggest, the delusional character of ideal ego. Vanheule and Verhaeghe refer to Lacan as suggesting, "The drawback he links to assuming an Ego by mirroring with an Ideal Ego is that this deludes the human subject: the feeling of unity the Ego provides is an illusion that blinds us to everything that does not fit the image."[24] The grand effect of primary representation is thus what Lacan called "mihilism," or what Vanheule and Verhaeghe call "the violent tendency to consider everything from the perspective of me."[25] Narcissism thus comes alive in the self-centering dynamics of ideal ego. But this occurs at a frightful cost, the price of conscious vulnerability but also of unconscious dread and despair embedded in anxiety and manifested by ever-present sensations of imminent physical dissipation and psychic dissolution.

Ego formations in the Imaginary consist of the "*objects*" of subject and otherness, sometimes blended together in part or in whole to form the self-deceptions from which identificatory processes emerge. Bice Benvenuto encapsulates this by depicting a kind of visualized "gaze" that peers into and out from the "infantile mirror." She writes, "This is the image Narcissus fell in love with; this is the image of completeness of the child held by another in front of the mirror . . . if love is always narcissistic, it is only as other, before the mirror." She adds, "It is in the pupil of the other that we see ourselves in its gaze."[26] The mirror image becomes a site of multiple refractions so that the subject becomes the image of the other as others recognize it. Benvenuto adds, "after the separation from the other's face which the mirror achieves, the other's gaze is on our face; we are identified with our mirror's upholders.[27] In this, Benvenuto's psychosocial theory is aligned with the performative social psychology advanced by Erving Goffman. The pervasive grasp of narcissist, as well as perfectionist, trajectories in the personalities of perpetrators is the consequence.

But herein lie appropriate claims to perpetrator "normality," "banality," and "ordinariness." Once these narcissist theoretical assertions become accepted as existentially valid, these conceptions of the Imaginary register become analytically potent in explaining hatred. Hatred and narcissism are never far apart in the psychodynamic registers of the Imaginary. Both sets of impulses reverberate in the fertile ground of an identitarian perfectionism that originates from outside the subject but becomes internalized in ways that divide subjects, including political subjects, from themselves. This is the analytical significance of self-reification suggested by the metaphor of the rival self-other. The rival self-other is constituted in the unconscious gaze of the political subject relative to itself. Benvenuto writes, "The mirror inaugurates a rivalry with oneself: the object of objectification also becomes an object of hatred and aggression."[28] In such psychodynamics, akratic disorders of motivation, will, and willfulness foment, though they remain for the most part misrecognized, individually and collectively, in particular, on the part of perpetrators.

As Adrian Johnston states, "All instances of (self) recognition, any and every possible moment of identification, are ego-level misrecognitions." Johnston describes primordial reification in terms of psychic layers of misrecognition and misrepresentation that are manifest in an "enveloping series" of "imaginary identifications" making up structures of psychic "sedimentation."[29] In Johnston's view, this impedes the capacities of transcendental imagination to progress beyond narcissism.[30] Žižek, for his part, writes, "[T]he paradox of self-consciousness is that *it is possible only against the background of its own impossibility*: I am conscious of myself only insofar as I am out of reach to myself qua the real kernel of my being."[31] The consequence is a kind of primary paranoia borne by profound insufficiencies. The effects of this resound not only during infantile development but beyond, into mature life. Frosh suggests, for example, "Identity fades away here. According to Lacan, the structure of human knowledge and ego functioning is a delusional one, finding in the spectral image a misleading promise of integrity."[32] Lacan interprets this "as a paranoid sensation." Frosh adds, "The negativity and persecutory associations of the paranoic are to do in part with the aggressivity of the drives." In this perspective, delusions of physical holism in ideal ego formations instill psychic impulses favoring paranoid fantasy. Frosh encapsulates the implications, "But it is also connected with the haunting of this satisfying image of the integrated self by the specter or memory of something else: somewhere inside, each of us knows that we are not really whole, that this seeming self is a bare cover for something disturbing." Thus ideal ego is presented in theory as a way to interpret patterns of primary representation that are held in the grips of absence and incompletion. As such, the ideal ego becomes a kind of "a home for lost desires and forsaken objects; its character is formed along the line of these objects, which are introjected and absorbed" but are also a "precipitate of abandoned object cathexes."[33] Such imprints wax in and out of political cultures in elusive but sometimes influential ways, as perhaps detected by a wide cross-cultural range of liminal practices dealing with initiation and confirmation rites that literally cut into the body and skin but in order to make a person "whole again" by becoming fully integral within the identifying group.

Primacy of Cultural Influences

In time, the primary formations of ideal ego gradually become contoured around maturational ego-ideals. These are said also to be reflective of the cultural and attitudinal dispositions of parents and caregivers. Lacanian perspectives sometimes represent these impacts as those of the *(m)Other*. This construction is meant to suggest that cultural intrusions begin to form within infantile unconsciousness as a consequence of the earliest interpersonal relationships between infants and caregivers. Cultural influences and impacts are theorized in Lacanian psychoanalytic theory as playing a significant role in individual development. This tends to belie assumptions alleging that psychosocial theory must necessarily be ahistorical or envision human behavior as being overly determined by interior psychic forces or drives. On the contrary, the priority granted to cultural influences in shaping ego-ideal development historicizes not only individual psychic development but also the role and impacts of collective culture and social environment. The concept of ego-ideal is critical to an understanding of post-Freudian and Lacanian and conceptions of the Imaginary. The developmental psychodynamics from ideal ego to ego-ideals, all associated with primary representations, are not predetermined along predictable lines; instead, they develop as a result of parental or caregiver nurture that is itself a conveyer of cultural identificatory influences. Such retroactive, retrospective overlays in shaping the unconscious mind help to "produce" human subjectivities mired in infantile fantasies of reified selfhood and otherness. The former fosters development of ideal ego; the latter, ego-ideals through the double mirroring effects of caregiver desire relative to what infantile unconscious gradually learns to recognize and imitate as the desire to be desired—that is, the desirable in desiring.[34] Throughout the transitions from ideal ego to ego-ideal the imagistic grips of primary imagos or Gestalts of originary pre-Oedipal infantile experience become reinforced. But the process is not necessarily placid. On the contrary, the primary representations in ideal ego that foster early narcissism sketched by primordial fantasies of wholeness are soon challenged by the emergence of ego-ideals beyond the ideal ego. This, too, has relevance to psychosocial theory as it interprets the relationship of political culture to collective violence.

The Political Subject as Lack: Learning How, as well as What, to Desire

The holistic bodily imagos or representations of ideal ego become challenged by interactions between infant and nurturer. The imago of the nurturer is the very object incorporated into the infantile psychic structure as internal to itself. Lacan differentiates "need" and "demand" to emphasize the contrasts between physical need and infantile demand, the former with limits, the latter beyond bounds, in order to claim that "desire" grows out from the tensions between each. Desire reflects biological "needs" but also reveals a demand for satisfaction beyond limitations. The consequence is to position desire, in particular, infantile "desires" to be desirable—that is, to be m(Other)'s or caregiver's desire—represents a critical vector in the formations of ego-ideal. The concept of ego-ideal as unconscious primary representation or imago is theoretically constructed around interpretations of how and to what degree infantile unconsciousness becomes shaped around desires as defined by what is communicated through nurture as culturally "desirable."

It is in the very nature of desires, therefore, to be learned. As a consequence, desires tend to be experienced in myriad ways. Unconscious desires do not directly determine behaviors, but they retain influence. Freudian and Lacanian theories of desire frame the psychic formation of ego-ideals as the initial benchmark for assessing the influences of the nurturing m(Other), but not in analytical ways that suggest consistent, predictive, or overly determined behavioral outcomes. If such were the case, ego-ideal as an analytical concept would render both human personality and cultural character automatic, absolutely predictable. Ego-ideal provides a conceptualization of how human subjectivation occurs as the outcome of a process of identification with the m(Other). This psychodynamic process is embedded in desires. Desires are reciprocal between the infant and the caregiver. How desires come to be expressed or are made known or experienced is the result of individual personalities, relationships, and interactions. Concepts of ego-ideal underscore that desire comes to be known and processed in infantile psychic development as the result of what Freud termed *Anlehnung*, or attachment.[35] But a main element of the environmental factors that shape the interior contours of desires is culture. Thus ego-ideal as a psychic formation or representation develops from its outset a range of features and characteristics reflective of cultural milieu, mores, and morality.

Many interpretations exist with respect to this process, particularly within the part-object school of psychoanalytic theory. The phenomenon of splitting (discussed in the chapter 6) begins to depict the turbulent processes which the ego-ideals as psychic formations are said to undergo. In the present context, the unconscious formations of ego-ideals are understood to go beyond the immediacy of parental or caregiver nurture. They congeal into primary unconscious representations formatted around what is culturally considered to be desirable. But this generates its own unconscious problematics concerning what is desirable, how it is signified, and in a metaphoric sense, over what it "demands" by way of its own "needs." For these reasons, many psychoanalytic theorists prefer to conflate ego-ideal with the superego, the placemat of moral judgment and conscience. In my view, this misrecognizes the discrete developmental process of ego-ideal contoured around the psychodynamics of what I would suggest is "transposed alterity" by which external imago become internally incorporated as representations of the desirable in whatever form. As Vanheule and Verhaeghe comment,[36] however, "Lacan starts from the axiom that the other's desire is essentially enigmatic to a subject. It comes across as a threatening riddle."[37] Psychic formations conceptualized as ego-ideals become forged through identificatory psychodynamics to resolve this fourfold conundrum: what does the m(Other) desire; what does the m(Other) want of me; what does the m(Other) recognize as desirable; how do I become what is desirable *in myself*? In response, persons learn how and what to desire. These tensions are mediated in pre-Oedipal infantile unconsciousness. They are nurtured in and by the pulsations of give and take and what Freud famously observed as the "to and fro" of infant and caregiver interactions. "By molding one's own Ego, and by observing the way the other reacts to it, a subject tries to see which object it is in relation to the other's desire, and tries to make sure that the other desires the content one tries to be identical with."[38] In this, Vanheule and Verhaeghe anticipate Lacanian theories of lack, the lack in maternal desire theorized as "want-of-being."

Metaphorically speaking, to want to be the desire desired by another is to accept desire on terms denoted by want-of-being—linking subject and m(Other). Desire functions in the unconscious in search of itself, a search defined by lack, absence and the evanescent between what is or has and what is lost, taken or never grasped. This places the m(Other) culture at the front and center of the ego-ideal in the unconscious, not only by shaping representations of what is desirable, but in fostering the virtually never-ending quest to be, find, and incorporate it as well. Vanheule and Verhaeghe declare, "Ego-Ideals are symbolic elements that a subject takes from the discourse of the other. This means that they are nothing but privileged discursive elements: specific traits and characteristics of others that arrest a subject's attention, and are unconsciously adopted to the extent that they are considered to imply an answer to the riddle of the other's desire."[39] The exterior force and internal impacts of desire thus become forged within the psychic functioning of the ego in formations of ego-ideals that establish primary representations. But the theoretical implications ripple far and wide since they are viewed as influences that not only stem from political cultures but which emanate from human personality in ways indicative of political culture, even at times when it is most under pressure of change.

Together, ideal ego and ego-ideals foster the illusions of completion and of closure. But the psychic imprints of desire provoke dissatisfaction and profound alienation. For the social ontologies of desire do not function to sustain psychic illusions of fulfillment but, on the contrary, to promote social fantasies of emptiness, alienation, lack and absence. Frosh, referring to Lacan, states,

> Instead, he evokes an empty subject, constituted through lack and marked by the impossibility of fulfillment or of recognition of the actuality of the other. For that is the register of "identity" in the Lacanian scheme: it is an aspect of the fantasy of fulfillment that is split apart by the discovery that the subject is produced by, rather than generative of, the signifying chain.[40]

Frosh adds that the "The child is thus 'seduced' by enigmatic signifiers that arise from the external other and yet are constitutive of the child's own unconscious, in a never-ending cycle from generation to generation, laying a mystery, an alienness, at the center of psychic life."[41] Ideal ego formations are thus molded around the self-representations of wholeness but are immediately subjected to imagistic formations that involve both splitting and fragmentation (as discussed in terms of Kleinian conceptions of infantile sadism). Ego-ideals center around the psychodynamics of desire but serve as psychic structures for chronic discontent. Ideal ego and ego-ideals are thus interpreted as the seeds of congenital narcissism in the case of the former, and perfectionism or extremism in the latter. Nurture plays a crucial role in extending or diffusing these characterological proclivities. Political cultures play important roles as influences in this, and for such reasons become elements in determining the dramaturgical and aesthetic styles adopted and instrumentalized in the macabresque.

IDENTIFICATORY INVESTMENTS

The basic proposition is that the psychodynamics of identification represent a central feature of the unconscious. In their classic compendium of psychoanalytic terms, Laplanche and Pontalis state, "In Freud's work the concept of identification comes little by little to have the central importance which makes it, not simply one psychical mechanism among others, but the operation itself whereby the human subject is constituted."[42] The identification process of development "internalizes intersubjective *relations*."[43] This occurs, but not without considerable turbulence and contradiction. "A subject's identifications viewed as a whole are in no way a coherent relational system," Jean Laplanche and Jean-Bertrand Pontalis observe. "Demands coexist within an agency like the super-ego, for instance, which are diverse, conflicting and disorderly. Similarly, the ego-ideal is composed of identifications with cultural ideals that are not necessarily harmonious."[44] This psychoanalytic perspective on ego-ideal formations during infantile psychic development thus becomes featured in psychosocial theory as the repercussive effects sensed within identity constructions whenever in-group and out-group interactions swirl around fixed political, social, or cultural reifications, or what Young-Bruehl preferred to call orectic ideologies. Glynos and Stavrakakis emphasize how ego-ideal formations promote an "ex-centric subject, a subject structured around a radical split."[45] This split grounded in the lack at the *core* of psychic desire establishes identity and identitarian constructions as the *core* of political culture.

Political culture operates to imbue identity with a sense of endowment that is borne, of necessity, by ego-ideal formations that help to center the political subject, who, in turn, is anchored by collective meanings or ideologies that are themselves configured around constitutive lack or absence. Glynos and Stavrakakis state, "The subject as lack cannot be separated from the subject's attempts to cover over this constitutive lack at the level of representation by affirming its positive (symbolic imaginary) identity or, when this fails, through continuous identificatory acts aiming to re-institute an identity." They continue, "This lack necessitates the constitution of every identity through processes of identification with socially available traits of identification found, for example, in political ideologies."[46]

The assumption of identity through unconscious identificatory acts can over time nurture diachronic risks of political reification through what Jeffrey Murer has described as "proxy narratives." Glynos and Stavrakakis indicate, "The inability of identificatory acts to produce a full identity by subsuming subjective division (re)produces the radical ex-centricity of the subject and, along with it, a whole negative dialectics of partial fixation." *Political or ideological reifications inhere in the psychodynamics of partial fixation.* For such reasons, Glynos and Stavrakakis speak of the psychodynamics of "*imaginariza- tion*," which, yet again, is suggestive of the forms that self-deception assumes when psychosocial dynamics veer toward the disordered desire to force "others" to be different so that in-groups can be made to feel stronger or confirmed in their difference. Frosh, for example, writes, "The process of racist ideation is therefore one in which unwanted or feared aspects of the self are experienced as having the power to disturb the personality in so damaging a way that they have to be repudiated and evacuated and projected into the racialized other, chosen for this purpose both because of pre-existing social prejudices and because, as a fantasy category, racial 'otherness' can be employed to mean virtually anything."[47] At the core of political reification revolves the psychodynamics of what Frosh calls "the lie," that is, reified formats of otherness "willed" as objects of difference, even hate, to sustain the sense of the self as integral to "the collective subject." Such psychodynamics may be theoretically interpreted as demonstrations of the paranoia originating in formations of ego-ideals.

Seen in this perspective, prejudice, hatred, even the violations occurring in the macabresque stem from self-deception now theorized as the "lie" fertilized in the compost of paranoid social fantasy. Such lies are not cosmetic conveniences that some persons wear as superficial dress. They serve as psychic compensations to make up for the lack that bars the subject from the fullnesses of desire. As Frosh observes, "The lie becomes something central to the preservation of the individual's personality and identity, deeply invested in and relied upon as a source of support to the self. The more strongly it is held, the more it is needed; the subject comes to be in love with the lie and fearful of anything that challenges it. 'The lie' in the system of personality organization becomes positively valued."[48] For such reasons, Freud insisted on the term *investment* as the critical element in interpreting how personality develops through identification.

Vanheule, in turn, indicates that Lacan's mature work was devoted in part to explorations of the lingering effects of primary representations conceived in terms of the " 'imaginary mode' of relating to the world."[49] Lacan concluded that the identificatory overlays formed during the pre-Oedipal phases were critical to an understanding of such psychic phenomena as paranoia and psychosis. Vanheule states, "By making this claim Lacan suggests that the core characteristic of madness concerns an identificatory structure. The essence of psychosis is, in other words, not made up by a frailty or an unfortunate event, but by a mode of identification." Or later, "The basic structure of paranoia is present in a person's functioning before the outbreak of psychosis, and . . . it concerns a mode of identification in social relationships. This identification is not necessarily indicative of a disorder and can be recognized as an aspect of human functioning."[50] Vanheule suggests that Lacan used two neologisms to encapsulate aspects of primary representation: *hainamorization* and *jealouissance*. Each combines contradictory feelings or emotions—the first, hatred and adoration; the second, jealousy—with what Lacan refers to as *jouissance*, an overabundance of desire and yearning that cannot be psychically contained. Lacan envisions the emergence of *hainamorization* and *jealouissance* as intrinsic to the pre-Oedipal development of ideal ego and of ego-ideal formations. Vanheule describes this in terms of mimetic rivalry and competition. He states, "Lacan indicates that in the mirror stage hate actually has three faces. The first way in which hate can manifest is via intrusion. Intrusion is experienced in relation to those who disturb the cherished relation between ego and its ideal image. The ego's typical reaction is to hate the intruder. Second, hate can manifest rivalry. Rivalry is experienced when an ego compares itself with a semblable and when both are perceived to relate to the same ideal."[51]

Vanheule situates such rivalry within an analytical context that links mimetic desire, rivalry, and competition to primary psychic formations. "This provokes competition around being the best in fulfilling the ideal, and gives rise to a desire to eliminate the rival other." The implications for psychosocial theory are thus made clear in terms of a psychic potential, indeed, predilection for violence. He adds, "The third way in which hate manifests is jealousy. Jealousy is experienced when the ego concludes that the semblable with which one is competing has the advantage, and something one lacks. Jealousy reflects the desire to have this advantageous position for oneself, and the wish to eradicate the frustrating other."[52] I shall refer to these extrapolations of psychoanalytic theory in subsequent chapters to suggest possible psychosocial implications for examining mimetic rivalry in both the Rwandan and Cambodian genocides.

Certainly, the concept of mimetic rivalry is highly suggestive of the psychodynamics of intergroup competition in which rivals in a competition over the desire to be the desire of another end up attempting to eliminate the rival. Beyond this, the psychodynamics of mimetic desire and rivalry indicate why the macabresque often turns into a dramaturgy of confession in which the sins or crimes to be confessed are merely those of desiring to be the most desirable. Vanheule concludes, "The concept jealouissance, which stresses the experience of enjoyment-beyond-lust that comes with jealousy, indicates that the imaginary experience of hate is more than a simple psychological reaction. Jealousy and hate put the body into a state of uproar; acts of revenge provide an unequalled satisfaction and any symbolic compromise will be experienced as frustration."[53] This sense of the ineluctable allures of revenge and hatred and envy and jealousy begin to etch out how honor and the shamefulness of shame play out as integral to the psychodynamics of the macabresque.

IDENTICALITY AND THE FANTASMATIC TYRANNY
OF MINOR DIFFERENCE AS KEY TO MIMETIC RIVALRY

This examination underscores the relevance of the well-known Freudian concept of "minor differences." One can parse this issue in a number of ways. For example, during instances of collective violence among competing groups, why does it appear necessary for protagonist groups to "manufacture" the differences between themselves and the others, such as the Nazi demand that Stars of David in yellow be sown on the outer garments of German Jews or the Pol Pot regime requirement that blue scarves be worn by those categorized by as "base people" during the Cambodian genocide. Ostensibly, this served as a way of ensuring that minor differences became accentuated. So why are small differences written so extensively in the history of vengeful violence among large groups? Why the hatred, the calumny reflective of merely "small" contrasts? Answers are suggested by the primacy of exteriority and otherness at the psychic core of human personality as indicated by the formative processes of ideal ego and ego-ideal. For if the "m(Other)" is "me," it must become installed and guard against the pretensions of "fraudulent" rivals. Social and political imposters must be fended off and destroyed. More than this, they must be "seen" to be destroyed, hence the macabresque. Behind acts of sadistic cruelty in the macabresque of genocide and mass atrocity, stands the narcissism of perpetrators driven by the inducements of "self-adoration." What greater forms of self-deception? Political self-adoration reflects disordered will, possessive, envious of rival claimants. Rivals who enter such claims who may appear to be the "same" but for "minor" differences threaten to eliminate difference and distinction. This threatens to defile the ego-ideal of existential "mihilism" and its demands for perfectionism. The "crime" of rivals is ultimately existential: they come too close to removing distinction in favor of identitarian identicality. Cultural forms of "sameness" that appear to operate in denial of difference threaten to erode the desire, nay, the demand to be "different."

Such threats, if realized, threaten claims for recognition. These claims are varied depending on political culture. People, nation, religion, and so on, stand in for the (vain) glorious narcissist schemes of "historic" and/or "divine" self-adoration. Minor identitarian difference thus becomes reified as the political justification of hatred because it and it alone looms as the prophylactic protection capable of shielding against the intrusions of "the dissolute other" who masquerades (too effectively) as the same as "us." Narcissistic self-adoration turns into fascistic hatred at moments when reified (paranoid) threats of lost difference or of the seeming incursions of cultural identicality become intertwined with a collective sense on the part of a mimetic group that lost distinction brings with it the sins of shame, humiliation, and lost honor. Anton Blok, in reviewing numerous conflicts, in Japan, the American South, in the Balkans, Rwanda, and Sri Lanka, for example, counterintuitively concludes that episodes of large-group political violence break out once political unity becomes threatened by loss of social or identitarian distinctions. Blok frames his analysis with a host of references. These include Girard's claim that "it is not these distinctions but the loss of them that gives birth to fierce rivalries."[54] Additionally, Blok[55] cites Pierre Bourdieu's conclusion that "social identity lies in difference, and difference is asserted against what is closest, which represents the greatest threat."[56] Blok speaks of "overdetermination" in the linkages between extreme violence and threats to collective identity and concludes, "The theoretical purport of the narcissism of minor differences suggests that identity—who you are, what you represent or stand for, whence you derive your self-esteem—is based on subtle distinctions that are emphasized, defended, and reinforced against what is closest because that is what poses the greatest threat."[57] Here again, we see how transposed alterity between the putative m(Other) and the political subject supports the social fantasies of difference against onslaughts of fantasized identicality. Such fantasies represent threats precisely because they appear to disentangle the ties that bind the political subject to what Murer, we shall see, calls the sense of "group-self."

THE RAGE OF PRE-OEDIPAL BLOOD FANTASIES

An additional way to interpret the social fantasies that percolate unconsciously in the formats of ego-ideals is to frame them as pre-Oedipal outcomes of failed personality or ego integration. Frosh for example, observes how "anti-Semitism is characterized by regression to preoedipal levels of functioning, and hence is associated with a wish for a narcissistic solution to the problems of reality, in which everything will be 'at one' with the self and no challenging differences will exist."[58] This social fantasy is indicative of psychosocial akrasia that "wills" collective existence to be based on "purity" and that "foreign," "polluting," "disgusting," "threatening," "intruding," "hateful," and so on, elements be destroyed or eliminated. Such disordered will fosters the political reifications and ideologies that in turn serve as interpellative calls for supremacist and exclusivist behaviors, particularly during instances of genocide and mass atrocity. Such appeals are readily incorporated into perpetrator justifications of the macabresque. Thus there is an Oedipal dimension to social fantasies of totalized "purity" of relevance to demands for cultural exclusivism and political supremacism. This is implied by Frosh's analysis of the anti-Semitic blood libel against the Jews. Frosh states, "The rigidity of formulaic but *unintegrated moralism* amounting to no more than a 'respect for force.' Oral and anal—that is, regressive and preoedipal—components dominate the mind and are revealed vividly in the accusations that the anti-Semite produces against the Jews. Thus, for example, oral aggression is witnessed in the accusation of the blood libel."[59] Frosh's reference to "unintegrated moralism" reminds one of the concept developed by Fonagy and colleagues with respect to secondary representations in which the imago of "the mother" or caregiver is dysfunctionally incorporated into the psychic development of an infant leaving the child unable to relate to both the object as real or the object as imago in ways that bring about genuine cathexis. Oedipal appeals conjuring up images of "blood fantasies" appear similar to the extent that they represent savage imaginaries imbued with the fixations of reification that have little or no bearing with "reality" but serve to embolden perpetrators unable to distinguish object from symbol.

The irony is that what is unconsciously despised is identitarian identicality conjured as difference in otherness. The social fantasy on which this regressive process pertains is also suggestive of the psychoanalytic metaphor of the phallus or the paternal law. Theoretically, this framework permits analysis of how human imaginative capacities to express symbolic meaning and to develop semiotic understanding develop by and through "entry into language" beyond the psychic structures of ideal ego and ego-ideal. Here again, Frosh's,[60] and indirectly Béla Grunberger's,[61] analysis of unrelenting Western anti-Semitism is instructive. Frosh suggests that the hated imaginaries reflected in the reification of Jews and the attitudinal predispositions toward internalized imagos of an all-knowing but authoritarian "father" are complementary. The Jew as the despised object becomes introjected, the imago of the perfect father is projected. Frosh writes, "Here the Jew is . . . acting as the recipient of hatred and split-off projections that attack the restrictive, Oedipal character of the father and yet allow the anti-Semite to maintain a loyalty to a loved father who is coded into various kinds of idealized absolutes: 'God, ideals, country and fatherland, etc.'" Such political reifications are readily formatted into ideological logics of illogic beholden to exclusivist and supremacist demands.

The psychodynamics of perpetrators' sadomasochism, therefore, reveal the mental mechanisms of introjection and projection. As Lacan noted with a question, "*At what moment, says Freud, do we see the possibility of pain introduced into the sado-masochistic drive?*—the possibility of pain undergone by him who has become, at that moment, the subject of the drive."[62] Lacan traces the theoretical loop of retroactive reversal when the object of sadistic hurt becomes the subject of masochistic pain. "At this moment, pain comes into play in so far as the subject experiences it from the other." Lacan elaborates, "The subject assuming this role of the object is precisely what sustains the reality of the situation of what is called the sado-masochistic drive . . . . It is in so far as the subject makes himself the object of another will that the sado-masochistic drive not only closes up, but constitutes itself." This formulation reconfigures but also reaffirms the validity of recursive explanations of the psychodynamics of transposed alterity linking perpetrators' motivations to "extimate" or external imprints on psychic formations of ego-ideal.

POLITICAL REIFICATIONS AS SUPEREROGATORY IDEALS

Political reifications thus become anchored to the self-deceptions deemed to "sanctify" macabresque violation by making them appear to perpetrators as supererogatory obligation. This is what Monroe observed and interpreted as Nazi supporters' ideals. The psychodynamics of perpetrators' hatred and reification often adhere to demonic kinds of political and eschatological theologies. Perpetrators, from the docks of the Nuremberg trials to the ranks of the accused and convicted in tribunals of transitional justice, consistently attest to their innocence. Often, they claim that the violations they fomented and often directed were done in the pursuit of noble calling. Such individual self-rationalizations emerge in case after case of genocide and mass atrocity, across the political spectrum. Perpetrators appear to "will" themselves into believing that they are the agents of high principle, inexorable cause, treasured history, goodness that is truth, and so on. In psychosocial perspectives, desire for the enjoyment of the macabresque arises within the mimetic interstices between collective political culture and individual perpetrator personality. This is also suggestive of Lacanian emphases on prosopopoeia, a phenomenon in which the speaker who speaks is psychically, ideologically, "absent," yet all the while appearing to be autonomous as an agent. From this perspective, speech becomes the product of the enunciations of address originating in third-person formats. Psychic processes of introjection and projection swing back and forth in the unconscious economies of self-deception and social fantasy, gripped by desire and manifested by ideologies of hate, at once masochistic and sadistic.

The very conceptual nomenclature of *ideal* ego and ego-*ideal* is not tangential to the significance of these ego formations in infantile unconsciousness. Ideal ego and ego-ideal emerge as the unconscious simulacra of wholeness and unity, integrity and completion, bonding and fulfillment. Primary psychic representations invested in the ideal ego are

precisely primordial in their subservience to bodily holism; similarly, the primary formations given to the ego-ideal are primordial in their proclivity toward bonding through
nurture and belonging on the basis of cultural affiliations. The intimate and inextricable
inter(*twin*)ing of body, parental bonding, and group belonging becomes fixed, indeed,
narcissistically fixated, in post-Oedipal ego formations. These appear to predispose
human subjects unconsciously to adore the body, "whole" and emotionally, under certain conditions that are conducive to conformity and obedience. This is transformed
into a want to imbibe the bonded group as a "whole." Ideal ego and ego-ideal formation
transfixes relations of subject to the self, so that the self is able to become not only a subject but also an object unto itself. The image of body as ideal ego is culturally molded so
that in time it will come to serve as the core symbol of the subject—objectified or reified.

On account of the body, subjects become symbols unto themselves. But the body is
not merely symbolic to the subject—that is, a body-self to itself. Rather, it acts as a testa-
ment to the meanings of physicality and meta-physicality as interpreted through the lens
of culture. Perhaps for such reasons, when mass atrocities and hate in the macabresque
occur, the means of assault often entail variations of bodily violation, for example, dismemberment, disemboweling, and evisceration, all meant to produce torment and agony
but in keeping with cultural significations. Additionally, ego-ideals appear to ground
social fantasies in pools of desires for self-identification through affiliation with large
groups, especially those associated with larger meanings, purposes, and designs. Such
groups take on the symbolic aura of the body of the subject and as such are transformed
into identities commensurate with the notion of a group-self that represents the incarnated ego-ideal. The body thus becomes a mastiff of cultural meanings and attitudes,
especially with respect to desire.

AGGRESSIVITY IN NARCISSIST FORMATIONS

During its earliest phases, human physicality is characterized by its frailties, premature
dependencies, and inability to control functional coordinates. Centripetal drives and
influences at progressive levels of consciousness counter physical but also psychic experiences of being enmeshed in centrifugal disaggregation. As a result, infants develop a
sense of their individuated wholeness, but only by renouncing the "realities" of the condition that Lacan describes as the *morcelized* body. For Lacan, this process of renunciation is primarily imagistic and "specular." Infants begin to develop an imago, that is,
self-reflexive capacities, as they come to know or recognize themselves according to the
reactions of others. Such representations serve as initial antidote against primary disabilities. Lacan's conception of aggressivity posits the psychic tensions between specular wholeness and physical fragmentation as keys to the initial or pre-Oedipal phases
of ego development in infantile consciousness. And because care is (or is not) given
at moments of wanting, needing, or at times of infant demands, pre-Oedipal experience across relational possibilities turns into disciplines of desire. Such reactions are

theorized as intrinsic to ego formations in the Imaginary. The ego remains gripped by the imago within what Lacan theorized as the psychic register of the Imaginary. The "normal" psychic and emotional task in human development is to break out of this hold in the Imaginary by "entry into language" with emergent capacities for symbolic expression and imaginative meaning in what Lacan also theorizes as the register of the Symbolic.

The psychodynamics of nurture, molded in the plays of desire and transpositions of alterity between infants and caregivers, in time inform how the ideal ego and ego-ideals become psychically constituted. Primary imago or representations in the Imaginary in structures of ideal ego and ego-ideals privilege congenital forms of narcissism, omnipotence, or "perfectionism." This is the import of psychic formations that cohere into "ideals." The body as a whole, the m(Other) as a unitary presence, each are transformed into lustrous apparitions that haunt human consciousness. These materialize into lifelong visceral insistence on the quest for "self-identification." Narcissist perfectionism gradually becomes modified by life's experiences. Aggressivity remains to the extent that the infantile quest for omnipotent demand assails individual personality. Such demands for idealized "identity" become nested at the core of earliest pre-Oedipal ego formations. They arise within the templates of primary psychic formations. These idealizations frame the identificatory acts attached to desire and to the transpositions of alterity in desire. The narcissism of ideal ego and ego-ideal formations resists moderation. As Chiesa writes, for example, "From the beginning of his psychic life, the subject both eroticizes and vies with his own self image since it constitutes the ideal perfection which the subject does not have."[63] Herein originate the theoretical grounds for suggesting the psychosocial linkages between primary representation in human personality and political ideology in mass atrocity and hate. What remains constant is a kind of narcissistic perfectionism attached to the psychodynamics of self-identification. From this psychosocial theoretical perspective, collective-identity constructions and ego formations are forged together in narcissism.

Narcissism represents the outcome of pre-Oedipal experience. The question in psychosocial terms is how and to what extent ego formations generate lingering effects in collective behavior. Some interpretations claim that the identificatory effects of ego-ideals contribute to identitarian conflict once large-group interactions become competitive or rivalrous. Identificatory patterns manifest narcissist demands for "difference" in otherness. Perhaps for these reasons, the psychodynamics of large-group behaviors often devolve into adversarial forms of opposition and conflict. Loss of status or distinction becomes an endemic risk to collective peace and toleration in the life of large groups, from city gangs to nation-states. *This is not to suggest that ideal ego and ego-ideal formations in infantile unconsciousness are somehow directly causal of large-group conflict, let alone of mass atrocity.* Rather, the Lacanian Imaginary as a theoretical perspective on infantile development suggests, first, that pre-Oedipal ego formations mutate into ideal ego and ego-ideals that usher in various psychic proclivities. These lend primacy to narcissist forms of bonding and to the desire for affiliations that bestow meaning and significance to the passage of life according to cultural disciplines.

But the Lacanian Imaginary also envisions this process in terms of the psychodynamics of transposed alterity in which what is exterior to the ego becomes intrinsic to its inner core. Although the cultural disciplines of desire are transmitted externally, they become the intimate artifacts of the interiorized human personality. As a result, desire resists satiation, while remaining psychically contrived and forever elusive. The subsequent narcissist search for completion in bodily wholeness and group bonding becomes a quest to quench the unquenchable. Denial of this under certain conditions of conflict, chaos, or threat culminates in disordered will and self-deception. Psychosocial theory and cultural perspectives thus can together be brought to bear in explaining the inexplicable in the macabresque beyond strategic or political necessity. This speaks to the tragic inevitability of the wide range of extremist and fascistic manifestations in political hate, from dark nationalist supremacism to terrorist violence, from racist extremism and popular authoritarianism to patriarchal misogyny.

The narcissism in the macabresque is detected in the arrogance of group aggression, but also in the insecurities of extreme defensiveness and paranoia. Narcissism in the human personality signifies a kind of psychic hollowness that invades the political subject and taunts it into behaviors recognizable by their anomic forms of paranoia and ego defensiveness. The more extreme the narcissism, the more unrelenting the psychosocial akrasia, and the greater the psychic and emotional pathology of what Fonagy and his colleagues called secondary representations. The theoretical argument from a psychosocial perspective is that narcissism is a basic feature of the psychodynamics of large groups. For such reasons, large-group behaviors tend toward infantilism and often shift toward paranoia or swerve toward aggression in ways that make them prone to violence. But the narcissism and the infantile aggression demonstrate the ineluctable grasp of ideal ego and ego-ideal formations in social fantasy—and the psychic unconscious demands that they be supported by means of ideological reification.

Narcissism and aggressivity represent the twin sides of the same psychic coin. Chiesa states, "Narcissism and aggressivity are thus one and the same thing . . . aggressivity differs from sheer aggression which is merely violent acting: the latter is just one of aggressivity's possible outcomes . . . aggressivity itself is, rather, a precondition of the subject's imaginary dimension, and can never be completely eliminated."[64] Narcissism and aggressivity, the pulsations between them as framed in these perspectives of psychosocial theory help to explain how and why some groups, acting under the influences of social fantasies molded by ego-ideals, engage in sadistic violence. Chiesa notes, "Aggressivity is the correlative tendency of a mode of identification that we call narcissistic, and which determines the formal structure of a man's ego and of the register of entities characteristic of his world." He continues, "As a consequence, the augmentation of aggressivity will be proportional to the narcissistic intensity of the subject's relationship with his own ideal image."[65] Aggressivity, then, is a function of the ego in the Imaginary and of the psychodynamics of transposed alterity in the formations of ego-ideals. Chiesa indicates, "The subject who, when considered as an ego is nothing but the consequence of an alienating identification with the imaginary other, wants to be where the other is; he loves the other only insofar as he wants aggressively to be in his place."[66] At primordial psychodynamic levels, where identifications of the subject tend to coil around reified images of ideal ego, as well as ego-ideals, narcissist aggressivity may indirectly influence disorders of collective will in large-group conflicts. Desire becomes the critical currency in such conflicts. Transpositions of alterity may provoke tensions regarding the psychodynamics of desire motivated by each group's claim to be the desire by which all desire is defined. As Chiesa adds, "The subject claims the other's place as the (unattainable) place of his own perfection."[67] This, in part, is what is meant by psychosocial akrasia, that is, demanding what cannot be granted, insisting that contingency become necessity, that in-group desire attain that status of desire in itself.

Willed forms of akratic motivation percolate out from the crucibles of primordial aggressivity gripped by the drive of ego-ideals and driven to control the seats of unconscious judgment, where the subject stands in judgment of the self. The psychic benchmarks of the akratic motivations and disordered willfulness caught in the ferocious grip of ego-ideals are measured in the metrics of the self-destructiveness stemming from aggressivity that has been laminated by overlays of narcissist vanity. "It goes without saying," Chiesa concludes, "that, for the same reason, this *ambivalent* relationship is also self-destructive."[68] This reveals the connections between transposed alterity in desire and supererogatory obligation or the moralistic excesses of political reification, contempt, and hatred. The so-called narcissism of small or minor differences refers, therefore, to variations in the rage experienced by members of groups, particularly, by perpetrators who identify themselves by what they deem to be the contrasts between them, but are assailed, sometimes even outraged—consciously or otherwise—by the very closeness or proximities in their perceived identities that render them more alike than different. It is this unwanted sense of sameness or identicality that transforms minor sociocultural or racial differences into powerful political reifications. These give expression to the misrecognized yearnings for the sensations of existential difference and, in extreme cases, to the akratic desires for supremacist nationalism or exclusivist racism or both. That this occurs becomes more likely once social fantasies are subjected to reinforcements of collective behaviors in genocide and mass atrocity that "normalize" the violence, thereby inviting the shift toward human violation in the macabresque.

Paranoia and Ego Defensiveness in Large-Group Conflicts

To what do identitarian differences across the social and political constructions of large groups refer? The answer points to the eponymous role of culture, to the substrata of cultural values and institutions that impart meaning and bestow significance in both personal and collective life. Culture is so much a part of what is mediated between social fantasy and political ideology in the composites of ego-ideals: social groups and political collectivities "live" in culture. The result is what Paul W. Kahn has labeled "political theology," that is, the composite of doctrines calling forth collective self-sacrifice in the name of national values and group identity.[69] In this view, individual subjectivities and group identities grow out of the inscriptions in social fantasy that foster political and ideological reifications. Sverre Varvin, for example, in his examination of xenophobia and Islamism, refers to an entire range of phenomena on the basis of psychosocial concepts and assumptions applied along these lines: "unconscious mental forces"; "primitive mental levels (undifferentiated and not well structured)"; social fantasies "related to common life themes"; "the collective memory of groups and nations of past traumatizations and humiliations"; "projection screens for the individual's and the groups fantasies which, in turn, take on a more violent form marked by primitive mechanisms such as splitting and projections," and so on.[70] If accepted as valid explanatory concepts and approaches, such psychodynamics appear manifest in the cultural values and associations established by ego formations during pre-Oedipal phases of infantile development; the second inference is that these psychodynamics are narcissistically driven and thus reveal the motivational features of disordered or akratic willfulness. How, then, to theorize this set of relationships, which are ultimately between influences of ego-ideal psychic structures and adversarial forms of political reification, in the psychodynamics of large-group conflict?

One set of possible responses is provided by reviewing the analysis of large-group conflicts suggested, first, by Hanna Segal and, secondly, by Jeffrey Murer. Each provides an alternative example of a psychosocial theoretical framework organized around the concept of ego-ideals; each presents an analytical version of the relationship between primary representation and political reification in large-group conflict. Together they illustrate the strength but also the limitations of focusing on the psychodynamics of primary structures in explaining large-group adversarial behaviors. Segal's analysis explicitly focuses on large-group paranoia and projection; Murer's examination, in turn, implicitly describes the unfolding of large-group conflict within analytical frames featuring group ego-defensiveness and introjection. Segal's concept of group paranoia and Murer's concept of ego-defensiveness both theoretically develop the implications of desire and transposed alterity in large-group conflict, but from opposing interior-exterior vantage points. Together they point toward the role of narcissist inscriptions in cultural manifestations of identity, and thus underscore the disordered motivational processes at work in the psychodynamics of mass atrocity, hate, and the macabresque.

GROUPS AS PSYCHOPATHS

Segal, for her part, embeds her analysis in the theoretical work of Wilfred Bion, whose studies expostulated a bimodal division in the internal psychodynamics of groups. Bion theorized the first set as that of a "work group" oriented to means-ends rationalities in task performance; but, in addition, he postulated the psychodynamics of what he named the "basic assumption group." The purpose of the basic assumption function was to manage the group's psychotic anxieties, which, he argued, inevitably arise in tandem with any group's task orientation. Segal thus turns her attention to the question of how the psychotic proclivities of large groups are manifested, in particular, how groups both reveal but control paranoid fantasies. She claims, for example, "Groups behave in a way which in an individual would be considered mad; for instance, almost invariably groups are self-idealizing, grandiose and paranoid."[71] In this, and citing Freud, she attributes the behavioral features of infantile identificatory aggression to large groups. She argues that members of groups project their ego-ideal and convert it into an idealized image that conflates the group with its leader, or in cases of leaderless groups, with a salient idea in order to relieve themselves of a pervasive sense of guilt, especially in cases of destructive activity that appears to demand the approval of a joint ego-ideal incarnated by the group itself.[72] Segal's interpretative language and approach bear direct resemblances to those of social and political psychology, particularly with respect to the dynamics of prototypicality. But her emphasis is on the unconscious forces at play within group dynamics, which in her view harken back to the psychic structures of ego-ideal. She thus speaks of the capacity to invest feelings of selfhood and "me-ness" into the groups with which participants identify and, as a result, for members to become submerged in group sentiments, feelings, or beliefs, especially if they inhere in vituperation and hate. "Our psychotic parts are merged into our group identity, and we do not feel mad since our views are sanctioned by the group."[73] Segal accepts the theoretical formulation of "group ego-ideal" and that it functions on the basis of a "tie being libidinal and linked with identifications." She, in effect, attests to the combined regressive-aggressive features of large-group behaviors and thus to the role played by such behaviors as supports for the fantasies in the Imaginary centered in ego-ideals.

In her view, ego-ideals tend to become suffused by the perfectionist demands that fire the psychotic and paranoid dimensions of large-group conflict. She states, "Such psychotic premises underlie, for instance, our sense of superiority to other groups, our unwarrantable hostility or fear of them, etc." Segal underscores the phenomenon of "splitting" to emphasize the parallel functioning of psychotic and non-psychotic behavior within large groups. "A large group, such as a state or nation, can also delegate such psychotic functions to subgroups, which are kept under control by the groups as a whole, for instance, the army." Segal warns of the dangers of "political groupings, whether national or ideological" and of their "paranoid mechanisms." She anticipates the so-called "monster theory" perspective on the collective need for enemies, such as Cold War fellow-travelers or internal subversives, and, more recently, dread of terrorists, who in these analytical frameworks are represented as the self-fulfilling prophesies conjured as a result of paranoid anxiety. "The enemy," Segal concludes, "must be presented as an inhuman monster. In genocide another element is added—that of contempt. The victim of genocide must be presented as not only inhuman, but as subhuman."

In Segal's psychosocial perspective, the very thrust of paranoid projection is, first, to externalize the fears, dread, and uncertainty internally experienced within groups; and, secondly, to give them a concrete form so that the sensations of internal dread can be projected back outward and thus onto the adversarial grouping now reified as "the enemy." Group identity thus appears to demand reification of the "other" so that in "willing" it to be "the enemy," the group sustains its own identity; this represents exercises in enemy-making. Paranoid fantasy is propelled outward. But the effects of such projection are to maintain internal solidarity within the group by envisioning the external enemy as its greatest threat. The enemy that is bedeviling the group fantasy is seen as a ghost that "returns," not from within the psychic parameters of the group, but rather from outside them. Such "ghosts" emerge out from the social fantasies motivated by primary representations that are thus ultimately sustained by the perfectionism of ego-ideals. This is the basic assertion of Bion's theory, as represented by Segal in her analysis of large-group behavior. "Basic assumption" large groups, in the sense Bion theorized, tend to transform ego-ideals into the paranoia of "group self-identities." The consequence of combined paranoia and projection is to risk transforming the transpositions of desire and alterity into the psychodynamics of dread, hatred, and political reification. Group cultures of "us-against -them" are projected outward and become reconstituted into paranoid mystifications of "them- against-us." This reinforces the psychodynamic conditions of denial and self-deceptions in ways that lend support to the group's social fantasies embedded in the perfectionisms of ego-ideal. This occludes understanding that the dread aimed against "the Other" originates within the interior psychodynamics of the large-group itself.

GROUPS AS SOCIOPATHS

Murer, for his part, examines the psychodynamics of large-group conflict by focusing on "the consequences of reifying projection." Murer privileges external interactions and influences during and after conflicts in the processes of large-group identity constructions. He rejects assertions that impute permanence or necessity to large-group identities. In contrast, he stresses change, fluidity, and the transformative potential of groups as a consequence of their interactions with each other—admittedly for bad, but also, Murer claims, for good. "Identity," he writes, "is a dynamic process that resounds to crisis; in other words, endangerment is often a significant source of identity formation. Individuals and collectivities form their identity through a series of threats, responses, and the narrative structures that chronicle those responses."[74] In so saying, Murer lends analytical primacy to external influences veering in on the conflicts among large groups relative to their internalized conceptions of self-identity. He suggests that the "continuities" of historical memory or narratives are thus subject to change and revision as a result of exterior intrusions. "Events provide information that either reinforces or alters individual or collective identity. Thus, the disruption of fundamental patterns of myths, symbols and collective memory affects the necessary notion of the continuity of collective narrative."[75] Murer, like Segal, remains analytically attached to the concept of ego-ideal as an explanatory device regarding large-group identity formations and perpetrator motivations, particularly in response to perceived external threats. He writes, "Large-group identity functions as an ego-ideal; it provides identity security whereby individuals can measure themselves against standards and attitudes that assess their level of social belonging."[76] Or later, "Reproducing the ego ideal is the condition of group entry . . . The adoption of the ego ideal is the development of the group ideal, the basis of group solidarity."[77] Murer indicates that the process of externalization extends from introjection back to projection so that "ego ideal is reinforced; shared identification is amplified."[78] Murer's analysis of "perpetrators of violence" underscores the role of self-deception in performative transgression. He points to "public enactment of identity," the aim of "committing 'heroic' acts under the economy of identity, the enactment of violent debasement" that "demonstrates the commitment of the individual self to the larger collective self through exposure to violence and to the enemy-other in oneself."[79]

Murer's view thus contrasts with that which Segal proposes via Bion and Freud. Instead of paranoid dread projected onto the adversarial Other at the behest of the influences of ego-ideal, the external Other becomes the enemy, so that, in Murer's words, "the individual ego is strengthened through the creation of protective barriers behind which the vulnerable ego can be reorganized, and the ego is validated through superegoistic validation that the individual self has done well."[80] Contrary to Segal's psychodynamics fueled by the processes of "Them-Against-Us," Murer envisions a process of "*Them In Us*," where the "Us" is the "self-enemy" constituting an interiorized "Them." This is introjected back onto the ego-ideal of the group to support internal cohesion and solidarity. Both Segal and Murer capture some of the essence of paranoid projection; whereas in the case of Segal, the primary dynamic is that of internal paranoid projection outward, in Murer's analysis the process entails social fantasy nurtured on the basis of external forces that internally sustain group identity and solidarity. Segal and Murer each suggests a variation in the polarity of transposed alterity, that is, "outside-in" (*Them Against Us*), or "inside-out (*Us Against Them*); but both subscribe to the psychodynamic analysis of large-group violence at structural levels denoted by ego-ideals. Whereas Segal indicates the centrality of projection outward, Murer emphasizes the significance of a psychic protective shield.

SEMIOTIC INITIATION AND ENTRY INTO LANGUAGE

How far do psychosocial explanations tied to ego formations help to explain large-group conflicts leading to atrocity, hate, and the macabresque? In psychosocial perspectives, the narcissism attached to ideal ego and the perfectionism of the ego-ideal appear to endow early ego formations with powerful associative effects in the psychodrama of social and political interactions. But beyond identificatory endowments, they are insufficient as units of analysis to establish the psychic or psychosocial characteristics of large groups consumed by hatred and political reification becoming the willing instruments of transgressive violence. This is in keeping with Lacanian theory that consistently subsumed ego formations in the Imaginary under the analytical primacy of the Symbolic realm or register. From this Lacanian perspective, the endpoint of Oedipal and post-Oedipal experience is precisely to struggle against the ego, to resist the narcissist and perfectionist blandishments of infantile omnipotence and anxiety. This is the precise psychoanalytic significance of Oedipal aggressivity, that it fosters emancipatory accession into the realm of creativity, language and semiotic signification and spontaneity.

ACCESSION INTO LANGUAGE AND THE STRUGGLE
FOR SUBJECTIVATION IN THE SYMBOLIC

The imago of self-unity borne by the fascination of the subject relative to bodily presence and physical integrity threatens to "kidnap" infantile ego development. So do the pre-Oedipal (partial) object(s) of nurture. Separation from the imagistic containments of primordial reification becomes a psychic exercise in the cosmic schemes of infantile self-worth. And this project is grounded in the modalities of what Lacan privileged as the Symbolic register. Primary representations in the Imaginary are viewed theoretically as inhibiting capacities for symbolization. The ego in the Imaginary creates but also battles against its imagistic captures of ideal ego and ego-ideals. The outcomes appear eventually to influence individual and collective capacities for moral and creative imagination. The question remains to what extent this allows individuals in groups to move beyond the isms of social and political reification. Primary representations are moored by infantile imagos. For this reason, Lacan declares, "The ego is structured exactly like a symptom. At the heart of the subject, it is only a privileged symptom par excellence, the mental illness of man."[81] Or as Richard Boothby extrapolating on Lacanian theory writes, "The imaginary institution of the ego is stabilized only at the price of a profound alienation of the subject from its own desire. The effect of this alienation is a profound misrecognition, or *méconnaissance*."[82] The tensions between the ego in the Imaginary and the desiring nature of the unconscious subject over and beyond the Imaginary results in chronic self-alienation but also in salutary engagement with the intrusions of the Symbolic.

Lacanian notions of aggressivity, therefore, suggest that ego formations struggle against infantile imagistic capture to open the way toward Symbolism and linguistic capacity in unconscious social fantasy. In keeping with Lacanian theory, language enters the unconscious capacities of the infantile subject and subjects' ego formations in the Imaginary, according to the rhythms and devices of the Symbolic register that produce meaning. The ego becomes transformed into a force or mechanism to challenge the circumscribed Imaginary. The consequence is that infantile unconscious progresses beyond the holds of ideal ego and ego-ideals.

But why leave the embrace of the Imaginary given its imagistic narcissistic or perfectionist comforts? The answer points to aggressivity in ego psychodynamics that function in ways that generate turbulence in the Imaginary. The ego is a function of the Imaginary but one that wrestles against the grasps of primordial reification. The ego defies the imagos and its overlays in primary representation. It seeks to decompose the imago of bodily unity and to reconstitute the binds of belonging imagistically sustained by ego-ideals. To enable infantile unconsciousness to process formations beyond those of ideal ego and ego-ideals is the precise task of the ego, but one which it resists. In such tempestuous ways, capacities for linguistic expression gradually replace the imagistic tyranny of primordial reification.

Several definitions and psychoanalytic approaches apply to the concept of "death drive." In the present context, it refers to the "death" of the imago, the hold of narcissist imagistic forms of physical omnipotence and bodily perfectionism. As Juliet Brough Rogers states, "In acts of violence we can say that there is no uncertainty—or there is a wish for no uncertainty. And it is for this reason that, in their performance, acts of violence to the self or to others bear the very definition of psychosis. For Lacan, the state of psychosis is a definitive alignment with, or submission to, the pure functioning of the death drive, to the point of *knowing* a singular reality. The performance of the psychotic act is then an enactment of *that knowing*, as an effort to produce *that reality* as a reality for all."[83] The death drive gives way to a life of living by opening the path to the Symbolic. Boothby indicates, "Thought is guided by structures belonging not to the perceptual register of imaginary forms but to the system of signifiers and the rules that govern it."[84] The failure of the death drive is the failure of what Lacan calls "the Letter" of the sign to become adequately inscribed in infantile consciousness. Such failures suppress critical capacities. Symbols represent renunciation, more than this, they provide the very possibilities for renunciation of the imagistic grasp of (m)Other. They hold out the promise of fulfillments beyond unitary completion and enchantment. Such renunciations in the Symbolic take shape during processes of turbulent mediation across the registers of the Imaginary and the Symbolic by inscribing signification to particular units of sensation in the body and across nurturing relationships. The undifferentiated plasticity of the Imaginary gradually gives way to the masochistic roughness of signifiers that in turn will open the way toward flexibilities of language and the discordant melodies of the Symbolic. If the Imaginary realm is one of smooth plasticity, the Symbolic realm is one of punctuation composed of the stop-and-go of linguistic percussion. Boothby indicates, "The coming-to-be of the subject beyond the imaginative entails the enactment of a certain primordial masochism that for Lacan is concomitant with the acquisition of the subject to a symbolic mediation."[85]

In this, Lacan is beginning to introduce the concept of the phallic and the psychodynamics of castration in terms of the struggle against the formations of the Imaginary, in order to allow accession into language, a process located at the juncture between the Imaginary and Symbolic.

From a Lacanian point of view, castration is the central moment of the child's acquisition of language not in the sense of its becoming able to voice words or to use them in some way (of this both the pre-Oedipal child and the psychotic are capable) but rather in the sense of becoming able to dwell in language, to rely on language for the guidance of thought and action, genuinely to appropriate language and to be appropriated by it. In and through castration, the speaking subject comes into being by becoming *subject*, by being *subjected*, to language.[86]

As Bruce Fink also indicates "[Lacan's] work on the relationship between words and the world (signifiers and 'reality'), and on the movements and displacements within language itself (metaphor and metonymy), provides the necessary linguistic basis for understanding the crucial role of the Freudian father." He adds, "The paternal function served by the latter is grounded in linguistics; his function is a symbolic one. His crucial role is not to provide love-as the politically correct popular mind is so likely to sustain to the exclusion of all else-but to represent, embody, and name something about the mother's desire and her sexual difference: to metaphorize it. Serving a symbolic function, he need not be the biological father, or even a man. It is the symbolic function itself that is essential."[87] At its core, primordial desire is sexual and forbidden, barred but substituted, sensed as deeply personally but entirely of an impersonal causality framed by an understanding of the transindividuation of human capacities for symbolism and for the abilities of symbolization embodied by and through words and speech.

The ego psychodynamics here tend to be partially effective, and only to varying degrees. The reasons for this underscore the limited abilities of some subjects to develop enveloping capacities for symbolization. Boothby, interpreting Lacan on this score, envisions these tensions between the registers of the Imaginary and of the Symbolic as the "axes" along which unconscious desire circulates. He contends, for example, that, "It is the conflict between the demands of the narcissistic ego, formed in the mirror phase and always tending toward the reestablishment of an imaginary coherence, and the resources of the symbolic system, in which is circuited the unconscious desire of the subject." Boothby adds, "The intersection between the two axes can therefore be taken to represent the necessity of symbolic castration; the necessity, that is, that the narcissistic bond of the ego and its objects must give way before the emergence of a speaking subject determined by its reliance on a symbolic code, a discourse of the Other."[88] Critical to the exercise are the pulsations of desire. The answer as to why primordial reification in the Imaginary accedes to the priority of Symbolic is the recompense offered or at least promised by the possibilities of desire that only come through the Symbolic.

Primordial reification in the Imaginary, therefore, provides a kind of constituted impediment to the Symbolic, a blockage that resists signification and surrenders its hold only reluctantly. The cost of psychic capitulation to the Symbolic comes high and remains fraught with incompletion. As Boothby observes, "But the work of castration that installs the subject in a symbolic function is never complete. The narcissistic substructure of the personality forever exerts its own gravity, drawing the symbolic process into the orbit of imaginary formations."[89] This tension or intrapsychic conflict between discrete individuated symbolism in language and speech, on the one hand, and unconscious holistic constructions, on the other, represent critical elements in framing how and in what ways cultural and ideological categories embedded in desire become converted into the psychodynamics of human development.

The Lacanian Symbolic, an Imperfect Route to Moral Autonomy

Lacanian theory posits the Symbolic as an artesian well for the in-sourcing and outpour-ings of desire. Simultaneously, it privileges the cultural impacts of the exterior m(Other). The lodestone of desire is always its otherness, its alterity; and language is its vehicu-lar instrumentality. Indeed, desire and its origins in alterity, language and its sources in otherness or transpersonality, are conjoined in Lacanian psychosocial theory as parallel, simultaneous, and mutually indispensable. Without desire, the language of the uncon-scious would not speak; and in the absence of language the unconscious could not desire. Since desire and language emerge in "m(Otherness)," Lacanian perspectives emphasize "extimacy" in the psychodynamics of desire and in the structures of language critical to subjectivity and the emergence of subjectivation. Desire is more than a stance toward the exterior universe beyond the subject of the self. For the world intrudes on infantile consciousness before the subject learns how to know itself through desire. External desir-ing is internally learned. It stems from the desiring of others who make their desires felt through nurture and by means of the impositions of language. Frosh cites contemporary psychoanalytic theory to stress this.

> Laplanche's theory has a range of connections with other psychoanalytic approaches, from the Lacanian mirror phase through Winnicottian notions of containment to recent developments on mentalizing such as of Mary Target and Peter Fonagy, who write, 'Unconsciously and pervasively, the caregiver ascribes a mental state to the child with her behavior; this is gradually internalized by the child, and lays the foundations of a core sense of mental selfhood.' They thereby insist on the primacy of the other in creating the child's sense of psychic reality. But what Laplanche achieves most profoundly is to indicate that the other is not just a container or mirror, in the Winnicottian sense, nor a purveyor of narcissistic fan-tasy, as Lacan suggests, but is *causal* in the constitution of subjectivity, profoundly passionate yet utterly mysterious, and right there at the center of psychic life. The parent no more intends this seductive message than does the child invent it; both are ensnared by it, as a continuing disruption in the unconscious."[90]

This is the great task of infantile development, how to learn to interpret "this seductive message."

Identity construction is an exercise in interpretation initially of caregiver or maternal actions, presence and departures, attentiveness and disappearances. The denominator is desire, the challenge is how to name it. The process of framing ideal ego and ego-ideals in the Imaginary engages infantile unconscious in naming the desire of the m(Other). The critical component in Oedipal theory of development is the functional indispensability of the third factor, the phallic or paternal metaphor. This serves as a signpost to subjectivation based on separation and individuation as bellwether to the cultural milieu that embeds familial relationships and social affiliations. A key component in this dynamic are the structures of language that in turn help to structure infantile unconsciousness in ways that support the gradual disciplining of desire, one's own as well as of others.

This process is also fraught with psychosocial implications. In 1967 Lacan presented a series of lectures on desire and the unconscious as a language. "The register of desire," he wrote, "must of necessity be constituted at the level of Table O, or in other words that desire is always what is inscribed as a repercussion of the articulation of language at the level of the Other." He adds, "Which basically means that we are always asking the Other what he desires." The desire to desire like capacities for language arise on a transpersonal basis. In this light, desire arises from the desiring of the Other, from what they "are" as desire. Transposed desire of the m(Other), particularly the Other's desire relative to Oedipal desire, anchors ego development in infantile unconscious. Lacanian conceptions of desire envision alterity as not only radical but also alienating on account of transpersonal impacts on the infantile subject. Alterity in desire thus privileges the transpenetration of exterior cultural and social forces in Oedipal psychodynamics over energetic physiology. Desire emerges through transposition; what is externally propelled becomes an inner compulsion. Transpersonal surrogates of desire masquerade as the "reality" of subjectivity in the unconscious. In the wake of the m(Other), the subject in some sense evaporates unto itself, a ship sunken, perhaps still visible but only as a glimmer from the depths. Butler, in her examination of Hegelian conceptions of desire, suggests, "This subject's desire is structured by philosophical aims: it wants to know itself, but wants to find within the confines of the self the entirety of the external world; indeed, its desire is to discover the entire domain of alterity as a *reflection* of itself, not merely to incorporate the world but to externalize and enhance the borders of its very self."[91] For Lacan, to the contrary, "dialectical" alterity functions *outward-in* through the positioning of language and its principal signifiers in the psychic structures of infantile consciousness.

Lacanian conceptions thus underscore the transpersonal processes of psychic development and cultural acculturation. The progenitors of Lacanian perspectives bear the marks of Ferdinand Saussure and Roman Jacobsen, but also Claude Lévi-Strauss. The basic proposition, as Anthony Wilden comments, is "to rebut the notion of the unconscious as an individual, intra-psychic entity, and to restore it as a function to the collectivity which in fact creates and sustains it." As Ian Parker has noted, "A Lacanian analysis of language emphasizes *form* over content. The interpretation of a text does not aim to uncover unconscious meaning that lies hidden beneath the surface, or even to retrieve the 'signified' content, the 'concepts' that Ferdinand de Saussure assumed to be attached to the 'signifiers' (the sound images). Rather, it is the organization of these signifiers in the text as such that is the object of study, and the formal structures of a text are decomposed by treating language, as Saussure did, as a 'system of difference *without positive terms.*"⁹² Lacan's view of the Other envisions it as a kind of cultural repository. Wilden states, "Lacan's point is surely that even outside the formal necessity of a collective unconscious as constituted through the objectively determined code of language itself, the unconscious, as the repository of personal and social myths, as the locus of socially approved hostilities, illusions, and identifications, could not be otherwise than collective." The grasp of the ego in the Lacanian Imaginary thus transmutes into the chains of the Symbolic in ways reflective of the collective metrics of culturally defined desire.

Language is the accompaniment that lends signature to subjectivity. Social fantasy is etched through semantic and phonemic constellations originating in otherness and desire. *Desire is epiphenomenal, the consequence of the transpersonality of cultures. But language is the phenomenon by which culture disciplines desire, and in so doing permits subjectivation to occur.* Desire and language are mutually implicated in infantile development. Lacan, referring to Heidegger, observes, "It means that language was there before man, and that is obvious. Not only is man born into language in precisely the way he is born into the world; he is born through language." Desire "speaks to itself" in linguistic formats molded by culture. Oedipal and post-Oedipal entry into language allows the infantile ego to cast ideal ego and ego-ideals aside and thus to slide beyond the immediacies of primordial reification. The Lacanian "subject" disengages from the Imaginary of the unconscious by means of language in the Symbolic register or order. Language is the lifeline of self-definition derived first and foremost from relations with others. Language is the currency, and desire the charge in this process. Acquisition of language represents a partial separation from primordial reification in the ego-ideals, but this is also a pyrrhic victory or, at least, a battle that must be constantly waged. In a sense, language joins the battle lines of the ego against the armor locked around the infantile imago of primordial reification. Linguistic mechanisms allow the subject of the unconscious to emerge beyond the blockages of ideal ego and ego-ideals. As a result of language and its constructions, the weapons of desire emerge by means of inscriptions wrought through signifiers.

What carries heft and weight in learning how and what to desire is the psychic invasion of what others desire, made known to the subject through language. The infringements of others' desire are conveyed by means of language; language captures desire as desire captures the unconscious. Desire adheres to symbolic parameters communicated through language and linguistic tropes, such as condensed metaphoric substitutions and metonymic chains of displaced associations. For these reasons, they give rise to the possibilities of creativity and imagination in desire. But even semantic freedom and creativity in and through language can become controlled by imagistic fixations in desire. When this occurs, political, specifically ideological conditions become readied for collective forms of akratic political behaviors that are distorted by the logic of illogics in reification.

This is often manifested in cases of racism, ethno-nationalism, and far-right extremist hatred. In such instances, constructions of collective identity become psychically distorted by the anamorphic refractions of ideal ego and ego-ideals. This translates into the flattening of the meanings of language. Segal refers to this as a "symbolic equation," concretized by means of political and social ideologies, or reified forms of language that narcissistically endow human physicality—that is, bodily, skin, or corporeal difference in general—with hatred, often in ways parallel to discursive or ideologically constituted forms of political self-adoration. In such instances, the interpretive capacities originating in the metaphors of language in the Symbolic are insufficient to counter the holds of ego-ideals in the Imaginary. Once social fantasy receives too much support from collective ideology, desire becomes realized or expressed in conformist ways reflective of ego-ideal.

Efforts to extrapolate psychosocial explanations on the basis of Lacanian theory begin with reference to pre-Oedipal mental figurations of ideal ego and ego-ideals in the Imaginary of primary representations. They culminate with emphasis on the Symbolic register, specifically, on how ensembles of signifiers comprise the unconscious. In this perspective, the unconscious represents a "mentalized" incarnation of signifiers. Signifiers are acoustic distillations based on the imagistic facsimiles of sound. They are comparable to the clefs of music, symbols on staffs indicating the names and pitches of the symbols that correspond to harmonic bars on a page of music. The unconscious is constituted in rivers of sound pictographs that undulate across the psychological or mental apparatus of mind and personality in sets of sequences. In Lacanian epistemological theory, signifiers are theoretically alleged to anchor human personality by forming around linguistic ensembles critical to the functioning of human psyche. As Fink points out, Lacan conceives of signifiers in terms of Freudian *vorstellungsreprasentänzen,* "ideational representatives," or what Lacan translates as *représentants de la représentants* (representatives of representatives) to refer to psychic representations initially of the libidinal Real, but later of *objet a* or desire that assume linguistic structures in social fantasy. Signifiers compose mentalized representations. They congeal around Oedipal desires; they are punctuated by separation fantasies. These transmute within the unconscious into sequential patterns of signifier-to-signifier "syntagms." Syntagms form "chains" characterized by diachronic elements, anterior associations that become retrospectively relevant to the unconscious fantasy in the present; synchronic elements are bracketed associations in the selection of sounds, images, and eventually, words that reveal the status of certain signifiers relative to others in unconscious processes of translating desire into speech.

Signifiers thus form mental associations indicating how and to what extent desire has become shaped in the unconscious. The general import of this approach is to underscore the role and impacts of associative chains in linguistic sequences for what Calum Neill aptly calls "the assumption of subjectivity."[93] Signifiers retain their capacity to represent the unconscious mind even after speech competency has been attained. Vanheule, in describing Lacanian linguistic theory, observes, "In the tradition of Saussure, the signifier is merely an element of differentiality that obtains identity in relation to other signifiers. What Lacan adds is that the speaker's use of the signifying chain has a further effect: the differentiality of the signifier determines human subjectivity."[94] From this perspective, (political) subjectivity becomes the retrospective outcome of syntagistic processes. Vanheule following Lacan adds, "This means that the subject is not conceptualized as a psychological entity that is articulated via speech, but as an 'emptity' resulting from references within the network of signifiers that make up someone's discourse: 'There's no other scientific definition of subjectivity than one that proceeds from the possibility of handling the signifier for purely signifying, not significant ends.'"[95] Lacan thus distinguishes the person who speaks of desire from the speaker whose speech "speaks" desire. The former remains partially blind or occluded from the structure of desire constituted by signifiers in the unconscious. As Dylan Evans indicates, "In designating the enunciation as unconscious, Lacan affirms that the source of ideological speech is not the ego, nor consciousness, but the unconscious; language comes from the Other, and the idea that 'I' am master of my discourse is only an illusion. The very word 'I' (*Je*) is ambiguous; as SHIFTER, it is both a signifier acting as subject of the statement, and an index which designates, but does not signify, the subject of the enunciation. The subject is thus split between these two levels, divided in the very act of articulating the *I* that presents the illusion of unity."[96] The central focus of Lacanian theory is not speech of the utterance. This obfuscates what desire is; it succeeds in prevarication; it gives birth to myriad self-deceptions; it gives rise to political and ideological reification. As Wilden comments, in his classic interpretation, "Lacan's point is surely that even outside the formal necessity of a collective unconscious as constituted through the objectively determined code of language itself, the unconscious, as the repository of personal and social myths, as the locus of socially approved hostilities, illusions, and identifications, could not be otherwise than collective."[97] As Lacan declares, "The communication function has never been the most important aspect of language." In this, the content of speech becomes relevant to psychosocial analysis for reasons of *what it hides* rather than in terms of what it is explicitly articulates. Rather, what counts theoretically is "the site of speech," "the subject not insofar as it produces discourse but insofar as it is produced [*fait*] . . . discourse . . . 'the signifier is that which represents the subject for another signifier', not for another subject." Vanheule summarizes this point by suggesting, "At the level of the message, speech functions to build images regarding who we are. These images make up the ego, but are selective imaginary self-presentations that exclude certain signifiers. The notion of the subject refers to these 'forgotten signifiers, across which it is fundamentally scattered;' hence the idea that the subject is divided."[98] Herein lies the core of the Lacanian philosophy of speech.

IMPURE QUESTS FOR PURITY

In this light, inquiry turns to the perplexing question of human "motivation," how it functions and with what effects. So many sectarian divisions and so much ethnic or racialized hatred inhere within the psychodynamics of disordered will that is manifested by political reifications of purity. Difference in otherness is deplored; illegal aliens, boat people, and economic refugees, as well as domestic minorities across many multiethnic societies are "willed" to be inferior, subordinate, marginalized or exploited, and, ultimately, existentially damned or politically condemned and thus subjected to the devices of hatred— all in the name of a willed essentialism that reifies "purity." Purity is an assertion of the essence of essence, as it were, in denial of open contingency. Purity as an essentialism insists that social and cultural categories become naturalized and thus transformed into axiomatic absolutes rather than sociological probabilities. Such essentialism reveals the psychodynamics of disordered will. During mass atrocity, relationships between fantasies of "purity" and illogics of hatred are illustrated by Robbie Duschinsky's analysis of the cultural implications of "purity." Duschinsky begins his examination with implied reference to the phenomenon of introjection and projection by pointing to Julia Kristeva's concept of "the abject." The abject represents the impure that must be flushed away from the body, and thus from any corporeal system, including the "body politic." Duschinsky, following Kristeva, writes, "subjects strive to achieve a state of purity, wholeness and autonomy by symbolically closing up the body through the categorical divisions of language." He continues, "In the maintenance of our 'clean and proper' categorical divisions, we engage in a continual attempt to sequester or destroy the hated bodily matter that necessarily underlies but also disturbs our experience of the world. Kristeva terms this 'jettisoned' matter out of place 'the abject.'"[99]

The concept of the abject plays out in the analysis of the psychodynamics of hate and political violence. But Duschinsky lays the groundwork for assessing how "purity" relates to the process of subjectivation, particularly in relation to the overlays of primordial and political reification, from formations of ideal ego to ego-ideal and beyond into the register of the Symbolic. He states, "Purity as a discourse is irreducibly tied to processes of *subjectivation*, the material and discursive factors that organize the assemblage of social and psychological relations that constitute an individual actor." He adds that "when mobilized, purity discourses arrange and shape the experience, knowledge and desires of actors, managing or resisting existing forms of meaning, emotion and power–relations."[100]

A silent code of power pervades the discursive representations of purity. Purity implies inclusion based on exclusion; and the exercise of exclusionary doctrines demands that power be used to ensure that "inclusivity" remains "pure." Purity transformed into ideological doctrine in mass atrocity or genocide demands the supremacist domination of the state, internally within sovereign borders or externally with respect to boundaries or perceived threats to national security and nationalist supremacy. Purity doctrines cast in terms of exclusivism demand unsullied forms of inclusivity that eradicate "impure" polluting influences or corroding forces. Political or collective imaginaries beholden to purity enthrone the status of those within the metaphysical "circle" of "the chosen" whether canonically contrived or ethnically constituted. Duschinsky comments, "The ascription of purity or impurity is a contingent discourse mobilized by subjects or institutions in order to enact a covert form of metaphysics." He adds that this "places the speaker in the position of being able to legitimately judge between the essential and the inessential."[101] This provides a kind of remit "for occluding the contingency of an essential ideal, and for regulating those physical and social elements thereby classified as essential or inessential."[102] In the psychodynamics of hatred, the power of purity is asserted as nothing less than the right, nay, obligation, to determine, in Judith Butler's terms, whose life is grievable

and whose life is entirely dispensable. "To gain access to a felt sense of justification or absolution in the face of the judging ideal, purity can mandate an agonized, incremental work
on the self—or *on others*.[103] Essentialist purity thus becomes transformed into reified versions of ideological validation for "work on others" that includes performative violation
in the macabresque spaces of hate and mass atrocity. As Duschinsky concludes, "What is
erected through appeal to purity is, rather, *a spectrum of subjectivities embedded in a matrix
of power-relations*" that guarantee the sense of superiority perpetrators narcissistically
demand. Perpetrator motivations intersect with such unwillable demands for a freedom
to exert power over others as a symbolic end in itself, beyond purpose or objective, except
for that emanating from delusions that conflate power and purity.

SELF-CONSTITUTIVE CRITICALITY OF THE SUBJECT RELATIVE TO THE SELF AS THE BASIS OF PRACTICAL ETHICS AND "IDEALS"

Psychosocial akrasia, however, does not mean to suggest that the capacity of perpetrators to engage in symbolic meanings in ways that presuppose moral autonomy are totally
diminished. Conceptions of moral autonomy framed by Lacanian interpretations of
existential "lack" posit a radically self-constitutive ethical subject, notwithstanding the
imagistic tyranny of ego-ideals. Neill envisions human subjectivity and capacity for ethical judgment as morally autonomous. But he also suggests that the exercise of moral
autonomy must be constantly tempered by a dedication to radical self-inquiry. Herein
lies the nature and significance of the Symbolic register and of language and meaning. It
permits purposive motivation oriented to critical self-reflection rather than self-deception as a measure of the qualities of not only the imaginative life, but also the political.
This underscores the possibility of ethical subjectivity that is revealed in constant self-
questioning, in a kind of profound humility toward normative certainties and unfailing
skepticism toward reified absolutes. Neill, echoing Christine Korsgaard's Kantian moral
ontology, proposes a Lacanian ethical sensitivity chastened by perpetual self-reflection,
a morality that constitutes itself by and through its self-interrogation. "The moment of
subjective assumption, as we have seen, is the possibility of the ethical precisely because it
is without guarantee," Neill declares. "In the pure assumption of subjectivity, the subject
so assumed necessarily assumes the weight of responsibility not only for its own constitution but also the parameters and configuration of that which it would experience."
A morally autonomous imagination and spirit thus seeks to problematize its encounters with the other, conceived of as other persons, but also as "the m(Other)" of cultural values, attitudes and shared beliefs. Boundaries between the ethical subject and the
m(Other) in ethical encounter become open, permeable, characterized by porous inner
and outer pathways of interiority and exteriority, open to revision, permeated by lack and
the absence of foreclosure. These qualities revel in the precise opposition to reification at
all levels of "overlay."[104] For reification adheres to its absolute certainties, absolutes, attitudinal closures, and ideological foreclosures. Reification, especially political reification,

reveals a diminished capacity for ethical imagination and a willed denial of the possibilities of ethical subjectivity and moral autonomy. Neill continues, "If the subject is irreversibly responsible for not only the position it would itself assume but, inseparable from this, it is responsible for that which it would encounter, then any conception of the other the subject would seek to maintain is necessarily *of the subject*. That is to say, it would be the subject's conception, and would, thus, neither be adequate nor inherent to the other." Neill adds, "And yet, so dislocated, the subject emerges as the possibility of that which would experience the Other, that which would encounter the other without any such experience or encounter ever being definitive."[105]

Neill thus outlines how Lacanian conceptions of ethical subjectivity adhere to notions of self-examination and self-constituting doubt in opposition to the political reifications of perpetrators, whose infantile narcissism and political perversity in skewed absolutizing forms of desire inflame social fantasies of exclusivism and supremacism that are formatted in racist terms and configured around the ideological logics of illogic. Such reifications admit of no uncertainty, but on the contrary, become configured around totalized, absolutized certitude. Neill citing Lacan indicates, "The 'normal subject' . . . is not concerned with certainty, only the psychotic is concerned with certainty. Which is precisely to mark certainty as a delusion." But is delusional fantasy on which political reifications depend necessarily psychotic? Neill establishes the basis for investigation when he states, "Where the psychotic subject would be characterized by the structure of foreclosure such that it would admit of no lack in the Other . . . such, that is, that it would attain to a certainty, the neurotic subject . . . would precisely encounter the Other as lacking, as incapable of providing that ultimate guarantee for the symbolic order in which the subject would find itself." From this perspective, perpetrators act with the ideological certitude that erodes moral autonomy. This is in the very character of political reification permeated by hatred. Perpetrators behave in willful denial of the lack in the Symbolic order as if the lack in victims, once destroyed, would alleviate existential lack for all time. Perpetrators of the macabresque act in willful denial, to repeat a Lacanian refrain, "of the lack that is the lack of the Other." And thus, from the perspective of Lacanian and ethical subjectivity, mass atrocity, political extremism, and hatred represent the violent behaviors gripped by absolutized social fantasies and constructed around ideological formats and iconic imagistic certitudes that are "infantile" in their quest for Oedipal, indeed, phallic omnipotence. This is their ultimate pathos, the infantilism of perpetrators motivated by absolute power and perverse desire for sadistic transgressions and thus the macabresque of performative transgressions.

EVACUATION OF THE SIGNIFIER IN THE SYMBOL

But such infantilism seeks to reduce semiotics to "bare" object without symbolic reference. As Boothby observes, "what is primordial to the birth of symbols." He writes, "Unlike the perceptual gestalt, which offers to consciousness an enduring and unitary form in the midst of a surrounding field, the linguistic sign must evacuate its own status

as an image in order to fulfill its signifying function." He later adds, "The child's accession to language requires a measure of escape from anchorage in the imaginary, an escape
that results in a general qualification of the force of images in favor of signs and the system in which they are imbricated."[106] Signification is the basis for mental, cognitive, and
imaginative activities. But the key is that it fosters mobility by negating its own status as
a system of signs and accedes to linguistic systems that surrender to the Symbolic. How
this is accomplished depends on cultural articulations imported through and by means
of the impacts of nurture and the extent to which such expressions foster certain kinds
of developmental capacities, in particular the ability to symbolize beyond the immediacy of images. "The perceptual body of the sign," Boothby states, "is merely the jumping
off point, for a structured reverberation across the network of relations that constitutes
the sign system." He continues, "The power of the sign to signify thus requires that the
sign not be seen as an image. The life of the sign is predicated upon the death of its own
image."[107] *The death of its own image is ultimately constituted by the birth of mystifications,
particularly concerning the body and desire. In instances of ideology and collective political
reification, demagogic "logics of illogic" spew imagistic constraints on any symbolic or ideological system. The symbolic system becomes a cover-up of ideological reifications that obscure
the closures and contradictions that beset social fantasy (and reality). The word becomes the
image, the image the symbol, the symbol, the reality, the reality, the word. It is a lethal exercise in symbolic equation or compression.*

This is what "hate speech," what Butler calls "excitable speech," is and does. Hate
speech incarnates the image in the word as a symbol. The symbol becomes constrained
by the action intended by the word such that the "action" *is* the word. Thus the word
becomes action. Hate speech represents a performative speech act, in Austinian terms,
a commissive designed to "do" hate. The intentionality that inheres within the word
becomes actionable by virtue of the image that the word "is" in itself. Hate words give
offense: they hurt, humiliate, cause others to suffer—but all on account of the collapse
between word, symbol and, meaning into the molds of specific images, symbolically conveyed but communicated in a scheme of fixed or reified cultural reality. Lacan theorizes
identity and subjectivity as a series of "events" denoted in the appearances and disappearances of signifier-to-signifier chains. This harkens back to Murer's point that identity is
constant but only to the extent that it is given over to flux and reformation. This helps to
mark the points of unconscious resistance undertaken by perpetrators as well as by large
groups caught by fixations of political or ideological reification or both.

Here again the effects of psychosocial akrasia is to "will" identity to be fixated by and
through binaries that occlude recognition of the epiphenomenal status of collective as
well as personal identities. Vanheule encapsulates Lacan's "parasitical" concept of language.
"Lacan affirms its status as a foreign body for the speaker. It is something that has an effect
on the speaker's being, largely beyond consciousness and intentional control. As a consequence, words inaugurate a deluded stance towards oneself: 'It is from language that we hold
this madness that there is being.' "[108] Vanheule draws the implication, "By using language we

fictionalize our being and live with a fictionalized account of ourselves as if we were a character in a story; it therefore creates a generalized form of madness in everyone."[109] Madness in the forms of psychosocial akrasia thus defines the relationship of Lacanian conceptions of language and primordial reification to the psychodynamics of political and ideological reification. On this basis, it would appear, Lacan would have no difficulty in describing large-group conflict, let alone mass atrocity, hate, and genocide, as outcomes of "the madness" of "fictionalized identity" constructed by and through accession into the Symbolic but beholden to the languages of social fantasy, the realm of signifier assembly.

Lacanian theory, therefore, stresses that the unconscious is structured "as a language." This analytical perspective juxtaposes the psychic role of metaphoric distinction, grammatical syntax, and punctuation and of metynomic chains of signification in the Symbolic realm of language. Lacanian theory proceeds to connect alterity of desire, transpersonality, and linguistic signifiers with social fantasy on the basis of the role and impact of Oedipal psychodynamics articulated through and by means of metonymic substitutions and metaphoric condensations. The origins of identity stem from the cultural modalities imprinted in the unconscious by the signifiers of language and its tropes framed in and by metaphoric constructions and metonymic chains. Lacanian theory suggests that desire as social fantasy functions across a set of displacements from one signifier to another to another in metonymic sequences; it also operates in metaphors "buttoned" by "master-signifiers" as the result of condensations where particular signifiers become foregrounded in the unconscious. Metaphors punctuate transpersonal desires by riveting certain pivots that Lacanian theory associates with a "quilting" process in the unconscious. This involves Oedipal "castration" by means of which the unconscious grapples with psychic distantiation in relationships of desire. The shift from ideological personality to character in political integrity is the shift from imagistic value certainty to symbolic ethical criticality.

We must now focus on sadism and the psychodynamics of phallic separation. This yields Lacanian interpretations of *jouissance* and *objet a*, both of which are critical to an understanding of perpetrators actions of displayed cruelty in the macabresque. As Lacan concludes, "The sadist himself occupies the place of the object without knowing it, to the benefit of another, for whose *jouissance* he exercises his action as sadistic pervert." Perpetrators thus envision themselves as acting in the name of personal self-sacrifice while psychically gripped by perverse sadism. Palacios encapsulates this by stating, "Lacan enters his *Lacanian-twist* here, however, and adds that anxiety is not 'without an object'. What he seems to have meant by this is that anxiety is not related to lack, incertitude or the fear of losing something; on the contrary, anxiety (as in the case of the uncanny) is related to the experience of 'excess', of something being 'too much', a 'too close' presence of the object."[110] This orientation to *jouissance* features the power of excess, or too much, relative to primordial desire and return to forbidden ecstasy. The irony, here, is that the impact on subsequent subjectivation is a yearning for the lost object that appears first in fantasmatic forms, but out of which spin a range of ideological supports driving the sadistic excesses in the macabresque.

6

Perversity in the Performative

SADISM AND SHAME IN THE MACABRESQUE

DRAMATURGY AS METHOD

What does it mean to take performativity seriously? As we have seen, much of social–political psychology in the study of genocide, hate, and mass atrocity steels itself against the methodological risks of casting inner or personality features of the self as causal dimensions of agential or subject behaviors. What appears to be most methodologically dreaded is explaining what subjects do or say based on the presumed overdeterminations that might be derived if any set of political or social motivations were attributed analytically to the unconscious. In my view, this distorts the character of political behavior and renders political and social psychology epistemologically suspect, not merely despite—but precisely on account of—the nature of their empirical assumptions and methods, as I sought to demonstrate in chapter 2. This avoidance of psychosocial phenomena results in analytical overreliance on cognitive processes of self-rationalization, as demonstrated by the repeated references to processes of self-identification and prototypicality. That said, the group dynamics so critical to social psychology are highly suggestive of an alternate set of analytical perspectives, focused on dramaturgy and theatrical performance not as secondary to the daily interactions of everyday lifeworlds, but as representative of the very core nature of all quotidian social relations.

To live is to live among others and to assemble and participate in relationships organized into clusters and categories in and through what Erving Goffman called the "presentation of self in everyday life." Indeed, Goffman has much to say about performativity as an epistemological approach and methodology that is relevant to the study of macabresque. "Perpetrators" are first and foremost perpetrators who operate at the behest of each other. What they do tends to be filtered through the refracted perceptions of each other on stage and on display. Such behaviors may be likened to "performances" for the benefits of other perpetrators who constitute a body of witnesses as well as a "command" audience. The macabresque does not cause mass atrocity. Once mass atrocity breaks out, however, the macabresque becomes an end in itself. Mass atrocity is thus the means toward the staging and the execution of transgressions. Taking performativity seriously thus demands an exploration of the theoretical or explanatory implications of this. And one clue is the tendency to transform collective violence into intense individual personal bodily violation. Sado-intimacy in the macabresque situates perpetrators and victims on the stages of performative transgression time and again during episodes of genocide, hate, and mass atrocity. Performativity represents an approach to examining these and similar social behaviors, particularly those that are staged, as in the macabresque, with emphasis on how actors perform and why.

In the present context, performativity focuses on the "interiorities" of desire, anxiety, and fantasy in relation to the "exteriorities" of political power, social hierarchies, cultural hegemonies, and collective ideologies. Performativity as a methodology stresses the recursive psychodynamic factors connecting human personality and the social and the political: the incentives, or "pulls," of collective violence and the "push" of human desire. Richard Ned Lebow identifies what he calls "three fundamental motives that reflect universal human needs—appetite, spirit and reason." Lebow notes that the concept of "spirit" represents "the motive more or less ignored by political science." Lebow defines spirit in contrast to reason as "the universal drive for self-esteem." He suggests, "By excelling at activities valued by society we win the approbation of those who matter and we feel good about ourselves. Institutions and states have neither psyche nor emotions. However, the people who comprise and run them do. They often project their psychological needs on to their political units, and feel better about themselves when those units win victories or perform well."[1] Performativity focuses on such political "spirits"; in instances of mass atrocity it would examine, for example, how capacities for self-esteem becomes transformed by dysfunctional psychic and emotional economies that combine variations in the psychodynamics of narcissism, shame, sadistic cruelty, self-deception, hatred, and political reification, etc. How and why these processes occur requires analysis of group dynamics with stress on the linkages between social fantasies and political ideologies. Performativity as an analytical methodology thus takes us beyond reason, rationality, and even rationalization, in ways that underscore the relationship of human personality to the dark aesthetics of shame and sadistic cruelty.

To study the staged or performative transgressions of victims, to explain the systematic processes of sadistic cruelty borne by the apparent desire on the part of perpetrators to be participant in or witness to the collective dying of victims, requires analytical orientations beyond those focused exclusively on motivations cast in rational or rationalizing, cognitive or purposive strategic terms. Concepts of motivation framed in terms of impulse-cognitive-strategic rationalities or purposive rationalizations may be methodologically appropriate in certain analytical contexts. But they are insufficient in relation to mass atrocity, hate, and the study of genocide, because they fail to examine motivations in methodological frames beyond those limited to notions of rationalist or rationalizing calculations within groups or command structures. Performativity as a theoretical perspective establishes the explanatory relevance of the unconscious in appraising the dynamics of desire, shame, and sadistic cruelty among perpetrators. Various psychosocial perspectives may be adopted in this regard. Indeed, there may be gains in analytical insight that derive from application of multiple perspectives, since any single one is limited in scope. Which psychosocial theory to apply in any given instance depends on explanatory emphasis and the pertinent questions. With respect to the macabresque, for reasons I suggested in chapter 5, distinctions between ideal ego and ego-ideal, as well as discussion of the psychodynamics of Oedipal development and the laws of phallic separation, are especially relevant. To illustrate this, I applied Lacanian approaches to desire and extrapolated from his perspectives on the psychic registers of the Imaginary, the Real, and Symbolic to derive certain interpretations of the vectors of narcissism. Building on this, I now focus on sadomasochism and shame in the macabresque of genocide, hate, and mass atrocity.

Sadistic behaviors are not only cruel; they also demand that the cruelty be displayed in the name of the laws of prohibition that are aimed at keeping what Lacan called *jouissance* away. The sado-intimacy at the core of human degradation in the macabresque may in part be explained in psychosocial perspectives as precisely this: the demand that victims declare the phallic law of separation from *jouissance* by dramatizing how human personality becomes grasped by torments of desire. This suggests how situational and cultural factors influence perpetrator behaviors. For the situational features that influence the demands for sadistic cruelty are those in which social disintegration, humiliation, and loss appear to threaten the stability of social order in ways that promise the release of what is most dreaded, *jouissance* itself, and thus dissolution into a plenitude beyond human capacities to know or experience. Perpetrator behaviors in mass atrocity demonstrate the psychic elements of emotionality and fantasy, paranoia and obsession. Group dynamics in the macabresque ebb and flow in the subterranean tides of anxiety and psychic desire made manifest by reifications and sadistic hate, a central focus of study in the analysis of perpetrator performativity.

Core methodological issues here pertain to the psychosocial study of groups, in particular, of perpetrators in the macabresque given over to sadistic forms of violent cruelty and of the victims made to suffer: what are "groups"; how are they named, framed, and constituted; what are the critical bonds of belonging and shared association in sadism that comprise the "group life" of perpetrators; what are the psychodynamics of intergroup hostility, and why do certain groups become perceived as threats and subject to sadistic victimization by means of the macabresque? To explore this, I begin with Goffman's theory of performativity and a brief review of Feldman's discussion of reciprocated violence in the H-Block wing of the Belfast prison at a pivotal moment of the Northern Ireland conflict. I then examine Kleinian and post-Kleinian interpretations of infantile sadism, and conclude by focusing on Lacanian perspectives on sadism and its demand that the law of prohibition be declared. This discussion anticipates Part III, which analyzes case studies in which cultural values and meanings shape the ways sadistic cruelties are made to occur in the macabresque.

PERFORMATIVITY ACCORDING TO ERVING GOFFMAN

For Goffman, to be human in a social sense is to be an actor on stage, constituted by our developmental history of experience on that stage, open to its blandishments, disciplined by its punishments, constrained by its values and ideologies, beholden to its structures of power. The histories we recount, the stories we tell, the narratives we cast into the shapes of our autobiographies do not merely represent the products of our lives; rather, they are how we transform the sense of self and of an *I* into the means by which we produce our identities, that is, the many *me*'s in the world in which we struggle for cosmic value. We stage these struggles, and we bear witness to our own and to those of others, and as we do so, mimetic comparisons are never far away. For Goffman, therefore, subjectivity is artifice; the subject is an artifact. We may hide away behind closed curtains of the self, but as human subjects the curtain is always open to self-judgment, to the assessments of others, to recognitions of success but also of failure, to the impulses of honor as well as to the compulsions of shame. Our personality traits and moral features are reflections of the normative order of society introjected into the roles we play and, in particular, into how we play them as we project ourselves, our "faciality," into the public places of social inter-action. Goffman aligns his self-presentation theory to the comedic traditions originating with the oeuvre of Molière; identity is but a "mask" each person chooses to wear. But the choice of the masks to present depends not entirely on the self. The masks themselves take shape according to how society molds them. Social norms and personal moralities are attached to what individuals do in and by means of social performances, and they retain significance against the background of the meanings attributed to them by others. We "frame" meanings, but "meanings" are framed for us by social orders and the posi-tional arrangements or structures within them. Goffman speaks of "dramatic realization" to underscore the many ways persons behave to add greater definition to how they wish to be perceived and understood. Dramatic realization often leads to gratuitous or extra-neous actions to reinforce self-identities at the intersections of group relations.

Goffman, like Foucault, attempted to define the degradations experienced in situations of confinement when the latitudes for choice and action become spatially compressed. He developed an analytical lexicon to describe what happens when persons are subjected to institutional or carceral conditions in which their autonomy for self-presentation becomes highly or severely restricted. These include "*role-dispossession*" and the enforced elimination of role-playing and the absence of possible identity constructions based on roles; *"programming an identity trimming"* so that the past autobiography or a sense of personal life continuity becomes disrupted; *"dispossession of name, property, and 'identity kit'"* occurring whenever personal identity becomes subsumed or secondary to the superimpositions of the personal markers inscribed on the incarcerated as prescribed by institutional powers; *"imposition of degrading postures, stances, and deference patterns"*; *"contaminative exposure"*; *"disruption of usual relation of individual actor and his acts"*; and *"restrictions on self-determination, autonomy, and freedom of action."*² Goffman, in outlining these processes of degradation and theft of dignified personhood, traces the effects of subordination at the initial phases of dramaturgical performance. He underscores the relevance of group dynamics among staff "performers" as they impose themselves on the confined. These include what he names as "dramaturgical loyalty"—that is, how staff signal their loyalty and their clandestine purposes to each other to protect against outside intrusions; "dramaturgical disciplines" to maintain consistency in behaviors and "dramaturgical circumspection" with respect to what is done inside the institution relative to what is seen to be done from the outside.³

MORTIFIED IN THE QUASI-MACABRESQUE OF "SYMBOLIC GENOCIDE"

In cases of penal and other carceral institutions, dramaturgical dynamics on the part of correctional or institutional staff often produce among inmates what Goffman describes as *the mortified self.* The subject of the self withers and struggles for a refraction of itself under circumstances in which intrusive personal violation represents the daily norm.⁴ Goffman's vision of social performativity has thus brought us to the edge of the macabresque. But is there a kind of performativity that approximates the macabresque but does not enter its dramaturgical universe. In cases of political imprisonment or torture, prison or guard brutality assumes a quality of wanton violation, tantamount to the symbolic weight of the sadistic cruelty we witness in the macabresque. The extent to which political imprisonment represents life and death in the macabresque, however, depends on whether or not and the extent to which latitude is available for prisoner autonomy even under conditions of violent duress.

Allen Feldman's study of terror violence in Northern Ireland, for example, addresses the question of "symbolic genocide" as narrated by those caught up in the "war-zone Communities of Belfast," and of the vile and violent interactions between prisoners and guards that reveal how groups subject to "mortification" can sometimes enter a performative dynamic of body and sinew, of muscle and excretion, close to pure animality yet seized by the possibility of political testimony and emboldened by the dignity of resistance. For those caught up by the exigencies of resistance, "Death has its oral history that is organized around the allegory of symbolic genocide. The genocidal allegory is constituted by part objects and part narratives that refer back to the absent whole, the completed erasure of ethnicity and ethnic spaces."⁵ He adds, "The metaphor is built death by death, and each death expands the negation of ethnicity from the household, to the street, to the neighborhood, until the outer limits of ethnic identity are made to coincide with the outer limits of ethnic erasure."[6] But in posing the question in this way, Feldman helps us to understand what may be the unique quality of the macabresque; and in this context the numbers of victims do matter. It is in the very inability of large numbers of innocents to engage in reciprocated violence against perpetrators or counter their egregious malevolence by engaging in self-sacrificial actions to oppose it that lends victimization in the macabresque its peculiar quality.

Feldman cites Girard's theory of sacrificial violence. "For Girard, the passage out of mimetic violence is the repetition of violence via a circumscribed form that terminates uncontrolled desymbolization. Because mimetic violence has dominated collective representation, the new modality resymbolizes by reorganizing social representation."[7] But does the macabresque in mass atrocity allow for resymbolization of violence in the absence of reciprocal exchanges of violence in which self-sacrifice is able to promote a new social order? Arguably, one of the core features of the macabresque is that it suffocates any capacity for reciprocity on the part of those subjected to it, not because victims go to slaughter "like sheep," but on account of the horror experienced in the macabresque that paralyzes the soul and the spirit of resistance. Feldman continues, "Girard links the mythic code of sacrificial expulsion, exile, or differentiation to cosmogenic rites, salvation myths, and origin narratives. These narrative codes point to the formation of polity around excluded negativity or absence." But forging new kinds of political legitimacy is impeded by the incapacity of victims to formulate reciprocated rituals of response. This is in the nature of the macabresque, to paralyze victims by the torments of their death and thus to inhibit the mutuality of reciprocated, let alone ritualized violence. Feldman comments, "The sacrificial act can only sublate other forms of violence and transgression by the ritual repetition of violence. It can only expel and delegitimize violence by legitimizing violence in a culturally encysted form which culminates in a double interiorization of violence: its containment and its reinscription as a cultural institution."[8] This is precisely what the macabresque is designed to prevent. Reciprocity does not exist in the macabresque. Time as temporality stops; space no longer conveys the sense of place.

And yet, in contrast to the macabresque, Feldman depicts the behaviors of the prisoners of H-Block whose identity as mortified subjects, despite their agonies, included ways of resisting authority even as subaltern objects. As a result, they held on to at least a prayer of continuity, resistance and resilience. "The H-Blocks became a site of intensive culture-building by the prisoners," Feldman writes.[9] Within the enclosure of the prison, further partitions were mapped out, dialogical domains defined by the antagonistic and intersecting ideological imaginations of the inmates and the prison guards. The prison became a bifurcated space . . . divided the prisoners and the guards to the very depths of their bodies and being."[10] These spatial barriers and cellblock bifurcations crisscrossed in multiple ways that evoked incessant testing of will and might that became ritualized and codified. Out of these hellish reciprocities a culture was born that feigned the reinstatement of the status of prisoners but at the costs of their deepening brutalization.

Feldman continues, "The H-Blocks became the scene for the development of dramatic biological and semantic reorganizations of the human body, secret languages, ritualized temporalities, surreal ecosystems, and unique technological adaptations. The H-Blocks had their myths, local histories, performance spaces, carnivals of violence, symbolic kinship, death rituals and animal totems." Prisoners developed a culture of resistance that permitted them, despite the pain they experienced, a sense that their bodies were sites of resilience even as their cells became excrementalized. Feldman describes the performativity of bodily intrusion. "The bodily interior of the inmate was detached from his control and transferred to the skeletal machinery of the administration. This established a correspondence between institutional performance and biological performance. Two systems of penological training converged—coercive economic exchange and optical exposure of the body."[11] Shame and humiliation became the ultimate weapon. Feldman describes it as follows: "The rectal mirror examination was a ceremony of defilement and the highest expression of the prison regime's optical colon-ization of the captive body . . . the central theater of observation." But the dramaturgy did not cease with this form of performative transgression, because prisoners adapted their fluids and bodily issues as weapons of their reciprocated contempt.

THEORIZING TRANSGRESSIVE PERFORMATIVITY IN PSYCHOSOCIAL PERSPECTIVE: INFANTILE SADISM AND REPARATIVE GUILT

Thus far I have developed two related themes: first, the macabresque exists as a problematic over and beyond genocide, hate, mass murder, and killing or annihilation; secondly, analytical approaches in social psychology and political psychology shed useful and important light especially on group dynamics in mass atrocity, but the explanations framed within these fields also tend to associate perpetrator identity with prototypicality in groups and thus treat self-rationalization as the equivalent of motivation. As a result, social psychology and political psychology are unable to account for the extraneous forms of staged human violation according to the dynamics of performative transgression. As we have just recounted, however, self-sacrificial forms of violence emerge under conditions of "symbolic genocide." This points toward symbolic practices and to the role and influences of cultural prescriptions with respect to the macabresque in mass atrocity. The dramaturgical and aesthetic elements of the macabresque invite us to focus on sadistic cruelty with emphasis on its performative features.

That surplus cruelty in the noir ecstasy of performative transgression, staged performatively and aesthetically in the macabresque transgressions of mass atrocity, is "sadistic" is a given. But what is sadism? How does this psychoanalytic concept apply to an examination of perpetrators who evince capacities for extraordinary cruelty but who also appear capable of a wide range of opposing emotions and behaviors, depending on immediate situation, overall context, and general circumstances? I shall address this question from a Lacanian perspective. But first, I review the psychoanalytic work of Melanie

Klein and a number of post-Kleinian theorists, particularly, C. Fred Alford, Thomas H. Ogden, and Arne Johan Vetlesen. I do so on the basis of a selective reading of their "part-object relations" approach to infantile sadism in order to examine its relevance to psychosocial explanations of perpetrator behaviors. What this examination demonstrates is the narcissist self-victimization or masochism of perpetrators. Thus our analysis shifts from the psychodynamics of self-deception and self-sacrifice to self-punishment and self-victimization. This is in keeping with a wide range of psychoanalytic theories that demonstrate the inextricable linkages between masochism and sadism. Klein sought to demonstrate the connections of primary sadism to human development. She argued that infantile psychic development progresses along pathways identified with what she famously labeled as "depressive" and "paranoid-schizoid" "positions." Ogden subsequently proposed a third, the "autistic-contiguous" position, which Alford and Vetlesen apply to the analysis of sadism, particularly within analytical contexts framed by criminality and its psychopathic linkages to sadistic violence.

Kleinian "positions" are not comparable to temporal "stages," developmental phases, or transformative periods. They serve as structural concepts that are alleged to show how the ego and superego emerge. Kleinian "positions" are theorized as fostering broad divergences among adults, from those who are able to learn how to play, love, and grow imaginatively to those who become enclosed within the corsets of mental rigidity and emotional narrowness. Applied as units of analysis, they point toward the particular ways in which the human personality relates to dread and anxiety and, additionally, how the psyche defends (or fails to defend) against such incursions, psychologically and emotionally. Kleinian constructivism emphasizes how the imaginations and emotional capacities of children become configured around external imagos or figurative representations that are not perceived to be external but that become internalized as "objects" by infants.

Infants experience relational dynamics that recognize no distinction between internal and external, between what is inner or beyond. What is outside the child becomes incorporated within; what stems from within is projected outward. Caretakers, the objects of childhood relationships, become parcelized into good and bad part-objects; these are disembodied and internalized emotionally but, in turn, become projected back onto the objects themselves according to fantasized features. Faces, bodies, body parts, anatomical vehicles, all collide in fantasy and confusion. Gradually, they take hold and become molded in ways connecting childhood fantasy to material reality. Kleinian psychoanalytic approaches emphasized subjects and objects, love and hate, anger and sadism, guilt and reparation, anxiety, and more anger. Her focus increasingly emphasized infantile sadism and interior responses to it. Klein came to believe that infantile sadism and childhood anxiety were mutually generative. She stated, "Thus the child's sadistic attacks have for their object both father and mother, who are in phantasy bitten, torn, cut or stamped to bits. The attacks give rise to anxiety lest the subject should be punished by the united parents, and this anxiety also becomes internalized in consequence of the oral-sadistic introjection of the objects and is thus already directed to the early super-ego."[12] Klein represents "orality" with the taking in of external objects of nurture, the attempt to possess the maternal object, and, thus, with aggression. But she also underscores the role of infantile guilt and children's innate capacities to experience guilt in response to their own possessiveness, a kind of guilt that exacerbates their anxiety. These sensations of anxiety become internalized within the psychic economy of children in a structural or topological "position" that Klein eventually determined was paranoid and schizoid.

The key to Klein's theoretical posture was that the resulting paranoid-schizoid position within children represented a defensive reaction to their own sadism toward caretakers. "The excess of sadism gives rise to anxiety and sets in motion the ego's earliest modes of defense," Klein averred. Klein's findings helped to establish the "object relations" school, theory, and tradition. This theoretical and clinical orientation emphasizes how infants relate to the authorities in their social universe, and how these figures become transformed into "partial objects," that is, the objects of infantile sadism and aggression, and, consequently, the objects of guilt, "depression," and the need to "repair" relationships. These and related generalizations fostered controversy across the entire field of psychoanalysis, but they also promoted analysis of the psychodynamics of separation that is at the core of Freudian Oedipal models and thus at the frontier of psychosocial theory.[13]

Klein's approach to part-objects, therefore, suggests that those who care for infants are readily transformed into the internalized objects that anchor how infants develop, and that the psychodynamics of this process inheres in "splitting" (*spaltung*). Infantile aggression, anger, and, ultimately, a sadistic impulse toward caretakers arise on account of "persecutory" fantasies, which are within children, but which appear to them to arise not from within but externally. This leads Klein to theoretically depict paranoia as an essential standpoint in infantile fantasy. Such interior persecutory and paranoid fantasies assume such powerful forms that they threaten to overwhelm children. The consequence is that they must be pushed out again, recursively, and become attached to external objects. The emotional tasks confronting children require them to deplete these fantasies of persecution and to reduce them to shapes amenable to psychic containment.

For such reasons, infants appear able to cut fantasies down to size by dividing and dismembering them. The external figures that loom as all powerful are fantasized as parts rather than wholes, "good" parts and "bad" parts, the "good" breast and the "bad" breast, a process of diminution that relieves the sense of persecution but retains the primary presence of infantile sadism. Just as reparation represents a delimiting or soothing device, so does cutting and dissecting. Infants delimit the threats posed by their own sense of persecution and their sadistic anger by strategies that involve the fantasized splitting of primary "partial objects." In infancy, the psychic economy thus latches onto a strategy of schizoid dissection. Wholes and parts of wholes, of good objects and bad ones, become transformed into fantasized "morsels." The "morselized" body of the nurturing other, particularly of the mothering "object," keeps existential anxiety, the anxiety over dissolution, contained within the limits endurable by infants. Thus, Klein concluded that the "schizoid" or splitting process attends infantile sadism and paranoia as a palliative.

THE SCHIZOID IN SPLITTING

The term *schizoid* originates in applications of the term *spaltung* (splitting). Splitting, as applied by Freud, referred to the psychic capacity to separate out fantasies, including scenarios of desire, from other mental activities in ways that held the fantasies constant but independent of each other—and with contradictory effects. In splitting, subjects become fixated by alternative "psychic positions" relative to external reality, each constant but covariant, both functioning within the human personality as givens, but with one accepting reality as emotionally apart, and the other disavowing (*Verleugnung*) this apartness by rejecting reality except in reified, mystified, or fetishized forms. Splitting thus permits the psychic economy to follow incompatible pathways relative to desire, one having little or no apparent effect on the other: one position accepts reality as distinct from one's own inner demands or cravings; the other position incorporates a reality that exists in disordered and fetishized forms that are converted emotionally into objects, eventually, of mimetic desire. In the Freudian/Kleinian perspective, splitting refers to a doubling of psychic defenses, one in relation to external reality, the other regarding the interiorities of drive and desire.

Klein adopted the term *schizoid* to refer to the recursivity in splitting that specifically involves "projective identification" with objects of nurture. Projective identification involves the projection of interior anger, aggression, and persecutory fantasies onto external objects. Schizoid splitting represented a kind of existential duplicity for Klein, one impelling sadistic desire to dominate infantile emotions, the other imposing "depressive" acceptance of reparation as an appropriate response to nurture. In positing the dynamics of schizoid splitting, Klein was interpreting how anxiety and the experience of being encumbered by fantasies of dissolution and disintegration played out from the earliest moments of infancy. She argued that at birth infants enjoyed sufficient psychic capacity to sense their own vulnerability and the anxiety that attends it. But as a consequence of splitting, they were able to project anxiety onto the external environment through projective identifications that separated out the distinct positions of love and hate.

Klein maintained many theoretical disagreements with Lacan, but like him she stressed the absolute importance for self-individuation of entry into language, culture, and symbolic meanings. She argued that entry into the symbolic universe offered a solution to the problem of infantile sadism, in the form of relief of anxiety. Through language and meaning, an infant could begin on the long road to selfhood as an alternative to sadism. "The sadism becomes a source of danger because it offers an occasion for the liberation of anxiety and also because the weapons employed to destroy the object are felt by the subject to be leveled at his own self as well." To underscore the importance of self-individuation against all the odds imposed by anxiety and sadism, she later adds, "Thus, the wholly undeveloped ego is faced with a task which at this stage is quite beyond it—the task of mastering the severest anxiety." In this, Kleinian theory and succeeding generations of objects-relations approaches establish a functional role for infantile sadism, anxiety, and childhood paranoia as a psychic threshold across which human personality struggles against throughout a lifetime. The ability to tolerate anxiety, and to incorporate and absorb it while going beyond sadistic tendencies by means of imaginative capacities denoted by symbolic dexterity, is critical to human self-realization. When these developmental dynamics become distorted, human personality may tend toward structural positions that are unable to experience empathy or compassion. In terms of psychosocial theory, this situates certain explanations of anomic and violent behaviors within the locus of normality, but gripped by combinations of sadistic impulses, lack of empathic capacity, and self-deceptions susceptible to dynamics of peer-group conformity and hierarchical command.

According to Klein, the superego develops out of these relationships, influenced by the elements present in the paranoid-schizoid position, as well as in the depressive position. Klein demonstrates how a malignant or maligned superego, formed in the primordial heat of infantile anxiety and by the primal responses to it, can—but does not have to—lead to the potential for destructive behaviors throughout adulthood. "The vicious circle that is thus set up," she writes, "in which the child's anxiety impels it to destroy its object, results in an increase of its own anxiety, and this once again urges it on against its object, and constitutes a psychological mechanism which, in my view, is at the bottom of asocial and criminal tendencies in the individual." This suggests that there exists a critical linkage between the superego, ego, and the management of anxiety and sadism. I suggest that this bears, however indirectly, on the macabresque. *Performative transgressions punish victims as objects; but such punishments are also aimed at perpetrators themselves as their own self-victimizers.* Another way to express this is to refer to the psychodynamics of rival self-other, the site of unconscious judgment structured in ways that promote an unconscious sense of shamefulness. A person as the subject becomes a self-object to itself.

This is the very character of the psychodynamics of reification, to attribute substantiality to the identities of others on the basis of closed categories but, in so doing, to relate to oneself as a "thing," and thus, in effect, to "thingify" one's freedom. This prompts an effort to "will the unwillable." How psychic structures and economies develop, how shame and anxiety become intertwined within human personality, points toward a congenital tug of war between anxiety and sadism, guilt and shame. Shame resides in ego formations, whereas guilt tends to emerge as a consequence of the overriding dynamics of the superego. Klein, relates guilt to the functioning of the superego in stating, for example, "Thus we must assume that it is the excessive severity of and overpowering cruelty of the superego, not the weakness or want of it, as is usually supposed, which is responsible for the behavior of asocial and criminal persons."[14] Klein's concept of the superego, like the Freudian concept, therefore, stresses its ultimate dysfunctionality in disordered willfulness. First, it provokes greater not lesser anxiety; secondly, it promotes the very anomic, alienated, and aggressive behaviors that it is often alleged to counter. As a result, Kleinian analytical theory has helped to establish the psychodynamic processes connecting superegotistical transgression and guilt linked to anxiety.

Also lurking in the recesses of ego dynamics are the sensations of shamefulness. Shamefulness is utterly personal, interior, and profoundly self-corrosive. Often experienced as an internal gaze originating from outside the self, it fosters a paralyzing combination of excessive self-disgust and self-condemnation over those fundamental fantasies, which are gripped by deepest forms of drive and desire, including those that are incestuous and libidinal. As a consequence of these psychodynamics sadistic, even, violent behaviors emerge aimed at countering the corrosive sensations of shame and shamefulness. Fantasies of shame and shamefulness in sadistic violence tend to be assuaged, in keeping with Kleinian theory, by means of projection outward and in ways that mask shame and self-disgust by seemingly serving "higher" purposes. Such purposes become oriented by political and ideological reifications toward identitarian otherness during instances of genocide, mass atrocity, and hate. The consequences are fateful. Perpetrators capable of the most squalid forms of violent behavior come to understand their acts of cruelty as obligations performed in the name and at the behest of noble causes. Fantasies of shame become transformed into the psychic and emotional energies leading perpetrators to self-deceive themselves into believing that they are the servants of supererogatory action grounded in transformative projects larger than the self. Shame always makes subjects sense themselves as small.[15] But sadistic cruelty galvanized by the political projects of genocide, hate, and mass atrocity and mobilized within the macabresque permits perpetrators to delude themselves into thinking that they are larger than life. This helps to explain why demands for absolute power became so compelling in the Nazi concentration camps. But shame as a unit of analysis and the shamefulness of shame as a framework of interpretation of perpetrator behaviors in the macabresque permits examination of the pervasive objective in the macabresque—that is, to humiliate victims before they die. Humiliation assumes multiple forms, and victims suffer in many ways, from torture, and in torments and agony. But the aims of perpetrators remain constant, however strange and manifestly diabolical, to project shame onto the bodies, minds, spirits of victims by means of humiliation; and the spaces, places, and time sequesters in which this process occurs is the macabresque. This also explains the macabresque dramaturgies of terrorism and the lurid signs and symbolisms of hate-group dynamics.

PSYCHIC POSITIONS

Ogden recasts Kleinian conceptions of "position," providing a theoretical basis for explanations of sadomasochism, a task taken up by Alford on the basis of Ogden's approach. Ogden considers the analytical concept of "position" to refer to processes of symbolization through which "perception is attributed meaning." Ogden's theory establishes the modalities of a third position, the "autistic-contiguous position."[16] Alford and others, including Vetlesen, adopt this concept in examining sadistic behaviors. Ogden emphasizes simultaneous or synchronic trifunctionality of "positions" in symbolic experience; each balances the other, but in varying ways with respect to how subjects constitute symbolic interpretations of "reality." Ogden states, "Because the paranoid-schizoid mode never exists in isolation from the depressive mode (and the autistic-contiguous mode), the concept of the self-as-object (completely disassociated from the experience of self as subject) is phenomenologically meaningless." He continues, "Due to the dialectical structure of experience, self-experience is never completely devoid of 'I-ness,' and one's objects are never simply objects altogether devoid of subjectivity." Ogden emphasizes psychic splitting, a process he describes as involving the sequestration of disturbing, dread-filled, and hate-filled "objects" by means of introjection and projection given to modes of defense.[17] Ogden declares, "This is the psychological meaning of splitting. All defenses in a paranoid-schizoid mode are derived from this principle; for example, projection is an effort to place an endangering (or endangered) aspect of self or object outside of the self while retaining the endangered (or endangering) aspect of the self or object within."[18] Ogden's interpretation of the depressive position speaks to variations in the capacities of persons: first, to engage in symbolic imagination; secondly, to engage in practices that reflect symbolic meanings. He introduces "symbol formation proper" and the symbolic imagination or capacity for symbolization as critical to the emergence of "an interpreting subject," to "a capacity for subjectivity," to the "experience of 'I-ness.'"[19] Ogden's stress is on psychic distance and perceptual space, on the differentiation between what he calls symbol and subjectivity in the depressive position.[20] He claims that it is this capacity that promotes emotional, moral, and intellectual capacities for autonomy, responsibility, and creativity. In distance and differentiation between self and symbol, a person learns self-acceptance and experiences "one's 'objects' as also being subjects." In the mediations of *autonomous* self and *autonomous* otherness, social imagination becomes relational. The "subjective" universe of social relations is thus psychically empowered to consist of "whole object" relations. Other persons come to be granted the same accommodations to think, feel, know, and experience all that one attributes to oneself; thus they come to be valued as persons armed with subjectivities, sentiments, and sensibilities of their own. Such relational capacities open up to the entire range of human exchange and intercourse based on mutuality and reciprocities that include ambiguity and ambivalence, the full panoply of emotions, hate and love.

　　Herein lies the contrast between those beholden to the depressive position and those in the paranoid-schizoid position. Those who relate to their social universe from a position of "whole object relations" can experience history and time, can recognize that "the individual exists as more or less the same person over time, in relation to other people who also continue to be the same people despite powerful affective shifts and mixtures of effect."[21] Experience compounds upon experience in ways that diffuse the need for "omnipotent defenses" against anxiety, dread, and emotional pain.[22] Similarly, others become defined not as symbolic of their omnipresence or power, but as persons open to all the frailties and vulnerabilities that one recognizes in one's own humanity and condition.

The psychic resonances of imaginative and emotional experiences in a paranoid-schizoid position erode these capacities that depressive modes permit: distance and relation between subjectivity and symbolization; autonomy of self and of otherness; reciprocity in exchanges and mutuality in relationships; a sense of time that combines change and continuity, ambiguity and ambivalences; openness to redemptive guilt and compassion. In the paranoid-schizoid position the relationship of self to the symbols constituted by others and the lifeworld becomes collapsed, rigidified, and subject to judgmental absolutes that revolve around "black and white," "all or nothing at all," by reified categories of "us" and "them," configured by the dynamics of enemy-making. Social relations and temporal conceptions become perceived as essentially "discontinuous": subjects of relationship become objects only good as "their last act."

Ogden refers to Segal's concept of "symbolic equation" to describe the ensuing psychic and perceptual condition in which perpetrators find it difficult or impossible to distinguish between object, symbol, and symbolization. And the implications for explaining political reification and the macabresque become clear. When perpetrators reify others or otherness, they reify themselves, so that the freedom and autonomy of self and that of "otherness" become elided and thus glued together in a common state of petrified concreteness. As Ogden comments, "Since one's objects, like oneself, are perceived . . . as objects rather than as subjects, one cannot care about them or have concern for them. There is little to empathize with since one's objects are not experienced as people with thoughts and feelings, but rather as loved, hated, or feared forces or things that impinge on oneself."[23] In political reification one attributes substantiality to that which is not a thing precisely because what is reified is the freedom, the humanity that partakes of the essence of personhood. Narcissism and sadistic desires for displayed cruelty emerge within these structural dynamics. Unlike subjects in depressive modes, who learn how to manage emotional and psychic pain, those in paranoid-schizoid positions "evacuate" pain "through the defensive use of omnipotent thinking, denial and the creation of discontinuities of experience."[24] Splitting operates to sequester feelings in ways designed to defend against ambiguous experiences that include measures of doubt and uncertainty with respect to other persons. Ogden writes, for example, "Each time a good object is disappointing, it is no longer experienced as a disappointing good object—but as the discovery of a bad object in what had been masquerading as a good one."[25] Time and truth come to a psychic "halt." "Instead of the experience of ambivalence, there is the experience of unmasking 'the truth.' This results in a continual rewriting of history such that the present experience of the object is projected backward and forward in time creating an eternal present."

The forms this takes in perpetrators of mass atrocity and hate gripped by perverse desire and ideological reification become manifest in the logics of illogic that ideologically construct justifications for efforts to "will" the macabresque, often in the name of various dystopian futures: absolute social exclusion, totalized purity, and unbounded security. All represent the fantasmatic plays demonstrating the influences of shame and shamefulness as they become transmuted into ideological and political reifications that are eventually projected onto victims, who, as a consequence, are humiliated in the macabresque by means of sadistic cruelty. Often, the ideologies that justify genocide, hate, and mass atrocity conjure up the notion of an eternal present, forever threatened unless supremacist and exclusivist conditions can be "restored," in ways that never existed but do exist in fantasy, as we saw in the cases of Nazi and Nazi collaborators described by Monroe. Ogden's analysis of the paranoid-schizoid position frames theoretical perspectives on political reification grounded in disordered efforts to will the unattainable, and thus to satisfy narcissistic yearnings composted in the psychodynamics of shamefulness. In political reification, emotional objectives and strategies become brittle, manipulative, and contemptuous. "Other people can be valued for what they can do for one, but one does not have *concern* for them . . . . An object can be damaged or used up, but only a subject can be hurt or injured."[26] The consequence is chronic "two-dimensionality" across the range of relational and emotional, perceptual and ideational experiences. "In the absence of the capacity to mediate between oneself and one's experience, a very limited form of subjectivity is generated," Ogden observes. "In a paranoid-schizoid mode, the self is predominantly a self as object, a self that is buffeted by thoughts, feelings, and perceptions as if they were external forces or physical objects occupying or bombarding oneself."[27]

This, then, points toward how the subject, the perpetrator, as the rival self-other, that is, the rival-self object, becomes conceptually theorized. Does application of the paranoid-schizoid concept permit the development of analytical linkages between psychoanalytic and psychosocial theory with respect to the behaviors of perpetrators? Does the paranoid-schizoid position as a theoretical perspective contribute to our understanding of why and how the dramaturgical aspects at the core of the macabresque function over and above mass killing in episodes of genocide and mass atrocity? Does it enable us to explain how group dynamics foment supremacist and exclusivist notions of hatred inherent within enemy-making? Ogden diagnoses disordered willfulness and resulting forms of political reification as symptomatic of the paranoid-schizoid posture. In this perspective, political reification becomes an indicator of the inability to mediate on the basis of symbolic extrapolation. Whereas ideology may be conceived as an exercise in symbolism, within this context it becomes a sign of semiotic weakness or failure.

Ogden's analysis includes focus on the primary experiences of infancy, a state he refers to as autistic-contiguous to emphasize "unboundedness" of skin, touch and feel experienced between mother and child, nurturer and infant. Alford recognizes in Ogden's formulations a way to interpret sadomasochism. In designating the term, autistic-contiguous, Ogden refers to "a psychological organization in which sensory modes of generating experience are organized into defensive processes in the face of perceived danger."[28] Ogden's application of the term "autistic" does not refer to disablement but, rather, to "the specific features of a universal sensory-dominated mode of experience."[29] Ogden thus posits the juxtaposition of autistic with contiguous to explore the immediacy of "non-reflective" physicality in infancy and its relationship to how the self becomes "organized" in and through the "most elemental forms of human experience."[30] He stresses "surface contiguity" and "sensory rhythmicity" along with the "sequences, symmetries, periodicity, skin-to-skin 'molding'" that he suggests provide "examples of contiguities that are the ingredients out of which the beginnings of rudimentary self-experience arise."[31]

The contiguities of infant and caretaker work initially to dissolve separations of both skin and spirit. "Contiguity of surfaces (e.g., 'molded' skin surfaces, harmonic sounds, rhythmic rocking or sucking, symmetrical shapes) generate the experience of sensory surface rather than the feeling of two surfaces coming together in mutually differentiating opposition or merger."[32] In the autistic-contiguous space there is only raw and unfiltered spatiality. Ogden states, "There is practically no sense of inside and outside of self and other; rather, what is important is the pattern, boundedness, shape, rhythm, texture, hardness, softness, warmth, coldness, and so on."[33] This emphasis on skin suggests the influential role played by insignias, uniforms, body art and cutting, leather, and tattoos in the bonding rituals and dramaturgies of anomic orders of all kinds, from skinheads to motorcycle gangs, from quasi-fascist hate groups to organized criminal networks. In the present context, it is also indicative of the desires for *bonding* on the part of perpetrators of the macabresque. The phenomenological role of skin as experienced by those who deploy it for purposes of social statement demonstrate what skin symbolism of all kinds is designed to deny, an inner emotional core gripped by the psychodynamics of shamefulness. As Kilborne observes, "Reliance upon appearances entails hiding whatever appearances one finds unacceptable, a reaction we associate with shame."

Interestingly, the word *shame* is derived from the Indo-European root *skam* or *skem*, meaning "to hide." From this same root come our two words *skin* and *hide*.[34] Skin represents the shield against embarrassment. Skin once deployed as social weapon serves as a template for shame and shamefulness projected outward. Shamefulness in shame turns toward humiliation against others by attacking their skin. Thus torture and a wide range of torments in the macabresque concentrate on the skin of victims. For these reasons, "whiteness" becomes associated with a wide range of supremacist ideologies and logics of illogic: from Aryanism to a wide range of cultural experiences in racializing ethnic identity, as well as in molding the casts of "dark nationalisms." Prejudice and the ideological doctrines that justify the linkages between prejudice and discrimination tend to be grounded in the reifications of skin and pigmentation. The colorations of skin serve as the basis for patterns of exploitation, domination, and, above all, cultural modes of subordination, leading to the historic production of subaltern groups. The structures of power across history situate groups according to how skin pigmentation becomes racialized. The question arises as to why the linkage between shamefulness and sadistic cruelty suggests an analytical avenue of explanation.

Sadistic cruelty in the macabresque tends to be exacted between perpetrators and victims in the most personal and intimate ways, since the nearly indescribable acts of sadistic horror pit the skin of perpetrators against the skin of victims. Shamefulness and sadistic cruelty, the one interior, the other exterior, both adhere to the politics of skin, one hidden, the other public, both beholden to the designs of humiliation. Shamefulness is not merely about how one sees oneself superficially; shamefulness resides within the interiorities of psychic and emotional fantasy because of the psychodynamics of the rival self-other, the shamefulness that derives from fantasies of shame wrought by an externalized gaze generated within. Kilborne describes this in terms of grace and disgrace. "Just as the notion of 'grace' designates a feeling that God approves of what he sees, the concept of 'dis-grace' designates a feeling of disapproval, an experience that others—who have seen how we have disgraced ourselves—are looking on with contempt and scorn."[35] But there is no "other" in the other, the other is the subject as the rival self-other or self-object. In hatred, the other is a displaced self. And in these instances, the inner object of the self is fantasized as shame-filled; in a profound sense this is correct, for it helps to explain the sadomasochism of perpetrators.

SADOMASOCHISM: VICTIMIZER AS VICTIM

Alford's theory of sadomasochism incorporates Ogden's theory of infantile sensory contiguity and dependency and Klein's theoretical constructions of the paranoid-schizoid position. Alford defines sadism as "the pleasure obtained from hurting others." He stresses projective identification as its essential characteristic. "What distinguishes sadism from aggression is not the sexualization of domination and destruction but the sadist's intense identification with his victim."[36] For Alford, the difference between sadism and masochism is less significant than the cruelty itself as a psychic instrument in self-defense against the demons of death, dying, and decay. He writes, "The issue is not whether cruelty is external or internal, but the form of cruelty, its shape and structure."[37] This by implication underscores how the macabresque serves as the vehicle of sadism in mass atrocity. Omnipotent fantasies combined with idealized narratives of shame and loss prompt perpetrators to want to project their dread onto others. "It is not accidental but central to the logic of sadomasochism that the idealization of one's own suffering becomes the idealization of inflicting suffering on others."[38] A forbidden sado-intimacy grafts victimizers onto the bodies and beings of their victims. "Above all, sadomasochism is about fusion, and confusion: identification with the victim's suffering so profound that the victim must be destroyed in order to protect the sadist's separate existence."[39] He adds, "Why sadism is properly called sadomasochism is apparent: identification with the victim is central to the act, without which it would be pointless."[40] In this perspective, the pain and sense of dissolution that victims must be made to feel in sadistic violation functions as a psychodynamic defense against the pain and sense of shame that perpetrators seek to nullify and evacuate. "*Sadism is the form that aggression takes when it is fleeing its doom.*"[41] The sadism in masochism and the masochism in sadism derive from this sense of conflation. "Here is an explanation of the much otherwise-incomprehensible violence, the victimizer feeling as though he were the victim."[42] Alford cites Janine Chasseguet-Smirgel in stating that "the telos of sadomasochism isn't pleasure or pain but the destruction, of individuality, of fate."[43] For these reasons, sadistic cruelty, virtually by definition, must be performed. Sadism inheres not merely in cruelty but in performative transgressions. Only the cruelty displayed *performatively* gratifies sadistic demand. Perpetrators of mass atrocity create the macabresque because they demand that an audience be present so that they and their victims are conjoined on the ghastly stages of sado-intimacy. Hate groups gripped by the yearnings of sadistic cruelty yield themselves unto the gods of enemy-making so as to act out the hatred toward others inherent in the shame within themselves. Alford indicates, "It is no accident because the logic [of sadism and of masochism] is the same, to control suffering at any cost. Only the locus changes, from self to other and back again."[44] Sadists in the macabresque want proof of the suffering they inflict to be inscribed on the bodies of victims whether by dismemberment in Rwanda or by step-by-step torture in Cambodia. Sadistic domination in the macabresque over others' suffering is the "evidence of control." Alford ruminates, "If I can't make my suffering yours for a while, how could I know I really control it? Here is the logic of sadomasochism in a nutshell."[45] During genocide and mass atrocity and hate, macabresque proximity of staged theatricality permits forbidden intimacy, skin on skin, flesh on flesh, so that what separates victims and victimizers appears only membrane-thin or as thick as the veneer of flesh. Violator and violated are brought together in merciless agony, one to void it, the other to suffer it in ways that allow perpetrators to know that victims know they are suffering it.

In these collisions of body against body Alford detects the relevance of Ogden's conceptualization of the autistic-contiguous position to sadistic violence. "Wonder at the intimacy of the sadistic relationship, a contact across boundaries which can only be called autistic-contiguous, like a vampire sucking blood."[46] The aesthetics of the macabresque are executed in theaters of sado-intimacy wherever performative transgressions in mass atrocity occur. Perpetrators and their victims each play (or are made to play) a part in the suturing of skin onto the bones of agony. "It is the psychologic of the autistic-continuous position, in which feeling someone else . . . and being felt by them are one," Alford writes. The intimacy in sadism serves as a means to a sense of domination and control. Nonetheless, victimizers remain victims of their own desire.[47] As Alford comments, "To stick to the other who now contains one's doom is hardly a solution. Shared doom is still doom. A violent separation is necessary, sadism a scratch across the autistic-contiguous surface to separate the parties, damaging the other so as to know who really has the power, who really contains the doom, and who's in charge."[48]

Alford's depiction of the "humanity" of perpetrators, very much in keeping with Dominick LaCapra's call for the same emphasizes their psychic and fantasmatic paralysis gripped by inner torments. This provokes Alford to refer to "precategorical dread" he describes as a manifestation of primordial anxiety, "the ambiguity of surfaces, the feeling of doom which arises when surfaces no longer contain," "the ineffable, experiences that involve not loss of others, not even loss of hope, but loss of self."[49] Alford suggests that perpetrators tend to be unable to give voice or lend symbolic expression to their own sense of anguish over what he calls "three terrors," by which he means "pain, abandonment and helplessness," to which might be added, shame and humiliation. Alford attaches self-victimization of perpetrators to this very "precategorical experience of evil," the "fear of a living death," the sense of "abstract doom."[50] From his perspective, perpetrators undertake the macabresque practices of sadistic cruelty "to inflict one's doom on others, becoming doom, rather than living subject to it." "Evil is bad faith," the living "lie" that one escapes "fate by inflicting it on others." He adds, "Evil inflicts pain, abandonment, and helplessness on others, so that the evildoer will not have to experience them himself. It is that simple, and that complicated."[51] Sadistic cruelty is performative since, as one informant cited by Alford comments, "Evil people don't just want to hurt you, they want to hurt you from the inside, so it's like you're hurting yourself."[52] Sadistic cruelty is violation, not mere violence. Its purpose is to violate the physicality of another, not only to invade their skin but to occupy their soul.

If sadistic cruelty is the means, performative transgression in the macabresque is the mechanism transmuted into an end for itself. This prompts Alford to observe, "It is why torture is the paradigm of evil, master of all three terrors at once. All evil has the quality of torture, inflicting dread on another so as to escape it oneself. Hence, all evil has the quality of sadism defined . . . as the joy of having taken control of an experience of victimhood by inflicting it on another."[53] Such "enjoyment" depends upon the collapse of victims' lifeworlds into the confines of raw and ravaged physicality. "Torture is reverse animism," Alford declares. "It reduces the world to the human body," as we saw in Feldman's graphic depictions of Belfast prison strife. This process of collapse into confinement of the self within the body stands in contrast to the entire life of symbolization. "Rather than nonbody symbolizing body, body comes to symbolize a world reduced to its bare essentials, pain and power." Alford adds, "Evil is uncreative because it abandons the quest to translate dread into abstract form and instead translates dread into the body and minds of others. Evil is the failure of creativity, and banality is its slogan."[54] This, too, echoes Feldman's analysis, and that of Elaine Scarry as well.[55]

In the torments and tortures of performative transgression, the boundaries of self and otherness between victims and perpetrators elide and become interpenetrated. The threats posed by unconscious dread and fears of social and of self-disintegration assail perpetrators. Skin becomes a vehicle for their disordered will. Perpetrators desire the unwillable to efface the delimitations of one body against another body. Performative transgression permits sadistic cruelty to be applied by destroying physical boundaries between perpetrators and victims in ways staged and performed in order for it to be made doubly visible to both victim and victimizer, doubly palpable, yet doubly permeable, by means of cutting, dismemberment, and invasive contusion. The surfaces of skin become the superficial reality that perpetrators plunge into as if they could invade the interior of a person's humanity by cutting into their surface. "Evil is a version of cutting," Alford observes.[56] The flailing of perpetrators is against physical boundaries and existential confinements. To violate the skin of another "is to implant our dread within another, and so define its boundaries, its limits, containing the uncontainable in the form of another so we might live."[57] For such reasons, perpetrators of genocide and mass atrocity may be aligned analytically along a spectrum that includes members of hate groups beholden to various forms of ideological racism, exclusivism, and supremacism, especially those that demonstrate their commitments to maligned purposes by means of skin tattoo and cutting.

Alford indicates that the conceptual distinction between sadism and masochism, between brutalizing oneself and brutalizing another, is of secondary significance. Sadistically to hurt another, masochistically to harm oneself, resides in the same sets of "psychologics" that are designed to contain the boundaries of the self while also destroying them. "In evil we scratch the surface of the other in order to mark the separation. At the same time we do the opposite, acting as if there are no boundaries, no limits, my access to your body limited not even by the envelop of your skin, which I slice open before you even feel the pain."[58] *Just as the importance of difference in otherness becomes emphasized in enemy-making as a device for shielding the dread of loss of distinction over identitarian identicality, so must the skin of perpetrators become exaggerated by the imprints and insignia of hate identifications in ways designed to protect against the absence of domination relative to the suborned other. Perpetrators are thus engaged in practices that work along the contours of skin and bounded physicality aimed at the utter humiliation and absolute domination of others.* When the violations of sado-intimacy are done the relational distance between perpetrators and victims is not far; the closeness in sadomasochism is always intimate in its absolute *impersonality*.

What Is Feared Is Dreaded

The theoretical strength of the analyses framed by Ogden and Alford emerges within their interpretations of "formless dread" or anxiety that inheres within unconscious displacements involving corporeal containments and configurations of fragmentation, dismemberment and ultimate dissolution, "the fear of formlessness, the loss of context, meaning, and containment, where boundaries fail."[59] What might be admired becomes feared; what is feared becomes dreaded. The dread is outside but inside. Symbolic representations of interiority and exteriority cave in. Confusion turns into conflation; the structures of autistic-contiguous positions now become reinforced by the fantasmatic constructions of the paranoid-schizoid position. In the absence or weakness of the depressive position, the autistic-contiguous and the paranoid-schizoid positions become amalgamated. Alford comments, "The dread that leads to evil takes place along . . . the side that connects autistic-contiguous with paranoid-schizoid experience . . . as these two positions collapse into one."[60] The sado-intimacies of bodily interpenetration generated under the psychic conditions held by the autistic-contiguous position now give way to the forms of conflicted symbolization produced within the fantasy frames of the paranoid-schizoid position. Symbolization becomes gripped by social fantasies and ultimately by akratic desires of disordered will. The sense of imaginative distance from actions based on self-aware symbolic meanings and values collapses into the "can-do-must-do" of injunctions to "enjoy" though self-deception and reification.

Alford raises the psychosocial question as to whether sadism and evil emerge more or less in one position rather than the other. His response proceeds along a fine ridge. He comments, "Violence, whether physical or mental, that has the quality of evacutive attachment—in which one connects with the other forcibly to share an unbearable feeling so as to communicate it and be rid of it—would come closer to the paranoid-schizoid position." On the other hand, he continues, "Violence that seeks to create an edge, a boundary, as though to say you must suffer and die so that I can live, would come closer to the autistic-contiguous position, violence a defense against merger."[61] Given weakness in the depressive position "evil operates through both positions at once, and it is not terribly important to sort them out. Important is the principle, the way in which paranoid-schizoid anxiety expresses and defends against autistic-contiguous dread."[62] The consequence is that what perpetrators fear, they dread, and what they dread most is precategorical and thus nameless. Such is in the nature of perpetrator bonding in the macabresque. But this analytical collapse of the paranoid-schizoid with the autistic-contiguous points, first, to the relevance of the phallic laws of separation and *jouissance*, and to the prevailing influences of culture, and especially of political culture, in shaping how the macabresque unfolds.

THE DIMENSIONS OF MACABRESQUE SADISM

The concept of sadism has entered vernacular English as a synonym for cruelty. It arises, of course, as a consequence of its literary heritage and is associated with a set of behaviors linked to those depicted in the writings of the Marquis de Sade. The concept of sadism is of special relevance to an interpretation of the macabresque, first, because of the intrinsic cruelty that defines what it is and how it comes about in the agonies of the victims. But, even more than the simple fact of its cruelty, macabresque sadism is cruelty displayed. Sadistic cruelty is by definition cruelty displayed, the very feature that distinguishes sadistic cruelty from other forms or versions. For this alone, it gains particular traction in the present study as an endeavor in coming to terms with why victims of genocide and mass atrocity are made to suffer the dramaturgies and aesthetics of surplus cruelty. It is its performativity that renders cruelty its surplus and thus its distinguishing feature as sadism. There yet remains a third dimension to sadistic cruelty of direct relevance to its performativity in the macabresque: its non-sensual sexuality. Sadistic cruelty is not about pleasure of any kind; rather it concerns power, the assertion of control by one person over the other's body. Here, too, the relevance of sadistic cruelty of this sort to the macabresque becomes self-evident. What is not so obvious, however, is why. This harkens back to the discussion adumbrated earlier in the context of Sofsky's interpretation of absolute power and how Nazi concentration camp guards relentlessly pursued it over hapless victims. It is also present in the macabresque prisons of the Cambodian genocide and on the roadblocks of the Rwandan genocide. It emerges wherever, and whenever, mass atrocity arises; it is inherent within the yearnings of extremist and fanatacist hatred; it propels enemy-making across diverse political cultures.

The drive for absolute power indicates the essential dimensions of macabresque sadism, its cruelty and performativity, but also its drive or thrust to violate the bodies of victims in order that victims experience the power of another over them. This is at the core of the macabresque, that victims experience the sadistic cruelty leveled against them. The dramaturgies and aesthetic "styles" of the macabresque appear in the course of various genocides and mass atrocities in ways that are reflective of the cultural traditions of the societies in which they occur. The question concerning the central feature of macabresque arises, what it is that perpetrators seek or "will" by means of absolute power or sadism displayed and thus manifestly experienced by victims?

Lacanian theory is of particular importance in this regard, first, for its emphasis on phallic fantasy as the quest for psychic stability and identity on the part of individuals, and, secondly, on account of the relevance of the concept of phallic fantasy for a psychosocial interpretation of macabresque sadism. Macabresque sadism demonstrates a collective, often a regressive or reactionary drive to restore whatever is ideologically constituted as "lost," "stolen," or "threatened." This, in turn, reflects (deflects) collective anxiety fueled by social fantasies of decay, disarray, disorder, and even demise, brought on by any subset of events or "proxy narratives" concerning loss of territory, status, honor or glory, common heritage or ancestors, national solidarity, ethnic or racial purity. But the logics of illogic intrinsic to political reification and ideology serve as cognitive buttresses for the psychodynamics of macabresque sadism or surplus cruelty designed to make victims "confess" to crimes, or to recognize their violations as a right bestowed on perpetrators to execute.

From this perspective, restoration fantasies partake of the character of phallic fantasies aimed at making victims "declare" the law of paternal or phallic separation from *jouissance* in *objet a*. Lacanian psychoanalytic theory thus becomes reconfigured into a psychosocial interpretation of performative transgression, now understood as macabresque sadism, to emphasize the relevance of phallic restoration fantasies so central to the political ideologies used to justify genocide, mass atrocity, and hatred in enemy-making. The point here is not to suggest that fantasies of any kind, phallic or restoration, cause genocide or mass atrocity. When perpetrators act, they do so within the contexts of the situations and groups in which they find themselves. In this sense, the behavioral pressures induced by and through the dynamics of prototypicality apply at the levels of self-rationalization, in keeping with the observations rendered by both political and social psychology. But once perpetrators become situated within the time, spaces, and places demarcating the macabresque from its exterior realms, perpetrators undertake to exact sadistic cruelties on victims not merely to fulfill the logics of illogic of political reification, but to gratify the restoration fantasies that are phallic in origin. This is implied by Lacanian theory, and it represents the critical explanatory dimension of the surplus cruelty in performative transgression at the heart of macabresque sadism.

METAPHORIC CONDENSATION AND THE ENIGMATIC SIGNIFIER IN THE UNCONSCIOUS

Lacan viewed the unconscious as antediluvian scroll made up of chains of linguistic signifiers that would appear, like the clustered traces of vestigial memory across the malleable pages of the mind, to congeal into social fantasy and thus to help structure human subjectivity. But Lacan theorized that the scrolling effects of mentalized tropes did not only include metonymic constructions framed in and by horizontal displacements. They involved metaphor and metaphoric structures as well; these function vertically, as it were, to condense disparate signifiers of desire into master signifiers. Otherwise, human personality could not stabilize (fictionalize) ego formations in the unconscious to the point that infantile fantasy would grow toward mature identity construction. In this perspective, subjectivation occurs precisely on account of metaphoric chains in which the signifiers, again, mental representations of desire, became anchored or established. Metaphors inhere in nonliteral comparisons or exchanges in which a host of diffused objects and experiences become condensed into a singular form. Metaphoric chains are said to compress the flows of indistinct realities in the infantile unconscious; thus they work to transform nondescript experience into iconic devices for purposes of earliest forms of impressionistic interpretation. This occurs through the mechanisms of allegory. Metaphoric chains comprised of master signifiers turn into representative configurations. These transform spiritual and abstract or non-material meanings, specifically experiences of desire, into concrete representations as filtered by infantile unconscious. Allegorization thus permits nonfigurative relations of desire to assume shape. Such concretions are interpretable by infants in ways rudimentary but critical to ego psychodynamics and identity formations.

The great Freudian allegory of infantile unconscious and its progression is, of course, that of the Oedipal complex or process of transcending the fundamental fantasy of incestuous return. As previously suggested, numerous depictions exist to divine what this great yearning that Lacan features as *jouissance* is, including the ecstasy of womb-like dependence and security. Lacan dutifully avoided the substance of the Oedipal story as recounted by Freud, but he remained committed to structuralist understandings of the unconscious as represented in the Oedipal account. And what counted in the Oedipal story was not so much its content but its structural arrangements, the trimodal fantasy arrangement rather than a two-party structure configured only around the relationship between two, that is, between mother or caregiver and child. Structural trimodality theoretically implied that the bilateral relationships between caregiver and infant, though deeply suffused by desire, could come to be processed by the infantile unconscious in ways other than as if it were merely bathed in the reciprocated desiring of two. Lacanian theory emphasizes "phallic separation" or "the name-of-the-father"—that is, the "paternal" metaphor—as the psychic mechanism that installs human subjectivity by intruding on the symbiosis of maternal-child cathexis. The paternal metaphor as master signifier represents a structural position that, contrary to vast misinterpretation, does not require a single person, a male, even a father, to perform.[63] The phallic as metaphor is neither sign nor symbol, and thus does not refer to male appendages or female organs, or to genitality as such, or to the sex of any specific caregiver. Caregivers, in "reality," come in multiple forms, shapes, attitudes, and dispositions. Relatives, strangers, a single female, group of females, small mixed families, entire tribes or segmented groups, cousins, aunts, uncles, in-laws, endogamous or exogamous figures, or groups of figures, each and all can and do play out the phallic function. This function is defined metaphorically to denote the structural role played by whomever or whatever acts on the infantile unconscious to sever the smothering demand for return to *jouissance* or incestuous desire that threatens ego development, and thus ultimately cultivating the emergence of human subjectivity in any single person. The basic proposition is that the phallic function (again, as represented metaphorically by the paternal metaphor) fosters a grounding process in ego formation and subjectivation. Subjectivation and ego formation are seen to be anchored by phallic signifiers. Lacan represented these as the *name-of-the-father*, to which he ironically referred as *le non-du-pere*. This propping up of the unconscious proceeds on account of the phallic signifier, inscribing paternalized separation from incest-laden desires, conveyed through maternal signifiers and infantile reactions to them. The psychodynamics of Oedipal separation enable infants to begin the task of interpreting their own position relative to their own demands, needs, and, above all, desires.

The phallic signifier is thus theorized as critical to an understanding of how subjectivation across all cultural settings operates, even in cultures in which the trimodal structure does not involve the standard nuclear family as posited in traditional Western industrial society (which in many ways is itself becoming eroded in contemporary culture). The triangular relationship of the basic family unit as unconscious fantasy is *structural* in the mentalistic sense that it does not depend on the specific contents of nurture, nor does it require any one structural pattern of parents or caregivers. The structural trimodalities of birth, nurture, and Oedipal separation are conceived as meta-psychoanalytic unconscious arrangements allegorized by infants, and transformed on the basis of metaphoric capacities instated in fantasy by the operations of linguistic tropes. For heuristic purposes of psychosocial analysis, the phallic metaphor serves as a way to allegorize the unconscious process of separation and individuation in human development. The paternal metaphor is allegorized as an ordering principle or arrangement in the unconscious. As metaphorical allegory, it becomes formally amenable to theoretical applications, including for the heuristic purposes of psychosocial theory. This permits analytical explorations of how infants as split subjects barred from *jouissance* in their desiring (*the first signifier, split and barred*) fantasize maternal desire (*the second signifier, in lack or want-of-being*) against the intrusion of the phallic or paternal metaphor (*the third signifier, phallic loss*). As in all cases of structural psychoanalytic interpretation, emphasis is on the ordering principles and their consequences as structured arrangements on processes of interaction and their outcomes.

Questions arise concerning the impacts of these structures and their influences in the unconscious of any desiring subject relative to social fantasy and political order. In Lacanian terms, Oedipal trimodality signifies metonymic slides across synchronic (horizontal) scales of displacement and the possibility that these can be positioned or arrested by means of metaphoric condensations. This is the essential role of the phallic or paternal metaphor, to help the infantile unconscious renounce *jouissance* by developing "phallic" capacities *for desire after loss* that are critical to subjective autonomy. To signify this, Lacan consistently refers to *objet a*—the alternative object—that inheres in fantasies of desire that are alternative to *jouissance*, but toward which the unconscious remains attracted. Clearly, sexuality and sexual objects and schemes partake of *objet a*, but so do the "objects" of power, greed, fame, and glory, as well as of honor, bonding, and rank, including divine authority—that is, in particular, the stuff and substance of society that readily becomes fantasized in terms of political power but also eschatological salvation.[64]

The "objects" of *objet a* are subjected to disorders of will and thus the kinds of desiring that involve *willing the unwillable*. This sets the stage for mimetic rivalries and conflicts. In cases where rivals are fantasized as having access to *jouissance*, as is so often the case in instances of genocide, mass atrocity, and enemy-making, rivals become reified, objectified and willed as objects of contempt, even, hatred. Their sin is to become in social fantasy the incarnation of *jouissance*, the very threat that invites enjoyment but at the risk of self-destruction. For all the reasons given in political ideology and posited by hate speech for why victims should be despised and purged, there remains the hidden narrative that imputes to them a kind of desire that embodies all of what is desirous. The stage is thus set for the macabresque. Sadistic cruelty emerges in the macabresque because victims must be made to pronounce the laws of separation and of prohibitions, in relation to what—*jouissance*. The macabresque serves this essential purpose: to allow perpetrators to force victims to renounce *joiussance* and, in so doing, transfer *objet a* to the spirit of the victimizers, the perpetrators. For these reasons, perpetrators seek absolute power; to achieve anything less serves as an unconscious reminder that *jouissance* remains with the victims, that *objet a* has yet to be transferred.

The phallic or paternal metaphor anchors desire in infantile unconscious development so that desiring facilitates the fundamental task of self-definition, individuation, autonomy, however the attributes of desirability are defined or configured in any specific family or culture. As Fink indicates, "Understood as involving two distinct logical moments, as instating the symbolic order as such, the paternal metaphor can be usefully understood as providing a subject with an 'explanatory principle,' an explanation of the why and wherefore of its having been brought into the world, an interpretation of the constellation of its parents' desire (and sometimes grandparents' desire, as well) that led to its being born."[65] The phallic signifier permits unconscious subjectivation to emerge by positioning the paternal metaphor (*third-party signifier defined as phallic loss*) relative to maternal desire (*second-party signifier defined as maternal lack*), so that infantile desire (*first-party signifier, defined as split and barred*) is able to develop its own individuated capacities.

This is what Lacan meant when he emphasized the importance of signifier chains in metaphoric constructions of language as the keys to infantile fantasy over and beyond the content or substance of whatever is constituted as the signified. "*Objet petit a* is any object which sets desire in motion, especially the partial objects which define the drives. The drives do not seek to attain the *objet petit a*, but rather circle round it. *Objet petit a* is both the object of anxiety, and the final irreducible reserve of libido."[66] This conveys the meaning and significance of the phallic as signifier relative to libidinal drive, and ultimately, unconscious desire. A bridging process occurs through inscriptions of the body, its parts and its discharges, that offer themselves up to consciousness as the primordial "matrix of signification, the ground upon which the synchrony of the most elemental signifying system" occurs.[67] As a result, mastery of language develops through an Oedipal phase of simple mimesis toward, metaphorically speaking, "castration" in and beyond Oedipal dynamics. Castration and self-definition, entry into language, and the paternal signifier of law and its instatement are keyed together in psychic development. On account of the paternal signifier, self-individuation through language and intentionality can proceed beyond pre-Oedipal triangulations, not as the separation to be feared but as the social identity to be welcomed. The paternal metaphor or name-of-the-father phallic metaphor means that infantile fantasy becomes configured around meanings of maternal or caregiver care—specifically, the desire conveyed through the maternal signifier—in ways permitting them to assume the mantle of individuated subjectivity. The task set before the infantile unconscious renders metaphoric assimilation of the experience of desire, nay, of relations permeated by desire, fundamental to ego formation. To enable infantile imagination to develop interpretive capacities represents a primary objective of Oedipal dynamics. But what is it that infantile unconscious can interpret through metaphoric forms of signification structured in fantasy like the scrolls of language that roll out mental representations of triadic relationships? The answer is desire in combinations of signifier chains that give access not only to immediate family relations but also to the whole host of cultural meanings and attitudes into which all infants are born.

Lacanian theory applies ethnographic structuralism in its psycho-anthropology by emphasizing the positionality endured by infantile consciousness in the course of receiving "a name," a family constellation of relationships, an inheritance of values and mindsets. This legacy is also the gift of the phallic, and it comes endowed with the fundamental mores of culture; the taboo against incest; the norms of liminal passage, particularly marriage, sexuality, and reproduction; guidance concerning economic exchanges; and political standing. But the phallic does not confer identity on subjects; rather, it lends space for the interpretation of desire within the network of cultural relations that position second- and third-party signifiers in particular ways relative to first-party signifiers of desire. Triadic relations permit the entry into language but from contradictory infantile positions of certainty and strength, weakness or instability, reflecting the vagaries of early nurture. The inexorable consequence of the three party signifiers at play during Oedipal inscriptions is that it sets in motion patterns of competition and rivalry, of envy and jealousy.

These patterns conduce to unconscious learning with respect to the rank held by the political subject in the ordering of society. Additionally, they induce a sense of echelon in the pecking orders of relations into which subjects are born. Above all, triadic structures alter the disciplines of desire, how they become dispensed and released, accepted or rejected. The paternal metaphor prescribes cultural and moral laws with respect to maternal second signifier representations of desire. In doing this, the phallic signifier opens up "liberating" space for the distantiation of relationships by positioning signifiers of desire in networks of three and beyond three to include the entire network of family and interfamilial relations from siblings to in-laws, consanguineal as well as affinal. This provides expanse for shifts in caring, attention and inaction and scope for interpreting the intent of such variations, their designs and import. The phallic as signifier does not confer identity but identifies the signifier of maternal desire. It thus sets in motion the quest for identificatory signature that connects ego formations with identity constructions.

But the price of freedom in relational structures means loss of totalized security wrought from the amalgamations with the partial objects (maternal signifiers); and, secondly, it locates ego formation and subjectivation within a contentious battle for desire that, if not met or surmounted, would incapacitate the quest for identity on which it is premised. The phallic signifier subscribes to answers, but only in the form of questions. Answers do come but in forms of symptomatic features definitive of human character, for example, the devices of akratic intentionality and disfigured forms of motivation. The political subject is thus the resultant outcome of a phallic freedom in which identity constructions reflect a grab bag of interiorized signifiers that are unable to bestow definitive identity on the desire of an infant or the first-party signifier, split and barred. Since the third-party signifier in phallic loss does not confer identity, but merely names second-party maternal desire in lack, the signifier of the first party, split and barred, remains indeterminate. First-party signifiers remain forever elusive; they, too, constitute an enigmatic signifier that sets in motion the quest for identity. On this account, identity, indeed, subjectivation as a process, becomes an exercise in the bricolage of indentificatory acts, different for each person, but congenitally fraught with the risks that come from improvisation. This bears on political identity and formations.

RESTORATION FANTASIES

The ravages of sadistic cruelty in the macabresque occur as the response to fantasized loss, on the one hand, and the ideological constructions of collective memory as articulated by and in political logics of illogic calling for the return and restoration of what was stolen or illicitly taken. Social fantasies enticed by memory or threats of loss corrode the stability of political order and promote waves of ideological reification often configured around: legitimacy; regime elites; the body politic; leadership; the sacredness of territory; political/cultural glory; collective survival; "face" and national solidarity; security; ethnic continuity; security supremacism; liberty in exclusionary freedom, etc. Erosion of political legitimacy and/or demise of traditional symbolic systems of political order lend support to demands for the restoration of what is often reified as historic necessity. For example, during the United States presidential campaign of 2016, the Trumpist slogan "Make America Great Again" resonated with the refrains of restoration fantasy, replete with alienated reifications of numerous groupings, such as the radical/ "alt" right, Ku Klux Klan, Neo-Nazi, and White/Aryan Supremacist identities made to bear "threats" of loss.

Derek Hook importantly stresses the analytical importance of levels of analysis in theorizing the relationship implied here between the psychical and the political grounded in an understanding of akratic willfulness made manifest by reification. He states, for example:

> In other words, the stereotype is a potent kind of reification, a type of re-evidencing, a making of one's own truth. Put differently, we are dealing with a game of ongoing re-'discovery' whereby one's racist notions are projected upon actual people, situations and events, which are then perceived as objective, factual incidents of racial inferiority. This, it seems, is a prime ideological operation, the imposition of what one wants to be the case upon the objects of the world, a continual reconfirmation of what one already 'knows' in the spiraling repetitions of the stereotype which precisely attempts to actualize a certain ideological apparatus of ideas. *The psychical process of condensation provides a means of understanding how the discursive operation of reification might work on an unconscious level.* Two crucial elements of ideological construction then: *essentialization* (reduction to minimal caricatured elements) and *reification* (a constant reaffirmation of what one wants to be the case), two means of protecting against the castration of difference.[68]

In this, however, he cautions against a crude theoretical conflation of the psychic and the political. He states, "In metonymic displacement and metaphoric condensation we have two concepts that pertain as much to the functioning of ideology as to the primary-process operations of the psyche. This, it would seem, is one way of conceptualizing the closeness of practices of discourse and mechanisms of psychical processing (indeed, the functioning of the unconscious) without simply conflating them." Applications of the concepts of akratic willfulness, disorders of will, and reification in racism and political hate do not suggest the analytical viability of a collective mind. On the contrary, as Hook concludes, it becomes critical for purposes of explanation to avoid simplistic, reduction-ist extrapolations linking psychic and emotional phenomena to collective political, in particular extremist, behaviors. Hook adds here, "We see here the possibility of a polit-ical functioning of psychical mechanisms that is not reducible to psychical procedures alone—evidenced as they are in the everyday use of language—and, likewise, a psychical functioning of political discourse not reducible merely to an ideological play of repre-sentations, to the force of discourse alone." He concludes "In these bridges between the psychical and the political—between primary processes of displacement and condensa-tion and ideological operations of reification and essentialization—we have certain [evi-dence] of the relay components, the 'go-between' mechanisms."[69] Psychosocial theory of human violation focused on desire and the psychodynamics of lack and loss help to frame an interpretation of precisely these sets of go-between mechanisms at work during epi-sodes of the macabresque.

The consequence in cases of genocide, hate, and mass atrocity is to permit macabr-esque sadism, that is, theatrical violence, by means of performative transgressions aimed at human violation to the point where perpetrators attempt to exert absolute power. Victims, especially citizen-victims reified as alien, are made to feel that their dying counts for nothing, that in death, their memory, their culture, their humanity goes with them. Victims are made to *perform* so that they live in interminable anxiety. It is this that is "willed" by perpetrators in mimetic desire. Macabresque sadism may be the-oretically represented as a "stand-in" psychic impediment against surplus enjoyment in *jouissance*, but in surrender to the *objet a* of performative transgression. To seek to impose on society "a new collective order" by means of the macabresque of mass atroc-ity represents a fantasmatic means of reinstating the paternal prohibitions relative to the anxieties of collective disintegration, by forestalling access to the forbidden obscenity of thing-enjoyment. Threats to the foundational artifacts of a collective order constructed around the fantasized paternal prohibitions risk weakening the psychic and emotional barriers to "thing-enjoyment." These kinds of psychodynamics, under certain political and economic conditions, appear to complement extremist efforts, especially if they are already in play, to impose retrogressive political regimes often articulated in ideologies of supremacist nationalism and exclusivist demands for cultural, ethnic, or racist purity in enemy-making.

Macabresque sadism arises from historical or cultural circumstances, or both, seized by conflicts over political legitimacy. Such conflicts trigger sadistic desires attached to mimetic rivalries. In cases of mass atrocity, this leads not only to collective political vio-lence but to human violation. The mimetic quality inheres in the disordered designs aimed at "stealing" enjoyment from the suffering of others—all in the name of prevent-ing "them" from stealing "enjoyment" from "us." Sadistic cruelty lives by its prophylactic desires to want human suffering as a protective shield. This operates along axes defined in allegories of parental attachment, demand and desire against the emotional intimidations threatened by cultural erosion of the moral, normative or spiritual standing of the collective sense of foundational order. In terms of social fantasy such desires are fostered by the dread of *jouissance* or thing-enjoyment that threatens the stability of psychic existence. Political reifications when grafted onto the psychic and emotional drives of sadistic cruelty impute *jouissance* or the enchantments of lost ecstasy in thing-enjoyment to others deemed "different" in their "otherness." The sadistic defeat of *jouissance* in others provides a psychic strategy and an emotional outlet for keeping *jouissance* at bay, the very *jouissance* that threatens to engulf collective order, even legitimacy, whenever the paternal prohibition seems on the brink of disintegration. Perpetrators who are gripped by psychic economies of macabresque sadism are in profound ways paralyzed despite their willfulness.

The psychodynamics of macabresque sadism illuminate the reasons for the repetitive nature of human violation during mass atrocity constituted by repeated demands for human suffering in order to install the paternal prohibition permeating the legitimacy of law. This also provides an explanatory basis in psychosocial theory with respect to why supremacism and exclusivism arise repeatedly in the dynamics of enemy-making. According to this framework of interpretation, the drive for "supremacism" in social fantasy signifies disordered attempts by perpetrators, hate groups, and their acquiescent minions to ideologically resurrect the paternal prohibition, metaphor, or law grounded in "phallic loss"; in turn, exclusivism—that is, ideological calls to "inclusivist purity"— represent disordered efforts to foreground psychic surrogates that block *jouissance* by means of access to the lack in *objet a* that remains psychically *present* by virtue of its existential *absence*. Together, supremacism and exclusivism help to constitute the ideological logic of illogics that come together in disordered calls for purity and absolute or totalized security, the very subsets of political reification that are typically evoked to justify hatred, mass atrocity, and genocide.

This helps to explain the relationship of human violation to political ideology and of ideology to sadistic cruelty. During the Rwandan genocide, radical or extremist Hutus imbibed the ideology of the Hamitic myth of Tutsi. This alleged that "Tutsi-ness" represented a form of racial "deformity" inveterately "alien" to Rwanda. This confirmed what the Hutu extremist class wanted to believe about the Tutsi. The consequence was that all of Rwanda became transformed into a macabresque theater of sadistic violation, where restoration was perversely demanded of the lost paternal symbol incarnated in the name of the Rwandan president killed in a plane crash. Social fantasies circulating around Hutu nativist exclusivism, became transformed into disordered aspirations for a kind of Hutu kinship that would be racialized and then executed to bring not only supremacist "honor" to the patrimonial ancestors but communal exclusivism to the now politicized society. This, then, is perverse desire in sadistic action at the core of the macabresque in mass atrocity, to torment victims held hostage in ways that lead to the repetition of violation over and over again in order to prevent the anxiety fired by a *jouissance* in social fantasy but triggered by political reification and ideology that avers, collective disarray is but a step away.

PERVERSION AND SADISTIC CRUELTY, OVER AND OVER

At one level of Freudian/Lacanian psychoanalytic explanation, perversity relates to the ways in which individuals seek pleasure in nongenital sexuality. Traditional definitions refer to five performative forms of "perversion": fetishism, transvestism, voyeurism, exhibitionism, and, of particular interest in the present context, sadomasochism.[70] These performative formats all are relevant to macabresque sadism given its combinations of surplus cruelty, human violations often of a quasi-sexual nature, and clear desire for voyeuristic and exhibitionist forms of dramaturgical display. Freud fought vehemently against the notion that perversion was in any sense "abnormal." The broad markings of incipient perversity reveal themselves across a wide cross-section of individuals, which led Freud to conclude that "the disposition to perversions is itself of no great rarity but must form a part of what passes as the normal constitution."[71] In the Freudian/Lacanian perspective, therefore, seeking pleasure in perverse desires has little to do with "abnormality" but, rather, represents a widely shared experience to be "overcome," not by "treatment" as such, but by means of transcendence into symbolic meanings and values. This becomes relevant to a discussion concerning whether or not perpetrators are normal human beings caught in unusual circumstances. The answer as implied by Freudian perspectives is that perpetrators are indeed "normal"; but they are rendered abnormal not only by virtue of the circumstances surrounding genocide, mass atrocity, and the dynamics of enemy-making, but also by the resilience of their self-deceptions. Why do "ordinary," dare one say, "normal" individuals engage in practices that are humanly revolting and morally repellent? Possible explanation derives from the nature of political perversity itself, from the fantasies that generate it, from the psychic structures it reveals, and, in particular, from the macabresque theatricality that is its very essence. Macabresque sadism seethes with desires for domination by means of theatrical enactments of absolute control over human anxiety, to satisfy the desire for a kind of political theater in which horror can be sensuously witnessed. For reasons of dramaturgy, victims become identified with dark and grotesque embodiment. Otherness becomes represented as the incarnations of monsters, zombies, cyborgs, and vampires: blood sucking or blood curdling animality. Cultural differences are made to take shape in gross imageries, from vampires and vermin to cockroaches. To enhance the theatrical sense of bare corporeality, victims are said to portray excremental waste or scatological impurity.

Not all the scripts run the same course. Theaters need not occur in single orgiastic moments involving mass strategies of displacement, agony, or elimination, although they often do; they can be sustained over long periods of time by means of sadistic torments imposed on individuals, small groups, or specified segments of any population. The curtains on macabresque sadism are never meant to fall. What is perversely desired is the systematic and controlled domination of victims as a kind of "surplus entertainment" (entertainment, literally, *entre tenir*, "to hold between") where "normal" life goes on with business as usual, untouched and unaffected, alongside the "Dirty War," the ethnic cleansing, the Holocaust, etc. One of the most vivid images of this is the death and dying by starvation taking place inside the Warsaw ghetto as the denizens of the city went about their daily routines. The "real action" is within the macabresque, where perpetrators come to feel that they dominate both space and time on the stages of history.

In these "spaces of exception," this sense of sequestered time and space allows perpetrators to be their own audiences, to applaud the executions of their own power, to enjoy their own sadistic capacities to violate the humanity of others, "to desire what the Other as law desires," as witnessed by Feldman in the H-Block of the Belfast political prison wing. Alford emphasizes the dramaturgical dimensions of torture in contrast to the realm of genuine drama based on imaginative creativity. "Evil and creativity come so terribly close that it is important to grasp the crucial difference," he writes. "Torture is a good place to start, particularly because torture is frequently couched in the language of drama, a work of art." The "art" of torture is in performance, and torture as performance thrives in its theatricality-given euphemistic names, to enhance the excitements of perpetrators. "The torture chamber is called the 'production room' in the Philippines, the 'cinema room' in South Vietnam, and the 'blue lit stage' in Chile," as Alford, citing the research of others, observes. But one should never conflate drama with torture, for the former is of the essence of creativity, whereas the latter is the essence of what is craven. As Alford declares, "In fact, torture is the reverse of drama. In drama, a transformed world is acted out on small stage. In torture, the world is reduced to the body of the victim, the difference between creativity and evil in a nutshell."[72]

THE SADEAN LAW OF PROHIBITION ON DISPLAY

Lacan depicts sadism alongside "the categorical imperative" by linking Kantian transcendental reason guided by universalizable normative principles with Sadean execrations. At first, this seems strange. Lacan's point, however, is not to judge either Kantian ethics or Sadean anti-ethics but to explore the relevance of how each system of ethics conceives of "universal law," both in relation to Freudian conceptions of the universal law of prohibition against incestuous return or what Lacan himself conceptualized as *jouissance*. In Lacan's view, just as Kantian principles of transcendental as well as practical reason are based on notions of the categorical imperative, that is, to act in accordance with normative principles that are universally applicable, Sade, too, makes claims to principles of universalizability, but ones grounded in control—cold and without mercy except as devices for dominance without empathy. Sade's enjoyment is that of the devil's emptiness, unyielding and demanding that the spirit of the victim be made to renounce its own soul.

Perpetrators in macabresque sadism seek libertine freedom to act with impunity on the bodies of their victims. The actions of sadists do not reflect, require, or serve the interests of erotic sensuality or sexuality as such, nor are they meant to result in some meaningful relationship, sexual or otherwise. The objectives of perpetrators beholden to sadistic desire in the macabresque is to empty out the personhood of victims through a series of violations, but in order to permit victimizers to represent themselves as law incarnate. Lacan's theoretical analysis of sadistic normativity explores desire, *jouissance* and *objet a* as the constitutive elements in strategies of control designed to make victims declare the law of domination, the law in fantasy that is the phallic law of restoration against anxieties of dissolution. To cite Silvia Ons, "Sade unmasks this object when he enunciates the right to enjoyment as a universal rule—this is how Lacan reconstructs the implicit basic premises of Sade's ethics: 'I have the right to enjoy your body,' anybody can tell me, 'and I will exercise that right, without limits preventing me from the whimsical exactions I feel like satisfying.' "[73] But what is the basis of such a law of enjoyment, a law that operates not as a personal "voice of conscience" but in the sense of "anybody can tell me" and thus exterior to subjectivity, beyond selfhood.[74] With respect to the macabresque and, by extension, the "law" imposed on victims is a fantasized law of phallic law, the law of prohibition imposed on victims by perpetrators who self-deceive themselves into believing that they are the voice of law incarnated. Macabresque sadism represents a psychic "locational strategy" for dealing with an inability to exert independence in the Symbolic when caught by fantasized desire to serve as the object of *jouissance* by becoming the cause of the m(Other)'s desire. In this, mimetic ideology in the Symbolic register plays out in ways that reinforce fantasized desire in the Imaginary register. Evans, following Lacan declares, "The pervert assumes the position of the object-instrument of the 'will-to-enjoy' (*volonté-de-jouissance*) which is not his own will but that of the 'big Other.' The pervert does not pursue his activity for his own pleasure, but for the enjoyment of the Other." Those who seek to be the object instrument of the "enjoyment of the big Other" seek to perform sadistic "enjoyment" by instrumentalizing it all in fantasy to bring about "enjoyment of the Other. In so doing, perpetrators become transmuted into the "instrument of the Other's jouissance."[75]

Perpetrators invariably claim that they are the (un)willing instruments of noble causes and inexorable fate. The willful legions that volunteer in the service of the macabresque do so as vehicles of the m(Other)'s *jouissance*. Ons speaks of the "voices" that call (interpellate) subjects that come from outside them, the voices of what Jacques-Alain Miller called "extimacy". This refers to the inner voices that reverberate as if outside of consciousness (as well as of conscience) demanding sadistic "enjoyment" through applications of merciless law. "In sadism/masochism, the subject locates himself as the object of the invocatory drive. The pervert is the person in whom the structure of the drive is most clearly revealed, and also the person who carries the attempt to go beyond the pleasure principle to the limit, 'he who goes as far as he can along the path of jouissance.' "[76] Or as Ons observes, it is to stand "for the voice in the mouth of the Other, as an object which is different from the objects that appear in the field of phenomena." Such a "voice," aligned with what we have called, the gaze of the rival self-other, speaks not of meaningful relationship or even of the vagaries of desire but, rather, of strict morality and of the strictures of law, sanctioned by fantasies of legitimacy that disavow limits or boundaries.

This is the significance of Sade's normative exhortations for the character of maca-bresque sadism, for an interpretation of performativity in mass atrocity. In the case of Kantian ethics, universalizability serves the deontological objectives of practical rea-son; in Sade's "decreative" constructions, universalist excesses service the supererogatory aims of satanic (perpetrator) desire permeated by the impulses to dominate and to do so in the name of a law "within" law. The sadist is one who gives way to the law, becomes its vessel and vassal, the law incarnate in its libertine abandon. Sadism is always about the inscriptions of law by extralegal means. In macabresque sadism, victims must be reduced to the instrumentalities of violation, done in the name of non-joyous "surplus enjoyment" one claimed as a "right" and "obligation" bestowed on perpetrators. As Ons comments, "The pervert wants to eliminate the unexpected event that shakes a previous assumption: his desire to break the law conceals the pervert's deepest wish: to substitute himself for it."[77]

Macabresque sadism often takes on a legalistic hue of codification. Perpetrators in the macabresque perform rituals of order, legality, and military command. The victims in the Omarska killing were made to march as if they were combatant prisoners. Nazi camp guards performed daily rituals of military review to insure "attendance," while they strutted in full regalia. The prisons of the Cambodian genocide were the sites of precise rules for how prisoners were to behave under torture: that included punctilious formulae for extracting confessions from them. As Ons indicates, "Sadeian society is a codified one, with guidelines and rules but devoid of eroticism, if by eroticism we mean allusive, ambiguous, suggestive language that is home to the unexpected."[78] Ons features Lacan's comparison between Kant and Sade in order to illustrate the contradictory objective in sadism to avoid *jouissance* by giving into *objet a,* "The law imposes itself as autonomous order, independent of the material nature of the desired object." In sadism, the "material nature of the desired object" includes the reified victim whose "personhood" is of no concern except that of a vehicle for the release of desire cruelly displayed. "In this opera-tion, however, another object appears as an intimidating agent. We know that whatever imposes itself, compels, and coerces frequently takes the form of a voice in the conscience, which arises as if from outside the subject." This external voice may be explained as the inflection of sadistic desires to impose surplus "enjoyment" by means of performative transgression. Ons declares, in describing the theatrical space of the macabresque, "as in other Sadeian scenes . . . the agent is not fundamentally the one who has the power or the pleasure, but the one who is in control of the scene and the phrase, or further still, the direction of meaning . . . . We can thus detect that there is repression in so-called lib-ertinage, repression of the non-prescribed, of the unframed, of *tyche.*"[79] The unpredict-able and the inconstant, the creative and the "spontaneous surprise" in human exchange must be brought under control since they become anathema to sadistic aims that detest all forms of singularity and autonomy, difference and otherness. As Ons concludes, "Strengthening morality implies appealing to a voice that does not tire the ear, reaching a definitive agreement between behavior and the law; a copula, then, between jouissance and morality. Such an amalgam will make jouissance take on the character of an unavoidable universal law, valid in all cases."[80]

In Lacanian perspectives, macabresque sadism seeks repeated re-enactment of efforts to reassert the primacy of paternal law against anxieties or dread, which are collectively fantasized as the threats to phallic prohibition, but which are ideologically constructed as the threats posed by demonized enemies inside or outside. Social fantasy and political reification do not cause each other. But they germinate the psychic seeds on which macabresque sadism feeds, perhaps in elusive nonlinear and indirect ways, but nonetheless, with terrible consequence once genocide and mass atrocity occur. Those who engage in practices of sadistic political evil are in a sense captured in fantasies of perverse desire to serve as the instrumentalities of *jouissance* while simultaneously "enjoying" *jouissance* by suppressing it by means of *objet a* and desire. This translates into disavowal and endless repetition that never satisfies. Lacanian perspectives on sadism help to explain the effete histrionics of Hitler's performative style and the megalomaniacal ruthlessness of Stalin's; it also helps to explain why both, each in his period and culture, found so many who were willing to accept. Both were styles designed to attract a mimetic following in support of ideologies and policies that succeeded in meeting the social fantasies provoked by disarray in the political order. This does not signify their justification; on the contrary, it illuminates the dangers posed by regimes headed by leaders able to personify the phallic prescriptions in social fantasy based on the illusions of power, especially once connected to political reification and hatred.

In this, a process of psychic transmutation occurs in which a kind of quarantine against *jouissance* is accomplished through a series of partial transformations often realized in and by metonymic displacements: jouissance into *objet a; objet a* into sadistic desire; macabresque forms of sado-intimacy staged for purposes of human violation justified by mimetic ideologies; ultimately, political reifications in the logics of illogic metaphorically articulated in thematic streams of supremacism and exclusivism. As Lacan once observed, "Desire is a defense, a defense against going beyond a limit in jouissance."[81] Sadistic "participation" in the macabresque on the part of perpetrators who "appear" normal demonstrates how wide the swath is of those who *desire* in social fantasy to support the paternal function relative to the threats of *jouissance* by in effect taking the "law" into their own hands, by becoming the law of desire that prohibits *jouissance*.

Ideology as an interpellative mechanism operates to galvanize the energies originating in the desire to stage or to enact the paternal prohibition or function and to direct them toward their target victims as ways of balancing psychic fantasy with external realities. This occurs across a wide range of circumstances of duress. Mimetic ideologies of desire are the lies that perpetrators may know full well to be self-deceptions but misrecognize and disavow *as lies* in willful denial. This permits the staging of sadistic violation to be repeated over and over.

The staging of macabresque sadism is "effective" only to the extent that those who become reified for reasons of the *jouissance* they are alleged to embody or "threaten," are violated in the anxiety reducing strategy that arises in order to confront "*the inadequacy of the paternal function.*"[82] Macabresque sadism and performative transgressions represent "an attempt to make the Other pronounce the law . . . so that the anxiety-relieving separation can come about."[83] Mimetic supremacist and exclusivist political ideologies transforming legal nationality and the rights of citizenship into totalized notions of purity, security, and freedom are in effect engaged in what Bruce Fink describes as "supplementation." Supremacist and fascistic ideology, in particular, supplements the fantasmatic yearning that the paternal law be reinstated in whatever ways social fantasies appear to want—but without recognizing the unfulfilled fantasy. But separation anxiety is a double-edged sword that cuts the human psyche in a variety of ways and directions. In Lacanian perspectives, the route to resolving such psychic and emotional tensions must pass through the realm of the Symbolic by means of "entry into language," which Lacan terms symbolic "castration" precisely because it suppresses the desire to serve as the phallic in the fantasy of the Imaginary register.

Language and symbolic imagination provide the instrumentalities in the psychic economy enabling subjects to "neutralize" the struggle over *jouissance* and desire. Thus existential, as well as political, freedom turns on a capacity for symbolization. Fink describes this process as a kind of cultural or experiential dynamic in language and symbolic meaning. "Once that which the mOther is missing is named, the *object* the child was for his mOther can no longer exist. For once desire is articulated in words, it does not sit still, but displaces, drifting metonymically from one thing to the next." He adds, "Desire is a product of language and cannot be satisfied with an [imagistic] object."[84] Thus a Lacanian-grounded psychosocial theory indicates that a primary psychic task in social fantasy is to leap into desire through symbolization and language. As Fink declares, "The mOther's lack has to be named or symbolized for the child to come into being as a full-fledged subject." Subjects must learn to live in the real world of symbolic meanings in which disordered reification reflective of lack, or what Klein called the paranoid-schizoid position, gives ways to distantiation, critical evaluation, and partial acceptance. This is precisely what does not and cannot occur in macabresque sadism. The subject remains caught in phallic fantasies of the Imaginary. Fink continues, "In perversion this does not occur: no signifier is provided that can make this lack *come into being at the level of thought*, easing its real weight."[85] Symbolic language and meanings represent the escape hatches toward processes of individuation based on promises of self-realization that pull away from the engulfing blankets of undifferentiated demands. As Fink comments, "Perversion can be understood as owing to the absence or failure of symbolization."[86]

And in this failure originate the patterns of disavowals that explain the cast assumed by political ideologies of mimetic desire in the macabresque of mass atrocity; the phenomena of "empty" speech; the desperation in attempts to constitute political order as a form of supremacist security and exclusivist purity; the refusal to accept difference or otherness as a basis for identitarian constructions. Performative transgressions in collective reification and mimetic ideology play the role of a giant cover-up of social fantasy, however unintended they may be, derives from the refusal to accept symbolic meanings. This again demonstrates the fundamental dimensions of disordered will and self-deception in political and ideological reification, especially during episodes of mass atrocity and genocide.

ENACTMENTS OF SYMBOLIC CASTRATION
IN GENOCIDE AND MASS ATROCITY

At certain historic junctures, genocidal "eliminationism," demands for totalized purity and freedom and absolute supremacism in fascistic reifications, tolerate nothing less than the extinction of a cultural genre and the groups who symbolize it. To understand this core phenomenon in mass atrocity and hatred requires an interpretation of the symbolic meanings and significance of Oedipal or symbolic castration. Symbolic castration refers to developmental capacity to participate in symbolic life and cultural meanings on an autonomous basis, even to the point of an ethical self-definition that contradict the demands for *objet a* in the social fantasy of phallic ambiguity. Symbolic castration represents the measure of Oedipal autonomy evoked by "the entry into language." It involves the psychic, emotional, and imaginative abilities to convert self-defeating "holds" of Oedipal attachments into positive forms of human subjectivity.

But the incapacity to achieve this and to be gripped by what Fonagy and associates called secondary representations condemns those who labor under such psychic and emotional weights to live repeatedly in what Fink calls "the enactment of castration."[87] Evans underscores how the "prohibition of jouissance (the pleasure principle) is inherent in the structure of language." He adds, "The subject's entry into the symbolic is conditional upon a certain initial renunciation of jouissance in the castration complex, when the subject gives up his attempts to be the imaginary phallus for the mother." Castration represents the precise psychic mechanism that refuses or rejects *jouissance* in favor of desire, the desire for life in the autonomy of mature self-individuation. If the lines between desire or "the pleasure principle" and the drive to reconstitute lost ecstasy by means of transgressive enjoyment of *jouissance* is not or cannot be successfully negotiated: first, by means of Oedipal castration, and secondly, by entry into the fullness of language and symbolization, the result, according to multiple psychoanalytic accounts, is perverse desires, narcissist fantasies of self-glorification, and sadistic yearnings for the enactment of law, the law of prohibition or castration. Perversity results from the failures of Oedipal castration to elicit mature emotionality. But this occurs under the illusions that *jouissance* is the lost ecstasy that can be retrieved through surrogacy or *objet a* according to psychic laws of paternal prohibition.

This perspective is highly suggestive of the psychodynamics of the Chinese Maoist Cultural Revolution (discussed in chapter 7). Evans comments, "The symbolic prohibition of enjoyment in the Oedipus complex (the incest taboo) is thus, paradox-ically, the prohibition of something which is already impossible . . . to sustain the . . . illusion that enjoyment would be attainable if it were not forbidden." Evans describes the ensuing existential paradox. "The very prohibition creates the desire to transgress it, and jouissance is therefore fundamentally transgressive." Oedipal castration enables the formation of psychic and emotion capacities to "go beyond desire" and past what Freud called, "the pleasure principle," and thus to renounce in fantasy the phallic *jouissance* that is "the Thing" (*das Ding*) of lost ecstasy suffused by the entrapments of primary maternal lack of lack. These insights are critical to a psychosocial analysis of the transi-tion from traditional Confucian culture to a communist revolutionary one that rejected everything associated with the "old" in favor of "youth," at the behest of the cadres of Red Guards, who helped to perpetrate one of the paramount genocides in all of human history: macabresque sadism was intrinsic to the process. To cite Evans, "The DEATH DRIVE is the name given to that constant desire in the subject to break through the pleas-ure principle towards the THING and a certain excess of jouissance; thus jouissance is 'the path towards death.'"[88] Evans further suggests, "Insofar as the drives are attempts to break through the pleasure principle in search of jouissance, every drive is a death drive." Failed Oedipal castration functionally provokes transgressive desires toward metaphori-cal "death" by impeding progressive capacities for imaginative symbolization. Failures in Oedipal castration take shape in the forms of perverse delight repeatedly brought to the fore in macabresque sadistic theaters of mass atrocity. These serve as the means or mecha-nisms to enact and reenact the Oedipal castration that might enable perpetrators to "feel free" in some psychic or emotional sense. But the result is sadism in perversity. Victims are made to suffer because perpetrators cannot live in the desires of symbolic gratification but, rather, find themselves doomed to relive the failures of Oedipal castration by repeat-ing them over and over again. And once genocide and mass atrocity are over, perpetrators are able to return to "normal" lives under conditions of normalcy in which desires exist but are captured by the (de)vices of symbolic compression and equation. Simply stated, imagistic reifications tend to continue to replace symbolic depth or flexibility relative to mass atrocity and its consequences, resulting in hollow shells of speech that are absent redemptive guilt. The victims of sadistic "enjoyment" serve as "displacements" for the symbolic meanings and values that most perpetrators are able to experience for so long as transgressive forms of psychic closure swirl around their political reifications battling with and against anxiety and lack, *jouissance* and loss.

POLITICAL EVIL AND FAILED PSYCHIC INDIVIDUATION: PERPETRATORS AS SELF-DECEIVED VICTIMS

The qualitative demand in political evil is to diminish the humanity of specific groups of citizen-victims by stealing their *jouissance* before *jouissance* destroys all. The political objective is to convert politics and the political into vehicles for social transformation to accommodate ideological notions of supremacism and exclusivism, in ways that are reflective of political reifications in relation to fundamental Oedipal fantasies. Perverse desire to destroy the *jouissance* attributed to others provokes unwillable supererogatory demand to protect the social order, but by methods that lead sadistically to the catastrophes of genocide and mass atrocity. Victims, whose lives are about to be torn asunder, often fall under a preliminary siege of "statelessness" aimed at alienating their citizenship. Statelessness becomes a means for devalorizing what is existentially human *in them*. Explanation for why the statelessness of victims is so valued points to the fantasy desires of perpetrators with respect to a surplus enjoyment that is aimed at stealing the *objet a* in victims so that they, too, might be separated from their *objet a*, that is, from the obscene supplements derived from *jouissance*. It is victims' reified freedom to desire that makes them so vulnerable to sadistic violation. They must become deprived of their rights to desire so that they may no longer live in any desire for desire. They "must be stripped" of their *objet a* so that they "may no longer revel" in *jouissance*. "Exclusivist purity" and supremacist security or freedom stands in for the *objet a*, the "be all" in desire, the diamond against glass in all signification, the master signifier in the psychic economies of specularity and the rival self-other that is the subject of the self in political reification. As Evans comments, "In the discourse of the master, one signifier attempts to represent the subject for all other signifiers, but inevitably a surplus is always produced; this surplus is *objet petit a*, a surplus meaning, and a surplus enjoyment (*plus-de-jouir*). This component in human subjectivity demands vindication in either desire/pleasure or *objet a*, ultimately death drive against symbolization."[89]

For this, victims must suffer. They threaten the *objet a* of surplus enjoyment when enjoyment is demanded and cannot be attained through achievement propelled by symbolic achievements. This also provides explanation for the tyranny of small differences in mimetic desire. Why is it that perverse forms of hatred arise amid histories of past cultural acceptance? Nazi contempt for Germany's Jewish citizens, Rwandan Hutu reprisals against Rwandan Tutsi, Serbian "cleansing" of Bosnian/Muslim communal members, so many other instances of "identity-based" episodes of genocide and mass atrocity spin on the lathes of small, even miniscule differences to what I have referred as the forms of identarian identicality. Fink, following Lacan, states that anxiety, unlike fantasy, never "deceives" (*ne trompe pas*). "Anxiety never lies. The sadist's aim is thus not anxiety itself, what it attests to: the object to which the law applies."[90] But fantasy by its very nature plays tricks. The object to which the law applies is the dreaded *jouissance* in the perpetrators as subject, not the *objet a* in the victim. "The sadist believes that it would be the symbolic Other's will to wrest the object from him, to take away his jouissance, if only the Other really existed," Fink writes. He continues, "The sadist, for whom the law has not operated, plays the part of the Other in his scenario *in order to make the Other exist*, and seeks to isolate for his victim the object to which the law applies."[91]

Sadistic perpetrators in the macabresque act as judge and jury. Sadistic violation serves as a means to reconstitute external reality by attempting to reinstate the symbolic meanings that reflect the Imaginary realms of "fundamental fantasies." *Mimetic ideology and social fantasy or frames work in tandem relative to existential maternal lack and phallic loss. This in turn calls forth surplus enjoyment in* objet a *as defense against threatening jouissance by means of surrogate forms of desire.* This proposition anchors any attempted adaptation of Lacanian psychoanalysis to psychosocial theory related to explanations of sadistic cruelty and the macabresque aesthetics of performative transgression. Fink declares, "The pervert himself is, in fact, a defense of sorts: the attempt to bring into being a law that restrains the pervert's jouissance, that bridles or checks him on the road to jouissance."[92]

This is the game that is played out in macabresque sadism: to obtain *jouissance* but to push its way through perverse desire that must be disavowed as desire so that the game of *jouissance* and thus surplus enjoyment in the sadistic theatricalities of victimage can continue. "The pervert's will to jouissance (pursuit of satisfaction) encounters its limit in a law of its own making—a law he makes the Other lay down, stipulate, mandate (even if, as in the case of sadism, the sadist himself plays the role of Other and victim simultaneously." For these reasons, perpetrators of all kinds, stripes, and ideological convictions, from Gestapo camp guards and commanders to Serbian thugs in the rape camps of Bosnia-Herzegovina, whenever they are forced to give testimony are prone to describe themselves the "victims."[93] As Fink states, "In a sense, the sadist plays both parts: legislator and the subject of the law, lawgiver and the one on whom the exaction or limit is imposed. To the sadist, the victim's anxiety over the isolation or designation of the object about to be lost is proof of the enunciation of the law, proof that the law requiring separation has been pronounced." But the mutuality between victim and victimizer continues, as Alford claims. "It seems to be a moot point," Fink comments, "whether the law thus enunciated applies to the other or to himself, since at a certain level he identifies with his own victim."[94] In so saying, Fink confirms Alford's observations with respect to victimizer as victim.

Since fantasies are in some sense control mechanisms, they are guided by shame as well as guilt disciplines in the economies of ego and superego functions. The superego is in some sense a control of fantasy-controls, and thus a major factor in desire, perversity and in sadistic forms of behavior where transgressions related to *jouissance,* surplus enjoyment and *objet a* lend themselves to fantasizing in ways conducive to political evil. Mimetic ideologies receive support from unconscious as well as disordered forms of intentionality in fluid and plastic ways, in a manner aimed at sustaining the stabilities of human personality and collective order. Social fantasies shape ideological confrontations with the social and political world; how and in what ways are critical to an understanding of the processes through which entire societies become prone to genocide and mass atrocity, as well as susceptible to the blandishments of ideological racism, political extremism, fascist fanaticism, and a wide range of canonical fundamentalisms. Mutuality between ideology and social fantasy is in turn reflected in the reciprocal dynamics between conscious and unconscious fantasies. These are subject to shifts in all the ways that human and social needs and demands, drives and desires become convoluted. Questions thus arise as to the extent to which social fantasy shape constructions of mimetic ideology or alternatively how and in what way mimetic ideologies intrude on social fantasy.

Fantasies point toward the most intimate of personal experiences of the self as subject; yet fantasies play out in social and political lifeworlds. Lacanian theory applied to an analysis of mimetic ideology incorporates the basic proposition regarding fantasy in the Imaginary; that is, it functions to maintain the phallic or paternal law as metaphor. This leads to the basic proposition derived from Lacanian theory as applied to a psychosocial perspective attempting to explain the macabresque of performative transgression by means of human violation: perpetrators in the macabresque "live" in the unwillable attempt to violate the bodies of victims as ways of reinstating the paternal metaphor that proscribes *jouissance* or ecstatic rapture. Lacanian theory suggests that the paternal metaphor, the paternal law, is the universal principle that renders all law possible through its prohibitions against incest, *jouissance*, and ecstatic rapture. Collective order coheres around paternal metaphors constituted by master signifiers establishing law itself. As Fink suggests, the paternal function is Symbolic, based in language that punctuates difference and distinction, it operates against the *jouissance* and fantasies of lost ecstasy. Its function is to permit resurrection of the legitimacy of law by separating the phallic from maternal desire. For this reason, perverse desires and the bio-politics of sadistic cruelty become mutually reinforcing: *through total domination provoked by sadistic violation of the bodies of others alleged and reified to possess "the object, the objet petit a" that is the stand-in for maternal desire, perpetrators can repeatedly stage the re-enactment of the paternal laws of prohibition while simultaneously servicing their need for maternal jouissance through possession of "otherness."* All fantasy is ultimately about beginnings, but so is mimetic ideology. Through mimesis we learn to speak and through mimetic speech we come to learn who we are and who we are for others among others. The paternal function grounds us in the constituted realities of culture and meanings, but not necessarily as captives. To erode the traditional functions of the paternal metaphor in honor and kinship cultures organized around segmented lineage and descent as has been the case throughout the entire process of colonialism, postcolonialism, so-called Westernization, and modernization has historically threatened the very basis on which law in the sense of legitimacy has depended in community after community. The displacements, dislocations, and disarticulations of political cultures can and sometimes have resulted in outbreaks of mass atrocity, often attributed in the West to "failed" or "fragile" states.

But such forms of collective violence indirectly originate in the devaluation of traditional forms of legitimacy anchored to communal forms of phallic law and prohibition. The paternal law as the fundamental fantasy of prohibition and Oedipal separation functions within but also outside the law. It prohibits access to *jouissance*, but once debilitated, it fuels perverse desire for the *objet a* that resists retrieval. The tragic consequence is that this demise in paternal legitimacy can and does assume sadistic force: first, by becoming enclosed within the psychic structures of perversity and perverse desires; and, secondly, by becoming turned against those who, however innocent, are reified as surrogates of the *jouissance* that must now be tethered by perverse desire and subjected to sadististic theatricalities and macabresque dramaturgies of performative transgression.

PSYCHIC SURROGACY IN FABRICATIONS OF DIFFERENCE

The *jouissance* of political victims is the surrogate for the *jouissance* that must be enjoyed but controlled by being transformed into perverse desire. Desire to destroy the *jouissance* of victims is a surrogate for the desire to manage the *jouissance* that threatens to destroy the self. In tormenting and eliminating *jouissant* victims, the perverse perpetrators of political evil and the macabresque are symbolically eliminating the threatened grasp of *jouissance*. In the psychic economies of political perversity, however, this is the grasp that can never be released. Psychic closure spins on disordered willfulness and spits out political reification as a substitute for symbolic flexibility and fulfillment. For these reasons, political reification is "empty" speech and the normative vehemence displayed by disordered willfulness in perverse desire represents adherence to "empty law" and "empty meaning." The psychodynamics in perverse desires lend themselves to sadomasochism as a supererogatory form of theatricality once genocide and mass atrocity give way to the macabresque. Sadistic violation is an enactment of the desire for desire when desire is a surrogate for *jouissance*, a surrogate that cries out for paternal prohibition in sadistic modes of castration, in which the laws of prohibition can and are performed by victims made to be participants in their own degradation. The psychic economies of sadomasochism and of sado-intimacy in the macabresque thus pervade mass atrocity that is oriented to an extremist restoration of the paternal metaphor through supremacism and exclusivism.

Perverse desires in the blandishments of *objet a* serve as diabolical ways of defending against *jouissance*, the ecstatic enchantment that can never be. And *for these precise reasons*, victims must suffer. Their *jouissance* must decline and be annihilated by means of sadistic torment and performative transgression. For it is the *jouissance* of victims, their desire for desire, that provokes the sense of mimetic rivalry in perpetrators that knows no relief except in *self-deceptions* contoured around political reification. It is as if victims possessed a magic that once destroyed would allow society to return to normalcy since the magic would be distributed among "the chosen" giving legitimacy to the phallic law of the paternal metaphor however it is fantasized and converted into ideology. Political perversity as phenomenological experiences revels in ideological doctrines that incentivize desire for exclusivist bonding and supremacist forms of belonging. Ideological and political reifications represent ways of giving symbolic form to the imagistic realms of exclusionary desire by means of contrived or fabricated identitarian differences.

In instances of political evil, this includes invented markers designating race, ethnicity, and religion that come to represent the surrogate signifiers grounding political and ideological reification. This is a central dynamic in the narcissism of perverse desire for sadistic instatements of phallic law. Surrogates or substitutions sustain and in turn nurture narcissist desire for self-glorification. By means of supremacist and exclusivist ideological reifications, narcissist desire can serve to contain or limit the grip of *jouissance* through surrogate forms of desire. It is as if the desire to fulfill maternal desire in lack of lack takes ideological or symbolic form as a way of avoiding the *jouissance* of thing-enjoyment and lost ecstasy that, if ever actually recovered, would destroy human personality itself. Supremacist and exclusivist reifications serve as the vainglorious substitutions in *objet a* and desire to impede *jouissant* rapture by becoming psychically aligned to ideological formations aimed at the desire to "project" desire imbedded in psychic structures of the rival self-other in ways that appear to offer solace from shame. As a result, during outbreaks of genocide and mass atrocity, ideological themes redolent with supremacist symbols, fascistic meanings vibrate with chauvinistic revanchism in the name of collective freedom. What is ultimately reified, however, is the perpetrator as subject relative to the rival self-other that is now transformed into the prototypical evildoer. Herein lies at least a partial basis for explanation of the "escape from freedom." Under the "right" set of external conditions shaped by extreme collective "anxiety" or threatening circumstances of social or political disarray in fact or in "fancy" and promulgated under states of duress, calls for ideological purity and supremacist freedom provoke perverse demands that give way to sadistic desire. The result is human hell on earth.

PART III

Cultural Contexts

CASE STUDIES OF PERFORMATIVITY IN THE MACABRESQUE

7

The Lurid and Ludic in the Chinese Cultural Revolution

ORAL DISCIPLINES AND OEDIPAL AGGRESSION

IN MAO'S RE-EDUCATION CAMPS

FROM INFANTILE SADISM TO SADISTIC INFANTILISM

Methodological problems arise once psychodynamic frameworks are applied to the study of genocide and mass atrocity, given the multiple levels of causality; related complexities of individual, group, and collective behaviors that operate simultaneously; and the often varying influences of culture, and socioeconomic and political factors, case to case. The ever-present analytical danger is to analyze groups as if they were individuals and to treat groups as if they were individual persons. This chapter examines the Chinese Cultural Revolution as a case study not so much to "explain" *why* it happened. Rather, I demonstrate the relevance of traditional values and certain child-rearing practices to psychosocial explanations of *how* mass atrocities were perpetrated. I focus on the genocide of the Maoist revolution and its dystopian project of peasant collectivization. The Cultural Revolution was political in its imposition of the Communist Party structure throughout China; but it was also socioeconomic and thus essentially about food, its production and distribution at macro levels of social organization and mobilization. Implementations of the party apparatus and of collectivized farming at meso levels within communities and at micro levels on the part of individuals involved lurid or sadistic displays of performative transgression.

The macabresque now included shame disciplines publicly administered as food punishments to the point of communal starvation. Such macabresque performances were often aimed as retributions against the elderly or whomever or whatever was deemed to be old and obsolescent. The combined patterns of ludic shame, performative transgression, and food deprivations or punishments reflected renunciation of the ingestive-digestive cultural traditions nurtured by Confucian values that emphasized Oedipal orality. Confucian traditions of oral—that is, food and shame—discipline, had been designed to instill expectations of obedience and obeisance, fealty and filial loyalty. Once these were challenged, the ensuing rage ravaged Chinese peasant society in ways that were indicative of a cultural crisis beset by conflict over its very core cultural identity. In psychosocial perspective, this identificatory crisis combined elements suggestive of the psychodynamics of perfectionism (ego-ideal) and fanaticism (superego). This led to genocidal violence, as well as mass atrocity. Here, too, performative transgression became an instrumentality of enormous human suffering. In this case, the macabresque was justified as a form of social re-education. This "re-education" project, propelled by cadres of Red Guards made up mostly of university students from various competing campuses and by rural peasants against their own neighbors, often employed village trials as the setting on which to stage shame or public punishments. It was Mao's political and diabolical genius to capture these malevolent energies and to direct them at those now deemed to be the enemy of the revolution but in so doing to transform Chinese peasant society. The macabresque in mass atrocity thus plays a central role in the Maoist revolution and thus in the emergence of modern Chinese society. But the dramaturgical and aesthetic form this assumed during the Cultural Revolution and Great Leap Forward was very much a reflection of the Confucian tradition and way of life.

Psychosocial theory in general, as in the case of much psychoanalysis, is sometimes critiqued on the grounds of being nonhistoric and noncultural in its analytical orientations. In studying genocide or mass atrocity, this would prove to be a fatal methodological error. Perpetrators operate within concrete situations delimited in time and space. In terms of mass atrocity, the macabresque would have no meaning in the absence of specific stage, setting, and audience brought together for limited periods of time—and then gone. Cultural factors become especially relevant in interpreting the macabresque at times of mass atrocity, given the influence of cultural values and meanings, as well as of identitarian constructions, in shaping the dramaturgical and aesthetic variations in how the macabresque becomes fashioned and applied. The theatricality and aesthetic forms of the surplus or sadistic cruelty applied in mass atrocities all entail unspeakable degrees of violence exacted in the name of human degradation. But how this occurs differs in specific cases, be it during the Holocaust, in Cambodia, Rwanda, Sri Lanka, or Guatemala, just to name a few instances, across different regional and cultural domains. These contrasts reflect the historic, including the postcolonial residues of social values, as well as the artifacts of economic systems, including structures of production and wealth and income distributions, along with religious, kinship, and ethnic traditions. The organization of political power and aggregation also play a role, particularly during the modern era, with respect to the centralized administrative state in relation to the structures of governance at regional or local levels. This, too, has important bearing on the consolidation of kinship, ethnic, or communal lineages into national political formations. All these factors, including internal movement of people from one location to others with the resulting social conflict, have relevance to the story of how the macabresque in mass atrocity became the main instrumentality of social change in China.

I demonstrate this with reference to the Chinese Cultural Revolution and the Great Leap Forward, genocidal movements that combined massive lethality with mass atrocity. This occurred across Chinese cities and villages, but especially within certain peasant districts or farming villages and communities. These settings were turned into centers for the "re-education" of the peasantry. The trope of re-education represents the particular cultural form of the macabresque. This was hardly accidental; it is, rather, reflective of certain traditional Chinese Confucian traditions and values and how these came to be virulently rejected during the Maoist revolution. To understand the loathing among segments of Chinese youth leveled against Confucian traditional values, I examine its origins in infantile sadism and relate this to the psychodynamics of sadistic infantilism that ran amok during the Cultural Revolution and Great Leap Forward. Sadistic infantilism infused the efforts of a generation of Chinese to throw off the shackles of the past, specifically, of the elderly and of what now came to be considered the old and, thus, obsolescent traditions. For these reasons, they deployed macabresque dramaturgies of cultural re-education. The weapon of choice was food. In this, the orality that Kleinian perspectives associate with infantile sadism becomes transformed into the oral aggression of sadistic infantilism that is critical to an understanding of the Red Revolution against Confucian filial piety.

OEDIPAL ORALITY AND THE RAGE OF YOUTH: FOOD AND EXPURGATION AS PERFORMATIVE TRANSGRESSION

During the mid-twentieth century, civil war within the People's Republic of China caused massive genocidal suffering on scales unique in modern times, perhaps throughout the history of recorded time. Political objectives became contoured around dystopian visions of collectivized perfection and the systematic leveling of rural peasant society. Class distinctions, in whatever guise, were seen as manifestations of dialectical contradiction. Social history was now ideologized as the unfolding of collective purity measured by the destruction of class enemies en masse. Criteria were arbitrary; accusations of guilt, capricious; but the consequences culminated in indiscriminate, yet systematic, mass murder of tens of millions. The means included didactic forms of "thought reform" and "self-criticism." The project involved nothing less than the creation of a dystopian faultless society in which class egalitarianism would result from existential instruction. The name given to this was "re-education." During the Communist Cultural Revolution and Great Leap Forward, this meant imposition of a pedagogy of perfectionism that did not stop at the mental borders of cognition. Class enemies were considered to be existential adversaries. The politics of class warfare carried the freight of political ontological meanings.

And those labeled as imperfect or incorrigible had their shame written on their faces, bodies, and spirits for all to see, community to community.

In the development of a historiography devoted to genocide, crimes against humanity, and mass atrocity, no greater burden has fallen on those seeking to document and interpret the pathways to human suffering than on those devoted to the story of the emergence of modern China during the past half century. It is a story told in red: red for blood, red for ideology, and red for the cadres of the rage-filled Red Guard youth who perpetrated killings and exacted revenge-filled torments, especially on "their" elders, in the name of proletarian egalitarianism. The consequence was a localized violent geography that ravaged Chinese communities. It was often the youth against the peasants in the rural areas and youth against the urban educated classes that brought tragedy to the Cultural Revolution.

The complexity of the Maoist genocide and history of massive murder and mass atrocity derives from several factors, not least of which stem from the various degrees to which the central committees of the Chinese Communist Party did or did not direct the widespread yet localized killings. Sets of entangled relationships among such forces as centralized political officials or representatives; agents of the Communist Party or military or police; localized clans with their own identities and traditions; generational conflicts; degrees of ideological excesses among youth; migration movements within China; regional, community, and local administrative and judicial controls, and so on, all played a role, but differently in contrasting regions. The major question in assessing the pathways to genocide and mass atrocity during the Chinese Cultural Revolution concerns top-down, bottom-up structural dynamics with respect to community killings. This issue raises not only important issues in historiography but also theoretical concerns regarding explanations of how genocide occurs and why mass atrocities, particularly in the form of performative transgression, play such a prominent role.

In the case of the Chinese Cultural Revolution and Great Leap Forward, once political power and dystopian ideology congealed into a fixed and frozen imaginary, "newness" was readily fetishized as all good, "oldness" as all bad. A pervasive sense emerged among youth, who were all too willing to become radicalized, that they had been betrayed on account of the obsolescence of the "old." All that was identified as old became reified as objects of disgust and vituperation, despised for what they represented, obstacles to vitality, renewal, reform, revolutionary transformation, and so on. "Things" old included persons, of any note or quality, of mature age. They now appeared as rivals whose presence impeded release of new generational desire to imbibe from the sources that promised liberation from a demeaning and retrogressive past. In the case of the Chinese revolution, it was the young who most wanted to imbibe the ideological elixirs held out by Maoism and Communist Party militancy.

Ideological militancy and performative transgression in mass atrocity were the revolutionary chalices that held the psychic and emotional waters of desire, channeling something akin to what Lacan called *jouissance*—in this case, a kind of libidinal yearning charged with the aura of pain in forbidden ecstasy, the very dystopian ecstasy that the Red Guards longed for as they drained Chinese peasant communities of their blood and sense of communal belonging. The fateful consequence resulted in lurid executions of sadistic violence combined with perverse yearnings for the physical violation of those community members now exposed as "enemies." "Enemy-making" during this period manifested all the characteristics of transforming minor differences into egregious faults, mostly conceived as "errors." But more than this, error was associated with "thinking" that had to be "corrected" by and through ludic performance. Victimage became transformed into transgressive community performance; trial by jury descended into a process of arbitrary but often staged expurgation. Thus, the macabresque took on the semblances of its unique form, sculpted, as it were, to suit the needs, demands, and desires of Chinese youth now transformed into perpetrators.

Purges went on ceaselessly during the Cultural Revolution and Great Leap Forward. But purgation took on semblances of Oedipal orality and also of a decompositive fecal symbolism in the shame punishments exacted during the phases of the Great Famine, the Great Terror, and the Great Leap Forward. In the punitive symbolism of the Chinese Cultural Revolution, Oedipalized forms of ingestive-disgestive purgative action permeated the dishing out of mass atrocity. It was not only that those who were insufficiently stalwart, unable to work, or guilty of the most minor of infractions in times of extreme duress denoted by massive levels of chronic malnutrition had to be purged from the rank and file of the Communist Party. The agents of revolution, often self-appointed or officially anointed by virtue of their zeal, repeatedly meted out luridly purgative shame punishments suffused by excremental kinds of symbolism: persons buried alive covered in excrement or bodies decomposed as fertilizer, or, in some cases, cannibalized in mashed forms.

The Chinese Communist Revolution was first and foremost about food, its production and distribution. The means used to achieve its designs included forced rural massification in accordance with dystopian conceptions of the ideal agrarian society, mimetically etched by Maoist attempts to impose Soviet-style collectivization on traditional Chinese peasant society. And, as in the case of Stalinist purges, the targeted enemy number one were the "rich" peasants: the *kulaks* in the Soviet case, landowners in the Chinese case. Overwhelmingly, however, peasant landowners in China were anything but rich. That they became the victims of vicious campaigns demonstrates some of the sadistic ways the Chinese Cultural Revolution became instrumentalized in the name of cultural re-education.

The process is now well documented. First, desire for *jouissant* "ecstasy" in mass violations against those deemed the enemy classes became triangulated; the Maoist movement and centralized Communist Party officials vied against various protagonists that included local cadres of Communist officials and community leaders, as well as the Red Guards, each rivaling the other to see how far and how effectively they could eliminate the impediments to egalitarian nirvana. Jonathan Spence describes the confusing array of multiple sets of adversaries called on to demonstrate loyalty to Mao, to the Communist Party and its ideology, but in competitive relationships to each other. He writes, "The

Red Guards were told to view the Cultural Revolution as the struggle of one class to over-throw another, to exempt no one in that struggle."[1] He adds, "The result was a bewildering situation in which varieties of radical groups, not coordinated by any central leadership, struggled with party leaders and with each other. The battles at the provincial level show this best."[2] Exterminatory violence accompanied by range of public and "correctional" forms of shame in the torments and agonies of mass atrocity were handed out on a com-petitive basis in ways not altogether different from the competitive sadism of the camp guards in Nazi concentration camps, as described by Sofsky. The Red Guards, like the Nazi camp guards, acted to outdo each other in the devil's game of absolute power.

What is especially relevant here is the sometimes on, sometimes off, influence of cen-tralized control and the consequent variability in how and when a macabresque stag-ing of shame discipline and punishment occurred. Performative transgression may have resulted from a central-government command or from Communist authority, but it became tied to community initiatives, even communal actions. In the Chinese Cultural Revolution and Great Leap Forward, the predominant thematic turns on ideological mystifications of youthfulness and subsequent exhortations of the young to destroy the vestiges of the old in the name of social change and transformation. Spence describes the call issued by the leaders of the Cultural Revolution "for a comprehensive attack on the 'four old' elements within Chinese society—old customs, old habits, old culture, and old thinking." Such generality and vagueness in interpellation, moreover, granted enormous latitude in implementation. Spence observes, "Red Guards eager to prove their revolutionary integrity turned on anyone who tried to hold them in check, any-one . . . who could be charged with 'feudal' or 'reactionary' modes of thinking."[3] The Cultural Revolution of the Communist Great Leap Forward was inspired by Mao, who "stood above this fray, all-wise and all-knowing."[4] But its implementation was designed by the Red Guards, who were given the go-ahead to engage in the kinds of generational warfare of young against old rarely seen in human history, when youth "rise up against their parents, teachers, party cadres, and the elderly." Spence explains this in ways that hint at psychosocial explanation. He writes, "For years the young had been called on to lead lives of revolutionary sacrifice, sexual restraint, and absolute obedience to the state, all under conditions of perpetual supervision. They were repressed, angry, and aware of their powerlessness."[5] Socioeconomic deprivations, puritanical limitations on sexuality and its expression, combined with the dread that is inexorably embalmed in the sense of powerlessness, represents a heady brew on which to become drunk "on the order to throw off all restraint" and to attack those vilified as responsible, especially the elders.

TEACHING TRUTH BY REFORMING THOUGHT THROUGH
SPEECH ACTS OF TORMENT

Herein lies a kernel of explanation into the reasons why the pathways to genocide in the Chinese Cultural Revolution entailed the ludic, dramaturgical, and aestheticized forms of macabresque performative transgression. It was not only that the objectified, reified obsolescent classes had to suffer, they had *to be made to be seen* to suffer. This is in the very nature of shame punishment, a key to its rationale but also to its sometime underlying perversity and sadism. During the Maoist revolution, macabresque transgressions had to be displayed, that is, performed before audiences who comprised not only perpetrators but also community witnesses; otherwise, the victims would not be given "the lessons" they "deserved." Communal desire for vengeance over whatever was dramatized as "lost" represents a form of motivation relevant to explanations of sadism and its execution. The yearning for displayed violation, its ludic performativity, as an end in itself, prompts the *sadistic* in sadism, the perversity in performative transgression, the ludic in lurid executions and punishments. This also suggests why Austinian speech act theory enables us to frame gratuitous cruelty in genocide and mass atrocity as forms of instructional speech act performativity. Spence, for example, describes the aesthetics of public transgression and performativity during the Chinese Cultural Revolution, "The techniques of public humiliation grew more and more complex and painful as the identified victims were forced to parade through the streets in dunce caps or with self-incriminatory placards around their necks, to declaim their public self-criticisms before great jeering crowds, and to stand for hours on end with backs agonizingly bent and arms outstretched in what was called 'the airplane' position."[6]

From a psychosocial perspective, what are we to make of this gratuitous, nonstrategic, nonpurposive "sadism"? Why the public display of humiliation and shame, why the trials, why the jeering audience? The aesthetics of performative transgression are sadistic, but not only on account of the lethality that results. The sadism resides in the cruelty of the aesthetics that include performance, dramaturgy, and public display. In the Chinese case, as in other instances of ideologically extremist movements, particularly on the left, including in Stalinist Russia and Pol Pot's Cambodia, public displays of shame punishments do have a purpose, but a manufactured one with no ultimate strategic aim. They are designed to exact confessions or admissions of guilt with respect to ideological doctrine or official policy. In the case of the Chinese Cultural Revolution, Confucian traditions built around honor codes and shame disciplines readily acceded to the macabresque during the campaigns of political re-education. Such aestheticized performative transgressions were meted out to serve the demand to teach victims "hard" lessons. In psychosocial perspective, this points toward a critical component of sadism and of what prompts sadistic behavior, including those framed in macabresque dramaturgies and aesthetics: to teach lessons, to instill the law, to declare the law. What is the law? In psychoanalytic terms, the law refers, in one way or another, to the phallic law of separation from the maternal "object" and loss of incestuous ecstasy, the ecstasy that can never be and thus never is or was. Those who engage in sadistic behaviors act as if they are in the service of the laws of separation, thus revealing profound psychic ambiguities and emotional ambivalences. Here again, we see a case of akratic willfulness covering over a weakness, not strength, of will and volition. Sadistic behaviors became paramount during the Chinese Cultural Revolution precisely because of the frail separation dynamics at the core of Confucian family life.

The Maoist revolution generated the circumstances of a perfect marriage, but the marriage was one forged in sadistic fantasies, bringing into conflict traditional ambivalence over maternal separation with unconscious demand that the bearers of the old declare the law of separation. This represents one of the central secrets of the communist reform effort and a key to its viciousness. Such is the meaning of cultural reform in the context of the Maoist revolution. Sons would declare themselves free of mothers and maternal care and nurture, specifically, of the cultural modes of traditional maternal nurture through eating, ingestion, and thus by means of oral desires and disciplines. As this occurred, the traditional "fathers" had to be destroyed, but not before being subjected to the sadistic display of shame and confession that was so much in keeping with Confucian values and traditions, but now transformed into Maoist styles of the macabresque. To achieve this, Mao had to preside over the process in fact as well as in fantasy. And when he did so, he became not so much the "father of his country" but its mother, the mother of nurture, who took away from all the mothers of China something of their traditional role and ambivalent status, thus permitting the law of separation finally to occur.

WHEN THE OLD MET THE NEW: OEDIPAL ORALITY AND TRANSGRESSIVE VIOLATION DURING THE CULTURAL REVOLUTION

In the Chinese Cultural Revolution sadistic desire became embedded in the Chinese traditions of cultural orality, first, in relation to dystopian visions centered around Mao as Chairman and leader, the Communist Party, its revolution and cadres; but secondly, relative to food production and consumption, as well as its disposal and decomposition. Orality meant more than mere ingestion; rather, it represented the cultural instrumentality through which the complex of family and social relations were established, including love, affection, respect, discipline, punishment, honor, shame, and face. Once the Cultural Revolution began in earnest, this influenced the psychodynamics of sadistic aggression, performative transgression, and mass atrocity. Sadism and performative transgression reveal the psychosocial character of disordered akratic willfulness. Orality in the Chinese tradition provides an example, and thus insight, into why. Sadistic cruelty is repetitive. It may seek greater and greater degrees of transgressive violation, since it re-enacts manifest dominance—over and again. But its aim is to never end violating its victims; its purpose is not the fulfillment of any rational (as opposed to rationalized) objectives. Sadistic cruelty and absolute power are related; both are sustained only so long as they remain ends for and in themselves. Once they become means to other ends or objectives, they tend to be dissipated. This is the case given their counterproductive strategic effects. What motivates sadism, and thus performative transgression or mass atrocity as such, cannot be understood in frames of strategic rationality. Again, purpose is not identical to motivation. This observation is critical to the uses of psychosocial analysis of political violence.

Sadistic cruelty and performative transgression cohere around what the linguistic philosopher J. L. Austin called instructional speech acts, speech acts that are illocutionary and performative, that assert certain givens as axiomatic truths that must be learned and accepted as such. Here, too, collective self-deceptions play a role. Such assertions readily lend themselves to the performative speech of hate, racist, or essentialized reification, as examined by Judith Butler in terms of "excitable speech." Sadistic acts are not only wrapped up in physical behaviors as such, but emanate from the rhetorical aesthetics in which speech, laughter, jokes, slander, slurs, and profanations of all kinds are the core elements of the surplus or sadistic cruelties themselves. And the process fed on itself during the Cultural Revolution as thousands became victimized by brainwashing exercises in confessional self-purification. As Spence indicates, "With the euphoria, fear, excitement and tension that gripped the country, violence grew apace." Solitary confinements for countless thousands over periods lasting for years and massive relocations to re-education labor camps for purposes of "purification," became commonplace.[7]

Re-education camps, like concentration camps or torture detention centers, represent the stylized spaces of the macabresque, where instructional speech turns into the modes of humiliation and degradation. At such times, speech act performativity and performative transgression unify the physicality of sadism with the ludic mechanisms and lurid methods of macabresque. In the macabresque, instructional speech act performativity becomes transformed into an instructional ethics that is dedicated to sadistic torments in the name of perpetuating the laws of separation—but in ways ultimately designed never to succeed or become finalized.

Instructional speech act performativity tends to be embedded in honor cultures disciplined by shame in which "saving face" becomes the main denominator of community standing. Honor is beholden to ancestors or to the cultural artifacts of tradition and communal values. For this reason, betrayal of honor amounts to more than the violations arising between one person and another in a dyadic or bilateral relationship. Rather, betrayal of honor is invariably a betrayal of the community, of the collective. Shame discipline represents a form of communal faciality. It is a "face" imposed on, or "made to be worn" by, those deemed to violate honor who are as a result required to suffer communal retribution through public forms of humiliation and punishment. The core dimension of the Maoist revolutionary project, then, was to link "emancipatory" ideologies of youth-driven collective egalitarianism onto the traditions of instructional speech act disciplines of honor and shame. The consequence was a Cultural Revolution that retrogressively sought to punish all and anyone who was deemed to represent the old order.

But punishments alone were not enough, because institutional reforms were insufficient to satisfy the desires fostered by the sadistic motivations. Revolution meant social transformation. During the Chinese Cultural Revolution, this appeared to demand the "re-education" of those identified as the recalcitrant classes. The means was performative transgression, but the end was to permit desire for sadistic cruelty to become endlessly engaged. Ideology became instructional, but in ways that were not merely cognitive, or even rational. Instructional pedagogy became sadistic because the lessons, which had to be learned by countless numbers, could only occur if village or highly localized communities suffered and were made to suffer in ways that staged speech act performativity so that youth could teach the old the lessons Mao wanted them to learn, and in the hard way. To demonstrate this against the background of traditional Chinese family life, I present a selective outline of Confucian family values and traditions. This serves as a case study for purposes of framing the psychosocial dimensions of mass atrocity during the Cultural Revolution. Emphasis on family traditions illustrates the psychodynamics of ego-ideal and superego relative to sadistic performative transgression and the macabresque of shame punishments, its aesthetics and dramaturgies.

FEALTY AND FILIALITY IN CONFUCIAN FAMILY LIFE

Confucian order was traditionally infused by notions of the centrality of the extended family as the core formation of society. Submission and acquiescence to parents and family elders served as the paradigmatic configuration around which the legitimacy of governance was modeled. In this cultural schematic, filial piety represented the primary virtue, one that was transferable to the successive echelons of feudal, and later regional, rulership that long predominated over Chinese political structures and traditions. Lifelong dependency and fealty, obedience and obeisance, represented consummate values; sons and daughters acceded to the legitimacies of parental authority, to their demands for commitments of succor and support, to their needs for security throughout their lifetimes and into the late adulthoods of successive generations of children. Richard Solomon provides an exposition of Chinese Confucian cultural values relative to Chinese political culture, including the values involving child-raising practices, that complements Spence's analysis of the cult of youthfulness and sadistic desire in Red Guard fanaticism.[8]

Solomon describes the Confucian life cycle as a reciprocated pattern of exchange, obedience toward elders and a lifetime of self-denial, especially during adulthood, as the price paid for the same in reverse during one's elderly years. He writes, "In childhood one depends on one's parents, and in old age on one's children; thus for the filial individual, life comes full circle." Solomon stresses the pathos that such renunciations bring. He continues, "The filial son in this sense remains a 'son' as long as he lives; he never breaks out of his original social matrix to establish an independent life. But he bears the pain and injustice which tradition tells him is an unavoidable part of childhood because he knows in time he will become a father while remaining a son."[9] Accordingly, personal identity became a function of subservience to family identity and to an acceptance of the demands for a "life-long prolongation" of "dependency" on parental authority and largess, especially on the part of male children, who were forever embedded in and bound by those Oedipal obligations.

The Strict Paternal Role and Weak Influence

Solomon makes the case that Oedipal psychodynamics, modeled in accordance with Western cultural concepts, including infantile separation, gradual adolescent self-individuation, and eventual adult self-definition, did not exist as such in traditional Confucian culture. The primary Oedipal process of distantiation between the subject and the maternal object, what Freud called *das Ding*, remained weak or ambivalent in concrete emotional life. This was the consequence of restrained, often removed paternal influences. These influences functioned in ways that fostered distant father-child relationships through a combination of weak paternal care and severe disciplinary postures. This tended to inculcate the values of deferential submissiveness to authority. Solomon outlines this by suggesting, "Chinese parents developed in their children considerable anxiety about disobeying their instructions, and indeed fear of direct contact with a stern father."[10] In psychodynamic terms, the role of the paternal law of prohibition and phallic separation is to assist in fostering mental and emotional capacities that avoid slavish acquiescence to authority. This proved difficult precisely on account of the severity of paternal authority.[11] Solomon observes, "The legacy of this pattern of childhood punishments and anxiety in the face of family authority which it developed was that the child acquired an attitude of passivity toward those with power over him. He tended to follow their guidance *rather than to internalize their standards of behavior* so that he might act independently of their control."[12] Solomon, in a thematic forecasting the research of Fonagy et al. on infantile emotional development, indicates that these patterns of psychic passivity and emotional acquiescence generated an authoritarian personality. He states, "From such a childhood pattern of relations with family authority seems to grow the adult concern for the presence of a strict, personalized, and unambiguous source of (political) authority who will impose order on potentially unruly peers and provide a clear source of guidance for all."[13] His basic argument is the Oedipal separation project appears fragile at best in Confucian traditions. Solomon states, "Put in more direct terms, there was no 'Oedipus complex' in traditional Chinese culture in the sense that this tradition explicitly told a son that it was both proper and morally virtuous for him to love his mother. This was not love in its sexual sense, of course, but love in the same form of *oral nurturing* by which the mother had loved the son as a child."[14] Nurturing orality relative to the psychic economies of the breast of the m(Other) represented the primordial denominator in a culture that featured dependency and fealty, and that honored these above the values of personal autonomy and individual self-definition. The role of the mother as a mediator between the father and the son, and as a consoler throughout life, remained paramount. Solomon states, "Evidence suggests that the mother could play a particularly critical role in the constellation of family relationships in giving her son the encouragement to respond to the demands of the father."[15] Paternal attention tended to be contradictory; at once, reserved, distant, judgmental, and invariably condemnatory; or on the other, suffocatingly affectionate. The result was that "the relationship between mother and son could be particularly close. When a mother found that her needs for affection, respect, or security were not fulfilled by her husband—who was very likely committed to fulfilling his filial obligation to his mother—she would seek solace in her relationship to her son. Mothers often were able to achieve a certain dominance with respect to family matters by using their sons as a 'narcissistic tool' in strategically influencing their husbands and his parents."

Oedipus the Son, Oedipus the Daughter

This presented certain openings, or what might be regarded as opportunities, for female children; but these also brought fateful dangers during later adult or married life. Solomon suggests that in several important ways, daughters were the true "Oedipus" of the traditional Chinese family.[16] But a feminized Oedipus condemned to servitude was unable to scale the heights of freedom or political power before the fall into tragedy, as in the original myth. Daughters were often sold or abandoned, given the low esteem bestowed on them, particularly on the part of poverty stricken peasant families. Solomon draws a parallel between the swollen foot, which helped bestow the name Oedipus on Sophocles's dramatic figure, with female foot-binding practices performed in accordance with traditional Chinese conceptions of beauty. As in many peasant cultures, once females married in Confucian China, they were forced to live with and to serve the needs of the parents of their husbands. Daughters thus feared what Solomon describes as the "dreaded harshness of the mother-in-law." Here again, maternalized authority became predominant, since the affinal mother was often determined to maintain the filial "affection which filiality said was her due."[17]

Mouths to Feed in Metrics of Jen-k'ou

The ligatures of consummate obligation and filial bonds of all-consuming loyalty to parents were benchmarked by levels of oral intake that were in turn regulated by oral forms of dispensation and discipline. Solomon states, "The considerable indulgence accorded a male child in infancy and early childhood, affection expressed above all through the giving of food, seems to be the basis of an 'oral' calculus in the way that Chinese approach interpersonal relations throughout life."[18] He continues, "The reckoning of their family or population size in terms of 'mouths' (jen-k'ou) rather than 'heads' . . . [is] only part of a view of life in which oral forms of pleasure and pain predominate."[19] Orality meant mealtime discipline. But kindness and loving care quickly, often abruptly, turned into instructional forms of deprivation. In due course, the familial love expressed during infancy by the giving of food turned into a device for teaching abstinence. Orality became a mechanism for learning the importance of abstemious disavowal of anything excessive, not only in material forms, but also with respect to emotional expressivity.

"Drowning" a Child with Love, or Ni-ai

Confucian practices of parenting centered on the disciplines associated with eating food. A prescriptive orality with respect to the taking in of food became an instrumentality of not only loving care, but also parental discipline, and was widely shared among peasant families and communities. Oedipal dependency retained its hold but became coded by the amounts of food given or supplied at any moment. Food restriction was a weapon of choice in teaching not only physical abstinence and fortitude in the face of deprivations, but also emotional control to the point of self-abnegation. Such self-denial was considered as a positive virtue, appropriate for the kinds of fealty recognized as highly virtuous. Solomon describes the way food acted as an instrumentality of personality development by referring to "taking in" as a disciplinary pattern adopted by traditional families. He writes, "For China's peasant millions, however, concern with 'taking in' was developed through the most basic discipline of all, an adequate food supply."[20] *Taking in* represents a cultural metaphor that conveys the stress caused by emotional restraint in traditional Chinese culture. Solomon states, "Also, the child learns from observing the ways in which adults handle their own feelings that reserve and emotional impassiveness are appropriate ways to discipline these inner urges."[21] But taking in related first and foremost to intake of food, which thereby tended to become infused by overlays of stress and anxiety. Solomon observes, "The handling and consuming of food thus, for Chinese of all economic levels, becomes an activity associated with considerable anxiety."[22]

Solomon infers from this a pattern of dependency and passivity toward authority. "The growing child soon learns that emotional expressiveness is dangerous because he lays himself open to manipulation by adults or older siblings." He adds, "If avoidance of contact with these offending family elders is not possible, then at least a *holding in* of the feelings by which they seek to use him becomes the most effective way to prevent humiliation or the pain of a rage."[23] Restrained emotionality and oral discipline represented twin components of efforts to ensure that children never became "spoiled" to the point that they would be so self-indulgent they would "eat" the family out of house and home. This fear often prevailed in peasant families, where excessive consumption on the part of younger generations spelled chronic malnutrition on the part of the elderly. This led to cultural mores that admonished against "spoiling" (*ni-ai*) children and thus warned against efforts "to drown them in love." As Solomon comments, "Drowning is an 'oral' kind of death; suffocation by taking too much in through the mouth."[24] Food, the currency of love during infancy, became the coin of scarcity in childhood. This had a double aim: to teach self-restraint to insure not only oral frugality during adulthood; but also to ensure that oral generosity toward elders would be forthcoming once they no longer were in a position to provide for themselves.

Eating Bitterness (Ch'ih-k'u)

In due course, the Cultural Revolution would give license for the release of contempt and hate against the old. Traditional emotional impassiveness among cadres of youth turned into a kind of intergenerational rage; once this occurred, the ravages of sadistic cruelty knew no bounds and recognized no conventional boundaries. Such sadistic release came on top of traditions that not only reinforced emotional passivity and self-restraint but also patterns of self-abnegation that required that the outward expression of frustration, anger, hurt, and pain be held within. Tantrums and rage did occur and were deemed permissible during early childhood. But they were regarded as profound failings once a person reached adolescence or early adulthood. This norm applied especially in relation to authority figures and became identified as "eating bitterness" (*ch'ih-k'u*), perhaps with similar connotations to the phrase often used by contemporary American youth and military personnel, to the effect of "sucking it in." Within the context of Confucian Chinese family life, yet again, the metaphoric language for disagreement and tension turned toward orality and ingestive-digestive associations. For things that were considered bitter were metaphorically recognized as being held "in the stomach."[25]

Speaking Bitterness (Su-k'u)

Orality is denoted not only by taking in but also by speaking out, and "speaking bitterness" became a rallying call among the cadres once the Cultural Revolution challenged traditional Confucian order. Solomon emphasizes the role of "*speaking bitterness*" (*su-k'u*), during the Chinese Cultural Revolution. Speaking bitterness represented a kind of collective shibboleth that mobilized mostly aggrieved youth by encouraging them to vent their frustrations and hostility in public, before audiences made up of community members across certain districts and regions. Speaking bitterness led to enemy-labeling. Labeling became a revolutionary tool meant to teach lessons about the indelible fault of some, and the possibility of ontological perfectionism for others. Solomon suggests that Mao's political effectiveness stemmed from his success at transforming personal bitterness into a political slogan directed against those labeled or reified as class enemies. Solomon recounts Mao's appreciation of anger and frustration in galvanizing the rural peasantry. He writes, "Combining ridicule of formal education with a recital of the power of slogans to focus peasant anger, Mao revealed that he had grasped what is perhaps his most basic insight into the process of politicizing peasants."[26] Solomon continues, "Mao perceived that *the anxiety before authority which underlay the millennial political passivity of China's peasants could be overcome if it were transformed into anger and directed outward through the force of ideology expressed in a political slogan.*"[27]

Solomon specifically cites Mao's revelations, given to André Malraux, in which Mao indicated that the "momentum" for the Cultural Revolution came from the pervasive sense of bitterness experienced across a wide swath of the rural peasantry. Mao told Malraux, "You know I've proclaimed for a long time: we must teach the masses *clearly* what we have received from them *confusedly*. What was it that won over most villages to us? The expositions of bitterness [*su-k'u*] . . . . We organized these expositions in every village . . . but we didn't invent them."[28] Loss and bitterness consolidated what Solomon describes as the "power to mobilize." Remediation for loss and bitterness are motivations, but not in the same sense as a set of purposive objectives to obtain particular ends or to achieve specific goals. This distinction appears to have been recognized as significant for the success of the Cultural Revolution. As Solomon states, "Ideology thus had the power to fuse passion and political purpose."[29] The critical component was repressed emotion experienced among those now bold enough and sufficiently inspired to transform haphazard or sporadic resentment into a unified political movement. But the motive force or element was neither land nor economic wealth in itself. Greed may have served as an influence; but it was resentment over the perceived greed of others, in combination with powerlessness to do anything about it, that led eventually to the prodigious violence.

Within the frameworks of psychosocial methodology, we encounter a cultural explanation of motivation that envisions anxiety, powerlessness, and passivity as counterparts to ideological justifications for the release of reification, hatred, and, ultimately, unrestrained forms of sadistic cruelty. The psychodynamics of desire and loss become salient forces in consolidating ideological mobilization and collective emotion. Solomon suggests, "This combination of ideological study and organized class struggle makes people politically 'conscious' in the sense of bringing together the perception of mistreatment and injustice with the repressed emotion."[30] What Mao succeeded in doing was to sanction a kind of grafting of unconscious emotionality onto the self-conscious awareness of bitterness due to grievous material circumstances, including property and land reform. But more than this, he also recognized that the promise to remedy these conditions *in themselves* would be inadequate to the tasks of cultural revolutionary violence. Sadistic cruelty and instructional performativity do not adhere exclusively to material or purposive objectives, as in the trope of not living by bread alone. Solomon indicates, "In developing this form of political mobilization, Mao began with the belief that simply redistributing land to poor peasants was insufficient . . . . *The peasants could sustain their commitment to the revolution only if they participated directly in the humiliation of those who represented the traditional system of authority.*"[31] Purposive and sadistic motivations differ and the peasants who brought about the Cultural Revolution were motivated by desires beyond the materiality of land redistribution, powerful as such objectives might seem. What they "willed" to be was what they historically produced, a cultural revolution of paramount cruelty written in metrics of revenge, contempt, and hatred. Powerlessness, obedience, and filial piety turned poisonous by provoking a rampage of sadistic violence. Villages became theaters, and theaters turned into the macabresque trials of mass atrocity. And by the time the Chinese Cultural Reform had ended, the traditional Chinese way of life was devastated.

COMMUNITY KILLING IN RED FOR RED BY RED: PERFORMATIVE TRANSGRESSION BY INSTRUCTIONAL SPEECH

The twelve-year history of the Chinese revolution, during the years 1945–1957, became drowned in death and dying, torments beyond measure, misery without limits.

Concentration camps and slave labor; a Soviet-style collectivization of peasant agriculture and the consequent famine and widespread chronic malnutrition; massive killing campaigns targeted at specific populations, including both rural land-owning and urban educated classes, at unprecedented rates—all characterize the mechanisms and methods of the Chinese Communist revolution. But, as previously noted, the means of the violence became ends in themselves. Sadistic cruelty was now represented as a public good; it was not merely a means of social and political change but a transformative device for collective transfiguration. What the Cultural Revolution wanted to achieve was existential purification through learning. Re-education meant mass atrocity; mass atrocity became the insignia of didactic reform; didactic reform became defined by the macabresque. Suffering was taken to represent remediation for past sins; subservience to the Communist Party a sign of transcendence, the coming of salvation, the final promise of ideological formation, the Parousia itself. At the center of this eschatological dystopia was Mao Zedong, who commanded that death be carried to thousands in multiples of tens upon tens, scored by district, regions, and communities until the benchmarks reached into the millions. In this, he succeeded. State terror and mass atrocity became a way of life. In ways imitative of the scourges brought by Stalin and the Communist Party of the Soviet Union, the Chinese Communist Party introduced new sets of social markers and imposed new kinds of identitarian categories on traditional society, in particular in agrarian areas. Identities were no longer to be demarcated in the natal categories of descent or lineage, of family or clan, or in terms of socioeconomic or geographical background. What counted was the relationship to the Chinese Communist Party: loyal or not, and to what degree, as manifested by what sets of actions or commitments.

Food distribution became an intermediate lever between class status and survival. Beginning in 1945, the registration of household units was required in relation to rationing. Frank Dikötter describes how the process of labeling and rationing worked. "On top of household registration, every individual was given a class label (*chengfen*), including his or her 'family background,' 'occupation,' and 'individual status.' There were sixty of these labels, which were further divided into broader class categories. These, in turn, were ranked as 'good,' 'middle' and 'bad' on the basis of their presumed loyalty towards the revolution." The so-called bad classes included, not surprisingly, "landlords," "rich peasants" and "capitalists."[32] Studies of genocide and mass atrocity repeatedly underscore the fact that identitarian categories in themselves do not cause violence; rather, they are the effects of other causes, particularly the result of political conflicts, war, and the drive to or exercise of power. Dikötter points to the process of category-making and the dynamics of reification that laminate new existential categories on groups and communities in ways that transform communal and social distinctions into integers of contempt, hatred and violence. One need only to recall the numerology inscribed on the skin of concentration camp victims during the Holocaust. In the case of the Chinese Cultural Revolution *category-making* relative to *enemy-making* was directed from the centralized structures of the Communist Party that now sought to promote mass atrocity violence through the creation of an enemy class consisting of thousands of those who inhabited the personal subjectivities and cultural identities of traditional China, including clan, peasant, land-owning, and more.

But what the contrasts across divergent pathways to mass atrocity reveal is that the semantic horizons of identitarian categories that stake out the contrasting parameters of difference and commonality, belonging and exclusion, and solidarity and suprema-cism emerge from within the cultural fabric of particular societies. For these reasons, cul-tural formats help to determine whether the dynamics of enemy-making congeal around race, class, sectarian differences, sexism and genderized categories, majority national-ism, or social exclusion based on physical or cultural markers, and so forth. To illustrate this, I distinguish ideological from culturally grounded identitarian categories; that is, I would differentiate ideological reifications from cultural values and meanings. In cases of ideology, categories of identity become transmogrified into the reified incarnations of identity. These can and often are used as political justifications for mass atrocity. Cultural constructions of collective identity in themselves do not cause genocide or mass atrocity; but ideological identitarian constructions become readily deployed, sometimes explicitly, sometimes tacitly, by political movements and their leaders to justify mass atrocity.

This, in turn, speaks to the relationship of ideological constructions in reification to social fantasy in disordered will. This question of the relationship between ideology and fantasy thus further devolves into an inquiry about what leads to akrasia: why ideological reification, why collective self-deception, and why the logics of illogic to justify sadistic aggression? In part, the answer points toward the relationship between ideology, reifica-tion, hatred, and social fantasies of existential purity or collective supremacism or both. Such instances tap into ideological logics of illogic that claim to predict political disarray and discontinuity, a cultural decline of values and traditions, social decay, and decadence. Often, social fantasy becomes instrumentalized by means of willful desire, played out in mass atrocity as an end in itself. However it may appear to seek consummation in con-scious or material reality, its psychic and emotional character prevents or inhibits fulfill-ment. But the costs can and do become very high once willful desire becomes released. This is reflected in the ferocious Maoist programs of re-education. Re-education in the name of cultural reform was an ideological exercise in class enemy-making by means of collective reification, and it became the didactic tool inscribed on those deemed to be class enemies.

For example, Dikötter describes the re-education process in the village of Yuanbao east of the city of Harbin in the 1940s. The modalities of the Chinese Cultural Revolution emerged, including: dystopian dreams; cultural and political polarities between perpetra-tors and victims; the communal dynamics of "speaking bitterness;" temporal processes of enemy-making; spatialized concentrations of victims; ideological reifications manifested by class identitarian categories; imposition of the artifacts of difference in material forms to contrast otherness; instructional speech act performatives with a vengeance; confes-sional narratives; and public humiliations and physical/spiritual transgression. Dikötter describes the scene, "After months of patient work, the communists managed to turn the poor against the village leaders. A once closely knit community was polarized into two extremes. The communists armed the poor, sometimes with guns, more often with pikes, sticks and hoes. The victims were denounced as 'landlords', 'tyrants', and 'traitors', rounded up and held in cowsheds. Armed militia sealed off the village; nobody was allowed to leave."[33] Ideological reification was designed to provoke a sense of personal meaning, significance, or power through missionary commitment and sacrifice. Dikötter observes, "Weeks of indoctrination also produced true believers who no longer needed prodding along from the work team. Some people were transformed into revolutionary zealots, ready to break the bonds of family and friendship for the cause . . . . They no longer felt themselves mere farmers plodding along in a forlorn village, at the mercy of the seasons, but instead believed they were part of something new that endowed their lives with meaning."[34] This sense of newness against oldness was vitalized by marking victims physically, first so that they could be reified as enemies, and secondly, by parading them across the village landscapes of macabresque trial and communal transgressions. "Everybody had to wear a strip of cloth identifying their class background." A reified color code emerged and was applied according to class identitarian category. "The landlords had a white strip, rich peasants a pink one while middle peasants wore yellow. The poor proudly displayed red."[35]

The production of enemies by marking them with the insignia of reified or objectified difference was but the first stage in a process of macabresque theatricality. Perverse akratic desire demanded sadistic dramaturgies in the case of the Chinese Cultural revolution to instate the laws of phallic separation. The "law" was thus sadistically seared into the flesh, bodies, and beings of those whose subjectivity rendered them objects, not merely of desire but of the desire to reenact desire in the macabresque so that the law might be performed. Dikötter describes the cultural style of performative transgression in peasant communities during the early phases of the Chinese Cultural revolution. He writes, "One by one the class enemies were dragged out on to a stage where they were denounced by the crowd, assembled in their hundreds, screaming for blood, demanding that accounts be settled in an atmosphere charged with hatred. Victims were mercilessly denounced, mocked, humiliated, beaten, and killed in these 'struggle sessions.'"[36] And so performative transgression during the time of the Great Terror, 1945–1951, was brought full circle: from "speaking bitterness" to "struggle sessions", from dystopia to instructional re-education, from akratic reifications of difference in otherness to sadistic cruelty, and from sadistic cruelty to macabresque trial by torture and torment. The psychodrama of hatred projected onto victims fed into the introjected ideological logics of illogic, and vice versa, to fuel a process in which inside/outside individual personality had lost its theoretical significance.

STYLES OF MACABRESQUE IN MASS ATROCITY

Ian Buruma, in commenting on Dikötter's examination of the aesthetics of performative transgression during the Communist Revolution, observes, "Since the 1920s Mao had reveled in violence for its own sake, as a cleansing expression of revolutionary zeal. As was true of Fascism, collective brutality had an aesthetic appeal."[37] But sadism is its own call to arms; its victims must pronounce the law. Sadistic cruelties in performative transgression differ depending on cultural constructions and specific ideological formats of identity. Pathways to mass atrocity rent by fascistic forms of racist or genderized reifications, for example, tend not to demand confessional rituals, public displays of "sincerity," as do the re-educative projects of dystopian communism. The reasons seem clear: race and gender tend to be reified as given by "nature"; the going presumption in such ideological logics of illogic is that no basis exists for victim self-re-examination. Fascist ideological reifications become grounded in notions of difference in otherness for which victims are branded forever, without the possibilities of remediation or redemption. *Victims do what they are.* Their presence amid the "select," "pure," or "chosen" is taken as defilement of a racialized liberty, the liberty fascistic ideology construes as necessarily supreme by virtue of nature or destiny. But on *pathways* to mass atrocity in cases of totalized communist domination, performative transgression often turns into sadistic torture and torment dedicated to forced confessional admissions of guilt. Class, after all, is based on material circumstances; "false consciousness" does not pertain to "nature" but to class. *Thus victims are what they do.* Their presence amid the "innocent" who are free from false class consciousness is taken as defilement of a totalized, essentialized equality, the reified equality communist ideology construes as historical necessity. In cases of fascist reifications, the normative justifications for genocide, mass killing, or mass atrocity tend to be denoted by an ideological determinism that is often sketched in corporeal or pseudo-genetic terms; in instances of communist reifications, the normative justifications for genocide, mass killing, and mass atrocity become devoted to ideological moralism, typically sketched in class-enemy or pseudo-structural and positional terms.

The dialectical contradictions that arise on account of false consciousness provide ideological impetus for transgressive performativity in which demands for confessional sincerity heap salt on the wounds of mass atrocity. Dikötter describes how during the twelve-year period of the Great Terror, China became a living theater of the damned. In the macabresque aesthetics of sadistic transgression, irony becomes encoded by hellish torments designed to demand behaviors that run contrary to anything resembling "decent" or even "normal" human emotion. Victims must perform in ways opposite to "ordinary" benevolence. They must smile as they are stripped of possessions, dignity, humanity; they must laugh as family members are brutalized. While articulating confessions for being enemies of "socialist thought," they must reach new heights of whatever their tormentors regard as "sincerity." As in other instances, irony became the fate of victims subjected to "re-education." The reasons are clear in psychodynamic frames: sadistic desire revels in parodies of excruciation. Buruma, on the basis of Dikötter's analysis, emphasizes how such sustained torments work over time to evacuate the mind and sense of self. He writes, "After days, months, years of mental torture there is no longer a self to retreat into. Besides self-abasement, victims were made to show their sincerity by persecuting others, sometimes friends or relatives. In many cases, suicide was the only way out." This seems altogether reminiscent of the ghastly *Sonderkommando* experience in Nazi concentration camps, when Jewish inmates were made to undertake horrific duties relative to other Jews and thus made complicit in how deaths and dying in the camps were being implemented. Existential self-abasement serves as a reminder of the aims of sadistic cruelty and performative transgression: to inscribe the laws of prohibition and desire into the spirit and psyche of those *subjected* to such *objectifications*. If a victim survived, the person within had died. Once the confessions became real, the re-educated victim entered the cadre of the "reinvented." But the cost was to evacuate all semblances of the self. Buruma concludes, "The process ended, in the phrase of a Chinese former victim, with 'the physical and mental liquidation of oneself by oneself.' The theater had become real."[38] The goal of sadistic cruelty is performative transgression, staged over time so as to allow akratic perpetrator desire to feed on itself, as in the case of attempts to attain absolute power. When this happens in some ludic sense, time on the stages of the macabresque stops since all reality is no longer a sequential process but only a moment of frozen presence.

LEVELS OF ANALYSIS IN SADISTIC
PERFORMATIVITY: A BREAKDOWN THEORY

Vexatious questions persist: To what extent is performative transgression and mass atrocity the result of command structures that direct the pathways to genocide? To what extent do orders issuing top down determine on-the-ground atrocities at regional, district, or community levels? How and under what conditions does sadistic cruelty become normatively acceptable within communities that previously had not witnessed such behaviors? What are the implications for a critical understanding of how time and space become transformed once sadistic aggression and performative transgression are made to occur within the camps, prisons, killing fields, neighborhoods and communities that in effect come to comprise a kind of exceptional spatiality and temporality? Yang Su frames these questions within a theoretical model designed to inquire about the relationship of the centralized national state to community collective killings. His analysis underscores the inadequacy of exclusive analytical stress either on top-down centralized state command structures or, by contrast, on bottom-up communal autonomy. Su provides a sociological framework of analysis that reveals how cultural perceptions and formats of identity become transformed into the ideological vectors of otherness based on minor differences.

The history of community killings begins with the process of ethnicizing traditional clan identities. Su writes, for example, "To explain the Chinese collective killings, I trace the long history of south-bound immigration to southern provinces and highlight the group identities based on surname lineage or family clan."[39] He further indicates, "Group boundaries were drawn within the Han ethnic population rather than between ethnic or subethnic groups." Su emphasizes the role of "blood relations" and clan based conflicts fueled in part by competition for resources as influences in shaping the dynamics "for imagining out-group members as potential targets of violence." He also stresses the importance of the role played by local leaders "motivated by their fear of being deemed politically lapse or by their ambition for career advancement."[40] Another critical factor was what Su describes as "the demobilization of moral constraints by framing war in a peacetime community."[41] Su demonstrates that the effects of these dynamics effected violent outcomes in two major provinces during the period 1967–1968, namely, Guangdong and Guangxi. He suggests that there were three factors: "designating the enemy, motivating potential killers, and demobilizing the law." But in the provinces most affected by community killings, two other factors were present as well. The first points to "immigration history" in these provinces that meant that the inhabitants were "more immersed in the culture of clan identities and competition"; the second underscores what Su describes as "the depth and salience of the war-framing."[42] Accordingly, culturally formatted identitarian perceptions combined with ideological visions of out-group conflict and war influenced community dynamics and culminated in killings. Su proceeds to embed his analysis within four theoretical frameworks of "collective identity, resource mobilization, political opportunity structure, and framing."[43] He adds a fifth he describes as the "community model." This community model focuses on what Su represents as the "structural breakdowns within the mobilization apparatus."[44]

Mobilization in collective killing results from state policy and centralized structures; but mass atrocity in community killings also derives from the discontinuities and gaps in those structures and the subsequent failures to control behavioral outcomes. In this view, the elites and upper echelons promoted the violence in the name of the Cultural Revolution; but they lost control of the actions within communities in various ways, including "organizational and informational." In response, group leaders and individual-level agents within communities assumed the mantle of excessive zealotry. Su describes this in structural and organizational terms. He states, for example, "Therefore the breakdown I refer to herein is structural rather than psychological." Su's breakdown theory thus focuses on patterns of community killing that resulted from the tension between "state sponsorship and state failure."[45] Community killings reflect the possibilities not only of state rationale and policy but, in addition, demonstrate how the "organizational pathology built into the system" may foster the pathways to what Su calls "eliminationist intent."[46]

Su suggests that his "breakdown" model stands in contrast to the hierarchical command structure framework often offered in explanations of the Holocaust. But his analysis veers toward Sofsky's examination of how individual camp guards, acting at their own behest, wielded absolute power in concentration camp environments isolated from exterior influences. His depictions are reminiscent of Jan Gross's analysis of neighbor-on-neighbor killing in Jedwabne, Poland. Su refers to the Dongshang Commune in Guangxi province, when, on October 2, 1967, village elderly, women, and the young were forced to jump off a mountain to their deaths and the fact that the "killers and victims were neighbors."[47] He describes this as typical of "a self-contained environment in which extraordinary acts of public killings met with no condemnation, intervention, or punishment." Law and order, restraint and decency, had become eroded to the point that performative transgression and community killing had now become a kind of "new normal." Su indicates, "For a sustained period, their extraordinariness had been neutralized by new perceptions of law and order as morality."[48] The macabresque had now eerily entered into neighborhood relationships and identities.

In the end, Su remains perplexed by what motivates localities to engage in the hellish torments of mass atrocity against victims who are distinguished by their lack of or minor forms of identitarian distinction. "The local governments at the county, commune, and village levels were clearly the direct sponsor of the mass killings, although the motivation is not clear." Su's entire point, however, is that power to decide who lived and who died and under what circumstances during the Chinese Cultural revolution fell to community governments and local bureaucrats and their adherents once centralized authority and power had broken down. This resulted in power flowing into the hands of trumped-up local authorities. As a result, they "zealously showed their compliance or they many have perceived terror as a convenient way to solidify their power hold on the local community."[49]

Su resists yielding to a psychosocial analysis by avoiding sadistic fantasies of retribution and revenge as units of analysis. His analysis points out that outrages were triggered by dystopian visions at the top, cast in molds shaped around ethnicized regional and local identities, endowed with the force of ideological reifications in terms of class warfare, and so on. His sociological emphasis on political and administrative structures leans toward situational explanations. "Hence, I also stress the importance of disaggregating state apparatuses into different levels and parts." He adds, "The result is a sociological model that stresses not only political and institutional variables at the nation-state level but also political, social, and cultural factors at local levels. As important, the model considers local processes of interaction between state and society."[50] He summarizes his position by stating, "Instead, one must explain why this choice may be available to the actors in the first place. This explanation is less about the actors themselves and more about the environment, or a community, as a whole."[51] The question persists as to why. Su admits, "By definition, collective killing is an irrational choice."[52] But his theoretical model of analysis disavows the significance of irrationality as an explanatory construct in favor of his emphasis on how "a diverse set mobilizations that are often in conflict with one another," play out in creating the space and time for collective killing particularly given the "conflicting interests" within the mobilization apparatus.[53]

Su specifically links his breakdown model to structural causes and their effects in that he frames the explanation of mass atrocity by pointing toward "collective action resulting from a dual process of mobilization and breakdown"—that is, "a condition in which actors evade discipline and punishment, whereas the classic models invoke psychological breakdowns."[54] He distinguishes this perspective from others, such as those "in traditional theories, [where] what is 'broken' is the 'normal' state of mind of actors within the community, who take unusual actions to address psychological needs." He contrasts this to the one he represents as novel, that is, the one with emphasis on "what is 'broken.'" And what is broken "is the linkage *between* the upper levels of government and the community at issue."[55] It is not my point to discount the usefulness of Su's breakdown model of mobilization, which adds richness even to Dikötter's historical analysis or Spence's political history or Solomon's cultural historiography. Rather, the question becomes broader still: what is it about human personality, ontological character, psychic economies or the psychodynamics of emotionality that makes these features seemingly inaccessible as contributing factors in explaining mass atrocity? Surely, psychic economies of mind, the topologies of human unconsciousness, the psychodynamics of fantasy and desire provide clues.

BEATINGS UNTIL ALL THE WATER COMES OUT: MASS ATROCITY DURING THE GREAT FAMINE

In the end, when famine came over the land and its inhabitants that had been devastated by mass atrocity, traditions of oral frugality did not save them. The life-sustaining scepters of wheat and rice turned into the macabresque scepters of death. Millions died from starvation, mostly in accordance with Maoist strategic design. It was what he had designed as the crucial path to social transformation. But as before, mass atrocity treaded alongside the pathway to genocide. Food insecurity and deprivation used as a weapon of war and as a means of executing mass atrocity carries the obligation to describe and remember but brings a sense of silence, one that veers against the capacity of words to measure the extent of human misery. In the case of the Chinese Cultural revolution, extreme brutality was used on wretched peasant communities that were already in the throes of starvation. Dikötter describes the unfolding violence of "Mao's Great Famine" during the years 1958 to 1962 to underscore the brutalities, mostly beatings by sticks and burials alive, performed on peasant victims *in addition* to their starvation. It appears that death by chronic malnutrition was too slow to meet the demands of Maoist Cultural revolution. Dikötter indicates that the cadres of Communist Party members preferred beatings above all and that the stick or baton was their "weapon of choice." Here is a sample depiction: "As famished villagers often suffered from oedema, liquid seeped through their pores with every stroke of the stick. It was a common expression that someone 'was beaten until all the water came out.'"[56] Dikötter cites the advice given to "new recruits," "If you want to be a party member you must know how to beat people."[57] Dikötter indicates, "Overall, across the country, maybe as many as half of all cadres regularly pummeled or caned the people they were meant to serve."[58] In certain provinces throughout Hunan, an estimated 10 percent of the already starving were buried alive or locked in basements or cellars and "left to die in eerie silence."[59] The methods used to torment and murder victims over and above making them die of starvation attest to the macabresque nature of the violence: widespread mutilations, deaths by live burial, by drowning, by being stripped naked to freeze, by means of dousing with boiling water, or by oil, by fire, or by branding. Many were buried in heaps of excrement or made to eat manure or drink urine. Dikötter adds, "The worst form of desecration was to chop up the body and use it as fertilizer."[60] Re-education in the name of cultural reform had entered a decompositive phase in which the integrity of revolution depended upon excremental decay.

FOR LOVE OF THE MOTHER: FROM FILIAL PIETY TO REVOLUTIONARY SHAME AND RAGE

This analysis has focused on the 1958–1961 Great Leap Forward pursued by the Chinese Communist Party and the subsequent 1966–1976 campaign referred to as the Chinese Cultural revolution. I have attempted to show how these murderous campaigns aimed at social transformation reveal patterns of revulsion against traditional Confucian values and child-rearing practices, and that this facilitates psychosocial explanations, not of the causes of genocide, but rather of *how* mass atrocities were perpetrated. In particular, I featured Su's analysis of the Communist Party command structure and its gaps and inefficiencies, as well as the situational variables at play at the middle or group level and at the ground level in towns, villages, and districts, which bore directly on the mass killing during the Chinese Cultural revolution. I presented my interpretation of Su's political sociology to underscore its importance but also to demonstrate its limitations, which arise with respect to the core set of issues and questions I have raised. These concern, first, why it is that macabresque performativity in genocide and mass atrocity occurs as a discrete phenomenon parallel to or in tandem with, but not identical to mass murder and killing; and, secondly, why when genocide and mass atrocity happen, they take on their own unique set of mechanisms, methods, and modalities. These include means and instrumentalities, the sum total of which I have described as consisting of dramaturgical and aesthetic ensembles in the macabresque. These are enacted during "frozen" periods of time; external temporality loses all meaning. They occur within confined spaces, prisons, concentration camps, torture centers, killing fields, and so on, to engage in highly particularized forms of torture, pain, and agony, and in accordance with specific styles that vary culture to culture. I have thus indicated that in the specific case of the Chinese Cultural revolution, Confucian traditions are clearly implicated in how mass atrocity was perpetrated.

The Great Leap Forward, modeled after Stalinist collectivization of the Russian and Crimean agricultural peasantry, was designed to transform an agrarian economy into a socialist order. The consequence was the Great Chinese Famine leading to an estimated number of deaths between eighteen and forty-five million persons. The subsequent Chinese Cultural revolution propelled by Mao Zedong represented itself ideologically as a reaction against bourgeois revisionism and a drive to return to the "purity" of Maoist "thought." Largely executed by Red Guard groups made up of urban youth and rural villagers who were responsive to Mao's call and his cult of personality, the campaign resulted in mass atrocity. To repeat, the essential question focuses on how and in what ways longstanding Chinese Confucian values and family traditions played a role or helped to determine the modes of performative transgression, and thus human violation, in Maoist cultural revolutionary violence. One dimension appears salient, the utter opprobrium and destructive contempt aimed at anything considered old or traditional. The Maoist Cultural Revolution ideologically rejected Confucian familial sensibilities and concepts of seniority. Vengeful campaigns on the part of galvanized Red Guard youth exacted retribution against all those deemed old or to represent Confucian family traditions. These had employed food/ingestive or oral/shame punishments as standard disciplines. In psychosocial perspective, introjected Confucian oral/shame traditions were now projected outward as a rejection of the filial dependency inculcated within the cultural core of Confucian family life and relations. When the "sons" of China revolted, they defied the very norms that linked infantile oral disciplines and food intake with shame discipline and parental authority. Maoist revolutionary ageism turned internalized infantile shame into externalized shaming vengeance. Its means was shame "re-education"; its weapon of choice was public punishment and violent transgression as performance; its consequences were mass atrocity and massive starvation.

Maoist implementations of collectivized farming entailed lurid or sadistic displays of performative transgression aimed at those labeled as enemies of the revolution, who became the victims subjected to shame disciplines. Perversely transgressive ludic performances served as retributions against the elderly or whomever or whatever was deemed to be old or obsolescent. These shame disciplines provoking publically displayed punishments reflected renunciation of the ingestive-digestive cultural traditions nurtured by Confucian values. These had been designed to instill expectations of obedience and obeisance, of fealty and filial loyalty. Once these values were challenged, the ensuing Oedipal shame and rage ravaged Chinese peasant society. Perhaps such shame rage demonstrated a kind of "relief" from the self-contempt experienced by mobilized Red Guard youth, who were set ablaze by Maoist rejections of the humiliations of the past, including the traditions of filial piety. These were typified by the intense role and emotionality associated with maternal care and presence lingering into the adult lives of countless Chinese families in accordance with Confucian traditions. Fervent rejection of familial interdependencies and ensuing shame rage against the old help explain the combination of sadistic infantilism and excessive moralism leading to ideological extremism and performative or ludic transgression throughout the Maoist Cultural Revolution. The psychodynamics thus also explain the perverse efforts of Red Guards to throw off the shackles of Confucian tradition symbolized by the old and the elderly by engaging in macabre dramaturgies of cultural re-education. In this, the orality that Kleinian perspectives, for example, tend to associate with infantile sadism became transformed into the perverse kinds of oral aggression that rejected the oral symbiosis often present in the psychodynamics of shame.

HONOR CODES AND SHAME DISCIPLINES

How was it that cadres of Red Guard youth, as they fomented horrific violence often across local and regional jurisdictions, particularly in rural China, demonstrated capacities for extreme retribution as the other side of their capacity for honor-bound obligations within the frames of shame and performative transgression? Honor adheres to bonds of belonging grounded in commonalities of blood, family, kinship, ancestry, and segmented lineage; aristocratic, chivalric, or noble orders; exclusivist sectarian, confessional, or devotional organizations; military and paramilitary brigades and "companies"; as well as throughout the many multiples of secret or clandestine, extremist or fundamentalist, radical or ideological groupings that exist within and across national and regional borders. Honor arises whenever risk, danger, or death especially by means of stealth, murder, or killings appear likely or near. It galvanizes modes of discipline over entire communities wherever they confront structural forms of scarcity, most especially food. Honor clings to shared perceptions rather than inner voices. It emphasizes exterior practices and outward performances in contrast to interior conscience. It enacts what Austinian performative language theory classifies as *instructional rules*, such as saving face, and reciprocal forms of retribution, such as an "eye for an eye," rather than adherence to the forms of law that require formal jurisprudence and rules of juridical procedure. It eschews the rule of law based on *commitment rules* governing voluntary behaviors grounded in notions of independent individuality, market relationships, and liberal values of freedom or liberty.

On the contrary, honor-bound regimes establish obligations among their adherents to defy social prescriptions based on rule of law, juridical legality, or political or economic justice. By those beholden to them, honor obligations often are seen to transcend personal conscience and ethical or legal normative restraints in favor of utter conformity to whatever undergirds "faith" and "faithfulness" to the code of honor incarnated by the social order. Betrayal and treason represent cardinal sins. Such social psychological dynamics imbued by honor obligations suffuse the specific or localized cultures based on "patron-client" relations. Thus honor disciplines tend to be grounded in the "natural" ties of kinship and clan, as well as on familial and blood ties and cultural traditions. Disciplinary codes of honor often reveal patriarchal, fraternal, or nepotistic beliefs. These in turn sometimes become embedded in rivalries over territory or control over distribution systems. Such codes of honor disciplines tend to reveal deeply valued social constructions based on ideological convictions; social etiquette or fealty; or attitudes regarding class, gender, religion, ethnicity, and so on. Honor codes and shame disciplines, moreover, tend to be patriarchal to the core. Honor codes and disciplines fall heavily on women and girls everywhere, since they tend overwhelmingly to glorify male dominance and in ways that serve to justify female subservience often in brutal ways to underscore the righteousness of female servility.

Shame and its affects serve to anchor honor codes attached to the disciplines of self as the rival self-other. Shame as a psychodynamic straddles ego-ideal and superego structures and formations.[61] Shame refers to either the conscious or unconscious sense of failures drafted onto the self in relation to sets of self-ideals. Often, shame includes narcissist elements, but it arises in the crucibles of personal self-rejection. It tends to be corrosive. In shame, the self becomes a rival to itself, a kind of rival self-other. Thus shame affects include integers of self-condemnation, not so much for reasons of actions taken, as in guilt, but on account of who one or "what" one is, for example: defective, dirty, disgusting, disgraceful, damaged, or degraded. Responses to shame include psychic and emotional efforts at disavowal.[62] As Léon Wurmser suggests, shame can be powerful in its affects (and effects) since it serves as a "screen" for deeper anxieties over castration and separation, as in the case depicted here. Shame is especially compelling when it arises in relation to parents and families.[63] The dynamics of familial symbiosis—that is, of separation and self-individuation—are especially prone to shame affects.[64] As Wurmser comments, "It is my impression that shame emerges particularly in family relationships that are involved in mutual power struggles and degradations."[65] Finally, a person's objective in shame is to become rid of it: shame introjected and experienced internally often becomes transmuted into shame affects projected outwardly. This psychodynamic was manifested by the Red Guards during the Chinese Cultural revolution.

THE LOST PRIMARY OBJECT AND SHAME PUNISHMENTS AGAINST THE OLD

The specific macabresque features of mass atrocity during the Chinese Cultural revolution underscore the particularities of culture and ideology mobilized by the Maoist revolutionary forces. These features include the psychodynamics of oral aggression and food disciplines. Of particular relevance is the strategic role played by Mao and of the Chinese Communist Party to galvanize the energies generated by mass resentment and fanatic opportunism among rural/agrarian youth. This resulted in the formation of decentralized cadres ready at the quick to mete out arbitrary on-the-spot indictments and capricious forms of abject cruelty, often on the basis of mere finger pointing. How, then, to apply a psychosocial analysis focused on these Red Guard and Maoist perpetrators as they engaged in mass atrocity at the local levels?

Janine Chasseguet-Smirgel's theoretical contributions are suggestive in this regard. Chasseguet-Smirgel focuses on the relationship between Oedipal separation and oral dependency with respect to developmental capacities for creative, ethical, imaginative, and thus symbolic forms of self-definition. She associates these features in human development with autonomy and individuation and thus with abilities relevant to social relationships characterized by mutuality of respect, reciprocity in self-esteem, and interdependence. Such characteristics cut against the delusions of omnipotence and dynamics of self-absorption that lend themselves to authoritarian behaviors combining excessive deference to authority and the capacity for ideological and political extremism. In her rendering, sadistic and narcissist demands associated with ego-ideal psychic defenses and economies of narcissist perfectionism result when the psychodynamics of caregiving and separation become deeply conflicted. When the psychic process of separation and renunciation is weak or ambivalent, the psychodynamics of personality development become narcissistic, perverse, and potentially sadomasochistic—that is, self-punishing—but also seeks to ground itself in forms of subjective stability rendered in part through exactions of cruelty enacted on others as a means of establishing a sense of personal individuation. Peter Fonagy and his colleagues observed how persons subjected to "the brutalization of affectional bonds" turn to violence in order to externalize the "basic affect of pain." "The act of violence, whether impulsive or calculated, is rarely one of blind rage," they write. "Rather it is a desperate attempt to protect the fragile self against the onslaught of shame, often innocently triggered by another. The experience of humiliation, which the individual tries to contain within the alien part of the self, comes to represent an existential threat and is therefore abruptly externalized."[66] Chassequet-Smirguel draws certain psychosocial inferences on similar theoretical grounds. The blandishments of ego-ideal and the unconscious desire for omnipotent perfectionism become readily moored to the psychodynamics of groups within certain cultures and at particular times. She states, "Temporally the group has a tendency to regress to primary narcissism; topographically, the ego and the superego can no longer exercise their control."[67] She continues, "The id takes possession of the psychic apparatus with the ideal ego which seeks fusion with the introjective restorations of the omnipotent mother the lost primary object."[68] This is highly suggestive for an understanding of the role gangs, hate groups, and terrorist organizations play in the psychodynamics of their participants. Such groups, networks, and constellations come to represent forms of psychic surrogacy. Chasseguet-Smirgel extends this analysis by applying it to an interpretation of the psychodynamics of ideology and political leadership. "Models, in so far as there are any, would be distant and abstract. When they are personified, it would not be in someone representing an idealized father substitute but in someone, precisely, who had himself succeeded in avoiding introjective conflicts and conferring upon himself a magic, autonomous phallus or someone who promises this to his followers whilst sparing them the painful process of development."[69]

In this, Chasseguet-Smirgel's analytical perspective is suggestive of the *maternalized* paternal role personified by Mao during the Cultural Revolution over which he presided—always as the unsullied model, the "magus" of the "ideological" leader—most significantly as the very incarnation of *Mother China*. Chasseguet-Smirgel states unequivocally, "Therefore the ruler partakes more of the omnipotent mother than of the father."[70] Chasseguet-Smirgel's psychosocial perspective offers explanations indicative of how Mao, as an ideological leader, functioned in social fantasy, beset by omnipotent or narcissist group ego-ideal formations, as mother figure or stand-in for the personification of China as maternal matriarch. Chasseguet-Smirgel states, in cases of primary fusion, leaders do arise but they "cannot, to my mind, be equated with the father. In this instance the leader is the person who activates the primitive wish for the union of ego and ideal." She comments, "He is the promoter of illusion, he who makes it shimmer before men's dazzled eyes, he who will bring it to fruition." She adds, "The group thirsts less for a leader than for illusions. And it will choose as leader whomsoever promises the union of ego and ego ideal."[71] Under such circumstances, social fantasy promises the retrieval of omnipotent perfection by becoming submerged in and by ideological groups now endowed with the prowess of primary fusion. This is evocative of the psychodynamics of weak but hyper disorders of will and desire made manifest by demands for heroic or salvific action by means of group action among the perpetrators of mass atrocity. Chasseguet-Smirgel hypothesizes, "It is as if the group formation represented of itself the hallucinatory realization of the wish to take possession of the mother by the sibship, through a very regressive mode, that of primary fusion."[72] As I have theorized such regression during the Chinese Cultural revolution took shape in the macabresque aesthetics of oral deprivation and the sadistic dramaturgies perpetrated by cadres of young Maoist zealots. Oedipal ego psychodynamics associated with oral aggression and the infantile fusional effort to resist the loss of the primary object through identification with a grand or idealized m(Other), as personified by Mao and Mother China, help define the unique character of the macabresque. Psychosocial perspectives thus provide insight into the unique features of the macabresque during the entire Cultural revolution that witnessed unprecedented levels of mass atrocity in the course of genocide.

Political reifications and hatred reveal forms of primary narcissism borne in and by yearnings for return to the omnipotence of the lost "Thing," a form of thing-enjoyment in ideological perfectionism that is fascistic, violent, and violative. It is as if, in the shift from infantile sadism to sadistic infantilism, there is a kind of tantrum of rage and revenge against the m(Other) that invites the primary illusions of return to ecstatic enjoyment but permits only a sense of partial return to placental omnipotence. This provides one form of explanation of the psychodynamics of self-deception. Caught by the psychodynamics of the ego-ideal, ideological groups assume cultural realities of their own, gripped by the fantasized grand self-deceptions of alignment with the good breast (orality) of the omnipotent mother. Psychically, the paternal figure of the phallic metaphor is "chased away" and excluded from group dynamics in ways that result in weakness of will but also disordered desire and demand. The hallucinatory desire is to eliminate the paternal signifier of castration that psychically poses the phallic barrier to *jouissance* in order to take possession of the group, or political movement, or social order, or, even the entire society as personified by a nation, in the present case, by the fantasized notion of Mother China.

Here again, the issue devolves into the psychodynamics of mature psychic and emotional development under the various conditions of culture, child-rearing practices, emphasis on individual autonomy and guilt disciplines, as opposed to honor and shame disciplines that tend to reinforce the primacy of groups, communal order, and survival, as well as the sanctity of ancestral, blood, and segmentary or totemic lineages. As Chasseguet-Smirgel indicates, "In groups based upon 'the Illusion,' the leader fulfills, in relation to the members of the group, the role that the mother of the future pervert plays in relation to her child when she gives him to believe that he has no need either to grow up, or to identify himself with his father, thus causing his incomplete maturation to coincide with his ego ideal."[73] Disordered or perverse desire demands of the self that it be omnipotent. Under the conditions of war, social disarray, genocide and massive violence, this can trigger or convert infantile sadism into the kinds of sadistic infantilism properly associated with self-deception, as Walter Kaufmann understood so well. In the social fantasies rooted in willed forms of self-deception, "knowing" operates in denial and thus unconsciously demands that phallic castration be a lie; that genuine renunciation of infantile thing-enjoyment be avoided; and that existential mourning of maternalized ecstasy or *jouissance* not be fully renounced in favor of symbolic values and meanings linked to human creativity and compassion invariably permeated by humility and limitation, rather than omnipotence and perfectionism.

Disordered desire in perversity originating in infantile sadism and manifested by outbreaks of sadistic cruelty in part represents a psychic strategy of evasion, based on fantasized attachments, that prevent the kinds of risk-taking in life that make living a quest for genuine self-realization, however defined. Chassequet-Smirgel comments, "As I see it, the pervert's 'creation' achieves this end: it represents his own glorified phallus which for want of an adequate identification with the father, cannot but be factitious, that is, a fetish."[74] This underscores the fetishistic behaviors of perpetrators, especially relative to sexual violence. "The pervert, and those with a related structure, will always be trying in one way or another to bring about a realization of the phantasy that lies behind the infantile sexual theory of sexual phallic monism, that is, the dual negation of the difference between the sexes and between the generations. The theory of sexual phallic monism is the infantile prototype of their adult ideologies. It is an attempt on their part to spare themselves the process of development."[75] Chasseguet-Smirgel's reference to inhibited genitality and perverse sexuality experienced in and as a consequence of repressed maturation points toward the ambiguous family relationships that are triangulated but centered around the maternal figure in traditional Confucian family life and roles. Perhaps no single metaphor captures the aesthetics of the macabresque, in any instance of mass atrocity, as does Chassequet-Smirgel's concept of the "fecal penis" that she represents as the fantasized outcome of the denial that genuine sexuality requires maturation in human and personal development. Throughout the Chinese Cultural revolution, the weapon of choice, beyond famine, used in thousands upon thousands of instances to beat, pulverize, and cannibalize victims was the stick. The stick stands as the symbolic emblem of how the macabresque aesthetics and dramaturgies became the distinctive instrumentality in performative transgression during the days of the Cultural revolution. It is perhaps not too much of an analytical leap to suggest that the stick as a symbol is precisely what Chasseguet-Smirgel means by reference to the fantasmatic instrument or obstacle that seeks to prevent accession to a future born of intergenerational hope and reverence on the part of a generation that is determined to destroy everything good and decent of the past.

In the end, the Maoist revolution, with its stress on China's youth over the elderly, collective agriculture over peasant farming, the communal law of arbitrary trials over the legality of the community, fostered the illusions of new birth, but in dystopic mass atrocity. Mao is the mother figure building on Confucian traditions of orality and social anxiety, who presided over the process as a distant father to some but an omnipresent mother to all. This forecasts the relationship between primordial and political reification. Chasseguet-Smirgel declares, "There is no absolute ruler who is not the bearer of an ideology. He is in fact the intermediary between the masses and the ideological illusion and behind the ideology there is always a phantasy of narcissistic assumption."[76] And the costs paid by the Chinese people on the alters of these grotesque fantasies and illusions of didactic revolutionary absolutism forever remain beyond moral or metaphoric measure.

POLITICAL IMAGINARIES AND METAPHOR: MOTHER CHINA, FICTION AS FACT

Political imaginaries arise at the conjunction of social fantasy and political ideology. They reveal what "a people" know, believe, and desire but also what they *want* to know, believe, and desire. Political imaginaries lend concrete form to collective life and social organization. They define what holds a people together, but also what divides them. In the modern world, they have helped transform populations into peoples, peoples into nations, nations into sovereign nation-states, collections of political agencies into the collective politics of "us" and "them." But what political imaginaries do or have done can also be undone. For the shifting sands of the imaginary reveal alternating currents. These pulsate differently at different times, especially with respect to political power, its exercise and justification. The struggles of political legitimacy are thus never far from the political imaginary. How does belief become transformed into political faith, how does political trust become subscribed and converted into a common virtue? How does political legitimacy become attached to forms of political power and authority governance, and, in turn, on what basis do governing elites and authoritative institutions establish claims and obligations, particularly those that call forth "popular" sacrifice in blood and treasure? Political imaginaries evoke and inspire belief and action; but they also reflect how collective belief becomes validated or legitimated through metaphoric condensations. These reduce truth to image and anchor the imagery to the emotive forces and ideological doctrines that drive the semiotics of political imaginaries. This process of metaphoric condensation becomes *more* rather than less critical in cases of coercive power, when regimes of ruling elites seek to mobilize a people into the grand designs of historic transformation, but at times when the principles of popular sovereignty are not clearly linked to democratic, authoritative, or constitutional procedures or have as yet taken hold in terms of "power to the people."

Metaphors distill, and like all distillation processes create residues that reflect the original properties of the materials that went into them, but with greater—that is, more concentrated—intensity. Metaphors thus transform constituted realities from one mode or model into another, usually in ways leading to the intensification of the antecedent or initial referent as its progresses along the symbolic chain. Often during metaphorization, one concept or idea comes to be represented by another, but not neutrally, as it were, in a trade-off of equivalent images. Metaphoric symbols strengthen the meanings of concepts by reconstituting them not merely as analogous or comparative configurations but as figurative representations of the images that "speak" or give expression to what is believed or desired most ardently or to the opposite, to what is most deeply condemned or deemed most abhorrent.

Such is the relationship of the nation to its metaphoric representations in the political imaginary of modern times. Perhaps no concept lends greater definition to contemporary struggles over what constitutes peoplehood and what grounds the legitimacy of political power and authority than the "nation." Such struggles lend themselves to metaphorization, in particular, to the personification of a nation and its people by means of anthropomorphical transformation. The complexities of divided, diverse, or diffuse national existence become at once reduced but also intensified by means of imagistic condensations to a person, an individual, a patriarch, a matriarch, a family, and so on. Such personifications are often depicted with attributed features (commonly, as in the present case, as the mother country) to mold belief into ideology but to ensure that ideology is molded in belief grounded in desire. Patrick Colm Hogan indicates, for example, "*The nation is a family structure* has several important functions. The first is to enhance affectivity. Especially when embedded in narratives, the metaphors of this type may recall feelings one has toward parents or siblings and direct those feelings toward the nation." He continues, "A second function is to enhance the sense of durability. Insofar as the nation extends back through ancestral generations, it has clearly endured in the past; insofar as it stretches forward through descendants, it promises to endure in the future."[77] Family metaphors provoke sentiments of belonging that are made to seem profound by virtue of common birth, blood, and nurture. Metaphors of motherhood evoke nationalist forms of patriotic loyalty, sentimental forms of fealty, pious forms of self-abnegation to what gives life and to which one's life is owed. Perhaps for these reasons, many nations adopt symbols of mother as the personification of themselves: Mother Russia, Mother Armenia, Mother Bulgaria, Bharat Mata (Mother India), or even Mother Svea (Mother Sweden). Such metaphors resonate with meanings, significations, and attributes that reflect the semiotic nature of the political cultures in which they arise.

Mother China emerged as part of the Communist iconography in the decades leading to the Chinese Cultural revolution. It served as a metaphoric representation or compressed image of the maladies afflicting Chinese society. As such, Mother China acquired revolutionary metaphoric features that stood for the external oppression and internal corruption that had to be ejected or overthrown before the Chinese people could stand tall. Lung-Kee Sun points toward the "ubiquitous evocation of an immaculate mother image of China" at this time. He interprets this to suggest that "the Chinese are less inhibited than Westerners when revealing their emotions concerning an anaclitically cathected mother figure." He also indicates, "Postwar Freudian studies of the Chinese personality have alluded to the de-emphasis of 'genital primacy' in Chinese personality development." Sun extrapolates important theoretical implications from this with respect to the psychodynamics of the Oedipal process, which is so often taken as a universal given or, at least, as being without cultural variation. To the contrary, Sun demonstrates that Chinese emotionality and affectivity toward the maternal was both intense and non-genital, and thus not wrapped around anxieties over separation and incest. He states, "By implication, a Chinese son, as a non-genital personality, could avoid oedipal conflict with his father while maintaining closeness with his mother in a way inconceivable to Westerners living under the haunting shadow of incest."[78] Although I largely agree with the thrust of Sun's argument, I suggest that the metaphor of Mother China served as a transcendent device enabling cadres of the Red Guard to reject repressive traditional familial and filial relationships with both fathers and mothers. Once the country, party, or Mao himself took on the semblances of Motherhood, cadres of youth felt enjoined to rebel against the "old" ways that had repressed them, including filial devotion to parents. The immaculate *reconception* of a transcendent Mother China generated by Communist insurgents was thus replete with a call to incitement in order to revenge the shame that had emasculated the sons of China. This call was not in the name of the mothers or even the fathers of China; on the contrary, the metaphor of Mother China helped to disengage familial obligations to both. Nonetheless the oral disciplines associated with shame and humiliation remained intact. The political semiotics associated with Mother China retained their oral allusions in forms that confirmed their fantasmatic ideological illusions in ways that heavily influenced the aesthetics of the macabresque during the Great Terror and Great Leap Forward.

As evidence, Sun cites the revolutionary tracts of Fang Zhimin, a major figure in the early days of the communist movement. He served as chairman of the Fujian-Zhejiang-Jiangxi Labor and Peasants Democratic Government and, in 1928, as a member of the Communist Party Central Committee. In 1934, he became "the commander of the vanguard forces" of the Red Army during the Long March, but was betrayed, captured, held in prison, and executed in 1935 by the regime of Chiang Kai-shek. He wrote several tracts while in prison that were smuggled out and preserved, including one entitled *Beloved China*. Fang's expressive imagery is redolent with rapturous affection and sensuous feeling toward a maternal figure he depicts with erotic flare and abandon but also deep shame and a sense of humiliation at "her" state of destitution and "beggary," having been ravaged by the West. He describes the topographical contours of China's terrain in terms of female physicality and applies such terms as "robust," "healthy figure," "dimples," and "abundant milk" as emblematic of their mother's body. He writes, "China is our mother who has given birth to and nurtured us . . . . This is like our mother by nature beautiful and adorable in every part of her body. China's coastline is long and curved, and from the point of view of the modern artist, it could be symbolic of our mother's having a beautiful figure." This paean to motherhood is disrupted, however, by the shame of "her" current state. "But our beautiful mother whom we love so dearly has been oppressed and exploited . . . . That is why she looks so haggard, shabby, and dirty. Yes, our poor mother, born a dazzling beauty, has now been reduced to beggary." As if to add injury to insult, Fang decries that fact, "She cannot compare with those fine ladies from the West and even feels put to shame by the Japanese girl."[79] But this is a call to arms, to revolution, a revolution described as return to honor in the wake of a shame that Fang portrays in the vivid terms of physical violation, including oral ingestion, cannibalism, rape, and dismemberment. "See friends, what devils those imperialists are! No monster, or demon in Chinese folklore was as savage as these hairy, cannibalistic orangoutangs. When they open their bloody mouths, like bottomless pits, they can swallow up tens of millions of people." Fang introduces the maternal imagery to propel the metaphor's emotive force. "Friends, look! Don't you see? They have taken mother in their arms to press their bloody mouths against her lips and cheeks, pawing roughly at her nipples and lovely skin." He demonstrates a certain racism in identifying the perpetrator. "And see what that devil in a white mask is doing!" he proclaims. Immediately, again, Fang's imagery turns toward the violence of oral ingestion. "He has thrust a golden pipe into her heart and is desperately sucking out her blood. Her lips have turned pale with trauma." He adds that other such "devils" are busy at the task designed "to suck the blood with might and main. Surely they will soon have drained all the blood from her veins." Fang's narrative is thus told in images of good and evil in which mother's "goodness" or virtue is depicted in frames of physical beauty while the evil of the West is described as ghoulish and black. Fang conjures up an imagery comprised of "devils," he implicitly associates with vampires who suck the blood out of China's capacities for maternal nurture. Fang, in conclusion, of course, rails against the domestic forces that he envisions as permitting these ravages to occur. "We have only ourselves to blame, because there are degenerates among us who oppress our people, so that we can only look on while our kindly, beautiful mother is humiliated and cruelly molested." Fang concludes with images of maternal dismemberment.[80]

Literary tracts such as Fang's facilitate understanding of psychosocial forces but do not prove them. At most, they serve to illustrate and confirm other forms of evidence. In the present instance, Fang's framing of Mother China represents a way of confirming the political imaginary that proved so powerful during the Chinese Cultural revolution, in two ways. It demonstrates the fact that the social fantasy of "mother" was being displaced in ways that permitted it eventually to serve as a transcendent metaphor mobilizing the sons of the revolution to take arms against Mother China's violators; secondly, that the metaphor of Mother China was necessarily linked to forms of violation that reflected the oral disciplines and traditions of Confucian family life. Sun infers from this, "In the area of political semiotics . . . modernization, especially the revolutionary process, has displaced the 'emperor-father' figure and has enshrined that of the 'mother'—applicable to Country, Party, and People alike . . . . The Chinese Communist party has been by far the more successful in fusing the maternal image of the Country with its own."[81] But the tragic irony of the Chinese Cultural Revolutions is that those who acted in the name of Mother China were the very same who devoured her children.

8

Cultural Case Studies in the Macabresque

VARIATIONS OF HUMAN VIOLATION IN THE TWENTIETH CENTURY

INTRODUCTION

Desire in the Study of Organized Human Violation

Thus far, I have emphasized the contrasts in inquiry between attempts to explain genocide and mass atrocity in terms of collective violence or by focusing on performative human violation. The first tends to examine the vectors and metrics of deaths; the second analyzes modalities of killing. These perspectives veer toward each other once attention turns toward war as a precipitant condition of genocide and mass atrocity. Wars, especially civil wars and cross-border conflicts, introduce multiplier effects leading to increasingly higher scales of lethality. Additionally, such accelerations prompt heightened campaigns of performative transgression. These are aimed at stylized suffering, but not as a side effect or collateral consequence of violence. Rather, they are established as a discrete organized process, in support of war aims when relevant, but meant to extract victim suffering through violation in massive, systematic, virtually systemic amplitudes. The question is why. If wars represent collective violence galvanized by political purposes and pressed into service by force for strategic gain, why alight the conditions that devolve into the macabresque? If collective violence, in the absence of war aims, is aggression, such as ethnic cleansing, why do perpetrators engage in methods that generate revulsion and widespread opposition that time and again prove to be self-defeating? What, then, is the allure of the macabresque? Why does it appear and reappear? It does not succeed in contributing to enhanced political power or strategic victory in anything like the long-term. In each of the cases studied below, the macabresque is relatively short-lived, its perpetrators thankfully vanquished, despite the egregious harm and hurt they have caused.

To respond, I examine seven prototypical vignette case studies of the dramaturgical horror definitive of macabresque sadism throughout the twentieth century in the political evil of genocide, mass atrocity and enemy-making. They are the following:

- *The Desert March of Young Turk Predatory Horror*: Young Turk post-imperial campaign of deportation, starvation, predation, and death against Armenian and Greek minorities in the aftermath of the fall of the Ottoman Empire, 1915–1916;
- *Stalin's Ideological Purgatory*: Collectivization, ideological fundamentalism, and the Great Purge and Moscow Show Trials, 1934–1938, in the aftermath of Russian mass dekulakization and collectivization and Ukrainian starvation in the Holodomor;
- *Hitler's Diabolical Laboratory*: Aryan eugenicist and Nazi physiological experimentation at Auschwitz and elsewhere during the Holocaust, 1942–1945;
- *The Hell of Blood Trauma in the Days of Hutu Power*: Physiological and natural flows, blood trauma, and stylized mutilation during Rwandan genocide 1974;
- *The Confessional Archive and the Facial Aesthetics of Ângkar's Torture*: Honor and shame, interrogational torture, confessional narratives, photographs of silent faces and death during the Cambodian genocide, 1975–1979;
- *The Junta's Neo-Inquisitional Operating Theaters*: Torture, state hypersecurity, and fantasies of heresy and apostasy during the Argentinean "Dirty War," 1976–1978;
- *The Bosnian Shame-Camps*: Genderized/sexualized humiliation and confinement, mass rape, and collective dying during Serb genocidal atrocity against Bosniak (Muslim) civilians, 1992–1995.

These case studies of the macabresque spanning the entire twentieth century and occurring across most of the major continents present a composite profile of the macabresque. My purpose is not to provide a comprehensive review of the causes or consequences of each. I do not necessarily focus on the major aspects of the genocide or mass atrocity in each, for example, the gas chambers, crematoria, and industrial methods of death on the assembly lines of the Nazi death camps. Nor do I thoroughly examine the political circumstances leading to genocide or mass atrocity, although historical context is relevant to an interpretation of the cultural dynamics influencing the variations that determine the macabresque. That said, I seek to portray the macabresque within each by adopting the "vignette" as a narrative form. A vignette is a patch, a semiotic sign, that stands in these cases of the macabresque as representative of a "mentality" that endows genocide and mass atrocity with a "noble" cause or "moral" if not, indeed, a "sacred" purpose. Similarities across cases of the macabresque emerge given the presence of human violation, almost by virtue of definition. But contrasts also appear that demonstrate major political, cultural, ideological, and attitudinal differences. I argue that these contrasts are not incidental side effects of violence. They reveal the relationships of social fantasy, specifically "thing-enjoyment" and mimetic desire and rivalry, in shaping not only ideological constructions of otherness but also the psychodynamics of a political ontology in which *ideology is ontology*. Thus, the modes of human violation are different because perpetrators in each instance of the macabresque are themselves different in ways that help illustrate how cultural environments and social acculturation influence the character of beliefs, attitudes, and psychological predispositions, including unconscious social fantasy during instances of genocide and mass atrocity.

And yet a central theme emerges across the case studies: perpetrators engage in diabolical sadistic shame punishments not merely to cause unbearable pain but to wound by means of abject forms of humiliation. It is as if unconscious fantasies over the dread of theft of thing-enjoyment become gripped by demands that mimetic rivals suffer the shame of sadistic degradation so as to impede their access to *jouissance*. Perpetrators in the macabresque play to the tunes of sadistic fantasies. In the course of the mimetic desires released by each case of the macabresque, this becomes orchestrated to the sounds of satanic honor. Sacred honor becomes satanic once it upholds a paternalized imago that demands that honor be performatively satiated through the excruciation of innocent citizens for sins against honor they never committed but are made to confess or yield. Satanic honor demands that victims be made to admit or recognize their shame, that they have dishonored the sacred ground of collective order, so that they do admit what they can never believe, that they deserve the shame and humiliation they are made to feel. Satanic honor demands that victims not only experience pain but that they performatively live through shaming; this is to restore the sense of lost or besmirched honor to the perpetrators. Honor is "losable," and once lost is only returnable through the "lessons" of shame punishment, or so it is experienced by perpetrators beholden to it.

But honor codes that manifest instructional rule orientations require normative guidelines and axiomatic principles to ground them. What is the psychosocial "rock" on which honor codes stand? This is the critical issue in the study of the macabresque. The paternal imago and the thing-enjoyment that ground the satanic honor of perpetrators in each case of the macabresque differs. They include:

- Turkified ethnicism (post-Ottoman Turkey);
- Stalinist totalitarian purgatorial ideology (Soviet Union);
- Nazi/Aryan eugenicist supremacism (Germany);
- Hutu nativist revanchism (Rwanda);
- Khmer racism and collectivist nationalism (Cambodia);
- Ultramontane Catholicism and military fascism (Argentina); and
- Serbian Orthodox nationalist extremism (Bosnia).

Ideational forms of ideology; religion; and racialized notions of blood, ethnicity, and nation all contribute to the dramaturgies and aesthetics of the macabresque. The consequence is that the sadistic shame punishments victims are made to endure differ; thus, the modalities of the macabresque differ in each instance. Nonetheless, the psychodynamics of satanic honor and sadistic shame prevails, with striking similarities, across the cases. The repeated intensity of sheer gratuitous cruelty against victims in theatrical modes of human violation, time, and again across historical episodes in the twentieth century of genocide and mass atrocity, at first make them appear as psychopathologically driven; but one is tempted to categorize them as a normative phenomenon if one correlates occurrence with normalcy.

To return to my central theme, it is difficult if not impossible to explain the macabresque in the absence of analytical perspectives that include the unconscious and its mimetic psychodynamics gripped by thing-enjoyment, desire, and its demands. Desire and thing-enjoyment represent a kind of "particle of anti-matter" that "must" exist in theory, if actual behaviors are to be explained. To demonstrate this, I turn to case studies in the macabresque to illustrate how or in what ways social fantasy, mimetic desire, and thing-enjoyment or *jouissance* influence perpetrators' behaviors with respect to modes of producing victim suffering. Each vignette features certain aspects of human violation at the core of each case of the macabresque, for example: the long marches, military-style predation and murder, as well as starvation during the Armenian genocide; the intra–Communist Party confessional campaigns of the Moscow Show Trials and Great Purge; the eugenic fantasies and experimental sadism in the laboratories of torment in the Holocaust; the mug shots and confessional archives in the torture cells and killing fields of the Cambodian genocide; and the agony of dismembered bodies and stylized cutting at the roadblocks of the Rwandan genocide. I also briefly refer to the neo-inquisitional torture chambers of the so-called Dirty War in Argentina; the cell-block torments by beating and group suffocation of the Omarska shame-camp that were mostly carried out against men and boys, as well as the multiple Serbian shame-camp sites of mass or genocidal rape, mostly against women and girls during the Serbian ethnic-cleansing campaign against the Bosniaks in Bosnia-Herzegovina.

The thrust of these case studies is, first, to illustrate why studies of genocide and mass atrocity should look beyond purposive motivations depicted in rational, strategic, or even ideological terms. Secondly, my objective is to emphasize the explanatory relevance of analytical linkages between political culture and social fantasies in examining extreme cases of sustained human violation. This also suggests that a focus on lethality in collective violence proves insufficient to explain the actual practices that occur during episodes of genocide and mass atrocity. The question remains, why does suffering over and beyond death appear so compelling to perpetrators? In raising this issue, I hope, finally, to demonstrate the analytical gains gleaned by adopting certain psychosocial approaches to mimetic desire and what is often framed as "thing-enjoyment" or *jouissance* and *objet a*. My attempt is not to "prove" that these factors are "causal" as such. The issues are far too complex for single causal explanations to apply. Explanatory rigor, however, sometimes derives not from the richness of answers provided by theoretical discourses, but stems from the richness of the questions they provoke.

That said, I argue that case studies of the macabresque require the application of psychosocial frameworks of explanation focused on the psychodynamics of mimetic desire, social fantasy, and thing-enjoyment in cultural constructions of collective identity, all as units of analysis that contribute to our understanding of the relationship between political culture and mass atrocity. Reasons point in part toward the relevance of honor and shame as forms of emotionality that influence or play out as the dynamics of mimetic desire unfold. Social fantasy and the psychodynamics of "thing-enjoyment," as well its fantasized loss or "theft" by the rivalrous "other," assume concrete forms through expressions of mimetic desires. What distinguishes the political study of mass atrocity as collective violence from case-study analysis of the macabresque are the psychosocial explorations of mimetic desire, "thing-enjoyment," and social fantasy. The shift, therefore, from analysis of collective violence to human violation entails a recalibration of the explanatory or theoretical approach, one that moves from cognitive rationalism (critiqued earlier as it is applied in social and political psychology[1]), to psychosocial perspectives on emotionality and desire. In particular, honor and shame become integral to the psychodynamics of mimetic desire, influencing the distinct performative character of mass atrocity in the macabresque, culture to culture, with fateful consequences for the victims.

Pain is universal, but how victims are made to suffer in each instance of the macabresque provides insights on culture in relation to cruelty and both with respect to the sadistic fantasy in mimetic desire. These factors become germane to explanations of the dramaturgies and aesthetics of each instance of the macabresque, and thus require appropriate methodological frameworks of analysis. Modes of performativity service perpetrator desires within the mimetic frames of culture that influence how human violations occur. The consequence is that the actual staging of performative transgression differs across cases. The macabresque is everywhere the same, yet different. The relationship of the macabresque to mass atrocity is in the instrumentalizing of how pain is caused or administered at the hands of others. All pain is *pain*, but is it possible to distinguish the suffering caused within the macabresque according to its performativity, execution, and modalities—that is, in how *torture, torment*, and *agony* are inflicted. Such factors reveal the cultural meanings and values and the ideological reifications that attend genocide and mass atrocity. The sufferings of *torment, torture*, and *agony* each demonstrate something specific about the cultural and ideological environment or milieu in which they made to occur. As Edward Peters, in his classic examination of torture, states, "There seems to be culturally-favored forms of torture in different societies."[2] How torture violations occur indicates more than incidental preferences. What victims are expected to confess, yield, or experience in the pain of their suffering is embedded in specific cultural meanings and values. Peters underscores this when he writes, "Every ideology presupposes an anthropology—an idea of what human beings are and how they are to be treated in order to create the society that each ideology requires."[3] Peters also detects in the twentieth century an emergent relationship between torture and cultural conceptions or yearnings for transcendence. The result is that ideology has now become grafted onto an eschatology or search for transcendent meanings in the anthropology of victim torture. "The new anthropology subordinates individual human beings to a new transcendent good," he concludes, and in ways that demonstrate "the human capacity to place supreme values upon transcendental ideas and to deduce an anthropology from them."[4] Such observations are critical to an understanding not only of the macabresque as such, but of its variations as demonstrated by the case studies presented here.

The Desert March of Young Turk Predatory Horror—Young Turk
Post-imperial Campaigns against Armenians and Greeks of Asia Minor

Deportation, Starvation, Predation, and Death in the Syrian Desert
and in the Euphrates and Black Sea, 1915–1917

Many of the theoretical perspectives relative to the macabresque I have so far developed
apply to an analysis of the massive crimes perpetrated against the resident Armenian people who suffered genocidal atrocity during the declining era of the Ottoman Empire.
Distinction between genocide and mass atrocity perhaps carries no greater significance
than in this case, given the jurisprudential and historic debates over perpetrator intent
and the methods of execution employed at the time. The historical record shows that
the post-Ottoman government of Young Turks, in the years immediately prior to and
during the establishment of the Turkish Republic, committed genocide against minority Armenian and Greek subjects in Eastern Anatolia, in what is today modern Turkey,
and in parts of Syria. The macabresque that ensued was a predatory horror in which a
regime that was powerless against the prevailing forces fantasized the possibility of social
purification and dreamed of the political possibility of new imperium. The results were
catastrophic for the Armenian and Greek minorities. The reasons it occurred serve to
validate several of the explanatory frames mentioned previously: political opportunity
in the face of declining power, mimetic rivalry, and armed power organizations acting
against noncombatant civilian populations. A kind of end-of-era political atmosphere
took hold of the Ottoman regime exulting in centuries of increasingly decadent rule, but
still able to bask in the memories of such imperial leaders as Suleiman the Great (1520–
1566). Ronald Grigor Suny describes the ideological imaginary at the time by indicating
the mutual influences at play between the corrosion of the Ottoman imperial dynastic
mode of governance, on the one hand, and the urgencies experienced on the part of the
Young Turks that prompted them to undertake a mission, however futile, aimed not only
at restoring but extending the empire based on Turkic and Islamic legitimacy.[5] At the very
instant of perceived loss of Ottoman imperial control, the Young Turk movement set in
motion a sequence of genocidal actions aimed at retrieving what had already become part
of the past. In a sense, the Armenia genocide represents an example of an extremist prena-
tionalism, one that combined an embryonic conception of nationalism and religion, but
on ethnic terms that were still vague but nonetheless lethal. Decline of power, loss of traditional identity, the presence of mimetic rivals, including the Russian imperial authority
with its military power (and the perceived cultural affiliations between Russians and the
Armenians as well as the Greek orthodoxy) set in place a move that Suny depicts as "state
imperialism." Competitive rivalry between the Turkic and the Armenian peoples gradually assumed nationalistic and racialized identitarian features, over and beyond religious
conflicts, as the need for a revitalized post-Ottoman Turkic and pan-Turanian political
entity emerged. It was this vision, this desire for a Turkic post-imperium that worked
its way into the policies of the Committee of Union and Progress (CUP), or *Ittihad ve*

Terakki Cemiyeti, terms with fateful meaning. What *union and progress* seemed to imply among the Turkic elites was that Armenians, now perceived to be "grasping and mercenary, subversive and disloyal,"[6] would constitute an impediment to both.

The fateful combination of glorious memory and contemporary weakness was made very much real by the Ottoman defeat at the hands of Russian army at Sarikamish in December 1914, which had sealed the fate of the Ottoman lands that were ceded to the Russians after the Russo-Turkish War of 1877–1878. As we have seen, the loss of land, the threatened loss of power, and abject defeat at the hands of traditional enemies stirs a vicious brew of resentment and revenge. This does not on any account justify bestial reactions, but it does help to explain the dynamics leading to the Armenian genocide. The initial signals occurred within the military with the release of the Ottoman General Staff Directive 8682, on February 15, 1915, only six weeks after the Sarikamish defeat, calling for the immediate removal of all ethnic Armenians from all military units. The process of "othering" and of purging the ranks of those who were about to be demonized had begun. Donald Bloxham observes, for example, "In general terms, genocide developed out of an Ottoman policy of ethnic 'reprisal'—meaning deliberately collective 'punitive' measures—informed partly by experience and knowledge of links between Armenian nationalists and Entente sponsors, but, more importantly, by simple ethnic stereotypes of Armenian disloyalty."[7] The Ottoman justification was that the Armenians represented what would come to be called a "fifth column" of those who operate and appear loyal from within, but only to betray and disrupt. Thus began the slide toward genocide and mass atrocity. The excuse was always that the Armenians represented an insidious element that would side with the Russians, a rumor lent support by Russia's aid of Armenians during the Ottoman military siege, in April 1915, of the Kurdish city of Van. The Ottoman response was to capture and later to assassinate Armenian leaders and intellectuals in Constantinople, beginning on April 24, 1914, a day memorialized as Red Sunday and Genocide Remembrance Day. On May 29, 1915, the Ottoman government issued a decree called "the Tehcir Law," the Temporary Law of Deportation, invoking the need to enact security measures and to sequester anyone it believed to represent a risk to security. The death marches and massive confiscation of Armenian property thus began. Bloxham refers to the role of the so-called punishment units pressed into service against the Armenians. He writes, "Ottoman forces had no compunction about rationalizing the severest methods to 'completely crush' any incidents . . . including taking 'rigorous measures against the families of deserters and traitors,' and punishing 'severely peasants who support these outlaws.'"[8]

In 1915, the Armenians were marched into the Syrian desert without any advance precautions taken for their safety or survival. The macabresque is denoted by processions of innocents, men and women, children, the elderly, the infirm, all made to walk into an abyss of exilic nowhere, without shelter, provisions, or other modes of transportation— all on foot. The eliminationist pogrom pursued by the Young Turks was implemented in ways to ensure that even if victims temporarily survived the long march into the desert, they would be murdered. The authorities set up a network of concentration camps and transfer points that permitted gendarmerie units to attack groups of Armenians as they walked. In addition to massive starvation, the Armenians were subjected to brutal abuse, at the hands of several hundreds of prisoners who were released to form a brigade called "the Special Organization," which operated in ways that anticipated the Nazi *Einsatzgruppen* in the Ukraine. This facilitated extermination under the guise of deportation. The evidence also indicates that the modes of atrocity in the march to the desert included burning and mass drowning, when columns of victims approached the tributaries of the Tigris and Euphrates. Bloxham suggests, "Much of the killing, rape, and dispossession of the Armenian deportees, parenthetically was the preserve of the irregular, paramilitary *Teskilati Mahsusa*, or Special Organization." He adds, "The epithet *genocide* is applicable in the Armenian case specifically because of the combination of the two elements of wholesale deportation, or 'ethnic cleansing,' and purposive physical destruction by systematic massacre."[9]

It is easy but simplistic to attribute the Armenian genocide to religious or sectarian conflicts or differences. As Taner Akçam indicates, massive numbers of Armenians accepted the offer to become Muslims if it meant their lives would be spared. He writes, "The policy of forced Islamicization was abandoned, however, when it turned out that most Armenians were to convert to escape death."[10] The religious divide between Muslims and Christians as an ideological force fails to explain the macabresque, since many Armenians did, under duress to avoid deportation and starvation, accept the offer to convert. Surely, this would have been sufficient to prevent further abuses if religious heresy had been at the core of the issue. Religion as an explanation becomes irrelevant given the Armenians' willingness, as death loomed, to convert to Islam.

An alternative dubious explanation also presents itself, in that large-scale confiscations and transfers of property occurred once Armenians had been forcibly removed from their places of residence. This was not unlike the events during the Holocaust when neighbors in certain towns or villages in Poland, for example, immediately moved into the homes of Jewish families after the Jews had been transferred to the concentrations camps or killed. Akçam lists the several reasons that were given at the time to justify the theft and transfer of property: to expand a bourgeois Muslim middle class, to meet the requirements of the immigrants resettling in areas that had been forcibly abandoned by the Armenians, to support the military, to help cover the costs of the deportations, and other needs of the authorities.[11] Political opportunity models, mimetic desire, and civil war as theories of explanation could now be complemented by an additional theory: the powerful allure of human greed. But greed alone does not explain the macabresque.

Within the explanatory frames of desire, and thus from the perspective of thing-enjoyment, Turkic (they were not yet Turkish) elites trying to salvage power amid the imperial disarray began to envision a new kind of domain, one "purified" of the Armenians, who were also beginning to imagine the possibilities of a new political situation, though from a position of greater weakness than even that of the Turks. This concatenation of factors is highly volatile and always potentially lethal. In keeping with the political opportunity models, declines in power and fears of loss generate movement toward genocide and mass atrocity. Those who are targeted because of their vulnerability become the victims of perpetrators who sense their own vulnerability, first in power terms, but also as a result of the shame of lost honor. In the face of social and cultural decline precipitated by the loss of empire, mimetic desire on the part of the Turks became tantalized by a dream of a post-Ottoman state for the Anatolian Turkic peoples alone, devoid of Christians as well as Greeks. The term "Turkish" had traditionally been considered a pejorative on account of its reference to the people inhabiting the Anatolian mountains. It would not be used to refer to a Turkish nation until the founding of the Turkish Republic and sovereign nation-state in 1923 under the Kemalist revolution. But the genocide and mass atrocity against the Armenians and Greeks demonstrate the essentialized cultural constructions of collective identity that manifest exclusionist principles of ethnic nationalism. This is demonstrated by the mass atrocities committed against the Greeks of Asia Minor, including the Ionians, Pontians, and Cappadocians, an estimated one million of whom lost their lives, many on forced death marches through the Syrian desert and its frigid mountainous regions. Assyrian peoples, including Chaldeans and Nestorians, were also exiled and attacked on these death marches.[12] As Bloxham concludes, "'Security' only assumed significance because of the linkage in CUP thought with the drive for ethnic homogeneity and national territorial integrity in the Ottoman 'heartlands,' and for political and economic independence for Turks as an ethnic-national group."[13] This represents a fateful turning point in the history of identitarian constructions, for the price of modernity includes the cost of ethnic nationalism and exclusivism.

The Ottoman Empire had been many things to many peoples; its millet system recognized many "peoples of the book" and had permitted a certain tolerance with respect to a range of complex cultural expressions. But the modern Turkish state was to be for the Turks alone. Even Islamic Kurdish citizens would have to struggle for recognition and status. The macabresque arose in the Armenian and Greek genocide. Mass atrocities in performative transgressions are forever symbolized by the forced marches of civilian populations into an abyss of torment and agony. In ideological terms linked to social fantasy, it was a purification scheme on the part of those grasping onto the lingering elements of failed glory and honor. But it will stand as the moment when the birth of political modernity became forever morally sullied.

****

Stalin's Ideological Purgatory

Collectivization, Ideological Fundamentalism, and the Great Purge and Moscow Show Trials of the Communist Party of the Soviet Union (CPSU), 1921–1938

The Macabresque of Stalin's Purgatory

What could possibly be more "macabresqian" than the following: class warfare by means of starvation and chronic malnutrition involving the elimination of the kulaks, an entire social category of peasant farmers and their families; sustained eradication of legions of Bolshevik revolutionary warriors and Russian patriotic heroes, who in massive numbers had led and supported the transformation of the Tzarist society, but who were destroyed on the grounds of insufficient ideological correctness—that is, for having loved Russia or the revolution too much; a series of great purges of cadres of Communist Party of the Soviet Union (CPSU; hereafter "the Party") faithful for failing to be good, true, or earnest enough—or the opposite, that is, too good, true, earnest, or faithful; and contrived show trials of core historic figures in which rules of evidence and procedure required their personal incantations of guilt, fault, and deviance based on ontological criteria benchmarked to standards of ideological "authenticity"—and immediate death for having failed to meet the criteria. These dynamics demonstrate the very essence of the macabresque, exhibitionist in its dramaturgy, systematic in its aesthetics of violation, and systemic in its exertions of the power to do evil. Stalin may not have known the word *macabresque*, but in giving Stalinism its essence, he revealed a diabolical mastery of the concept.

Stalin's success was to meld political surrealism into the coins of modern politics. His macabresque is a personal one. His autobiographical and political personality became fused in Bolshevik and Party games of ideological truth and political consequences, played ultimately for Stalin's benefit alone. This did not come in one fell swoop but developed over years of debate and confrontation within the hermetic cubicles of Party ideological debate and confrontation. Stephen Kotkin writes, "Stalin's role as guardian of the ideology was as important in his ascendancy as brute bureaucratic force. In the 1920s, Communist party plenums, conferences, and congresses constituted the core of Soviet political life and of Stalin's biography; the political brawling shaped not just his methods of rule, but also his character, and image."[14] There exists a strange and horrible absurdity to Stalinism, a kind of absurd surrealism that represents a "take" on realism but only as an echo in the hollow sounds of the Party line and thinking. Stalin's purgatory in the macabresque is exclusively focused on the canon of Marx and Lenin, in particular, on how to implement Lenin's transformational drives and ambitions in a fast-changing world of revolution and depression, of liberal markets and fascist power. Stalinist fundamentalism becomes totalitarian once words become perceived not merely as concepts but as material realities, while concrete reality is treated as entirely ideological. Fundamentalist disagreements in Bolshevik and Communist Russia become lethal because the laws of history are seen to be riding on how the Party derives and implements its resolutions. Tzvetan Todorov captures the rapturous qualities associated with ideology in a totalitarian society, even for those oppressed by it, "It seems to be little more than empty words and window dressing." He adds, "However, the interference produced by the regime's lies and double-speak risks obscuring the actual function of ideology," namely, and "most important . . . the recourse to ideology—regardless of its content—is an essential ritual." Ideology is thus in some sense performative, and its very performativity demands that it becomes ritualized. As Todorov states, "This point is critical. Ideological discourse is like an empty shell, but without that shell, the state would collapse."[15] The macabresque of Stalin's purgatory consisted of that empty shell, in which the empty speech of ideology became performatively ritualized to keep the emptiness of terror alive.

Fundamentalism is always about the interpretation of texts and their meanings regarding the "laws": the laws of divine will or of nature and, in the case of Stalinism, of the contrasts between a progressive versus reactionary interpretation of the dialectical "laws of motion." Stalin's purgatorial world is one framed by conflicts over the policy implications of dialectical materialism and Leninist theories of class rule. Party debates become consolidated into a singular realm of ideological interpretation—that is, one in which disagreements over intertextual interpretation no longer comprise a language game over normative theory but confrontations over the laws of social transformation and how they were foreordained to be realized. The reality of Stalinism as the embodiment of the macabresque was not in actions alone; on the contrary, Stalin's words, thoughts, and policies not only "represented" reality, they *were* reality. Soviet Russia, all Soviet social history and future, had to be brought into alignment with them. If reality in the incidental shape of daily events did not conform, words as the performatives of Party will had to ensure that they did.

The career that made Stalin was one immersed in words, permeated by ideological debates, submerged by factional conflicts, and dominated by his intellectual acuity, strategic cunning, and utter ruthlessness. The purgatorial macabresque eventually became shaped around his personality alone. The shift from collective violence to human violation in the 1920s and 1930s demonstrated his ideological convictions. But even more than this, the Great Purge and Show Trials following on the extermination of the kulak class provide insight into what Stalin would take to be his alone to enjoy or, at least, what he would allow others to "enjoy" but only on his terms. Stalin's universe was a purgatorial world cast in the molds of a proletarian ideological perfectionism as a form of thing-enjoyment. And in this purgatory, the winners and the losers constantly interchanged, from the one to the other. The Party members debated with fundamentalist conviction, but gradually, inexorably, Stalinism prevailed, not only in terms of what Stalin said or thought but also on account of how the cadres interpreted what they believed he said or thought. In this arena, no one was guaranteed safe passage, as the brutal fate of Stalin's adversaries, Trotsky on the "left" and Bukharin on the "right," reveal. They were not alone. What cadres believed yesterday might very well become painfully unacceptable at a later point. Thousands were beaten into submission, into confession, and, eventually, into death often with bullets to the head. Spontaneity in politics gave way to a kind of fundamentalist hermeneutic in which terror and ideology defined the logics of illogic but in ways that never guaranteed personal survival. Stalinism demanded conformity in thought and action, but always in orthogonal contradiction to what ideology or orthodoxy had once appeared to demand.

This defines the distinct character of Stalin's purgatory as a case study of the macabresque. And what Stalin's purgatory was designed to ensure was that his major protagonists, potential adversaries, along with the cadres of old guard Bolsheviks and many others, were coerced into submission, made openly to confess to crimes of deviation against the Party and its movement, all in order to make theme complicit in their own condemnation. Stalin's purges were purgatorial in this precise sense that they demanded those who stood accused, and thus automatically convicted, participate in their own self-betrayal, not only by confessing their guilt but, in addition, by implicating former comrades in crimes against the Party they had never committed. Victims of Stalin's terror were made to admit to ideological deviation in order to engage in the betrayal of others who had been active in the Party during and in the aftermath of the revolution and civil war. Accusation served as a critical mechanism in the process of purging Party cadres of victims transformed into ideological "deviants." Many held out for the truth of their innocence. But they were interrogated and beaten until physical and mental exhaustion made them submit not merely to death but to the indignity of having to declare that they deserved it.

Stalin's purgatory, therefore, involved a dramaturgy perhaps unique in the history of the macabresque in which the art of self-betrayal was perfected by a system of terror and self-abnegation on the part of many who had previously been devoted to the Party and its role in Soviet Russian society. In Stalin's purgatory, self-humiliation became transformed into an art form, a kind of theater of self-accusation and self-immolation staged publicly to ensure that those who confessed would be perceived as having required their fate. Resistance became dangerous. Increasingly, Stalinist designs and objectives rewarded only those from the lower ranks of the movement. The ephemeral nature of ideological discourses became transformed into a kind of totality, deadly, uniform, and unsparing. Terror enforced by secret police became increasingly arbitrary, absolutely capricious. What counted first and foremost were ideas, but nonideational ideas and thus those framed by the will of the Party as determined by Stalin. Kotkin observes, "To an extraordinary extent, it was skirmishes over *ideas* not solely personal power that preoccupied him and his rivals in the struggle to define the revolution going forward. Ideology was Bolshevik reality."[16] During such processes of ideological discursivity, shades of truth and falsity lose significance. The power to render the verdict is what matters most. This is the basic feature of purgatorial fundamentalism, "truth" becomes a dimension of verdictive judgment imposed on the Party rank and file. For many, this meant the difference between life and death.

Eventually, all debates caved in under the weight of Party orthodoxy as the dialectical, and Bolshevik ideology of Leninist revolution developed into Communist dogma dominated by Stalin and Stalin's dystopian visions, particularly concerning agricultural production and the agrarian sector. Stalin waged war against his own people and showed no mercy toward those who demurred, let alone objected. What he wanted was to use the agricultural sector as a means to industrialize Russia over and beyond the necessities of food production and distribution. He pursued this aim with absolute determination without concern, let alone care, for the consequences. And the historic results proved dire: first, came famine; and then the elimination of the most productive class of farmers; and then starvation again; and, next collectivization; and, finally, resistance and rebellion. The overall impact was genocide and mass atrocity. These circumstances served as background to the reality that counted most to Stalin, Party and cadre conformity to collectivization whatever the cause of doubt, hesitation, or disagreement. His method of ensuring this was the terror of the macabresque, with its dramaturgies of expurgation and show trial. Purgatory is sometimes represented as a place of limbo and suspension before souls are permitted to enter heaven. But Stalin's objective was to create a Soviet heaven on earth, and as a result the Russian and Ukrainian earth became a living hell, its immediate manifestation was Stalin's purgatory in the macabresque.

Dekulakization as Mass Atrocity

To understand the macabresque of Stalin's purgatory, one must recount, however briefly, the early story of the Bolshevik war on peasant communal agriculture, specifically against the kulak agricultural class. Those who toil the earth are sometimes either revered or reviled. In Stalin's view, profoundly influenced by Leninist perceptions and attitudes, those perceived as wealthy off the land were to be considered as rich on the land, and thus as primary obstacles to the immediate proletarianization of Russian society and the rapid industrialization of the communist economy and, therefore, as a major impediment to the precipitous rise of what would eventually be conceived as Soviet power. The Russian word *kulak* refers to a "fist," or the grip of wealthy peasants who constituted what Leninism-Stalinism ideologically constructed as the rural bourgeoisie that had to be destroyed by means of forced collectivization. The consequence was dekulakization; the means included genocide and mass atrocity. Tzarist Russia and the Ukraine had been mostly agricultural societies, with a system of production made up of peasant village communes in Russia but that also included individual farms throughout the Ukraine. From the very beginning, the Bolsheviks waged war against both. During the Russian civil war, they engaged in large-scale grain and food "requisitioning" to feed the revolutionary army and urban populations. The kulak class became the immediate targets. The vast majority of peasants had been poor; a middle class of peasants had emerged who were relatively well off and economically self-sustaining. In addition, a small minority of kulaks had grown wealthy enough to produce enough food so as to generate profits sufficient to hire other peasants and to lease farm equipment to the village communes.

This would prove fatal. They immediately became categorized as the "class enemies" of the revolution.

Systems of agriculture demarcated by peasant or small-scale farming consistently confront the problem of how to generate sufficient profits over and above what it takes to invest in producing annual crops, which is especially difficult under economic conditions in which markets function poorly with respect to price valuations relative to scarcity or supply and demand. The period 1921–1923 witnessed failures in agricultural policy and practices that led to famine and widespread malnutrition. Lenin was forced to accept the New Economic Policy (NEP), later identified, to his enormous detriment, with Nikolai Bukharin who temporarily favored market solutions as a "one-step backward, two steps forward" method for dealing with food shortages. The kulaks and large landowners gained some leeway for a period, but the year 1927 proved to be a major turning point. The fulcrum was failure in food and grain procurement. In response, the Bolshevik government reinstituted policies of re-acquisition and imposed crushing taxes and other oppressive measures. The reaction of the kulaks was to resist by liquidating assets, selling off land, livestock, and equipment, and by moving to town centers. This dynamic has been referred to as "self-dekulakization." But it did not take long for real dekulakization to occur.

On December 27, 1929, Stalin announced a full-fledged war against traditional forms of agriculture aimed at the systematic decimation of kulak holdings and widespread collectivization. Mass atrocity ensued. Politicized security police of the Organization of State Political Administration (OGPU) divided the kulak class into three groups: the first, regarded as counterrevolutionary, were subjected to arrest, transfer to concentration or work camps, and eventual execution; the second, open opponents of collectivization, were deported to other farming regions; and the third were resettled on less productive lands. These processes of dekulakization occurred in waves, one in 1930 and the second in 1931, when large numbers of kulaks and their families were deported to Siberia, the Ural Mountains, and Kazakhstan, as well as to Northern Russia, and many of them died on the way. State workers from urban areas were seconded to rural areas to assist the security police and local party loyalists to round up kulak families. Incalculable levels of wealth denominated in metrics of land and equipment were transferred to collectives. Abuse became rampant; for example, poor peasants often became profiteers by appropriating kulak property and transferring it to the collectives as if it had been their own. Russian and Ukrainian agriculture suffered the economic consequences. The devastation of Ukrainian agriculture, for example, meant large-scale disruptions that led to the Ukrainian famine of 1931–1932 (the Holodomor, or hunger extermination) in which an estimated five million persons died, as well as to the eventual ethnic Russification of the eastern Ukrainian region. There was massive resistance to collectivization during the early 1930s. But these rebellions met with prompt and crushing defeat.

In the days leading to Stalin's purgatory, Stalinism became a "cult of personality." In terms of thing-enjoyment and mimetic rivalry, Stalinism fostered conformity to personality worship; Stalin's "personality" became represented as the origin of all that was desirable. This, in turn, had major political effects. The mass atrocity perpetrated by dekulakization fostered starvation and malnutrition. But this became part of an ideological proposition that somehow defended against the loss of what the Party had achieved under Lenin's and Stalin's leadership. This set the stage for the mimetic rivalry embodied by ideological wars waged within the Party. Toward the end of the decade, Stalin was ready to assert absolute control over the ideological debates centering on the role and status of the peasantry in postrevolutionary Russia. His mechanism became the purgatory of the great purges and show trials. Stalin would now demonstrate on the world stage, as well as on the Russian stage, what Stalinism really meant. Kotkin concludes his biography of Stalin, covering the early years of Stalin's rule, by observing, "Stalin made history, rearranging the entire socioeconomic landscape of one-sixth of the earth. Right through mass rebellion, mass starvation, cannibalism, the destruction of the country's livestock, and unprecedented political destabilization, Stalin did not flinch."[17] Stalin had been warned of the consequence of his policies against the peasant class. But as Kotkin indicates, "Feints in the form of tactical retreats notwithstanding, he would keep going even when told to his face by officials in the inner regime that a catastrophe was unfolding— full speed to socialism." This is what is meant by the sacrifice of an entire generation. And Stalin never wavered. His will was the macabresque; his method was purgatorial; his desire, the source of Party desire.

The Great Purges and Show Trials

The Great Purge of 1936–1938 occurred during an historic phase when Stalinist state terror became entrenched as a way of life in the Soviet Union. The Great Terror, sometimes called the Red Terror, was a political condition in which civil rights disappeared and private space collapsed under the duress of an official campaign aimed against all those labeled as "dissidents," "saboteurs," "counterrevolutionaries," or "enemies of the people." The particular targets were senior members of the Communist Party, the government bureaucracy, and the armed forces, but the net widened to include specified categories, such as the intellectual class or intelligentsia, particular ethnic minorities, and, eventually, all Soviet citizens. Police surveillance and political repression and arbitrary detentions and immediate executions became the way of life. More than a million people were expelled from official positions, or arrested, or murdered. The key to Stalinist terror was its capriciousness; one never knew when the long hand of the NKVD (People's Commissariat for Internal Affairs) or Soviet secret police would strike, or whom. Even the first head of the Great Purge campaign, Genrikh Yagoda, would fall victim to it after being replaced by Nikolai Yezhov, who would gain historic notoriety by lending his name to the Great Purge—that is, the *Yezhovshchina*, the "Time of Yezhov." This period witnessed Stalin's consolidation of power at a time of possible widespread dissent as well as social disruption caused by collectivization and large-scale movements of peasants from farms into the cities.

Social control and engineering became the orders of the day. But the focus of the Great Purge was the Party, its leading members and the thousands of its cadres who were eliminated. Justification for the Great Purges came in the form of the Moscow Show Trials, between 1936–1938.

The steps leading to the Show Trials included: devastation of the agricultural economy; elimination of the kulak class; collectivization; famine; mass movements of peasants off the farms; resistance and rebellion; Party debates and ideological dissent; consolidation of power by and around Stalin; state terror; the purges; and, finally, the Show Trials. Together, these dynamics provide a case study of mimetic rivalry fueled by the psychodynamics of thing-enjoyment, fantasies of its loss, and subsequent social antagonism leading to the rejection and elimination of those forced into becoming "the threatening other." The Show Trials were designed to provide justification for everything leading up to them, from collectivization to terror. Their aim was to provide ideological validation for Stalinist fundamentalism, a way to demonstrate what ideological truth meant. They were didactic and instructional to their core because they taught Soviet citizens what to think and how to "desire." But more than this, they revealed that even loyal Party apparatchiks could desire wrongly, could yearn for what had to be proscribed, could want what must be prohibited. It all depended on Stalin. But Stalin himself was presented as but an instrument of the laws of dialectical change incarnated by and through the Soviet utopian vision. Those accused in the Moscow Show Trials had violated this vision. What counted above all is that they would publicly confess to their transgressions. And thus, performative transgression in the macabresque of the Party took on a new dimension in which victims were made to perform transgressions upon themselves as a form of penance for the sins they had never committed. This is the import of Stalin's purgatory in the macabresque.

Three trials were held, in August 1936, January 1937, and in June 1937: the first, against the so-called Trotskyite-Kamenevite-Zinovievite-Leftist-Counter-Revolutionary Bloc, involved important Bolshevik associates of Lenin; the second, of the so-called Anti-Soviet Trotskyite-Center included a number of cadre members; and the third and final, the Trial of the Twenty-One, of those listed as the "Bloc of Rightists and Trotskyites," including Nikolai Bukharin, who symbolized the consequences of ideological deviation. Bukharin famously resisted making a confession for a period of several months. But after intense psychological and physical torture, he did offer a confession, rendered in the most general terms possible, and not etched in personal terms regarding specific crimes. Since he had supported the NEP, he admitted to having wanted to restore "capitalism." Bukharin's now legendary effort to preserve a certain element of dignity by refusing to perform what was tantamount to a self-betrayal continued until the end. But it did not save him. His confession was personally vetted by Stalin, who found it insufficient and rejected it. At the end, the horrors of the macabresque dissolved even the fortitude that Bukharin had been able to maintain in the face of inhuman torment. He eventually caved under intolerable torture by recanting his support for the NEP, but his recantation only culminated in his eventual execution at Stalin's hands.

Stalin's purgatory of the Great Purge and Show Trials defies logical analysis because on its face it was profoundly irrational to wage a war against the ruling elite and the cadres of Party loyalists and government bureaucrats, when a looming war in Europe and domestic social chaos appeared to demand all they might contribute. The mimetic rivalry and theft of thing-enjoyment that introduce concepts linked to the psychodynamics of social fantasy, antagonism, and ideology provide a perspective that helps in part to explain what otherwise remains inexplicable. Igal Halfin describes the Great Purge and Show Trials as a "pervasive mystery," a "war of all against all," "a chaotic seesaw of mutual incriminations," "a morbid carnival." Halfin's analysis provides certain clues for purposes of explanation. This includes, first, the sadistic abstinence of Stalin and of his henchmen in the Party, denoted by what he calls their "hypermorality." Halfin writes, "A radical instrumentalization of their subjectivities rendered Party members selfless. Modern ascetics, they worked around the clock, forfeiting riches and recreation—recall Stalin's famous frugality, the modest dress of Communist leaders."[18] Stalinist Party executioners converted their self-deceptions into "hypermoral behavior" in keeping with sadistic fantasy. Halfin continues, "Dedicated to the emancipation of humanity, the perpetrators of the Great Purge regarded themselves as vehicles of history."[19] In this regard, Halfin might have written, *vehicles of the law*. He adds, "Having shaken off all petit bourgeois squeamishness, they were proud to denounce, torture, and kill. All this was morally justified." Sadism exists in those who self-deceive themselves into believing that they and they alone act as instruments of law, of history, or of higher purposes, however defined. The Communists who acted in the macabresque of Stalin's purgatory did so in the delusionary belief that they were working to the benefit of humanity. They wanted to think of themselves as agents of the Marxist dialectic that would transform the economic base, and therefore, superstructure. Halfin comments, "It is important to distinguish here between immoral behavior, instigated by egotism, and the hypermoral behavior of the Communists who transgressed for the sake of humanity . . . . Titanically destructive, the Communist moved beyond good and evil. First he annihilated the institutions created by centuries of tsarist rule, dismantling every state institution. But this was only the beginning: his next step was to abrogate not just positive law but also moral law."[20] Sadism inheres in fantasies of transcendence beyond moral or normative categories because its impulses adhere to the psychodynamics of desire and fantasmatic dread over the loss of thing-enjoyment, in this case, the dread of those deemed ideological deviants who had strayed from Stalinist desires. Stalinism and sadism thus became fused in a combined social fantasy and ideology that justified the near-suicidal purification of rank-and-file loyalists on the grounds that their desire and that of Stalin's were incompatible on the road to class power.

The "problem" was that one could not always tell who the deviants were. They had to be ferreted out by terror. Halfin also implies the dread of identicality in mimetic rivalry and the psychic impacts of resentment felt as hatred against those who appear to threaten loss of distinction. This represents a fantasized form of theft of thing-enjoyment. Stalin's purgatory emerged as a kind of defense mechanism. This helps to explain why it operated not merely against apostates or political nonbelievers but, instead, against the heretics of the Communist Party, that is, those who did believe, who did desire what Leninism and Stalinism desired—but *wrongly*. Perpetrators of the Great Terror and the purges, Halfin indicates, "killed the similar, not the different. The other could never be terribly threatening because he or she could be converted, while those from within—traitors and spies, ubiquitous and undetectable—stood to besmirch revolution itself." True believers treat mimetic rivals who deviate from the strict dictates of the logocentric truth with special vengeance. "NKVD interrogators fell on such suspects with terrible violence, anxious that the enemy was undetectable because undistinguishable from the faithful."[21] For such reasons, the Bolshevik Revolution, like the French Revolution, devoured its own children in the thousands, the very "children" who believed but whose aspirations appeared to threaten the power structure Stalin had perched himself atop. This, then, is the second element in Stalin's purgatory, to determine who among the Party faithful were not in solidarity with those who truly stood among the faithful, not merely in terms of ideology but with respect to mimetic desire over power. Stalinism destroyed many of the most dedicated, talented, and experienced Party loyalists, because the sole criteria of survival in Stalin's purgatory was the extent to which anyone threatened the status of Stalin as the sole possessor of the power to desire. It was a fool's errand, but it succeeded because it was done at Stalin's bidding.

The two initial features of Stalin's purgatory, therefore, were sadistic indifference to lived pleasure in the name of sacrifice to a Stalinism experienced as a form of moral(istic) desire; and, second, dread over lack of distinction fostered by fantasies of mimetic rivalry and theft of thing-enjoyment that promoted campaigns to distinguish the "best" from those who were merely "good" and thus not good enough on the scales of threat to power. These aspects were combined with a third feature: brutal implementation of Party judgment ostensibly in a search of ideological or political "authenticity." In its essence, this constituted a modern-day witch-hunt replete with public or shame punishments. Ideology turned lethal when converted into a basis for determining the ontological "truth" of a loyalist's nature measured against benchmarks of faithfulness to Party. Epistemological truth no longer mattered as such; in the quest to prove or disprove "authenticity" Party perpetrators drilled into the secret realms of human desire to show not merely incorrect *thinking* but rather "incorrect" *being*. When ideology becomes an exercise in judging the correctness of human ontology, the political exercise becomes one aimed at defining the distinctions between ideological propriety and the existential obscene. This further illustrates how totalitarian disciplines operate. Halfin refers to this as "a peculiar form of state instrumentality, a modern type of soul shepherding."[22] In Stalinism, ideological deviance became conceived as a condition of human personality, "something fundamental and intrinsic to a person—a quality that could never be transformed, only concealed, and that thus could be rooted out only using techniques of inquisition."[23]

In their effort to defend Stalinism, the Apparatchiks of the party campaigned against ideological deviation and doctrinal deviance by pursuing putative authenticity in the guise of defending the party against criticism and rejection through the modes of sadistic moralism. Terror filtered into public discourse and the victim was language itself. An additional feature of Stalin's purgatory was the defeat of signification by sanitizing shades of meaning from linguistic expression. Stalinism took the richness of the Russian language and made it the enemy of political imagination. For these reasons, many literary figures fell victim to Stalinist terror, including, among others, the poet Osip Mandelstam. Sadistic messianic fervor, dread over identicality among mimetic groups, and ontological authenticity therefore combined with this fourth feature of Stalin's purgatory in the macabresque, the reduction of language and linguistic meanings into set patterns illustrative of what Daniel called "informativeness." As Halfin observes, "This entailed the erasure of narrative from autobiographies; the transcendence of the body; and a death sentence imposed on metaphor, irony, and wordplay."[24] In Stalinism, language became reduced to the production of nonsignificant meaning aimed at imparting, not information but pretentious self-displays of ritualized discourses on a "bible" of Party truth repeated over and over again. Halfin indicates, "One might describe the Stalinist discourse of the time as flat, but its apparent simplicity was accompanied by verbosity and obsessive repetitiveness." The result was that, as Halfin suggests, "analysis could be jettisoned: texts and utterances were self-evident, open to just one interpretation."[25] The syntax of ideological necessity took over from the grammars of discovery and infinite probability. Halfin writes, "Once contingency had been excluded as a possible aspect of interpretation, it reappeared as the gatekeeper of language; the limits of language (what had meaning and what did not, what was just and what was unjust, who was to live and who was to die) became arbitrary, a state of things with no motivation or explanation, an extension with no intention."[26] Informativeness in Stalinist ideology was aimed at serving the Party in a very precise way: to extract confessions as acts of self-betrayal and as a method of instilling absolute conformity across Party adherents.

Language and performative transgression thus become intermingled in the grotesque of Stalin's purgatorial macabresque. This represents one of the core features of Stalinist technique of shame discipline, language became instrumentalized not merely for purposes of violence but as a weapon of human violation by means of self-betrayal. Halfin declares:

> The Party's determination to overcome transcendence made language itself messianic. In claiming to have described reality fully, language met its outer limits: everything that remained on the outside had to be foreclosed, condemned, and exterminated. Paradoxically, even as it rejected rhetoric, pragmatics, everything that normally alludes to the gap between words and things, the language of Stalinism deployed its performative dimension with a vengeance: *annihilation resulted from the act of pointing—a borderline linguistic phenomenon.*[27]

Confessions demonstrate the performativity of transgression in which human subjects are made to betray themselves by means of grandiose narratives unattached to their own lives but suited to the interests of perpetrators who see ghosts and demons in the shapes of specific persons. It appears that even self-betrayal was insufficient to satisfy the beasts of the Stalinist truth mongers. Halfin captures this essential feature of the Stalinist purgatory, that in self-betrayal victims implicate others who might also be identified, isolated, interrogated, and thus subjected to the confessional process of Party purification.

There remained one redoubt to which victims could escape in order to preserve a precious iota of personal self-respect—namely, a confession presented in the morbid styles of "magic surrealism," or the grotesque. This represents the fifth aspect in the macabresque of Stalin's purgatory, the confessional as a literary form manifested by a performative act of resistance by means of the grotesque. Compilations of confessions in effect created a literary form that depicted the political universe of Party ideology in ways that accentuated the grotesque nature of deviation and thus in vague and angular ways was tantamount to a form of surrealism. Halfin comments, "If the interrogator was thus a soothsayer divining essence, not to say an artist making things up, his creations may be examined in the light of the theory of literature."[28] Confessions should be read not as individual statements but collectively, as a whole, and as such "emerge as morbid works of art." Halfin advises, "A holistic approach that examines the form of prisoners' confessions is in some ways more fruitful than exclusive preoccupation with their content." Halfin describes this confessional "art form" as follows: "The plot is usually ghoulish but abstract—its images are magnified but not developed. This was a work of fictional criminological writing inscribed upon the Stalinist slate."[29] Confessions embedded within the morbidity of magic surrealism attempt to "say" something by revealing nothing. Halfin illustrates this by suggesting their, "wooden character and lack of precise setting reflect the fact that much of the action indeed took place in the chamber of the investigators' minds." Such "minds" demand that social fantasy be confirmed by a nonexistent reality repeated under pressure of torture and interrogational torments in formats of the grotesque more real than real, that is, in forms of magic surrealism. Halfin further illustrates this confessional form by stating, "Its situations were not ones in which the accused had actually existed, instead based in a world full of sinister connections, ploys, and nightmarish images."[30] But magic surrealism is realism nonetheless and the critical component of confession in Stalin's purgatory is its verisimilitude, its plausibility, and thus to the extent to which surrealist fantasy appeared to confirm ideologically manufactured "facts."

The means to confession was thus the grotesque in keeping with magic surrealism, but confessions were not ends in themselves. Rather, they served the Party interest to purify its ranks ultimately by means of human violation. This represents the sixth characteristic of Stalinist purgatorial invention: the language of ideological informativeness in confessional magic surrealism seamlessly converted into the performativity of victim violation. Halfin declares, "Torture, mockery, and ritual humiliation were the only ways to communicate with prisoners—truncated forms of address that assume that truth can be imprinted on the other, not imparted to him."[31] But even this was not enough. In the battle over dignity, those excluded from the blessings of Party affiliation not only had to lose, they had to be seen to lose completely. What that meant was their very presence as individual actors and as Party agents had to be erased as if they had never existed. The very aim of informativeness was to wipe out any possibility of remembrance of the victims. They were lumped together, demonized as a whole, and transformed into what Halfin calls the "'*pharmakos*', dangerous creatures whose killing was mandatory."[32] Critical to an understanding of the macabresque is to grasp the linkages between mass atrocity and the performativity of transgression, including the styles of dying and killing it imposes on innocent victims. The macabresque of Stalin's purgatory is no exception.

The battle over dignity in confession as exhibited in the magic surrealism of the grotesque culminated in battles over the extent to which victims might die as sacrificial martyrs to the Soviet Communist and Party cause. Ideological deviants found to be ontologically "incorrect," however, discovered no mercy in this purgatory, where any sense of human tragedy was washed away by comedic derision. As we have seen earlier, the "laugh" of non-humor—the laugh of shame discipline—derides the meaning, significance, and even the validity of victims' suffering as they approach death. This is what macabresque performativity in human violation attempts to do—deny torment and agony their moral stature. The purification schemes in Stalin's purgatory enlisted shame disciplines. The means were humiliating laughter aimed against victims who had confessed to crimes of deviation in the hopes that their dignity might attenuate the import of their forced self-betrayal. For the most part, this did not work. As Halfin observes, "In a sense, the rhetorical battle during the Great Purge was over plot." Perpetrators "insisted on the comic, portraying the accused as laughable and their death as a joke."[33] This is shame discipline to its core, to humiliate through laughter, to shame through the discipline of public derision. Victims were not allowed to experience an antidote to shame, the sense of tragedy in the human condition, a belief that they had contributed to the cause, or that their lives had represented a genuine self-sacrifice at the behest of higher purposes. This forced self-abnegation, too, represents a feature of the consequences of the macabresque.

At the end, even shame was not enough, since after all, shame is nothing if not intensely personal. In Stalin's purgatory, the grammars of informativeness aimed to subtract the person from the personality. Halfin declares, "The absence of the symbolic dimension from the death of counterrevolutionaries must be seen against the background of the elimination of the figurative from Stalinist messianic semiotics of the late 1930s. . . . the death of enemies of the Party had to be literal. The oppositionist was reduced to pure body—a pharmakos that absorbed the dirt and, in dying, took it away."[34] And death did come to thousands, and when it did it was done in a vile manner, by firing squads or bullets to the brain in gestures of pure anti-ceremony, the final humiliation. This represents an eighth feature of the macabresque of Stalin's purgatory: to kill human beings as if they were less than human. The macabresque of performative transgression thus moves from shame punishment and humiliation to disgust. As they are murdered, they are made to experience their own physicality as if they were animals, a final gesture of the disgust that perpetrators want to experience in distancing themselves from the humanness of victims.

Stalin's purgatory, therefore, denotes the shift from collective violence to human violation by demonstrating eight features and techniques of performative transgression in the modern macabresque:

- sadism;
- dread of identicality;
- ideological quest for (ontological) or moral "authenticity";
- informativeness in linguistic usage;
- confessional surrealism;
- self-betrayal and complicity of victims in their torments;
- shame punishments; and
- death by methods designed to reduce victims to the status of animality as a final gesture of shame, humiliation, and disgust.

Stalin's rule led to the death of tens of millions, an estimated ten million from famine, millions of innocents who were killed for their ideological "crimes," several millions in the Gulag. Indeed, the Gulag itself represents a macabresque formation framing the Show Trials of the 1930s, with roots back to the nineteenth century. Anne Applebaum notes with respect to "state slavery" in the Gulag, the origins of the macabresque within the Tzarist state, "What is so striking about the reports is their very repetitiveness: they call to mind the absurd culture of phony inspection so beautifully described by the nineteenth century Russian writer Nikolai Gogol. It is as if the forms were observed, the reports filed, the ritual anger expressed—and the real effects on human beings were ignored."[35] The Gulag would play an important role in the Holocaust as well, since the Nazi work-to-death camps were modeled after the Gulag camps. Work-to-death features would be repeated in various ways during successive transmutations of the macabresque. But explanations of the macabresque point beyond political exigencies or strategic goals. The "absurdity" of which Applebaum writes derides explanations of work-to-death camps either in the Gulag or in Nazi Germany if they are based exclusively on assumptions of rational behavior. On the contrary, such absurdity is intrinsic to the macabresque.

What the macabresque reveals, what Stalin's purgatory demonstrates, are the influences of social fantasy in ideology. Glyn Daly describes this in the following way: "Thus the central paradox of ideology is that it cannot affirm a notion of unity without simultaneously producing the idea of a threat to that unity."[36] This is demonstrated in almost clinical ways by the features characteristic of Stalin's purgatory in which the ideology of the Party is fantasized as threatened, thus meriting political purification as a prophylactic defense. Daly adds, "Such an effect is rather the result of a broader process in which antagonisms and otherness are articulated as a positive support for the fantasy of a consummate encounter with the Thing of closure." Daly's analysis thus connects with that of Palacios's understanding of social antagonism. Both embed their analysis in Lacanian theory with respect to *jouissance* and thing-enjoyment. Daly encapsulates this, "In this way, ideology endeavors to resolve what might be called an existential out-of-jointness through a phantasmatic translation of lack into a particular experience of loss and the historical determination of those deemed responsible for the loss/theft of enjoyment."[37] How costly are the social fantasies of theft-enjoyment played out in the mimetic rivalries of desire, status, and power once arrayed within the macabresque. The distinctions between the political "right" and "left" seem to lose some measure of significance once Stalin's purgatory and Hitler's laboratory are both explained by common sets of psychodynamic processes, however different their fantasies and fears, not to mention their ideological constructions.

****

Hitler's Diabolical Laboratory

Aryan Eugenicist and Nazi Satanic "Scientistic" Experimentations on Live Human Subjects, 1942–1945

White Uniforms in Noir Ecstasy: Aryan Eugenicist Fantasy and German Physiological Experimentation

Throughout this study, I have described the macabresque as a singular phenomenon functioning differently in contrasting cultures. There are many *macabresques* in the macabresque. Perhaps none are so shocking, so morally repugnant, as that of Hitler's diabolical laboratory entailing Nazi eugenicist and physiological experimentation. And just as the forms of informativeness are projected onto victims by means of excruciating pain, desires for the Faustian bargain, as the great dramatist Goethe understood so well, become introjected into those, in particular, into the Nazi "doctors," who willfully sold their souls to the devil. How else to understand the perversions of physiological science and eugenicist research in the Nazi macabresque of Hitler's diabolical laboratory?

Isabel V. Hull has written, "I believe that understanding how genocide develops is easier if one focuses not on the killing but on the final, or total, aspect of the goal."[38] I have suggested to the contrary that the process of killing in genocide and mass atrocity is performative and thus shaped by desires for certain kinds of theatricalities, dramaturgies, and aesthetics in relation to thing-enjoyment or *jouissance*. This often leads to a misguided and profoundly misrecognized quest for what Daniel has named informativeness devoid of information. As we have just recounted, torture represents one form of performativity, with its own style of weaponry, euphemistic language, and mode of delivering pain, all in search of informativeness but mostly against victims without information to provide. One speaks of torture as a process of inducing pain, and of pain itself as a means of suffering but also as the outcome or end of torture, as in "a person is tortured by pain." Suffering interrogational torture is thus both a means and the end in the macabresque, a form of suffering as the result of what one might call "performativity of informativeness." But there exist other forms of informativeness. In the macabresque of transgressive performativity, perpetrator drive for informativeness leads to *torment* as well as *agony* and none more horrifying than ersatz eugenic and medical/physiological experimentation. Whenever sadistic desire turns toward the laws of science, the bodies of victims become transformed into the sources of informativeness in ways that no longer require victims' voices or confessions. This observation yields a major distinction between *torture* and *torment*. Both define human suffering under the duress of macabresque sadistic transgressions; both are fantasmatically designed to permit access to the insidious lures of *jouissance* by sadistically shutting down victims' capacities for desire. *But if torture aims at informativeness through the mechanism of victim confessional speech, the torments of errant physiological and fraudulent quasi-scientific eugenicist research seek answers through the mechanisms of physical disfiguration and implosion.*

Pain is pain, suffering is suffering, all ineffable, all beyond our descriptive capacities. In the macabresque, the distinction between interrogational torture and coercive torment does not settle facile questions such as which is qualitatively or morally "worse" in metrics of more or less; rather, it permits an examination of the self-deceptions emboldening different sets of perpetrators who are acting under alternative cultural compulsions and social fantasies, and who demand that suffering be inflicted *in particular ways and forms*. This is suggestive of why the macabresque as an analytical perspective provides opportunity for insight and explanation that a theoretical focus on genocidal lethality alone does not permit. What, for example, does Nazi eugenic, physiological, and medical experimentation indicate about the mystifications leading German so-called doctors and clinical researchers to violate their professional oaths as doctors and scientists by producing indescribable torment instead of seeking to ameliorate it? Nazi eugenicist and medical/physiological experiments were not aimed at confessional forms of interrogation. In this precise meaning, they were not torture. Nonetheless, they were aimed at the informativeness of the human body and, as Daniel might suggest, they were simultaneously coherent but *nonsensical* and thus devoid of methodological, epistemological verity. That they caused unspeakable torment is a given. But a more compelling set of challenges is presented by questions about the relationship among the social fantasies, ideological self-delusions, and sadistic impulses of perpetrators with respect to this transgressive mode of violation. Simply stated, what is the significance of eugenicist, physiological, and medical sadism as a specific performative motif, aesthetic, and dramaturgy in the macabresque of the Holocaust?

I suggest that the answers point toward German cultural traditions of honor and the challenges to those cultural values and pretensions throughout the first half of the twentieth century. The sense of humiliation felt across Germany in the aftermath of World War I is, of course, well known. But insufficient attention is paid to the psychodynamics of shame and honor as analytical concepts that help to explain the Nazi glorification of Aryan racial superiority or German national supremacism. As analytical concepts, honor and shame help to underscore the fantasmatic influences of human physicality, anatomy, and conceptions of beauty in helping to foment the self-deceptions in the logical (coherent) illogics (fantasmatic) of the Nazi ideological imaginary. This is well documented in certain ways. Felicity Rash, for example, in her study of linguistic usage in Hitler's *Mein Kampf*, stresses the metaphoric centrality of the body, the body as container, the body as state, and *volk* as body in Hitler's literary allusions. "The metaphor A STATE IS A CONTAINER was fundamental to Hitler's political vision," Rash writes.[39] This metaphor of container and containment helped spew a series of associations dealing with blood and heart, sickness and health, purity and beauty. Beauty is associated with sanitation, hygiene, and collective heath; bodily disease is affiliated with threat, decline, and the disintegration of Germany, indeed, of the Teutonic cultural and Aryan racial expression. Rash cites numerous examples, "The cure of a sickness can only be achieved if its cause is known, and the same is true of curing political evils."[40] In this context, imagery of Jews assumed an especially lurid quality as they become demonized in terms of reified physicality in a sense contrasting the blond "whiteness" of Aryanism with the dark "blackness" of African racial descent imputed to the Jews.

A shame leitmotif is at work here in demonized forms of disgust thrust against the Jews as the impurity threatening Aryan whiteness and thus the health and beauty of a racialized *Volk*. Idolized or iconic notions of beauty are never far from acting as a normative standard of ideological *truth*. Alastair Sooke has indicated, for example, Hitler's special fascination with a Roman marble replica of the Discobolus classical statue that he had purchased in 1938. The original, sculpted in the fifth century by a Greek master named Myron, was renowned for the immediacy and power of its realism relative to the representation of this male nude athletic figure.[41] Clearly, this is that standard Hitler sought to impose on the German people as the master race. All this is well documented. What concerns me in the present context are the psychodynamics of social fantasy and ideology in influencing Nazi eugenicist and physiological experiments. The true irony here is, of course, that the bodies of Jews, among other sets of victims, in particular, twins, dwarfs, and others physically shaped by what was depicted by Nazi ideologues as abnormality and thus those features so reviled by the Nazis and their propagandists, were the focus, nay, the objects of informativeness for the purposes of what was ostensibly represented as the eugenic laboratory to achieve Aryan perfectionism. In psychosocial terms, narcissism constituted by the social fantasies of ego-ideal perfectionism became suffused by the psychodynamics of sadistic cruelty. The result was the satanic horror of eugenicist and "scientistic" sadism in the macabresque.

Sadistic cruelty seeks restoration of the laws of fantasized desire in accordance with the dynamics of identification associated in Freudian and Lacanian terms with the Oedipal process of separation from maternalized lost *jouissance*. Sadists seek victims to inscribe fantasmatic notions of law and law's desire on the bodies of victims. Sadists self-deceive themselves into believing that they alone serve as the embodiment of law destined or called on to defend collective culture and social identification against the thefts of *jouissance* or thing-enjoyment that threaten to erode the order on which such identification or thing-enjoyment depends. Sadism is always about defending against demons threatening dissolution and decay. Political fascism and the psychodynamics of sadism are in a constant process of mutual reinforcement, and the larger the demons loom, the greater the drive for perverse cruelty. As mentioned earlier, sadism is dispositive in aim; those caught by its fantasies act out in ways that permit them to believe that they control the controls over others' desires. Sadistic cruelty is disciplined cruelty, not random or entirely licentious precisely because it is aimed at the reenactment of the fantasmatic laws that revolve around stabilization of social order. The fantasmatic forms and social or political ideologies that such reenactments assume depend on collective constructions of political culture and identity. In the present instance, the case history of Nazi Germany, eugenicist science and physiological experimentation played a critical ideological role precisely on account of the social fantasies swirling around desire, desire for absolute narcissist perfection idolized in terms of Aryan beauty and racialized in terms of desire to destroy, in particular, Jewish capacities for desire. Such fantasies and the ideological reifications they fostered led to the *medicalization of the macabresque*, a hellish and "scientistically" staged confinement of performative transgression customized to the fantasies of its perpetrators, who willed themselves into believing that sadistic torment would yield return to thing-enjoyment or the *jouissance* of noir ecstasy by means of a eugenic paradise in which Aryan perfectionism would forever be on display.

In Hitler's laboratory, the diabolical exercise was clinical, but what the clinic performed was an exercise of purest satanic sadism. Sadistic cruelty is never about pleasure per se, but is rather the result of impassionate, indifferent, nonempathetic efforts to identify with a paternal imago or fantasized wholeness that keeps dissolution, and thus shame, away by restoring stability, even honor or glory. Nazi doctors and researchers provide an example of such a sadistic group enraptured by delusions of narcissist perfectionism but indifferent to the human costs and tormented suffering their sadistic invasive procedures caused. Their "scientistic" self-deceptions were vivified in hollow experimentations; victim torment was the supposed necessary byproduct of a scientifically designed quest for truth. But the pain of the victims who suffered the torment *was not the object* of these self-styled scientific researchers. Rather, in the torments of macabresque sadism these perpetrators envisioned themselves as the vanguard of a new human and political order, an order populated by perfected specimens of blood and beauty. Against such diabolical delusions, the satanic torments of eugenicist experimentation seemed of little concern.

The purpose of such eugenicist sadism under the guise of medical experimentation is equivalent to the informativeness sought by torturers who know full well that their victims do not possess information. Performativity in the macabresque becomes pressed into the service of non-truth by means, in a literal sense, of methodological *make-believe*. Nazi doctors in the macabresque may have performed experiments to obtain information from the bodies of victims in the make-believe of self-delusion. Perhaps the information may have been deemed to be relevant to the creation a master Aryan race, but at the self-evident price that the process violated all standards of moral decency, humane care, or ethical treatment. As in the case of torture, therefore, the torments resulted not merely from self-deceptions but from the combination of self-deception and disordered will. The consequence was that eugenicist experimentation became an end in itself, a form of absolute power, with so-called doctors and researchers competing for "truth," using the currency of torment as its standard.

Gradually, ineluctably, victims began to lose their individuality as human persons. They became abstracted as physical specimens fantasized as necessary "cargo" for the higher purpose of German physiological superiority and eugenic supremacy. Such abstractions fed the self-deceptions of those in the medical and scientific research professions who wanted to believe that in their professionalism they could contribute to cultural if not, indeed, human salvation. But these are the kinds of delusions carried by those captivated by shame and humiliation who seek a return to honor in sadistic methods framed by shared blood and destiny. Wherever there is "honor" as binding value in social fantasy there tend to arise collective tropes or metaphoric constructions of "blood" in ways representative of the *jouissance* of belonging; and the medical and "scientistic" criminals of Nazi Germany who participated in the hellish experiments extracted blood torments from victims in sadistic ways in order to live in the shared desire for the blood of German or Aryan honor—as a fantasmatic form of thing-enjoyment. This is what they willed as a way of protecting themselves against the shame of threatened anxiety and dread of dissolution. For these reasons, they remained indifferent, however great the pain of tormented suffering they caused. Impeccable in dress and procedure, cruel in method, dishonorable to their core, even as they deluded themselves into believing that they were acting out of the noblest of purposes, they manifested the prototypical features of sadistic personalities, their names forever damned in the very hell of their own making. That their fantasmatic self-delusions and subsequent ideological extrapolations would mistakenly be cast by some authors in contemporary scholarship as a form of adherence to morality norms or principles represents profound confusion between moral discourses and ideology. At its core, such conflation, as I suggest later, demonstrates the continuing failure to distinguish genuine quests for information from the sadistic performativities of informativeness.

Timothy Snyder depicts the profound epistemological circularity in the Nazi scientistic method that limited any "truth" stemming from inductive or experimental methodology to those sets of absolute axioms or principles deductively derived on the basis of ideology—that is, the logic of illogic. He writes, "Hitler's views of human life and the natural order were total and circular. All questions about politics were answered as if they were questions about nature; all questions about nature were answered by reference back to politics. The circle was drawn by Hitler himself."[42] Scientific methods framed by absolutized conceptions of nature enable the circular pursuit of "truth," one that reduces truth to essence and essence to absolute principles. No truth exists except *Truth* given by nature and discernible only by those who in *essence* are naturally endowed to know it. "For Hitler," Snyder suggests, "science was a completed revelation of the law of racial struggle, a finished gospel of bloodshed, not a process of hypothesis and experiment. It provided a vocabulary about zoological conflict, not a fount of concepts and procedures that allowed ever more extensive understanding." Snyder concludes, "It had an answer but no questions."[43] This helps to define the core methodological feature of Hitler's diabolical laboratory: to ask nonquestions in the quest for nonanswers by reducing human persons to creature-like status in order to dominate not merely racialized "inferiors" but *Nature* itself in the name of *Truth*. Snyder has gone far toward describing the particular rendition of informativeness within the procedures of Hitler's diabolical laboratory. But in each and every instance of the macabresque, a specific version of informativeness emerges. To its perpetrators, genocide and mass atrocity are always about Truth; and the macabresque, in all its tragic permutations, demonstrates the psychosocial akrasia of perpetrators who combine self-deception and disordered will at the behest of a sadistic and narcissistic desire to capture, control, and forever instantiate it—however futile the exercise in reality.

Doctors and Researchers in the Satanic Inferno of Hitler's Diabolical Laboratory

The name that is most notorious in this regard is that of Josef Mengele, but as the titles of such firsthand accounts as Alexander Mitscherlich and Fred Mielke's *Doctors of Infamy: The Story of the Nazi Medical Crimes* or Vivien Spitz's *Doctors from Hell* suggest, there were many, many others.[44] Spitz served as a court reporter during the Nuremberg War Crimes trials. Her subsequent book recounts in all too graphic detail the doctors and researchers, their experiments, their trials and convictions, and, of special interest here, their final statements in defense of what they did.[45] In similar fashion, Gerald l. Posner and John Ware recount the details of Mengele's role at Auschwitz between May 1943 and January 1945.[46] Mengele's behaviors are well known and do not require extensive description here. But certain features are especially relevant: his hands-on capacities for cruelty, rage, and revulsion; his sometimes calm and "tender" demeanor; sadistic indifference to the torments of victims; his presiding role in the *selektion* process by which many new camp arrivals were sent to their immediate deaths, while others were remaindered, according to the flick of his wrist and the point of his walking stick; his obsessive commitment to experimentation on live subjects however excruciating the pain; his dissection of victims before their deaths; his manic focus on twins; his efforts to classify the organs, eyes, body builds, facial features, and blood of twins, dwarfs, and others whom he regarded as genetically inferior, including especially Jews, but also Gypsies, who by virtue of their appearance provoked his belief that they were relevant as scientific material; and, finally, his unquestioned belief in the eugenic possibilities of a new race. Additionally, his personal fastidiousness and vain displays of uniform, medals, boots, cane, and so on, is integral to assessments of his role and personal behaviors. But so is his apparent disquiet over the "dark" features of his outward appearance. This, too, deserves examination, however brief, since it concerns the psychodynamics of shame.

Throughout his life and career as a Nazi officer, Mengele was assailed by his looks and genetic status within the Nazi racial taxonomy. Posner and Ware observe, "The irony was that Mengele himself was sometimes known to remark on his own un-Aryan looks. . . . Mengele's own classification by the SS had put him in the *Dynarisch-Ostisch* category, which meant that his predominant features were of 'Eastern' origin."[47] In Mengele's case the ridicule stemmed from alleged physical similarity to the Roma. Analysis of the import and effects of these early shame experiences do not provide evidence of psychological causality. Such forms of self-consciousness, however, do require an exploration of shame dynamics, as I later suggest. In Mengele's case, an unconscious shame-filled sense of self would have played into his narcissistic self-presentation as an officer with combat experience, as he had to a minor extent been. In any case, his vanity, lack of empathy, self-delusion as an eugenic trailblazer focused on those whose appearance assailed him precisely because, like Heydrich, he had been identified as less than pure. For Mengele, the malignant associations were with the so-called Gypsies. Mengele's utter fascination with what he regarded as genetic aberration thus included Gypsies as well as Jews. Posner and Ware comment, "Since childhood he had been self-conscious about his slightly tawny skin, his penetrating brown-green eyes, and his dark brown hair. At school, he had endured mild taunts from his classmates about his Gypsy looks. And in Bavaria, where Mengele grew up, the word for 'Gypsy' had a derogatory meaning." In due time, Gypsies or Roma would be rounded up throughout occupied Europe and brought to Auschwitz, where they would pay a frightful price in Mengele's inferno.[48] Miklos Nyiszli, a Hungarian and Jewish pathologist dragooned by Mengele to provide laboratory assistance, survived the war to write an eyewitness account of Mengele's personality and behavior, including a description Mengele's treatment of those incarcerated at Auschwitz in what came to be called "Camp Gypsy." Nyiszli writes that several thousands of Gypsies were "herded" together and subjected to "unimaginable cruelty."[49] Once Mengele decided the time for their extermination had arrived, the Gypsies were sent to their deaths with dispatch. Nyiszli describes how SS guards with dogs chased them out their barracks and made them "line up"; they were fed rations, as Nyiszli dryly comments, "a very easy and efficacious way of calming their fears. No one thought of the crematoriums, for then why would rations of food have been distributed."[50] Mengele's aim was neither "pity nor a regard" but rather moving humans toward their death expeditiously, and, as Nyiszli remarks, "the strategy worked to perfection."[51] Nyiszli describes how the gas chambers and crematoria were kept going throughout the night, sending "flames roaring skyward, so that the entire camp was lighted with a sinister glow."[52] With acerbic contempt, Nyiszli declares, "Once again Europe's pyromaniacs had organized a gigantic display of fireworks."[53] Nyiszli pays homage to the ensuing silence, "Next day the Gypsy Camp, once so noisy, lay silent and deserted." Nyiszli concludes, "The only sound was the monotonous chant of the barbed wires rubbing together, while the doors and windows left open banged and squeaked endlessly under the powerful wind of the Volhynian steppes."[54] Mengele, however, remained true to his unrelenting eugenicist sadism. The bodies of a dozen sets of twins among the Gypsy population were not sent to the crematoria but marked for experimentation as "rare and precious specimens."[55]

Mengele's sadism was demonstrated repeatedly, not the least on account of the numerous instances of vivisection performed on miserable victims. To cite just one example, Posner and Ware observe that after dissecting "a one-year old while the child was still alive," Mengele displayed the typical sadistic reaction of complete indifference. In noting this Posner and Ware appear perplexed by what witnesses of the scene report to have actually seen. These authors comment, "At such times it might seem that Mengele was motivated by sheer sadism, although most witnesses have remarked not at his pleasure at watching or inflicting suffering but at his *total detachment* from it."[56] But *this is* the very central feature of sadistic torment—that is, its very detachment. Sadistic behavior *does not seek* pleasure, at least not in the ways implied by Posner and Ware. The witnesses are altogether correct in reporting Mengele's profound indifference to human pain and suffering, for in the mind of this eugenicist sadist, torment was the key to informativeness, that is, to this disordered quest for "truth" framed by Mengele's self-delusions. Posner and Ware include the analysis of Tobias Brocher, a psychoanalyst who actually practiced near Mengele's home town in Germany. Brocher concluded that Mengele's behavior did not exhibit sadism itself but rather the "narcissistic component of sadism." Brocher bases his conclusion on the grounds that "he didn't take pleasure in inflicting pain, but in the power he exerted by being the man who had to decide between life and death within the ideology of a concentration camp doctor."[57] But the combination of cruelty and calm, outbursts of temper and outbreaks of momentary tenderness, exhibited by Mengele reveals the behavioral features of clinical sadism, psychopathological in its satanic and depraved indifference to the torments of others, but normalized by the systemic evil of the diabolical conditions in which it occurred.

Robert Jay Lifton, in his study of Nazi doctors, has famously proposed "doubling" as a way of explaining a duality in Mengele's personality, "an Auschwitz self" and "a prior self" each of which operated "as a functioning whole." Lifton indicates, for example, "the Auschwitz self enabling him to function in that murderous environment and to exploit its human resources with considerable efficiency; the prior self enabling him to maintain a sense of decency. His powerful commitment to Nazi ideology served as a bridge,' a necessary connection between the two."[58] Lifton appears to conceive "doubling" as a kind of defense mechanism by which otherwise decent human beings protect themselves against the psychic costs of inflicting pain on others by nurturing a sense of self that remains somehow inviolate. On analytical grounds, I find this interpretation profoundly misleading. It fails to grasp the essential features of sadism. Mengele did not have to become "enabled" to function in the murderous environment of Auschwitz, he reveled in it, presided over it, gave definition to a major aspect of its particular macabresque style of torment and suffering. In doing so, he did not act with efficiency. On the contrary, his methods were depraved, crude, and altogether haphazard despite the fury of his determination and obsessive dedication to them. He did not need to "maintain a sense of decency" since decency was not his concern or objective. And the notion that ideology served as a "bridge" between a decent self and an evil self misinterprets the relationship of social fantasy, sadistic personality, and the psychodynamics of shame and humiliation in forging Nazi racism and the eugenicist codes of Aryan ideological illogic that guided it.

Such so-called doctors as Mengele are the "true believers" who "self-sacrifice" themselves to an eschatological enterprise in order to bring fantasized purity and glory to the human condition. Purity, too, is a way of fantasizing *jouissance* and thing-enjoyment. I suggest that the fantasmatic influence of "purity" represents a reaction to shame, indeed, is itself a way of fending off an inveterate sense of shame by projecting it outward in forms of disgust against those who, in Mengele's case, became the victims of sadistic experimentation. I also argue that the glory fantasized in terms of eugenic perfectionism and beauty reflects a distorted fantasy of honor stemming from cultural traditions that were perceived as being devalued but which were assumed to be resurrected through eugenic science. Performativity in the macabresque devolves into the sadistic because the bodies of victims are made to suffer on the basis of what they contain, the truth of *jouissance* and thus the power to determine not merely what to desire but how to desire. Sadistic desire invariably attempts to transform epistemology into performance, as if truth can through power be willed over performativity, particularly in the macabresque. Sadistic exertions of power in performativity become recast according to cultural artifacts and ideological artifice. In the Nazi case, the control over the power to control desire became suffused with the eugenicist illusions in ways personified by Mengele's evil. Such epistemological illusions nurtured self-delusionary forms of narcissist grandeur among an entire German scientific class that helped propel them to assume that the secrets of Aryan purity and the keys to German glory could be found in the torments of those exposed to extremes of temperature, pressure, and disease. Posner and Ware include the testimony of Martina Puzyna, a Polish inmate in Auschwitz, who stated, "I found Mengele a picture of what can only be described as a maniac. He turned truth on its head. He believed you could create a new super-race as though you were breeding horses. He thought it was possible to gain absolute control over a whole race."[59] But the racial component of eugenicist sadism is desire over control of what is fantasized as most desirable in desire. And in this respect, there is no psychological "doubling" but rather a full throttle effort to control evolution, and in this sense, to enter into systemic sin.

This is made clear in Spitz's account of the Nazi doctors who were actually brought to justice in the Nuremberg judicial process. She lists "distinguished" scientists, head medical doctors, and chief surgeons as well as clinicians with former careers across Germany who "performed or participated in grisly medical experiments at Auschwitz, Dachau, Buchenwald, Ravensbrueck, Sachsenhausen, Naatzweiler, Bergen-Belsen, Treblinka, and others."[60] Not all physiological experiments were designed for eugenicist purposes, at least not in an immediate way. As their names and titles indicate, the doctors and medical assistants who practiced medical experimentation were sometimes guided by a military rationale, especially by military aviation. Experiments thus included high-altitude endurance; freezing; malaria; bone, muscle, and nerve regeneration, as well as bone transplantation; mustard gas; sulfanilamide; sea water endurance; epidemic jaundice; sterilization; typhus; poison; incendiary bomb; and phlegmon, polygal, and phenol experiments.

The names of these doctors and their assistants, along with their titles and eventual penalties include *seven defendants sentenced to death*: Karl Brandt, Major General in the SS and Hitler's personal physician and chief architect of the program of eugenic experimentation (death); Karl Gebhardt, Major General in the Waffen SS and President of the German Red Cross (death); Joachim Mrugowsky, Chief of the Institute of Hygiene of the Waffen-SS, responsible for maintaining and distributing the Zyklon-B gas used at the death camps, including Auschwitz (death); Rudolf Brandt, Personal Administrative Officer to Himmler (death); Wolfram Sievers, Reich Manager of the Ahnenerbe Society (death); Waldmar Hoven, Chief Doctor, Buchenwald Concentration Camp (death); and Viktor Brack, Chief Administrative Officer in Hitler's Chancellery (death); *five defendants sentenced to life imprisonment*: Siegfried Handloser, Lieutenant General Medical Services (life); Oskar Schroeder, Chief of the Medical Services of the Luftwaffe (life); Gerhard Rose, Brigadier General of the Medical Service of the Air Force (life); Fritz Fischer, Assistant Physician to Karl Gebhardt (life); Karl Genzken, Chief of the Medical Department of the Waffen SS (life); *four defendants sentenced to years in prison*, Hermann Becker-Freyseng, Chief of the Department for Aviation Medicine (20 years); Herta Oberheuser, Physician in the Ravenbrueck Concentration Camp (20 years); Wilhelm Beiglboeck, Consulting Physician to Air Force (15 years); Helmut Poppendick, Chief of the Personal Staff of the Reich Medical SS (10 years).

Despite differences in their roles and responsibilities, not one of these individuals, who were found guilty of the most heinous crimes imaginable, uttered a single shred of remorse, doubt, or even regret in the face of overwhelming testimony in their trial as to the torments they caused within the confines and delusions of Hitler's laboratory, in the name of science. Each demonstrates the precise same set of fantasmatic self-delusions at the heart of sadism in the macabresque:

- *Karl Brandt* states, for example, "It is immaterial for the experiment whether it is done with or against the person concerned . . . The meaning is the motive— devotion to the community." A sadist's cry could hardly be more precisely artic- ulated than the shibboleth "the meaning is the motive"; that is, the law of desire must be declared so that the perpetrator assumes the mantel of law itself.
- *Karl Genzken* stated, "I am proud to have been their leader," referring to "decent and brave doctors and medical attendants," and, he adds, "a leader of those who sacrificed their lives and blood with unceasing fervor." In moments of sadistic excess, blood and honor tend to be recurrent themes, especially when communal loyalty is at issue.
- *Joachim Mrugowsky* proclaimed, "My life, my actions, and my aims were clean." Sadist behaviors tend often to distinguish obscenity from what is demanded to sustain a social and/or a personal sense of order.
- *Wolfram Sievers* declared, "I devoted myself to resistance, continued it undaunted, and never abandoned it." Dedication to cause is a sadist's creed.
- *Victor Brack* indicated, "Euthanasia has always been an endeavor of mankind and was morally as well as medically justified." Purity is a form of exclusion that appears to anchor the sadistic personality.
- *Herta Oberheurser* demurs by saying, "In administering therapeutical care, fol- lowing established medical principles, as a woman in a difficult position, I did the best I could."[61]

Thus the curtain on the macabresque of Aryan eugenic and German experimentation sadism closes with a whimper, "I did the best I could." At the end, *no "doubling"* in per- sonality, remorse, or ethical or moral recognition is to be found among these sadistic criminals. They continued to believe in the rightness of what they did, in part because they believed in the genetic cause and racial superiority that enabled them to constitute their sense of personal honor, but even more than this, the honor of the Aryan race that they associated with the purity of blood and kin, their fantasmatic form of thing-enjoyment, the core of their guiding ideology.

On the Epistemological Dangers of Ethical Relativism Combined with Moral Situationism

I have dwelt on the specific combinations of social fantasy, ideology, and sadism in the eugenicist and sadistic experimentation of the Nazi macabresque in the Holocaust to illustrate the failings or inadequacies of analytical interpretation that excludes the psychodynamics of the unconscious in attempting to explain why and how the macabresque functions. Killing may be strategically purposive; performativity *is not* in the same sense, since it reveals the social fantasies of mimetic desires. The question is why the macabresque emerges to torture, torment, and agonize victims if simply killing them would serve the same sets of political objectives. Framing the inquiry in this way requires alternative explanatory frameworks and perspectives. In the sections that immediately follow, I wish to demonstrate the analytical consequences of failing to include some conception of the unconscious in explanations of perpetrator behaviors. I have previously demonstrated the incomplete versions presented by social and political psychology. Now, I examine how a failure to recognize the intimate connections between ideology and social fantasy in psychosocial terms leads to the mistaken conclusion that popular ideological delusions, having once contributed to the self-deceptions of perpetrators, could in their aftermath be considered to have satisfied the standards of moral discourse.

Harald Welzer argues for a dual conception of morality, the first constituted by "super-individual and super-situational values"; the second, by normative standards guiding interpersonal conduct. He does so to present the case that the behaviors of the Nazi elite reflected inherited cultural beliefs, attitudes, and values of their era for which they were not directly responsible. At the same time, Welzer indicates, many of them comported themselves according to high standards of interpersonal conduct, for which they were responsible. Welzer applies what he calls "a social-psychological axiom" to the effect that "if people define situations as real, they are real in their consequences." This permits him to abjure universalizable norms in moral argumentation in favor of standards influenced by cultural mores in situ, so that "it is the variability of the given framework which permits sometimes one and at other times another action to appear to be right." Welzer complements this moral relativism with a situationist logic. He distinguishes moral codes that support "society's standpoint" from moral interpretations guiding "interpersonal agreement or motives directed towards particular individuals."[62] On this basis, Welzer concludes, first, that the super-situational moral code reinforced rather than inhibited the capacity of the Nazi elite to preside over mass murder; secondly, however, they proceeded in good conscience so long as they felt that they were acting interpersonally on the basis of their personal honor and integrity, or what Welzer calls "the personal dimensions of their actions."[63]

Welzer's argument thus combines several elements: moral relativism in terms of what is culturally constructed during specific historical periods; prototypicality or interpersonal situationism in the sense that group values and norms guide or influence individual actions; and, thirdly, a kind of ethical doubling, in the sense that individuals act according to different ethical standards with respect to public obligations as opposed to those of private life and personal integrity. Welzer bases his case on the prominence of what he calls, citing the work of Norbert Elias, the prominence of the honor canon among the German elite and suggests that the Nazi elite manifested "ideals" inherited from Wilhelmian society. This included "pre-conceptions" "on questions of honor, blood, nations and race" that were "complemented by a scientific racism and dreams of the complete malleability of the world."[64] Welzer claims that a "national socialist moral code" emerged within these cultural frames to present individuals with "super-individual and super-situational values." These promoted the adoption of mass murder as "morally acceptable." At the same, time, the honor canon fostered a personal code of "moral integrity" that was scrupulously followed.

Welzer's case in point is Franz Stangl, the commandant of Treblinka, who presided over its death camp but who appears to have simultaneously maintained fastidious attention to what Welzer indicates was "moral integrity in his personal dealings." Welzer associates this with "an ethics of decency"[65] or "super-personal correctitude." Welzer infers from this that Stangl, as a prototypical case, "did nothing else, on the one hand, than behave within the framework of contemporary normative paradigms, academic teachings, military conceptions of duty and canonized definitions of 'decency.' "[66] But does any of this constitute morality or a "moral code"? Welzer responds by indicating, "The relationship between mass murder and moral code needs to be discussed in a manner which reverses that normally adopted. The question is not how the erosion or overcoming of moral inhibitions can explain perpetrator behavior; it is rather how particular moral commitments and principles gave the perpetrators a sense of moral integrity which enabled them to carry out the deeds they performed."[67] Welzer concludes, "Mass murder could not have been carried out with amoral perpetrators."[68] Welzer's entire argument, therefore, suffers from a profound confusion between morality and ideology.

Welzer ignores the extent to which Nazi perpetrator behaviors were the inflections of social fantasy anchored to Aryan codes of honor and self-sacrifice masquerading as moral discipline and principle. Welzer's case fails to recognize the role that social fantasy, thing-enjoyment, *jouissance*, and desire played in cultural constructions of Teutonic honor. It also refuses to recognize the extraordinary narcissism being played out in the examples he provides of Stangl's fastidious attention to interpersonal exchanges in which the power to decide life and death remains exclusively with the one who is telling himself how fastidious he can be. Welzer's case comes close to a "national guilt" argument, although this is manifestly not what he intended, since he places blame on the collective self-delusions of what is clearly an example of popular nationalism virulent enough to prompt world war. But to associate moral discourses with such ideological mystifications or to conflate moral codes with uncritical illogic, however logical the appearance, is to deplete the meaning of the term "morality" and to misconstrue the nature of ideology as a form of political ontology combining self-deception with disordered willfulness. Welzer's argument does succeed, however, in demonstrating how difficult it is to prosecute those whose crimes bridge collective violence and human violation, in part, because of the moral patina that appears to emerge in cases of the macabresque in which honor and a quest for what Daniel calls "informativeness" predominate to constitute a kind of perpetrator alibi. Mengele escaped justice; so do many perpetrators. The connections between collective violation and human violation tend to be forged by sets of perpetrators, both major and those less important, who give every evidence of having been sane, indeed, morally composed, but for their sadistic cruelty. Repeatedly, we have been made to witness examples of "normal" persons undertaking to engage in sadistic cruelty once placed under the tents of the macabresque. In part, this stems from the fact that perpetrators themselves represent what is in effect the macabresque as having been made necessary on account of exigencies at times of duress. *Morality, epistemology, and aesthetics become transformed into elements of willed self-justification.* That this is seductive is self-evident as Welzer's arguments demonstrate, but for these reasons it is all the more insidious, as Anne Harrington, in her examination of "Nazi medicine," demonstrates.

Her analysis places the macabresque of what she calls "Nazi medicine" into a context that encompasses the history of German science and describes what she calls "Nazi biomedicine as objectivity run amok." Her reference point is the account by Alexander Mitscherlich and Fred Mielke, *Doctors of Infamy*, in which they indicate that "the most pernicious energy driving the engine of Nazi medical science" was not political or racial or anti-Semitic illusion, but rather "its perverse fidelity to an obscene *objectivity*."[69] Harrington also mentions Benno Muller-Hill as a scientist who powerfully condemned Nazi conceptions of objectivity, but who also rejected objectivity in science on the basis of a "moral act of witness-bearing, of authentic *seeing*, [who] became associated with an epistemological stance that denied scientific objectivity the capacity to *see* humanity."[70] But "objectivity" in scientific endeavor is profoundly misrepresented by such a formulation just as "morality" was in Welzer's analysis. The case against objectivity illustrates yet again an epistemological confusion between scientific and scientistic research, between scientific discovery using human subjects that debases the human spirit, and methodological inquiry regulated by an abiding commitment to protect the sanctity of the living even at the point when human subjects are included in medical experimentation. In this confusion, we see once more the conflation of informativeness with information within the context of judging perpetrator behaviors in the macabresque. What the macabresque thus demonstrates is how to distinguish misconstructions of truth or truth-making grounded in social fantasy and ideology, from moral discourses, scientific inquiry, and aesthetic creativity. Properly named morality and scientific research is grounded in theoretical, analytical, and logical commitments to what epistemology genuinely demands: reasoned criticality, empathetically open to a multiplicity of perspectives and contradictory debate. None of this is to be found in so-called Nazi moral codes or Nazi scientistic research. Such is never present in the macabresque of desire and supremacist, exclusivist hate, whatever the guises of honor or morality.

****

The Hell of Blood Trauma in the Days of Hutu Power

Physiological and Natural Flows, Blood Trauma, and Stylized
Mutilation during the Rwandan Genocide, 1974

Scripted Narratives, Physiological and Natural Flows, Blood Trauma,
and Weapons of Choice in the Rwandan Genocide

Numerous examples of dramaturgical and aesthetic styles (and their cultural meanings) in the production of agony exist, but one in particular illustrates the problem of
evaluating culpability when many "normal" persons become transformed into sadistic
genocidaires. The case in point is the Rwandan genocide when large numbers of people
undertook mass killings. The predicament raised by Mark J. Osiel in the context of judicial rules of evidence and procedures (discussed later in this chapter) extends beyond the
use of torture as such but also beyond the question of the moral and legal culpability of
a few or of even delimited groups of perpetrators. The issue here concerns the dozens
of cadres who become transfixed by the political momentum of the macabresque and
willfully transformed into sadistic warriors. In the Rwandan case, as in Nazi Germany,
the call to arms assumed the form of racialized purity and restoration of honor. During
the Rwandan genocide, the main weapons were machetés and, to a lesser extent, firearms. The key to the aesthetic and dramaturgical modes of massacre and misery in the
Rwandan macabresque was agony due to dismemberment and evisceration, what was, in
effect, the agony of blood trauma.

To emphasize cultural influences on forms of suffering in the macabresque, I propose
the following distinctions: *torture represents a mechanism designed to cause pain and suffering for reasons of revenge, political re-education, social engineering, or coercion under conditions of interrogation and confession; torment arises as the consequence of extreme physical,
psychological, and emotional pain, including that resulting from rape or sadistic medical
experimentation, that causes extended suffering but in the absence of interrogation and confession; agony results from suffering caused by blood trauma, that is, violations of the physical
integrity or wholeness of the human body, such as impalement, dismemberment, evisceration, and disemboweling. Such distinctions sometimes dissolve on sites of the macabresque.*
Victims are made sometimes to suffer in all three ways. Some instances of the macabresque engage in the production of all three. This conceptual distinction does serve one
analytical purpose, however. It illustrates how various instances of human violation demonstrate the role, influence, and impact of culture in the performativity of transgression
and thus on how sadistic cruelty becomes deployed.

The Rwandan genocide consisted of a mass slaughter of Tutsis and moderate Hutus by
vast numbers of the Hutu majority. During the hundred-day period between April 7 and
July 15, 1974, an estimated 800,000 persons lost their lives, representing approximately
70 percent of Rwandan Tutsi and about 20 percent of Rwanda's total population. The
leaders of the genocide consisted of an elite group, positioned mostly at the top of the
national government, called the *akazu*; whereas the actual perpetrators, initially, came

from the national police or gendarmerie and government-supported militias, including the *Interahamwe* and *Impuzamugambi*. Most of the perpetrators emerged, however, from the ranks of the citizenry—that is, from the Hutu civilian population. The genocide occurred in some sense predictably given political conditions that were framed by the civil war between the Hutu-led central government in Kigali and the Rwandan Patriotic Front (RPF), which mainly comprised Tutsi refugees who had escaped to Uganda to avoid previous outbursts of Hutu violence. The 1993 Arusha Accords had created a power-sharing arrangement, but it provoked increasing resentment among major segments of the Hutu population. This resentment fueled the widespread ideological acceptance of "Hutu power," with its assertions of the need to purify Rwanda of Tutsi aliens, who were bent on the occupation of Rwanda and the oppression of all Rwandan Hutu. Here, again, we are witness to the psychodynamics of political mimetic rivalry, in which the threat of the loss of power and consequent social antagonism burst into genocidal violence, and in ways that demonstrate how social fantasies of theft-enjoyment lead to the macabresque in mass atrocity.

The unfolding of the Rwandan genocide violence is especially poignant given the large numbers of perpetrators involved.[71] Lee Ann Fujii has examined how the genocide unfolded. She concluded that no single conception of ethnicity or unified image of hatred determined perpetrator behaviors. Rather, scripted narratives containing virulent allegations unfolded that, in turn, prompted violent groups to form, leading eventually to the acceleration of genocidal behaviors. Fujii states, "Put simply, killing produced groups and groups produced killings." Or, as she observes, "Ethnic hatreds seemed to have been a consequence of the genocide, not a cause."[72] Scripted narratives turned into demands for exclusion and purity, but not on account of prior fixed identitarian constructions. Fujii writes, "Preexisting hatreds tended to be personal and individual, not collectively aimed at an entire ethnic group."[73] Fujii emphasizes the mutuality felt and the reciprocities experienced among the perpetrators.[74] She outlines a "social interaction" model by suggesting that "Joiners did not kill because they hated or feared Tutsi as a group; rather, Joiners killed because of more immediate, and less abstract, reasons," identified as "local ties" and "group dynamics." She elaborates, "People did not kill over ethnicity, they killed with scripted ethnic claims."[75] The murderous exercise Fujii describes is one of shifting identities on the ground level at the Rwanda roadblocks. "Scripted ethnic claims were accusations and statements people made about another person's ethnic identity. The most common was that the accused was Tutsi, looked Tutsi, or supported the Tutsi. Any one of these claims made the accused a legitimate target for killing."[76] Fujii stresses the role of those in leadership positions in fomenting the violence. "Most of the time, the targeted person was whatever those in power said she was," Fujii observes. "It was leaders' subjective interpretations of who was Tutsi and their determinations of when ethnicity mattered that shaped how the genocide was performed." And it appears there existed latitude for perpetrators to decide how actively engaged in the killing they might be. Fujii indicates,

"Joiners, too, made the decisions about how faithful they would be to the script during a given performance. In coercive situations, they spoke their lines and followed stage directions carefully. In less coercive or less public moments, they were able to deviate from the script or drop it completely."[77]

Fujii's analysis thus implicitly turns toward an examination of the performative in the macabresque of the Rwandan genocide, specifically how performative transgression gained traction and fueled what was in effect momentum killing. Fujii's observations thus underscore the role of situational context. Her analysis suggests how identities emerge and re-emerge within group contexts, where they are played out in theaters of blood and agony. Once the stage for violence is set, agents assume their parts, and the parts become realized through group identities that in turn become solidified around the very performance of violence and violation. Fujii indicates that examination of genocide "should start with the assumption that ethnicity (or any type of identity) is not an objective thing out there, easily observed and analyzed from outside, but a shared and complex set of understandings that become reconstructed and deconstructed through processes of violence."[78] In this, Fujii warns against methodological representations of ethnicity as causal. "Rather than drawing a straight line from ethnicity as a precondition to violence as outcome, we would draw a double arrow that would show how performing violence reconstitutes the identities of performers."[79] She adds, "Focusing on endogenously generated dynamics does not rob actors of agency; rather it points to how people help to reproduce the very contexts they initially confront. People do so not through blind obedience or deference to authority, but through actions taken."[80] Thus, the macabresque becomes theorized as itself the crucible for identity constructions. Fujii emphasizes the recursivity that obtains between group violence and identitarian character or personality; and she demonstrates the recursivity between the decision to engage in collective violence and the situational conditions in which human violation occurs in the macabresque.

The question of leadership in collective violence in relation to ground-level human violation becomes a salient one in the context of the Rwandan genocide. The late Alison Desforges observed, in her report for Human Rights Watch, "The genocide resulted from the deliberate choice of a modern elite to foster hatred and fear to keep itself in power." In addition, she comments on how the Rwandan leadership fostered interethnic divisions that in effect objectified, essentialized, and thus racialized inter-group relations. She adds, "This small, privileged group first set the majority against the minority to counter a growing political opposition within Rwanda."[81] This observation suggests that it was not elite power but, rather, the threat of the loss of elite power that set in motion the conditions, first, for the manipulation of identitarian constructions, and secondly, for outbreaks of genocidal violence or mass atrocity. But the question here concerns the dramaturgical and aesthetic style of the Rwandan genocide and the degree to which power elites inscribed traditional or communal values onto the process of killing to gain the support of willing perpetrators.

This question is especially pertinent to the Rwandan genocide given the exceptionally high numbers of participant perpetrators. Simply put, why did the macheté become the weapon of choice in the macabresque of the Rwandan genocide? Scarry's analysis of torture features the significance of specific weapons, modes, and methods for interrogating victims and emphasizes contrasts that appear in this regard within various cultural environments. If we take the macheté to be emblematic of the Rwandan genocide, how does this reflect the cultural meanings and values of Rwandan society, if at all? Posing the question in this way presents us with the critical relationship between performativity in the macabresque and the cultural traditions in which it occurs. If aesthetic and dramaturgical styles in the macabresque vary, and if these variations in performative transgressions do indeed reveal and reflect the cultural milieu in which they happen, how is this demonstrated in the Rwandan case by the instrumentalization and widespread use of the macheté? Before turning to these questions, however, we must question whether this image of the macheté as the symbol of the Rwandan genocide is historically correct. To begin, several studies have confirmed Desforges's assessment as to the role of elite leadership in fomenting genocide and, in particular, in giving rise to the organized, marauding armed groups that operated at the roadblocks and killing fields.

This bears on the question of weaponry. Philip Verwimp, for example, has undertaken an empirical analysis of the use of different weapons, particularly firearms and machetés in different regions during the Rwandan genocide. He also took into account such factors as age, gender, and the occupation of victims in relation to how they died. On the basis of his findings, Verwimp concludes, "The genocide had an organized nature and was not a random killing spree."[82] He states unequivocally, "This does not mean there were no local initiatives, but it offers strong indications of central command and central organization. As it happens, local initiatives could take place only with central approval, either implicit or explicit."[83] He bases these conclusions, first, on the fact that "in the sample, in 17.7% of all cases where the weapon is known, the weapon is a firearm." He adds, "In the absence of any organization behind the genocide, we would not observe clusters of victims gathered in schools, churches and stadiums where many (in several massacres, 60–80%) of the victims were killed by firearms instead of traditional weapons."[84] Verwimp also found that young Tutsi and men "in the modern sector of the economy" were more likely to be killed by firearms. Verwimp infers from this that perpetrators "used firearms only against those people who could mount resistance."[85] What Verwimp thus confirms is first, the primacy of leadership, and secondly the central role of armed power organizations in determining not only the extent but also the modalities of violence. That said, these findings also suggest that in certain geographic regions primarily inhabited by Tutsi or mixed Tutsi and Hutu communities, the use of machetés in the killing process became extensive.

Once again, the human body and the concept of the body politic become analogous to each other in the shift from collective violence to human violation. Liisa H. Malkki contributed to the development of perspectives on performativity and human violation in her ethnographic study of what she describes as the "mythico-history" in the atrocity accounts of the Hutu refugees of the Tutsi violence that occurred in Burundi in 1972. "But what made the refugees' narrative mythical, in the anthropological sense," she writes, "was not its truth or falsity, but the fact that it was concerned with order in a fundamental, cosmological sense."[86] Malkkii's approach to the question of memory is very much in keeping with the concept of the macabresque. "The first thing to be examined in the present case," she writes, "is the extent to which the techniques of cruelty actually used were already symbolically meaningful, already mythico-historical."[87] She adds, "Acts of cruelty and violence, after all, often take on conventions readily. They become stylized and mythologically meaningful even in their perpetration."[88] Malkkii's additional point is to suggest that the stylization of cruelty helps shape not only how such acts are enacted but also how they are remembered. "Thus, acts of atrocity are not only enacted and perpetrated symbolically, they are also, after the fact, stylized or narratively constituted symbolically."[89] In the macabresque, the modalities of death and the means of suffering become linked in ways that humiliate and shame. The weapon of choice used by the Tutsi minority against the Hutu were bamboo poles, which Malkkii indicates were "themselves stereotypically emblems of Tutsi categorical identity" and thus "sometimes specified to be 1.8 or 2 meters long," the length stereotypically associated with Tutsi height. Memories of this were not recounted randomly. Malkkii indicates that, on the contrary, they "operated through certain routinized symbolic schemes of nightmarish cruelty."[90] In the macabresque of Tutsi violation, the bamboo pole was used as weapon and became symbolically associated with impalement at the apertures of human physicality, including entry into the womb in a war waged against Hutu reproduction.[91] The social fantasy at work appears aimed at the elimination of Hutu capacities for desire. But the legacy was its opposite, as is so often the case with mimetic desire. Hutu memory would instill a legacy of hatred and resentment contributing to the Rwanda genocide of 1994. Here, too, violence turned into violation; and once it did, the macabresque returned with vengeance, this time not with bamboo poles but with the macheté, mostly imported from China.

Christopher C. Taylor, in examining human violation in the Rwandan genocide, asserts, "Much of the violence, I maintain, followed a cultural patterning, a structured and structuring logic . . . . It was overwhelmingly Tutsi who were the sacrificial victims in what [in] many respects was a massive ritual of purification, a ritual intended to purge the nation of 'obstructing beings,' as the threat of obstruction was imagined through a Rwandan ontology that situates the body politic in analogical relation to the individual human body."[92] Taylor is quick not to impute causality to such representations, but he envisions them, following Bourdieu,[93] as "generative schemes" that become "internalized during early socialization," and thus attain a "nearly unconscious" way of knowing even if not formally articulated as such.[94] This massive ritual of purification facilitated the Rwandan genocide of 1994; the specific style of suffering was agony. The mode of producing agony throughout was cutting and blood trauma that Taylor, among others, indicates included "impalement, evisceration of pregnant women, forced incest, forced cannibalism of family members," as well as "the severing of the Achilles tendons of human and cattle victims; emasculation of men; and breast oblation of women."[95] Many died of dismemberment but were in countless instances forced to remain alive while the perpetrators gloated, specifically, with respect to their production of agony.

Blood trauma by means of incision represents the form of violation assumed during the Rwandan genocide and thus the macheté as the instrumental symbol of the macabresque. The question that Taylor asks is, why? His answer is to refer to the "specific ontologies" in which "myths, legends and other traditions" exist and become "constitutive of being and personhood."[96] Taylor's analytical perspective within anthropology parallels psychosocial analysis of social fantasy relative to ideological reifications. He stresses "prereflective dimensions of ontology" in order to feature what he calls "the structures of thought that underlie the construction of the moral person in Rwanda," which in turn appear to help explain what he suggests is the "practical logic of being in the world."[97] In so doing, Taylor is well aware of the analytical risks of attributing national character to Rwandan society. He obviates this by seeking to identify what he calls the "logic of ordinary sociality."[98] His observations derive from study of Rwandan medical practices and suggest that the "root metaphor" is "bodily flow" and that "flow/blockage symbolism mediates between physiological, sociological, and cosmological levels of causality."[99] Whatever flows can be blocked; and the means to blockage is rupture, impediment, and immobility. The leap between social fantasy and political imaginary eventually became transmuted into a strategy for genocide. The means became an end in itself. Dismemberment, the cutting of limbs and tendons, and the invasive severance of organic flows, defined the modes of performative transgressions in the macabresque of the Rwandan genocide. This was neither incidental nor coincidental; on the contrary, naturalized as well as metaphysical concepts of fluency denoted "realities" in axiomatic ways and thus in terms of what was assumed to define "truth." Flow and fluidity, blockage and obstruction, represented the metaphoric polarities between personal health and sickness, as well as communal order or disruption. Life and living, collective existence and the natural world, cosmic order and the metaphysical universe appeared to be suspended between these extremes.

At the core of such cultural constructions of collective identity stands the human body with its anatomical flows. Taylor describes, in effect, the basic Oedipal ritual of grounding human consciousness in the unconscious structures of psychic separation on which cultural identity and collective identification depend. The ritualized process stresses family and communal participation in an examination of the body of the newborn infant to ensure that the physicality of the child is an "open conduit." This is deemed critical to the eventual emergence of the child as a full-fledged member of the community able to "give and receive."[100] The digestive, reproductive, and other cyclical physiological processes of flow become analogized in ways emphasizing the cultural importance of reciprocity. This is grounded in Rwandan cosmological traditions, but I suggest that reciprocity represents a conceptual approach for apprising shame and honor in general terms that are relevant, not only to the Rwandan genocide but to that of the Holocaust and the Cambodian genocide, as well. With respect to Rwandan cultural constructions, Taylor observes, "By analogical extension the concern with unobstructed connection and unimpeded movement characterizes earlier Rwandan symbolic thought about the topography of the land, its rivers, roads, and pathways in general."[101]

Taylor's analysis becomes especially relevant by virtue of the explicit connections he theorizes between Rwandan traditional cosmology and the macabresque during the Rwandan genocide. He states, for example, "In Rwanda of 1994 torturers manifested a certain proclivity *to employ violent methods with specific forms.* These forms betrayed a preoccupation with the movement of persons and substances and with the canals, arteries, and conduits along which persons and substances flow: rivers, roadways, pathways, and even the conduits of the human body, such as the reproductive and digestive systems."[102] Taylor's analysis is especially noteworthy in the present context since it raises the question of the linkages between cultural constructions and dramaturgical and aesthetic styles of the macabresque by recognizing that the means of killing cannot be explained simply by reference to instrumental purposes or strategic motivation. "Killing one's adversaries while communicating powerful messages about them and oneself are not mutually exclusive," he comments. "Pragmatic explanations alone, however, cannot account for the sheer number of roadblocks that refugees reported to me that they had encountered. There was certainly a point of diminishing returns where adding new barriers was concerned, and it would appear that this point had been more than surpassed."[103] Taylor's analysis thus becomes foisted against the problems we have previously encountered with respect to performative transgression in mass atrocity: the self-defeating quest for absolute power as an end in itself, for itself. This illustrates the futility of interpreting the macabresque in mass atrocity in terms of purposive, instrumental, strategic, or even tactical calculations, let alone in moral or ethical normative perspectives.

The macabresque may support the designs and devices of means and ends in political decision-making, but its role is also to help fulfill a desire to re-establish control over shared desire. In the case of genocidal Hutu Rwanda, the demand was to control the desire of the mimetic rival, the Tutsi, along with those unfortunate Hutu who were classified as somehow contaminated by their Tutsi desire. The psychodynamics of mimetic desire also predominated in Nazi hatred against the Jews, as well as in the Khmer Rouge regime's fulminations against the Vietnamese during the Cambodian genocide. But in the case of the Rwandan genocide, the cosmological and the crisis in political imaginary became linked in the macabresque by the precise use of mass rape as a form of torment during the genocide, as well as of the macheté in blood trauma as the ultimate lethal weapon. This led to indescribable suffering, but of a specific kind, blood trauma agony from physical invasion, cutting and dismemberment, incision and impalement. This represents the emblematic style in the aesthetics and dramaturgies of the Rwandan macabresque. It reveals the cultural constructions of collective identity grounded in conceptions of flow and fluidity in human physicality as well as in a communal order subject to fantasized barriers, but also to the material ways victims were culled together at the fatal roadblocks where much of the genocide unfolded.

One of the critical components of the macabresque, as I have previously observed, is the forced complicity of victims in their humiliation and suffering. This points to the core element of performativity, that victims be made to declare the law of desire and thus, in psychosocial terms, the law of separation from *jouissance* so that perpetrators can come to believe they control desire. This helps to explain the relationship of interrogation to torture or torment in the modalities of eugenic sadism. In order to be forced to renounce their capacities for desire, victims must be made to experience the psychic agonies of self-betrayal. This also helps to explain why victims were sometimes forced into becoming complicit "collaborators" at the roadblocks of the Rwandan genocide. Taylor describes this by referring to the reports of those who were able to escape that they had been "forced to bludgeon a captured Tutsi with a hammer before being allowed to move on." Taylor indicates that some had been made to repeat the blows "for lack of enthusiasm." Now, the question arises as to why. Taylor's response is to interpret this as an attempt to generalize the sacrifice of the perpetrator in a manner aimed at ensuring that order is preserved. These acts of forced complicity, Taylor indicates, "served a useful psychological function," in that they assisted in "removing the ambivalence of the sacrificial act and the stigma of the sacrifice/executioner."[104] Taylor's perspective follows Bourdieu's conception of the foundational nature of order. Taylor indirectly references Bourdieu when he states the following, "The magical protections that are set to work whenever the reproduction of the vital order requires transgression of the limits that are the foundation of that order. Especially whenever it is necessary to cut or kill, in short, to interrupt the normal course of life."[105] Within the present context, to turn victims into perpetrators is to lend performativity to mimetic rivalry so that the control over the control of desire is performed by innocents who are impressed into the service of sadistic cruelty. Ultimately, the price is communal self-betrayal and the cost is to the continuities of segmented lineage that is the basis of both time and flow in Rwandan cultural traditions.

****

The Confessional Archive and the Facial Aesthetics of Ângkar's Torture

Interrogational Torture and Confessional Narratives, Honor and Shame, Visibility and Faciality in the Genocide of Democratic Kampuchea (DK), 1975–1979

Intertwines of Cultural Tradition and Ideological Revolution

In 1975, the Khmer Rouge gained political control of Cambodia. As a communist guerilla movement, it manifested influences of Marxist/Leninist/Stalinist/Maoist ideologies. It held racist hatred of the Vietnamese, designated *yuon*, or "barbarian"; while adulating French communism. This combination fostered a form of anticolonialism oriented to visions of classless agrarian society culminating with a radical version of agrarian communism. The end result was totalitarian in its extremist dystopian visions of societal transformation. The official name of the Khmer Rouge was the Communist Party of Cambodia, later the Communist Party of Democratic Kampuchea (CPK). The immediate political context in which the Khmer Rouge came to power was civil war, the fall of the Lon Nol government on April 17, 1975, and the Cambodian-Vietnamese War beginning in May 1975. Within hours of taking control of Phnom Penh, this revolutionary communist movement, under the leadership of the Standing Committee of the Central Committee or Party Center, or the *Ângkar*, "Organization," set in motion one of the most lethal tragic episodes of genocide and mass atrocity in a century punctuated by collective violence. The consequence was that an estimated 1.7 to 2.2 million persons died, within a relatively brief period, approximately half from intentional murder, the others from starvation or forced labor. The means included deportations from the cities combined with the massive dislocations brought on by forced collectivized agriculture and forced labor, in addition to widespread executions and forced starvation. The CPK combined communist ideological perspectives with Khmer cultural traditions that fostered a range of self-deceptions: territorial irredentism or expansionism; glorification of the rural peasantry; condemnation of family units in favor of romanticized notions of communal life and agricultural production; and advocacy and implementation of economic self-reliance and autarkic policies and practices. A critical political objective of the regime was irredentist and openly dedicated to efforts to regain territory around Cambodia's borders, especially the "retaking" of Vietnam's Mekong Delta and parts of Northeastern Thailand that the CPK identified by as Kampuchea Krom. The regime was also intensely racist and focused not only on the ethnic Khmer majority for collectivization, but as well on the effective elimination of all minorities, especially the Vietnamese and the Cham Muslims.

The *Ângkar* differed from its Soviet counterpart, the CPSU, in at least two major ways: first, it partially avoided the cult of personality; secondly, its radical egalitarian designs devastated urban centers. Once the DK regime was in control of the central government apparatus, it depopulated the major cities. The CPK culled all persons associated with cosmopolitan urbanism; the educated; the professional class; the creative; the devout or religiously affiliated; the commercial class; anyone with honorific status;

those identified with the previous regime; all ethnic Vietnamese, Chinese, Laotians, Muslim Cham; other ethnic minorities, the disabled; Buddhist monks; populations in the Eastern provinces; and anyone else alleged to suffer from "regressive consciousness." These groups were instantly ideologically reified as enemies of their own people. Draconian repression was manifold: the economy became collectivized; private property and farms were abolished; Buddhism and its ceremonial traditions and other forms of religious worship and expression were proscribed. Any semblance of personal freedom was eliminated, including civil liberties pertaining to residence, work, travel, speech, and creative expression. Formal education was abolished except for forms of cultural literacy that supported CPK propaganda with respect to the so-called Khmer agrarian revolution; books were confiscated and journalist publications were prohibited; banking, financial, monetary, market, industrial, and judicial systems were suppressed or annihilated. Black pajamas became mandatory for all citizens as a gesture of solidarity with the peasant revolution, supposedly beginning at "Year Zero."

Along with forcible evacuations, massive dislocations, starvation, destitution, and fear, the *Ångkar* engaged in the systematic *Khemrification* in inverse ways: the young, poor, and relatively uneducated gained a powerful status, just as those with higher standing were systematically murdered. Identitarian constructions became artifacts of ideology so that "base," "new," and "depositees" became the categories of existential difference on which life and death depended. Depositees, those deposited, literally, from the cities, were marked for death, and many suffered first from meager nutrition and gradual starvation and, in countless cases, by having to dig their own graves while shackled together and beaten to death or buried alive. Their remains symbolize the meaning of "the killing fields." Those who were selected for imprisonment and murder, such as Cham Muslims and people living in the Eastern zone, who were imputed to have "Khmer bodies but Vietnamese heads," were all classified as "new" people. Sign techniques aimed at marking identitarian differences in "otherness" where identicality pressed against the political instincts of the *Ångkar*, which was anxious to exaggerate the categories of political and social distinction, were applied throughout the Eastern zone. Like the Jews in Nazi Germany, who were forced to wear yellow Davidic stars, people in the Eastern zone were required to wear blue and white checked scarfs, the *kroma*, the ultimate sign that death was imminent.[106] Language became a tool to reinforce the "classless" society: people were to refer to each other as "comrade" (*mitt*); to "forge" (*lot dam*) new forms of political character; to become the instruments (*opokar*) of the revolution; and, at all cost, to avoid sentimental yearning for the prerevolutionary era, or "memory sickness" (*choeu stek arom*).[107]

A distinguishing feature of the *Ångkar* was its explicit designations of status and positionality in the "pecking order" of power, authority, and rank. For all that it was a radical egalitarian movement, it was fastidious with respect to the rankings among the leaders of the Party Center. Many had known each other for years, since their graduate days in Paris and, in some cases even earlier, during the colonialist era. This sense of family, bonding plus honorific seniority, was indicated by the term "Brother" and included Pol Pot (Saloth Sar), "Brother Number 1," who took his nom de guerre from the French by reference to *politique potentielle*; Nuon Chea (Long Bunrot), "Brother Number 2"; and Ieng Sary, "Brother Number 3"; and Ta Mok (Chhit Chhoeun), "Brother Number 4"; and Khieu Samphan, "Brother Number 5"; and others farther down the ladder, step by step. This system of rank designation reflected a culture of honor that would influence the style of macabreseque.

The usage of the term "Brother" to designate the members of the Party Center seems ironic given that the Khmer Rouge represented itself as a replacement of the traditional family. Family structures became subordinated to the *Ângkar*. Parents were represented as intrinsically reactionary. Youth became the wards of the Party Center, often trained to engage in torture through initial use of animals as objects, eventually serving as an important CPK cadre and thus as murderers in the killing fields and as perpetrators in the macabresque of interrogational torture. Familial affiliations, family associations, were prohibited at the risk of death; family members were often relocated to different areas of the country as modes of internal communication such as postal and telephone services were disbanded. Children were reared in communal ways. Residences became transformed into tenements for dozens, homesteads into the casernes of regimental order. Kaylanee Mam comments, "These irrational policies prove that collective dining was enforced not because of lack of food, but because the regime feared that allowing families to produce their own food would encourage family interests and distract loyalty from Angkar." Mam thus focuses on the critical dimension of transfer of loyalty to centralized authority but within the ideological frames of collectivist agrarianism. Mam continues, "As with other policies implemented by the regime, the purpose of collectivizing food and property was to eliminate individual dependency on the family and force individuals to project this dependency toward the organization.[108] In the case of the *Ângkar*, "forced dependency" represented a technique to promote its legitimation by grounding its totalitarian disciplines in codes of honor reflective of Cambodian dynastic traditions. This helps to explain certain features of the macabresque in the Cambodian genocide, in particular, the eerie emphasis on the archivization of precisely contrived confessions and photographs of prisoners.

The core linkage between ideology and tradition in the case of the CPK regime lies in its efforts to impose an extreme discriminatory or exclusivist but egalitarian agrarian communal communism by means of a quasi-dynastic dictatorial regime. Dynasties represent political formations that struggle with the tensions between national political formations based on central forms of governance, on the one hand, and, on the other, with various forms of familial, blood, ancestral or segmented lineage, that is, formations that tend to disaggregate national or collective governance. From this perspective, dynastic rule concentrates power in centralizing authority relevant to national governance but retains its legitimacy in values derived from kinship/descent orders of segmented lineage. In this sense, dynastic rule demonstrates transitional tensions between tribal, clan, or lineage chiefdoms and centralized kingships of governance. What the CPK regime attempted was to transform itself into a dynastic form of national or centralized political rule, anchored to the Party Center or *Ângkar*, which comprised leaders ranked by echelons of "Brotherhood," who were nonetheless legitimated on the basis of a radical communist ideology that sought to create a revolutionary order by devastating civil society and the economy, and thus in ways that exacerbated cultural divisions.

Dynastic systems partake, therefore, of the features of kingships legitimated by honor codes of fealty in which blood, family, and ancestry designate authoritative status or power position. The CPK *Ângkar* however, sought to destroy family and blood ties within Cambodian society in order to assert its own role as "family," thus exclusively deserving of the honorific affirmation traditionally accorded Cambodian royalty and those of honorific standing. This influenced how the macabresque of the Cambodian genocide was perpetrated, with its stress on interrogational torture, confession, and archivization, of both the confessional statements and the mug shots taken day after day, prisoner by prisoner, in the macabresque hell of S-21. Ben Kiernan encapsulates the ideological intertwining of international communism and traditional dynasticism at the core of the *Ângkar's* logic of illogic. He writes, "With Pol Pot's victory in 1975, however, the re-emergence of dynastic internationalism in the clothing of official nationalism was symbolized by the return to the dynastic name of the country. Its title was now 'Democratic *Kampuchea*,' an apt combination of pre-nationalist tradition with international communist usage."[109] But this *Ângkar* hybrid of dynastic communism within the Cambodian national context meant that traditional mythologies would be politically converted into the legitimizing supports for the revolutionary endeavor. Kiernan states, "Two 'transnational' ideologies—one traditional and dynastic, one modern and communist—provided the high culture from which Democratic Kampuchea's ultra-nationalism actually derived." He later concludes, "The unique historical amalgam was also an important factor in the hierarchical DK conception of its international relations, and in the genocidal outcome for Cambodia's both 'foreign' minorities and the Khmer majority."[110] The hierarchical DK conception to which Kiernan refers was permeated by fantasies of honor and shame that in turn influenced how collective violence was transmuted into the practices of human violations in distinctive ways during the macabresque of the Cambodian genocide and mass atrocity.

Honor, Shame, and Revenge in Tradition and in Genocidal Ideology

Attempts to define "honor" confront the double-sidedness or bipartite character of how the concept tends to be constructed; it partakes of the interiority of the self in relation to others, but represents how others or the external social universe perceive, recognize or treat persons, alone or in their capacities as members of the groups with which they become identified. The concept honor refers to extrinsic factors, such as the social status, esteem, or recognition accorded those perceived as deserving of measures of fealty, as well as to those intrinsic features guiding behaviors based on codes of conduct or socially accepted rules. Frank Henderson Stewart defines honor as "a claim-right," that is, that others act in particular ways regarding the claim to honor. He states, "On the one side is the bearer, who has something about him that gives him the right to respect; and on the other is the world, which has a duty to treat the bearer with respect."[111] For such reasons, "insult," is never far from the social dynamics of honor. Julian Pitt-Rivers suggests that honor codes guide personal behaviors, influence normative evaluations of others and reflect degrees of social status in communal cultures in which social standing depends on social image.[112] Valeschka Martins Guerra and colleagues summarize some of the empirical findings in this regard by stating, "The association between the individual's worth and his or her social image is stronger in cultures that abide by honor codes. Honor might be especially important for collectivist cultures where family values, harmony, and respect are emphasized, and honor is not just a trait of the individual but his or her family and other collective groupings."[113] These authors thus underscore "honor-based collectivism," that does not stress modest demeanor or subservience to notions of harmony, but rather "the public nature of self-worth and the need to protect and maintain honor through positive presentation of oneself and in-group members."[114] Collectivism, communal codes, self-imagery as a function of social imaginaries all provoke emphasis on face and facility, on saving face and seeking revenge or recompense if "face" becomes, literally, *defaced*.

Emotionality is thus intrinsic to honor codes. In cases of insult or offense, anger and shame often occur in discordant, disruptive, or dysfunctional ways. In cultures in which honor-based collectivism influences values and behaviors, shame becomes a function of what others do, rather than what the individual alone experiences.[115] Shame thus represents an emotional condition that provokes the right-claim described by Stewart, a right-claim that makes demands on others for rectification. It is at this juncture that violence, feud, or collective punishment might ensue. This helps to explain the dramaturgical and aesthetic style tragically witnessed during the Cambodian genocide under the Pol Pot regime.

Austinian speech act performativity and its distinctions among directive, commissive, and, in particular, instructional speech acts illustrate the critical role played by cultural values of honor and shame disciplines in the macabresque of the Cambodian genocide. Speech act performativity becomes embedded in certain cultural environments on account of society's normative behavioral activity. Arguably, and in broad terms, market economies, for example, adhere to commissive speech acts since they are grounded in cultures that emphasize incentives that reward or punish on the basis of individual agency, personal as well as group commitments, voluntary competition or contractual obligations. In such cultural settings, which are typically associated with liberalism and possessive individualism, agency commitments become normative: in commercial activity, fault, tort, and liability operate; in both personal and in civil and penal realms, guilt becomes a principle of discipline, particularly with respect to agentic failure to satisfy commitments or to meet standards. Commissives are thus speech acts in which promise and promissory obligation represent normative forms of performativity the outcomes of which often determine status based on achievement. Alternatively, directive speech acts perform in settings denoted by ascribed rank and echelon in which social order tends to depend on the normative acceptance of rule by dictatorial governance, including authoritative, hierarchical, or command.

As discussed earlier in the context of Chinese Confucianism, instructional speech act performativity flows from cultures beholden to the values of honor in which ascribed standing based on segmented lineage, blood, or ancestral heritage rather than achieved status represents the normative standard. The values of honor impose vast obligations on those beholden to them, not the least of which is to uphold the ties of intergenerational continuity. To lose honor is to dishonor the linkages in which familial or tribal groups embed their collective life and history. Dishonor is rarely felt as personal but rather as familial or communal. Although it may in some cultures be experienced as an insult to a single, often a male, person, it tends not to function as an individual blemish. And thus honor or dishonor function weakly as values in cultures of individualism and guilt. Honor values do sometimes arise in such cultures within highly specific groups, settings, or milieus, such as within the ranks of the military and law enforcement or among members of organized crime or other exclusive organizations, especially those that face risk or require secrecy and involve clandestine activity. This is the case whenever group survivability depends on individual behaviors and restraints. For these reasons, heroism is often associated with honor, since heroic acts tend to be self-sacrificial on behalf of a group. Dishonor, therefore, tends to be experienced as a stain against one's standing in relation to ancestral lineage or with respect to identificatory groups, however conceived or constructed. Such groups may be interpreted in psychosocial terms as those very same groups that impress Oedipal identifications onto neonates.

For all these reasons, shame punishments and disciplines differ from the penalties of guilt and the individualism of guilt punishments. Shame is experienced in intensely personal ways, to be sure, but shame punishments are public precisely because they are designed to *instruct* those who violate group norms or traditions in ways that return normative justice or stability to the social order as a whole. Shame disciplines are thus scopic and exhibitionist, unlike those of guilt, which tend to function silently or personally in relation to individuals alone. In shame punishments, the operative principle is the gaze of an externalized other, that is, the gaze of the totemic ancestral order or of the patrimonial authority, or of some superegotistical force that demands that subjects be "taught" how to live in compliance with the honor of the group. Shame dynamics and disciplines function differently across cultures steeped in traditions of honor. They help to explain caste systems, feuds, honor killings, and so on. In general, however, they explain why saving face represents the core feature of shame discipline. Those who incarnate the external "gaze" of authority address the "face" of those who have brought dishonor; they do so in a public manner so that the group that punishes is able to "see" and recognize the face of the ones who are being taught the "lessons." Faciality, its retention, loss, and restoration, therefore, represents a cultural mechanism for the mediation of wrongs whenever traditional values and group behaviors embedded in honor codes intersect with individuals whose behaviors are seen to demand shame punishments. In the present context, honor and shame disciplines help frame an understanding of the Cambodian genocide.

During the era of DK genocide, faciality and the confessional came to represent some of the distinguishing features of its macabresque. When victims were killed, therefore, the final blow was often to the head or an act of beheading. Prisoners in the Cambodian torture centers were confined en masse in unhygienic conditions with little access to food and water until their bodies became ravaged by disease, parasites, hunger, and filth. By the time they were interrogated under torture, they often were "in an already dehumanized and impure state"; they no longer "appear[ed] quite human."[116] As Alexander Laban Hinton observes, "A person who stinks, has skin diseases and lice, and is emaciated is marked as different."[117] Prisoners who had succumbed to bodily torment and ideological pressure "confessed" their crimes against the nation, party, and state, thereby justifying their executions.[118] Having been tortured with "truncheons, electric wire, plastic bags, whips, shackles, pliers, needles, tanks of water, ropes and pulleys," Hinton writes, "These contaminating beings were eradicated in a desolate field, clubbed on the back of the head with an iron bar and dumped into a ditch that was eventually covered over—the final step in the recoding and containment of these dangerous, and now dead, bodies."[119] Mass atrocity during the Cambodian genocide involved decapitation as a preferred execution technique because of the symbolic significance of the human head with respect to cultural notions of honor and shame. Hinton observes:

> The head is thus symbolically linked to issues of status and reciprocity that are at the core of disproportionate revenge . . . to strike off the head of an adversary is to "completely defeat" them by obliterating their honor, their capacity to engage in social interactions, their ability to seek revenge in turn, and their life itself . . . it sends a powerful message to potential enemies . . . [and] manufactures difference, transforming a human being into a headless corpse—an enemy whose body has been inscribed with a message stating that the person is no longer fully human and is completely different from the pure "us."[120]

To dishonor the "enemy" by beheading him not only humiliates the person, it serves the added aim of social "purification.

"Face-Work" in "Defensive" versus "Offensive" Honor Competition

To examine why and how these unique features operated raises major questions concerning the relationship of culture to genocide, and of both with respect to the macabresque. As Hinton has stated, "Genocidal regimes will draw on preexisting cultural models to motivate their minions." He refers to "behavioral templates for violence," to the fact that "cultural models often persevere despite historical and structural change" and that in the specific case of the DK, the genocidal regime of the *Ângkar* "both initiated sociopolitical transformations that undermined traditional constraints on violence and incorporated preexisting cultural models into their genocidal ideology."[121] Honor-bound cultures envision intergenerational linkages in terms of totemic, ancestral, or familial verticality; in a metaphoric sense, the communal "gaze" vertically focuses on each of its members. Hinton states, "When a schema is highly elaborated in a given society, it becomes a 'foundational schema' that is part of the local cultural ethos. In Cambodia, the 'up-down' or 'vertical' orientation constitutes just such a foundational schema that serves as a template for Cambodian cultural models."[122] Hinton, in describing honor within the Cambodian tradition indicates that the Khmer word for honor, *ketteyos*, connotes character or moral excellence "primarily focused on the external recognition of one's glory, prestige, and splendid reputation." Hinton stresses that Khmer usage of the term, *ketteyos* connotes "a stronger sociocentric emphasis" than the term, honor, whenever applied in English.[123] The vernacular applications of honor thus impute not merely verticality but externality to the judgmental gaze by and through which a person understands his or her own standing as a member of Cambodian society. Given such honor dynamics the operative principle in social relations attaches to the mirror image; people's self-images depend on how they perceive themselves against how they perceive others to perceive them. In other words, "I am *what I think you think* I am." Faciality becomes, literally, the critical interface or boundary between external assessment and internal self-evaluation. Hinton links honor to faciality suggesting that faciality is "predicated on the evaluation of others" and is "performative." In the context of Cambodian culture, one acts or performs in accordance with others' expectations and utterly in "fear of exposure and shame." Hinton describes processes of "face-work" aimed at enhancing one's standing in terms of honor and of what he calls "mutual face-saving" or "the shield," involving tacit understandings aimed at reciprocated actions to avoid the embarrassments or humiliations that might cause hurt or shame. Whenever persons act outside this realm of propriety, anomic behaviors can result in ways "likely to disregard face norms."[124] This occurs in instances of violence or crime and became normative during the genocide and mass atrocity perpetrated by the DK regime in terms of what represents *performative faciality*.

During the DK regime, honor values and shame disciplines were reinscribed onto the body politic in ways indicative of how the macabresque of genocide and mass atrocity was implemented. Hinton outlines some of the wider social norms. "People were constantly evaluated," he writes. "Given these dangers, it was imperative for people to keep up 'the shield' at all times. Public meetings, for example, constituted a form of ideological face promotion."[125] People engaged in "face-work" by competing for honor through displays of loyalty in formats of political celebration. In keeping with honor values, and to counter the "shield" as a form of propriety, "blood sacrifice" against "enemies" became a trope repeated in "political speeches, revolutionary songs and slogans, and even the national anthem."[126] Ideological vehemence became prescriptive and called forth what Hinton calls "performative competence" and "role commitment" to the Khmer cause including "renunciation of individualistic ties, behaviors, and ways of thinking."[127] The political effectiveness of the *Ângkar* in perpetrating its unique macabresque of torture and torment in the course of genocide and mass atrocity demonstrates its capacities to convert the Cambodian cultural traditions of honor and face into core ideological motivations for collective violence and justifications for the shift to human violation. Honor codes imbue action with meanings that derive from how persons understand themselves as perceived by others. This represents the critical process in the psychodynamic transformation of youthful peasants into willing perpetrators. Face-consciousness represented the metric of honorability: the more revolutionary, the more honorable; the more "detached" from family and tradition, the greater the nobility; the more able and willing to torture and kill, the more luminous the face. "Ultimately," Hinton writes, "revolutionary consciousness was evinced through behavior. Face and revolutionary consciousness converged in social performance . . . a desire to prove beyond a doubt that one was loyal to and willing to fulfill any duty for the DK regime. In many contexts, this proof consisted of a demonstrated willingness to kill."[128] The psychodynamic linkages between desire, ego-ideal, prototypicality in group dynamics toward peers and leaders we have previously discussed appear to have remained constant, just as the quest for honor and higher status denoted by "face" remained constant, especially among the young peasantry youth now swept along by the DK's ideological promise of collective glory. What had changed was the currency by which actions would be evaluated and recorded, and what counted was where one stood on the scales of CPK cruelty that was represented as necessary and therefore good. Hinton concludes in this regard, "Face and honor continued to have ontological resonance. Face remained a self-implicating, embodied locus of social visibility, communication, and public standing."[129] Whenever honor codes influence behavior, shame performativity soon follows. In the case of interrogators this appears to have functioned in two distinct but related ways: within the emotional interiorities of the perpetrators as an experience to be avoided, and as a motivation for greater degrees of cruelty. Hinton indicates, "Shame was likely an ontologically resonant undercurrent of interpersonal interactions that motivated violence . . . first, by pressuring cadres who wanted to avoid shame . . . and, second, by moving cadres who had lost face to perpetrate brutal excesses."[130]

This led to what Hinton depicts as competitive killing. It is as if the cultural mechanism of the gaze had to become institutionalized as genocide and mass atrocity unfolded. At first, this meant that killing had to be witnessed. "Executions usually took place in front of a perpetrator's peers and/or superiors. Within this structured setting, the killers attempted to gain honor through the positive evaluations of others."[131] Hinton distinguishes two forms of structured honor competitions: *defensive* versus *offensive*. In instances of defensive honor, perpetrators killed to protect themselves against losing face and the risk of being killed themselves, lest they were perceived as reluctant or unwilling to murder for the cause; in cases of competitive honor, cadres from different regions competed for honor by demonstrating greater enthusiasm or ability in killing class enemies. Betrayal also became integral to offensive honor competitions in that "reporting on one's rivals was a common strategy . . . it was encouraged by the DK regime and constitutes one of the reasons purges and paranoia were so rampant."[132] The DK regime, itself a product of mimetic rivalry between itself, the French, and the Vietnamese, now encouraged mimetic rivalry among those who competed for the honor of becoming the most virulent of perpetrators.

Honor codes and shame disciplines often exact the prices of revenge as the costs of slights or insults. Instructional speech act performativity means that those party to exchanges that carry dishonor must ultimately come to resolution through repayments of an honorific "debt" owed not only to the individuals involved but as well to the social groupings or communities with which they identify. This is the meaning of *"instruction"* within the context of speech act performativity, to avenge wrongs by "teaching" lessons through the restitution of honor, however extracted. Saving face often means preserving the "name" of family or clan by paying off the debts owed on account of individual infractions by means of revenge on a group-to-group basis. Instructional speech act performativity and honor codes and shame disciplines function in cultural settings where centralized authority is legitimated through dynastic rule and thus in societies in which mimetic rivalry tends to be organized along tribal or segmented lineage lines. Honor codes of revenge demand retribution across time and generations and thus maintain their hold over families for extended periods of escalating violence unless conciliation processes are introduced. The DK regime built on this cultural mode of reciprocated revenge by severing the connections between "instructional" revenge and blood or familial lineages and reconnecting it to the *Ångkar*. As suggested earlier, the reason given was to renounce family ties as the fundamental unit of social life in favor of the DK regime and its movement. This partially explains why the DK regime became associated with the color, red, and thus with blood. Honor was thus to be transferred from traditional forms of Oedipal cathexis to the DK regime as the presumed embodiment of nurture. This was in keeping with a tradition of what Hinton calls, "disproportionate revenge" in which entire families would be executed as a preemptive device to prevent mutual acts of revenge on the part of family representatives over an extended period of time. Hinton indicates, "Much DK violence can be viewed as a modern example of 'cutting off a family line.'"[133] The DK regime, therefore, influenced perpetrator behaviors in accordance with the influences of honor codes rooted in notions of revenge: grudge and feud, payback, and the talion law of eye for an eye.

But Hinton stresses not mere reciprocity in feuds but the role played by cultural values of disproportionate revenge in dynamics he depicts as "a head for an eye." Revolutionary fervor combined with resentment by the rural poor of those reified as "new" people fostered a powerful ideological movement against those condemned as enemies by the DK regime. Hinton writes, "By drawing on preexisting resentment and focusing it on the city, Khmer Rouge ideology effectively fostered a rural class grudge (*kumnum vonnah*) against the urban population" in which the campaign to destroy completely (*phchanh phchal*) became the order of the day.[134] Hinton recounts that during these initial phases of collective violence, shibboleths against "new" people raged with images of red, blood and

revenge. "In fact, the color of blood, red, was a prominent theme in Khmer Rouge propaganda and provided a metaphoric call for revenge." In such a manner, honor tradition
had become grafted onto an ideology of modern class warfare and radical egalitarianism leading to the specific dramaturgies and aesthetics of *Ângkar's* hellish macabresque.
Modern interrogational torture was adopted to ensure controlled and tightly monitored
confession. This was an extension of the honor codes and traditions grounded in shame
punishment and reciprocated violence but customized to satisfy the cultures of gaze and
public punishment as well as disproportionate revenge. This culminated in reams upon
reams of confessions, carefully monitored, endlessly revised, stacked in piles on top of
piles and stored long after the confessors had ceased to exist. The macabresque of the DK
regime did more; it ensured that faciality would remain the essential boundary between
shame and vindication. This led to a unique feature of the DK macabresque, a photographic gallery of silent faces, covering up their fear and what would ultimately be their
agonized screams. Witnesses such as the S-21 photographer Nhem En or the guard Khieu
Lohr, interviewed by Alexander Hinton, or Kok Sros, interviewed by Douglas Niven, all
vividly recall the ever-present sounds of agonized screams, "especially at night," so loud
they could be heard "half a mile away."[135]

Ângkar's Tuol Sleng or S-21 Interrogational Torture Center: Paying Homage and Faciality in the CPK Macabresque Archive

For as long as the history of genocide and mass atrocity in the twentieth century is
recounted, the S-21 prison, torture and interrogation center, will stand in infamy as a
paradigmatic example of the macabresque. The four prison buildings, located in the Tuol
Sleng district of Phnom Penh and arranged in a quadrangle affronting onto a single open
area, had been formerly used as a secondary school facility but were now enclosed by a
corrugated tin wall and barbed wire, and surrounded by soldiers. Some classrooms were
converted into cells sometimes holding up to a hundred "low status" prisoners, all shackled together or bolted to the floor; whereas others, usually of greater prestige or importance, were incarcerated in cells on the bottom floors and were shackled to their beds.
Female prisoners accused of crimes or, in the case of the majority, imprisoned simply as a
consequence of being the wives or daughters of male prisoners were confined to a single
large area on the second floor. During the period 1977–1978, the prison held between
1,000 and 1,500 prisoners at any given time, some for a period of days, others for months
of torture and interrogations. An estimated 20,000 to 25,000 prisoners were channeled
through S-21 during this period; only seven survived.

According to David Chandler, the "S" stood for the word, *la salle* or "room," and 21
was the code term for the *santebal*, or security police, who ran the facility under the
indirect control of the *Ângkar* of the Communist Party Center (CPK) and the immediate direction of Kang Keck Ieu (Duch) from 1976 until the prison's liberation by the
Vietnamese. Once within its confines, prisoners were subjected to incarceration, interrogation, degradation, systematic torture, confession, and ultimately death. In the hands

of the santebal at S-21, the spectral gaze of honor and shame within traditional culture became transformed into a panoptical spectacle of mental, physical, and spiritual abuse and horror. It was as if the interiority of a prisoner's mind could be externalized by means of intense microscopic scrutiny under the duress of pain and torment. The ostensible aim was to protect the DK revolutionary future using the political souls of "enemies of the people" as a mechanism of political salvation. The result was macabresque sadism in the particular dramaturgy of S-21. David Chandler has recorded the methods of torture applied against prisoners in S-21 that included beatings, electric shocks, suffocation, water tortures, forced swallowing, standing with arms up or hanging upside down for hours, and other hideous violations, including evisceration and laceration.

One specific form of torture that perhaps conveys that specific style of the macabresque in the hell of S-21 was designated by perpetrators as "paying homage," including to images of Ho Chi Minh, "image(s) of dogs," "to the wall," "to the chair," or "to the table."[136] The DK regime, throughout Cambodian society, had proscribed traditional honorific gestures of formal recognition and propriety on the pain of death. This included a prohibition against bowing or paying homage. But inside S-21 paying homage became a style of torture, as if honor had to be transformed into a shame punishment by being enacted as mockery of itself. Chandler describes the *thvay bongkum* gesture, "raising the joined palms above one's head and also occasionally prostrating oneself," as a form of torture sufficiently painful so as "to induce a full confession."[137] And paying homage to dogs meant paying homage to the two main enemies of the DK regime, the Americans and the Vietnamese. Chandler comments, "'Paying homage' in this way introduced many prisoners abruptly to the power relations of S-21. It highlighted the contrast or contradiction in Khmer Rouge thinking between hidden, abject, foreign, and treasonous 'facts' on the one hand and the overwhelming 'truth' of the hidden but resplendent Organization [Angkar] on the other . . . . This particular torture also set out the discipline of the interrogation that was to follow and forced prisoners to identify themselves, even before they started talking, as traitors."[138] Hinton also comments on how "cultural knowledge helps structure the bodily inscription of violence" within the context of torture that reenact gestures of "paying homage" but in humiliating ways and positions.[139]

Paying homage represents another form of torture in the macabresque of genocide and mass atrocity. Its applications in S-21 help illustrate the critical linkages between cultural styles and symbolic values, on the one hand, and how the macabresque unfolds in any given instance of genocide and mass atrocity, on the other. As in numerous cases of genocide and mass atrocity, perpetrators engaged in the practice of interrogational torture. The goal or ostensible aim, as before, was to extract "truth" from prisoners who had no information to provide. The quest over informativeness thus remains a constant. *What differs, however, is how specific cultural values or traditions help shape the style or the aesthetics of the macabresque and how the dramaturgies of confession are cast in the molds of local symbolic or semiotic meanings.* In the case of S-21, paying homage represented a form of shame punishment aimed at reducing the standing of prisoner honor to the state of animality, that is, to a condition of disgust or ultimate shame. Chandler declares, ' "Paying homage' was one of a series of degradations designed to force prisoners to recognize their animal status." In the fantasmatic universe of the santebal tormentors, the Vietnamese became the mimetic rival threatening the theft of thing-enjoyment. Chandler adds, "Their foreign masters (*me*) were depicted as animals, and only animals would pay homage to them." Chandler describes how the illogic of human degradation became externalized performatively. "Once the patron-dogs' identities and the prisoners loyalty to them had been displayed, the prisoner was divested of revolutionary and human status, and the interrogation could proceed, majestically or at a fast clip, to unearth 'treacherous activities,' 'plans,' and 'strings of traitors.' " The victims were now "creatures tottering on all fours toward their deaths."[140] The practice of paying homage often induced prisoner confessions but confession itself did not mean the cessation of additional torture. Torture was also often applied after confession, another indication of the extent to which the psychodynamics of mimetic rivalry had fallen under the fantasmatic influences of social antagonism and dread of thing-enjoyment, particularly with respect to reifications of everything and anything imputed with essences of the Vietnamese. When death finally came, it was performed at the killing field Choeung Ek with blows to the spinal cords at the neck of kneeling prisoners at the edge of pits, that is, blows to the head as a sign of ultimate dishonor.

But the influences of cultural mores retained its grasp on the entire process. Chandler, like Kiernan as well as Hinton, stresses the verticality in honor-bound structures as critical to an understanding of how prisoners came to be treated in S-21. Chandler writes, "Hierarchies, patronage, and 'paying homage,' so characteristic of 'exploitative' society (the Cambodian phrase translated as 'exploit,' *chi choan*, literally means 'ride on and kick') had not be extinguished by the revolution." He adds, "In some ways, the 'new' society consisted of the same mixture as before and followed prerevolutionary patterns of authority and compliance."[141] This pattern in S-21 assumed a basic three-tier structure: "those who commanded or put others to use (*neak prao*) and those who 'listened' (*neak sdap*) and were put to use (*neak bomrao*), as well as prisoners.

Perhaps another unique feature of S-21 was the seemingly precarious status of those in the middle category, the guards, interrogators, and other perpetrators, who at times were given full and free range to torture, but who also consistently appear to have fallen under the vigilant "eye" of the senior members of the *Ângkar* regime. Guards were given strict rules to follow and were themselves under scrutiny with respect to their comportment and ability to follow elaborate procedures regarding the transfer of prisoners, the disposition of weapons of torture, and the extent to which they manifested revolutionary gravity. Chandler describes them as mostly young, poor, and from rural areas. "For many of them, the 'Organization' had replaced their mothers and fathers. Responding to its desires, filtered through the commands of their 'older brothers,' they were often capable of extreme cruelty."[142] Interrogators walked a fine line between being weak or too avid. If they failed to get the wanted confession or if a prisoner died before making or completing one, the guards themselves could fall under suspicion and become imprisoned. This, too, demonstrates the honor code and loss of face or shame disciplines that were operating within the culture at the time.

Hinton lists a nine-step procedure the CPK mandated interrogators to follow that outlined how "politics" and torture were to be applied to prisoners: "extract information"; "assemble as many points as possible to pin them down"; "pressure them with political propaganda"; "press on with questions and insults"; "torture"; "review and analyze the answers for additional questions"; "review and analyze for documentation"; "prevent them from dying"; and "keep things secret."[143] Prisoners were also held to sadistic rules of "propriety," such as "you must immediately answer my questions"; "while getting lashes or electrification you must not cry at all"; "do not make pretexts about Kampuchea Krom in order to hide your jaw of traitor"; "if you disobey any point of my regulations you shall get either ten lashes or five shocks of electric discharge."[144]

But it also demonstrates how ideological notions of party loyalty and of personal or cadre authenticity became transformed into sadistically performed "truth" standards in situations of interrogational torture when neither epistemological truth nor existential authenticity were even remotely possible. As in the case of Stalin's purgatory, particular force was leveled against former members of the CPK on the grounds of personal, political, and intellectual deviation. Kiernan provides an example, one among many others, with reference to the forced confession of Koy Thuon, a former CPK operative, whose confession was rejected by Duch on the grounds of "why is your belief so wholehearted?" Kiernan comments, "This letter encapsulates the process and mentality of S-21. . . . Prisoners were routinely forced to confess that they were not Cambodian political actors, but mere agents of foreign powers, motivated by greed or cowardice rather than conviction or dedication." Forced confessions confirming such motivations were deemed necessary "for propaganda purposes" and also to validate the CPK's rampant suspicions. The aim of obtaining the correct confessional language went beyond the requirements of propaganda. Perpetrators gripped by self-deception in the quest for "informativeness" without information believe in the lies told to them in the formats of truth they demand.

Thus, of the present case, Kiernan writes, "Duch still considered CPK dissenters to be *objectively* working in concert with foreign powers," so long as they did not provide confessions to this effect in the precise forms, tone, and detail demanded.[145] Thousands of confessions were produced that admit to a range of counterrevolutionary activities and that as well implicate "strings" or "networks of traitors." Here, again, the forced self-betrayal of victims was deemed unsatisfactory unless combined with the betrayal of other victims. At S-21 this sometimes led to lists of hundreds of names.[146] Confessional narratives assumed a kind of performativity of betrayal in which those alleged to be complicit with treason or treachery toward the revolution were categorized according to the vertical structures of honor and face. Chandler declares, "The world view of the [S-21] confession . . . includes the individual who is confessing, the people above him who persuaded him to betray the revolution and the people below him whom he persuaded to betray it. Everything is seen in terms of networks and forces."[147] At the core of such narratives was the indispensible presence of "self-criticism" in patterns similar to that developed by the NKVD at the time of the Soviet great purges and Show Trials. Self-betrayal and the betrayal of others appears to have required an art form consisting of a stylized form of self-revelation in which a victim turns against himself or herself in expiation for sins never committed to appease the Party agents who demand such confession as a way of defeating the enemies that hardly existed.

This process also represents a purification scheme originating in social fantasy and realized by systematic applications of power that are indicative of the theoretical linkages between the use of sadistic methods and situational contexts framed by political purposes. In this regard, Chandler uses Foucault's phrase, "the vengeance of the sovereign," to refer to the "coolness" with which torture was imposed. "What is striking about the imposition of torture (*tearunikam*) at the prison, however," he writes, "is not its brutality . . . but its use within a graduated, supposedly rational process. The coolness with which torture is chosen, inflicted, and written about is unnerving."[148] Chandler ponders the reasons for this and determines that "the tortures at S-21 were purposive and constrained." He envisions them as an effort "to display and rationalize the power of those inflicting it, especially when they are representative of the state."[149] This represents the precise objective of sadistic behavior, to empower its perpetrators to fantasize themselves into the delusional belief that they are the appointed agents of the law designated by fate or power to ensure that victims declare the law of desire by means of renunciation. The sadistic process of attaining "truth" by torture and torment at S-21 presents us with one of the prime examples in the psychosocial history of political sadism during the last century.

The Confessional Archive

Confession never led to dispensation; those who confessed were killed; many were tortured even after their confessions had been rendered and signed. Re-education and reform, the ostensible didactic nature of the macabresque in the case of the Chinese Cultural revolution, or, even, in the frames of Stalin's purgatory, played no part here. To confess was to admit shame, and shame was punishable by death. Shame punishments tend to be public but in this case the torture, shame, confession, and death by humiliating means or methods were only for the benefit of the senior members of the *Ångkar*. They were not only judge and jury; they were the sole audience, for whom confessions were made, recorded, culled, categorized, and archived. Prisoners were not placed on political trial, nor were their confessions released to the general public. In their grandiose episode of self-deception, the "top brothers" of the *Ångkar* sought to convince themselves that they could rewrite not merely the course of history but the human condition by forcing subordinates to record, transcribe, vet, and archive the written confessions of the "enemies" of their revolution. The logic of illogic appears to have been that the greater the number of confessions, the more lurid and specific the details of betrayal, the more history was being rewritten and humanity was being transformed. Ideological self-deception teetered on the brink of the delusional. Archivization of confessional narratives appears to have been designed to assuage any doubts that may have arisen with respect to the non-reality of the reality the *Ângkar* brothers wanted to believe. This produced the distinctive characteristics of the macabresque in the DK genocide.

The confessional, its narration and archivization, represents a central feature of the *Ângkar* macabresque. The several thousands of confessions extracted ranged from single pages to several hundred pages long, sometimes handwritten, often typed. Reams of confessions, totaling thousands of pages, well over 200,000 in all, reveal the care that was taken in transcribing, recording and processing prisoner statements.[150] Chandler reports that most of the confessions were "authenticated by being signed or thumbprinted and dated by the prisoner on each page," while those written by an interrogator were "countersigned by a document worker present at the interrogation." In addition, confessions tended to be formatted in a four-part sequence: "life stories," "history of [my] treasonous activities," "plans," and "strings of traitors."[151] Often, notational comments appear in the margins indicating approval or disapproval on the part of superiors, including Duch himself. The confessions of major political prisoners were sent on up to the top for review by senior national security figures or political leaders, including Son Sen and Pol Pot.

This demonstrates the purpose of such confessions. Why engage in the manufacture of narratives designed to confirm the validity of what never was if not for the benefit of those who seek to transform "reality" in accordance with what their fantasies of mimetic desire appear to demand; and mimesis demanded that "rivals" be destroyed before they could "steal" away with the thing-enjoyment of revolutionary fervor. Rivals had to be ideologically invented as a device to ensure that the revolution would proceed for the benefit of the leading figures in the *Ângkar* who needed a revolution to justify the destruction of mimetic rivals. In instances of mimetic rivalry, the rival represents the blockage that prevents access to thing-enjoyment; thus, in destroying the rival the theft of thing-enjoyment is in fantasy at least "forever" prevented. This helps to explain why the *Ângkar* focused on the significance of confessions as an indicator of success. Chandler describes the process of producing confessions. "For days or months, interrogators at S-21 invaded the prisoners' bodies, minds, and histories, teasing out, inducing, and inventing memories to coincide with prepackaged accusations and adjusted to the format of confessions. Prisoners and interrogators were engaged in shadow-boxing, with the interrogators trying to get at the 'truth' (without revealing what it was)."[152] But the purpose of confessional archives was to represent the history of the revolution as its leaders wanted the story to be told, so that they could recount the fantasized narrative as they wanted to tell it to themselves. Self-deception when akratically willed wants nothing more than to be confirmed by an "objective truth" however forcibly generated. Chandler concludes, "The prisoners at S-21 objectified these fantasies and brought their [Ângkar's leaders'] dreams to life just long enough for the dreamers to know that their enemies were being subdued."[153] Like Stalin, Pol Pot and his immediate entourage self-deceived themselves into believing that the socioeconomic failures that had resulted from their policies were the result of enemies within the cadres, including the fellow leaders who had been most devoted to the revolutionary and Party cause. The logic of illogic seems to have been, how else could the revolution fail if it were not for those most active within it? The consequence was that the Khmer revolution, like the French and the Bolshevik revolutions before it, began to devour its own children in ever widening circles of more and more innocent victims. But as is also consistently the case, the drive for power as an end itself leads to its own demise; in this case, at the behest of the enemy most dreaded in *Ângkar* ideology, the Vietnamese. The *Ângkar* had invaded Vietnam on several occasions since coming to power: in 1975 in an attack against the Vietnamese island of Phú Quốc as well as in 1977. But it was the massacre of approximately 3,000 civilians at Ba Chúc, in the An Giang province of southern Vietnam, by the DK regular army, among other cross-border invasions and atrocities, that provoked the Vietnamese into ridding the region of the DK. On December 25, 1978, 150,000 Vietnamese troops invaded Cambodia, a move that led to the establishment of the People's Republic of Kampuchea (PRK). Reality had finally set in.

The Archivized Mug Shot

Among the features of the Cambodian macabresque that most distinguish it is its photographic archive, comprising thousands of mug shots of prisoners, mostly taken upon their entry into S-21. What do these faces "say" as they silently stare out from the photographic portraiture taken inside the prison and framed according to the aesthetics of the criminal mug shot? Is it coincidental that faciality and honor, saving face and shame in traditional Cambodian culture, appear to have retained their influences given the faciality of the mug shot? Might we attribute the photographic archive to the modern emergence of biopower and the disciplinarity of the state, its panoptical gaze on citizens, as theorized by Foucault? The original technique of the mug shot was executed, first, by immobilizing the subject's face by placing it in the firm grip of a metal brace and, secondly, by photographing frontal as well as side profiles of what are for all intents and purposes expressionless faces. Critical to its initial conception was standardization and uniformity to facilitate in the identification of criminals. Originally designed in 1879 by a Parisian police official named Alphonse Bertillon, the mug shot aims at consistency in terms of pose, format, background, lighting, and so on. In the case of the *Ângkar* photographic archive, consistency was also abetted by the fact that one photographer, named Nhem En, who eventually escaped from S-21, took many if not most of them over the course of several years. Nhem En, an apparent favorite of the *Ângkar*, had been sent to Shanghai, China, in 1975–76, to receive formal training as a photographer. In an interview years later, Peter Maguire asks Nhem En about the reasons given for creating the photographic archive. Nhem En responded, "He [Son Sen] told me to keep track of the photos, because they might want to use them for conducting investigations on issues about the CIA spies, KGB, Vietnamese."[154] When asked if he had ever tried to communicate with the prisoners while photographing them or whether he felt for them knowing they would be killed, he replied, "I felt numb because I saw this every day and there was nothing I could do." Finally, he admitted that he undertook his work almost mindlessly. "I never had a thought what would happen to the photographs. I made them because I was ordered to."[155] Nhem En also indicated that the numerical system for identifying prisoners unfolded each day and thus was applied on a daily basis to the particular succession of prisoners lined up within that specific period of time. This explains how numbers substituted for the names of victims within the prison, as opposed to any other method of penal identification.

What, then, does the Cambodian photographic archive indicate about the macabresque in the Cambodian genocide; what does the central framing of prisoner faces reveal about the character of human violation in the mass atrocity of this genocide? Amy Ray Stewart, in her analysis of lynching photography in the South offers a suggestive analytical approach. She writes, with reference to photographic portrayals of racial lynching, "lynching photographs reveal the often unstable process of signification inasmuch as these archival objects signify both white supremacy and white anxiety, both social power and psychical fear."[156] She describes lynching photography as a form of "racial abjection," in which, as she puts it citing Lacan and Kristeva, "aggressivity turns into aggression."[157] She defines this process as follows, "Aggressivity surfaces when the Real threatens to collapse the Imaginary and, thereby, destabilize the subject's illusory identification that substantiates meaning in the symbolic."[158] In this perspective, the *Ângkar* photographic archive indicates the psychodynamic linkages operating between psychic aggressivity and social aggression, the latter to defend against the former and its attendant dread of fragmentation and dissolution. Iconic mug-shot representations demonstrate a psychosocial process that entails "a violent shift from collective psychical aggressivity to concerted social hatred."[159] Mug shots of prisoners thus constituted "an abject stain," which Stewart suggests "underpins the aggressivity when the subject of *meconnaissance* is caught by the photographic stain" that "literalizes the signification of hatred."[160] Mug-shot archivization represents the exertion of power. It is a way of stabilizing a sense of social or cultural order at times when mimetic rivalries appear to threaten not only political dissolution but psychic fragmentation as well.

Henry Krips further extends this reading by implicitly suggesting that a relationship pertained within the *Ângkar* between secrecy and voyeurism—that is, between the initial unwillingness of its top members to be "seen" or recognized as leaders of the revolution and the visuality intrinsic to S-21 mug-shot photography. Krips thus proceeds across the Lacanian terrain: from the emergence of a desiring subject through unconscious loss of thing-enjoyment to drive "concealment" by the unconscious. Krips features the process of concealment in terms of what he calls the scopic drive. He writes, "What Lacan calls 'the arms of the drive'—which, in the case of the scopic drive, correspond to the voyeuristic activity of looking and the exhibitionistic activity of being displayed/looked at—are *not* covered over. Instead it is their relation to each other . . . that is 'effaced or struck out/cut out.'"[161] In this concealment, the psychic origin of what I have called the rival self-other misrecognizes itself against fantasies of ego-ideal nurtured by what Krips describes as "a void corresponding to a point of failure/blank spot in the visual field that speaks to the subject's loss/lack and around which the scopic drive turns endlessly in fruitless pursuit of an imaginary ideal of total visibility by which it distracts itself from loss/lack." Krips encapsulates the psychodynamics of self-deception as it operates within the visual fields of self-recognition and psychic misrecognition. In such a psychosocial perspective, the secrecy of the *Ångkar* in relation to the mug-shot representations of mimetic rivals represents a way of creating "total visibility," a voyeuristic "arm" of the scopic drive in relation to the exhibitionist "arm," so that those who see are never seen, while those who are seen lose all interiority. Otherwise, total visibility would be impossible. The *Ångkar* photographic archive stands for the relationship of a universalizing and all-seeing gaze, the gaze of traditional honor, blood, and ancestral power, now transformed into a diabolical dystopian or revolutionary totalitarianism on the part of "top brothers." They become defaced but gaze in omnipotent, almost totemic distance for these precise reasons. Those who *see* engage in a lingering and totalized form of voyeurism in an attempt to make exterior what is most intimate and precious to a human person, one's soul. No greater perverse invasion exists than to try to possess what is secreted in any person's heart. Nothing less is the significance of the mug shot in the Cambodian macabresque. Its exhibitionism lay in its interrogational torture and in the killing fields. But its essence was its voyeuristic fetishism beholden to futile, fatalistic designs to facialize the sublime in the human condition.

The Archive in the Macabresque

The spectacle of the archive haunts the examination of the macabresque of the Cambodian genocide and the analysis of the dystopian fantasy of the *Ångkar*. This distinctive element or feature of what the *Ångkar* "Brothers" attempted was nothing short of controlling time and memory. Chronological time and political memory were meant to become one in hermetic closures of chronicled confession and mug-shot faciality. No reality was to exist beyond what was represented or portrayed in and by the *Ångkar* archive. What Jacques Derrida, in his examination of "archival fever" calls "the three actual presents," by which he means "past present, the present present, and the future present," were now defined by a process of "archivization" that conjoins temporality and the foundational anchors of law.[162] "*Arkhe*, we recall," Derrida writes, "names at once the *commencement* and the *commandment*. This name apparently coordinates two principles in one: the principle according to nature or history, *there* where things *commence*—physical, historical, or ontological principle—but also the principle according to the law, *there* where men and gods *command, there* where authority, social order are exercised, *in this place* where *order* is given—nomological principle.[163] The macabresque always possesses an address, a demarcated space in time and of confinement, a place where absolute power over human dignity, survival, and suffering is located and exercised. Its aim, as we have repeatedly seen, is in part to obtain from victims the non-truth of informativeness. Perpetrators' desire to immemorialize their quest, however depraved, leads to the archive in the macabresque.

The archive becomes fused with the macabresque once power becomes possessed of the aim to transform the human condition by means of purification; elimination; and extermination by means of the planned, deliberate, and sustained torture, torment, and agony of mimetic rivals—*and to inscribe these dynamics into the annals of history and memory.* To do so is to desire to control the *ends* of history by *means* of the power over memory. This is why genocide and mass atrocity are repeatedly accompanied by the macabresque: to make rivals suffer the ravages of sadistic humiliation but *also to record their degradation as a way of transforming how memory records political and social history. If one controls the past by dominating memory, one determines the future by obliterating history.*

This is in keeping with the origins of archivization. Derrida indicates, for example, that the etymological origins of the word "archive" reside in the classical Greek *arkheion*, "initially, a house, a domicile, an address, the residence of the superior magistrates, the *archons*, those who commanded . . . and signified political power." On account of their power and status, their homes, their residences, became the sites where documents were stored and filed. The authority to interpret the law, to speak to the meaning of the documents kept and maintained, belonged to archontic authority alone. This archontic authority was empowered to "speak the law" and thus not only to provide "security" for what was "deposited" but also to determine its "substrate" of meanings. Guardianship, domiciliation, and the hermeneutics of "right and competence" with respect to archival documents became historically fused by what Derrida metaphorically calls, "this house arrest."[164] Knowledge classifies, cultures codify, truth divides. Language signifies by means of punctuation and opposition. The power of the archive in the macabresque is that it appears to ground a unity that represents itself as oracular authority from which all linguistic and conceptual tension derive. The aim in the macabresque for the non-truth of the informativeness sought through the humiliation, degradation, and death of the victims is to generate ersatz data that then is recorded, often in precise detail. The precision with which the non-truth of such "information" is obtained is stored on the racks of the archive in the macabresque, whether it be Stalin's purgatory, or Hitler's (and Mengele's) diabolical laboratory, along with all the others in such cases, including *Ångkar's* archive. Such archives in the macabresque speak to the false unity of mimetic fantasy converted into the logics of illogics at the core of ideological reification. The macabresque archive stands as a monument, not only to the self-deceptions of the perpetrators, but also to their attempts to transform the memory of past events so that the future will confirm the truth of the very lies they told to themselves. The macabresque archive is thus an *epistemological* exercise in the "truth-ification" of falsity. It represents the effort to validate the fraudulent, not merely by means of propaganda, but by transforming victims and their suffering into ontological "data-points" for purposes of archival information. This is yet another means to assert power by means of the self-betrayal of victims.

Genocidal regimes and perpetrators of mass atrocity engage in sadistic cruelty in order to make victims speak the "law," the law Lacan theorized in terms of *jouissance* and *objet a*, and which other psychosocial analysts have analytically applied in terms of thing-enjoyment and *das Ding*. This represents a kind of eschatological endeavor, futile in its objectives, but for that reason all the more willfully implemented. The macabresque archive serves as an instrumentality in a denial of the futility of self-deception and, above all, of disordered will. Its purpose is to bestow material confirmation of the messianic ideologies of perpetrators by making victims bear false witness against themselves not only to mystify the past but to manipulate the future. Derrida observes, "The question of the archive is not, we repeat, a question of the past . . . . It is a question of the future, the question of the future itself, the question of a response, of a promise and of a responsibility for tomorrow." He adds, "A spectral messianicity is at work in the concept of the archive and ties it, like history, like science itself, to a very singular experience of the promise."[165] In this, Derrida distinguishes between messianicity and messianism. This distinction is relevant to the macabresque since the so-called promise of the macabresque is invariably that of a delusionary messianic spirit, omnipotent in its desires, sadistic in its drives, and, therefore, punctilious in its demands for exactitude in prevarication masquerading as truth.

****

The Junta's Neo-Inquisitional Operating Theaters

Torture, State Hypersecurity and Fantasies of Apostasy and Heresy during
Argentina's "Dirty War," 1976–1978

Marguerite Feitlowitz, in her study of the legacies of torture in the case of Argentinean junta, comments about the systematic deployment of a lexicon that substituted the term "torture" for an array of others such as "methods," "long established police procedures," and "physical maltreatment of their nature."[166] At La Perla, a major detention center, torture was routinely referred to as "work" and performed in five rooms designated as "operating theaters." Terms such as "useful" were applied to some prisoners who broke down or confessed in contrast to those who retained the hope of "freedom." In the latter instance, "freedom could be a synonym for self-destruction." The benchmark of effective torture was the extent to which prisoners had become "ideologically *normalized*." Feitlowitz, with clear reference to these and other aesthetic and dramaturgical effects, writes, "This theatricality—of which language was an integral part—served several purposes: as a torment for the prisoners, a sadistic pleasure for some enforcers, and as a distancing, enabling device for others in the chain of command."[167] Sadistic styles of shame performativity serve as surrogates for epistemological interrogations of truth. Sadistic cruelty, whether to produce suffering through torture, torment, or agony, is always done in the name of truth; this a critical element in the shift from collective violence to human violation, that truth be performed; only thus is the desire for another's desire captured and controlled in fantasy.

Some sets of perpetrators engage in torture as a way of causing suffering; others in the torment of victims absent interrogational purposes. Yet, fantasmatic illusions of exclusivist shame and purity and supremacist glory and honor are never far in the distance. This is demonstrated by the ability of elites to vent logics of illogic purporting to justify sadistic cruelty not only in the name of higher causes, including state security and national supremacy, but also at the behest of the many others, perpetrators of violation, collaborative supporters, bystanders who are quietly complicit, and so forth, who also believe in those causes cultivated around ideology, race, ethnicity, religious belief, and institutional affiliation. Religious faith and principle, like morality and scientific objectivity, become transmuted into exclusionary, self-righteous dictates, especially when combined with the power elites or governing regimes of modern nation-states. Such was the case during the Argentinean "Dirty War" in which major clerical authorities of the Roman Catholic Church in Argentina aligned themselves with the military junta while it was engaged in macabresque practices of the most horrific kind. To understand the Argentinian Dirty War, therefore, requires an investigation into the relationship of religion to politics, social fantasy, and the policy implementation of fascist ideology. During the Dirty War, Nazi ideology and Roman Catholic eschatology were mixed together in poisonous brews of macabresque fantasy and institutional paranoia. In the case of the Argentinean macabresque, systemic sin and the perversity of political evil met, intertwined, and became one with the other. The legacy of suffering continues today.

Again, language becomes a kind of front line of victimization in the macabresque, truth a mere ghost of itself. "Argentinians lived in an echo chamber," Feitlowitz writes. "With diabolical skill, the regime used language to: (1) shroud in mystery its true actions and intentions, (2) say the opposite of what it meant, (3) inspire trust, both home and abroad, (4) instill guilt, especially in mothers, *to seal their complicity*, and (5) sow paralyzing terror and confusion."[168] The Dirty War was very much waged against the "children" of Argentina, university students, representatives of the liberal generation whose secular cultural orientations appeared to threaten the sanctimonious spirit of the members of the Junta. To "seal the complicity of their mothers" represents one more example of how perpetrator regimes try to defile the dignity of victims by making them complicit in their very own shame and degradation. In this case, the means of self-betrayal ran through the torments of mothers and were presumably aimed at their silence in the face of disappearances.

Fascist ideologies romanticize blood and honor, self-sacrifice and salvation, purification by force, and sanctification by power. They see enemies everywhere. In the Argentinean macabresque, anyone, anywhere could be taken off and tortured or made to disappear. But the overall objective was to root out those who threatened what the military told itself was cultural, moral, ideological, and spiritual decay. It all depended on how individuals thought. Liberal modesty and the inducements of democratic decision-making seemed to threaten the erosion of what the regime wanted to believe was its tight-fisted pursuit of national security and grandeur. They assumed, and were in fact encouraged to believe by major figures of the Roman Catholic clergy of Argentina, that ardent desire was appropriate to maintain society's glorification of God, the God of love, peace, and reconciliation. It scarcely needs saying they the actions of the Junta defiled the theology, faith, and meaning of the Holy Spirit in Christian Catholicism. The fateful marriage of self-deception and akratic willfulness of Aristotelian inspiration was abused in this diabolical moment when piety became the enemy of faith and conviction the opposite of Christian love and charity. How did it happen? How could it have happened? In the Argentinean macabresque the fantasies of the regime and the ideologies of its political imaginary took shape around a reactionary brand of Roman Catholicism that was virulent and unrelenting in its determination to preserve Argentina from disintegration, thereby to save its soul from decay. The model was inquisitional Spain.

The Dirty War was a war waged against the phantoms of liberal thought and imagination in which extremist religious dogma combined with fascistic leitmotifs. The junta and its perpetrators adored Nazi models and allusions in speech and language. Dozens of references to the Nazi past become part of the ordinary vernacular. Feitlowitz, for example, reported that "hundreds of mutilated corpses, with limbs and parts deliberately confused—were buried in graves labeled 'NN', denoting 'no name'" but also standing for the Spanish translation of the German expression "Nacht und Nebel" or night and fog "drawn like a curtain in the collective mind."[169] She also indicates that torture was often undertaken before portraits of Hitler and "more than one concentration camp doctor was known as Mengele."[170] As in the Holocaust, language became a translation not of reality but of social fantasies of power made real by victim pain and human suffering. Feitlowitz provides an outline of how language recreated meaning in the Argentinean macabresque, a core feature of its aesthetic and dramaturgical qualities.

Examples paraphrased from Feitlowitz's "A Lexicon of Terror":

trasladar, meaning, prisoner about to be transferred in order to be killed; *asado*, barbeque, meaning corpses burned by bonfire to eliminate remains; *avenida de la felicidad*, the avenue of happiness, meaning the corridor from prisoner cell to torture chamber; *capucha*, hood, meaning *desparecidos* made to wear hoods over their heads as way of destroying their "faciality" and thus all social contacts; *chu-pado*, to suck, meaning, a person swallowed, kidnapped, disappeared; *comida de pescado*, fish food, meaning, victims thrown from planes; *enfermeria*, infirmary, a central hall used for torture covered with swastikas; *esculea de los mudos*, mean-ing, school for the mute, torturers name for their concentration camp; *hurvera*, egg carton, meaning, the walls covered with egg cartons in a torture chamber at ESMA aimed at blunting the sounds; *marcadores*, markers, victims who broke under torture who became willing to implicate friends and families as threats, another form of forced victim self-betrayal; *pacto de sangre*, blood pact, agreement among enforcers and torturers complicit in kidnap, murder and torture; *parilla*, Argentine grill for cooking meat, meaning metal table on which electric shocks were administered; *picana*, cattle prod, meaning torture weapon; *quirofano*, oper-ating theater, meaning, torture chamber; *rectoscope*, rectoscope, meaning, "anal torture device" invented by Julio Simon, the extremely sadistic anti-Semite know as Julian the Turk; *submarino*, meaning a form of waterboarding torture including being immersed until the point of near suffocation in excremental waste; *terapia intensiva*, intensive therapy, meaning torture; *trabajo*, work, meaning torture; *trat-amiento,* treatment, meaning, torture; *Tubo*, tube, meaning, tiny prison cell; *vuelo*, flight, meaning, death flight. Those who adopted this language assumed names that evoked the sadism of their tasks.[171]

This lexicon adds insight into the cultural illusions that influenced its formulations, including references to food and its preparation as well as the euphemistic naming of the instruments of torture. Perhaps the single most salient motif is that of disappearance, whether by kidnapping or transfer or removal, or on account of death after being cata-pulted alive from an airplane. The macabresque of performative transgression during the Argentinean "Dirty War," but during other instances of mass atrocity in Latin America as well, included an aesthetic of disappearance. In political evil, victims are sometimes made "to disappear." The word "disappear," commonly an intransitive verb, becomes conjugated as a transitive verb. This trope is designed linguistically to stress that victims *are made absent*, that their disappearance is *produced*. During the installments of fascist regimes in Latin America, specifically in Argentina, Chile, and Guatemala, victims included "the disappeared ones" (*los desaparecidos*). Thus, they are said to *have been disappeared* rather than to *have disappeared*; their governments *disappeared* them. The "disappeared" are thus deprived, not only of the rights of citizenship, but also of their identities—past, present, and future. Families are prevented from mourning the loss of their loved ones in any definitive sense. In many cases, the individuals who were "disappeared" were detained, enslaved, and tortured before they were killed, their bodies then hidden or destroyed to guarantee that remains would never be found. The "disappeared" are "made absent" forever, "neither living nor dead, neither here nor there."[172] As a survivor from Operation Condor in Argentina recalls, "They were always saying, 'You don't exist. You're no one .. . No one remembers you anymore.'"[173] In the words of another Argentinean *desaparecido*, "The first thing they told me was to forget who I was ... and that for me the outside world stopped right there."[174] These sadistic semantic horizons reveal the core fantasy sustaining them, that somehow what is demonized can be eradicated, that the corrosive threats to the spiritual sanctity and national security of the homeland could be purified. Torture and disappearance function together in a purification schema aimed at extricating heretics and apostates. But heretical and apostate thinking loomed as a threat in Argentinean theocratic culture because it became attached to a social fantasy linking state honor to the machismo of divine authority. In this, modernity as a cultural style was itself reified as a threat for which representative victims had to pay. It is as if victims of the Argentine macabresque had to experience what prisoners of the Spanish inquisition had been made to endure in the prisons of Queen Isabella's Spain when "the question was put to them." And as before, liberals of many stripes became subjected to the pain. As the heroic likes of Jacobo Timerman learned at tremendous cost, no one should entertain any doubt that the movement was deeply anti-Semitic, and the trope, as during the Inquisition, was that the Jewish cosmopolitan spirit violated God's will. And thus with each disappearance, the junta told itself that the body and blood of Argentina was safer and more pure.

One searches for explanation of the patterns of self-deception and ideological mystification that distinguishes these hallucinatory but very real events. Mark J. Osiel declares, "If academic social science does not yet offer us the tools by which to convey this intensity of belief on the cold printed page, this simply attests to the methodological limitations of such science."[175] But he also suggests a response when quoting a victim subjected to torture by the notorious naval member of the junta (Baby Face) Alfredo Astiz, who had made it practice to circulate among activist students in order to be able later target them. "He was a kind of 'worthy enemy' for us," this former prisoner recounted. "He wasn't corrupt. He didn't rape. He was fighting subversion and communism, not trying to get rich. His vision of the world was terribly Neanderthal, but he was convinced of what he was doing. He was there to 'save' his country."[176] The fascist pattern stretches across a time and place once suffused by sadistic fantasies of threat to honor and by allures of curative shame. *Perpetrators manifest the disciplines of law-like behaviors precisely because they are captivated by social fantasies conjured around the theft of thing-enjoyment and the exigencies of shame punishment as the bulwark of defense. Their complete indifference to the pain and suffering caused by shame and humiliation of victims, however brutally executed, demonstrates the intensity of unconscious fantasy. These are the true believers, who transform ideational forms of ideology into a way of being—that is, into a political ontology that masquerades as morality.* Osiel observes, "Most junta members and other high-ranking officers derived no private benefit from the antisubversive campaign, it is clear. Their stake in the disappearances was institutional, not personal." He adds, "They were willing to allow their junior subordinates free exercise of Dionysian will only as long as the destructive impulses thereby unleashed would be directed, substantially if not entirely, in service of regime goals."[177] Such dedication to a common cause, such discipline as professional practice is readily misperceived as conformity with a moral code.

To assume that perpetrators act according to a moral code, however, compounds the original harm, as I suggested in reference to the case made by Harald Welzer. Sadistic discipline in shame punishments at the behest of satanic honor is not morality but, on the contrary, its ultimate defilement. This renders the explanatory effort to interpret perpetrator behaviors from theoretical perspectives that include the unconscious and social fantasy as units of analysis critically important, using when appropriate qualitative ethnographic research, including archival documentary and interview materials, as evidenced by Osiel and other authors whose research is directly relevant to these case studies of the macabresque. Scholars such as Omer Bartov and Ian Kershaw have demonstrated the proclivity of power regimes under conditions of dramatic change to use divine or religious preaching as justifications for genocide and mass atrocity, such as in the Armenian genocide at the end of the Ottoman Empire and during the mass atrocities of the Bosnia conflict.[178] In the Argentinean case, the influence of Catholic clergy on the junta was immediate and direct. Sadistic intent in the macabresque is hardly limited to a few discernible members of elite regimes. This confounds jurisprudence, but more than this, it raises perplexing questions as to the moral and ethical status of non-elite perpetrators.

Osiel envisions the problem of sadistic torture as a kind of jurisprudential and, ultimately, philosophical no-man's land, a realm between guilt and innocence, reason and insanity. What is culpability, and on what grounds does posterity recognize the wrongdoing of perpetrators when it occurred under conditions shaped by attitudes and beliefs that were apparently subscribed to by many considered to be incidental bystanders or merely witnesses to the genocide or mass atrocity? An alternative way to pose this question is in social psychological terms, asking what constitutes "normality" when conditions become "pathological"? Osiel writes, "This is precisely the predicament presented by a defendant who perpetrates colossal wrongs with a mental state displaying neither standard indicia of culpability nor of exculpation. His legal mistakes cannot be reasonable, for then most agents of mass atrocity must be acquitted."[179] This is the problem macabresque sadism poses: the indifference to human suffering is in some sense pathological but is as often as not characterized by reasonableness, especially when the quest for "informativeness" is used as the excuse or validation. We saw this demonstrated in

Monroe's interview with Nazi sympathizers. It emerges often in the judicial testimonies of those accused of mass atrocity, crimes against humanity, even war crimes: sadism but in the seeming absence of sadistic personality; cruelty in the name of the (supererogatory) obligation to fend against demons. This leads Osiel to declare with respect to perpetrators, "If he is culpable, then he is so in some sense not yet cognizable within the law's doctrinal grid. But if he is *in*-culpable, it is for reasons other than those that millennia of human experience have led us to anticipate and codify in our laws."[180] And so ethical norms dissolve into a conundrum of juridical categorical confusion. Accordingly, Osiel describes the problem of classifying perpetrators as follows: "He must be found guilty or not guilty, crazy or sane. Yet here we seem to require a middle category that can mediate the binary opposition. . . . Within our legal culture, that is virtually a conceptual impossibility, however."[181] Osiel is writing within the context of the Argentinean Dirty War, but the problem of how to categorize and thus theorize sadistic cruelty in mass atrocity hardly ended there.

****

The Bosnian Shame-Camps

Genderized/Sexualized Humiliation and Confinement, Mass Rape, Beatings,
and Collective Dying in Genocidal Atrocity against the Bosnian Muslims
(Bosniaks) of Bosnia-Herzegovina, 1992–1995

The Bosnian Genocide

The Bosnian genocide refers to the sustained killings at Srebrenica and around the
nearby Zepa enclave that were executed by the Bosnian (Serb) army of the Republika
Srpska (VRS), under the command of General Ratko Mladić, in 1995, and the extensive "purification" campaign often referred to as "ethnic cleansing" aimed at non-
Serb populations throughout Bosnia-Herzegovina, spearheaded by the Bosnian
Serb military but also including Serb paramilitary, security, police, and irregular
"volunteer" forces. During the Bosnian war, April 6, 1992 to December 14, 1995,
the Bosnian army remained under the nominal control of the Yugoslav government
in Belgrade headed by President Slobodan Milošević, who was also the head of the
Socialist Party of Serbia. Despite political tensions between Milošević and the president of the VRS, Radovan Karadžić, the Bosnian army was partially manned, supplied, and heavily supported during the war by the Yugoslav People's Army (JNA).
In addition to Bosnian army units, Serb forces that engaged in ethnic cleansing
included VRS special police and national security units, elements from the so-called
Serb Territorial Defense of Bosnia and Herzegovina and Croatia, and the Military
of Serbian Krajina, as well as various Serb paramilitary forces and volunteer militia
units. These went by a variety of suggestive names: the Serbian Volunteer Guard,
or *Arkanovci* or Arkan's Tigers, named to represent the reputation of its leader,
Zeljko Ražnjatović; or the Chetniks or *cetnici* led by Vojislav Šešelj, also known as
Šešelj's men, or *Šešeljevci*. The overall objective of the VRS, its army, and the armed
organizations acting in support, was to establish and dominate a "Greater Serbia"
by means of the forced displacement of non-Serb majority populations, including
Muslim Bosnians, or Bosniaks, and Bosnian Catholic Croats. Their methods, historically associated with ethnic cleansing, involved rampaging through municipalities and other localities; illegal detention and forced confinement; beating; murder;
rape; sexual enslavement; inhumane and degrading treatment; coerced removal and
displacement of civilian populations; confiscation and destruction of property; and
desecration of religious places and destruction of buildings of worship. Historic fault
can be found on all sides and on the part of all too many perpetrators. Indeed, before
the Bosnian War had ended, the three major sectarian groups had become tainted by
the stains of extremist violence against civilians done in their names. Serb elements,
however, provoked genocidal or near genocidal atrocities across the region and, in
so doing, introduced the shift from collective violence to collective human violation. What follows below is an attempt to briefly describe the consequent Bosnian
macabresque against the background of the cultural values and meanings in which

it emerged and, additionally, to explain its performative dramaturgies in psychosocial perspectives focused on Serb shame-camps and the humiliations that occurred within them.

Pre-genocidal Conditions of Civil War and Political Opportunity

How might we approach explanations of mass murder and rape perpetrated mainly by Serb political elites and militia forces against the Muslim or Bosniak citizens of Bosnia-Herezegovina during the period 1992–1995? Depraved patterns of human degradation demonstrate the movements from violence to violation consistent with the macabresque, but why? What would prompt multiple levels of Serbian elites functioning within the Yugoslavian political context to pursue mass atrocity against a civilian population in response to the shifting nature of political legitimacy? The immediate answer points toward three Yugoslav "dissolution" wars: the first, a ten-day war that effectively brought about Slovenian secession from Yugoslavia in 1991; the second, a war waged during 1991–1995 between Croats and Serbs over Croatian independence and the meaning of national as opposed to ethnic identity and citizenship within a Croatian sovereign state; and the third, the Bosnian War of 1992–1995, a territorial and secessionist dispute over partition and ethnic composition in Bosnia-Herzegovina between the local Bosniaks and Croats, supported by the Croatian government in Zagreb, on the one hand, and local Bosnian Serbs backed by the Serbian-dominated Yugoslavian army and the Serbian central government in Belgrade. Sovereign disintegration resulted from the diplomatic machinations of national leaders whose political vision tended to be influenced by various ideological strains of ethnic nationalism and sectarian essentialism. In all, the demise of the legitimacy of the Yugoslavian state and the subsequent conflicts were in part a reflection of the intense ethnic conflicts and mimetic rivalries among the Serbs and, to a lesser extent, the Montenegrins, on the one hand, and among the Croats and Bosniaks and Slovenes, on the other, as well as among Serbs, Bosniaks, and Croats in Bosnia. The basic ingredients that set in motion the events leading to the Bosnian macabresque, therefore, were all in place: secessionist or territorial dreams and nationalist aspirations for sovereign statehood; disintegration of centralizing authority and the emergence of "political opportunity"; the threatened decline of power and dread of future domination by mimetically rivalrous or competitive groups; the fear of identicality resulting from the universal Slavic heritage combined with sectarian and religious contrasts and oppositions; and finally, the presence of extremist leaders who were willing and able to manipulate collective sectarian, religious, and ethnic identities for political purposes. Such factors provoked dread over the dissolution of territorial integrity and the dynamics of social antagonism configured around ethnicity and the possibilities of majority Bosniak domination over state power.

Patterns of collective violence of the Bosnian war included the siege or "ring" around Sarajevo, beginning in April 1992 and lasting forty-four months, whose aim was to terrorize the Bosniak majority into acceding to Serb demands. The war was also witness to widespread marauding on the part of the Serb forces throughout the municipalities, towns, and villages of eastern Bosnia. Bosniak homes and apartment complexes were looted and often razed or burned to the ground. Their occupants were rounded up, and families were segregated mostly according to gender and taken to detention sites or camps, where the men would mostly be massacred after enduring beatings, while the women and children were made to live in demeaning and unhygienic conditions and subjected repeatedly to mass or genocidal rape. Sometimes Bosniak women were raped in public view in front of neighbors before being taken to the camps. This points toward the essential dynamics of shame and humiliation, a core dimension of the Bosnian macabresque.

Does ethnic conflict as such explain the Bosnian macabresque? As we have seen in other cases of genocide and mass atrocity, ethnic or identitarian differences are often assumed to be causal but on empirical investigation turn out to be epiphenomenal or coincidental to the violence. Furthermore, ethno-conflicts at best only partially help to explain why and how the macabresque emerges. As I have repeatedly noted, the macabresque, its styles, dramaturgies, and aesthetics represents a discrete analytical problematic relative to genocide and mass atrocity that is distinct from the causes of collective violence per se. It thus behooves us to focus on the immediate conditions that prompted the shifts from collective violence to mass violation, creating the Bosnian macabresque of ethnic cleansing. Bosnian Serb reactions to the dissolution of Yugoslavia and to the potential control of the Bosnian government by the Muslim Bosniak majority were to indulge in a series of purification schemes widely referred to as ethnic cleansing. In psychosocial terms, threats of political dissolution and loss of communal standing or ethnic power provoked Serbian fantasmatic dread of a theft of thing-enjoyment that materialized into mimetic rivalries and envy and devolved into ideological or identitarian conflicts, and, eventually, into open hostilities, including in their extremes, mass atrocity and the macabresque. So much of what appears to be ethnic hatred is in psychosocial perspectives the result of envy borne by mimetic rivalries under conditions of the threatened loss of political power, socioeconomic status, or cultural standing.

The spark that fired the war in Bosnia-Herzegovina was a referendum of February 29, 1992, taken in the aftermath of the Slovenian and Croatian successions that favored Bosnian independence on terms that appeared favorable to the Muslim majority and were dearly opposed by Serb elements. Serb reactions were fierce and immediate. Serb perpetrators of ethnic cleansing thus appear to have had three major objectives: territorial consolidation of a sovereign Bosnia-Herzegovina, Serb political and communal dominance over those lands, and dramatic increases in Serb ethnic populations within these borders. Throughout the ensuing conflict, Serb partisans in Bosnia-Herzegovina led politically by Radovan Karadžić pursued ultranationalist policies aimed at insuring Serb domination of Bosnia by means of ethnic purification across the entire territorial span of Bosnia previously pocketed by Serb localities amid a demographic landscape dominated by the Bosniak majority. Serb military strategy thus led to pursuit of tactical forms of violence aimed at ethnic cleansing. Standard definitions or renditions of ethnic cleansing emphasize, first, its modes of violence, terror, or intimidation. These are designed, secondly, to bring about evacuations of territories by means of large-scale or communal displacements of residential populations and the confiscation/transfer of their property. This permits, thirdly, reoccupation by ethnic, sectarian, or religious civilian communities favored by the militia committing the violence. Norman Cigar describes these tactics as follows, "Although the Serbs often appeared to choose targets not having, strictly speaking any military significance, the targets did make sense in rewriting the demographic balance sheet."[182] Bosnian Serb forces pursued these tactics in especially rapacious ways against civilian populations. This resulted in mass atrocities that were tantamount to genocidal violence.

Genderized/Sexualized Shame-Camps: Means to an End or an End as the Means?

Moreover, the forms and modalities of Serb collective violence perpetrated massive human violation to degrees *far exceeding* presumed requirements of ethnic cleansing and *in particular ways*. This is indicative of the specific ways the Bosnian macabresque at the hands of the Serbs unfolded. The violations implemented during the Bosnian genocide and mass atrocity revealed set patterns. These arose despite apparent chaos and randomness. Serb forces adopted distinct tendencies to congregate Bosniak men together, to congregate Bosniak women together, each into demarcated and separated geographic areas, the former primarily for purposes of brutal beating and eventual murder, the latter primarily for purposes of mass rape. Such areas of congregation came to be called "camps." One of the initial camps was the Batković concentration camp, in the municipality of Bijeljina, in which both Bosniaks and Croat men, women, and children were held in two barns and subjected to inhumane treatment, including forced labor, beatings, rapes, starvation, and being forced to bury their own dead. On May 30, 1992, the local police in Prijedor publicly declared the establishment of four additional detention camps: Keraterm, Manjača, Omarska, and Trnopolje. These locations helped to stage the Bosnian macabresque. The Keraterm site, a death camp maintained by Serb military and police forces near the town of Prijedor, which strategically connects northwestern Bosnia with the so-called Republic of Serbian Krajina in Croatia, was located in a former ceramics factory and used to gather mostly Bosniak, but also a small percentage of Croat males. They were subsequently subjected to unrelenting physical violence that included brutal beatings with a range of blunt weapons as well as continual forms of humiliation. The Manjača death camp near the city of Banja Luka in northern Bosnia-Herzegovina held several thousands of Bosniak and Croatian men until liberated, but not before more than a thousand died of maltreatment and murder. The Trnopolje camp, also near Prijedor, served as a detention center mostly for Bosniak men and as a kind of "staging area" or transit point for women, children, and elderly men sent off to other camps. Between May and November 1992, approximately 30,000 prisoners were detained at the Trnopolje camp site, and it held roughly 4,000 to 7,000 prisoners at any given time. Photos of emaciated Bosniak men detained here helped establish the iconic images seen throughout the Western world that led to efforts to liberate the camp and end the war.

In addition, many Serb shame-campsites established exclusive zones in which detained Bosniak women and girls were subjected to nearly indescribable torments and agonies as a result of sex slavery and mass or gang rapes, often extending for several weeks, even, months, during which time they also endured public humiliation, physical brutality, and sometimes murder. One such location was the Vilina Vlas, a concentration and rape camp maintained in a hotel in the area around Višegrad by the Užice corps and used by such paramilitary forces as the White Eagles and by Arkan's Tigers, as well as units under the command and control of Vojislav Šešelj. Few women survived the ordeal, and several are alleged to have committed suicide. Similarly, numerous rape camps operated in and around the Foča municipality, also the site of many Bosniak massacres. One of the most notorious was the so-called Karaman's House. Bosniak women and underage minors were abused by gang rapes and sometimes sold into sex slavery, with the complicity of local Serb officials. Sites at Liplje and Uzamnica, as well as at Omarska, also witnessed mass rape and other forms of inhuman violation.

Norman M. Naimark captures some of the issue concerning the macabresque when he writes, "Ethnic cleansing is not just about attack, violence, and expulsion; in almost every case it also includes punishment. Those who are driven off are punished for their existence, for the very need to expel them."[183] Naimark mentions the same phenomenon of identitarian "othering" against Bosniaks as had occurred during the Holocaust, when Jews were forced to wear yellow stars on their garments, and when the so-called "base" people were compelled to sport blue and white scarves in the dystopic fantasies of the *Ângkar* genocide. In the case of Bosnian ethnic cleansing, non-Serb civilians in the Prijedor region were made to wear white armbands, leaving them vulnerable to detention and subsequent abuse. He stresses the systematic modes of abuse and implies their genderization. He writes, for example, "The Serb paramilitaries seem to have regular routines. They beat young men more than the old, men more than women." He adds, "All over Bosnia, young Muslim men were shot in groups and buried in mass graves."[184] As to Muslim women, Naimark comments, they were "also being punished for their very existence." He notes that in camps such as Trnopolje and in sites around Foča, "Serb soldiers and paramilitary fighters beat and assaulted the women as part of an evening's entertainment. They would shave the women's heads, tattoo their bodies with their persecutors' first names, and force them to submit to their alcohol-and drug-induced sexual-sadistic fantasies."[185] Naimark's observations thus point not toward Serb political ambitions or even toward strategic calculations with respect to the demographic composition of a fantasized future Republika Srpska. Rather, Serb transgressions at this time call forth the need for an explanatory approach to the Bosnian macabresque. Theoretical analyses of ethnic cleansing that refer exclusively to Serb territorial designs, even demographic ambitions, underscore what is necessary by way of explanation but remain insufficient. Before approaching this analytical task, I wish to describe Serb efforts at debasement of prisoners at the Omarska camp in order to illustrate how the dramaturgies and aesthetics of humiliation were a major component of the violation.

The Macabresque of Camp Rape: Sexual Violation, Sadistic Degradation, and Cultural Shame

The carnivalesque, with its aesthetics of ritualized irony aimed at the production of human torment and agony, and the macabresque, in its aesthetics of performative transgression theatricalized by means of dramaturgical displays of sadistic or surplus cruelty in concentrated spaces during a compressed period of time, devolved into the psychodrama of hideous humiliations in the concentration campsite at Omarska, where an estimated 4,000 to 5,000 mostly Bosniak males, but also Muslim women, suffered and perished. Let us recount the basic events. Bosniak victims were rounded up, brought together, tormented, brutalized, eventually killed, first, in a carnivalesque procession of marches, and, secondly, by means of macabresque atrocity staged for purposes of perpetrator sadistic "enjoyment." Omarska reveals how and in what ways the ravages of macabresque atrocity are perpetuated by willful desire for "revenge." The question becomes why there existed this desire for revenge on the part of certain elements in the Serbian elite at this time. Many causes have been attributed to Serb cruelties. Among them was the historic loss of Kosovo suffered by Serbs. In a sense, Serb testimonies of loss provide a basis for interpreting how unconscious desire fuels overt transgression. In the case of Bosnia-Herzegovina, the clues to performative transgression appear as a reflection of the cultural, social, and political constructions of "loss," a loss that exists as an artifact of ethnicized national identity. Its virulence as a shibboleth and call to arms speaks to something beyond a mere reading of history, to Serb sense of communal self-righteousness, the need for self-sacrifice, the demands for heroism, the unconscious desire for desire to unify the nation in some glorious fantasy of truth and belonging. This is in keeping with the character of performative transgression. It takes shape and form in attempts to impose the social fantasy that gives expression to desire in formats of ideological political reification. Such reifications also demonstrate the viability of willful desire as it travels from unconscious demand to conscious action, often in ways justified by notions of supererogatory heroism and sacrifice. "Ethnic cleansing" unfolded despite—perhaps on account of the threats posed by identicality, the fact that both the perpetrators and the victims shared in the same "Slavic" ethnic origins. They differed primarily on account of religious history having to do with Serbian Orthodox Christianity and the Islamic faith, a clear case of "the narcissism of small differences" with a religious twist.

As in many other cases of genocide and mass atrocity, the perpetrators of ethnic cleansing acted "authoritatively" at the behest of legitimated state institutions. The atrocities committed at Omarska were mandated by Serb and Bosnian government authorities and were thus endowed with the sanctity of law and legitimacy. In a process that is illustrative of the macabresque, Serb operatives, either in uniform or acting under officially sanctioned legal authority, fanned out throughout the region. They congregated mostly male Bosniak citizens and marched them into designated makeshift areas. Detainees were forced to parade in macabresque military-style columns to the Omarska detention center. On arrival, they were confined. Three buildings and an adjoining concrete courtyard incarcerated them. Each of these spaces possessed a name; each name designated a process; each process consisted of specifically prescribed torments. All led to intense torment and agony before dying. Perpetrators at the Omarska camp referred to each of its three buildings or spaces according to how victims would be made to suffer. In such a manner, surplus cruelty became suffused yet again with the aura of macabresque aesthetics. The Omarska courtyard came to be known as the "Pista," a place of "mass killings." A "crammed hangar building" was named the "White House" and housed the implementation of torture. Another building came to be called the "Red House" because it became the location of immediate execution. Another area came to be recognized as "the Garage" because it served as a carceral area crammed with prisoners. Victims placed in the Omarska garage overwhelmingly wilted, fading in the heat of their own sweat, and suffered eventual death by means of mass dehydration and suffocation from overcrowding. To describe such a place is to recount what it means to exist in living hell. "In the building known as the 'White House,' the rooms were crowded with 45 people in a room no larger than 20 square meters. The faces of the detainees were distorted and bloodstained and the walls were covered with blood." The role of the epidermal surface was erased as bodies become compressed, one against all the others. From the beginning, the detainees were beaten, with fists, rifle butts, and wooden and metal sticks. "The guards mostly hit the heart and the kidneys, when they had decided to beat someone to death. In the 'garage,' between 150–160 people were 'packed like sardines' and the heat was unbearable. . . . Men would suffocate during the night and their bodies were taken out the following morning." The account continues, "The detainees at Omarska had one meal a day. The food was spoiled and the process of getting the food, eating and returning the plate usually lasted around three minutes. Meals were usually accompanied by beatings. The toilets were blocked and there was human waste everywhere . . . . detainees drank from a river that was polluted with industrial waste." If the strategic purpose in ethnic cleansing were coerced removal of civilians, as often alleged, do such excesses serve such aims? Is this process of humiliation and death not gratuitous and unnecessary in any rational context? Macabresque aesthetics of performative transgression typically signify the ludic, a desire for theatricality. At Omarska, the desire for the macabresque appears to have decreed that when death came to prisoners it was deigned to arrive in the company of the many, who die not alone but together, literally, in a bunch. As a result, the victims felt, saw, and heard the death throbs of others, as they themselves were dying. In Omarska, "killings were usually by shooting, beating or cutting of throats, although on one night of frenzied killing, prisoners were incinerated on a pyre of burning tires." Macabresque theatricality lingers on the noir ecstasy of perverse desire realized through performative transgressions that include the near-dead being made to dig their own collective graves. This, too, became a part of the Omarska "routine." "The dead would be loaded on to trucks by their friends or with bulldozers. Sometimes prisoners were taken to dig the graves; they did not return." The victims at Omarska were overwhelmingly male. But Bosniak women were present at Omarska, and they did not escape the attempts at their own degradation. They were forced to clean "the interrogation rooms" used for torture and thus had to dispose of remaining "blood and pieces of skin and hair" after the euphemistically named "informative conversations" had ended. The women bore the pain of hearing "the moaning and wailing of people who were being beaten up." And they suffered the same fate of hearing themselves wail as they, too, were raped.[186]

How does one speak of Omarska? How do we bear witness? Is analytical language able to explain the metrics of human violation exacted here? Once again, we are made to confront the drive to absolute power by means of transgressive violations of human beings in the course of mass atrocity. In the case of Omarska, the standard macabresque pattern emerges:

- Perpetrators of the violence act under the authority of official or quasi-official sanctions issued from the legitimately constituted government of a sovereign state.
- Victims are national citizens.
- Criminal indictment and legal due processes are absent; victims are innocent of any crime; guilt derives from the "identity" of victims.
- Detainees are made to march in formal military formations as if they were in training, part of a ceremony, or the willing participants of some ritualized event; the staged quality is part of a carnivalesque performance.
- Confined incarceration of prisoners transforms mere crowding into the dynamics of human physical compression; the bodies of victims are squeezed; epidermal separation no longer demarcates personal presence or privacy; skin and breath both are made to disappear along with individual personhood.
- Torments and agonies are inflicted directly, person to person, and thus in the close proximity of perpetrators to their victims; perpetrators' hands, fists, boots, rifle butts, clubs go to the bodies and brains of victims; victims are beaten, bludgeoned, pummeled, mutilated, and burned; interrogations are the sites of sustained torment; food and water become the instrumentalities of degradation and demeaning treatment.
- Death occurs as a group dynamic shared among the living-dying who must live in each other's agony as they disappear into their own.
- Killing comes in waves of frenzy; frenzied perpetrators seek new forms of cruelty, more painful forms of excruciation, for example, the suffering of victims being burnt alive on pyres of smoldering tires.
- Cadaverous victims transport the cadavers of the dead and dig their own graves.
- Victims are made to share in the violence of their own violation.
- Ghastly vernacular masquerading as irony develops among perpetrators; this infuses the horror with the theatricality that links the carnivalesque to the macabresque aesthetics of performative transgression.[187]

These represent the elements of surplus cruelty, the concatenation of component features of the macabresque aesthetic and dramaturgy at the core of mass atrocity. Violence is systematic and spatialized. Its character, means, and depth violate the personhood of the victims. Again, let us assume for the moment that ethnic cleansing was the political objective sought by perpetrators at Omarska. Would the killing of the victims, fast and dramatic, not be sufficient to provoke the mass departure of the families whose identities apparently warranted their being cleansed from the regions in which they were living? Are the torments and agony ever-present at Omarska necessary to achieve the political objectives of ethnic cleansing? Is it necessary to demean, humiliate, and degrade the humanity of victims if what is sought is identitarian "cleansing" of space? Why must victims be transformed into bludgeoned corpse-like apparitions of themselves before death? Why must their death come either in the slowness of mass suffocation or in the frenzies of mass execution?

The violations of personhood at Omarska, as elsewhere, eventually proved counter to the ostensible aims or political objectives Serb perpetrators sought to achieve. Nevertheless, the Serb perpetrators acted with firmness and resolve in the strength of their conviction that cruelty was the better part of moral resolve. Mass atrocity is rarely about political, strategic, or even tactical objectives alone. Surplus cruelty does not stem from rational considerations. It is not about intelligence or reason or even primarily about rational thought let alone rational objectives, however rationalized. *Nor does it stem from banal "thoughtlessness."* Its roots are in the psyche and emotional character of human personality in its capacities for disordered will that take their toll when shame and humiliation become fueled by mimetic rivalry, envy, the dread of the theft of thing-enjoyment and, thus, the psychodynamics of social antagonism. And so the century of genocide and mass atrocity ended as it had begun with a mimetic struggle by the willful warriors ostensibly of religion but in actuality of their own self-mystifications, Serbian Orthodox against Bosniak Muslims, all futile and altogether self-defeating. But the task of explanation still remains; and in the case of the Bosnian genocide and mass atrocity, what requires explanation is the macabresque of the genderized/sexualized character of the Bosnian shame-camps. The macabresque of the Bosnian genocide and mass atrocity inheres in the shame-camps giving vent to Serb yearnings for what Heinz Kohut once called narcissistic grandiosity configured around social fantasies of genderized humiliation and formatted by sexualized sadistic desires.

Explaining the Bosnian Macabresque: Shame and Humiliation, Envy and Mimetic Rivalry

Serb genocidal atrocity assumed a *genderized and sexualized* geographic topology that lent specific features to the macabresque of the Bosnian war and genocide or mass atrocity. Hundreds of camps were established during the Bosnian war by perpetrators representing all three sectarian constituencies. But Serb camp topology reveals the core characteristic of the Bosnian macabresque. Serb camps were put down in areas such as mines, parks, or wherever formerly commercial or public facilities could be converted, including restaurants, schools, hospitals, hotels, factories, peacetime brothels, residential villas, and so on. Questions thus arise concerning the genderized/sexualized demarcations in the violations. One immediate answer emphasizes the Serb determination to reverse its minority status by increasing the numbers of Serb-ethnicity babies born. Ethnic cleansing aimed to satisfy not only territorial ambitions of Bosnian Serbs seeking to build a "Greater Serbia," but their desires to reverse their relatively low birthrates by forcibly making Bosniak women give birth to Serb children. This appears to be fully in keeping with Serb patrilineal laws of inheritance by which a child's ethnic identity is conditioned, not by nurture, but by paternity, literally, by the genetic substance of the father. Serb practices of impregnation, insemination, and incubation were consistent with systematic depersonalization of Bosniak men and women—that is to in effect de-spiritualize them to serve the interests of Serb repopulation. Slavenka Drakulić, in her novelist account of the rape of women during the Bosnian War, titled *S.*, depicts this by writing, "Perhaps that is the point, that it has to be all the same to them. The same wrong blood flows inside each of the women. The differences between them [Bosniak women] must be so small that the men can easily forget them."[188] Bosniak women experienced the horrors of depersonalization stemming from repeated sexual abuse and violation. Depersonalization did not result from mere anonymity, however. It was the consequence of shame violations or humiliations imposed on Bosniak men and women and without surceases of mercy by the Serb perpetrators.

Ethnic cleansing could well have occurred without the widespread violations associated with the shame and humiliation of Bosniak victims. That they did not illustrates what is particular to the shame-camp macabresque of the Bosnian mass atrocity, its depersonalization based on genderized and sexualized forms of violation reflective of envious desires to shame and humiliate mimetic rivals, thereby defending in a social fantasy against the dread of theft-enjoyment. Shame-camp macabresque provides perhaps a partial explanation as to why Bosniak women, whose apparent vulnerability stemmed from Serb desire to capture and to abuse their reproductive fecundity, were subjected to depraved cruelty and deeply degrading treatment, including sexual torture and slavery. Clearly, the Bosnian shame-camp macabresque emerged at a critical intersection linking the genderized topography of campsite violence with distinguishable patterns of sexualized violation. The shame-camps tended to be genderized—that is, some isolated mostly the men and boys; others, primarily the women and girls. These formats also predicted for certain kinds of violation. Men and boys suffered mostly physical brutality, starvation, and murder, whereas women and girls endured sexualized modes of violation, including mass rape and enslavement. It should be noted, these genderized demarcations in shame-campsite geography were not absolute and thus were often loosely maintained as were the patterns of sexualized violations. That is to say, Bosniak men and boys were also sexually abused, and Bosniak women were also subjected to brutal beatings. The fault lines of genderized campsite boundaries were thus never inviolately protected. Women were abused in the areas where Bosniak male prisoners were held; and men and boys also suffered sexual abuse in and around the rape camps designated for women. Nonetheless, the Bosnian shame-camp macabresque demonstrated a genderized divisional schematic linked to the modes of violation the victims experienced within them, in particular, stylized physical violation and mass murder against males, sexualized abuse against females. In all instances, shame and humiliation were integral to the process. This suggests the relevance of psychosocial analysis focused on desire and envy, shame and humiliation, within the context of mimetic rivalry, theft-enjoyment, and social antagonism.

This, then, points to the core issue in the search for explanations: how do we explain the genderizing/sexualizing of the Bosnian shame-camp macabresque? *I suggest the Bosnian shame-camp macabresque provides a cultural example of masculine hegemony or of extreme patriarchy aligned to ideological conceptions of honor beset by fantasmatic shame and thus gripped by psychic and emotional reifications or disorders of will in the form of mimetic rivalry and envy.* Loss of power, authority, prestige, and so on, all denoted by the demise of the Yugoslavian state and its sovereign legitimacy, fostered a pervasive shame reaction among the Serb elite and partisan elements. This fueled the psychodynamics of mimetic envy and the emotional demand that mimetic rivals be punished, their volitional autonomy degraded, their communal standing downgraded. As a result, Serbs adopted the practices of humiliation against the Bosniaks. Why, then, did the Serbian macabresque in Bosnia turn on the dramaturgies and aesthetics of genderized/sexualized violations? Within the cultural precepts of Serb society at the time, emphasis on ethnic honor codes, values, and traditions tended to be intensely suffused by notions of *masculinized supremacism* and thus pervaded by *hegemonic arrogations of patriarchy*; similarly, Serb cultural predispositions posited a gender hierarchy permeated by values that were tantamount to an idealization of femininity along traditional lines of chastity, if not passivity. To humiliate male rivals and "their" women conjured up a set of tactical aims and methods that led the Serb perpetrators to presume that violent subordination had to be pursued in distinct ways against each grouping—that is, men beaten, women raped.

The deployment of violence and rape against women as an instrument of policy was executed in rape camps throughout the period of ethnic cleansing in the Bosnian War but in different modes. The indictment that framed the proceedings of the International Criminal Tribunal for the former Yugoslavia (ICTFY) at the Hague specified five patterns of rape and sexual assault: that undertaken by "individuals or small groups" in the course of "looting and intimidation of the target ethnic group"; or "in conjunction with the fighting in an area, often including the rape of women in public"; or that which occurred against those held "in detention" after individuals had been "rounded up" and either killed or sent to camps based on their gender; or sexual assaults and rape "against women for the purpose of terrorizing and humiliating them, often as part of the policy of 'ethnic cleansing'"; and the final, fifth pattern, involving "detention of women in hotels or similar facilities for the sole purpose of sexually entertaining soldiers."[189] In numerous instances, the women subjected to this form of abuse were "more often killed than exchanged." The indictment emphasized the sadistic performativity of perpetrators in implementing modes of sexual violation in ways that were clearly designed to accentuate the humiliation of victims: rape "in front of adult and minor family members, in front of other detainees or in public places, or by forcing family members to rape each other." Forced pregnancies are common so that "perpetrators tell female victims that they will bear children of the perpetrator's ethnicity, that they must become pregnant, and then hold them in custody until it is too late for the victims to get an abortion." Men, too, were subjected to sadistic violations. Bosnian shame-camp macabresque thus demonstrated a core phenomenon manifested throughout the entire history of twentieth century genocide and mass atrocity—perpetrator desire to humiliate victims before, and thus in addition to, their annihilation, murder, or displacement in the name of purification.

Humiliation, an Alternate Perspective on "Absolute" Power

Humiliation originates in the imposition of forces exterior to victims or collective groups of people in ways that are profoundly affecting to the interiorities of the self. It adheres to unequal relationships of power and subordination. It aims at control over subaltern victims in ways that ultimately offend the dignity of their very personhood. It not only makes victims feel degraded, it renders them powerless to resist. In chapter 1, I examined Sofsky's analysis of absolute power. In a sense, what made power absolute in the concentration camps of the Holocaust, as it did throughout the history of macabresque torture, torment, and agony sites of pain and suffering, is this precise dimension of humiliation. Its exercise brings with it deep and abiding memories of harm, wrong, egregious injustice—that is, if its victims survive. It is thus readily associated with evil. It calls forth demands for recompense in the name of righteousness. Its victims, particularly in a cultural milieu of honor, often cry out for retribution and revenge. Conceptual distinctions between dehumanization and depersonalization help to characterize the specific ways humiliation operates. It is not so much that persons humiliated lose their humanity in the sense of dehumanization; on the contrary, their humanness is precisely that which renders them vulnerable to humiliation. What is taken from victims, however, is their latitude for volition, their vitality, their ability to act autonomously, the core elements that constitute social identity. In all, *humiliation depersonalizes precisely by robbing personhood and collective existence of the possibility of self-determination.*

Nationalist supremacism, patriarchy, and ethnic honor readily lend themselves to the promotion of cultural justification of the need to humiliate targeted groups in instances of mimetic rivalry and envy. Fantasy, ideology, and shame easily become allied in perpetuating the macabresque in which victims must not only be violated but must be made to signal their "inferiority" to their violators. This represents a critical component in shame-camp macabresque violence, not only is violation done, it must become recognized as a dimension of performativity. Avishai Margalit describes what he calls "the paradox of humiliation" in these precise terms. He writes, "An aspirant to omnipotence needs to have his absolute superiority recognized. Such recognition has value only if it comes from a free agent, that is, a full-fledged person. This being so, much treatment of humans as nonhumans is 'as-if.' This means that the treatment does not really deny the humanness of the other on an ontological level. It denies the other's freedom on the level of the concrete relations between them."[190] The Bosnian shame-camp macabresque was organized and deployed to execute the practices of humiliation by placing Bosniaks in spatial confinements to render them powerless to defend the values the Bosnian Serb perpetrators assumed they most deeply cherished—male honor, female virtue.

Humiliation derives not from personal fault or failings, as in guilt. For in suffering humiliation, victims know that it is not they who are guilty. The sting of humiliation stems from knowing that one is unable to stave off the violation to one's dignity and self-respect, to the stain of being incapable of defeating the defamations of the violators. Humiliations hurt because their afflictions cause harm to what one wants to believe about one's ability to defend oneself and those one most deeply cares about against the ravages of complete or totalized powerlessness. As Margalit indicates, "Humiliation involves an existential threat. It is based on the fact that the perpetrator . . . has the power. . . . This sense of defenselessness manifests itself in the victim's fear of impotence."[191] The Bosnian shame-camp topology appears to have confirmed the Serb social fantasy that Bosniaks would suffer shame and humiliation in experiencing group or collective impotence, in being unable to fend against brutal violations to their honor and virtue. The macabresque of the shame-camps was designed to operate in such a way that the victims would not only be brutally violated, *they would realize, and it would be seen by their violators, that, as a result of their torment and agony they had recognized, the profound violation leveled against them in their abject humiliation.* Perpetrators seek not merely to pulverize the human body by means of collective violence, they attempt to humiliate the human spirit in mass human violation.[192]

Critical to shame-rage spirals and humiliation in the Bosnian macabresque, furthermore, was how campsite genderization and the sexualization of violation tended toward spatial confinements in both male and female processes of depersonalization. The main element here is not so much the defacement of personality, as in the *Ángkar* mug-shot archive, but the figurative evisceration of skin as a boundary of personality, a border between self and other. The Bosnian macabresque attacked the epidermal surfaces of Bosniak victims in ways indicative of how shame punishments operate publicly. One form of ultimate humiliation is to suffer violent disregard for skin as a borderline between the self and one's social identity. What the Bosnian macabresque attempted to do was to eliminate the sense of Bosniak identity by attacking the epidermal surfaces of its victims. This, too, speaks of the experiential nature of shame. Jennifer Biddle writes, for example, that shame is performative, and its performativity attaches to the skin, which normally becomes discolored in shame. "That it is the skin which registers shame is not arbitrary. The skin, the epidermis, is . . . the outer covering of the material body . . . the mimetic interchangeability of ourselves with others as subject *and* object. In shame, the self expresses itself where it finds itself virtually, negatively differentiated, severed as it is from the other, naked, exposed, and replete with its vulnerability."[193] In the Bosnian macabresque, Bosniaks suffered the torments and agonies of humiliation by means of systematic depersonalization, men suffocating together in the confinements of Omarska, women repeatedly raped with brutalizing cruelty including that of sadistic indifference.

Victimizer as Victim, Again

Such linkages between shame and humiliation, as well as the connections between perpetrators and violated victims, represent critical features in the Bosnian macabresque. Humiliation fantasies and behaviors often demonstrate the outer effects of the interior psychodynamics of shame. These tend to operate through feedback dynamics; the outcomes of internal sensations of shame regulate external behaviors aimed at the humiliation of others. Shame arises within the inner recesses of what is deemed intimate and secret, hidden or clandestine. To humiliate another, that is, to shame them or to make them "feel" ashamed by humiliating them, often masks the projection outward onto others of one's own profound feelings of shame. To humiliate another often says much about those who engage in acts of humiliation. They seek to dishonor mimetic rivals in order to dissipate an inveterate sense of shame. Julien A. Deonna, Raffaele Rodogno, and Fabrice Teroni suggest, for example, "Shame, thus consists in taking an unfavorable third-person perspective upon ourselves." They add, "In shame, the relevant perspective is that of a particular imagined audience, necessary to provide the specific detached viewpoint that always features in shame." Again, the critical dimensions, or what Margalit named as the paradox of humiliation, inheres in the psychodynamics of shame-rage in which the omnipotence of perpetrators must be exercised to the point that the victims perceive themselves as powerless and thus depersonalized. Perpetrators become their own audience as witnesses to the humiliation they cause. This demonstrates not merely the shamelessness of perpetrators, however, but also the shamefulness that they project toward victims in efforts at omnipotence.[194] The recursive psychodynamics also help to explain the Bosnian shame-camp macabresque.

Helen Block Lewis, who pioneered contemporary studies of shame, writes, "Dishonor is the most serious shame state . . . signifying both a serious transgression and a personal failure." She continues, "*Shame is about the self; guilt is about things.* Shame thus appears to be a 'narcissistic' reaction evoked by a lapse from the ego ideal. An ego ideal is difficult to spell out rationally; shame thus can be a subjective 'irrational' reaction."[195] Thus the phenomenology of shame underscores the psychodynamics of the rival self-other, a condition or state of self-condemnation, but from a third-party perspective altogether devious, and thus hidden from conscious view. Lewis adds, "The experience of shame often occurs in the form of imagery, of looking at or being looked at. Shame may also be played out in the imagery of an internal colloquy, in which the whole self is condemned by the 'other.'" And later, "*Shame-rage, which originates in the self, is discharged upon the self.*"[196] The release or "discharge" of shame-rage when it is provoked by mimetic rivalry counters this internal shame by making the external or envied rival feel even less, smaller, more shameful or degraded than the self or one's group. The mimetic rival and the rival self-other become psychologically and emotionally fused. "So long as shame is experienced, it is the other who is experienced as the source of hostility. Hostility against the rejecting other is almost simultaneously evoked. But it is humiliated fury, or [introjected] shame-rage, and the self is still in part experienced as the [projected] object of the other's scorn."[197] Lewis concludes, "Hostility against the other is trapped in this directional bind."[198] Thomas J. Scheff adds two additional dimensions to the "directional bind" of shame-rage, first, that its psychodynamics often become psychologically and emotionally articulated in terms of "honor," and, secondly, these dynamics often provoke shame-rage spirals of ever increasing hostility or violence, such as feuds or vendettas or in acts of humiliation. Scheff, in this regard, emphasizes that rage dynamics or "shame-rage spirals" operate "at the societal level, as well as the interpersonal one."[199] "At the core of this issue," Scheff writes, "is the phenomenon of having emotional reactions to one's emotional reactions, which may become a closed loop."[200] Viewed from the explanatory perspective of shame-rage spirals and humiliation, Serb perpetrators became warped in a closed loop of honor and dishonor, shame and humiliation. Demeaning Bosniak males and females in ways designed to make them suffer the greatest humiliation given cultural presentiments and values, countered the dread of shameful loss attached to their own fantasies of theft of thing-enjoyment.

****

What the Macabresque Vignettes Demonstrate:
Psychosocial Perspectives

What do these case studies of twentieth century macabresque dramaturgies and aesthetics of performative transgression reveal? One theme that has emerged across such factors as time, location, political culture, and power structure is the omnipresence of humiliation as the modus operandi of perpetrators whenever, wherever they operate. Perpetrators want victims to feel shame, suffer humiliation, and recognize that they deserve the humiliation because they are shameful. This is the existential "truth" perpetrators seek in what I have examined as the willed efforts at informativeness by means of torture. The punitive methods of pain we have recounted that produce torture, torment and agony all exact sufferings that humiliate and thus shame victims in ways aimed as much at soul death as they do physical dying. They do not always succeed. Victims and their relatives or support constituencies sometimes find ways to return to life with their sense of dignity and political vindication intact, some by bearing witness, others by promoting new and favorable social or political conditions.

Bosniak Women as "Victims" and as Dignified "Survivors"

Indeed, some evidence suggests that this is true for many Bosniak women who were brutalized during the Bosnian War but who reasserted their rights to full social acceptance and unqualified respect as victims of war but, even beyond this, as honorable members of their faith and culture. Inger Skjelsbaek, in her study of the political psychology of war rape, states, "War *sexualizes other gendered as well as non-gendered identities for political purposes and thereby alters the ways in which masculinization and feminization are perceived.*"[201] Sexual violence during the Bosnian War "took the stigma away from the female victims. Her ethnicity determined whether she was 'eligible' for attack. Through the situating of victims of sexual violence as ethnic subjects, a sense of unity was created between men and women within the same ethnic group." Perceptions of ethnicity, gender, and sexual violence helped to generate conditions of postwar acceptance and forgiveness for the violence endured but not as a result of the victims' fault. The social dynamics of blaming the victims was thus, within limits, avoided. In part this was the consequence of the violence exacted against Bosniak males as well. They had been powerless to defend against the brutality, and thus they, too, had suffered humiliation as well as murder. After the violence had receded, this fostered a mutual recognition on the part of all parties of their innocence relative to the crimes committed against them. The critical factor here, as before, was power and the status that social and political power confers. For in bearing their suffering, as some did with self-understanding and reciprocated forgiveness, Bosniak women were able to challenge cultural constructions of their social standing as victims by becoming represented as "survivors." This distinction between *victim* and *survivor* underscores the role that self-interpretations and social narratives play in recounting the extent to which the humiliations of violation retain their "power" to invoke shame with respect to those who suffered abuse. Skjelsbaek concludes, "The political context shifted, and sexual violence became more a question of male and female power relations, less a question of ethnicity."[202] If humiliation is born of depersonalization, and if depersonalization is borne by powerlessness, the antidote is power and how it positions various groups in relation to each other at any given time and within any given political dynamic.

Humiliation as Residue of Perpetrator Self-Contempt in the Shame of Shamefulness

What about the perpetrators? How do we understand their attractions to depraved horrors of shame and humiliation, a veritable constant throughout the history of the macabresque. To pose the question in this manner is to discount in varying degrees many of the influences and indicators emphasized in the study of genocide and mass atrocity within social and political psychology that, as was noted at the beginning of this study, tend to stress such causal factors as civil war, leadership, command structures, group dynamics, prototypicality, ideology, a range of strategic objectives, and so on. These remain relevant to explanations of collective violence; but on the whole, they fail to allow us to penetrate the sadistic, narcissist behaviors of human violation. And they overwhelmingly ignore shame as an emotional, psychological, and psychic influence despite its centrality in case after case in the macabresque. Why do perpetrators, from the historically infamous to the abject and insignificant, appear consistently to yield to desires for the obscene cruelties of shame-rage and humiliation? It matters not whether the macabresque in genocide and mass atrocity emerges in political cultural contexts registered as fascist or communist, nationalist or ethnicist, racist or nativist, supremacist or exclusivist, totalitarian or collectivist, radical or authoritarian, honor and tradition bound or dystopian, fundamentalist or futurist, or agrarian or extremist. What perpetrators appear to want across all the case studies reported here is to shame and humiliate their victims. As we have seen, they did so with cunning, relish, and sustained contempt.

Contempt, moreover, seems to be the operative dynamic. It matters not whether one is examining genocidal tyrants or low-life thugs. Benjamin Kilborne stresses the etymological roots of the term *shame*, which derives from Old High German *scama,* as in "to cover" or "to hide" and indicates "the hiding of shame is about the *shame of shame.*"[203] The shame of shame helps to explain the psychodynamics of *self-deception* and of *the rival self-other*, that is, the willed denial of truth and the self-contempt that derives from viewing the self as if from a third-party gaze in ways in which the subject of the self becomes its own judge and jury on scales of *shamefulness*. This is what the shame of shame suggests theoretically. It speaks to the relationships of ego to ego-ideal and to both narcissistic and sadistic personality structures that are all too amenable, it would seem, to making others pay the price, as Naimark suggested with reference to Serb humiliation of Bosniak women, "for their very existence." This points toward the psychodynamics of self-contempt. Kilborne tells a revealing story about Stalin, in this regard, for example, how the dictator was ashamed of his diminutive stature. Kilborne points to Stalin's chronic insistence that all photos diminish the stature of others to make him "look wise and glowing, overshadowing all others in importance," where he is ' "in fact small and cunning, pockmarked and swarthy, lost in the crowd."[204] Kilborne concludes, "Not unlike the shame-ridden patients I have described, Stalin appears to have lived his entire life in terror of being exposed, a terror that drove his cruelty and sadism and that led him in uncompromising fashion to purge not only the past but, more ominously still, the future."[205]

Taking a similar perspective, Thomas J. Scheff and Suzanne M. Retzinger examine Hitler's shame-filled personality, and then emphasize the linkages between this and German popular response to him. Hitler was assailed by dread that "he would appear ridiculous" and by "feelings of inadequacy and inferiority."[206] This does not "explain Hitler," in the sense that Ron Rosenbaum critiqued, as discussed in an chapter 3. It establishes the relationship between shame and shame-rage, between interior, or psychic and emotional, sensations of shame and externalized projections of shame-rage, leading to the fury, however systematic and controlled, in the demands that victims suffer humiliation. Scheff and Retzinger observe, "Shame theory suggests that protracted and destructive anger is always generated by unacknowledged shame."[207] And it is this shame of shame or unacknowledged shame that helps explain why humiliation becomes the key to macabresque dramaturgies and aesthetics across the case studies of performative transgression regardless of culture, political circumstances, or time period.

Scheff and Retzinger also make the case that Hitler effectively absorbed, incarnated and redirected the national shame Germany experienced as humiliation for the *Dolschstoss*, or "stab-in-the-back" and losing the First World War. Reification of the Jews emerged as a contrived salve to mitigate German shame-rage over their powerlessness. Scheff and Retzinger associate this feat with Hitler's demagogic style that they cast in terms of "charisma." They write, following Harold Lasswell, "The secret of charisma may be that it is not the cognitive content of the message, but the emotional one, that is important. *The leader who is able to decrease the shame level of a group, interrupting the contagion of overt shame, no matter how briefly or at what cost, will be perceived as charismatic.*"[208] Scheff and Retzinger envision this charismatic process as a feedback outcome of cascading shame-rage spirals in which Germans "were ashamed, angry that they were ashamed, ashamed that they were angry, and so on, without limit."[209] Much violation in the macabresque results from sadistic indifference to suffering and systematically performed torture, torment, and agony. Does this comport with the notion of shame-rage? Scheff and Retzinger following other shame theorists distinguish "overt" from chronic or "bypassed" shame that is psychologically unrecognized. They imply the performative nature of chronic shame in that it influences behaviors by shaping how groups of others come to be perceived. Scheff and Retzinger infer from the changing nature of Hitler's behaviors "that Hitler may have been in a virtually permanent state of shame, manifested as either bypassed shame (the stare) or overt shame (avoiding eye contact). As his power increased, the bypassed shame was more and more in evidence, in the form of arrogance, extreme self-confidence, isolation, and obsession."[210] What appears pertinent to the sadistic violence originating in the psychodynamics of human violation is the hidden shame of perpetrators, major and small.

The relationship of the shame of shame and the psychological, emotional, and psychic etiologies of violence was famously examined by James Gilligan, who concluded, "The emotion of shame is the primary or ultimate cause of shame."[211] Gilligan, like Scheff and Retzinger, argued that the psychodynamics of shame revolve around the shame of shame, whether at the interpersonal or societal levels. With respect to perpetrators of violence, he writes, "The secret is that they feel ashamed—deeply ashamed, chronically ashamed, acutely ashamed, over matters that are so trivial that their very triviality makes it even more shameful to feel ashamed about them, so that they are ashamed even to reveal what shames them."[212] Gilligan thus elucidates the meaning of the shame of shame and in so doing asks, "And why are they so ashamed of feeling ashamed?" His answer, "Because nothing is more shameful than to feel ashamed." But the shamefulness of shame does not *cause* perpetrators behaviors in the macabresque. To suggest so, returns to the critiques of psychosocial theories such as that examined earlier by such scholars as Daniel Pick. Rather, it functions as a source that nurture predispositions for violence that can be triggered under the right circumstances, as demonstrated throughout this volume. Gilligan underscores the importance of lack of empathy or the absence of guilt and love in combination with shamefulness as critical to perpetrators' capacity for cruelty and implicitly anticipates the findings of such scholars as de Swaan, Fonagy, and Baron-Cohen, discussed earlier. Gilligan concludes, "A central precondition for committing violence, then, is the presence of overwhelming shame in the absence of either love or guilt."[213]

Heinz Kohut, in a well-known essay on shame, attributes the psychodynamics of shame and lack of empathy to narcissism, a kind of grandiosity inherent in the psychic and emotional structures of the rival self-other, in which the tensions between the self as subject and the self as object lead to merciless aggression toward others whenever provoked by insult or perceived hurt. Kohut writes, "Although everybody tends to react to narcissistic injuries with embarrassment and anger, the most violent forms of narcissistic rage arise in those individuals for whom a sense of absolute control over an archaic environment is indispensable because . . . the unconditional availability of the approving-mirroring functions of an admiring self-object" is critical. The macabresque creates the conditions Kohut refers to as "an archaic environment" in which the absoluteness of power and depersonalization sustains "the grandiosity and omnipotence of the self and self-object" of perpetrators.[214] This does not provide a congenital explanation for perpetrators' actions with respect to killing or murdering per se; rather it is suggestive of an approach focused on the causes of the macabresque and the reasons for the allure of performative transgression with its exhibitionist dramaturgies once conditions arise permitting the release of such desires. Kohut puts it in classical fashion, "But while the essential disturbance which underlies the experience of shame concerns the boundless *exhibitionism* of the grandiose self, the essential disturbance underlying rage relates to the *omnipotence* of this narcissistic structure."[215] Kohut thus returns our attention to Sofsky's observations concerning the idiosyncratic but competitive behaviors of Nazi concentration camp guard of wanton cruelty gripped by what he called the demands of "absolute power" and of the most exhibitionist kind. The humiliations suffered by victims bespeak what Kohut names as "insistence of the exercise of total control." This insistence functions across the boundaries of internal fantasies and externalized behaviors under the conditions he calls archaic, as in the macabresque. He concludes, "We are thus witnessing the gradual establishment of *chronic narcissistic rage,* one of the most pernicious afflictions of the human psyche—either, in its still endogenous and preliminary form, as grudge and spite; or, externalized and acted out, in disconnected vengeful acts or in a cunningly plotted vendetta."[216] The honor dramaturgies and aesthetics of humiliation that exhibit the plays of omnipotence strike at the core of the macabresque. And for such reasons, mimetic rivalry and the reifications of envy and contempt represent the basic psychodynamics of the macabresque.

The narcissism of the exhibitionist desire for omnipotent dominance over an archaic environment, and in relation to mimetic rivals who disturb the fantasy of absolute power, is readily reinforced by the psychodynamics of sadism, as also consistently demonstrated by the case studies of the macabresque. And sadism and desire for humiliation also become mutually reinforcing. To return to Stalin as a prime example, Erich Fromm points to "a particularly refined form of sadism," namely, Stalin's predilection for arresting and sending into the Gulag and labor camps the wives, and even the children, of the most senior of his government or Party entourage who "had to do their jobs and bow and scrape before Stalin without daring even to ask for their release."[217] Yet again we find a humiliation game indicative of supreme sadism. Fromm concludes, "I propose that the core of sadism, common to all its manifestations, is *the passion to have absolute and unrestricted control over a living human being.*"[218] At the end, it constitutes no part of a justification to indicate that despite desires for omnipotence, perpetrators reveal profound, indeed, intense forms of infantilism and primordial anxieties adherent to Lacanian conceptions of the Real and the Imaginary and thus to forms of shame gripped by the psychodynamic tensions described earlier in reference to Jeffrey Murer's and Hanna Segal's application of the psychoanalytic concept of ego-ideal.

In another classic study of shame, Gerhart Piers and Milton B. Singer relate shame to fantasies of failure with respect to ego-ideal to the extent that it emerges as "a severe unconscious threat to the ego."[219] The challenges provoked by civil war, mimetic rivalry, loss of power, declines in status or standing, and so on, typically present in outbreaks of genocide and mass atrocity, also appear to tantalize potential perpetrators. But the essential Lacanian observation retains its theoretical and analytical validity in that the essential psychosocial phenomenon does not revolve around hatred alone, as has repeatedly been documented by numerous genocide scholars who find that identitarian constructions do not predict for genocidal hostility or violence. The psychosocial dynamics of shame and humiliation provide insight into the anxiety or dread of the loss of the "thing"—that is, *das Ding* of *jouissance* and the quest in surrogacy for *objet a*—and to defend against the theft of thing-enjoyment. As Piers and Singer conclude, "Behind the feeling of shame stands not the fear of hatred, but the fear of *contempt* which, on an even deeper level of the unconscious, spells fear of *abandonment*, the death by emotional starvation."[220] *Mimetic rivalry, envy, and contempt, critical to the psychic and emotional dynamics of perpetrators of the macabresque, validate theoretical efforts to explain the desire for human violation by means of humiliation, not by reference to hatred, identity, let alone strategic or political objectives, but rather by stressing primordial dread of contempt, and thus the shame of shame. Perpetrators of all ideological stripes, power ranks, and political cultures dread the contempt of others above all, since it triggers the deep forebodings of one's own cosmic unworthiness and in so doing fuels the deepest dread of all—that is, of abandonment and, therefore, the fantasmatic specter of the theft of thing-enjoyment.* Thus we return to the frameworks of social psychology, specifically to the work of Peter Glick, who explained the dynamics of scapegoating within a perspective focused on what Glick calls "envious prejudice."[221]

Glick observes, "Thus, groups that are targets of *envious prejudice* are at particular risk of being viewed as intentionally causing economic and social problems." Glick also indicates, "Envious prejudices are likely to be at their most acute in situations in which majority groups members feel that their social status has shifted downward relative to the status of a minority."[222] For such reasons, illegal aliens, refugees, asylum-seekers, and migrants of all backgrounds are often conjured up as "enemies of the people" who threaten the survival of the nation. And if the question arises, why such fear, the answer points toward the dread of loss configured around ideological images of descending into a state of powerlessness and loss associated with minority status. Again, the dangers of violence turning into violation against members of minority groups attends a sense of loss or risk of loss of status, standing, or power relative to mimetic rivals and, above all, the shamefulness of shame.

The Triadic Structure of Evil

Ruth Stein's psychosocial analysis of what attracts individuals to terrorism emphasizes the collective nature of what she describes as the "triadic structure of evil."[223] That is, "the perpetrator, the victim, and the ideal."[224] Stein reserves the term "evil" for collective violence and envisions collective violence as evil once it "proceeds with the aid of *a corresponding ideology that articulates an ideal object*." This ideal object corresponds to "truth," the very truth that is taken to justify the normalization of collective violence, at least from the perspective of perpetrators. Stein observes, "The ideal mediates, ratifies, even sanctifies the action of the (collective) perpetrator on the (collective) victim."[225] Stein's analysis thus illustrates the problem of individual culpability when the origins of collective violence appear to inhere in collective beliefs, ideology, and, indeed, in collective forms of epistemology through which truth becomes evaluated. Stein's perspective thus situates evil at the core of what I have referred to as collective self-deception. At first glance, this appears to render motivational considerations in cases of human violation difficult to assess. This predicament tends to become framed, as we have also seen, in terms of normalcy versus psychopathology. Stein stresses the fact that the Nazis tended to "evict those members who might derive pleasure from what had to be done, lest their impulses would jeopardize the dependability and efficiency of their functioning."[226] That said, however, Stein develops a theory of perversity akin to the one I developed here in terms of sadism, one that eschews pleasure as a criterion of sadistic behavior. Indeed, the psychosocial linkages between perversity and sadistic cruelty are forged in and by means of the psychic and emotional mergers of self, one's self-sacrifice and the ideal, if one conceives of "the ideal" as law, its merger as a psychic demand to be the law in the psychodynamics of mimetic desire. As Stein indicates, "*Evil* is thus *a merger with an object that is both idealized and persecutory*, omnipotent and contemptuous of human vulnerability."[227]

The psychic phenomenon of "merger" with the "law" and social fantasies fostering the persecution of enemies in the collective "name" of the law is critical to the perversity and sadism operative in instances of the macabresque. The psychodynamics of "object ideal" in mimetic desire conjures up fantasies of the rival other, the enemies who "need to be liquidated in the service of this persecutoriness."[228] It is the ideal that solicits the persecution of mimetic enemies who become outsized on account of the characteristics attributed to their desire. For Stein, this represents the perversity of collective evil. "These two characteristics, the reversal of good and bad and the dehumanization or 'superhumanization' of the object of desire, are hallmarks of perversity."[229] Stein's examination of perversity veers toward an interpretation of sadistic cruelty as a result of its emphasis on what she calls "the superlaw." Contrary to first impressions," she declares, "a perverse person does not place himself outside the law, and the pervert's challenge to the law does not entail the will to abolish it." She adds, "Speaking in the context of social and political group dynamics, perversion will express itself within a political formation as the attempt to impose a preferred, 'superior' law to the conventional, ordinary one."[230] Stein speaks of the sense of "liberation" that derives from the sense of "self-abandonment" once one has committed to an unfolding of death at the behest of higher causes.

But at this critical juncture, in the absence of a clear definition of sadistic cruelty in mimetic desire, conceptual distinctions between good and evil, love and perversity, become lost. She writes, for example, "Nazi ethics is the oxymoron it appears to be, since what was done in Auschwitz was done in the name of the good, or, more precisely, a certain conception of the good for a certain community. It was done not as a deliberate denial of the moral code but as an intended affirmation of it."[231] But moral or ethical relativism of this sort fails to connect disorders of will with the self-deception that is critical to an understanding of sadistic cruelty beyond mere perversity. To demonstrate this is in fact Stein's very objective, to demonstrate that perpetrators self-delude themselves into believing their own lies, into believing that they represent incarnations of truth or beauty or goodness. Depraved behavior in human violation is always represented as the good in collective violence, as Stein's own triadic definition of evil makes clear. Once the collective designs of power become transformed into ends for themselves, discourses of morality or ethics become irrelevant. Power no longer serves as a means relative to collective purposes; its sole aim is dystopia beyond moral consideration or ethical embrace.

Collective violence in the macabresque is not intellectualistic or ideational alone; rather it is performative and, as we have repeatedly observed, demands that victims participate performatively in the process of their own violation. The evil in perverse desire once suffused by sadism is that it imposes suffering by willfully imposing torture, torment, or agony as a supplement to death. No conception of "good" based on *object as ideal* ethically or morally inscribes the performativity of suffering as an end itself—as a moral good. For such reasons, the macabresque and styles of macabresque sadism represent critical analytical perspectives with respect to human violation. In this sense, Berel Lang's observation (referred to in chapter 4) that evil is done *because it is evil*, is in my view, closer to the mark. Collective evil arises as a consequence of the systemic sin of indifference or lack of empathy with respect to human suffering, especially when caused by human hands. This is the critical feature of sadistic cruelty over and beyond the perverse desire to become the incarnation of any objectified ideal. In psychosocial terms, the dimension that is critical to both perversity and sadism is the threatened erosion of the paternal imago in ways favoring a fantasized fusion with "maternalized" *jouissance*, and thus the psychic emergence of anxieties that attend sadistic exercises to make the victim declare the law of desire as a defense against *jouissance*. Chasseguet-Smirgel describes this as a fusion of the ego with an ego-ideal aimed at the avoidance of the "paternalized" formations in the superego that might contribute to self-individuation and thus to moral or ethical behaviors relative to moral norms or ethical precepts, properly so called.

Mimetic Rivalry in Envy and Desire

Žižek, among others, explains the dynamics of mimetic desire in psychosocial terms. "The true opposite of egoist self-love is not altruism, a concern for common good, but envy, *ressentiment*, which makes me act *against* my own interests." He adds, "The true evil, which is death drive, involves self-sabotage. It makes us act against our own interests."[232] Envy is borne by social fantasies of disordered will and desire in ways captured by the notion of death drive that is so akin to the macabresque. In this realm, envy and desire, mimetic rivalries, and resentment are never far away. Žižek reaffirms what we have already observed, "The problem with human desire is that, as Lacan put it, it is always 'desire of the Other' in all senses of that term: desire for the Other, desire to be desired by the Other, and especially desire for what the Other desires. This last makes envy, which includes resentment, constitutive components of human desire, something Augustine knew well."[233] Envy and sadism are never distant in the intersections between the politics of collective violence and the psychodynamics of human violation. To envy is to reify not the objects of desire but rather to reify *how* the mimetic rival desires the desirable. On this account, sadism is driven not so much by desire as it is about the control of the rival's desire to the point of pain or death. "So what *is* envy?" Žižek asks. He answers, "The subject does not envy the Other's possession of the prized object as such, but rather the way the Other is able to *enjoy* this object, which is why it is not enough for him simply to steal and thus gain possession of the object." This influences why mimetic desire, envy, and sadistic cruelty play out in the macabresque. Victims must be made to act out the depletion of their desire so that perpetrators can come to "know" that they possess rival's desiring in itself. Žižek comments with respect to the envier, "His true aim is to destroy the Other's ability/capacity to enjoy the object."[234]

So often, the cries and shibboleths of those who incite others to undertake mass atrocities, evoke political imaginaries of past wrongs, collective loss, demands for justice. This, too, reveals the interpenetration of envy, desire, and mimetic rivalry in the sadistic cruelties of the macabresque. As Žižek concludes, "The demand for justice is thus ultimately the demand that the excessive enjoyment of the Other should be curtailed so that everyone's access to *jouissance* is equal."[235] But there exists no "thereness" in *jouissance* however great its allures. And like the sirens of myth and legend, it tantalizes perpetrators until their doom.

Ideology Again

Žižek rejects Louis Althusser's approach to how ideology influences collective behavior on the basis of his claim that Althusser fails to explain why political subjects cynically defend ideological assertions that at some level they know to be false, in my terms, why they articulate logics of illogic that they know at some level to be fraudulent. Žižek suggests that the political ontology outlined by Althusser assumes a certain hollowness or automaticity in how people believe and act ideologically based on what Althusser called the "Ideological State Apparatus" in keeping with his Marxist orientation to "false consciousness." Althusser's theoretical perspective emphasized chronic, collective, class-driven misunderstandings, and, most centrally, the malevolent impacts of the propaganda machines that make up the Ideological State Apparatus that include not only governmental structures but also a wide range of political processes, social norms, and cultural mores. In Althusserian social theory, the Ideological State Apparatus stands as a kind of "master signifier" or grand independent variable. As a consequence, what political subjects think and believe, act and do are overwhelmingly epiphenomenal and secondary to the state and class structures. Cognitive "realities" emerge from processes of socialization organized under the aegis of the Ideological State Apparatus. Individuals learn how to position themselves in relation to the entire complex of external institutions and cultural artifacts now constituted as material or social "reality." Althusser thus argued that the Ideological State Apparatus is "the Subject" that "invents" persons as political "subjects" precisely because persons as subjects learn how to confirm and reinforce the ideology promoted by "the Subject," even as they suppress the doubts that might arise as a result of critical distance from the social realities in which they are immersed. Throughout this chapter, I have demonstrated the risks of adopting this and similar analytical perspectives that conflate epistemological, moral, and scientific reasoning with ideological constructs on the basis of what appears to be an Althusserian approach to ideological dynamics.

Žižek, correctly in my view, as I have tried to illustrate, takes aim at Althusserian political ontology on the grounds that the political "subjects" of the Ideological State Apparatus have been theorized as devoid of interiority, as puppets on a stage marching blindly to the tunes of class consciousness. Žižek argues, to the contrary, that ideology is humanly or ontologically intrinsic to the political. It consists of the social fantasies and self-deceptions that strike at the heart of behavioral attitudes in political ontology. Žižek writes, for example, "the illusion is not on the side of knowledge, it is already on the side of reality itself, of what people are doing. What they do not know is that their social reality itself, their activity, is guided by an illusion, by fetishistic inversion."[236] How does this fetishistic inversion operate? "The illusion" he asserts, "is therefore double: it consists in overlooking the illusion which is structuring our real, effective relationship to reality. And this overlooked, unconscious illusion is what may be called the ideological fantasy." He later adds, "The fundamental level of ideology, however, is not of an illusion masking the real state of things but that of an (unconscious fantasy) structuring our social reality itself."[237] In Lacanian and psychosocial perspectives, as I have tried to represent them, ideology, then, does not represent a set of epistemological traps in false cognition or consciousness but rather distorted, even disordered social and political behaviors and attitudes skewed by fantasies of desire in service of *objet a* and the residues of *jouissance*. Ideology gives life, meaning, and specificity to desire by attaching to the emptiness of lack and the inducements to desire that have been left over from the injunctions of lost thing-enjoyment among those who sense within themselves a desire for shared desire in opposition to those excluded from the bonds of belonging. Ideologies reside in intersubjective social fantasies grounded in lack of lack *plus* existential loss and thus in the push and pull of psychic flows and polar tensions that spin and congeal into conscious forms of collective desire. The manifestation of this is ideology manifested by political reifications and skewed by disordered will. But disordered will ideologically experienced in collective desire is never about the individual in splendid isolation. Social fantasy and akratic intentionality in desire is tied to transpersonal dynamics. In a sense, desire speaks through persons as the agents seeking shared affiliations in collective life.

The problem of ideology is precisely that this grounding in solidarity is, for Žižek, a form of collective self-deception, a social fantasy designed to conceal the contradictions and antagonisms between the one and the many, the individual and the political. Adam Kotsko following Žižek observes, "The ideological fantasy, which serves as the 'interface' between the individual subject and the social order, provides a means of keeping *jouissance* at a safe distance. In exchange for renouncing access to the fullness of *jouissance*, the subject is 'interpellated' or brought under the symbolic order, which opens up the space of desire."[238] This process is on the order of Oedipal castration and the entry into language, and for this reason the legitimacy of law, order, stability, authority, hierarchy, and power are all central to outbreaks of the macabresque. State atrocity in the macabresque of sadistic and surplus cruelty is aimed at restoration of the paternal rock that blocks access to *jouissance* and thing-enjoyment. But as a result, desire becomes much more compelling, more voracious for shared desire in supererogatory norms or principles that resonate, that vibrate, with the desire for shared desire. During such instances, the essential aspect of ideology is to "live" in the pretense that "totality" is possible through the commonalities of the political when totality is the very fantasy that remains impossible in the commonalities of desire. Žižek declares, "Ideology is not a dreamlike illusion that we build to escape insupportable reality; in its basic dimension, it is a fantasy-construction which serves as a support for our 'reality' itself." Žižek's concept of ideology, therefore, represents a political ontology based on collective self-deception that both "structures our effective, real social relations" but also "masks some insupportable, real, impossible kernel," in *objet a*, and thus conceals the very "traumatic social division which cannot be symbolized" from which relief is sought through the blandishments of desire.[239] What political subjects seek in ideological practices is what they cannot attain, although the consequences of these practices are to sustain the social conditions that foster this impossibility. Žižek concludes, "In the Lacanian perspective ideology rather designates *a totality set on effacing the traces of its own impossibility.*"[240] This is demonstrated again and again in the macabresque, where profound disorders of will borne of akratic intentionality transform desire and turn into willfulness in volition and convert emotionality into the vain futilities of willing the unwillable. The consequence is suffering brought on by torture, torment, and agony made all the more tragic on account of the cultural illusions and perpetrators' self-delusions that inexorably attend them.

PART IV

Politics of the Unreal

9

On the Slippery Tropes of We-ness

REALITY AND THE UNREAL IN SOCIAL FANTASY

AND POLITICAL IDEOLOGY

ELUSIVE MIRRORS

Slavoj Žižek sees significance for a rendering of ideology in a detail of theatrical presentation contrasting Hitler and Stalin. "The Fascist Leader finishes his public speech and the crowd applauds," Žižek observes. "The Stalinist leader "*stands up himself and starts to applaud,* he continues."[1] "This change," Žižek suggests, "signals a fundamentally different discursive position: the Stalinist leader is compelled to applaud, since the true addressee of the people's applause is not himself, but the big Other of History." Žižek adds, "Insofar as—according to Lacan—the position of the object-instrument of the big Other's *jouissance* is what characterizes the pervert's economy, one can also say that the difference is the one between the Fascist paranoic and the Stalinist pervert."[2] Žižek repeats this theme by referring to Christopher Hitchens's effort to examine how and to what extent North Koreans "authentically" revere "Dear Leader." Žižek supports Hitchens's analysis on the grounds that the latter has "produced what is arguably the most succinct definition of ideology: 'mass delusion is the only thing that keeps a people sane.'" Žižek indicates, "The fetishistic split at the very heart of an effectively functioning ideology" demands that the members of a society bestow their desire for belief onto the "big Other." Žižek sees this as a tacit social device to avoid the necessity of having to affirm "love" for "Dear Leader"—as individuals. Once desire of the collective becomes lodged in the desire of the individual, personal desire becomes normalized in a way that indicates renunciation of *jouissance*. But this also reveals the functioning of the superego.

For it is the superego as a psychic agency that putatively permits failed congruence in desire to be asserted. "This necessary gap in identification enables us to locate the agency of the *superego*: the superego emerges as the outcome of failed interpellation," Žižek writes. "At a 'deeper' level, the superego gives expression to the guilt, to a betrayal, that pertains to the act of interpellation *as such*: interpellation qua symbolic identification with the Ego-Ideal is as such, in itself, a compromise, a way of 'giving up on one's desire.'"[3] Congenital forms of psychic "lack" and "loss" in formations of desire are thus imputed to shape political and ideological reification. Žižek writes, "Desire is constituted by 'symbolic castration,' the original loss of the *Thing*; the void of this loss is filled out by *objet petit a*, the fantasy-object; this loss occurs on account of our being 'embedded' in the symbolic universe which derails the 'natural' circuit of our needs."[4] Such derailments also transport demands for the macabresque to permit, what is in effect the renunciation of *jouissance*. The performative aesthetics of transgression occur as perpetrators "will" the unwillable desire of the introjected m(Other) experienced in fantasy in modes that include superegotistical enjoyment projected outward in forms of sadistic cruelty. Such macabresque pursuits assume surrogate forms of desire, in surplus cruelty, in the gratuitous sadism of absolute power. *Superegotistical desire and its "enjoyment" are sustained by supererogatory reifications that revel in moral masochism and sadistic moralism. This leads to macabresque aesthetics and theatricality of performative transgression since the laws of jouissance, its prohibition and pursuit in substitute forms, must be repeated again and again.* This is the significance of *objet a* in the study of desire with respect to perpetrators.

In Lacanian psychosocial perspectives, *objet a* represents the primary concupiscence that derives from Oedipal castration and entry into language. *Objet a*, as fantasy, inheres in a kind of psychic "obedience" to phallic proscriptions but it also fuels libidinous, even, surrogate desire, because paternal law demands renunciation of *jouissance* only to sustain its allures in mimetic desires. Because *jouissance* is barred to the subject, temptations to transgress in some sense never cease. Lacan associates the superego with the symbolic, with evocations of speech, and with censorious invocations of law. These are galvanized by unconscious energies positioned in the human psyche to oppose incest. But they also induce a kind of "extra-legal" fascination with the possibilities of transgression. Evans, citing Lacan, comments, for example, "The superego has a close relationship with the Law, but this relationship is paradoxical. On the one hand, the Law as such is a symbolic structure regulating subjectivity in ways preventing or inhibiting psychic disintegration. On the other hand, the law of the superego has a 'senseless, blind character, of pure imperativeness and simple tyranny."[5] Lacan points to this in his essay on Kant and Sade in which he joins them together at the hip of universalizable law, the Kantian by means of the "categorical imperative," the Sadean by means of the "Supreme Being-in Evil." Both devolve into supererogatory commandments to enjoy the law, to give into law, to be the law, the Kantian in the renunciation of desire, the Sadean in its transgressive fulfillments. In both cases, the superego is the psychic mechanism of a morality transformed into a moralism of desire.

The suffering of victims in the macabresque represents an instrumentality of super-egotistical desire "enjoyed" by means of supererogatory display. Žižek illustrates the concept of "surplus enjoyment." He connects surplus enjoyment with the psychodynamics of sadistic transgression grounded in ideologically justified performativity through which the perpetrator imposes agony and torments of human violation on the victim so that the victim might declare the law of historic necessity. Žižek thus helps to illustrate the critical linkages among the political dynamics connecting human violation, sadistic perversity, and ideological doctrines or political imaginaries that become attached to authoritarianism and its willing executioners at all levels of society:

> The Sadeian executioner has nothing whatsoever to do with pleasure: his activity is *stricto sensu* ethical, beyond any "pathological" motive, he only fulfils his duty—witness the lack of wit in Sade's work. The executioner works for the enjoyment of the Other, not for his own: he becomes a sole instrument of the Other's Will. And in so-called "totalitarianism", this illegal agent-instrument of the law, the Sadeian executioner, *appears as such* in the shape of the Party, agent-instrument of historical Will.[6]

Perpetrators do believe in their own lies. This is the very point of the banality of evil, that those who "do" evil *are* "ordinary" in seeking desire and its enjoyment. Perpetrators do believe that supererogatory moral norms and ethical standards matter. They do agree that the greater good of society counts; under interrogation they repeatedly argue that one must sacrifice personal interests on behalf of the good of society and that to do so is heroism, not villainy. Over and over again, high-profile perpetrators, from Hermann Göring to Ratko Mladić, challenge the legitimacy of transitional courts or international tribunals to sit in judgment of them. This is the case not because perpetrators tend to be merely deceitful (although they may well be), not only because they are perverse or sadistic (which they undoubtedly are), but because of the psychic economies of super-egotistical desire and perverse injunctions to transgressive desire—not as a crime but as a "duty"—that is, as a profound supererogatory obligation. As Žižek concludes: "Lacan's fundamental thesis is that superego in its most fundamental dimension is an *injunction* to *enjoyment*: the various forms of superego commands are nothing but variations on the same motif: 'Enjoy!' Therein consists the opposition between Law and superego: Law is the agency of prohibition which regulates the distribution of enjoyment on the basis of a common, shared renunciation (the 'symbolic castration'), whereas superego marks a point at which *permitted* enjoyment, freedom-to-enjoy, is reversed into *obligation* to enjoy—which, one must add, is the most effective way to block access to enjoyment."[7]

Moral Masochism and Sadistic Moralism

As Daniel Jonah Goldhagen recognizes, the macabresque is emblematic of mass atrocity. He observes how perpetrators invert human violation and open manifestations of

indescribable cruelty as forms of righteousness in which the measures of victims' suffering become ideologically mystified as an attempt to transform the world according to
the metrics of "good." The disordered willfulness that drives such behaviors is cast not
only around fantasies of return to the lost enchantments of the m(Other), but seek to re-
inscribe fantasized, laws of prohibition. Lacanian perspectives extrapolated for purposes
of psychosocial analysis demonstrates the profound structural role of *objet a* as fantasy
constructions. Paternal prohibition played out in fantasy fuels the fires of excess or surplus cruelty especially if collective anxiety becomes compelling over what anchors the
legitimacies of social solidarity, due to the decline of law and order, massive economic
shock or disintegration, shame and humiliation over national loss, and so forth. Here the
political is seen to intrude on social fantasy, before fantasy invades politics. The irony
is that the macabresque in mass atrocity, the most transgressive of all forms of political
action and behavior, is done in the name of law, sacred, inviolable, and inexorable.

Perpetrators of political evil in the macabresque will the unwillable by envisioning
themselves as the servants of law, sometimes even the unwilling instruments of law's
desire, but agents, nonetheless, acting nobly in the name of law's necessity. Herein,
again, the devices of self-deception become operative. Perpetrator motivations infused
by unconscious fantasy become cast around the desire, law's desire, to embody the desire
of the m(Other) and thus to be the cause of the m(Others') desiring. The desire of the
m(Other) is not the object but the cause of desire. And the cause is the desire for transgressive desire as substitute for forbidden *jouissance*. It is the superego, therefore, that
sanctions surplus enjoyment fantasized as self-sacrificiality and given over to the necessities of sacral violation in the name of the legitimacies of a law higher than law. But
superegotistical enjoyment is not the same as desire readily channeled and disciplined
by notions of rational self-interest. In cases of genocide and mass atrocity, superegotistical desire/supererogatory enjoyment leads to the transgression of law in the name
of higher law, a law perversely inscribed by *objet a* to project narcissistic masochism
outward toward victims and transform it into the perversity of sado-intimacy in the
macabresque.

SCREENS OF HORROR

Žižek captures something of this when he writes, "Horror is not simply and unambigu-
ously the unbearable Real masked by the fantasy-screen—the way it focuses our attention, imposing itself as the disavowed and, for that reason, all the more operative central
point of reference. The Horrible can also function as the screen itself, as the thing whose
fascinating effect conceals something 'more horrible than horror itself,' the primordial
void or antagonism."[8] The sources of political reification may reside here: the horror
over horror that is the void in the Real, experienced in the lack, and "positivized" by
and through the lack of lack, the double negativity; the horror that calls forth human
personality in the guise of "subjectivity" materialized by cultural and ideological norms

but inherent in fantasies of desire. These work to compensate against the lack by seeking impossible psychic satisfaction in the lost enchantments in the *objet a*. In Lacanian terms, psychic "journeys," from fantasized desires nested against the lack in the Real to the political reifications articulated in the Symbolic order, pass through screens of horror gripped by infantile flashes of corporeal disassembly and imagistic dismemberment in the Imaginary.

Cavarero, in her study on horrorism, distinguishes the concept of "horror" from terror and other forms of violence akin to what I suggest distinguishes surplus cruelty and the macabresque from other forms of violence.[9] She writes, "The work of horror does not concern imminent death from which one flees, trembling, but rather the effects of a violence that labors at slicing, at the undoing of the wounded body and then the corpse, at opening it up and dismembering it." She refers, within a context of Homeric historiography, to the desire of Achilles to cannibalize Hector's body and suggests, "Through the ceremony of the dragging of the body tied to the chariot, the offense to corporeal unity actually extends even to the outer surface that is the expression of a unique existence: the face, the physiognomy. There is no more life to rip away from the dead body, only the uniqueness of its figure." What transforms violence into the "horrorism" of human violation is fascination with corporeal disfiguration, the making visible of the hidden interiorities of the body, the disgorging of guts, the evisceration of bowels, the laceration of skin. Horror, Cavarero continues, "curdles the blood and provokes repugnance or a fright that petrifies" and adds, "the most authentic image of ontological crime, stripping them of any heroic pretext" that "goes beyond homicide, indeed it represents a killing that overshoots the elementary goal of taking a life and dedicates itself instead to destroying the living being as a singular body, such that repugnance . . . is, in a certain sense, nothing other than an organic repulsion with respect to the violent act that deforms it."[10] Cavarero's notion of horror, of "organic repulsion" in response to acts or scenes of violence, ones that elicit visceral repugnance, is all about disgust, the kind of deep phobic aversion to the representations of human physicality, its animality, that evoke horror. This is what human violation in the macabresque signifies, however, surplus overflow of omnipotent willfulness and self-righteous emotionality on the part of perpetrators. They enter the dramaturgy of the macabresque to defy the screens of horror in the name of honor and obligation but as the self-deceptions necessary to approach forbidden *jouissance* while all the time keeping it away.

This is suggestive of the origins of *desire* inherent in *demand* for the macabresque in mass atrocity. The demand is the demand for the desire of the victim, nay, to become the cause of desire in the victim as a way of approaching the *jouissance* of victim's desire. Perpetrators seek what Sofsky called absolute power; but what does "absolute power" over victims mean if not fantasmatic allures of *jouissance* in desire, the very desire that is the cause of all desiring, the *jouissance* of enchantments made accessible through the obscene supplements of thing-enjoyment? The macabresque partakes of the very essences of the obscene in its forbidden sado-intimacies. And for these reasons, at times of sensed collective shame and humiliation, calls to honor and for revenge can become the ideological shibboleths demanding return to "rightful order" and/or "righteous justice." But in social fantasy these demands represent the desires to reinstall, albeit on murderous terms, the phallic law of paternal order to keep *jouissance* away but also to imbibe it through violations of victims.

FIGURES IN FANTASY

The practices of the macabresque in mass atrocity appear to evoke desire for cruelty at one moment but provoke horror at the next. Žižek detects *jouissance* in the "surplus-obedience" of an Eichmann, whose banality was to execute bureaucratic discipline but "as a kind of obscene dirty secret" and thus the superegotistical desire of a person who gave every appearance at trial in believing his own self-deception, that he did not hate Jews, that he did not intend their annihilation. What this indicates, Žižek observes, is "how the very 'bureaucratization' of the crime was ambiguous in its libidinal impact," how it contributed to what Žižek calls the "obscene superego supplement" of enjoyment. "The executioners experienced their deeds as a kind of 'transgressive' activity, as a kind of pseudo-Bakhunian 'carnivalesque' activity," he comments, that added to rather than depleted its "surplus enjoyment." The very process of normalizing the administration of mass atrocity and genocide provided the *jouissance* intrinsic to "the perverse ritual" of killing by rationalized organizational methods.

Ideology can be made to perform a duplicitous role in this regard. On the one hand, it can maintain political "innocence" in sociocultural patterns of denial, while simultaneously acting to elevate the very sense of *jouissance* conveyed in performative transgression. In each instance of "no" a certain formulaic "yes" appears. A dialectical contradiction intervenes through the paternal signifier that inverts negativity with the "positivization" of consciousness. The paternal metaphor empowers subjectivation of the subject. The negativity of the paternal signifier is the very principle that "positivizes" self-individuation: psychic "castration" permitting traversal of the fundamental fantasy permits eventual entry into language. In saying no to the fundamental fantasy, the paternal signifier enacts capacities for symbolization. Žižek picks up on Lacan's play on words between the "name" and the "no" of the father. He describes this as "a kind of theoretical anamorphasis." He writes, "The shift from *Nom* to *Non*—that is, the insight which makes us discern, in the positive figure of Father as bearer of symbolic authority, merely the materialized/embodied negation . . . the Father's majestic presence becomes visible as a mere positivization of a negative gesture."[11] He adds a Kantian twist to "the anamorphic shift" that "enables us to discern an apparently positive object as a 'negative magnitude,' as a mere 'positivization of a void.'" Žižek links this to his concept of the "sublime object" of ideology, "the spectral object which has no positive ontological consistency, but merely fills in the gap of a certain constitutive impossibility."[12] Žižek likens this inversion to the "positivization of the opposing force of 'evil' whose activity explains why the order of the

Good can never fully win;" he suggests, "One of the most elementary definitions of ideology, therefore, is a symbolic field which contains such a filler holding the place of some
structural impossibility, while simultaneously disavowing this impossibility."[13] The lack,
the gap, the social contradictions come first in this scheme; desire always comes secondarily. The paternal signifier is the ultimate stopgap measure that lives in its inverse perversity, in other words, "its 'transgression' which in fact serves as its ultimate support."[14]
The ultimate form of transgression that instates, nurtures, and sustains the law of the
paternal signifier are the enticements of *objet a*, the object of lost ecstasy, "the Thing" of
enchantment, the artifacts of *jouissance*. These embolden the promises of supererogatory
"enjoyments" that work to transform superego "activity" into the sado-intimacies of the
macabresque. These cluster around the ideological illogics of political reification to justify the macabresque: to validate the "willed" notions of exclusivist purity and supremacist security and freedom.

*Thing-enjoyment is never so compelling as when it seems to those who live in its desires
as rightful vengeance in return for aggrieved loss. Thing-enjoyment translates into surplus
cruelty under cultural conditions gripped by social fantasies of reverberating against profound collective uncertainty regarding political institutions, the continuity of authority.*
Such crises of legitimacy often appear as the results of decay or disintegration of the
founding narratives of a society: in traditional communities, from the delegitimation of
ancestors, blood, tribal or segmented lineage and kinship honor as forms of governance;
within liberal societies a wide variety of forms, including transformations of republi-
can government, civic insurrections, rebellions, revolutions, martial law, constitutional
crises, extraction, taxation and conscription revolts; demise of the social fabric, poverty, anomic alienation, and so on. All these are said to reflect the breakdown in political stability that opens the way to a felt desire to reinstate the sense of law and order.
Such desire is both the symptom and cause of thing-enjoyment. It is symptom or effect
because whenever legitimacy appears as a guide to how to desire, what to desire becomes
fragile, with tensions that are often racialized.

The consequence is to render thing-enjoyment more of a demand—not less. Whenever
thing-enjoyment becomes threatened, the desire to reassert desire becomes more urgent,
and potentially more extreme, as we saw in reference to the case studies of the macabresque. This occurs because the erosion of political legitimacy makes thing-enjoyment
anchored to the fundamental fantasy of *jouissance* seem too close for comfort. Surplus
cruelty in the macabresque thus becomes a mechanism to keep thing-enjoyment at bay.
Such designs are aimed at restoration or recourse to the sense of prohibition, so that
desire and the phallic law of separation can both operate simultaneously. Thus political reification becomes embodied in performative aesthetics as ways of reenacting the
"play" of restoration. As Chiesa observes, "My final suggestion is that, in everyday life,
such a transformation of demand into pure desire is paradoxically achieved when, instead
of always demanding 'something else,' we contingently demand something specific in an
inflexible way, at any price."[15]

Surplus cruelty is the price of inflexibility of demand. Desire emerges in recompensatory fantasy-objects of displacement, substitution, or surrogacy over and beyond the loss of the fundamental fantasy; such objects never fully attain the full status of the "real thing." Chiesa states, for example, "the fundamental fantasy is nothing less than what structures the unconscious to be understood as primal repression: in this sense, it is both 'fundamental,' insofar as it constitutes the synchronic structure of the unconscious according to which the 'true articulation between desire and its object' should be understood.'"[16] Chiesa continues by citing Lacan's emphasis on the diachronic mobility of desire to situate itself in variable ways relative to the fundamental fantasy of *jouissance*. "The subject's desire is not adjusted to a pregiven object, but must learn to adjust itself to a phantasmatic object."[17] But the synchronic impact of this is both "lack" and "loss" that incites a primal uncertainty, perhaps a primordial skepticism, regarding "love" and its certainty as well as the possibilities of self-constitution. "The child," Chiesa writes, "is confronted with the fundamental lack in the (m)Other—with the fact that his own demands cannot ultimately be recognized by the Other—and thus 'fails in his certitude' of being the exclusive imaginary object of the (m)Other's love: at the same time, and for the same reason," Chiesa indicates, "the child is equally unable symbolically to 'name himself as subject,' he 'fails in his designation as subject' precisely inasmuch as there is no Other of the Other, there is no signifier that 'might guarantee the concrete consequences of any manifestation of the signifier,' that is, the child's symbolic demand for love."[18]

And it is here at this critical juncture between the fundamental fantasy and unconditional demand for love that desire emerges to be the lack that fulfills the desire of the (m)Other. It unfolds, first, in the constitution of the subject, and secondarily, in the directionality of human will and motivation. "The only way out of this impasse," Chiesa comments, "the only way to constitute himself as subject, is for the child precisely to locate himself at the level of lack of the Other as the failing/lacking subject."[19] Human personality thus develops in the form of "a desiring *manque-à-être*." Desire is born in the failure of psychosocial certitude. Ideology is the product of existential or incertitude that serves as a bulwark against lack and loss. Chiesa ironically cites Lacan in declaring, "Not giving up on one's desire, the well-known motto of Lacanian ethics, necessarily presupposes—and, in practice, problematically resolves itself into—not giving up on one's demand."[20] Political reification results from lack of lack and is nurtured by the quest for thing-enjoyment in *recompensatory* strategies seeking enchantment. As such, it derives from a depleted psychic process for acquiring the capacities for symbolization that point toward what Chiesa describes as "dialectic of frustration." He writes, "Therefore, in order to desire the lack that (the) desire (of the Other) is, desire has to remain fundamentally unsatisfied; it has to continue to desire, to desire to desire.[21]

Desire arises as a function of the double negativity *in lack of lack*. Castration and the renunciation of the fundamental fantasy of *jouissance* imply the lack of lack on account of a surplus left over from the absence—that is, from the "foundational hole" in the m(Other) that sustains desire. But the fundamental fantasy is never far away. Again,

Chiesa, indicates, "It is possible to desire the lack only insofar as it emerges as lack through the retroactive reification of the imaginary 'veil' in the fundamental fantasy. The desire of the Other cannot be *desired* directly, and so one *repeats* one's desire for it."[22] That desire relates to, but functions as distinct from, either physiological need or psychic demand is critical to an understanding of the operations of political reification. Reification inheres in desire and desire is surrogacy for both need and demand. As Lacan stated, "The desire for the mother cannot be satisfied because it is . . . the abolition of the whole world of demand, which is the one that at its deepest level structures man's unconscious."[23] Chiesa infers from this, "There is a perfect compatibility between the desire for incest as 'fundamental desire' and the repetition of the 'unsatisfied' desire for the Other's desire as 'mitigated' phantasmatic lack; the *desire* for incest, the desire for the mother as lost object (the Thing as hole), is indeed nothing but the desire to be desired by the (m)Other's desire as lack."[24] *Political reification adheres to skewed or "disordered" desire that spins over and again in pursuit of itself by condemning itself to pursue the unwillable in order to capture in fantasy the very jouissance that is itself sequestered in the pursuits of desire.* These psychodynamics come to ground perpetrator hate, contempt, and sadistic violations in the macabresque.

Lacan likened *objet a* to *agalma*, an ambrosia fit only for Gods, but also profane, a residue of titillation but not simply the object of desire since is it the "object-cause of desire," the pure desire of the desiring subject. Such are the motor forces of human motivation in the polar turbulences of lack of lack, the want of being, Being toward Death, the chronic yearning for return to lost enchantment. Here the quest of Don Quixote becomes emblematic, the Don Quixote whose very name stands for a love forever unrequited since its only reality resides in its impossibility. Lack of lack, lost ecstasy, the fantasies of rapturous return, skew human motivations in the quests for kinds of purification that resist the passions of desire, but in that very ambition give way to them.

This, too, is suggestive of perpetrators efforts to "purify" themselves and the cultures of those reified as impure by means of performativity. And the keys are the macabresque aesthetics of *surplus* cruelty aimed at capturing the excesses of thing-enjoyment by means of performativity. Simon Critchley adumbrates this when he writes, "It is, rather, that *the aesthetic intimates the excess of the ethical over the aesthetic.* In other terms, the real (as the realm of the ethical) exceeds the symbolic (the realm of the aesthetic) but the latter provides the only access to the former."[25] Critchley concludes, "Thus, access to the real or the ethical is only achieved through a form of symbolic sublimation that traces the excess within symbolization." Macabresque performativity and dramaturgy (aesthetics) in the surpluses of cruelty during mass atrocity provide the misbegotten avenues to the "ethical." In this perspective, reality and the non-real displace each other.

Memories of narrated history shape national fantasies of desire and what is desired turns into the ideologies of historical memory that justify collective desires in ways that reify "difference" to the point of mass atrocity. For such reasons, historical memory sometimes stands in the balance between honor and false rectitude. It was how the German nation "remembered" the Treaty of Versailles ending the First World War that allowed them to "accept" the Nazi allegation that it was Jews who had "stabbed Germany in the back" lead-ing led to the German defeat in World War I. The Serbian "memories" that led to eth-nic cleansing "remembered" Kosovo as shamefully lost. Thousands of Croats took to the streets of Zagreb and other cities to protest the conviction of Ante Gotovina, announced on April 15, 2011, by the International Criminal Court for the former Yugoslavia (ICCFY). Ante Gotovina had been the commanding officer of the "lightning" military campaign named Operation Storm. This 1995 campaign to retake land on Croatia's eastern border with Serbia that had been seized by the Serbs brutally expelled Serbs from the Krajina area of Croatia. The ICCFY found Gotovina guilty on seven of eight counts of war crimes, crimes against humanity, murder, deportation, and inhuman acts. In the immediate after-math of the conviction, vast majorities of Croats regarded him as a "national liberator" and a "popular folk hero," in effect, rejecting the guilty verdict of the ICCFY.[26] Gotovina him-self became transformed into a fantasy figure, an image designed to help shape Croatia's memory of itself as an "identity" harmed by loss, in a world of misunderstanding that only a Croatian could understand. This reflects the psychodynamics of melancholy in the col-lective mourning of a people unable to come to grips with its own past by letting go of its essentializing myths. But such desires exist because they are impossible to satisfy. That is, they exist as the object cause of desire not as the object of desire.

POLITICAL REIFICATION IN FACT AND FANTASY

Beyond the substantive content of what comprises historic memory, these reactions illus-trate the features of political ideology that combine unconscious fantasy with conscious reification:

- Ideology arises in fantasy, deploys "reality" as a support mechanism to maintain its symptoms of desire and "enjoyment."
- It impedes access to *jouissance* by becoming affixed to fantasy-objects.
- Fantasy-objects are objects of desire as well as phobic objects of disgust.
- Fantasy-objects are introjected psychic objects that become projected externally through psychodynamic processes of imagistic "objectification and reification."
- Ideology is "empty"; it is built into political disorders of self-deception; it mani-fests logics of illogic not open to confirmation, validation, or falsification.
- Interior fantasy-objects of desire and disgust represent the exterior reality trans-formed and projected outwardly in logics of illogic.
- Political reification destroys genuine "symbolization."
- Political reification tends to be transpersonal, culturally constructed, and collec-tively confirmed.

Reifications, or the externally reified images of "objectified" but internally constructed "partial objects," provoke behaviors that manifest disorders of will. Such behaviors often invoke self-righteous or litigious forms of justification. These demonstrate doctrinaire logics of illogic that are "empty" and devoid of critical or analytical substance. Kosovo became a kind of fantasy-object instructing Serbs on how to desire. But so, too, is it with other "national identities" that experience the fantasies that are misrecognized. Žižek describes fantasy with a Lacanian twist as "*the very screen that separates desire from drive*: it tells the story which allows the subject to (mis)perceive the void around which drive circulates as the primordial loss constitutive of desire."[27] In this perspective, reifications of "otherness" originate in the surrogacy of substitution and displacement.

This psychodynamic process invites collective strategies to scapegoat the victims who are reified as the agents of "embezzlement" about to steal *jouissance*, the thing-enjoyment of lost ecstasy or enchantment. The disorder of will in political reification circulates around its demand for the fulfillment of desire that can never be satisfied but deemed accessible if not for the "other" who steals it, possesses it, refuses to renounce it, and who therefore must be made to suffer. This is in the nature of the mimetic rivalry as we saw in the case of both the Cambodian and Rwandan genocides and in the other examples of the macabresque. "Fantasy provides a *rationale* for the inherent deadlock of desire: it constructs the scene in which the *jouissance* we are deprived of is concentrated in the Other who stole it from us." Žižek 's example is "the anti-Semitic ideological fantasy, social antagonism is explained away via reference to the Jew as the secret agent who is stealing social jouissance."[28] Political reification is thus a defense against drive, thing-enjoyment and the demand for *jouissance*. Nonetheless it functions as a comfort mechanism, fraudulent and misrecognized, but for all that, tempting. It soothes the voracious demand for a kind of fantasized magic longed for in avaricious quests to fill the existential void with the blood, body and being of others who now become victimized by virtue of their identification with lost or stolen *jouissance*. *From a Lacanian perspective, these represent the sources of ethnic-grievances, racism, ethnic hatred; these are the origins of the mystified forms of self and otherness among perpetrators that foster the surplus cruelty in cases of mass atrocity, and during the dynamics of enemy-making.* Under certain prevailing conditions, political reification targets social segments or cultural groupings in ways leading to the demand for surplus cruelty as a form of collective superegotistical "enjoyment" in the name of "higher" or supererogatory causes, as experienced by those caught or captured by the fantasy-objects or frames of images that allow no genuine forms of symbolization.

VISION WITHOUT SIGHT

Objectification, essentialization, and political reification represent akratic strategies designed to preserve psychic unity, stability, and wholeness but at the cost of self-deception, imaginative closure, and spiritual concealment. Political reification may be likened to a form of dysfunctional perception in which fantasies abound like the haze of dreams while vision becomes occluded. A way to understand political reification, therefore, is to conceive of it as a process of perception that precludes *insight*. It adheres to a psychodynamics of images, imagistic formations, collective imaginaries, all closed to self-reflexive or critical symbolization in ways that block collective understandings open to doubt, skepticism, and contestation.

To explore this, let us recall the making of silent film in the early days of photography technology. Film grew out of photographic alignments in which single photographs constituted a frame or image that when attached alongside others and focused in rapid succession created the illusions of movement. To watch silent film is to experience photography in motion, slide by slide, frame by frame. What one sees as reality is the colliding images of individual frames running together at a pace that tricks the eye into believing that motion is the reality when in fact the collective image is comprised of single frames that are in every sense of the word—motionless. This is suggestive of the very structural nature of political reification. The structural character of reification does not determine the substantive content of imagery any more than the rapidity of individual photographic frames in itself determines the content of the actualized film. The substance of reification varies as does the contents of silent film. What the structure in film as well as in reification reveals is the relationship between what is seen and what remains unseen, what is believed and what goes misrecognized or undetected in the production of collective images.

For heuristic purposes let's rework an interpretation of the static motion of silent film projection around an examination of the structure of collective political reification. In a sense, the film in silent film, what the viewing spectators (one hesitates to use the term, "audience," given the latter's etymological emphasis on hearing and thus on words rather than images) see are the fleeting frames of content in the film perceived as representative of reality. The film made from the sequence of frames constitutes in this heuristic example what we might understand as ideology, that is, collective orders of belief made from the content of framed images spun and sewn together invisibly to establish a sense of reality from the nonreality of each slide or frame constituted individually but projected together in rapid sequence. The slides or individual frames that constitute the film, the ideology, the sense of reality in the content of the film, provide a basis for interpreting fantasy-objects or frames that ground the ideological content. They are the partial objects of fantasy since they are partially visible, partially accessible to self-understanding, although their partiality, their fantasy "anchor," tends to be denied or rejected as reality. Nonetheless, they are representative of non-reality, the very non-reality that supports the fantasy reality of the film or ideology, that is, the non-reality that is perceived as reality, the reality of the film in motion. But both the film in motion and the set of individual slides or frames that comprise the film function in the concealed absence of the motor force in which reality and non-reality collide or coincide.

Lacan captures this in the struggle of the libidinal or Real in the Imaginary, in the battle of the ego in the Imaginary against the superego in the Symbolic and the conflict of the Symbolic to be free from the imagistic hold of both the Real and the Imaginary, that is, to be free of symptom, the symptom of lost *jouissance* in ideological or political reification. To extend the heuristic one step further, the relationship of film in motion and the motion of pictures framed in and by individual slides, that is, the relationship of ideology and the content of what is accepted as reality, on the one hand, and the partial fantasy-objects, on the other, is established by the light and energy of the projection mechanism that sets the process in motion but which is never seen or experienced. In Lacanian terms this mechanism originates in the "plus a minus" of *das Ding* in phallicized lost ecstasy and enchantment and in the maternalized double negativity of lack of lack.

Reification operates on the fault lines of the double negativity of lack of lack plus a minus of lost ecstasy relative to *das Ding* and the paternalized or phallic laws of prohibition. These are the defaults made up of *jouissance* and the demand for its enjoyment; of temptation and titillation distilled into the quest for *objet a* but coupled with dread if ever *jouissance* were to appear as actualized. These are the boundaries established between demand and desire, imagistic containments and supererogatory demands propelled by superegotistical and in extremist cases, perverse desire. These psychopolitical conditions are traced in the symptomatic political ontology of akratic willfulness. What motivates "the film" of ideology being taken as "reality" is the attempt to return to the source of projection, *das Ding*, through the circuitous route of fantasy-objects or isolated slides and frames that emanate out from *objet a* and *jouissance* but that in themselves prevent, block, and impede all efforts to enjoy them. Ideological demand grounded in akratic disorders of will trussed in superegotistical desire and trumpeted as supererogatory obligation configured by the collective disguises and self-deceptions of political reification represent the consequence. This represents the psychodynamics at the motivational core of what perpetrators *are* as they set about the task of performative violation in the macabresque. It is as if a single frame or a subset of slides locks in so that fewer and fewer images control the film as it projects the (non)reality of ideology. In disorders of will, the focus of desires narrows the perceptual field of understanding to a limited range of reified images, that is, to the slides that frame the fantasy-objects that float in non-logical sequences that nonetheless have become or are "willed" to be fixed and frozen as the non-reality of the film moves on. And for these reasons, the psychodynamics of disordered political reification combine elements not only of repetition but also of self-deception.

CATHECTIC HAUNTS

The concept of trauma framed within the analytical language of political reification underscores the larger methodological point that fantasy and the unconscious represent structures and dynamics of human personality relevant to the study of politics, and especially political ontology, once captured in extremist violence. The psychosocial perspective emphasizes the relationship of what is undetected in whatever is seen. Boothby places this methodological perspective within the context not only of psychoanalysis but also of ontological philosophy. He writes, for example, "The strangely compelling claims of certain memories, dream images, compulsive ideas, phobias, and fetishes in which the psychoanalyst discerns the workings of the unconscious are describable by the phenomenologist as the coming-to-presence of somehow exceptional or privileged appearances." Boothby adds, "The Freudian problematic particularly resembles Heideggerian phenomenology, for which every coming into appearance is correlative with a disappearance, every revealment conditioned by a concealment." Political reification in genocide and mass atrocity begins—not ends—with the frozen images of victims ideologically selected for degradation, dehumanization and demonization. It grows out of the imagistic grips of the split ego in the Imaginary structured by representations and secondary representations configured into ideal ego and ego-ideal. It resides in the supererogatory disciplines of sadistic excess. It proceeds through the primary patterns of moral masochism and unconscious forms of masochistic self-incrimination. It is driven by superegotistical fantasies emanating within the psychodynamics of the rival self-other in relation to the subject of the self. It revolves around the surpluses of thing-enjoyment guided by the forbidden proscriptions of *jouissance* and of *objet a*. It reflects the radical alterity of self, (m) Other and recursive cultural influences. These are some, hardly all, of the hidden psychic structures, influences and dynamics at work in the external outcomes we know and (mis) recognize as motivations in conscious thought that play out eventually in the political and ideological reifications rightly associated with hate speech and, in the present context, the macabresque. "It is what remains hidden in the heart of what is most manifest that interests Freud," observes Boothby. From this perspective, theoretical and empirical students of politics are not always the most effective forensic sleuths. "Freud is attracted by the way presence is haunted by absence. There is always an unconscious staging, an invisible, conditioning ground out of which the conscious rises up."[29]

This underscores the central relationship between words and images, between the Imaginary and the Symbolic, between the imagistic and the symbolic. Ideology gives way to what Freud might have called cathexis and anticathexis, a kind of *besetzung* or investment that includes repression, what Boothby suggests is "the unfolding of a symbolic process [that] has been submitted to the force of an imaginary effect . . . . that now functions to obstruct the further play of associations . . . bound to a particular representation . . . under the influence of a 'fixation.' "[30] Political reifications inhere in the repressions of the Imaginary and thus provide access to explanatory understandings of the relationship of psychic fixations to the "empty" words of ideology, in particular, those transformed into the shibboleths that call upon armed citizenry to serve as the warriors of political evil—all in the name of what is represented as "noble cause," "higher virtue," and "sacred honor." The psychodynamics reveal the structural commitment of psychoanalytic theory that envisions consciousness as a support system for the unconscious. As Boothby indicates, "For this reason, perceptual cathexis must be considered to be an indispensable moment in the constitution of the unconscious and the maintenance of repression." Boothby describes this as "the central enigma brought to light" by psychosocial theory: "it is in and through consciousness that the unconscious maintains itself."

Surplus cruelty in macabresque theatricality and aesthetics involving sustained and staged mass atrocity represents a process by and through which unconscious fantasy functions relative, first, to the various structural levels of reification and, secondly, to the collective fixations used to trigger systematic violations of political segments of domestic national populations. But the symbolic operates not merely according to the imagistic fixations of the Imaginary but as a network of signifiers open to endless shifts, metaphorical substitutions and sliding chains of metonymic meanings. Language and a genuine capacity for symbolization adhere not in imagistic foreclosure but to imaginative games and creative innovation to the extent that human personality is able to free itself of imagistic capture and to engage in the true work of imaginative play. "Every symbolic process," writes Boothby, "must take its point of departure from a perceptual registration but proceeds along the trajectory of signification only by evacuating the initial investment of attention in the perceptual contour of the sign."[31] Consciousness and unconsciousness travel along the pathways set by the words in the Symbolic and the imagistic in the Imaginary and their interplay and thus, "it is among the primary purposes of normal, waking consciousness to distinguish these two levels, to ensure that the subject does not mistake words for things"—the fundamental feature of self-deception and political reification in the macabresque.[32]

NORMALCY AND PSYCHOSIS: THE EXTERIORITY OF INNER VOICES

Perpetrators of genocide and mass atrocity, and those enlisted in service of enemy-making, tend to be considered theoretically and methodologically as "normal"—not abnormal in their perverse desires despite horrendous crimes against personhood and humanity. This represents the conundrum presented by perpetrators of mass atrocity that the entire discourse over the banality of evil fails to resolve. But the irony here is that the surplus cruelty performed by perpetrators is structurally akin to a psychotic state in one major sense. During psychotic delusions, the boundaries of self and externality are extinguished; interior psychic images turn into externalized "voices" that transmute into the voice of the self. These often exhort external behaviors relative to imagistic figures in ways that erode the capacities of any human personality to maintain its own continuity. In the case of the psychotic, it is the voices that overwhelm, the interior voices experienced as external calls, speaking in words that flow in tsunamic or tidal waves of sounds that become instantly transmuted into images beyond control. In such instances, reification haunts and taunts the mind with empty words or symbols; but these are experienced imagistically as things in themselves. This occurs in the absence of any imaginative or mental capacity for cognitive mediation or symbolic negotiation. This is the non-real form of reality in psychotic fantasies that threaten the very stability of the person so affected. One can only imagine the pain of it when words and images form collisions in the mind bereft of meaning on account of a surfeit of imagistic immediacy. "The relation between words and things breaks down," Boothby observes, "with the result that words are mistaken for things. The problem for the paranoid psychotic is that *everything* has become meaningful . . . .

Having lost its anchorage in the imaginary, the play of the signifier rushes over the falls of cascading associations."[33]

In this sense, the voices of ideology and political reifications resemble the voices of psychosis, voices absent meaning because of too much meaning, devoid of information, on account—not of too little—but of too much data. Reality is no longer a support for fantasy once fantasy and reality become fused in the reification of representations that conflate things with their images and images substitute for things in themselves. This is the essence of the symbolic compression or equation that operates most dangerously in psychosocial processes once identity becomes disfigured into naturalized identities and essentialized difference. Infantile experiences shape the fantasies associated with "identification." These psychosocial processes involve: identification of self in relation to others, particularly with respect to the "m(Other)" of culture; the (m)Other of the maternal signifier; the paternal signifier that makes symbolization possible beyond the fundamental fantasy; and the role of the phallic fatefully linking the inscription and stability of the law with desire to overcome the demand to be the lack in the (m)Other's lack thereby depleting demands to return to lost ecstasy or *jouissance*.

In the psychic and emotional processes marked by Oedipal resolutions, these dynamics devolve into structural forms of the "rival self-other" that is, ego structures in the Imaginary and superegotistical structures in the Symbolic. These generate the indelible marks or the "insignia" of the cultural fixations that serve as the platform of ideological constructions in human personality. Psychosocial theory suggests that fantasies grow out of the primary double negativity of lack of lack plus a minus of loss and thus they emerge as a kind of psychic "positivity" within the unconscious spaces and/or recesses beset by lack and loss. Fantasies work with varying degrees of efficacy or dysfunctionality to maintain social stability and continuity. Primary fantasies are in some sense control mechanisms partially guided by superegotistical functions. Since superegotistical dynamics are in a certain sense control of fantasy controls, fantasy and their objects represent a major factor in understanding the psychosocial nature of desire and how desire fuels ideological and political reification. In this perspective, fantasies and ideology may be viewed as mutually implicated replete with reciprocal interactions, influences and outcomes. Together they shape psychosocial and emotional life of perpetrators, with all its desiring, skewed purposes, and akratic forms of motivation and intentionality.

Parables of the Prodigal Brother

Ideologies receive support from unconscious fantasy in fluid and plastic ways, but also in a manner that sustains human personality and collective order. Social fantasies shape ideological confrontations with the political world and influence how and in what ways entire societies become collectively defensive or aggressive. Mutuality between ideology and fantasy is in turn reflected in the reciprocal dynamics between conscious thought and unconscious fantasies. These are subject to shifts according to human and social threats, demands, and desires. An adequate theoretical perspective on ideology would emphasize unconscious fantasy and the "reality" supports it provides relative to (mis)recognized ideological constructions. The question arises as to the extent to which fantasy shape constructions of ideology or alternatively how and in what way ideologies intrude on fantasy. As indicated earlier, some schools of psychoanalysis, including the "object relations school," distinguish phantasies (*ph*) from fantasies (*f*) to stress how daydreams in *conscious* thought differs from *unconscious* phantasies and phantasmatic scenarios consisting of narratives that position a subject around specific goals or objectives related to the fundamental "phantasy." The question in the present analysis concerns how fantasies formed out of the fodder of primary infantile experiences play a role or influence perpetrator behaviors in and during instances of genocide and mass atrocity. In this context, fantasies and fantasy objects of desire point toward intimate psychic experiences that play out in the transsubjective or transrelational social, cultural, and political lifeworlds. Žižek observes, "In every ideological edifice, there is a kind of 'trans-ideological' kernal, since, if an ideology is to become operative and effectively 'seize' individuals, it *has* to batten on and manipulate some kind of 'trans-ideological' vision." Thus, "*it is only [in] reference to such a trans-ideological kernal which makes an ideology 'workable.'*"[34] And in psychosocial perspectives, these so-called trans-ideological kernals flourish from the soil of double negativity plus a minus that lead to the quest for *jouissance* and *objet a* in the shells of desire that ground collective political identities in fantasies of self and otherness, belonging and difference, purity and freedom. Fantasy guides how and what to desire within the interiorities of human personality, whereas ideology instructs on how to realize desire in the material cultures that shape the lifeworld of collective existence.

Fantasy-objects of desire are realized in the "normative" range of choices, values and preferences ideologically available but which are as a result limited and foreclosed thus doomed to repetition. Lost wax methods of sculpture illustrate how political reifications and ideologies operate to restrict choices based in desire formatted culturally but that appear to be open or even universal. Lost wax involves a series of molds poured within an original model constructed of wax, clay or other material and amenable to sculptural form. Strong or rigid molds are poured within the original model or sculpture along with other softer molds that act as exact negatives of the original model. The final sculptural reality is formed by the molds based on the model. In some sense, fantasy is in the model that negotiates between the reality/ideology represented by the mold that takes shape around the fantasy and eventually emerges as the shape and form of the model, that is, the reality of the sculpture cast by and in fantasy but now constituted in ideology as the very reality that is the sculpture. Within the context of genocide and mass atrocity, political reifications and ideologies sustain illusions of choice at the very instance when collective intentionality becomes disordered by the nonchoices of perpetrators' motivations. Ideologies nurture attitudinal belief in the self-deceptions of perpetrators that they are uniquely called to greatness. As such, perpetrators of many stripes evidence proclivities for the appeals of covenantal selection. Ideologies of selection delude by

pandering to fantasies of desire for a sense of unique purpose or "chosenness." How tragically ironic it is that those who would assert their uniqueness in the name of selection so
often become the perpetrators of horrendous cruelty reified as "necessary" in the select
service of higher political aims. These self-serving personal self-deceptions and collective
delusions wrapped in the ideological constructions of select uniqueness, historic obligation, (dys-)utopian ideals, and so on, tend to become operative at the very political crossroads where ideology and desire combine to produce collective patterns not of unique
selection but, to the contrary, of utter conformity. This is what ideology is—collective
misrecognition—that provides the appearance of personal choice and absolute uniqueness, but at the critical junctures where fantasies of desire are most mimetically replicated
across a society. This is the meaning of totalitarianism, but it is also a reflection of the
modernist conditions of national political existence across the cultural and institutional
spectrum ranging from authoritarian to democratic.

Yet, again, we confront the significance of deliberative speech and symbolic openness
in the making of a political subject empowered by a capacity to diagnose critically the
symptoms of desire. Žižek refers "to the radical ambiguity of fantasy within an ideological space: fantasy works both ways, it simultaneously *closes the actual span of choices . . .*
and *maintains the false opening.*"[35] Mass atrocity and genocide situate their perpetrators
in the empty spaces of political evil, empty spaces with empty words and empty choices,
but where choices are made nonetheless. Mass atrocity is disordered and destined to fail
for all its power to hurt and cause grievous harm and pain. It shows how motivations
and intentionality based on fantasy-objects of desire tantalize through empty promises
of thing-enjoyment, but always in order to inflame the sense of loss and frustration. This
is, after all, what allows desire to remain desire.

Modern political formations constituted by identitarian constructions of collective
belonging, state sovereignty and ethnic (plus) differences have helped to generate modernist ideological "styles" of collective desire that inhere in fantasies of frustrated desire.
Frustrated desire lends itself, first, to self-blame not least on account of the guilt and
shame associated with notions of failed fulfillment, but also, secondly, to the projection
outward of blame onto to others who as a result become reified precisely in terms of
their "otherness." Society becomes like the Prodigal Brother who resents the Prodigal
Son for what he is, had, and wasted even though the Prodigal Father tells the brother to
forgive and forget and to become reconciled with the Prodigal Son since he, the Prodigal
Brother, is everything the Father is and has everything the Father possesses. This is the
story written over and over again in the annals of surplus cruelty and political evil in keeping with the character of the macabresque to perform its symptoms over and over again.

DISAPPEARING SIGNIFIERS, EVAPORATING LEGITIMACY:
METONYMIC DISPLACEMENTS IN THE UNCONSCIOUS

Lacanian theories of language envision a dual configuration of signifier chains. Signifiers
become arranged through a series of metonymic substitutions or displacements and/or

become organized around metaphoric singularities that condense diffuse elements and conflate them into intensive value-laden images. Lacanian structuralism thus theorizes the intersections of vertical and horizontal mental representations of desire in the unconscious: the first denoted by metonymy, the second by metaphor. In a sense, Lacan's philosophy of language establishes a kind of nonstructuralist structuralism by envisioning the unconscious as a process of formation anchored to and framed by the intrusions of the Other. Peter Klepec refers to this aspect of Lacanian theory by stating, "If he claims that discourse is the structure which goes beyond speech and which can subsist without words, he is, contrary to all appearances and conjunctions, not a structuralist. . . . from the very beginning we enter in *relations* with others through the medium of speech and language; that this medium (speech; language; symbolic order; structure) has a formative function for us and thus brings certain consequences (we are not masters of language, but on the contrary, we are spoken by it; the Other precedes the subject."[36] Metonymic constructions operate horizontally through the sequential ordering of displacements and substitutions. The subject learns to speak through fluid associations within contexts framed by "an enunciating subject" who engages in the surrogacy of displaced or substituted signifiers. From the perspective of subjectivation, metonymic constructions represent structural devices in the unconscious to conceal the subject's relationship to desire by substituting certain signifiers and displacing them with others. Identity slides across glaciers of fragility and indeterminacy.

Vanheule, following Lacan, indicates, "When metonymy is at work an illusion to the identity of the subject is present, but does not clearly define him. Through metonymy the speaking subject is connoted, without actually being defined in its identity."[37] Later, he adds, "Subjectivity fades under the signifying chain. In metonymy, an enunciating subject is at work, yet at the level of signification, no enunciated subject is produced. Metonymic speech does not attribute a clear position to the subject, and therefore it can be qualified as 'empty.' "[38] Linguistic fluidity functions in ways that challenge the relationship of speech to its full possibilities for meaning. Žižek illustrates the Lacanian implications of imagistic metonymy for an understanding of ideology with reference not to hate speech but to the empty word, "duck," in the Marx Brothers film, "Duck Soup" in which the words, "duck," "viaduct," and "bridge" have all become metonymically transposed. They thus symbolically refer to the same objective, to meet someone at the "bridge," at the "viaduct"—that is, at the "duck." Why the duck? The answer is that ducks swim under the bridge or viaduct. The "bridge" becomes the displaced word, the "duck" the word that performs or represents the displacement; each collapse into the other. Žižek concludes, "The key feature here is that *the question (about why this name) is inscribed into the name itself.*"[39] The word "encodes" sets of reified meanings willed to be true through imagistic closures that paradoxically operate by means of an open series of semantic displacements metonymically embedded in ideological logics that play on but also serve to obscure social reality.

Metonymic speech clustered into fantasies of surrogate associations as such is suggestive for psychosocial theory linking disorders of will and political reification. Overlays of reification adhere to empty forms of speech based on imagistic representations "willed" into presence or actuality and thus *akratically* represented as "reality." The "lie," as Frosh called it, becomes the image and the image becomes transformed into "truth" as truth becomes subservient to metonymic substitutions or displacements, in hate speech, prejudice, and stereotyping, as well as during times of genocide and mass atrocity, as well as in all instances of enemy-making. From this perspective, political reifications suffused by themes of hatred represent forms of metonymic displacement, the functional equivalent of signifier-to-signifier surrogacy. Victims are subjected to projection formatted into ideological reifications based on mental mechanisms of substitution on the part of perpetrators. These entail what Murer describes as "proxy narratives."

This psychosocial tradition takes its originating framework from Saussurean theories of language and combines it with Freudian psychoanalysis to develop a psychosocial perspective with respect to perpetrators of mass atrocity. Murer refers to "the politics of Trianon in post-communist Hungary" and the trauma of historic loss that fostered the sense of national humiliation and collective "debasement" resulting from the 1920 Trianon Treaty that ceded a major portion of what had been Hungary. Primary trauma over Trianon became reincarnated after the empty promises of the Cold War era led to downward socioeconomic mobility. The third wave of trauma occurred when the European Union failed to produce the rise in living standards some segments of the population had anticipated. Political reifications typical of far-right Magyar ethnonationalism exploded along with rampant rise of anti-Semitism. Murer's analysis demonstrates how metonymic displacements in Hungarian public discourses traveled from original trauma over loss to secondary disillusionment and from there into the depths of a kind of dread over the seemingly endless state of decline. The displacement process proceeded in ways that combined projection with abjection. Murer comments, "Further, through a process of abjection, the familiar foreigner, assimilated Jewry, was cast out, split off, as the enemy-other working to destroy 'true Hungarians.' "[40] Genuine targets of frustration were thus replaced. In their place, blameless victims now became "willed" as the "enemy-other" and thus reified by means of metonymic displacements through "empty speech" purporting to be "reality." Murer refers to this as "the linking cycle" of continuing associations that attribute new traits to "old enemies" and old traits to new enemies.[41] He writes, "The 'old' enemy-other is, therefore, responsible for 'new' losses. Successive generations may increase their union with earlier ones by invoking the narrative structures used first to create the abject. The renewed application of iconographic mechanisms, rhetorical structures, narrative imagery and shared ego representations provide the links to the past as well as appropriate structures for the present." He adds, "Hatred is particularly useful, as previously experienced rage and humiliation associated with victimization in the case of the Chosen Trauma is now validated in the new context."[42] At the core of these psychodynamics is the motivational phenomenon of abjection, a metonymic process of substitution in which the subject displaces a segment of itself, infuses it with hatred and projects it in ways external to itself, in order to establish a new and reborn "self" filled with a renewed sense of collective identity.

But the price comes high: collective self-deception. *The costs of substituting the abject for a genuine understanding of the forces prompting the trauma involve mystifications of complex reality by means of the simplistic displacements configured around the reverberations between social fantasy and political reification. Abjection and the ideologically constructed proxy narratives of hatred in ethno-exclusivism represent metonymic exercises in disordered willfulness that finds support for social fantasy in political reification.* This represents a prototypical instance of "willing the unwillable." There are many other cases of loss, trauma and metonymic displacement culminating in "proxy narratives" of political and ideological reification. Nazi vilifications of German Jews as the cause of Germany's loss in World War I, radical Hutu genocidal assaults against the Tutsis in Rwanda as revenge for perceived losses of status and power, Serb and Croat conflicts and attacks against the Bosniaks in the aftermath of the demise of Yugoslavia, and in numerous other instances of genocide and mass atrocity. All demonstrate how metonymic substitutions in social fantasy provoked by loss, trauma and/or humiliation help give rise to political and ideological reifications that employ hatred toward surrogate "abjects." The abject is a displacement mechanism permitting the rejected dimensions of the group-self to excise elements of self-disgust or shame and to push these rejected elements onto others.

THE MYSTIQUES AND MYSTIFICATIONS OF PEOPLE-AS-ONE

Homi K. Bhabha captures the essence of this when he writes, "Time and time again, the nation's pedagogical claim to a naturalistic beginning with the unchosen things of territory, gender, and parentage—*amor patriae*—turns into those anxious, ferocious moments of metonymic displacement that mark the fetishes of national discrimination and minorization—the racialized body, the homophobic defence, the single mother: the 'chosen' fixated objects of a projective paranoia that reveal, through their alien 'outsideness,' the fragile, indeterminate boundaries of the 'People-As-One.' "[43] This helps to redefine the traditional mediations associated with political legitimacy and the question of popular consent, namely the issue posed by "one and the many, the many and the one" in contexts dealing with the legitimacy of the nation-state and the congruence in political culture between top-down centralized institutions or apparatus of the state, in relation to bottom-up values, ideologies and subscriptions associated with national or massified cultures. Neill illuminates certain ethical implications of this set of political problematics.[44] He declares, "At the heart of Lacanian subjectivity is an ethical calling." He elaborates, "The *I* here is posited as purely contingent and this contingency, in turn, necessitates a certain responsibility. Faced with the 'forced' and impossible choice between meaning and being, the *I* arises in response to the *vel*, as that which assumes responsibility for the 'decision' (*de-caedere*; cutting away) taken. The Lacanian *I* is a response to the unknown and as such, insofar as it is assumed, it entails a responsibility for its own assumption."[45]

But this ethical project depends on a syntagmatic system of signification in which the subject struggles against its own fantasized defacement along the axes of lack of lack between first- and second-party signifiers and third-party phallic loss. Loss and lack are intrinsic to the passage from the Imaginary into the Symbolic. They result from the castration dynamic in which the paternal metaphor or third-party signifier establishes the "law" of separation from the "fundamental fantasy" of *jouissance* or return to completion by means of reincorporation into the body of the (m)Other. But in so doing, the paternal third-party signifier remains unable to "name" the first-party signifier of the subject beyond what desire defined in terms of *objet a* allows. And *objet a* represent the "things" of this world and thus permeated by incompletion, inadequacy, failure and doubt. In naming (m)aternal desire it bestows upon the subject a capacity to be the desire desired by the (m)Other—but only partially. Phallic loss thus becomes associated with maternal lack of being, a lack that in turn invades infantile unconscious. Lack and loss retain pervasive impact. The subject becomes divided unto itself, split and barred, only able to constitute the rival self-other of the subject relative to itself.

This is fundamental to the entire philosophical project addressed by Lacanian psychoanalysis and was subjected to a critique by Derrida on the grounds of circularity. William Egginton examines the debate between Lacan and Derrida on this issue and enters a plea in favor of Lacanian theory on this account of the grounding of human subjectivity in lack, loss, absence, and barred "splitness." Egginton begins:

> The impossibility of occupying this place becomes for Lacan the philosophical template for desire, and it is here that one of Derrida's most strident critiques can be heard because, as he points out, such a move reinstalls at the center of philosophical desire exactly the same structure that was always there, "the circular return of reappropriation toward what is most proper about the proper place, whose borders are circumscribed by lack, and so forth, through a handling of philosophical reference whose form, at least, was in the best of cases elliptical and aphoristic, and the worst, dogmatic."[46]

This critique appears to equate philosophical desire for truth with the circularity pursued in the macabresque with respect to informativeness. How to proceed out of the linguistic labyrinth of logical circularity in the quest for "truth" if it is merely propelled by the positivity generated psychically on account of existential lack. As Egginton admits, "In other words, Lacan's model seems to reinstall at the center of all searches a hole, a castration, whose filling in is what we all seek."[47] But this developmental process of subjectivation proceeds by becoming attached to another, in the Imaginary, later in the Symbolic, in ways that ground the absence, the sense of non-being or powerlessness. Egginton describes this in Lacanian terms, "The coming into being of a being who is in this way submitted to the dictates of signification, Lacan theorizes, involves a certain assumption of powerlessness: I wish to do such and such, I cannot, and so on. The proliferation of these utterances of powerlessness implicates, again, logically, the existence of an 'I' who can, who easily finds its vehicle in another party."[48]

At this juncture, moreover, analysis begins to enter a psychosocial theoretical universe. For the question becomes who or what "party" provides the constitutive dimensions to the truths of subjectivity. Egginton engages in a description of the dialogue between Lacan and Derrida to demonstrate the profound contradictions that arise in the tensions between powerlessness and plenitude, between the necessities and contingencies of truth and meaning. Egginton declares, "From the perspective of the 'castrated I' the father would thus appear to be the one who speaks from the position of plenitude, of total identity between his utterance and the body that utters it, so that his word is self-identical in the way that the word of the "I can never be." What is overlooked in many critiques of Lacanian theory, however, is that Lacan theorized this power as also modified by the inexorability of its own dependency. "The father, himself, on the other hand, or anyone who attains that position vis-à-vis another, cannot fail to know that he is just as powerless as the one who so regards him and that this point of power, this 'place of absolute master,' if it exists at all, must be occupied by someone else."[49] Egginton names this the "eternal deferral of authority of some big Other."

In this, we catch a glimpse of the profound akrasia of perpetrators who proceed on the basis of paternalized imagos and disordered will in order to execute the "law" of the big Other by means of sadistic cruelty. Such postures are ideological precisely because of their failure or inability to recognize the contingency and the powerlessness imbricated in the "plenitude" such willed self-deceptions grant to the legitimacy of power. This represents the error we have witnessed repeatedly in the macabresque of genocide and mass atrocity: the abhorrent obeisance paid to totalitarian, at best authoritarian, dictators who invest themselves and thereby become invested with the absolute "plenitude" of political power or what Derrida derided as the "privileging of the present" in a phallocentric way. Political values, liberty or equality, freedom or justice cannot be realized in ways that are absolute but only in constant tension, each against the others, in the name of what Egginton calls "that absolutely certain place of absolute uncertainty."

The aim of the macabresque, of its depraved efforts to assert absolute power over victims is to transform the contingent legitimacies of authority into the power of power, a power beyond modification and thus fated with inevitability. Such denials of the contingent dynamics of history also explain the historiographic efforts to distort history that were so central to Mao's Great Leap Forward and Cultural Revolution, Stalin's purgatory, Hitler's laboratory, and the *Ångkar* archive, as in the other instances of the macabresque. Here, too, Lacanian theory is suggestive in that it registers the psychosocial needs for the "plenitude" of power as the basis of political legitimacy. Such disorders of will in ideology deny or reject the impossibility of plenitude if and when attributed to any singular source, in particular, any single paternal imago. Egginton describes this as "the heart of the Lacanian theory of positionality," one that recognizes *"referral to an illusory position of plenitude."*[50] (Egginton attributes this to Lacan's reading of Hegel—that is, "to historicize being, to narrativize the contingencies" of life, existence, history, or truth, "one must speak as if there existed a position of absolute knowledge, of totality.") But this functions as an epistemological method of truth, *if and only if* it is modified by "the equal and opposing certainty that the existence of such a place coincides exactly with the impossibility of our ever occupying it." The macabresque, then, becomes the place where the delusions of totalized space and time become operationalized and barbarously executed in denial of the critical "as if" contingencies of life and living, history and politics. This, too, explains the drive for absoluteness in power and legitimacy.

Thus, the polar valences of loss and lack pulsate through social fantasy in discernable ways and in the macabresque with fateful consequences. Neill, for example, indicates, "Through the impossible choice of the *vel* of alienation, the subject comes to be divided from itself. In coming to be in and through the order of the symbolic, that is, the field of the Other, the subject can never be in its own place; it has no place of its own."[51] The subject is the product of dislocation. Lack and loss situate subjectivity in the interior folds of absolute, perhaps, terrifying, doubt about the signifiers of desire that enfold the subject in its triadic relationships to its life-world. The trilateral psychodynamics of Oedipal desire thus lead to the psychic loss and lack that become imprinted in infantile fantasy. Neill refers, first, to the imprint of loss relative to the maternal signifier. "In another sense, the subject's desire is of the Other insofar as it is the desire *for* the Other." He adds, "The subject desires the Other qua Other. It desires the Other in its otherness. Bound to this sense of otherness of the Other is the fact that the Other is always elsewhere. This links to a further sense in which the subject's desire is the desire *of* the Other, that is insofar as it is a desire which is always necessarily deferred."[52] The maternal as second-party signifier signifies *lack incarnate* in the representational presences of infantile unconscious.

This excites a sense of urgency in the question as to what does the desired Other want of the subject who yearns only to be the desire that is desired. Fantasy emerges in the quest for fulfillments through attempts to respond. But the triadic structure that embeds the paternal as third-party signifier fails to have the capacity or power to guarantee that the subject as first-party signifier will be the desire the (m)Other wants. The phallic third-party signifier comes with the trademarks of loss rather than with the patents of potency. *The paternal signifier thus signifies "loss" or inadequacy and situates desire on the ladders of narcissist demand, unrelenting frustration and lack of fulfillment.* The question of paternal potency, adequacy and rank permeates phallic relations precisely because it positions maternal desire in a network of competitive relations and, secondly, because it propels competitive and often conflictual jousting for recognition of desire and its legitimacy. "Who" gets "what" by way of satisfaction, "when" and "how" becomes suffused by dread and anxiety. And power often looms as a panacea even in primary schoolyards, where "My dad's—is bigger than your dad's—" becomes the prototypical mantra spoken out of the innocent mouth of babes that reveals the truth of the paternal metaphor. As a signifier it represents the mentalization of responses made necessary on account of demands that arise or are made "necessary" by structures of three.

For subjectivation to proceed, Oedipal separation, castration and entry into language require the political subject to learn how to navigate through the shoals of rivalrous desires. And power counts in this game. The paternal signifier stands for power but also its insufficiency in not being able to confer identity directly on infantile unconscious, let alone the guarantee that desire will be met at all times and in all ways. And because maternal desire becomes signified by lack and separation from maternal desire spells loss, pre-Oedipal ego formations in the Imaginary theorized as ideal ego and ego-ideal surrender to the Symbolic entry into language and human relationships fraught as they are with disappointment and risks.

This is the ultimate meaning of castration, the loss of interiorized ecstasy that derives from symbiotic bonding with exterior or externalized perfection. Inner narcissism is sustained by the illusions of return to the lost objects of desire that once were laminated onto the very fabric of embryonic skin. How quixotic is the search for the lost "thing" or the *das Ding* constituted by the unconscious fantasy of something stolen or taken as the price of being born. Desire exists as result but only in its negativity, experienced according to what it is not, never known for what it is. For these reasons, transgression of laws of desire appears to gain such allure. Thing-enjoyment becomes an incandescence that lasts throughout a lifetime and its trajectories live in the fantasies of individuals. These are contained for the most part but when triggered by situations of genocide and mass atrocity, they are released onto the stages of the macabresque.

Signifiers exist in relation to each other. The consequence of the phallic or paternal metaphor, therefore, is endless search denoted by lack or primordial want-of-being and by loss or primordial quest for lost ecstasy (that never was). Fantasized third and second-party signifiers inscribe loss and lack integers on infantile unconsciousness in different ways in different cultures. Human personality, as a result, is forever conflicted by the onslaughts of lack and loss built into the very language of the unconscious as the signifiers of fantasy becomes mentally scrolled. Language speaks through the subject; and the metonymic and metaphoric tropes that assemble into syntagmatic chains speechify the fantasies of subjects in formats that reflect but also struggle against ideal ego and ego-ideals. Neill concludes in this regard, "signifiers are not arsenal to be deployed between subjects, or, to oversimplify, words are not carriers of meaning between people, but, rather, it is the subject which is constituted in the movement of *significance* between signifiers . . . The soldier, the subject, is *given* his subjectivity through the mediating representation between one signifier, 'the flag', and other, 'the fatherland.'" Neill adds, "For Lacan signifiers operate as representations of drives."[53] But subjectivity is never satisfied with the deflections. The signifier of desire that is the first party structurally incarnated by the political subject, split and barred from *jouissance*, holds out only weak promises of satisfaction. In part, this is the consequence of the fundamental Lacanian proposition that, as Neill comments, "This signifier of the lack in the Other thus stands quite apart from other, 'normal' signifiers."[54]

This makes the quest for psychic accommodations in social fantasy ever more pressing. Signifiers relate to signifiers. The ultimate demand of human subjectivity is to ground

signification in the "button-holes" of meaning. That is what is meant by the desire to be
the desire of the desiring m(Other); but this is tempered by visceral crucibles bubbling
in unconscious signification. Phallic signifiers fail to designate the identity of the subject
relative to lack and loss, that is, with respect to the self as a subject that is split and barred
as well as in relation to second and third-party signifiers. The consequence is suggestive
for psychosocial interpretations of large-group conflict, especially in a post-colonial era
in which modern sovereign nation-states have become a near universal political formation, but also when political legitimacy of such entities remains highly contested, as evidenced by outbreaks of genocide and mass atrocity.

Third-party signifiers of phallic loss and second-party signifiers of maternal lack provides a basis for theoretical explanations of large-group violence and mass atrocity in
psychosocial perspectives. Fantasies of lack and loss consistently translate into political
reifications and ideologies to justify political conflict, enemy-making, and, in particular
mass atrocity. Correlation in itself does not constitute causality. But ideological consistencies do suggest consistent forms of social fantasy. This is revealed by political reifications that imply "loss" as a way of arguing for a *push* toward supremacist or totalized
state security, by contrast, on insisting on national "lack" as a *pull* to justify demands for
return to exclusivist national homogeneity or absolutized and thus "pure" social inclusivity. The fantasy configurations around lack and loss are not necessarily universal or
absolute any more than any single form of Oedipal triangularity is identical everywhere
for all time. But thematic consistencies appear when the "loss" in state security and the
"lack" of national identity together constitute the ideological and political reifications
constructed on the basis of unspoken fantasies of the insecurity of the "paternal" or "masculinized" state (subjected to phallic loss as pull) or the impurity and of the "maternal"
or "feminized" nation (subjected to maternal lack). These observations *do not* and *could
not* indicate direct forms of causality. These propositions comprise ways of theorizing
the relationships of social fantasy and political ideology in which the latter seeks support
through reifications aimed at buttressing fantasied fears of state dissolution, on the one
hand, and, on the other, social decadence and decay on terms that embrace anxieties or
dread over lack and loss.

During moments of extreme conflict, political and ideological loss pulls in the direction of return to the "purity" of maternal desire and physical incorporation with the
primary object of nurture. This translates into akratic desire for a kind of totalized exclusivism in cultural, social or ethnic bonding. This often leads to political reifications that
call for systematic elimination of segmented parts of the group-self now reified as foreign,
polluting, corrupting, and so on, and thus in terms of "the abject." The abject becomes
the enemy that is the obstacle to return to the lost ecstasy of completion in a collective
formation that is fantasized as potentially "pure"—except for the alien presence. The
near universal rejection of economic refugees is suggestive of such fantasies that arise
whenever specific groups are reified as alien, a concept that connotes the deepest meanings of social exclusion and vituperation. The abject represents a compensatory object

against the loss of the "Thing" of *jouissance* in the vain hopes that in exclusivism a form of bonding that is "pure" can ensue. Herein perhaps originate the forms of ideological eliminationism that would produce a paradise of totalized inclusivism by means of mass atrocity made known to its proponents by performativity in the macabresque. In turn, the role and impacts of paternalized signifiers "push" toward political reifications of power articulated in terms of fascistic state supremacism.

Perhaps herein lie the fantasmatic origins of ceaseless militarization. The social fantasy is loss of *jouissance* on account of phallic prohibition; in ideology, the state becomes threatened by loss of absolute security or power. The return to *jouissance* demands militarism. The push in lack, the pull in loss cover the void, the absence, the chronic "hole" in the register Lacan ironically named as the Real to represent the indeterminate qualities grounding the human condition. The question remains how to convert Lacanian psychoanalytic theory, in particular Lacanian structuralist theories of unconscious development, for purposes of psychosocial explanations of political reification and ideology as they become embroiled in genocide and mass atrocity. In my view, this raises a conclusionary set of issues pertaining to the nature and meaning of political legitimacy raised at the beginning of this book.

10

The Quest for the Never-Is

LEGITIMACY-GROUNDING AS ENEMY-MAKING

HYPHENATED LEGITIMACY AS ENIGMATIC SIGNIFIER

How might the first-party signifier, split and barred, be theorized in psychosocial perspectives relative the second-party signifier, maternal lack, and the third-party signifier, paternal loss or prohibition? If the subject of the first-party signifier is the product of identificatory schemes brought about in linguistic ensembles of social fantasy, how might psychosocial examination of genocide and mass atrocity be applied in particular to the study of the modern nation-state? Is it useful for heuristic and explanatory purposes to draw a homology between first-party signifiers, split and barred, with the nation-state, that is split and barred relative to sovereignty, and ultimately, legitimacy? Since its earliest days, modern international law has enshrined sovereignty as the primary subject of international discourse and the state as its main object. The linkage between sovereignty and statehood has been long forged in the irons of war and history. So, too, has the principle of self-determination and the rights of a nation or people who conceive of themselves as such to enjoy statehood. National sovereign states represent top-down forms of governance that centralize rule in terms of public goods, the obligations to defend, but also in terms of the right to conscript and tax by extracting blood and treasure from citizen populations. The nation, in turn, represents a bottom-up social formation that installs the state with the legitimacy to perform its functions in the name of popular sovereignty, particularly with respect to defending citizens, territorial boundaries, and ways of life. The nation thus represents a legitimating mechanism of the state that in turn gains its authority on the basis of popular consent. These normative principles form the three-point convergence among (second-party) nations, (third-party) states and (first-party) hyphenated constructions, the very glue of legitimacy indicated by "nation-state." First-party hyphens represent the critical signifier of incarnated collective identity concretized by nation-states and confirmed by the hyphens of legitimacy.

Problems arise, however, as a consequence anticipated by Sassurean linguistic theory and as subsequently elaborated by Lacan. Although master-signifiers buttonhole the slide across signifiers, they operate only in relation to other signifiers and are thus unable to contain the signifieds. What this suggests in terms of political analysis is that the question of legitimacy promulgated by and through hyphenated ligatures that purport to embrace nations and states in the wraps of historic necessity is always problematic. The first-party signifier of the hyphen always threatens to disappear. This risk makes political contingency appear forever threatening. The political desire for absolution of nationalist identity and for totalized statist attachments become all the more reified, all the more ideological. Third-party paternalized signifiers name the desire of second-party maternalized signifiers for purposes of interpretation on the part of the subject, split and barred as it is, but first-party signifiers are left to self-identify themselves since paternal metaphors of loss and prohibition cannot do it for them. Identity becomes the product of identificatory relationships rather than the effects of solitary confinement. Relational linkages are the keys to identity constructions in unconscious fantasy. Oedipal subjectivation situates first-party signifiers of the subject at the junctures between maternalized desire and its allures in lack and paternalized phallic separation through loss.

The subject of infantile fantasy is located at the apex of triangulated fantasized formations. These permit Oedipal dynamics to trump the evanescent grips of primordial reification. They allow infantile fantasy to enter the realm of the Symbolic; they also conduce to the illusions of originary unity. But first-party signifiers that denote the subject represent hyphenated constructions built on the shifting sands of desire, its lack and loss relative to signifiers representing the (m)Other. For such reasons, the subject tends to mythologize identity. It does so in denial of its fragile status as a signifier of the first-party. The triadic Oedipal structure that bestows upon the subject the somewhat dubious distinction of being signified merely by an "empty" hyphen hardly works to satisfy the desire for desire, particularly the drives and demands of desire for full recognition. The first-party signifier of the subject must then evacuate its own status as a hyphenated construction in favor of a consolidated signifier that appears to endow subjectivity with the convictions of purity (especially against lack) and the certitudes of necessity (especially against loss). The leap from fantasy to ideological reification results as a consequence. This tends toward a collective exercise in akratic confirmation. The hyphenated construction linking the first-party with its two structural counterparts is transformed into an akratic attempt to deny the impossibility of the subject qua unity by grounding it in a collective first-party signifier reified as natural, given and inexorable. For want of a better term, this first-party signifier may be referred to as ethnicity within the structural frames of the nation-state as a political formation that elicits support from social and collective fantasy. Just as identity construction of the subject is wrought through tripartite identificatory processes, so is the legitimacy of sovereign nation-states.

In a sense, legitimacy represents the first-party signifier linking second-party signifiers of the nation with third-party signifiers of the sovereign state. The state as third-party signifier "names" the nation as a second-party signifier across the multiple histories leading to sovereign rule, laws, defense, extraction dynamics and borders, and so on. Nations bestow upon states the recognitions of legitimacy through multifarious processes—not all democratic—but that together permit states to govern in the name of popular consent, that is, in the name of legitimacy. But the hyphenated status of state and nation in the historical constructions of the nation-state remains as dubious and problematic as the first-party signifiers of the subject. The question is: how is legitimacy, legitimated? The very posing of this question underscores the ephemeral qualities of legitimacy. It also points to reasons why it becomes charged with volatility whenever and however it is challenged. And contested it is throughout modern history, by civil wars and insurrections, secessionist insurgencies and separatist movements, by partitions and revolutions, many of which devolve into identitarian contests over ethnicity. A constant feature of struggles over legitimacy, especially those culminating in large-group conflicts, are identitarian rivalries constituted in and by what has come to be used as a generic term of identitarian differences—that is, ethnicity. The classical Greek term *ethnos* referred to "foreigner," a person originating beyond the city walls. Ethnicity in its etymological roots has always stood for the representations of "difference" in otherness.

Signifiers shift from signifier to signifier and whatever is signifieds slides under. The first-party signifier of collective identity risks becoming lost if the naming of nations by states depends on legal status alone. This is the problem that appears to confront national constituency after constituency, and the consequence is unceasing political anguish. What appears to be the problem in social fantasy may be described as follows: the paternal metaphor names maternal desire but what is the "desire" that is the "nation" if it is internally "diluted" (qua "polluted") by rivalrous "contestants" seeking privileged access to maternalized *jouissance*. If sovereign states represent third-party signifiers of paternalized security, nations represent second-party signifiers of commonality. But as we have seen the problem with commonality is that it runs into anxieties over identicality in ways that threaten what Lacan named as the lack of lack, the demise of desire, the end to the pursuits or pull of *objet a*.

Such tensions exist across the universe of nation-states in the postcolonial worlds of Africa, Asia, the Americas, and so on. In a sense, first-party signifiers work in fantasy to resist hyphenated identity constructions that would meld ethnic, racial, linguistic, and religious minorities together in blends of common desire denoted by the term "nationality." Nationality thus stands for the enjoyment of a common civic life and political membership in the community constituted by a sovereign state as a function of legal status, that is, citizenship. Citizenship is not existential; rather it is a legal status conferred by conferral of passports and other such rights and duties. Once nationality becomes conflated with existential ethnicity or race or religion or other such markers, the cultural possibilities of nationality to include citizen differences within the frames of a common nationality become limited. It readily leads to legitimacy crises, as witnessed today at the time of writing by failures in governance in the aftermath of the so-called Arab Spring, but also throughout modern history by sectarian conflicts. It is as if in the name of identity, identicality must be prevented by reifying difference by means of equating nationality with identitarian forms of particularism. This represents another way of maintaining fantasies of purity.

Ethnopolitical violence due to subnational conflicts over the nature of "purity" have been experienced virtually everywhere—in Rwanda, Yugoslavia, Cambodia, Burundi, and Darfur, to mention just a few instances. These serve as the permanent testaments to the human tragedy that occurs whenever the political/cultural linkages between nationality and ethnicity or the values of ethnic identity and difference collapse into a fantasized mindset that privileges one national identity group within a nation-state to the exclusion of all others. Excluded identity groups emerge in political cultures once citizenship or nationality becomes a kind of insignia to be possessed by one or bestowed on a few groups but denied to others, especially on the basis of objectified, sometimes racialized, ethnic difference. In many instances of mass atrocity when state or government legitimacy and ethnocultural values play a role, victims readily become marked as belonging to subnational identity group-objects. As a result, they are designated as the enemy within and thus denied the privileges and enjoyments of nationality. At times of sectarian conflict, first-party signifiers glide toward fraudulent signifiers that attempt to "naturalize" the hyphenated constructions of nation-state by eliminating the evacuated signifiers of hyphenated legitimacy. The collective insignia of the first-party signifier masks the contingencies and incertitude of nation-state legitimacy by coming to be materialized in reified formats of essentialized "blood," race and racialized markers, kinship lineage, linguistic and other particularistic features of culture, religious devotion, geographic or country of origin, and so on. These identitarian constructions become reified as the exclusive basis of nationality. Nationality becomes transfigured from an extension of historic contingency to an artifact of nature. The enigmatic signifier of legitimacy is now transmogrified into the collective insignia of reified essence.

The disappearance of difference in otherness at the level of hyphenated nationality (relative to ethnicity) means that the hyphenated constructions of legitimacy at the level of nation-state often become subjected to psychosocial akrasia. Collective disordered "will" begins to attribute substantiality to the enigmatic hyphen of the first-party signifier. Maternalized second-party signifiers of desire become the proprietary object of those who designate their identity in reified substantialist ways. And paternalized third-party signifiers of the state become reified as the instrumentality of law, which nominates some identity groups for the benedictions of citizenship in order to deny these for everyone else on the grounds that desire is only for the chosen. When social fantasies devolve into political reifications of nationality or citizenship, hyphenated constructions of collective identity become transformed. The enigmatic signifier of hyphenated legit-imacy that binds nation-states is reified; ethnicity that partakes of necessity and exclu-sionist purity becomes essentialized. Once the enigmatic signifier becomes transformed in this way by forms of psychosocial akrasia, transgressive performative violence in mass atrocity follows in the aftermath.

Just as identity is wrought by means of identificatory processes, so is the legitimacy of nation-states. The process is often burdened by a history of ethnopolitical conflict revolv-ing around questions of land, nationality, citizenship, and political authority. During such instances, victims become caught in political struggles rooted in failed notions of congruent legitimacy between nation and state. Political violence, terror, degradation, ethnic cleansing, mass atrocity, ultimately, genocide, all result from the phallic debili-ties of legitimacy. Perpetrators and victims vary. Sometimes agents of states seek national "purity" by means of long-term oppression against reified racial, ethnic, religious, or kin-ship minority groups. At other times, it is members of such groups that struggle against sovereign agents in the name of a takeover of the state or in order to establish a new state sovereignty over a land in the name of a renewed nationality now purged of its previous "corrupting" elements. An example of the former is the Rwandan genocide in which Hutu and Tutsi kinship groups became ethnicized in ways that set in motion the outbreak of genocidal violence; an example of the latter is first the secession of Pakistan from India and the later secession of Bangladesh from Pakistan. These events culminated in mass atrocities. The many additional examples include the attempted Tamil secession from Sri Lanka and the Chechen struggles to secede from the Russian Confederation of States. These conflicts generated high levels of brutal violence against civilian popula-tions and entry into the macabresque.

Especially volatile are those cases that emerge whenever national unity appears to be threatened or undermined by the presence of separatist or secessionist subnational groups. During these instances, the secessionist group rejects the legitimacy of central-ized state authority. The political alignment of statehood relative to cultural configura-tions of nationhood or peoplehood thus becomes challenged by an unwillingness of certain groups to accept the legitimacy of a nation-state. The history of modern nation-states bears witness to a series of such "long wars" between states and the so-called state-less nations within their borders: the Soviet Union and the Ukrainians, Ethiopia and the Eritreans, Nigeria and the Igbo, Indonesia and the East Timorese, Serbia and the Kosovars, the Palestinians and the Israelis. Although the particularities of political cul-ture and ideology make each example historically unique, each is characterized by the unleashing of mass political violence against citizens on account of their claims to the freedoms of self-determination in ways that challenge the legitimacy of compounded collective identity. In such instances, both friends and enemies appear to lend credence to the substantiality of ethnicity as the materialization of the enigmatic signifier. In such instances, ethnicity becomes reified as the fundament of collective identity, the basis for the hyphenated construction of legitimacy binding the nation-state. Nationality as a form of collective belonging, citizenship as a legal status, become conflated into the "naturalized" claims of ethnicity. Legitimacy is essentialized; the enigmatic signifier becomes reified.

The territorial dimensions of statehood ground powerful sentiments of the nation-state. Perhaps no resource serves to consolidate a sense of unity, common destiny, and national glory more than land, its boundaries, and limitations. The demarcations of national space delimit the political realm in material ways, but even more significantly, in cultural and ideological ways. Modern conceptions of sovereignty and patriotic attachments to "flag" and "country," denote collective desire to assert proprietary claims to territory as the basis for ways of life distinguished by nationality and conceptions of existential or group identity. For such reasons, challenges to the integrity of territorial or spatial understandings of what constitutes "statehood" appear to provoke profoundly violent responses and, under certain conditions, nationalist forms of rage that make mass atrocity possible. This occurs whenever counternationalist aspirations for autonomy become galvanized into a secessionist action. These separatist movements assume a wide variety of names: Liberation Fronts, People's Parties, National Fronts, Liberation Armies, Democratic Popular Fronts, National Movements, Civic Alliances, Autonomous Movements, Solidarity Movements, and so on. These legitimacy struggles represent some of the most brutal conflicts in modern history. Perhaps no form of large-group violence is as costly in terms of blood, treasure, and torment as civil war, as has been evidenced over and again, by the American, Russian, Chinese, and Korean civil wars, to name but a few.

Here, it seems, is a collective version of the narcissism of minor differences. Living hell falls upon earth whenever the former citizens or subjects of a single state sovereignty make claims for a separated legitimacy. First-party signifiers provoke violent rage in such cases perhaps because the claims strike close to home. The enigmatic signifier of collective identity that grounds common solidarity in nation-statehood must, it seems, be protected at all cost, lest mystifications of the social fantasy that prop ideological reifications of legitimacy be lost entirely. In addition to violation of physical integrity, ethnopolitical violence entails policies of forced relocation and internment designed to create concrete physical space between "us" and "them." The consequences adhere to the dynamics of enemy-making. From the Long Walk of the Armenian genocide to the concentration of European Jews in ghettos and concentration camps under the Nazi regime, forced deportation can be used to ethnically cleanse a national territory. In many examples, victims are concentrated spatially so that they might be more easily targeted, such as in Bosnia and in the displacement camps in Darfur. In this manner, the abject become territorially confined: in processes linking racialization with spatialization.

Sometimes conflicts arise as the consequence of attempts to divide the nation-state by means of territorial secession. Such efforts are often met with powerful resistance on the part of centralized authorities that make claims to an overweening legitimacy and use this as justification for supererogatory excesses that include genocidal and mass atrocity crimes. Postcolonial history is etched by incidences of collective violence within political contexts denoted by conflicts over territorial secession. The nation-state in effect becomes fantasized as the "property" of centralized ruling elites. Such mimetic rivalries once accentuated or fueled by ethnic, religious, sectarian, or identitarian conflicts and triggered into violence by secessionism under conditions of civil war often devolve into the macabresque of human violation. Tragic examples include the Nigerian Civil War, sometimes called the Nigerian-Biafran War, between 1967 and 1970, in which encirclement and food deprivation to the point of starvation became weapons of war; and Operation Searchlight, beginning in March 1971 and ending in December 1971, undertaken by the Pakistani central government and implemented by the Pakistani Army to defeat the Bengali nationalist movement, in what was East Pakistan and later became Bangladesh, but not before a military campaign that witnessed unbridled ferocious attacks against civilian populations that included mass rape. Secessionism also defined the political conditions provoking the mass atrocity crimes during the Sri Lanka Civil War. Related to secessionism are the territorial campaigns on the part of centralized or sovereign governments to incorporate the territories of previously self-governing political entities, such as the Indonesian invasion of East Timor, 1975–1976, to overthrow the popular Fretilin-led government that included so-called "final solution" campaigns involving macabresque tactics, such as encirclement of civilian populations and subsequent aerial bombardment, famine, and defoliation of land for resettlement, and the prevention of food cultivation. One of the basic features of the macabresque was ever-present: self-betrayal and forced complicity. Civilians in resettlement camps were forced to clasp hands and parade in front of military units; whenever members of Fretilin were discovered, they were singled out and made to shoot their own people on the threat of being killed and tortured themselves.

As we have seen, mass political disruptions originating from such ethnopolitical subnational conflict characterized the Balkanization of the former Yugoslavia throughout the 1990s and early 2000s. In the former Yugoslavia, Balkanization led to the creation of Slovenia, Croatia, Bosnia-Herzegovina, Montenegro, Macedonia, Serbia, and Kosovo. The violence was particularly brutal in Bosnia-Herzegovina, where Bosnian Serb military forces attempted to maintain control of Serb-dominated territory and ethnically cleanse it of minority populations. During this time, Croatian and Muslim Bosnian or Bosniak, as well as Kosovar forces were also complicit in crimes against humanity. The overall consequence was to create a set of national political cultures that tend to view each other from objectified perspectives of mutual contempt rather than from those of mutual recognition and reciprocated legitimacy.

Ethnocratic Politics

Gerard Toal and Carl T. Dahlman describe the human, cultural, and political consequences of the General Framework Agreement for Peace in Bosnia and Herzegovina, the so-called Dayton Peace Accords of 1995, negotiated in the aftermath of ethnic cleansing.

They begin, "Ethnic cleansing, in short, is a form of geopolitics. The 'geo' and 'politics' can be parsed to signify two interrelated practices: first the attempt to produce a new *ethno-territorial order of space*, and second the attempt to build an *ethnocratic political order* upon that space. The remaking of Bosnia through ethnic cleansing involved both."[1] These statements suggest that in the midst of some of the worst moments of performative violence seen in Europe since the end of the Second World War, social fantasies supported by political reifications attempted to reconstitute the nation-state on the basis of a revised ideological set of constructions regarding hyphenated legitimacy. During this ethnopolitical subnational conflict involving ethnic cleansing, the Serb objective was to transform Bosnian nationality into the "possession" of those who shared in Serb ethnicity—that is, birth or blood—to the exclusion of others, particularly Muslim Bosniaks.

In addition, the task was to consolidate state power on the basis of ethnicized legitimacy. To cite Toal and Dahlman, "That there is a now restored Islamic cultural landscape in Republika Srpska does not negate its origins as a secessionist project launched by figures that became indicted war criminals. The polity is founded on a racist Darwinian scenario, a hyperbolic Orientalist fear that 'Muslims' are 'conquering' Bosnia with their birthrate and planning to turn it into an Islamic state."[2] Toal and Dahlman describe the cultural process of objectifying "difference" in terms of "us" and "them" thereby transforming an ethnic identity-group into an essentialized identity-object for purposes of political subordination and exclusion. "Essentialized enemy construction was and is used to fix an equally essentialized self, a long suffering 'Bosnian Serb' community that requires its own exclusivist space to survive such a plot."[3] The birth of the Republic of Srpska as a nation-state is based on a political culture of ethno-nationalism that divides ethnic groups from each other in ways that reinforce the mutual dynamics of objectification. The Dayton agreement thus helped to foster a national political culture that "locks Bosnia into bipartite spatial division and tripartite ethnic division organized upon the spatial division." The result of the peace agreement is clear: "the ethnoterritorialism it institutionalized has entrapped Bosnia ever since."[4] The enigmatic signifier remains reified and thus ironically forever denied.

The most heinous forms of mass atrocity in the macabresque occur when states and their agents undertake to annihilate populations on the basis of reified traits. Policies of annihilation aim not only at political purity but also at a fantasized national ideal in which the hyphenated mediations between nationality and difference in the name of political sovereignty vanish. Each historical episode of genocide and mass atrocity manifests a unique combination of torture, torment, agony in modalities of concentration, human violation, and near-annihilation, all staged in the macabresque. These dynamics become apparent whenever and wherever the commonality of sovereign statehood and nationality fails to anchor difference and becomes transformed into an exclusivist, supremacist form of political reification. Mass atrocity thus becomes a public spectacle designed to purge the body politic and the nation of the contaminating "impurities" of those deemed representative of otherness, but who all too often provoke fantasized anxieties of the collapse of difference.

The Endless Return of the Absent Leviathan

A major political question in genocide and mass atrocity concerns the legitimacy of the hyphenated status in the relationship between state and nation as conveyed by the symbol of the nation-state. From whence does the legitimacy of state in relation to nation derive? How does the nation grant or confer legitimacy onto the state? Popular sovereignty may or may not depend on popular consent, but even in situations when it actually does, on what foundation is popular consent justified with respect to the hyphenated glue of nation-state? The hyphen of sovereignty linking second-party lack and third-party loss anchors the relationship of maternal desire and paternal disciplines. In psychosocial terms framed by Lacanian perspectives, where is the first-party signifier if it is forever condemned to be split and barred? Signifiers only speak to other signifiers. Signifieds of the nation-state slide under the signifiers of the first party; what this demonstrates is they are ultimately unable to confer absolute identity and thus cannot guarantee the validity of the hyphenated legitimacy that consolidates nation with state. The collective entity, like the individual subject, evacuates its own status as a grounded formation framed by desires for the materiality bounded state territory, as well as by the immateriality housed in the clandestine terrains of national "consciousness." For these reasons, territory, boundaries, and borders tend to become readily contested. It is the very dubious nature of legitimacy, the very incapacity of hyphenated signifiers to guarantee legitimacy that makes legitimacy more contestable, all the more amenable to serve as the basis of conflict. Just as desire for power acts as its own cause on account of its intrinsic attributes in lack and loss, so does the hyphenated legitimacy of the nation-state function as a primary cause of conflict. This is not because it is a strong signifier among others, but precisely because it cannot serve as a Petrinal foundation for it. The relationship of state and nation in the context of sovereignty is thus permeated by lack and loss. But more than this, the cultural constructions of collective identity in which the entire fabric of sovereignty is woven evaporates into the mystifications and self-glorifications of social fantasy, which are not altogether different from the narcissist or primordial self-mystifications of the Lacanian subject.

Another way to put this is to suggest that just as the signifier of the subject evaporates under the tropes of metonymic and metaphoric distillations that in turn become maternalized and paternalized on account of the transpositions of desire, so does the hyphen as signifier oscillate between nation and state. Just as identity becomes forged as it slides under the signified of paternalized and maternalized signifiers, so does the acceptance of the political legitimacy of sovereign mergers of nation with state once established. Despite this, doubt lingers often in ways that come to assail large-groups once, and if ever, caught by the coruscations of mimetic envy and hatred. Hate reflects uncertainty but as in all cases of desire, the consequent quest for certainty becomes all the more compelling, all the more subject to virulent forms of disordered will and collective self-deceptions that are characterized by psychosocial akrasia and political reification. Psychosocial theory and perspectives, with their emphases on the impacts of desire, appear to detect the imprints of political imaginaries embedded in *jouissance* and *objet a*. Fantasies of loss and lack leading to political hatred socially construct political desire in ways that give in to demands for self-sacrifice, often in the name of supererogatory moralism. As we see today, this occurs in the name of religious and clan honor. Political theology is thus used to justify superegotistical forms of sadomasochistic transgression. Often acts of human violation are videotaped and performatively presented through sophisticated media sources. Performativity of transgression in the macabresque has now gone digital. The aim appears to be to establish a grundnorm on the basis of a misrepresentation of Sharia law: a political imaginary that seeks to undergird all law, all bonding, all forms of solidarity against the presumed threats of enigmatic signifiers represented by Western political formations and nation-state legitimacy. With the transpositions of desire into law, the demand for *jouissance* devolves into a demand for performativity in which the aesthetics and dramaturgies of sadistic cruelty and transgression now are ideologically justified as supererogatory acts of highest moral imperative. Once this occurs, the maca-bresque of mass atrocity, disordered, depraved, and perverse, as it is, becomes aligned with the unconscious spirit and sets in motion the turn from political culture to the political evils of the macabresque. Ultimately, perpetrators must and can only be under-stood as human persons, not monsters, however monstrous their behaviors. In their inhumanity, they reveal their profound humanity. What perpetrators hate most when they hate their victims is not difference but sameness, not otherness but identicality. For such reasons, supremacism and exclusivism represent disordered aspirations for a totalized reality to counter the apparent anxieties provoked by any legitimacy based on cosmopolitan principles of shared humanity or dedicated to democratic modes of deliberative governance. For this, perpetrators bear full responsibility. And the costs are dear to the spirit of their own humanity. In all sadism lurks the masochism on the part of the rival self-other that condemns perpetrators to live in denial of the symbolic meanings of genuinely redemptive remorse, remorse, that is, not only for the harm done to others, but as well for the harms perpetrated unto themselves, to their souls, in the tragedy of the macabresque.

NOTES

INTRODUCTION

1. E. Valentine Daniel, *Charred Lullabies: Chapters in an Anthropography of Violence* (Princeton, NJ: Princeton University Press, 1996).

2. Tzvetan Todorov, *Hope and Memory: Lessons from the Twentieth Century* (Princeton, NJ: Princeton University Press, 2003), 20.

3. Ibid., 21.

4. Leslie Farber, *The Ways of the Will: Essays Towards a Psychology and Psychopathology of Will* (New York: Harper & Row, 1966).

CHAPTER 1

1. Daniel J. Goldhagen, *Worse than War: Genocide, Eliminationism, and the Ongoing Assault on Humanity* (New York: Public Affairs, 2009), 430–431; it should be noted that Goldhagen's study runs parallel to the one I develop here in no small measure, on account of Goldhagen's emphasis on the performative qualities of gratuitous cruelty exerted during episodes of what he calls "eliminationist" assaults.

2. Ruth Minsky Sender, *The Cage* (New York: Aladdin, 1986), 153–159.

3. Ibid.

4. Ibid.

5. Primo Levi, *Survival in Auschwitz: The Nazi Assault on Humanity,* trans. Stuart Woolf (New York: Touchstone, 1996), 42.

6. Anne Applebaum, *Gulag: A History* (New York: Doubleday, 2003), 334–335.

7. Arne Johan Vetlesen, *Evil and Human Agency: Understanding Collective Evildoing* (Cambridge: Cambridge University Press, 2005), 214.

8. Giorgio Agamben, *Remnants of Auschwitz: The Witness and the Archive*, trans. Daniel Heller-Roazen (New York: Zone Books, 2002), 107.

9. Inga Clendinnen, *Reading the Holocaust* (Cambridge: Cambridge University Press, 1999), 141.

10. Ibid., 145.

11. Ibid., 142.

12. Slavoj Žižek, *For They Know Not What They Do: Enjoyment as a Political Factor* (London: Verso, 2008), 71.

13. Ibid.

14. Ibid., 72.

15. Ibid.

16. Ibid., 93.

17. Aristotle Kallis, *Genocide and Fascism: The Eliminationist Drive in Fascist Europe* (New York: Routledge, 2009), 306–307.

18. Ibid., 307.

19. Ibid., 306.

20. Historical Clarification Commission, *Guatemala: Memory of Silence: Report of the Commission for Historical Clarification Conclusions and Recommendations* (Guatemala City: Historical Clarification Commission, 1999).

21. Ibid., 34; emphasis in the original.

22. Ibid.

23. Ibid.

24. Ibid.

25. Greg Grandin, "The Instruction of Great Catastrophe: Truth Commissions, National History, and State Formation in Argentina, Chile, and Guatemala," *The American Historical Review* 110, no. 1 (2005): 46–67, at 61.

26. Diane M. Nelson, *Reckoning: The Ends of War in Guatemala* (Durham, NC: Duke University Press, 2009), 95.

27. Ibid.

28. Michel Foucault, *Discipline and Punish: The Birth of the Prison*, trans. Alan Sheridan (New York: Vintage, 1995), 25–26.

29. Edward Weisband and Courtney I. P. Thomas, *Political Culture and the Making of Modern Nation-States* (Boulder, CO: Paradigm, 2015), 191.

30. "Sri Lanka: Government Abuses Intensify: Killings, Abductions, and Displacement Soar and Impunity Reigns," *Human Rights Watch*, August 5, 2007, http://www.hrw.org/en/news/2007/08/05/sri-lanka-government-abuses-intensify.

31. Eddy Isango, "Cannibalism Shock as Congo Atrocities Revealed," *The Age*, March 18, 2005, http://www.theage.com.au/news/World/Cannibalism-shock-as-Congo-atrocities-revealed/2005/03/17/1110913734387.html.

32. Ibid.

33. BBC News, "UN Condemns DR Congo Cannibalism," *BBC News World Edition*, January 15, 2003, http://news.bbc.co.uk/2/hi/africa/2661365.stm.

34. Stephanie Nolen, "Not Women Anymore: The Congo's Rape Survivors Face Pain, Shame, and AIDS," *Ms. Magazine*, Spring 2005, http://www.msmagazine.com/spring2005/congo.asp.

35. *Wikipedia*, "Sexual Violence in the Democratic Republic of the Congo," updated, March 11, 2017, https://en.wikipedia.org/wiki/Sexual_violence_in_the_Democratic_Republic_of_the_ Congo.

36. "War against Women: The Use of Rape as a Weapon in Congo's Civil War," *CBS News*, August 17, 2008, http://www.cbsnews.com/stories/2008/01/11/60minutes/main3701249.shtml.

37. Ibid.

38. Ann Jones, "Mass Rape in the Congo: A Crime against Society," *The Nation*, December 23, 2008. http://www.alternet.org/reproductivejustice/113782/mass_rape_in_the_congo:_a_ crime_against_society/?page=entire.

39. Nolen, "Not Women Anymore."

40. Ibid., 308.

41. Ibid.

42. For an elaboration of *jouissance* and "thing-enjoyment," see Jelica Šumič, "Politics and Psychoanalysis in the Times of the Inexistent Other," in *Jacques Lacan: Between Psychoanalysis and Politics*, ed. Samo Tomšič and Andreja Zevnik (London: Routledge, 2016), 28–42.

43. Bruce Fink, *The Lacanian Subject: Between Language and Jouissance* (Princeton, NJ: Princeton University Press, 1995), 59.

44. Ibid.

45. Ibid., 60.

46. Ibid.

47. Žižek, *They Know Not What They Do*, 98.

48. Ibid., 99.

49. Ibid., 308.

50. Ernst Klee, Willi Dressen, and Volker Riess, *Those Were the Days: The Holocaust as Seen by the Perpetrators and Bystanders* (London: Hamish Hamilton, 1991), 126.

51. Hugh Trevor-Roper, foreword to *"The Good Old Days": The Holocaust as Seen by Its Perpetrators and Bystanders*," ed. Willi Dressen, Ernst Klee, and Volker Riess, trans. Deborah Burnstone (Old Saybrook, CT: Konecky and Konecky, 1991), x–xvi.

52. Ibid.

53. Klee, Dressen, and Riess, *"Those Were the Days"*, 108.

54. Stephen Frosh, *For and against Psychoanalysis* (London: Routledge, 2006), 172.

55. Stephen Frosh, *Hauntings: Psychoanalysis and Ghostly Transmissions* (New York: Palgrave Macmillan, 2013).

56. Adriana Cavarero, *Horrorism: Naming Contemporary Violence*, trans. William McCuaig (New York: Columbia University Press, 2011).

57. Eric Zillmer, Molly Harrower, Barry A. Ritzler, and Rober P. Archer, *The Quest for the Nazi Personality: A Psychological Investigation of Nazi War Criminals* (New York: Routledge, 1995), 180.

58. Nancy Jay, *Throughout Your Generations Forever: Sacrifice, Religion, and Paternity* (Chicago: University of Chicago Press, 1992).

59. Dan Stone, "Biopower and Modern Genocide," in *Empire, Colony, Genocide: Conquest, Occupation, and Subaltern Resistance in World History*, ed. A. Dirk Moses (New York: Berghahn, 2008), 162–182, at 175.

Stone refers to Emile Durkheim, *Elementary Forms of Religious Life*, trans. Karen E. Fields (New York: Free Press, 1995); Roger Caillois, *Man and the Sacred*, trans. by Meyer Barash, 2nd ed. (Urbana: University of Illinois Press, 2001); and Saul Friedländer, *Memory, History, and the Extermination of the Jews of Europe* (Bloomington: Indiana University Press, 1993). See also Clendinnen's *Reading the Holocaust*, for a critical discussion of Friedländer's concept of *Rausch*, by which he meant the "rush" and high satisfactions of the mystical Führer-Bindung (Fuhrer-Bond) provoked by increasing the numbers of Jews killed as the fulfillment of the Fuhrer's will; Clendinnen's criticism is based on what she sees as the inherent mystifications of Friedländer's concept of *Rausch* as a unit of analysis to the degree it suggests that "the actions of its agents are not amenable to the analyst's intuitive comprehension of events." Clendinnen rejects any such imputation and writes, "This conclusion—indeed Friedländer's whole discussion—places us squarely in a conceptual field inhabited by words like 'evil,' which are of no use whatsoever when it comes to teasing out why people act as they do." (86–88)

60. Clendinnen, *Reading the Holocaust*, 57–58.

61. Ibid., 48–49.

62. Mark Levene, "Connecting Threads: Rwanda, the Holocaust, and the Pattern of Contemporary Genocide," in *The Genocide Studies Reader*, ed. Samuel Totten and Paul R. Bartrop (New York: Routledge, 2009), 258–286.

63. Ibid., 274–275.

64. Ibid.

65. Ibid., 197–198.

66. Linda Brakel, *Unconscious Knowing and Other Essays in Psycho-Philosophical Analysis* (Oxford: Oxford University Press, 2009), 165.

67. Amélie Oksenberg Rorty, "The Social and Political Sources of Akrasia," *Ethics* 107, no. 4 (1997): 644–657, at 651.

68. Ibid., 649.

69. Ibid., 652.

70. Farber, *Ways of the Will*, 6–7.

71. Ibid., 8.

72. Ibid., 48.

73. Ibid.

74. Ian Deweese-Boyd, "Self-Deception," *Stanford Encyclopedia of Philosophy*, Edward Zalta, ed. Winter 2016, http://plato.stanford.edu/entries/self-deception/.

75. Ibid.

76. Ronald Aronson, *The Dialectics of Disaster* (New York: Schocken, 1983), 193.

77. Ibid., 195.

78. Stone, "Biopower and Modern Genocide," 174.

79. Ibid.

80. Aronson, *Dialectics of Disaster*, 203–204.

81. Theodor W. Adorno, *Critical Models: Interventions and Catchwords*, trans. Henry W. Pickford (New York: Columbia University Press, 2005), 109.

82. Aronson, *Dialectics of Disaster*, 203.

83. Ibid., 204.

84. Michel Foucault, *"Society Must Be Defended": Lectures at the College de France 1975–1976*, trans. David Macey (New York: Picador, 1997), 239.

85. Ibid., 232.

86. Ibid., 255.

87. Ibid., 255–256.

88. Ibid., 257.

89. Ibid., 258.

90. Ibid., 260.

91. Ibid.

92. Walter Kaufmann, *Existentialism from Dostoevsky to Sartre* (New York: Meridian, 1957), 267.

93. Ibid.; emphasis in the original.

94. Jason J. Campbell, *On the Nature of Genocidal Intent* (Lanham, MD: Lexington, 2013), 154.

95. Wolfgang Sofsky, *The Order of Terror: The Concentration Camp*, trans. William Templer (Princeton, NJ: Princeton University Press, 1997), 13.

96. Ibid., 9.

97. Ibid.

98. Ibid.

99. Ibid.

100. Ibid., 10.

101. Ibid., 9–10.

102. Ibid., 13.

103. Ibid., 17.

104. Ibid., 18.

105. Ibid.

106. Ibid., 17.

107. Ibid., 19.

108. Jean-Paul Sartre, *Being and Nothingness*, trans. Hazel E. Barnes (New York: Washington Square Press, 1984), 616.

109. Sofsky, *Order of Terror*, 23.

110. Ibid.

111. Ibid., 223–258.

112. Ibid., 229.

113. Ibid.

114. Ibid.

115. Ibid., 229–230; emphasis added.

116. Ibid., 230.

117. Ibid., 228.

118. Ibid.

119. Ibid., 23.

120. Ibid.; emphasis in the original.

121. A. Dirk Moses, ed., *Empire, Colony, Genocide: Conquest, Occupation, and Subaltern Resistance in World History* (New York: Berghahn, 2008), esp. 229–270.

122. See Martha Nussbaum, "Objectification," *Philosophy and Public Affairs* 24, no. 4 (1995): 249–291; and Evangelia (Lina) Papadaki, "Feminist Perspectives on Objectification," *The Stanford Encyclopedia of Philosophy* (Winter 2015 Edition), Edward N. Zalta (ed.), https://plato.stanford.edu/archives/win2015/entries/feminism-objectification/.

123. See Howard Caygill, *Levinas and the Political* (London: Routledge, 2002), esp. chap. 4, "Prophetic Politics, or 'Otherwise than Freedom,' " 128–158.

124. Karl Figlio, "The Dread of Sameness: Social Hatred and Freud's 'Narcissism of Minor Differences,'" in *Psychoanalysis and Politics: Exclusion and the Politics of Representation*, ed. Lene Auestad (London: Karnac, 2012), 7.

125. Johannes Lang, "Questioning Dehumanization: Intersubjective Dimensions of Violence in the Nazi Concentration and Death Camps," *Holocaust and Genocide Studies* 24, no. 2 (2010): 225–246.

126. Ibid., 241.

127. Ibid., 237.

128. Ibid.

129. Ibid.

130. Ibid., 228. See also Alexander Laban Hinton, *Why Did They Kill? Cambodia in the Shadow of Genocide* (Berkeley: University of California Press, 2005).

131. Lang, "Questioning Dehumanization," 234.

132. Abraham Kaplan, *The Conduct of Inquiry: Methodology for Behavioral Science* (San Francisco: Chandler, 1964), 297.

133. Ibid.

134. Marguerite Feitlowitz, *A Lexicon of Terror: Argentina and the Legacies of Torture* (Oxford: Oxford University Press, 1998), 64.

135. Billig, Michael, "Humour and Hatred: The Racist Jokes of the Ku Klux Klan," *Discourse & Society* 12, no. 3 (2001): 267–289, at 279. See also Theodor Adorno and Max Horkheimer, *Dialectic of Enlightenment*, trans. John Cumming (London: Verso, 1997).

136. Hitler, quoted in Ron Rosenbaum, *Explaining Hitler: The Search for the Origins of his Evil* (New York: Macmillan, 1998), 385.

137. Ibid., 388.

138. Ibid., 388–389.

139. Ibid., 218–219.

140. Ibid., 215.

141. Ibid., 214.

CHAPTER 2

1. Simon Baron-Cohen, *The Science of Evil: On Empathy and the Origins of Cruelty* (New York: Basic, 2012), 45–47, 78–87.

2. Russell Jacoby, *Bloodlust: On the Roots of Violence from Cain and Abel to the Present* (New York: Free Press, 2011), 128–135, 151–152.

3. Léon Wurmser, *The Mask of Shame* (Baltimore: Johns Hopkins University Press, 1981), 161–162.

4. Greg Cashman, *What Causes War? An Introduction to Theories of International Conflict* (Lanham, MD: Rowman and Littlefield, 2014), 477–478.

5. Ibid., 478–479.

6. Ibid., 479.

7. Martin Shaw, *What Is Genocide?* (Cambridge: Polity, 2007), 140.

8. Ibid., 141.

9. Ibid., 110.

10. Ibid., 114.

11. Ibid., 111.

12. Ibid., 117; emphasis in the original.

13. Ibid., 147; emphasis in the original.

14. Ibid., 149; emphasis in the original.

15. Ibid.

16. Matthew Krain, "State-Sponsored Mass Murder the Onset and Severity of Genocides and Politicides," *Journal of Conflict Resolution* 41, no. 3 (1997): 331–360, at 333–334.

17. Ibid., 335.

18. Ibid., 346.

19. Ibid., 348.

20. James D. Fearon and David D. Laitin, "Ethnicity, Insurgency, and Civil War," *American Political Science Review* 97, no. 1 (2003): 75–90, at 75.

21. Ibid., 83.

22. Ibid., 75.

23. Ibid., 82.

24. Ibid., 88.

25. Ibid.

26. Hannibal Travis, *Genocide, Ethnonationalism, and the United Nations* (New York: Routledge, 2013), 39.

27. Ibid., 31.

28. Ben Kiernan, Holocaust and the United Nations Discussion Paper Series, Discussion paper #3, unpublished and undated.

29. Richard Rhodes, *Masters of Death: The SS-Einsatzgruppen and the Invention of the Holocaust* (New York: Vintage, 2003), xi.

30. Ibid., 4.

31. Ibid., 22.

32. Ibid., 25.

33. Ibid.

34. Ibid.

35. Ibid.

36. Stanley A. Renshon, "Lost in Plain Sight: The Cultural Foundations of Political Psychology," in *Political Psychology*, ed. Kristen Renwick Monroe (Mahwah, NJ: Lawrence Erlbaum, 2002), 123.

37. Kristen Renwick Monroe, *Ethics in an Age of Terror and Genocide: Identity and Moral Choice* (Princeton, NJ: Princeton University Press, 2012), 4.

38. Ibid., 26.

39. Ibid., 8.

40. Ibid., 19.

41. Ibid.

42. Ibid., 23.

43. Ibid., 190.

44. Ibid., 191.

45. Ibid., 217.

46. Ibid., 245.

47. Ibid., 231.

48. Ibid., 230.

49. Ibid.

50. Ibid.

51. Benjamin A. Valentino, *Final Solutions: Mass Killing and Genocide in the Twentieth Century*, Cornell Studies in Security Affairs (Ithaca, NY: Cornell University Press, 2004), 10.

52. Ibid., 25.

53. Ibid., 25–26.

54. Ibid., 9.

55. Ibid., 64.

56. Ibid., 39–40.

57. Ibid., 64.

58. Ibid.

59. Ibid., 60.

60. Ibid., 61.

61. Michael Mann, "Were the Perpetrators of Genocide 'Ordinary Men' or 'Real Nazis'? Results from Fifteen Hundred Biographies," *Holocaust and Genocide Studies* 14, no. 3 (2000): 331–366, at 331.

62. Michael Mann, *The Dark Side of Democracy: Explaining Ethnic Cleansing* (New York: Cambridge University Press, 2005), 27–29.

63. Mann, "Perpetrators of Genocide," 344.

64. Manus Midlarsky, *Origins of Political Extremism: Mass Violence in the Twentieth Century and Beyond* (Cambridge: Cambridge University Press, 2011), 289.

65. Mann, "Perpetrators of Genocide," 356–357.

66. Mann, *Dark Side of Democracy*, 8.

67. Ibid., 6.

68. Ibid.

69. Ibid., 7.

70. Daniel Bar-Tal, *Shared Beliefs in a Society: Social Psychological Analysis* (Thousand Oaks, CA: Sage, 2000), 164.

71. Alette Smeulers, "Perpetrators of International Crimes: Towards a Typology," in *Supranational Criminology: Towards a Criminology of International Crimes*, ed. Alette Smeulers and Roelof Haveman (Antwerpen: Intersentia), 234.

72. Ibid., 239.

73. Ibid.; Robert J. Lifton, *The Nazi Doctors: Medical Killing and the Psychology of Genocide* (New York: Basic Books, 1986).

74. Lifton, *Nazi Doctors*, 242.

75. Ibid., 235.

76. Ibid., 236–237.

77. Ibid., 264.

78. James Waller, *Becoming Evil: How Ordinary People Commit Genocide and Mass Killing* (Oxford: Oxford University Press, 2002), 111.

79. C. Fred Alford, *What Evil Means to Us* (Ithaca, NY: Cornell University Press, 1997), 129.

80. Ibid., 131.

81. Ibid.

82. Ibid., 132; emphasis in the original.

83. Philip Zimbardo, *The Lucifer Effect: Understanding How Good People Turn Evil* (New York: Random House, 2008), 7.

84. Ibid., 212.

85. Ibid., 221.

86. Ibid.

87. Ibid.

88. Ibid., 10–11.

89. Ibid., 221.

90. Ibid., 259.

91. Ibid.

92. Ibid., 226.

93. Ibid.

94. Ibid.

95. Waller, *Becoming Evil*, 225.

96. Waller, *Becoming Evil*, 225.

97. Christopher R. Browning, *Ordinary Men: Reserve Police Battalion 101 and the Final Solution in Poland* (New York: Harper Perennial, 1993), 166–167.

98. Ibid., 168.

99. Ibid., 174–175.

100. Ibid., 176.

101. Ibid., 216 and the afterword.

102. Ibid., 216.

103. Ibid., 216–217.

104. Ibid., 208; citing Katz.

105. Ibid., 208.

106. Roy F. Baumeister, *The Self in Social Psychology*, ed. Roy F. Baumeister (Philadelphia: Psychology Press, 1999), 8.

107. Ibid., 14.

108. Ibid., 186.

109. Ibid., 190.

110. Ibid., 195.

111. Ibid., 196.

112. Ervin Staub, *Overcoming Evil: Genocide, Violent Conflict, and Terrorism* (Oxford: Oxford University Press, 2011).

113. Ervin Staub, *The Roots of Evil: The Origins of Genocide and Other Group Violence* (Cambridge: Cambridge University Press, 1989), 15.

114. Ibid., 237.

115. Ibid., 238.

116. Staub, *Overcoming Evil*, 56.

117. Ibid., 56.

118. Ibid., 112–113.

119. Ibid.

120. Waller, *Becoming Evil*, 134.

121. Ibid., 272.

122. Daniel Chirot and Clark McCauley, *Why Not Kill them All? The Logic and Prevention of Mass Political Murder* (Princeton, NJ: Princeton University Press, 2006), 61.

123. Ibid.

124. Ibid., 62.

125. Ibid., 73.

126. Ibid.

127. Ibid., 74.

128. Ibid.

129. Ibid., 75.

130. Ibid., 77.

131. Ibid., 76.

132. Theodor W. Adorno, *Minima Moralia: Reflections on a Damaged Life*, trans. E. F. N. Jephcott (London: Verso, 2006), 105.

133. Ibid.

CHAPTER 3

1. Daniel Pick, *The Pursuit of the Nazi Mind: Hitler, Hess, and the Analysts* (Oxford: Oxford University Press, 2012), 3.

2. Ibid, 233.

3. Ibid., 6.

4. Ibid., 4.

5. Ibid.

6. Ibid., 3.

7. Ibid., 232.

8. Ibid.

9. Ibid., 237.

10. Ibid., 232.

11. Ibid., 238.

12. Rosenbaum, *Explaining Hitler*.

13. These range from Hitler's alleged perverse psychosexual development or paraphilia to his excretory perversions; from allegations concerning his anatomical anomalies in that he is rumored to have possessed one testicle, to suggestions of his latent predatory homosexuality as well as a host of maternal fixations; these and more are pressed into theoretical service as psycho-historical interpretations of Hitler's psyche, a psyche variously treated as obsessional, neurotic, psychotic, paranoid, and/or normal; in 2008, Rosenbaum criticized suggestions that Hitler's pathology was based on anatomical abnormality in that he had only one testicle; see Ron Rosenbaum, "Everything You Need to Know about Hitler's 'Missing' Testicle: And Why We're so Obsessed the Führer's Sex Life," posted November 28, 2008. http://www.slate.com/articles/life/the_spectator/2008/11/everything_you_need_to_know_about_hitlers_missing_testicle.html.

14. Pick, *Pursuit of the Nazi Mind*, 145.

15. Rosenbaum, *Explaining* Hitler, 136.

16. Ibid., 137.

17. Ibid.

18. Ibid., 138; emphasis added.

19. Ibid., 139.

20. Ibid., 138.

21. Ibid., 293; emphasis in the original.

22. Ibid.

23. Ibid., 138–139.

24. A careful reading of Bromberg and Small's interpretation of Hitler's psychopathology reveals a far more nuanced and subtle rendering than Rosenbaum's criticism allows; Bromberg and Small outline the major biographical events in Hitler's life that appear to have contributed to the development of various aspects of his perverse personality, particularly in relation to his mother and his father. I shall discuss these later. See Norbert Bromberg and Verna Volz Small, *Hitler's Psychopathology* (New York: International Universities Press, 1983), esp. "Psychoanalytic Speculations," chaps. 9 –14, pp. 203–318.

25. Elisabeth Young-Bruehl, *For Love of the World* (New Haven, CT: Yale University Press, 1996), 340.

26. Ibid., 341.

27. Ibid., 185; emphasis in the original.

28. Ibid.

29. Ibid., 189; emphasis in the original.

30. Ibid., 209.

31. Ibid., 194.

32. Ibid., 348.

33. Ibid.

34. Ibid., 349.

35. Ibid., 194.

36. Ibid., 193–194.

37. Ibid., 189.

38. Ibid., 190.

39. Ibid., 193. In this proposition, Young-Bruehl offers an alternate explanation to Lifton's notion of "doubling." See Lifton, *Nazi Doctors*. For a critical evaluation of Lifton's thesis, also see Waller, *Becoming Evil*, 111–123. Waller questions Lifton's "doubling" thesis when he writes, "If, by simply advocating a position in which we do not believe, we find the inner dissonance so intolerable that we will modify our previously held beliefs to be more consistent with that position, then the extreme dissonance required by Lifton's theory cannot be validated as a sustained form of adaptation to evildoing.

40. Fred Weinstein, *Freud, Psychoanalysis, Social Theory* (Albany: State University of New York Press, 2001).

41. Ibid., 96.

42. Ibid.

43. Ibid., 156.

44. Ibid.

45. Ibid., 155.

46. Ibid.

CHAPTER 4

1. Juliet Flower MacCannel, "Lacan's Imaginary: A Practical Guide," in Tomšič and Zevnik, *Jacques Lacan*, 72–85.

2. Jean-Michel Oughourlian, *The Genesis of Desire*, trans. Eugene Webb (East Lansing: Michigan State University Press, 2010), 18.

3. Ibid., 23.

4. Ibid., 19.

5. Ibid., 24.

6. Ibid., 23.

7. Ibid., 19; emphasis added.

8. Ibid., 33.

9. Scott Straus, *Making and Unmaking Nations: War, Leadership, and Genocide in Modern Africa* (Ithaca, NY: Cornell University Press, 2015).

10. Ibid., 275.

11. Ibid.

12. Ibid., 296.

13. Ibid.; emphasis added.

14. Ibid.

15. Mahmood Mamdani, *When Victims Become Killers: Colonialism, Nativism, and the Genocide in Rwanda* (Princeton, NJ: Princeton University Press, 2002), 190.

16. For an elaboration of the origins of desire, see Ari Hirvonen, "The Truth of Desire: Lack, Law, and Phallus," in Tomšič and Zevnik, *Jacques Lacan*, 202–216..

17. Oughourlian, *Genesis of Desire*, 63.

18. Ibid.

19. Ibid., 23.

20. Ibid.

21. Ibid., 57.

22. Ibid., 25.

23. Ibid., 35.

24. Jason Glynos, "The Grip of Ideology: A Lacanian Approach to the Theory of Ideology," *Journal of political ideologies* 6, no. 2 (2001): 191–214, at 197.

25. Ibid., 197.

26. Lorenzo Chiesa, *Subjectivity and Otherness: A Philosophical Reading of Lacan* (Cambridge, MA: MIT Press, 2007), 133; emphasis in the original.

27. Ibid., 132–133.

28. Ibid.

29. Adrian Johnston, "The Vicious Circle of the Super-Ego: The Pathological Trap of Guilt and the Beginning of Ethics," *Psychoanalytic Studies* 3, no. 3/4 (2001): 417.

30. Ibid.; italics in the original.

31. Derek Hook and Calum Neill, "Perspectives on 'Lacanian Subjectivities,'" *Subjectivity* 24, no. 1 (2008): 247–255, at 249.

32. Ibid.

33. Jason Glynos and Yannis Stavrakakis, "Lacan and Political Subjectivity: Fantasy and Enjoyment in Psychoanalysis and Political Theory," *Subjectivity* 24, no. 1 (2008): 256–274, at 261.

34. Ibid.

35. Ibid., 263.

36. Margarita Palacios, "On Sacredness and Transgression: Understanding Social Antagonism," *Psychoanalysis, Culture and Society* 9, no. 3 (2004): 284–297, at 285.

37. Ibid., 288–289.

38. Ibid., 285.

39. Ibid., 286.

40. Ibid., 289.

41. Ibid., 291.

42. Ibid., 293.

43. Elaine Scarry, *The Body in Pain: The Making and Unmaking of the World* (Oxford: Oxford University Press, 1985), 8–11.

44. Ibid., 27.

45. Ibid., 28.

46. Ibid., 31.

47. Ibid., 41.

48. Ibid., 47.

49. Ibid.; emphasis in the original.

50. Ibid.

51. Ibid., 44.

52. Ervand Abrahamian, *Tortured Confessions: Prisons and Public Recantations in Modern Iran* (Berkeley: University of California Press, 1999), 7.

53. Ibid., 6–8.

54. Ibid., 7.

55. Berel Lang, *Act and Idea in the Nazi Genocide* (Syracuse, NY: Syracuse University Press, 2003), 97; emphasis in the original; For a parallel analysis of the subversion of language in relation to social reality relevant to contemporaneous American governance in the era of the Trump administration, see *Brooke Gladstone, The Trouble with Reality: A Rumination on Moral Panic in our Time* (New York, NY: Workman Publishing Company, 2017).

56. Ibid., 89.

57. Ibid., 93.

58. Ibid., 101.

59. Ibid.

60. Ibid., 102; emphasis added.

61. Ibid.

62. Ibid.

63. Liah Greenfeld, "Using the Holocaust. Review Essay of *Metaphor, Nation and the Holocaust: The Concept of the Body Politic*," Library of Social Science, February, 23, 2015, 5; emphasis in the original. http://www.libraryofsocialscience.com/reviews/Greenfeld.html.

64. Ibid.

65. Daniel, *Charred Lullabies*, 121.

66. Ibid.

67. Ibid., 122.

68. Ibid., 123.

69. Ibid., 136.

70. Ibid.

71. Ibid.

72. Daniel, *Charred Lullabies*, 136; emphasis added.

73. Ibid.; emphasis in the original.

74. Ibid., 138.

75. Ibid., 137.

76. Ibid., 138.

CHAPTER 5

1. Hanna Segal, *The Work of Hanna Segal: A Kleinian Approach to Clinical Practice*, (Lanham, MD: Jason Aronson, 2007), 49–68.

2. Richard K. Ashley, "Critical Spirits/Realist Specters: Some Hypotheses on the Spectro-Poetics of International Relations," in *The Ashgate Research Companion to Modern Theory, Modern Power, World Politics*, ed. Scott G. Nelson and Nevzat Soguk (Surrey: Ashgate, 2016), 111, 114; emphasis in the original.

3. Ibid., 112–113.

4. Abram de Swaan, *The Killing Compartments: The Mentality of Mass Murder* (New Haven, CT: Yale University Press, 2015).

5. Ibid., 11.

6. Ibid., 239.

7. Ibid.

8. Irving L. Janis, *Victims of Groupthink: A Psychological Study of Foreign-Policy Decisions and Fiascoes* (New York: Houghton Mifflin, 1972).

9. Peter Fonagy, Gyorgy Gergely, Elliot Jurist, and Mary Target, *Affect Regulation, Mentalization, and the Development of the Self* (New York: Other Press, 2004), 3.

10. Ibid., 248.

11. Ibid., 266–267.

12. Ibid., 267.

13. Ibid., 254.

14. Ibid., 267.

15. Zillmer at al., *Quest for the Nazi Personality*, 180.

16. See Lene Auestad, *Respect, Plurality, and Prejudice: A Psychoanalytical and Philosophical Enquiry into the Dynamics of Social Exclusion and Discrimination* (London: Karnac, 2015), 246; emphasis in the original.

17. Ibid. This phrase is Auestad's.

18. Fonagy et al., *Affect Regulation*, 11; emphasis added.

19. Stijn Vanheule and Paul Verhaeghe, "Identity through a Psychoanalytic Looking Glass," *Theory and Psychology* 19, no. 3 (2009): 391–411, at 394–395.

20. Ibid., 395.

21. Ibid., 23.

22. Ibid.

23. Ibid., 396.

24. Ibid.

25. Ibid.

26. Bice Benvenuto, *Concerning the Rites of Psychoanalysis: Or the Villa of the Mysteries* (New York: Routledge, 1994), 82–83.

27. Ibid., 83.

28. Ibid.

29. Adrian Johnston, *Žižek's Ontology: A Transcendental Materialist Theory of Subjectivity*, Northwestern University Studies in Phenomenology and Existential Philosophy (Evanston, IL: Northwestern University Press, 2008), 8.

30. Ibid., 8–9.

31. Slavoj Žižek, *Tarrying with the Negative: Kant, Hegel, and the Critique of Ideology* (Durham, NC: Duke University Press, 1993), 15.

32. Frosh, *For and against Psychoanalysis*, 181–183.

33. Ibid., 181.

34. Vanheule and Verhaeghe, "Identity through a Psychoanalytic Looking Glass," 397.

35. Ibid., 394.

36. Ibid., 397.

37. Ibid.

38. Ibid.

39. Ibid.

40. Frosh, *For and against Psychoanalysis*, 185.

41. Ibid., 191.

42. Jean Laplanche and Jean-Bertrand Pontalis, *The Language of Psycho-Analysis*, trans. Donald Nicholson-Smith (New York: W. W. Norton, 1973), 206.

43. Ibid., 208; emphasis in the original.

44. Ibid.

45. Glynos and Stavrakakis, "Lacan and Political Subjectivity," 260.

46. Ibid., 261.

47. Frosh, *For and against Psychoanalysis*, 262.

48. Ibid.

49. Stijn Vanheule, *The Subject of Psychosis: A Lacanian Perspective* (New York: Palgrave Macmillan, 2011), 24.

50. Ibid., 25.

51. Ibid., 29.

52. Ibid.

53. Ibid.

54. René Girard, *Violence and the Sacred*, trans. Patrick Gregory (Baltimore: Johns Hopkins University Press, 1979), 49.

55. Anton Blok, "The Narcissism of Minor Differences," *European Journal of Social Theory* 1, no. 1 (1998): 39.

56. Pierre Bourdieu, *Distinction: A Social Critique of the Judgement of Taste*, trans. Richard Nice (Cambridge, MA: Harvard University Press, 1984), 479.

57. Blok, "Narcissism of Minor Differences," 48.

58. Richard Grunberger, *Germany: 1918–1945* (London: B. T. Batsford, 1964), 380–385, cited in Stephen Frosh, *Hate and the 'Jewish Science': Anti-Semitism, Nazism and Psychoanalysis* (New York: Palgrave Macmillan, 2009), 189.

59. Frosh, *For and against Psychoanalysis*, 189; emphasis added.

60. Ibid., 191.

61. Grunberger, *Germany:1918–1945*, 384.

62. Jacques Lacan, *The Four Fundamental Concepts of Psychoanalysis*, trans. Alan Sheridan (New York: W. W. Norton, 1998), 183–185; emphasis in the original.

63. Chiesa, *Subjectivity and Otherness*, 21.

64. Ibid., 20.

65. Ibid.

66. Ibid.

67. Ibid.

68. Ibid.

69. Paul W. Kahn, *Political Theology: Four New Chapters on the Concept of Sovereignty* (New York: Columbia University Press, 2011).

70. Sverre Varvin, "Islamism and Xenophobia," in *Psychoanalysis and Politics: Exclusion and the Politics of Representation*, ed. Lene Auestad (London: Karnac, 2012), 155–168.

71. Hanna Segal, *Psychoanalysis, Literature and War: Papers 1972–1995* (London: Routledge, 1995), 133.

72. Ibid., 129–151.

73. Ibid., 133.

74. Jeffrey Stevenson Murer, "Institutionalizing Enemies: The Consequences of Reifying Projection in Post-Conflict Environments," *Psychoanalysis, Culture and Society* 15, no. 1 (2010): 4.

75. Ibid., 5.

76. Ibid.

77. Ibid.

78. Ibid., 6.

79. Ibid., 8.

80. Ibid.

81. Jacques Lacan, *Écrits*, trans. Bruce Fink (New York: W. W. Norton, 2007), 12.

82. Richard Boothby, *Death and Desire: Psychoanalytic Theory in Lacan's Return to Freud* (New York: Routledge, 1991), 25.

83. Juliet Brough Rogers, "A Stranger Politics: Toward a Theory of Resistance in Psychoanalytic Thought and Practice," in *Jacques Lacan: Between Psychoanalysis and Politics*, ed. Samo Tomšič and Andreja Zevnik (London: Routledge, 2016), 189–190; emphasis in the original.

84. Richard Boothby, *Death and Desire*, 25.

85. Richard Boothby, *Freud as Philosopher: Metapsychology after Lacan* (New York: Routledge, 2001), 159.

86. Boothby, *Death and Desire*, 152; emphasis in the original.

87. Bruce Fink, *A Clinical Introduction to Lacanian Psychoanalysis: Theory and Technique* (Cambridge, MA: Harvard University Press, 1997), 196.

88. Boothby, *Freud as Philosopher*, 83.

89. Ibid., 84.

90. Frosh, *For and against Psychoanalysis*, 191.

91. Judith Butler, *Gender Trouble: Feminism and the Subversion of Identity* (New York: Routledge, 1999), xix–xx.

92. Ian Parker, "Lacanian Discourse Analysis in Psychology Seven Theoretical Elements," *Theory and Psychology* 15, no. 2 (2005): 163–182.

93. Calum Neill, *Lacanian Ethics and the Assumption of Subjectivity* (New York: Palgrave Macmillan, 2011).

94. Vanheule, *Subject of Psychosis*, 46.

95. Ibid., 46–47.

96. Evans, *Introductory Dictionary*, 55.

97. Jacques Lacan, *The Language of the Self: The Function of Language in Psychoanalysis*, trans. Anthony Wilden (Baltimore: The Johns Hopkins University Press, 1981), 266. See also Jacques Lacan, *The Four Fundamental Concepts of Psychoanalysis,* trans. Alan Sheridan (New York: W. W. Norton, 1998), 136–148.

98. Ibid., 44.

99. Robbie Duschinsky, "Ideal and Unsullied: Purity, Subjectivity, and Social Power," *Subjectivity* 4, no. 2 (2011): 151.

100. Ibid., 152; emphasis in the original.

101. Ibid., 153.

102. Ibid., 154.

103. Ibid, 158; emphasis in the original.

104. Neill, *Lacanian Ethics*; Christine M. Korsgaard, *Self-Constitution: Agency, Identity, and Integrity* (Oxford: Oxford University Press, 2009).

105. Neill, *Lacanian Ethics*, 3; emphasis in the original.

106. Boothby, *Death and Desire*, 25.

107. Ibid.

108. Vanheule, *Subject of Psychosis*, 42.

109. Ibid., 42.

110. Margarita Palacios, *Radical Sociality: On Disobedience, Violence and Belonging* (New York: Palgrave Macmillan, 2013), 42.

CHAPTER 6

1. Richard Ned Lebow, *A Cultural Theory of International Relations* (Cambridge: Cambridge University Press, 2008), 509.

2. Charles Lemert and Ann Branaman, ed., *The Goffmann Reader* (Malden: Blackwell, 1997), liv–lvi; emphasis in the original.

3. Ibid., lxvi.

4. Ibid., 55–71.

5. Allen Feldman, *Formations of Violence: The Narrative of the Body and Political Terror in Northern Ireland* (Chicago: University of Chicago Press, 1991), 65.

6. Ibid.

7. Ibid., 259.

8. Ibid., 260.

9. Ibid., 165.

10. Ibid., 165–166.

11. Ibid., 174.

12. Melanie Klein, *The Psychoanalysis of Children*, trans. Alix Strachey (New York: Delacorte Press, 1975), 219.

13. This analysis of the relationship between Confucian culture and the shame rage that ensued during the Maoist Cultural Revolution is theoretically framed by reference to the psychodynamics of Oedipal castration and separation. For a sustained critique of Freudian/Lacanian representations of the Oedipal dynamic, see Gilles Deleuze and Félix Guattari, *Anti-Oedipus: Capitalism*

and Schizophrenia, trans. Robert Hurley, Mark Seem, and Helen R. Lane (London: Penguin, 2009), 51–138.

14. Klein, *Psychoanalysis of Children*, 326.

15. Benjamin Kilborne, *Disappearing Persons: Shame and Appearance* (Albany: State University of New York Press, 2002).

16. Thomas H. Ogden, *The Primitive Edge of Experience* (Lanham, MD: Jason Aronson, 1989), 22.

17. Ibid., 22–23.

18. Ibid., 11.

19. Ibid., 12.

20. Ibid.

21. Ibid.

22. Ibid., 13.

23. Ibid., 21–22.

24. Ibid., 19.

25. Ibid.

26. Ibid., 21–22.

27. Ibid.

28. Ibid., 31.

29. Ibid.

30. Ibid.

31. Ibid., 32–35.

32. Ibid., 33.

33. Ibid.

34. Kilborne, *Disappearing Persons*, 6.

35. Ibid.

36. Alford, *What Evil Means to Us*, 27.

37. Ibid., 127.

38. Ibid., 127–128.

39. Ibid., 125.

40. Ibid.

41. Ibid., 27; italics in the original.

42. Ibid., 49.

43. Ibid., 128.

44. Ibid.

45. Ibid.

46. Ibid., 125.

47. Ibid., 49.

48. Ibid., 125.

49. Ibid., 53.

50. Ibid.

51. Ibid., 52.

52. Ibid., 21.

53. Ibid., 52.

54. Ibid., 104.

55. Scarry, *Body in Pain*.

56. Alford, *What Evil Means to Us*, 101.

57. Ibid.

58. Ibid.

59. Ibid., 39.

60. Ibid., 43.

61. Ibid., 44.

62. Ibid.

63. See Stephen Frosh's critical commentary on the masculinist conceptual imagery of the "phallic," "name-of-the-father," and related paternalized formulations: Stephen Frosh, "Masculine Mastery and Fantasy, or the Meaning of the Phallus," in *Psychoanalysis in Contexts: Paths Between Theory and Modern Culture*, ed. Anthony Elliott and Stephen Frosh (London: Routledge, 1995), 166–190.

64. For further discussion, see Dominiek Hoens, "Object A and Politics," in Tomšič and Zevnik, *Jacques Lacan*, 101–112.

65. Bruce Fink, *A Clinical Introduction to Lacanian Psychoanalysis: Theory and Technique* (Cambridge, MA: Harvard University Press, 1997), 197.

66. Evans, *Introductory Dictionary*, 125.

67. Boothby, *Freud as Philosopher*, 170.

68. Derek Hook, *A Critical Psychology of the Postcolonial: The Mind of Apartheid* (London: Psychology Press, 2012), 193.

69. Ibid.

70. Jean Laplanche and Jean-Bertrand Pontalis, *The Language of Psycho-Analysis,* translated by Donald Nicholson-Smith, (New York, W. W. Norton, 1973), 306–309.

71. Ibid., 307.

72. Alford, *What Evil Means to Us*, 103.

73. Ons in Žižek, *Silent Partners*, 79–89, at 82; see Jacques Lacan's chapter "Kant with Sade," in Lacan, *Écrits*, 645–670.

74. See Panu Minkkinen, "Lacan avec Bataille avec Nietzsche: A Politics of the Impossible?," in Tomšič and Zevnik, *Jacques Lacan*, 281–298.

75. Dylan Evans, *An Introductory Dictionary of Lacanian Psychoanalysis* (London: Routledge, 1996), 136; Lacan, *Écrits*, 320.

76. Evans, *Introductory Dictionary*, 139; Lacan, *Écrits*, 323.

77. Ons, "Nietzsche, Freud, Lacan," 83–84.

78. Ibid.

79. Ibid.

80. Ibid.; emphasis in the original.

81. Lacan, *Écrits*, 699.

82. Fink, *A Critical Introduction to Lacanian Psychoanalysis*, 174; emphasis in the original.

83. Ibid.

84. Ibid.

85. Ibid.; emphasis in the original.

86. Ibid.

87. Ibid., 192.

88. Evans, *Introductory Dictionary*, 92; emphasis in the original.

89. Ibid., 125.

90. Fink, *A Critical Introduction to Lacanian Psychoanalysis*, 191.

91. Ibid.

92. Ibid., 192.

93. Ibid.

94. Ibid.

CHAPTER 7

1. Jonathan D. Spence, *The Search for Modern China* (New York: W. W. Norton, 1990), 607.

2. Ibid.

3. Ibid., 606.

4. Ibid.

5. Ibid.

6. Ibid.

7. Ibid.

8. See Richard H. Solomon, *Mao's Revolution and the Chinese Political Culture* (Berkeley: University of California Press, 1971), esp. chap. 2, "Confucianism and the Chinese Life-Cycle," 28–39; chap. 4, "Emotional Control," 61–81; and chap. 5, "The Pain and Rewards of Education," 82–93.

9. Ibid., 37.

10. Ibid.

11. In this regard, Laplanche and Pontalis suggest, "Several authors, following in Freud's footsteps, have stressed that the character of the super-ego is very far removed from the prohibitions and precepts actually enunciated by parents and teachers—so much so, in fact, that the 'severity' of the super-ego may even be in inverse proportion to theirs." This would appear to be the case in the present example of strict paternal influences leading to weak psychic and emotional capacities for normative self-individuation. LaPlanche and Pontalis, *The Language of Psycho Analysis*.

12. Solomon, *Mao's Revolution*, 52; emphasis added.

13. Ibid.

14. Ibid., 37; emphasis added.

15. Ibid., 58–59.

16. Ibid., 36.

17. Ibid., 37.

18. Ibid., 42.

19. Ibid.

20. Ibid., 48.

21. Ibid., 62.

22. Ibid., 48.

23. Ibid., 62; emphasis added.

24. Ibid., 65.

25. Ibid., 70.

26. Ibid., 194.

27. Ibid.,194–195; emphasis in the original.

28. Ibid., 195.

29. Ibid.

30. Ibid., 196.

31. Ibid., 196; emphasis added.

32. Frank Dikötter, *The Tragedy of Liberation: A History of the Chinese Revolution 1945–1957* (New York: Bloomsbury, 2013), 47.

33. Ibid., 66–67.

34. Ibid., 66.

35. Ibid., 67.

36. Ibid.

37. Ian Buruma, *Year Zero: A History of 1945* (New York: Penguin, 2014), 39.

38. Ibid., 41.

39. Yang Su, *Collective Killings in Rural China during the Cultural Revolution* (Cambridge: Cambridge University Press, 2011), 14.

40. Ibid., 14–15.

41. Ibid., 16.

42. Ibid., 18.

43. Ibid., 19.

44. Ibid., 21.

45. Ibid., 24.

46. Ibid.

47. Ibid., 244.

48. Ibid.

49. Ibid., 249.

50. Ibid., 250.

51. Ibid., 254.

52. Ibid., 254–255.

53. Ibid., 254.

54. Ibid., 257.

55. Ibid.

56. Frank Dikötter, *Mao's Great Famine: The History of China's Most Devastating Catastrophe, 1958–1962* (New York: Walker, 2010), 293.

57. Ibid., 294.

58. Ibid.

59. Ibid., 296.

60. Ibid., 294–297.

61. Wurmser, *Mask of Shame*, 72–79.

62. Ibid., 27–28.

63. Ibid., 46.

64. Ibid., 64.

65. Ibid., 76.

66. Fonagy et al., *Affect Regulation*, 426–427.

67. Janine Chasseguet-Smirgel, *The Ego Ideal: A Psychoanalytic Essay on the Malady of the Ideal*, trans. Paul Barrrows (New York: W. W. Norton, 1985), 114.

68. Ibid.

69. Ibid.

70. Ibid., 83.

71. Ibid., 82.

72. Ibid., 83.

73. Ibid., 92–93.

74. Ibid., 105.

75. Ibid., 114.

76. Ibid., 82.

77. Patrick Colm Hogan, *Understanding Nationalism: On Narrative, Cognitive Science, and Identity* (Columbus: Ohio State University Press, 2009), 154–155; emphasis in the original.

78. Lung-kee Sun, "Beloved China: Imagery of 'Mother China' in Modern Chinese Political Thinking," in *The Psychodynamics of International Relationships*, vol. 1: *Concepts and Theories*, ed. Demetrios A. Julius, Vamik D. Volkan, and Joseph V. Montville (Lexington, MA: Lexington, 1991), 147.

79. Fang Zhimin, quoted in ibid., 144.

80. Fang Zhimin, quoted in ibid., 145–146.

81. Ibid., 152.

CHAPTER 8

1. See chapter 2.

2. Edward Peters, *Torture* (New York: Basil Blackwell, 1985), 171.

3. Ibid., 163.

4. Ibid., 164.

5. Ronald Grigor Suny, "Constructing Primordialism: Old Histories for New Nations," *Journal of Modern History* 73, no. 4 (2001): 862–896 and "Truth in Telling: Reconciling Realities in the Genocide of the Ottoman Armenians," *The American Historical Review* 114, no. 4 (2009): 930–946.

6. Ibid., 54.

7. Donald Bloxham, "Internal Colonization, Inter-imperial Conflict and the Armenian Genocide," in *Empire, Colony, Genocide: Conquest, Occupation, and Subaltern Resistance in World History*, ed. A. Dirk Moses, 325–342 (New York: Berghahn, 2008), 335.

8. Ibid., 336.

9. Ibid., 334.

10. Taner Akçam, *A Shameful Act: Armenian Genocide and the Question of Turkish Responsibility* (New York: Metropolitan Books, 2006), 175.

11. Ibid., 189–193.

12. Thea Halo, *Not Even My Name: A True Story* (New York: Picador, 2001), 131.

13. Bloxham, "Internal Colonization," 335–336.

14. Stephen Kotkin, *Stalin*, vol. 1: *Paradoxes of Power, 1878–1928* (New York: Penguin, 2014), 420.

15. Tzvetan Todorov, *Voices from the Gulag: Life and Death in Communist Bulgaria*, trans. Robert Zaretsky (University Park: Penn State University Press, 1999).

16. Kotkin, *Stalin*, vol. 1, 420.

17. Ibid., 739.

18. Igal Halfin, *Stalinist Confessions: Messianism and Terror at the Leningrad Communist University* (Pittsburgh, PA: University of Pittsburgh Press, 2009), 2.

19. Ibid.

20. Ibid.

21. Ibid., 3.

22. Ibid.

23. Ibid.

24. Ibid., 4.

25. Ibid.

26. Ibid., 8.

27. Ibid.; emphasis added.

28. Ibid., 9.

29. Ibid.

30. Ibid.

31. Ibid., 5.

32. Ibid., 359; emphasis added.

33. Ibid., 369.

34. Ibid., 370.

35. Anne Applebaum, *Gulag: A History* (New York: Doubleday, 2003), 279.

36. Glyn Daly, "Ideology and Its Paradoxes: Dimensions of Fantasy and Enjoyment," *Journal of Political Ideologies* 4, no. 2 (1999): 235.

37. Ibid.

38. Isabel V. Hull, "Military Culture and the Production of 'Final Solutions' in the Colonies," in *The Specter of Genocide: Mass Murder in Historical Perspective*, ed. Robert Gellately and Ben Kiernan (Cambridge: Cambridge University Press, 2003), 143.

39. Felicity Rash, *The Language of Violence: Adolf Hitler's Mein Kampf* (Bern: Peter Lang, 2006), 93.

40. Hitler, *Mein Kampf*, quoted in ibid., 95.

41. Alastair Sooke, "The Discobolus: Greeks, Nazis and the Body Beautiful," *BBC*, March 24, 2015. See also Johann Chapoutot, *Greeks, Romans, Germans: How the Nazis Usurped Europe's Classical Past*, trans. Richard R. Nybakken (Oakland: University of California Press, 2016).

42. Timothy Snyder, "Hitler's World," *New York Review of Books*, September 24, 2015, 10.

43. Ibid.

44. See Alexander Mitscherlich and Fred Mielke, *Doctors of Infamy: The Story of the Nazi Medical Crimes*, trans. Heinz Norden (New York: Henry Schuman, 1949); and Vivien Spitz *Doctors from Hell: The Horrific Account of Nazi Experiments on Humans* (Boulder: Sentient Publications, 2005).

45. Spitz, *Doctors from Hell*.

46. Gerald L. Posner and John Ware, *Mengele: The Complete Story* (New York: Cooper Square Press, 2000).

47. Ibid., 25. The self-consciousness as reported by Posner and Ware hardly appears unique to Mengele. The same sense of stain affected several major Nazis figures, including Reinhard Heydrich, who had to fight off the "persistent rumor" that he was part Jewish on account of his father's alleged family background, which may have included some Jewish ancestry. This appears to have prompted various incidents of ridicule when Heydrich was attending naval school, a curriculum he never completed. Specifically, Heydrich was called "Itsy" for Isadore. Mario R. Dederichs, *Heydrich: The Face of Evil*, trans. Geoffrey Brooks (Philadelphia, PA: Casemate, 2009), 37.

48. Posner and Ware, *Mengele*, 25.

49. Miklos Nyiszli, *Auschwitz: A Doctor's Eyewitness Account*, trans. Richard Seaver (New York: Arcade, 2011), 30.

50. Ibid., 131.

51. Ibid.

52. Ibid., 132.

53. Ibid.

54. Ibid.

55. Ibid.

56. Posner and Ware, *Mengele*, 44; emphasis added.

57. Tobias Brocher, quoted in ibid., 45.

58. Robert Jay Lifton, "What Made This Man Mengele," *New York Times Magazine*, July 21, 1985, 23; also see Posner and Wade, *Mengele*, 48–49; and Lifton, *Nazi Doctors*; also, Benno Muller-Hill, *Murderous Science: Elimination by Scientific Selection of Jews, Gypsies, and Others in Germany 1933–1945*, trans George R. Fraser (New York: Oxford University Press, 1984).

59. Martina Puzyna, quoted in Posner and Ware, *Mengele*, 43.

60. Spitz, *Doctors from Hell*, 47.

61. All statements are from Spitz, *Doctors from Hell*, 258–264.

62. Harald Welzer, "Mass Murder and Moral Code: Some Thoughts on an Easily Misunderstood Subject," *History of the Human Sciences* 17, no. 2/3 (2004): 21; citing the work of Lawrence Kohlberg.

63. Ibid., 29.

64. Ibid., 18.

65. Ibid., 23.

66. Ibid., 29.

67. Ibid., 30.

68. Ibid.

69. Anne Harrington, "Unmasking Suffering's Masks: Reflections on Old and New Memories of Nazi Medicine," in *Social Suffering*, ed. Veena Das, Arthur Kleinman, and Margaret Lock (Berkeley: University of California Press, 1997), 184; emphasis in the original.

70. Ibid., 184.

71. See Mahmood Mamdani, *When Victims Become Killers: Colonialism, Nativism, and the Genocide in Rwanda* (Princeton, NJ: Princeton University Press, 2002); Robert Melson, "Modern Genocide in Rwanda: Ideology, Revolution, War and Mass Murder in an African State," in *The Specter of Genocide: Mass Murder in Historical Perspective*, ed. Robert Gellately and Ben Kiernan (Cambridge: Cambridge University Press, 2003), 325–338; de Swaan, *Killing Compartments*.

72. Lee Ann Fujii, *Killing Neighbors: Webs of Violence in Rwanda* (Ithaca, NY: Cornell University Press, 2009), 185–189.

73. Ibid., 183.

74. Ibid., 187.

75. Ibid., 183, 185–186.

76. Ibid., 185.

77. Ibid., 187.

78. Ibid., 188.

79. Ibid.

80. Ibid.

81. Alison Des Forges, *"Leave None to Tell the Story": Genocide in Rwanda* (New York: Human Rights Watch, 1999), 1.

82. Philip Verwimp, "Machetes and Firearms: The Organization of Massacres in Rwanda," *Journal of Peace Research* 43, no. 1 (2006): 5–22, at 8.

83. Ibid.

84. Ibid., 19.

85. Ibid.

86. Liisa H. Malkii, *Purity and Exile: Violence, Memory, and National Cosmology among Hutu Refugees in Tanzania* (Chicago: University of Chicago Press, 1995), 55.

87. Ibid., 94.

88. Ibid.

89. Ibid., 95.

90. Ibid., 92.

91. Ibid.

92. Christopher C. Taylor, "The Cultural Face of Terror in the Rwandan Genocide of 1994," in *Annihilating Difference: The Anthropology of Genocide*, ed. Alexander Laban Hinton (Berkeley: University of California Press, 2002), 139.

93. Bourdieu, *Distinction*.

94. Taylor, "Cultural Face of Terror," 139.

95. Ibid., 141.

96. Ibid., 142.

97. Ibid., 146.

98. Ibid.

99. Ibid.

100. Ibid., 148.

101. Ibid.

102. Ibid.,158; emphasis added.

103. Ibid., 171–172.

104. Ibid., 161.

105. Ibid.

106. Gregory H. Stanton, "Blue Scarves and Yellow Stars: Classification and Symbolization in the Cambodian Genocide," *The Faulds Lecture* (1987).

107. *Wikipedia*, s.v., "Language reforms" in "Khmer Rouge," updated May 23, 2017, https://en.wikipedia.org/wiki/Khmer_Rouge#Language_reforms.

108. Kaylanee Mam, "The Endurance of the Cambodian Family Under the Khmer Rouge Regime: An Oral History," in *Genocide in Cambodia and Rwanda*, ed. Susan E. Cook (New Brunswick, NJ: Transaction, 2006), 134.

109. Ben Kiernan, "Myth, Nationalism and Genocide," *Journal of Genocide Research* 3, no. 2 (2001): 201.

110. Ibid., 203.

111. Frank Henderson Stewart, *Honor* (Chicago: University of Chicago Press, 1994), 21.

112. Julian Pitt-Rivers, "Honor," in *International Encyclopedia of the Social Sciences* (1968), 503–511; and "Honor and Social Status," in *Honour and Shame: The Values of Mediterranean Society*, ed. J. G. Peristiany (Chicago: University of Chicago Press, 1966), 19–78.

113. Valeschka Martins Guerra, Roger Giner-Sorolla, and Milica Vasiljevic, "The Importance of Honor Concerns across Eight Countries," *Group Process and Intergroup Relations* 16, no. 3 (2011): 299.

114. Ibid., 301.

115. George E. Marcus and Michael M. J. Fischer, *Anthropology as Cultural Critique: An Experimental Moment in the Human Sciences* (Chicago: University of Chicago Press, 1999).

116. Alexander Laban Hinton, *Why Did They Kill? Cambodia in the Shadow of Genocide* (Berkeley: University of California Press, 2005), 226.

117. Ibid., 226.

118. Ibid., 223.

119. Ibid., 229.

120. Ibid., 93.

121. Alexander Laban Hinton, "Why Did You Kill? The Cambodian Genocide and the Dark Side of Face and Honor," *Journal of Asian Studies* 57, no. 1 (1998): 96, 97n7.

122. Ibid., 98n9.

123. Ibid., 103n16.

124. See ibid., 101–104.

125. Ibid., 112. Donald J. Trump's insistence on the fealty display by his cabinet members represents a parallel.

126. Ibid., 115.

127. Ibid.

128. Ibid., 159–160.

129. Hinton, *Why Did They Kill?*, 274.

130. Ibid., 175.

131. Ibid.

132. Ibid., 116.

133. Alexander Laban Hinton, "A Head for an Eye: Revenge in the Cambodian Genocide," *American Ethnologist* 25, no. 3 (1998): 359.

134. Ibid., 363, 367.

135. David P. Chandler, *Voices from S-21: Terror and History in Pol Pot's Secret Prison* (Berkeley: University of California Press, 1999), 128.

136. Ibid., 130.

137. Ibid., 132.

138. Ibid., 133–134.

139. Ibid., 227.

140. Ibid., 134.

141. Ibid., 149.

142. Ibid., 33.

143. Hinton, *Why Did They Kill?*, 231–232; as abbreviated by the author.

144. Ibid., 232–233; as abbreviated by the author.

145. Ben Kiernan, *The Pol Pot Regime: Race, Power, and Genocide in Cambodia under the Khmer Rouge, 1975–1979* (New Haven, CT: Yale University Press, 1996), 349–350.

146. Chandler, *Voices from S-21*, 6.

147. Ibid., 81; Chandler quotes a statement from Steve Heder, see ibid., 81n15.

148. Ibid., 113.

149. Ibid.

150. Michelle Caswell, *Archiving the Unspeakable: Silence, Memory, and the Photographic Record in Cambodia* (Madison, WI: University of Wisconsin Press, 2014); more recently, see also James A. Tyner, Sokvisal Kimsroy, Chenjian Fu, Zheye Wang, and Xinyue Ye, "An Empirical Analysis of Arrests and Executions at S-21 Security-Center During the Cambodian Genocide," *Genocide Studies International* 10, no. 2 (2016): 268–286.

151. Chandler, *Voices from S-21*, 89.

152. Ibid., 79.

153. Ibid., 50.

154. Peter Maguire, *Facing Death in Cambodia* (New York: Columbia University Press, 2005), 120.

155. Ibid., 122.

156. Amy Ray Stewart, "Witnessing Horror: Psychoanalysis and the Abject Stain of Lynching Photography," *Psychoanalysis, Culture & Society* 19, no. 4 (2014): 422.

157. Ibid., 424.

158. Ibid.

159. Ibid., 427.

160. Ibid., 426, 424.

161. Henry Krips, "Politics of the Picture," *Psychoanalysis, Culture and Society* 18, no. 1 (2013): 27.

162. Jacques Derrida, *Archive Fever: A Freudian Impression*, trans. Eric Prenowitz (Chicago: University of Chicago Press, 1996), 80.

163. Ibid., 1; emphasis in the original.

164. Ibid., 2.

165. Ibid., 36.

166. Feitlowitz, *Lexicon of Terror*, 11.

167. Ibid., 11, 65.

168. Ibid., 20; emphasis added.

169. Ibid., 49.

170. Ibid.

171. Entire listing is from ibid., 51–62.

172. Ibid., 49.

173. Ibid., 51.

174. Ibid.

175. Mark J. Osiel, "Constructing Subversion in Argentina's Dirty War," *Representations* 75, no. 1 (2001): 119–158, at 131.

176. Ibid. Citing Tina Rosenberg, *Children of Cain: Violence and the Violent in Latin America* (London: Penguin, 1992), 97–98.

177. Osiel, "Constructing Subversion in Argentina's Dirty War," 141.

178. Omer Bartov and Phyllis Mack, introduction to *In God's Name: Genocide and Religion in the Twentieth Century*, ed. Omer Bartov and Phyllis Mack (New York: Berghahn, 2001).

179. Osiel, "Constructing Subversion," 157.

180. Ibid.; emphasis in the original.

181. Ibid.

182. Norman Cigar, *Genocide in Bosnia: The Policy of "Ethnic Cleansing"* (College Station: Texas A&M University Press, 1995).

183. Norman M. Naimark, *Fires of Hatred: Ethnic Cleansing in Twentieth-Century Europe* (Cambridge, MA: Harvard University Press, 2001), 160.

184. Ibid., 163.

185. Ibid., 168.

186. *Wikipedia*, s.v. "Omarska Camp," updated April 26, 2017, http://en.wikipedia.org/wiki/Omarska_camp.

187. The final report of the Commission of Experts distinguished between five different patterns of rape. For further elaboration on this critical issue, see Norman Cigar and Paul Williams, *Indictment at the Hague: The Milošević Regime and Crimes of the Balkan Wars* (New York: New York University Press, 2002), 235–241.

188. Slavenka Drakulić, *As if I Am Not There* (London: Abacus, 1999), 73.

189. Cigar and Williams, *Indictment at the Hague*, 236–239.

190. Avishai Margalit, *The Decent Society* (Cambridge, MA: Harvard University Press, 1996), 118.

191. Ibid., 122.

192. François Debrix, *Global Powers of Horror: Security, Politics, and the Body in Pieces*. Interventions (New York: Routledge, 2017), 56–84.

193. Jennifer Biddle, "Shame," in *Emotions: A Cultural Studies Reader*, ed. Jennifer Harding and E. Deidre Pribram (New York: Routledge, 2009), 115.

194. Julien A. Deonna, Raffaele Rodogno, and Fabrice Teroni, *In Defense of Shame: The Faces of an Emotion* (Oxford: Oxford University Press, 2012), 31–32.

195. Helen Block Lewis, "Introduction: Shame—the 'Sleeper' in Psychopathology," in *The Role of Shame in Symptom Formation*, ed. Helen Block Lewis (Hillsdale, NJ: Lawrence Erlbaum, 1987), 18–19; emphasis in the original.

196. Ibid., emphasis in the original.

197. Ibid., 19.

198. Ibid.

199. Ibid., 147.

200. Thomas J. Scheff, "The Shame-Rage Spiral: A Case Study of an Interminable Quarrel," in Lewis, *Role of Shame in Symptom Formation*, 112.

201. Inger Skjelsbaek, *The Political Psychology of War Rape: Studies from Bosnia and Herzegovina* (New York: Routledge, 2012), 141; emphasis in the original.

202. Ibid.

203. Kilborne, *Disappearing Persons*, 123–124; emphasis added.

204. Ibid., 123–124.

205. Ibid., 124.

206. Thomas Scheff and Suzanne M Retzinger, *Emotions and Violence: Shame and Rage in Destructive Conflicts* (Lexington: Lexington Books, 1991), 151–152.

207. Ibid., 152.

208. Ibid., 159; emphasis in the original.

209. Ibid.

210. Ibid., 153.

211. James Gilligan, *Violence: Our Deadly Epidemic and Its Causes* (New York: Putnam, 1996), 110.

212. Ibid., 111.

213. Ibid., 111, 113.

214. Heinz Kohut. *The Restoration of the Self* (New York: International Universities Press, 1973), 386.

215. Ibid., 395–396; emphasis in the original.

216. Ibid.; emphasis in the original.

217. Erich Fromm, *The Anatomy of Human Destructiveness* (New York: Holt, Rinehart and Winston, 1973), 288.

218. Ibid., 288–289.

219. Gerhart Piers and Milton B. Singer, *Shame and Guilt: A Psychoanalytic and a Cultural Study* (New York: W. W. Norton, 1971), 28.

220. Ibid., 29; emphasis in the original.

221. Peter Glick, "Sacrificial Lambs Dressed in Wolves' Clothing: Envious Prejudice, Ideology, and the Scapegoating of Jews." In *Understanding Genocide: The Social Psychology of the Holocaust*, ed. Leonard S. Newman and Ralph Erber (Oxford: Oxford University Press, 2002, 130; emphasis in the original.

222. Ibid.

223. Ruth Stein, *For Love of the Father: A Psychoanalytic Study of Religious Terrorism*, Meridian: Crossing Aesthetics (Stanford, CA: Stanford University Press, 2010), 106–109.

224. Ibid., 107.

225. Ibid.

226. Ibid., 109.

227. Ibid., 118.

228. Ibid.

229. Ibid.

230. Ibid., 121.

231. Ibid., 123.

232. Žižek, *For They Know Not What They Do*, 87; emphasis in the original.

233. Ibid., 87.

234. Ibid., 90.

235. Ibid.

236. Ibid., 30.

237. Ibid., 32–33; emphasis in the original.

238. Adam Kotsko, *Žižek and Theology* (London: T & T Clark, 2008), 35.

239. Slavoj Žižek, *The Sublime Object of Ideology* (London: Verso, 1989), 44–45.

240. Ibid., 49; emphasis in the original.

CHAPTER 9

1. Žižek, *For They Know Not What They Do*, 73; emphasis in the original.

2. Ibid., 73.

3. Slavoj Žižek, *Looking Awry: An Introduction to Jacques Lacan through Popular Culture.* (Cambridge, MA: MIT Press, 1991), lxx–lxxi.

4. Žižek, *Tarrying with the Negative*, 3.

5. Evans, *Introductory Dictionary*, 200–201.

6. Žižek, *For They Know Not What They Do*, 234.

7. Ibid., 237.

8. Žižek, *For They Know Not What They Do*, 7.

9. Cavarero, *Horrorism*, 6.

10. Ibid., 12–13.

11. Žižek, *For They Know Not What They Do*, 97.

12. Ibid.

13. Ibid., 98.

14. Ibid.

15. Chiesa, *Subjectivity and Otherness*, 156.

16. Ibid., 157.

17. Ibid.

18. Ibid.

19. Ibid.

20. Ibid., 156.

21. Ibid., 150.

22. Ibid.

23. Ibid., 169.

24. Ibid.; emphasis in the original.

25. Simon Critchley, *Ethics-Politics-Subjectivity: Essays on Derrida, Levinas and Contemporary French Thought* (London: Verso, 1999), 203.

26. http://www.telegraph.co.uk/news/worldnews/europe/croatia/9682855/Croatian-hero-Ante-Gotovina-acquitted-of-war-crimes.html.

27. Žižek, *For They Know Not What They Do*, 43; emphasis in the original.

28. Ibid.

29. Boothby, *Freud as Philosopher*, 66.

30. Ibid., 84.

31. Ibid., 120.

32. Ibid., 117.

33. Ibid., 122.

34. Žižek, *For They Know Not What They Do*, 28.

35. Ibid., 39.

36. Peter Klepec, "On the Mastery in the Four 'Discourses,'" in Tomšič and Zevnik, *Jacques Lacan*, 117–118.

37. Vanheule, *Subject of Psychosis*, 54.

38. Ibid., 54.

39. Žižek, *For They Know Not What They Do*, 71.

40. Jeffrey Stevenson Murer, "Constructing the Enemy-Other: Anxiety, Trauma, and Mourning in the Narratives of Political Conflict," *Psychoanalysis, Culture and Society* 14, no. 2 (2009): 122.

41. Ibid., 123.

42. Ibid., 124.

43. Homi K. Bhabha, *The Location of Culture* (New York: Routledge, 1994), 208.

44. Neill, *Lacanian Ethics*, 20.

45. Ibid., 29; emphasis in the original.

46. William Egginton, *The Philosopher's Desire: Psychoanalysis, Interpretation, and Truth* (Stanford, CA: Stanford University Press, 2007), 101.

47. Ibid.

48. Ibid.

49. Ibid., 102.

50. Ibid., 103; emphasis in the original.

51. Ibid., 31.

52. Ibid., 40.

53. Neill, *Lacanian Ethics*, 45.

54. Ibid.

CHAPTER 10

1. Gerard Toal and Carl T. Dahlman, *Bosnia Remade: Ethnic Cleansing and Its Reversal* (Oxford: Oxford University Press, 2011), 5.

2. Ibid., 307.

3. Ibid., 307–308.

4. Ibid., 308.

BIBLIOGRAPHY

Abrahamian, Ervand. *Tortured Confessions: Prisons and Public Recantatons in Modern Iran.* Berkeley: University of California Press, 1999.

Adorno, Theodor W. *Critical Models: Interventions and Catchwords.* Translated by Henry W. Pickford. New York: Columbia University Press, 2005.

———. *Minima Moralia: Reflections on a Damaged Life.* Translated by E. F. N. Jephcott. London: Verso, 2006.

———. With Max Horkheimer, *Dialectic of Enlightenment.* Translated by John Cumming. London: Verso, 1997.

Agamben, Giorgio. *Remnants of Auschwitz: The Witness and the Archive.* Translated by Daniel Heller-Roazen. New York: Zone Books, 2002.

Akçam, Taner. *A Shameful Act: Armenian Genocide and the Question of Turkish Responsibility.* New York: Metropolitan Books, 2006.

———. *The Young Turks' Crime against Humanity: The Armenian Genocide and Ethnic Cleansing in the Ottoman Empire.* Princeton, NJ: Princeton University Press, 2013.

Alford, C. Fred. "'Hitler's Willing Executioners': What Does 'Willing' Mean?" *Theory and Society* 26, no. 5 (1997): 719–738.

———. *Melanie Klein and Critical Social Theory: An Account of Politics, Art, and Reason Based on Her Psychoanalytic Theory.* New Haven, CT: Yale University Press, 1989.

———. *What Evil Means to Us.* Ithaca, NY: Cornell University Press, 1997.

Applebaum, Anne. *Gulag: A History.* New York: Doubleday, 2003.

Aronson, Ronald. *The Dialectics of Disaster.* New York: Schocken, 1983.

Ashley, Richard K. "Critical Spirits Realist Specters: Some Hypotheses on the Spectro-Poetics of International Relations." In *The Ashgate Research Companion to Modern Theory, Modern Power, World Politics*, edited by Scott G. Nelson and Nevzat Soguk, 105–126. Surrey: Ashgate, 2016.

Auestad, Lene. *Respect, Plurality, and Prejudice: A Psychoanalytical and Philosophical Enquiry into the Dynamics of Social Exclusion and Discrimination*. London: Karnac, 2015.

Autesserre, Severine. "Dangerous Tales: Dominant Narratives on the Congo and Their Unintended Consequences." *African Affairs* 111, no. 443 (2012): 202–222.

Baron-Cohen, Simon. *The Science of Evil: On Empathy and the Origins of Cruelty*. New York: Basic, 2012.

Bar-Tal, Daniel. *Shared Beliefs in a Society: Social Psychological Analysis*. Thousand Oaks, CA: Sage, 2000.

Bartov, Omer, and Phyllis Mack. Introduction to *In God's Name: Genocide and Religion in the Twentieth Century*, edited by Omer Bartov and Phyllis Mack, 1–22. New York: Berghahn, 2001.

Baumeister, Roy F. "The Nature and Structure of the Self: An Overview." In *The Self in Social Psychology*, edited by Roy F. Baumeister, 1–21. Philadelphia, PA: Psychology Press, 1999.

BBC News. "UN Condemns DR Congo Cannibalism." *BBC News World Edition*, January 15, 2003. http://news.bbc.co.uk/2/hi/africa/2661365.stm.

Bellamy, Alex J. *Massacres and Morality: Mass Atrocities in an Age of Civilian Immunity*. Oxford: Oxford University Press, 2012.

Benvenuto, Bice. *Concerning the Rites of Psychoanalysis: Or the Villa of the Mysteries*. New York: Routledge, 1994.

Bhabha, Homi K. *The Location of Culture*. New York: Routledge, 1994.

Biddle, Jennifer. "Shame." In *Emotions: A Cultural Studies Reader*, edited by Jennifer Harding and E. Deidre Pribram, 113–125. New York: Routledge, 2009.

Bikont, Anna. *The Crime and the Silence: Confronting the Massacre of Jews in Wartime Jedwabne*. Translated by Alissa Valles. New York: Farrar, Straus and Giroux, 2015.

Billig, Michael. "Humour and Hatred: The Racist Jokes of the Ku Klux Klan." *Discourse & Society* 12, no. 3 (2001): 267–289.

Blok, Anton. "The Narcissism of Minor Differences." *European Journal of Social Theory* 1, no. 1 (1998): 33–56.

Bloxham, Donald. "Internal Colonization, Inter-imperial Conflict and the Armenian Genocide." In *Empire, Colony, Genocide: Conquest, Occupation, and Subaltern Resistance in World History*, edited by A. Dirk Moses, 325–342. New York: Berghahn, 2008.

Boothby, Richard. *Death and Desire: Psychoanalytic Theory in Lacan's Return to Freud*. New York: Routledge, 1991.

———. *Freud as Philosopher: Metapsychology after Lacan*. New York: Routledge, 2001.

———. "The Psychical Meaning of Life and Death: Reflections on the Lacanian Imaginary, Symbolic, and Real." In *Disseminating Lacan*, edited by David Pettigrew and Francois Raffoul. Suny Series in Contemporary Continental Philosophy, 337–363. Albany: State University of New York Press, 1996.

Bourdieu, Pierre. *Distinction: A Social Critique of the Judgement of Taste*. Translated by Richard Nice. Cambridge, MA: Harvard University Press, 1984.

Brakel, Linda A. W. *Unconscious Knowing and Other Essays in Psycho-Philosophical Analysis*. Oxford: Oxford University Press, 2009.

Bromberg, Norbert, and Verna Volz Small. *Hitler's Psychopathology.* New York: International Universities Press, 1983.

Browning, Christopher R. *Ordinary Men: Reserve Police Battalion 101 and the Final Solution in Poland.* New York: Harper Perrenial, 1993.

Buruma, Ian. "China: Reeducation through Horror." *New York Review of Books,* January 9, 2014, 39–41.

———. *Year Zero: A History of 1945.* New York: Penguin, 2014.

Butler, Judith. *Gender Trouble: Feminism and the Subversion of Identity.* New York: Routledge, 1999.

Campbell, Jason J. *On the Nature of Genocidal Intent.* Plymouth, UK: Lexington, 2013.

Caillois, Roger. *Man and the Sacred.* Translated by Meyer Barash. 2nd ed. Urbana: University of Illinois Press, 2001. Originally published in 1959.

Cashman, Greg. *What Causes War? An Introduction to Theories of International Conflict.* Plymouth, UK: Rowman & Littlefield, 2014.

Caswell, Michelle. *Archiving the Unspeakable: Silence, Memory, and the Photographic Record in Cambodia.* Madison, WI: University of Wisconsin Press, 2014.

Cavarero, Adriana. *Horrorism: Naming Contemporary Violence.* Translated by William McCuaig. New York: Columbia University Press, 2011.

Caygill, Howard. *Levinas and the Political.* London: Routledge, 2002.

CBS News. "War against Women: The Use of Rape as a Weapon in Congo's Civil War." *60 Minutes,* August 17, 2008. http://www.cbsnews.com/stories/2008/01/11/60minutes/main3701249.shtml.

Chandler, David P. *Brother Number One: A Political Biography of Pol Pot.* Boulder, CO: Westview, 1999.

———. *Voices from S-21: Terror and History in Pol Pot's Secret Prison.* Berkeley: University of California Press, 1999.

Chapoutot, Johann. *Greeks, Romans, Germans: How the Nazis Usurped Europe's Classical Past.* Translated by Richard R. Nybakken. Oakland: University of California Press, 2016.

Chasseguet-Smirgel, Janine. *The Ego Ideal: A Psychoanalytic Essay on the Malady of the Ideal.* Translated by Paul Barrrows. New York: W. W. Norton, 1985.

Chiesa, Lorenzo. *Subjectivity and Otherness: A Philosophical Reading of Lacan.* Cambridge, MA: MIT Press, 2007.

Chirot, Daniel, and Clark McCauley. *Why Not Kill Them All? The Logic and Prevention of Mass Political Murder.* Princeton, NJ: Princeton University Press, 2006.

Cigar, Norman. *Genocide in Bosnia: The Policy of "Ethnic Cleansing."* College Station: Texas A&M University Press, 1995.

Clendinnen, Inga. *Reading the Holocaust.* Cambridge: Cambridge University Press, 1999.

Conley-Zilkic, Bridget K., ed. *How Mass Atrocities End: Studies from Guatemala, Burundi, Indonesia, the Sudans, Bosnia-Herzegovina, and Iraq.* New York: Cambridge University Press, 2016.

Critchley, Simon. *Ethics-Politics-Subjectivity: Essays on Derrida, Levinas and Contemporary French Thought.* London: Verso, 1999.

Daly, Glyn. "Ideology and Its Paradoxes: Dimensions of Fantasy and Enjoyment." *Journal of Political Ideologies* 4, no. 2 (1999): 219–238.

Daniel, E. Valentine. *Charred Lullabies: Chapters in an Anthropography of Violence.* Princeton, NJ: Princeton University Press, 1996.

de Swaan, Abram. *The Killing Compartments: The Mentality of Mass Murder.* New Haven, CT: Yale University Press, 2015.

Debrix, François. *Global Powers of Horror: Security, Politics, and the Body in Pieces.* Interventions. New York: Routledge, 2017.

———. *Tabloid Terror: War, Culture, and Geopolitics.* New York: Routledge, 2007.

Dederichs, Mario R. *Heydrich: The Face of Evil.* Translated by Geoffrey Brooks. Philadelphia, PA: Casemate, 2009.

Deleuze, Gilles, and Félix Guattari. *Anti-Oedipus: Capitalism and Schizophrenia.* Translated by Robert Hurley, Mark Seem, and Helen R. Lane. London: Penguin, 2009.

Deonna, Julien A., Raffaele Rodogno, and Fabrice Teroni. *In Defense of Shame: The Faces of an Emotion.* Oxford: Oxford University Press, 2012.

Derrida, Jacques. *Archive Fever: A Freudian Impression.* Translated by Eric Prenowitz. Chicago: University of Chicago Press, 1996.

———. *On the Name.* Translated by David Wood. Stanford, CA: Stanford University Press, 1995.

Des Forges, Alison. *"Leave None to Tell the Story": Genocide in Rwanda.* New York: Human Rights Watch, 1999.

Deweese-Boyd, Ian. "Self-Deception." *Stanford Encyclopedia of Philosophy.* Edward Zalta, ed. Winter 2016. http://plato.stanford.edu/entries/self-deception/.

Dikötter, Frank. *Mao's Great Famine: The History of China's Most Devastating Catastrophe, 1958–1962.* New York: Walker, 2010.

———. *The Tragedy of Liberation: A History of the Chinese Revolution, 1945–1957.* New York: Bloomsbury, 2013.

Drakulić, Slavenka. *S.: A Novel about the Balkans.* Translated by Marko Ivic. New York: Penguin, 1999. Originally published as *As if I Am Not There.* London: Abacus, 1999.

Drumbl, Mark A. *Atrocity, Punishment, and International Law.* Cambridge: Cambridge University Press, 2007.

Durkheim, Emile. *The Elementary Forms of Religious Life.* Translated by Karen E. Fields. New York: Free Press, 1995.

Duschinsky, Robbie. "Ideal and Unsullied: Purity, Subjectivity, and Social Power." *Subjectivity* 4, no. 2 (2011): 147–167.

Egginton, William. *The Philosopher's Desire: Psychoanalysis, Interpretation, and Truth.* Stanford, CA: Stanford University Press, 2007.

Evans, Dylan. *An Introductory Dictionary of Lacanian Psychoanalysis.* London: Routledge, 1996.

Farber, Leslie. *The Ways of the Will: Essays towards a Psychology and Psychopathology of Will.* New York: Harper & Row, 1966.

Fearon, James D., and David D. Laitin. "Ethnicity, Insurgency, and Civil War." *American Political Science Review* 97, no. 1 (2003): 75–90.

Feitlowitz, Marguerite. *A Lexicon of Terror: Argentina and the Legacies of Torture.* Oxford: Oxford University Press, 1998.

Feldman, Allen. *Formations of Violence: The Narrative of the Body and Political Terror in Northern Ireland.* Chicago: University of Chicago Press, 1991.

Figlio, Karl. "The Dread of Sameness: Social Hatred and Freud's 'Narcissism of Minor Differences.'" In *Psychoanalysis and Politics: Exclusion and the Politics of Representation*, edited by Lene Auestad, 7–24. London: Karnac, 2012.

Fink, Bruce. *A Clinical Introduction to Lacanian Psychoanalysis: Theory and Technique.* Cambridge, MA: Harvard University Press, 1997.

———. *The Lacanian Subject: Between Language and Jouissance.* Princeton, NJ: Princeton University Press, 1995.

Fonagy, Peter, Gyorgy Gergely, Elliot Jurist, and Mary Target. *Affect Regulation, Mentalization, and the Development of the Self.* New York: Other Press, 2004.

Foucault, Michel. *Discipline and Punish: The Birth of the Prison.* Translated by Alan Sheridan. New York: Vintage, 1995.

———. *"Society Must Be Defended": Lectures at the College de France 1975–1976.* Translated by David Macey. New York: Picador, 1997.

Friedländer, Saul. *Memory, History, and the Extermination of the Jews of Europe.* Bloomington: Indiana University Press, 1993.

Frijda, Nico H. *The Laws of Emotion.* Mahwah, NJ: Lawrence Erlbaum, 2007.

Fromm, Erich. *The Anatomy of Human Destructiveness.* New York: Holt, Rinehart and Winston, 1973.

Frosh, Stephen. *For and against Psychoanalysis.* London: Routledge, 2006.

———. *Hate and the "Jewish Science": Anti-Semitism, Nazism and Psychoanalysis.* New York: Palgrave Macmillan, 2009.

———. *Hauntings: Psychoanalysis and Ghostly Transmissions.* New York: Palgrave Macmillan, 2013.

———. "Masculine Mastery and Fantasy, or the Meaning of the Phallus." In *Psychoanalysis in Contexts: Paths Between Theory and Modern Culture*, edited by Anthony Elliott and Stephen Frosh, 166–190. London: Routledge, 1995.

Fujii, Lee Ann. *Killing Neighbors: Webs of Violence in Rwanda.* Ithaca, NY: Cornell University Press, 2009.

Gilligan, James. *Violence: Our Deadly Epidemic and Its Causes.* New York: Putnam, 1996.

Girard, René. *Violence and the Sacred.* Translated by Patrick Gregory. Baltimore: Johns Hopkins University Press, 1979.

Gladstone, Brooke. *The Trouble with Reality: A Rumination on Moral Panic in our Time.* New York: Workman Publishing Company, 2017.

Glick, Peter. "Sacrificial Lambs Dressed in Wolves' Clothing: Envious Prejudice, Ideology, and the Scapegoating of Jews." In *Understanding Genocide: The Social Psychology of the Holocaust*, edited by Leonard S. Newman and Ralph Erber, 113–142. Oxford: Oxford University Press, 2002.

Glynos, Jason. "The Grip of Ideology: A Lacanian Approach to the Theory of Ideology." *Journal of Political Ideologies* 6, no. 2 (2001): 191–214.

Glynos, Jason, and Yannis Stavrakakis. "Lacan and Political Subjectivity: Fantasy and Enjoyment in Psychoanalysis and Political Theory." *Subjectivity* 24, no. 1 (2008): 256–274.

Goffman, Erving. *The Goffman Reader.* Edited by Charles Lemert and Ann Branaman. Oxford: Blackwell, 1997.

Goldhagen, Daniel J. *Worse than War: Genocide, Eliminationism, and the Ongoing Assault on Humanity.* New York: Public Affairs, 2009.

Gourgouris, Stathis, ed. *Freud and Fundamentalism: The Psychical Politics of Knowledge.* New York: Fordham University Press, 2010.

Grandin, Greg. "History, Motive, Law, Intent: Combining Historical and Legal Methods in Understanding Guatemala's 1981–1983 Genocide." In *The Specter of Genocide: Mass Murder in Historical Perspective*, edited by Robert Gellately and Ben Kiernan, 339–352. Cambridge: Cambridge University Press, 2003.

——. "The Instruction of Great Catastrophe: Truth Commissions, National History, and State Formation in Argentina, Chile, and Guatemala." *The American Historical Review* 110, no. 1 (2005): 46–67.

Greenfeld, Liah. "Using the Holocaust. Review Essay of Metaphor, Nation and the Holocaust: The Concept of the Body Politic." Library of Social Science, 2015. http://www.libraryofsocialscience.com/reviews/Greenfeld.html.

Gross, Jan T. *Fear: Anti-Semitism in Poland after Auschwitz.* New York: Random House, 2007.

——. *Neighbors: The Destruction of the Jewish Community in Jedwabne, Poland.* New York: Penguin, 2002.

Grunberger, Richard. *Germany: 1918–1945.* London: B. T. Batsford, 1964.

Guerra, Valeschka Martins, Roger Giner-Sorolla, and Milica Vasiljevic. "The Importance of Honor Concerns across Eight Countries." *Group Process and Intergroup Relations* 16, no. 3 (2011): 298–318.

Halfin, Igal. *Stalinist Confessions: Messianism and Terror at the Leningrad Communist University.* Pittsburgh, PA: University of Pittsburgh Press, 2009.

Halo, Thea. *Not Even My Name: A True Story.* New York: Picador, 2001.

Harrington, Anne. "Unmasking Suffering's Masks: Reflections on Old and New Memories of Nazi Medicine." In *Social Suffering*, edited by Veena Das, Arthur Kleinman, and Margaret Lock, 181–206. Berkeley: University of California Press, 1997.

Hinton, Alexander Laban. "A Head for an Eye: Revenge in the Cambodian Genocide." *American Ethnologist* 25, no. 3 (1998): 352–377.

——. *Why Did They Kill? Cambodia in the Shadow of Genocide.* Berkeley: University of California Press, 2005.

——. "Why Did You Kill? The Cambodian Genocide and the Dark Side of Face and Honor." *Journal of Asian Studies* 57, no. 1 (1998): 93–122.

Hirvonen, Ari. "The Truth of Desire: Lack, Law, and Phallus." In *Jacques Lacan: Between Psychoanalysis and Politics*, edited by Samo Tomšič and Andreja Zevnik, 202–216. London: Routledge, 2016.

Historical Clarification Commission. *Guatemala: Memory of Silence: Report of the Commission for Historical Clarification Conclusions and Recommendations.* Guatemala City: Historical Clarification Commission, 1999.

Hoens, Dominiek. "Object a and Politics." In *Jacques Lacan: Between Psychoanalysis and Politics*, edited by Samo Tomšič and Andreja Zevnik, 101–112. London: Routledge, 2016.

Hogan, Patrick Colm. *Understanding Nationalism: On Narrative, Cognitive Science, and Identity.* Columbus: Ohio State University Press, 2009.

Hook, Derek. *A Critical Psychology of the Postcolonial: The Mind of Apartheid.* London: Psychology Press, 2012.

——. *Foucault, Psychology and the Analytics of Power.* Critical Theory and Practice in Psychology and the Human Sciences. New York: Palgrave Macmillan, 2007.

Hook, Derek, and Calum Neill. "Perspectives on 'Lacanian Subjectivities.'" *Subjectivity* 24, no. 1 (2008): 247–255.

Hull, Isabel V. "Military Culture and the Production of 'Final Solutions' in the Colonies." In *The Specter of Genocide: Mass Murder in Historical Perspective*, edited by Robert Gellately and Ben Kiernan, 141–162. Cambridge: Cambridge University Press, 2003.

Human Rights Watch. "Sri Lanka: Government Abuses Intensify: Killings, Abductions, and Displacement Soar and Impunity Reigns." *Human Rights Watch*, August 5, 2007. http://www.hrw.org/en/news/2007/08/05/sri-lanka-government-abuses-intensify.

Isango, Eddy. "Cannibalism Shock as Congo Atrocities Revealed." *The Age*, March 18, 2005. http://www.theage.com.au/news/World/Cannibalism-shock-as-Congo-atrocities-revealed/2005/03/17/1110913734387.html.

Jacoby, Russell. *Bloodlust: On the Roots of Violence from Cain and Abel to the Present*. New York: Free Press, 2011.

Janis, Irving L. *Victims of Groupthink: A Psychological Study of Foreign-Policy Decisions and Fiascoes*. New York: Houghton Mifflin, 1972.

Jay, Nancy. *Throughout Your Generations Forever: Sacrifice, Religion, and Paternity*. Chicago: University of Chicago Press, 1992.

Johnston, Adrian. "The Vicious Circle of the Super-Ego: The Pathological Trap of Guilt and the Beginning of Ethics." *Psychoanalytic Studies* 3, no. 3/4 (2001): 411–424.

———. *Žižek's Ontology: A Transcendental Materialist Theory of Subjectivity*. Northwestern University Studies in Phenomenology and Existential Philosophy. Evanston, IL: Northwestern University Press, 2008.

Jones, Ann. "Mass Rape in the Congo: A Crime against Society." *The Nation*, December 23, 2008. http://www.alternet.org/reproductivejustice/113782/mass_rape_in_the_congo:_a_crime_against_society/?page=entire.

Kallis, Aristotle. *Genocide and Fascism: The Eliminationist Drive in Fascist Europe*. New York: Routledge, 2009.

Kahn, Paul W. *Out of Eden*. Princeton, NJ: Princeton University Press, 2010.

———. *Political Theology: Four New Chapters on the Concept of Sovereignty*. New York: Columbia University Press, 2011.

Kaplan, Abraham. *The Conduct of Inquiry: Methodology for Behavioral Science*. San Francisco: Chandler, 1964.

Kaufmann, Walter. *Existentialism from Dostoevsky to Sartre*. New York: Meridian, 1957.

Kershaw, Ian. *The Nazi Dictatorship: Problems and Perspectives of Interpretation*. 3rd ed. London: Edward Arnold, 1993.

Kiernan, Ben. "Hitler, Pol Pot, and Hutu Power: Distinguishing Themes of Genocidal Ideology." *Holocaust and the United Nations Outreach Programme Discussion Papers Journal* 1 (2009): 19–32.

———. Holocaust and the United Nations Discussion Paper Series, Discussion paper #3, unpublished and undated.

———. "Myth, Nationalism and Genocide." *Journal of Genocide Research* 3, no. 2 (2001): 187–206.

———. *The Pol Pot Regime: Race, Power, and Genocide in Cambodia under the Khmer Rouge, 1975–1979*. New Haven, CT: Yale University Press, 1996.

Kilborne, Benjamin. *Disappearing Persons: Shame and Appearance*. Albany: State University of New York Press, 2002.

Klee, Ernst, Willi Dressen, and Volker Riess, eds. *Those Were the Days: The Holocaust as Seen by the Perpetrators and Bystanders*. London: Hamish Hamilton, 1991.

Klein, Melanie. *The Psychoanalysis of Children*. Translated by Alix Strachey. New York: Delacorte, 1975.

Klepec, Peter. "On the Mastery in the Four 'Discourses.'" In *Jacques Lacan: Between Psychoanalysis and Politics*. Edited by Samo Tomšič and Andreja Zevnik, 115–130. London: Routledge, 2016.

Kogon, Eugen. *The Theory and Practice of Hell: The German Concentration Camps and the System behind Them*. Translated by Heinz Norden. New York: Octagon, 1979.

Kohut, Heinz. *The Restoration of the Self*. Madison, CT: International Universities Press, 1973.

———. "Thoughts on Narcissism and Narcissistic Rage." In *The Psychoanalytic Study of the Child*, edited by Anna Freud, Ruth S. Eissler, Marianne Kris, and Albert J. Solnit. New York: Random House, 1973.

Korsgaard, Christine M. *Self-Constitution: Agency, Identity, and Integrity*. Oxford: Oxford University Press, 2009.

Kotkin, Stephen. *Stalin*. Vol. 1: *Paradoxes of Power, 1878–1928*. New York: Penguin, 2014.

Kotsko, Adam. *Žižek and Theology*. London: T & T Clark, 2008.

Krain, Matthew. "*J'accuse!* Does Naming and Shaming Perpetrators Reduce the Severity of Genocides or Politicides?" *International Studies Quarterly* 56, no. 3 (2012): 574–589.

———. "State-Sponsored Mass Murder: The Onset and Severity of Genocides and Politicides." *Journal of Conflict Resolution* 41, no. 3 (1997): 331–360.

Krampf, Thomas. *Taking Time Out: Poems in Remembrance of Madness*. Knockeven, Co. Clare, Ireland: Salmon Poetry, 2004.

Krips, Henry. "Politics of the Picture." *Psychoanalysis, Culture and Society* 18, no. 1 (2013): 17–34.

Lacan, Jacques. *Écrits*. Translated by Bruce Fink. New York: W. W. Norton, 2007.

———. *The Four Fundamental Concepts of Psychoanalysis*. Translated by Alan Sheridan. New York: W. W. Norton, 1998.

———. *The Language of the Self: The Function of Language in Psychoanalysis*. Translated with commentary by Anthony Wilden. Baltimore: The Johns Hopkins University Press, 1981.

Lang, Berel. *Act and Idea in the Nazi Genocide*. Syracuse, NY: Syracuse University Press, 2003.

———. "Intentions and 'the Final Solution.'" In *The Future of the Holocaust: Between History and Memory*, 65–76. Ithaca, NY: Cornell University Press, 1999.

Lang, Johannes. "Questioning Dehumanization: Intersubjective Dimensions of Violence in the Nazi Concentration and Death Camps." *Holocaust and Genocide Studies* 24, no. 2 (2010): 225–246.

Laplanche, Jean, and Jean-Bertrand Pontalis. *The Language of Psycho-Analysis*. Translated by Donald Nicholson-Smith. New York: W. W. Norton, 1973.

Lebow, Richard Ned. *A Cultural Theory of International Relations*. Cambridge: Cambridge University Press, 2008.

Lemert, Charles, and Ann Branaman, ed. *The Goffmann Reader*. Malden, MA: Blackwell, 1997.

Levene, Mark. "Connecting Threads: Rwanda, the Holocaust, and the Pattern of Contemporary Genocide." In *The Genocide Studies Reader*, edited by Samuel Totten and Paul R. Bartrop, 258–286. New York: Routledge, 2009.

———. *The Crisis of Genocide*. Vol. 1: *Devastation: The European Rimlands 1912–1938*. Oxford: Oxford University Press, 2013.

———. *The Crisis of Genocide*. Vol. 2: *Annihilation: The European Rimlands 1939–1953*. Oxford: Oxford University Press, 2013.

———. "Empires, Native Peoples, and Genocide." In *Empire, Colony, Genocide: Conquest, Occupation, and Subaltern Resistance in World History*, edited by A. Dirk Moses, 183–204. New York: Berghahn, 2008.

Levi, Primo. *Survival in Auschwitz: The Nazi Assault on Humanity*. Translated by Stuart Woolf. New York, Touchstone, 1996.

Levin, Paul Iganski, and Jack Levin. *Hate Crime: A Global Perspective*. New York: Routledge, 2015.

Lewis, Helen Block. "Introduction: Shame—the 'Sleeper' in Psychopathology." In *The Role of Shame in Symptom Formation*, edited by Helen Block Lewis. Hillsdale, NJ: Lawrence Erlbaum Associates, 1987.

Lifton, Robert J. *The Nazi Doctors: Medical Killing and the Psychology of Genocide*. New York: Basic, 1986.

———."What Made This Man Mengele." *New York Times Magazine*, July 21, 1985.

Locard, Henri. *Pol Pot's Little Red Book*. Suthep, Thailand: Silkworm Books, 2004.

Luke, Timothy W. *Screens of Power: Ideology, Domination, and Resistance in Informational Society*. Champaign: University of Illinois Press, 1990.

MacCannell, Juliet Flower. "Lacan's Imaginary: A Practical Guide." In *Jacques Lacan: Between Psychoanalysis and Politics*, edited by Samo Tomšič and Andreja Zevnik, 72–85. London: Routledge, 2016.

Maguire, Peter. *Facing Death in Cambodia*. New York: Columbia University Press, 2005.

Malkki, Liisa H. *Purity and Exile: Violence, Memory, and National Cosmology among Hutu Refugees in Tanzania*. Chicago: University of Chicago Press, 1995.

Mam, Kaylanee. "The Endurance of the Cambodian Family under the Khmer Rouge Regime: An Oral History." In *Genocide in Cambodia and Rwanda*, edited by Susan E. Cook, 127–171. New Brunswick, NJ: Transaction, 2006.

Mamdani, Mahmood. *When Victims Become Killers: Colonialism, Nativism, and the Genocide in Rwanda*. Princeton, NJ: Princeton University Press, 2002.

Mann, Michael. *The Dark Side of Democracy: Explaining Ethnic Cleansing*. New York: Cambridge University Press, 2005.

———. "Were the Perpetrators of Genocide "Ordinary Men" or "Real Nazis"? Results from Fifteen Hundred Biographies." *Holocaust and Genocide Studies* 14, no. 3 (2000): 331–366.

Marcus, George E., and Michael M. J. Fischer. *Anthropology as Cultural Critique: An Experimental Moment in the Human Sciences*. Chicago: University of Chicago Press, 1999.

Margalit, Avishai. *The Decent Society*. Cambridge, MA: Harvard University Press, 1996.

Mbembe, Achille. "Necropolitics." *Public Culture* 15, no. 1 (2003): 11–40.

McDermott, Rose. "Emotion: Why Do We Love to Hate?" In *Political Psychology in International Relations*, by Rose McDermott, chap. 6. Ann Arbor: University of Michigan Press, 2004.

Melson, Robert. "Modern genocide in Rwanda: Ideology, Revolution, War and Mass Murder in an African State." In *The Specter of Genocide: Mass Murder in Historical Perspective*, edited by Robert Gellately and Ben Kiernan, 325–338. Cambridge: Cambridge University Press, 2003.

Melvern, Linda. *Conspiracy to Murder: The Rwandan Genocide*. London: Verso, 2006.

Midlarsky, Manus. *Origins of Political Extremism: Mass Violence in the Twentieth Century and Beyond*. Cambridge: Cambridge University Press, 2011.

Miller, Jacques-Alain. "Extimité." In *Lacanian Theory of Discourse: Subject, Structure and Society*, edited by Mark Bracher, Marshall W. Alcorn, Jr., Ronald J. Corthell and Françoise Massardier-Kennedy, 74–87. New York: New York University Press, 1994.

Minkkinen, Panu. "Lacan avec Bataille avec Nietzsche: A Politics of the Impossible?" In *Jacques Lacan: Between Psychoanalysis and Politics*. Edited by Samo Tomšič and Andreja Zevnik, 281–298. London: Routledge, 2016.

Mitscherlich, Alexander, and Fred Mielke. *Doctors of Infamy: The Story of the Nazi Medical Crimes*. Translated by Heinz Norden. New York: Henry Schuman, 1949.

Monroe, Kristen Renwick. *Ethics in an Age of Terror and Genocide: Identity and Moral Choice*. Princeton, NJ: Princeton University Press, 2012.

Moses, A. Dirk, ed. *Empire, Colony, Genocide: Conquest, Occupation, and Subaltern Resistance in World History*. New York: Berghahn, 2008.

———. "Empire, Colony, Genocide: Keywords and the Philosophy of History." In *Empire, Colony, Genocide: Conquest, Occupation, and Subaltern Resistance in World History*, edited by A. Dirk Moses, 3–54. New York: Berghahn, 2008.

Muller-Hill, Benno. *Murderous Science: Elimination by Scientific Selection of Jews, Gypsies, and Others in Germany 1933–1945*. Translated by George R. Fraser. New York: Oxford University Press, 1984.

Murer, Jeffrey Stevenson. "Constructing the Enemy-Other: Anxiety, Trauma, and Mourning in the Narratives of Political Conflict." *Psychoanalysis, Culture and Society* 14, no. 2 (2009): 109–130.

———. "Institutionalizing Enemies: The Consequences of Reifying Projection in Post-Conflict Environments." *Psychoanalysis, Culture and Society* 15, no. 1 (2010): 1–19.

Musolff, Andreas. *Metaphor, Nation and the Holocaust: The Concept of the Body Politic*. New York: Routledge, 2010.

Naimark, Norman M. *Fires of Hatred: Ethnic Cleansing in Twentieth-Century Europe*. Cambridge, MA: Harvard University Press, 2001.

Neill, Calum. *Lacanian Ethics and the Assumption of Subjectivity*. New York: Palgrave Macmillan, 2011.

Neiman, Susan. *Evil in Modern Thought: An Alternative History of Philosophy*. Princeton, NJ: Princeton University Press, 2004.

Nelson, Diane M. *Reckoning: The Ends of War in Guatemala*. Durham, NC: Duke University Press, 2009.

Nolen, Stephanie, "Not Women Anymore: The Congo's Rape Survivors Face Pain, Shame, and AIDS." *Ms. Magazine*, 2005. http://www.msmagazine.com/spring2005/congo.asp.

Nussbaum, Martha C. "Objectification." *Philosophy and Public Affairs* 24, no. 4 (1995): 249–291.

Nyiszli, Miklos. *Auschwitz: A Doctor's Eyewitness Account*. Translated by Richard Seaver. New York: Arcade, 2011.

Ogden, Thomas H. *The Primitive Edge of Experience*. Lanham, MD: Jason Aronson, 1989.

Ons, Silvia. "Nietzsche, Freud, Lacan." In *The Silent Partners*, edited by Slavoj Žižek, 79–89. London: Verso 2006.

Osiel, Mark J. "Constructing Subversion in Argentina's Dirty War." *Representations* 75, no. 1 (2001): 119–158.

Oughourlian, Jean-Michel. *The Genesis of Desire*. Translated by Eugene Webb. East Lansing: Michigan State University Press, 2010.

Owens, Peter B., Yang Su, and David A. Snow. "Social Scientific Inquiry into Genocide and Mass Killing: From Unitary Outcome to Complex Processes." *Annual Review of Sociology* 39, no. 4 (2013): 69–84.

Palacios, Margarita. "On Sacredness and Transgression: Understanding Social Antagonism." *Psychoanalysis, Culture and Society* 9, no. 3 (2004): 284–297.

———. *Radical Sociality: On Disobedience, Violence and Belonging*. New York: Palgrave Macmillan, 2013.

Papadaki, Evangelia (Lina). "Feminist Perspectives on Objectification." *The Stanford Encyclopedia of Philosophy* (Winter 2015 Edition). Edward N. Zalta (ed.), https://plato.stanford.edu/archives/win2015/entries/feminism-objectification.

Parker, Ian. "Lacanian Discourse Analysis in Psychology: Seven Theoretical Elements." *Theory and Psychology* 15, no. 2 (2005): 163–182.

Peters, Edward. *Torture*. New York: Basil Blackwell, 1985.

Pick, Daniel. *The Pursuit of the Nazi Mind: Hitler, Hess, and the Analysts*. Oxford: Oxford University Press, 2012.

Piers, Gerhart, and Milton B. Singer. *Shame and Guilt: A Psychoanalytic and a Cultural Study*. New York: W. W. Norton, 1971.

Pitt-Rivers, Julian. "Honor." In *International Encyclopedia of the Social Sciences*, vol. 6, 503–511, 1968.

———. "Honor and Social Status." In *Honour and Shame: The Values of Mediterranean Society*, edited by J. G. Peristiany, 19–78. Chicago: University of Chicago Press, 1966.

Smeulers, Alette. "Perpetrators of International Crimes: Towards a Typology." In *Supranational Criminology: Towards a Criminology of International Crimes*, edited by Alette Smeulers and Roelof Haveman, 233–265. Antwerpen: Intersentia.

Snyder, Timothy. *Black Earth: The Holocaust as History and Warning*. New York: Tim Duggan, 2015.

———. *Bloodlands: Europe between Hitler and Stalin*. New York: Basic, 2010.

Posner, Gerald L., and John Ware. *Mengele: The Complete Story*. New York: Cooper Square Press, 2000.

Power, Samantha. *"A Problem from Hell": America and the Age of Genocide*. New York: Basic, 2002.

Rash, Felicity. *The Language of Violence: Adolf Hitler's* Mein Kampf. Bern: Peter Lang, 2006.

Renshon, Stanley A. "Lost in Plain Sight: The Cultural Foundations of Political Psychology." In *Political Psychology*, edited by Kristen Renwick Monroe, 121–140. Mahwah, NJ: Lawrence Erlbaum, 2002.

Rhodes, Richard. *Masters of Death: The SS-Einsatzgruppen and the Invention of the Holocaust*. New York: Vintage, 2003.

Rogers, Juliet Brough. "A Stranger Politics: Toward a Theory of Resistance in Psychoanalytic Thought and Practice." In *Jacques Lacan: Between Psychoanalysis and Politics*, edited by Samo Tomšič and Andreja Zevnik, 183–201. London: Routledge, 2016.

Rorty, Amélie Oksenberg. "The Social and Political Sources of Akrasia." *Ethics* 107, no. 4 (1997): 644–657.

Rosenbaum, Ron. "Everything You Need to Know About Hitler's 'Missing' Testicle: And Why We're so Obsessed the Führer's Sex Life." Posted November 28, 2008. http://www.slate.com/articles/life/the_spectator/2008/11/everything_you_need_to_know_about_hitlers_missing_testicle.html.

———. *Explaining Hitler: The Search for the Origins of His Evil*. New York: Macmillan, 1998.

Rosenberg, Tina. *Children of Cain: Violence and the Violent in Latin America*. London: Penguin, 1992.

Sands, Philippe. *East West Street: On the Origins of "Genocide" and "Crimes against Humanity."* New York: Knopf, 2016, especially section 135.

Sartre, Jean-Paul. *Being and Nothingness.* Translated by Hazel E. Barnes. New York: Washington Square Press, 1984.

Saussure, Ferdinand de. *Course in General Linguistics.* Translated by Roy Harris. Chicago: Open Court, 1983.

Scarry, Elaine. *The Body in Pain: The Making and Unmaking of the World.* Oxford: Oxford University Press, 1985.

Scheff, Thomas J. "The Shame-Rage Spiral: A Case Study of an Interminable Quarrel." In *The Role of Shame in Symptom Formation,* edited by Helen Block Lewis, 109–149. Hillsdale, NJ: Lawrence Erlbaum, 1987.

Scheff, Thomas J., and Suzanne M. Retzinger. *Emotions and Violence: Shame and Rage in Destructive Conflicts.* Lexington, MA: Lexington, 1991.

Segal, Hanna. *Psychoanalysis, Literature and War: Papers 1972–1995.* London: Routledge, 1995.

———. *The Work of Hanna Segal: A Kleinian Approach to Clinical Practice.* Lanham, MD: Jason Aronson, 2007.

Sender, Ruth Minsky. *The Cage.* New York: Aladdin, 1986.

Shapiro, Michael J. "Justice and the Archives: 'The Method of Dramatization.'" In *International Politics and Performance: Critical Aesthetics and Creative Practice,* edited by Jenny Edkins and Adrian Kear 63–77. London: Routledge, 2013.

———. *Violent Cartographies.* Minneapolis: University of Minnesota Press, 1997.

———. *War Crimes: Atrocity, and Justice.* Cambridge: Polity, 2015.

Shaw, Martin. *What Is Genocide?* Cambridge: Polity, 2007.

Skjelsbaek, Inger. *The Political Psychology of War Rape: Studies from Bosnia and Herzegovina.* New York: Routledge, 2012.

Smale, Alison, and Steven Erlanger. "As Obama Exits World Stage, Angela Merkel May Be the Liberal West's Last Defender." *New York Times,* November 12, 2016.

Smeulers, A. "Perpetrators of International Crimes: Towards a Typology." In *Supranational Criminology: Towards a Criminology of International Crimes,* edited by A. Smeulers and R. Haveman, 233–265. Antwerp: Intersentia, 2008.

Snyder, Timothy. "Hitler's World." *New York Review of Books,* September 24, 2015.

Sofsky, Wolfgang. *The Order of Terror: The Concentration Camp.* Translated by William Templer. Princeton, NJ: Princeton University Press, 1997.

Solomon, Richard H. *Mao's Revolution and the Chinese Political Culture.* Berkeley: University of California Press, 1971.

Sooke, Alastair. "The Discobolus: Greeks, Nazis and the Body Beautiful." *BBC,* March 24, 2015.

Spence, Jonathan D. *The Search for Modern China.* New York: W. W. Norton, 1990.

Spitz, Vivien. *Doctors from Hell: The Horrific Account of Nazi Experiments on Humans.* Boulder, CO: Sentient, 2005.

Sri Lankan Ministry of Defense, *LTTE Defeated; Sri Lanka Liberated from Terror.* May 18, 2009. http://www.defence.lk/new.asp?fname=20090518_10.

Stanton, Gregory H. "Blue Scarves and Yellow Stars: Classification and Symbolization in the Cambodian Genocide." *The Faulds Lecture* (1987).

Staub, Ervin. *Overcoming Evil: Genocide, Violent Conflict, and Terrorism.* Oxford: Oxford University Press, 2011.

———. *The Roots of Evil: The Origins of Genocide and Other Group Violence.* Cambridge: Cambridge University Press, 1989.

Steele, Brent J. *Alternative Accountabilities in Global Politics: The Scars of Violence.* New York: Routledge, 2012.

Stein, Ruth. *For Love of the Father: A Psychoanalytic Study of Religious Terrorism.* Meridian: Crossing Aesthetics. Stanford, CA: Stanford University Press, 2010.

Stewart, Amy Ray. "Witnessing horror: Psychoanalysis and the Abject Stain of Lynching Photography." *Psychoanalysis, Culture & Society* 19, no. 4 (2014): 413–434.

Stewart, Frank Henderson. *Honor.* Chicago: University of Chicago Press, 1994.

Stone, Dan. "Biopower and Modern Genocide." In *Empire, Colony, Genocide: Conquest, Occupation, and Subaltern Resistance in World History,* edited by A. Dirk Moses, 162–182. New York: Berghahn, 2008.

———. "Genocide as Transgression." *European Journal of Social Theory* 7, no. 1 (2004): 45–65.

Straus, Scott. *Making and Unmaking Nations: War, Leadership, and Genocide in Modern Africa.* Ithaca, NY: Cornell University Press, 2015.

Su, Yang. *Collective Killings in Rural China during the Cultural Revolution.* Cambridge: Cambridge University Press, 2011.

Šumič, Jelica. "Politics and Psychoanalysis in the Time of the Inexistent Other." In *Jacques Lacan: Between Psychoanalysis and Politics.* Edited by Samo Tomšič and Andreja Zevnik, 28–42. London: Routledge, 2016.

Sun, Lung-kee. "Beloved China: Imagery of 'Mother China' in Modern Chinese Political Thinking." In *The Psychodynamics of International Relationships.* Vol. 1: *Concepts and Theories,* edited by Demetrios A. Julius, Vamik D. Volkan, and Joseph V. Montville, 56–68. Lexington, MA: Lexington, 1991.

Suny, Ronald Grigor. "Constructing Primordialism: Old Histories for New Nations." *Journal of Modern History* 73, no. 4 (2001): 862–896.

———. "Truth in Telling: Reconciling Realities in the Genocide of the Ottoman Armenians." *The American Historical Review* 114, no. 4 (2009): 930–946.

Taylor, Christopher C. "The Cultural Face of Terror in the Rwandan Genocide of 1994." In *Annihilating Difference: The Anthropology of Genocide,* edited by Alexander Laban Hinton, 137–178. Berkeley: University of California Press, 2002.

Toal, Gerard, and Carl T. Dahlman. *Bosnia Remade: Ethnic Cleansing and Its Reversal.* Oxford: Oxford University Press, 2011.

Todorov, Tzvetan. *Hope and Memory: Lessons from the Twentieth Century.* Princeton, NJ: Princeton University Press, 2003.

———. *Voices from the Gulag: Life and Death in Communist Bulgaria.* Translated by Robert Zaretsky. University Park: Penn State University Press, 1999.

Travis, Hannibal. "The Assyrian Genocide: A Tale of Oblivion and Denial." In *Forgotten Genocides: Oblivion, Denial, and Memory,* edited by Rene Lemarchand, 123–136. Philadelphia: University of Pennsylvania Press, 2011.

———. *Genocide, Ethnonationalism, and the United Nations.* New York: Routledge, 2013.

Trevor-Roper, Hugh. Foreword to *"The Good Old Days": The Holocaust as Seen by Its Perpetrators and Bystanders,* edited by Willi Dressen, Ernst Klee, and Volker Riess, translated by Deborah Burnstone, x–xvi. Old Saybrook, CT: Konecky and Konecky, 1991.

Tyner, James A., Sokvisal Kimsroy, Chenjian Fu, Zheye Wang, and Xinyue Ye. "An Empirical Analysis of Arrests and Executions at S-21 Security-Center During the Cambodian Genocide." *Genocide Studies International* 10, no. 2 (2016): 268–286.

Valentino, Benjamin A. *Final Solutions: Mass Killing and Genocide in the Twentieth Century.* Cornell Studies in Security Affairs. Ithaca, NY: Cornell University Press, 2004.

Vanheule, Stijn. *The Subject of Psychosis: A Lacanian Perspective.* New York: Palgrave Macmillan, 2011.

Vanheule, Stijn, and Paul Verhaeghe. "Identity through a Psychoanalytic Looking Glass." *Theory and Psychology* 19, no. 3 (2009): 391–411.

Varvin, Sverre. "Islamism and Xenophobia." In *Psychoanalysis and Politics: Exclusion and the Politics of Representation,* edited by Lene Auestad, 155–168. London: Karnac, 2012.

Verdeja, Ernesto. "The Political Science of Genocide: Outlines of an Emerging Research Agenda." *Perspectives on Politics* 10, no. 2 (2012): 307–321.

Verhaeghe, Paul. "The Riddle of Castration Anxiety: Lacan beyond Freud." In *The Letter: Lacanian Perspectives on Psychoanalysis* 6 (Spring 1996): 44–54. Originally a paper presented at the Second Annual Congress of the APPI: "Anxiety and Its Coordinates." Dublin, November, 1995.

Verwimp, Philip. "Machetes and Firearms: The Organization of Massacres in Rwanda." *Journal of Peace Research* 43, no. 1 (2006): 5–22.

Vetlesen, Arne Johan. *Evil and Human Agency: Understanding Collective Evildoing.* Cambridge: Cambridge University Press, 2005.

Volkan, Vamik. *Bloodlines: From Ethnic Pride to Ethnic Terrorism.* Boulder, CO: Westview, 1997.

Waller, James. *Becoming Evil: How Ordinary People Commit Genocide and Mass Killing.* Oxford: Oxford University Press, 2002.

Weinstein, Fred. *Freud, Psychoanalysis, Social Theory.* Albany: State University of New York Press, 2001.

Weisband, Edward, and Courtney I. P. Thomas. *Political Culture and the Making of Modern Nation-States.* Boulder, CO: Paradigm, 2015.

Welaratna, Usha. *Beyond the Killing Fields: Voices of Nine Cambodian Survivors in America.* Asian America. Stanford, CA: Stanford University Press, 1993.

Welzer, Harald. "Mass Murder and Moral Code: Some Thoughts on an Easily Misunderstood Subject." *History of the Human Sciences* 17, no. 2/3 (2004): 15–32.

Wikipedia. s.v. "Language reforms" in "Khmer Rouge." Updated May 23, 2017. https://en.wikipedia.org/wiki/Khmer_Rouge#Language_reforms.

———. "Omarska camp." Updated April 26, 2017. http://en.wikipedia.org/w/index.php?title=Omarska_camp&oldid=755021740.

———. "Sexual Violence in the Democratic Republic of the Congo." Updated March 11, 2017. https://en.wikipedia.org/wiki/Sexual_violence_in_the_Democratic_Republic_of_the_Congo.

Wurmser, Léon. *The Mask of Shame.* Baltimore: Johns Hopkins University Press, 1981.

Young-Bruehl, Elisabeth. *For Love of the World.* New Haven, CT: Yale University Press, 1996.

Zillmer, Eric, Molly Harrower, Barry A. Ritzler, and Rober P. Archer. *The Quest for the Nazi Personality: A Psychological Investigation of Nazi War Criminals.* New York: Routledge, 1995.

Zimbardo, Philip. *The Lucifer Effect: Understanding How Good People Turn Evil.* New York: Random House, 2008.

Žižek, Slavoj. *For They Know Not What They Do: Enjoyment as a Political Factor.* London: Verso, 2008.

———. *Looking Awry: An Introduction to Jacques Lacan through Popular Culture.* Cambridge, MA: MIT Press, 1991.

———. *The Plague of Fantasies.* London: Verso, 2009.

———. *The Sublime Object of Ideology.* London: Verso, 1989.

———. *Tarrying with the Negative: Kant, Hegel, and the Critique of Ideology.* Durham, NC: Duke University Press, 1993.

INDEX